POPULATION REFERENCE BUREAU, INC.

(REVISED EDITION) AUGUST 1971

D1541197

Region or Country	Population Estimates Mid-1971 (millions)†	Annual Births per 1,000 Population‡	Annual Deaths per 1,000 Population‡	Annual Rate of Population Growth (percent)°	Number of Years to Double Population□	Annual Inf...			Pe Na
SOUTHERN AFRICA	23	41	17	2.4	29	—	40	34	
Botswana	0.6	44	23	2.2	32	—	43	0.9	100
Lesotho	1.1	40	23	1.8	39	181	43	1.4	80
South Africa	20.6	40	16	2.4	29	—	40	29.7	}650
Namibia (Southwest Africa)*	0.6	44	25	2.0	35	—	40	0.9	
Swaziland	0.4	52	22	3.0	24	—		0.7	200
ASIA	2,104²	38	15	2.3	31	—	40	2,874	—
SOUTHWEST ASIA	79	44	15	2.9	24	—	43	121	—
Cyprus	0.6	23	8	0.9	78	27	35	0.7	830
Iraq	10.0	49	15	3.4	21	—	45	16.7	260
Israel	3.0	26	7	2.4	29	23	33	4.0	1,360
Jordan	2.4	48	16	3.3	21	—	46	3.9	260
Kuwait	0.8	43	7	8.2	9	36	38	2.4	3,540
Lebanon	2.9	—	—	3.0	24	—	—	4.3	560
Muscat and Oman	0.7	42	11	3.1	23	—	—	1.1	250
Saudi Arabia	8.0	50	23	2.8	25	—	—	12.2	360
Southern Yemen	1.3	—	—	2.8	25	—	—	2.0	120
Syria	6.4	47	15	3.3	21	—	46	10.5	210
Turkey	36.5	43	16	2.7	26	155	44	52.8	310
Yemen (Arab Republic)	5.9	50	23	2.8	25	—	—	9.1	70
MIDDLE SOUTH ASIA	783	44	16	2.7	26	—	43	1,137	—
Afghanistan	17.4	50	26	2.5	28	—	—	25.0	80
Bhutan	0.9	—	—	2.2	32	—	—	1.2	60
Ceylon	12.9	32	8	2.4	29	48	41	17.7	180
India	569.5⁴	42	17	2.6	27	139	41	807.6	100
Iran	29.2	48	18	3.0	24	—	46	45.0	310
Nepal	11.5	45	23	2.2	32	—	40	15.8	80
Pakistan	141.6	50	18	3.3	21	142	45	224.2	100
SOUTHEAST ASIA	295	43	15	2.8	25	—	44	434	—
Burma	28.4	40	17	2.3	31	—	40	39.2	70
Cambodia	7.3	45	16	3.0	24	127	44	11.3	120
Indonesia	124.9	47	19	2.9	24	125	42	183.8	100
Laos	3.1	42	17	2.5	28	—	—	4.4	100
Malaysia	11.1	37	8	2.8	25	—	44	16.4	330
Philippines	39.4	46	12	3.4	21	72	47	64.0	180
Singapore	2.2	25	5	2.4	29	—	43	3.0	700
Thailand	37.4	42	10	3.3	21	—	43	57.7	150
Vietnam (Dem. Republic of)	21.6	—	—	2.1	33	—	—	28.2	90
Vietnam (Republic of)	18.3	—	—	2.1	33	—	—	23.9	130
EAST ASIA	946.	30	13	1.8	39	—	36	1,182	—
China (Mainland)	772.9	33	15	1.8	39	—	—	964.6	90
China (Taiwan)	14.3	26	5	2.3	31	19	44	19.4	270
Hong Kong*	4.3	21	5	2.5	28	21	40	6.0	710
Japan	104.7	18	7	1.1	63	15	25	121.3	1,190
Korea (Dem. People's Rep. of)	14.3	39	11	2.8	25	—	—	20.7	250
Korea (Republic of)	32.9	36	11	2.5	28	—	42	45.9	180
Mongolia	1.3	42	10	3.1	23	—	44	2.0	430
Ryukyu Islands*	1.0	22	5	1.7	41	11	39	1.3	580

Population Reference Bureau, Inc., 1755 Massachusetts Avenue, N.W., Washington, D. C. 20036 (202) 232-2288

POPULATIONS
AND
SOCIETIES

PRENTICE-HALL SERIES IN SOCIOLOGY

Neil J. Smelser, *Editor*

POPULATIONS AND SOCIETIES

JUDAH MATRAS

Hebrew University

PRENTICE-HALL, INC., Englewood Cliffs, New Jersey

Library of Congress Cataloging in Publication Data

MATRAS, JUDAH.
  Populations and societies.

  Bibliography: p.
  1. Population. 2. Social structure. I. Title.
HB851.M37   301.4   72-8951
ISBN 0-13-684563-0

Printed in the United States of America

10 9 8 7 6 5 4 3 2 1

ACKNOWLEDGMENTS
Cover photograph by Harold M. Lambert.
Photograph, p. xiv, by Jim Jowers, from Nancy Palmer Photo Agency.
Photograph, p. 228, from Wide World Photos.
Photograph, p. 420, of Tapiola, Finland, Courtesy of the
Consulate General of Finland, in New York.
Endpapers reprinted with permission from Population Reference
Bureau, Inc., Washington, D.C.

Prentice-Hall International, Inc., London
Prentice-Hall of Australia, Pty. Ltd., Sydney
Prentice-Hall of Canada, Ltd., Toronto
Prentice-Hall of India Private Limited, New Delhi
Prentice-Hall of Japan, Inc., Tokyo

For Hagit, Yaron, and Gilat

Contents

Preface

This book is a theoretical, methodological, and substantive introduction to the study of human populations, their structures, variations, and changes; and to the social structural causes, correlates, and consequences of population trends. It summarizes world population history, reviews recent growth trends and variations, and considers the background and meaning of the current world population "explosion." Materials presented in the book describe and illustrate sources of demographic data, methods of measurement, and basic techniques of analysis. I have tried to synthesize current research issues and recent research findings concerning social factors affecting fertility, mortality, migration, and mobility, and I discuss the effects of population change upon social relationships and upon economic, political, and social organization.

Books on population and demography typically deal with similar topics—adequately or less adequately, as the case may be. But, beyond this task, I have tried in this book to argue and demonstrate that the central determinants of variations and changes in populations are *social structural* determinants; that population structure itself is an important aspect of social structure which bounds all other aspects of social structure; and that population processes and transformations per se constitute change in social structure and are at the same time direct causes of other major social structural and cultural changes. And, indeed, I have tried to build the text, discussion, examples, and analysis explicitly around these central ideas and arguments. Although this is a point of view which has informed a long and distinguished tradition of teaching, research, and writing both in population studies and in sociology, it has not previously found its way into introductory books on population. It is my hope that this book will comprise a modest contribution towards filling this need.

Virtually every author carries a heavy debt to his predecessors and peers, known and unknown. I owe a special intellectual debt to my teachers, classmates, colleagues, students, and friends at the University of Chicago, the Hebrew University of Jerusalem, and the University of Wisconsin. It was at the University of Chicago that I first had the privilege of studying sociology with distinguished demographers and demography with distinguished sociologists. The Hebrew University offered me my first concrete research challenge and opportunity and continues to provide ever more exciting challenges and opportunities. Two visits at the University of Wisconsin have afforded me not only those crucial resources, time and library facilities, but also a variety of teaching experiences, a breadth of collegial and student encounters and feedback, and both window and gateway to current American sociology and population studies.

Special acknowledgements are due to Philip M. Hauser and Alexander J. Morin, who read the very earliest memos, outlines, and sketches and encouraged me to undertake writing the book; and to Yehudi A. Cohen, Julian Simon, Alma F. Taeuber, and Don Treiman for critical readings of parts or all of the first draft. Calvin E. Goldscheider and Robert W. Hodge first brought me to the crucial insights leading to revision of the first draft and its trajectory, and thereby rendering the book accessible to a wider audience of students and colleagues without compromising its central ideas. Hal H. Winsborough and an anonymous reader provided helpful suggestions to a revised draft.

Credit for conversion of a ponderous manuscript to a readable book is due to Neil J. Smelser, consulting editor of the Prentice-Hall Sociology Series, and to Barbara Phillips, who performed wonders in editing the manuscript. Credit for all remaining ponderousness is jealously retained by the author. The first drafts of the manuscript were typed by Barbara Zaleski, who also provided early research and editorial assistance and prepared the bibliography in Jerusalem. Joann Miller provided later research assistance, Pat Blair edited and typed the final bibliography, and Janice Deneen provided all manner of secretarial and administrative assistance in Madison. The task of typing the final version of a manuscript whose author is several thousand miles away fell upon Diane Stanford, whose efficiency and ingenuity in managing it left the author feeling entirely redundant. Suffering the responsibility—or enjoying the freedom —of a similar distance from the author, Ann Torbert managed the details and intricacies of production of the book. The patience, fortitude, care, and pampering provided by Edward H. Stanford, Sociology Editor of Prentice-Hall, have been far in excess of the call of duty, and his good-humored mind and hand lie behind and alongside a very considerable part of the entire enterprise.

No adequate homage can be paid the home front, not even the dedication.

JUDAH MATRAS

Jerusalem, The Hebrew University

one

POPULATION
AND
SOCIAL STRUCTURE

1

Introduction:

World Population

and

Populations of the World

1. MAN'S NUMBERS AND HIS CHANGING SOCIETIES

The "population explosion," the "human zoo," the "population bomb," "standing room only," "zero population growth," the "garbage explosion," "cities without space"—these and other apocalyptic phrases have been showered upon the public by the popular media and in learned forums and publications. The public generally, and social scientists in particular, are now being alerted to the "menace" of rapid world population growth and its "dire consequences" for the well-being—indeed, the survival—of the individual and society.

Remarkably enough, only a generation ago a flurry of phrases warned about the dire consequences of "population decline" and "demographic, social, and economic stagnation." What, then, is the basis for the present alarm? What are the facts of population growth, and how are they to be interpreted?

The present population of the world—just under four billion people (about 3.5 billion in 1969)—could have been produced from an initial population of two dozen persons increasing at the rate of 0.02 percent per year over a period of 100,000 years. But we know that almost all of the increase in the earth's population has occurred during the three cen-

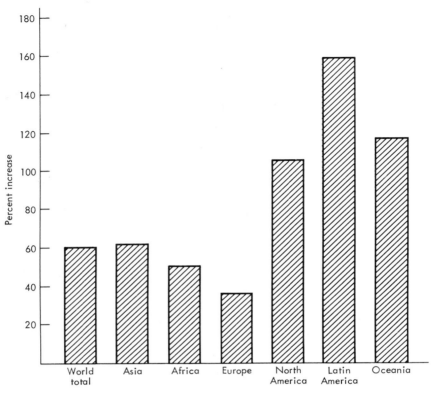

FIGURE 1.1.   Percent increase in world population, by continent, 1900–
1950. Source: Endpapers.

turies of the modern era, 1650–1950. Moreover, it is estimated that in the
decade 1950–1960, world population grew at a rate of 1.0 percent annually
—a rate which would double a population about every 70 years. And in
the period around 1970–1971, world population was increasing at the
rate of 2.0 percent annually—a rate which would double it about every
35 years. It is very easy to show mathematically that so large a rate of
growth cannot have characterized the world's population for very many
years in the past and that it cannot continue to do so for very many
years in the future. Thus, the current growth is quite justifiably termed
a "population explosion."

If world population continues to increase at its present rate, it will
probably reach seven billion persons by the year 2000. In other words, it
will virtually double its 1969 total during the remainder of the century.

Implications of Population Growth

At least three types of consequences may be anticipated from such an enormous rate of growth. First, there is likely to be increased pressure upon food, space, and other resources and upon the social and community relationships organizing their allocation; and, following from this, there is likely to be increased economic hardship, poor nutrition or malnutrition, and perhaps increasing rates of mortality. In 1960, the population density of New York's Manhattan Island already exceeded 77,000 persons per square mile; the pressures resulting from a doubling of that density hardly seem imaginable. And for example at the national level, one estimate holds that the fossil fuel resources of the United States may be exhausted in 75 years. In the second place, the efforts of new or underdeveloped nations to accelerate development may be largely frustrated by the continued drain on resources resulting from rapid population increases (Coale 1963). Thus, if India's growth rate is not reduced, her population will probably double in the next generation from 560 million to about 1100 million, with no comparable growth of national product. Finally, the differences in rates of growth among the different areas of the world (see column 3 of end papers) will produce a redistribution of the world's population which will probably have major implications for international politics. Europe's population, which accounted for an estimated 15 percent of the world population in the year 1000, increased to almost 26 percent by 1900. But 50 years later it was reduced to 23 percent of the total, and by 1971 to only 12.6 percent.

These three types of consequences of population growth recur in many guises, in many social and cultural settings, and they evoke a variety of responses. Thus, the problem of the amounts and distribution of the earth's resources is also the problem of poverty and want; of space and clean air and environment; of equality of opportunity and of segregation of residences, schools, and employment; of health and of access to care and treatment; and of the way in which national goods, air and environment, health and medical care, entertainment, leisure, culture, and all manner of resources are distributed, made freely available, guarded, hoarded, or stolen in our society or in other societies.

A crucial twentieth-century—perhaps post-World War II—development is that the various parts of the world have discovered one another to an extent previously unknown in human history. All are increasingly aware of how "the other half lives," and, in particular, the "have-not" peoples, nations, and societies are no longer ignorant of the worlds and the pleasures of the "haves." Leaders and governments increasingly are seeking to better the lives and conditions of their "have-not" constituents; the "have-nots" make increasing demands upon their own rulers and leaders and upon the "haves." But knowing about the "haves" is not the same as being one! And the political commitment of rulers and of the elites to development and to increased levels of living is not the same as its achievement. Whether the "have-not" peoples can hope to become "haves"—and by what means—is a central issue in which population growth patterns have a crucial influence.

In the modern world homogeneous societies are the exception rather than the rule. Most large-scale societies maintain a balance between two or more quite distinct population groups. Whites and blacks, Catholics and Protestants, Czechs and Slovaks, Hindus and Moslems, Spanish and Indians, Jews and Arabs, Swedes and Finns may coexist in a more or less delicately balanced, more or less equalitarian, more or less segregated, more or less open, pluralistic society. In many societies such coexistence is a matter of tradition, pride, and harmonious cooperation and mutual respect. But increasingly, under the new visibility afforded by the revolution in communication, literacy, and information, pluralism has come to be synonymous with inequality. In all societies and all communities, the ongoing *balance* between majority and minority populations, between dominant and subordinate population groups, or between groups of divergent interests, outlooks, traditions, or needs is *always* rendered problematic and of doubtful stability by the differentials in growth patterns among the different groups.

What are the chances that the world population will continue to increase at its present rate? And what are the likely consequences of any continued growth or of changing rates of growth? As we shall see in the chapters that follow, the population's size, rates and components of growth, structure and composition, and patterns of settlement have changed historically, and at any moment in time vary in geographic and social space.

Population Growth and Social Change in History

The prehistoric period was characterized by an extremely slow population growth, generally small population groupings, very low population density, no permanent settlement, and a small total population. According to archaeological evidence, sustenance in this period was obtained almost entirely by food-gathering and simple hunting.

The neolithic period witnessed a much more rapid population growth and the appearance of much larger, often more permanent, densely settled population groupings. (Whether the latter came about through migration or natural increase is not generally known.) In addition, there was a much larger total population. These developments evidently occurred simultaneously with the development of agriculture—indeed, the period is credited with the "food production revolution"—and with some domestication of animals, some division of labor, some exchange and trade, the beginnings of writing and literacy, religion and government, and the extension of political and economic integration over progressively larger population groupings.

Finally, the "modern" or "industrial" period—our own period—has been characterized by extremely rapid population growth, increased longevity, and more recently, the widespread and effective control of population growth. These developments have been accompanied by highly rationalized food production; by very large, densely settled, population agglomerations of great social and economic differentiation; by the extensive development of transportation and communication; and by very large-scale systems of exchange, trade, economic and political integration, and mutual interdependence.

It is possible that a *similar* historical sociodemographic process has taken place at different *rates* in different areas or historical settings, or, alternatively, that *different* processes have taken place historically. We shall consider this in chapter 3 and again in Part III. In any event, today we encounter a large variety of populations which differ from one another with respect to size, growth characteristics, density, structure, and composition. These variations are, in turn, accompanied by societal variations. For example, small high-fertility–high-mortality populations—such as those of Laos, Chad, and Nepal—belong to nonurban societies characterized by low levels of differentiation and localized economies and polities. Conversely, large low-fertility–low-mortality populations—such as those of the United States, Japan, and Great Britain—are typically highly urbanized, industrialized, and characterized by intensive specialization and division of labor.

How and why are populations and societies related? Under what conditions do they vary or change together and under what conditions independently of one another? How can we account for change, and how, indeed, can we account for the *absence* of change? How can we explain variations in the direction of change, in the path of change, or in the rate of change in populations and societies? A scientific theory of populations and societies seeks to answer these questions by developing propositions that are empirically verifiable. It is the beginning and outline of such a theory that we intend to develop in this book.

Curiosity and speculation about man's numbers on earth may be as ancient as man himself. But it is the recognition that man's numbers are related to, and influence, his safety, his well-being, his social relations and community organization, and perhaps his very survival that has given impetus to the modern systematic study of populations, their structures, and their transformations. Unfortunately, such studies have too often been obscured by a spate of statistical tables, graphs, and charts which portray populations in extreme detail. In this book we shall attempt to make such relationships explicit and explore them in some depth. At the same time we shall attempt to introduce, as a multidisciplined scientific enterprise, the study of populations, their variations, and their relationships with social structure as they vary over space and time.

We shall try to show, on the one hand, that the central determinants of variations and changes in population size, composition, and distribution are *social structural,* and that it is to sociology, social anthropology, and human ecology that we must turn for fundamental theoretical and analytical concepts and research tools. However, we shall also argue that population structure is itself an important aspect of social structure, bounding all its other aspects; that populations naturally tend to grow and change in the absence of constraints; and that population processes and transformations constitute change in social structure in and of themselves and are direct causes of other major social structural and cultural changes.

A number of concepts and fairly complex ideas are introduced—but treated only briefly—in this section and in the sections which follow. Our purpose here is to provide an overview of the subject matter and objectives of this book and to indicate briefly the scope of demography and population studies. We return in much more detail to concepts of population, population structure, population transformations, social structure, community organization, and relationships between them in later sections and chapters.

2. DEMOGRAPHY AND POPULATION STUDIES

Two areas of concern comprehended by demography are formal demography and population studies. We shall begin the discussion in this section by explaining what demography is, what distinguishes formal demography from population studies, and what aspect of demography receives relatively greater emphasis in this book.

We follow P. M. Hauser and O. D. Duncan (1959a) in defining *demography* as the scientific study of the size, territorial distribution, and composition of population, of changes therein, and of the components of such changes, which may be identified as natality, mortality, territorial movement, and social mobility (or change of status).

"Composition of population" has reference to (1) such traits as age, sex, race, place of birth, and ethnic origin (the so-called "biological," or fixed, traits), (2) such "life-cycle" attributes as educational level and marital and household status, and (3) such variable characteristics as occupation, social class, and other social roles or categories. When one investigates the components of growth and change in the distribution and composition of a population, one studies not only such vital events as birth, death, marriage, and divorce, but also migration, geographic mobility, and all manner of social mobility and change in social role or status.

Demography studies population size and composition in terms of geographic variation and historical trend. The analysis of spatial and historical variations in the size, structure, and growth of populations is brought to bear upon the formulation of hypotheses concerning factors affecting population and factors affected by population trends. Demography characteristically treats a large variety of social, economic, political, biological, and physical factors, insofar as they may affect population size, distribution, and composition, or be affected themselves by population and population trends.

It is worth noting that demography is not concerned exclusively, nor even primarily, with developing population predictions or forecasts. Demography does have techniques for projecting population growth and compositional change, that is, for computing the population size and composition implied by sets of explicit assumptions regarding natality, mortality, migration, and mobility. But the major area of modern demographic inquiry is not the simple computation of what is implied by an assumed set of conditions. Rather, it is the analysis of the causes and consequences of trends found to be occurring in the various components of population growth and change.

Demography seeks to identify and abstract facets of human populations which recur over a large range and variety of real populations. For example, a population's size, age structure, geographic distribution, and growth characteristics are all facets which demography seeks to identify and whose variations it wishes to analyze and explain. In accounting for variations in population size and characteristics, demography necessarily draws upon such related social sciences as sociology, economics, and history, as well as upon the biological sciences, geography, and geomorphology. The consequences of population structure and its changes are fundamentally economic, social, historical, and political, no less than demographic. *Demographic theory*, then, identifies those recurring facets of populations which comprise its subject matter, formulates statements concerning the range and nature of variations in these facets, and formulates generalizations concerning, first, the factors affecting these variations and, second, the consequences of these variations. *Demographic research* observes real populations, analyzes its observations, and seeks thereby to test theoretical formulations and expand them.

Among the specific variables included in the subject matter of demography are mortality and differential mortality; family formation, including patterns of marriage and child-bearing; population settlement; migration; and a full range of factors presumed to be related to these variables. For example, it is widely known that birth rates historically have varied quite considerably, and that at any moment in time they vary among different countries or societies and, indeed, within any given society. Taking birth rate as a facet of all populations, demography observes its variations and inquires about their range, their causes, and their consequences.

Certain of the causes and consequences of birth-rate variations are inherent in the structure of the population itself. For example, populations with a relatively large number of young adult women will have relatively higher birth rates than populations with relatively few young adult women. Populations with high birth rates will tend to grow faster than populations with low birth rates. The study of interrelationships between different components of a given population, and between components of a population and the pattern of population growth, is called *formal demography.* In the case of the birth rate, formal demography would study the structure of the population as related to the birth rate and the growth of the population as affected by the birth rate.

In this book we shall place relatively less emphasis upon formal demography and relatively more upon *population studies,* the investigation of the factors and consequences of population trends. More specifically, population studies concern (1) social, economic, historical, and other determinants of population trends and movements, and (2) social, economic, political, cultural, and other consequences of population trends and changes. With reference to the birth rate, in population studies we would study the social and economic factors connected with variations in the birth rate and the social and economic consequences of those variations.

The Emergence of Demography as a Scientific Discipline

Historically, four major factors account for the emergence of demography as a scientific discipline. These are:

1. Interest in population processes as *natural phenomena* which have recurring regularities and which are deserving of observation and speculation.
2. The introduction and development of systems of reporting vital events and population counts for purposes of civil status, taxation, and administration. This took place in Europe, largely in the nineteenth century.

3. Publicly and privately initiated movements to study, measure, and control morbidity and mortality, beginning in Western Europe in the first half of the nineteenth century.

4. Recognition of—and attempts to formulate and apply—generalizations concerning relationships between population change and economic, social, and political change, with T. R. Malthus (1766–1834) the central figure of this sequence.

GRAUNT AND SÜSSMILCH. The key names associated with the promotion of inquiry into population and vital events as natural phenomena with recurring regularities are those of John Graunt, an Englishman whose findings from a study of deaths and births were first published in London in 1662 (Graunt 1662), and Johann Süssmilch, a German whose essay on population sizes, structures, components of growth, and their interrelations was first published in Berlin in 1741 (Süssmilch 1761–1762). Graunt, a merchant with close ties to personalities in London's midseventeenth century intellectual circles, conceived the idea of using summaries of parish records of burials and christenings to study mortality and fertility in London and in a rural English parish, presenting his findings and analysis to the newly founded Royal Society of Philosophers. Graunt used these data to measure variations in mortality, fertility, and nuptiality, and in population size, growth, and composition, and it was he who first discovered, or at least drew attention to, the significance of the recurrence, uniformity, and predictability of important biological phenomena viewed in the aggregate. Indeed, the American demographer and pioneer social scientist W. F. Willcox views Graunt as the real founder of statistics (Willcox 1939).

A theological interpretation of the kinds of population "regularities" discovered by Graunt was advanced by Johann Süssmilch. Süssmilch, a Lutheran clergyman, viewed the orderliness of vital events and population phenomena as an expression of the divine mind and will. To prove and expand this proposition, he set about accumulating and analyzing masses of observations and data on populations, publishing a first edition of his essays on "divine order" in 1741, a second in two volumes in 1761–1762, and a third in 1765. In his essays, Süssmilch made careful estimates of the world's population and studied the sex ratios at birth, at marriage age, and at advanced age. He also studied ratios of population to births, deaths, and marriages, ratios of births to marriages, ratios of deaths at given ages to all deaths. Moreover, he studied empirically some factors affecting marriage, birth, and death.

Thus, Graunt and Süssmilch saw population phenomena as subject matter for systematic, empirically based, investigation. These convictions were shared by their contemporaries and inherited by their successors.

VITAL STATISTICS AND POPULATION CENSUSES. The routine recording of births, deaths, and marriages dates from the middle ages and was carried out originally by ecclesiastical authorities for purposes of explicating such matters as an individual's civil and religious status and the inheritance of property. In many periods these activities were reinforced by the concern with disease, epidemics, and mortality. Church registers were the principal source of demographic information throughout Europe through the eighteenth century and were then gradually replaced by civil registration systems. Toward the close of the seventeenth century, summaries and compilations of vital statistics were published periodically in several countries of Europe.

Population censuses are known to have been carried out in ancient Israel, Rome, China, and elsewhere for purposes of administration, taxation, or military recruitment. However, these were generally only partial enumerations and were not repeated in comparable forms.

According to Wolfenden (Wolfenden 1954, pp. 4–6), population counts were carried out in various European cities and provinces as early as the sixteenth and seventeenth centuries. In the eighteenth century national census programs were initiated in several countries, including the United States, with a constitutionally prescribed decennial census. But full national census enumerations were made only around 1800 in England, France, and Iceland, and they were not fully tabulated or analyzed. National censuses have subsequently become much more common, elaborate, and comprehensive.

In the nineteenth century, the collection and publication of censuses and vital statistics expanded and intensified, both in Europe and in North America. Between 1830 and 1849, a series of international meetings and congresses on the organization, standards, and comparability of official statistics were held, initiated largely by Adolphe Quetelet, a Belgian statistician of remarkable initiative and strong theoretical interests (Lorimer 1959). By the close of the nineteenth century, the collection, compilation, and publication of official population statistics had generated interest in population trends and in many countries had mobilized cadres of professional personnel engaged in describing and analyzing population size, distribution, and dynamics.

The rise of insurance companies and societies, which in many countries coincided approximately with the entrance of governments and public bodies into activities promoting or safeguarding public health, created a strong demand for mortality data during the nineteenth century. Probably the central figure in the mobilization of official vital statistics for purposes of mortality and morbidity control was William Farr, who was employed in the British Registrar General Office from 1839 to 1880, first as a compiler of abstracts and ultimately as superintendent of statistics. He himself did pioneering work in the study of occupational mortality, contributed to demographic methodology, and was a prime mover in the development of British census and vital statistics services (Grebenik 1959). But Farr is to be credited most of all for having drawn the attention of the general public to the high mortality existing in certain districts and trades as a result of unsanitary conditions and dangerous work. It was Farr's use of population data in mortality analysis that paved the way for the social legislation instrumental in the great reductions in mortality that were eventually achieved in Great Britain (Cox 1959). The demand in this period for more direct control over disease and mortality was increasingly reflected in public intervention via legislation and specialized institutions. These, in turn, created an increasing demand for data and analyses concerning population phenomena generally and mortality in particular.

MALTHUS.   The central historical personality in the recognition and formulation of a theory of interrelationships between population and social and economic change was Thomas Robert Malthus. Malthus is immortalized in demographic history both for his *Essay on the Principle of Population* (1958), which ran through no fewer than seven editions from 1798 to 1872, and for the controversy which raged and continues to rage around his ideas (Glass 1953). The main ideas of Malthus's analysis are:

1. Since population tends to increase faster than food resources do, there is always tension between population and subsistence.
2. This tension is resolved by the "positive checks" of mortality. That is, the increase in population to a level close to the limits of subsistence produces poverty, misery, vice, disease, and ultimately the mortality operating to restrain population growth.
3. But, Malthus allowed in the second and subsequent editions of his *Essay,* a measure of population balance can be obtained by the "preventive checks" of "moral restraint," i.e., by delayed marriage or continence in marriage, which could replace the "positive checks" described above.

Malthus felt that several of the social reforms advocated in his day would, if adopted, result only in increased population and as high, or higher, a level of poverty, misery, and disease, and at the same time would diminish industry and thrift. He advocated "preventive checks" and, indeed, observed with approval the institutionalization of delayed marriage in increasingly broad sectors of the population (Malthus 1829).

The timing of its appearance and its polemical character made Malthus's essay a topic of lively and sometimes bitter controversy between advocates of a variety of social reforms and their opponents. Malthus's essay appeared at a period when two opposing schools of thought, mercantilism and revolutionary utopianism, dominated European ideas about population. Both mercantilism and revolutionary utopianism advocated pro-natalist policies (i.e., policies supporting high fertility and population growth), but with vastly different objectives and with different visions of society's social and economic state.

According to mercantilist theory, population was one facet of a state's resources and population increase was desirable as a means of furthering the production of goods and armies for the greater power of the state. Revolutionary utopianism advocated state intervention to enhance health and living conditions and support family life. Misery, poverty, and inequality of opportunity were all seen as institutionally based, and the reforms proposed to eliminate them were expected to lead to population growth on a bountiful earth. While far from supporting mercantilist ideas concerning population, Malthus's essay was a direct attack on revolutionary utopianism (Beshers 1967, chap. 1; Petersen 1969, chap. 5).

From the point of view of the subsequent development of population studies and theory, Malthus's work may usefully be viewed as a deliberate, direct assertion and analysis of relationships between population and economy, and as an indirect, perhaps less deliberate, assertion and analysis of relationships between population change and social structure. These relationships still form the core of the subject matter treated by theories of populations and societies, and the questions which Malthus raised even now remain subjects of study and controversy. Moreover, it is the recognized and understood relationships between population and economy, between population and polity, and between population and society which stimulate the ongoing demand for population data, analyses, and projections. In the chapters which follow, we shall refer again to Malthus, his analyses of populations and societies, and his supporters and critics.

3. A BRIEF SKETCH OF WORLD POPULATION HISTORY

In this section we shall review briefly the growth of the world's population and the background of the recent "population explosion." Then, in the following section, we shall sketch the variations in size and structure that obtain among populations in different places and different historical settings. Later in the book we shall try to show that population variations over space and population transformations over time are always accompanied by changes and variations in societies and in social structure. In the chapter which follows, we shall outline a theory which seeks to explain why these concomitant variations occur and how populations and societies are linked.

There are two areas of concern in the study of population history. The first is that of description and analysis—the description of world population, the description of the development of populations in various areas of the world, the description of patterns of settlement, and the analysis of factors involved in population change and growth. Included also is the problem of determining what population setting attends the social, economic, and political history of any area at any given time. "Population setting" refers to the size and composition of a population. Thus, what was the population setting of colonial America? Of Ancient Rome at various stages of its growth and decline? Of England on the eve of the Industrial Revolution? Of France at the time of Louis XIV? Of Japan at the beginning of World War II? The answers are crucial if we are to understand the events of the periods indicated and their causes and consequences.

The second area concerns the scientific interest in population per se. Demography has presented observations on many populations, observations which can indicate much about variations in population size and structure, about factors associated with such variations, about change, types of change, and patterns of change in populations, and about factors that accompany, cause, or result from population change. Thus, the study of colonial America's population growth, expansion of settlement, and changing social institutions may suggest something about the interaction between the geographical and social-structural consequences of population growth generally, with applications for the analysis of current demographic and social change in, say, Australia, the Middle East, or Asiatic Russia. Similarly, the study of marriage patterns in Medieval European towns is instructive about relationships between urbanization, matchmaking, and family formation in general. Unfortunately, as we shall see later, this second area has been largely neglected by all but a few students of population history.

Prehistoric Populations

Almost nothing is known about the world's prehistoric populations. It has been possible to identify human habitation in certain areas from about the early paleolithic through the late neolithic periods, but at most this has indicated only the existence of human activity and given some general insight into the kinds of technological adaptations characteristic of the human groupings found. Accordingly, the earliest identifiable human beings are generally presumed to have lived in nomadic groups, quite small in size, and to have engaged primarily in elementary sustenance activities, such as food-gathering and perhaps hunting or fishing. Humans identified as belonging to later periods are presumed to have engaged in some domestication of animals, some pastoral activity, and eventually some crude agriculture. These inferences derive fundamentally from tools, implements, relics, and drawings found by archaeologists and anthropologists.

However, there is almost never any indication of the size of the human grouping, or of birth and death processes, nor is there much concern with the group's identity or, indeed, with whether the same or different human groupings are found in any given area. Sometimes histories of populations tend to impute certain characteristics of size and structure to prehistoric populations. For example, the groupings of the nomadic hunting and gathering populations are believed to have been very small, while those characterized by some animal domestication or crude agriculture are supposed to have been slightly larger. However, these imputations are based fundamentally on the more contemporary study of so-called primitive or preliterate populations or on that of small-scale nomadic tribes or population groups (McNeil 1963, p. 6; Reinhard and Armengaud 1961, pp. 18-20; Peterson 1961, p. 314; Clark 1947, pp. 274-80), or else they derive from theoretical calculations concerning the size of populations supportable by certain types of economies (Grauman 1959).

We may cite the recent attempt by E. S. Deevey, Jr. to arrive at a quantitative representation of prehistoric population growth (Deevey 1960). According to Deevey's calculations, the total population of the world a million years ago—at around the beginning of human habitation on earth and corresponding to the Lower Paleolithic period in archaeological prehistoric chronology—was about 125,000 persons. Seven hundred thousand years later, in the Middle Paleolithic period, the population of the world reached one million persons, and some 275,000 years after that, in the Upper Paleolithic period (the close of the Paleolithic periods), it reached 3,340,000.

By about 8000 B.C., at approximately the beginning of the Bronze Age or Mesolithic Period, the human population of the planet had reached some 5,320,000 persons. Four thousand years later—by about 4000 B.C., the onset of the Neolithic Period, or Iron Age, which also witnessed the beginnings of agriculture—it reached some 86 million. And by the time of Christ, with a plurality of ancient civilizations based on both agricultural and urban settlements, world population amounted to some 133 million (see table 1.1).

THE NEED FOR MORE INFORMATION. The relative neglect of prehistoric populations and the absence of all but the most modest information or speculation concerning them represents a much more serious lacuna in population history than is generally admitted or recognized. In the first place, although it is true that most of the increase in total world population has taken place in the last three hundred years, nevertheless the great majority of all persons ever alive lived before this period.

TABLE 1.1
Estimated Prehistoric World Population

Years Ago	Cultural Stage	Estimated Population
1,000,000	Lower Paleolithic	125,000
300,000	Middle Paleolithic	1,000,000
25,000	Upper Paleolithic	3,340,000
10,000	Mesolithic (Bronze Age)	5,320,000
6,000	Neolithic (Iron Age)	86,000,000
2,000	C. E.	133,000,000

Thus, the great bulk of population history is in fact the history of pre-1650 populations. An estimate by Deevey suggests that there were as many as *36 billion* Paleolithic hunters and gatherers, i.e. 36 billion persons living sometime in the Paleolithic Period, from about 1,000,000 years ago until about five to ten thousand years ago.[1]

In the second place, there is a broad agreement among archaeologists and anthropologists that some fundamental cultural and technological transformations—such as the beginnings of agriculture, urban settlement, and writing—can be identified and located in prehistoric time and space. Regardless of whether the advent of such developments in a given place reflects their origins, or whether it reflects only their diffusion, arrival, and adoption in the area, the *fact* of such transformations, and of at least some of their effects and ramifications, seems to be well established. Thus, for example, the beginnings of agriculture have been identified in Palestine (Albright 1965; Watson 1965) and in Mesopotamia (Braidwood 1960; Greene 1962, chap. 4; Adams 1964; Child 1951, chap. 5) as having occurred in the ninth to seventh millenniums B.C. Similarly, the beginnings of urban settlement and sociopolitical organization have been traced in early Mesopotamia to the beginning of the fifth millennium B.C. and, apparently of independent origin, in prehistoric central Mexico around 100 B.C. (Adams 1966). Other prehistoric and protohistoric urban settlements which have been identified include those in Crete in the second millennium B.C., in the Nile and Indus valleys in the third millennium B.C., in Etruscan Italy in the first millennium B.C., and in China in the second millennium B.C. (Clark 1967; Braidwood and Willey 1962; Duncan 1964).

Much earlier than the origins of agriculture or urban settlement, climatological and other environmental changes are known to have taken place. These must have affected prehistoric man and his ways of survival

---

[1] On the basis of more recent computations by Keyfitz (C. F. Keyfitz 1966), it can be estimated that about 14 billion persons were born from the beginning of human existence some one million years ago until about 5000 B.C. But, by Keyfitz's calculations, this figure also represents some 20 percent of all the persons ever born on earth and just under the number living in the 310 years from 1650 through 1960.

and sustenance. Moreover, prehistoric technologies are known to have undergone changes and development, with man accumulating both knowledge and implements over time (Butzer 1964, chap. 28).

These prehistorical transformations were multitudinous, and each of them—whether societal, technological, or cultural—affected population or was affected by it, or both, but of this virtually nothing is known. Tentatively, we hypothesize that many of the transformations originated as innovations invented or adopted in response to the pressures of population growth. Also, there is good reason to assume that the central demographic process of prehistory was migration. Many of the aforementioned transformations may have resulted from migratory movements, the latter in turn occurring in response to pressures of sustenance and survival.

The lives and times of prehistoric populations—whether the number of people was 14 billion or 36 billion—stretch over a period of hundreds of thousands of years to comprise a multitude of population histories, even the barest outline of which are still entirely unknown. There is little doubt that scientific population studies would be greatly advanced by the study of prehistoric relationships between populations and societies: surely such studies could suggest or test hypotheses about both the causes and consequences of population change—hypotheses which would be relatively less qualified and restricted by the considerations that characterize the more complex social, economic, and political relationships of later periods. This awaits primarily the *interest* of archaeologists and other specialists in prehistory in population studies and in the development of approaches and techniques for estimating population, composition, and movement. An outstanding example of what is needed is Nougier's study of prehistoric France (Nougier 1954).

Population in the Ancient World and Middle Ages

Compared to the information available on prehistoric populations, much more is known about those of the ancient world. For example, we have more comparatively substantial information on ancient populations of the Mediterranean, the Indian peninsula, China, and Middle and South America. Many of these populations seem to have been characterized by political and economic integration on a considerable scale, and many numbered in the thousands and even more. A population of four or five million has been attributed to the region of ancient Mesopotamia, and it has been estimated that the population of Ancient Egypt reached some seven or eight million, roughly equivalent to a density of 200 persons per square kilometer.

Historians have estimated the population of ancient Athens in the fifth century B.C. at about 200,000 (Clark 1967; Reinhard and Armengaud 1961). The population of Rome was about 130,000 in 508 B.C., 337,000 in 164 B.C., and 900,000 in 70 B.C. One author, Tenny Frank, has estimated the population of all of ancient Italy around 19 B.C. to be 3.5 million (cited in Clark 1967) while the best-known historian of Roman population, Julius Beloch, has estimated the same population at six million (Beloch 1886). Ancient Gaul, according to near-contemporary scholars, had a population of between five and 8.9 million. Despite these estimates, however, the gaps in our knowledge of population and settlement patterns in ancient and premodern times are so great as to render almost impossible any attempt to estimate the total population of the world for dates prior to around 1650, much less to trace the development and growth of world population and its components.

Estimates of the total population of the world in Roman times, ranging from 200 to 256 million, are cited by J. J. Spengler and O. D. Duncan (1956, p. 1), by W. S. Woytinsky and E. S. Woytinsky (1953, p. 34), and by Colin Clark (1967, chap. 3). There is evidence that population declines of considerable scale occurred in the transition from the beginning of the Roman Empire in Europe to the more localized polities and societies of the Middle Ages (Clark 1967; Reinhard and Armengaud 1961).

In the course of the Middle Ages populations grew, but very slowly, and often the growth was wiped out or reversed by recurring famines, wars, or plagues. Great famines were experienced throughout India in 650 A.D.; over the entire world in 879; in India in 941, 1022, and 1033; in England in 1005; and in all of Europe in 1016. A seven-year famine depopulated Egypt between 1064 and 1072, and many of the German lands are said to have lost half their population from hunger in 1125. From 1148 to 1159, a period of eleven years, there was famine in India, and 1162 witnessed a universal famine (Ross 1927, chap. 3). Malaria is believed to have been primarily responsible for the reduction in the size of ancient Near Eastern populations, and the Black Death of 1348-1375 is thought to have reduced the population of England from about 5 million to 2.3 million (Clark 1967). Spain suffered continuous warfare from the eighth to the fifteenth centuries, and her population declined from a peak of about eight million in the second century A.D. to 3.6 million in 600; it took until late in the thirteenth century for the population to reach the eight-million mark again (Clark 1967).

Such patterns characterized a considerable part of the world until very recently. At the same time, however, there was some improvement in agriculture, food preservation, and transport and communication, and this, combined with the increasing use of money generated the production of food for markets rather than for subsistence only. Also, a considerable number of ancient cities—such as Lacydon (Marseilles), Alexandria, Rome, Athens, and Byzantium—were revived and rebuilt, and many new cities were founded (for example, London, Paris, Bruges, Cologne, Venice, Florence, Genoa, and Milan). By 1650, the onset of the modern period of population growth, world population had reached about 500 million.

World Population Since 1650

Two sets of estimates of the population of the world and its continents from 1650 to 1900 have achieved wide acceptance and are conventionally quoted as the best available ones for the period. The first is by W. F. Willcox (1931) and is reproduced in table 1.2, with earlier dates as well and the second is by A. M. Carr-Saunders (1936a).[2] The usually accepted estimates of world population in the twentieth century are those prepared by the United Nations; these are also reproduced in table 1.2.

Table 1.2 shows that world population increased almost eightfold from 1650 to 1971—from under 470 million to just over 3,700 million. Thus, while it took all of human history prior to 1650 to reach a world population of one-half billion, the second half-billion was achieved in less than 200 years, the third in fifty years, the fourth in only 30 years, the fifth in just over 20 years, the sixth in a little more than a decade, and the seventh in eight or nine years. The growth rate of the world's population has increased from about 0.3 percent per annum in the period from 1650 to 1750, to 2.0 percent per annum around 1971.

From the same table it is evident that population growth has not taken place uniformly in the several continents of the globe. In the two centuries from 1650 to 1850, the population of the area of European settlement—including Europe, Asiatic Russia, North and South America, and Oceania—virtually tripled, while the population of Asia, excluding Russia, increased by about 150 percent and the population of Africa did not increase at all, and may even have decreased. However, in the period from 1900 to 1971, the population of Europe increased by only 68 percent, while that of Africa grew by 151 percent, that of Asia by 146 percent, that of North America by 182 percent, and that of Latin America by 362 percent. In 1971, the total population of the world was growing at an annual rate of 2.0 percent, but the rate for Europe was only about 0.8 percent, while that of Asia was 2.3 percent (a rate at which the population doubles every 31 years), that of Africa was 2.7 percent, and that of Latin America was about 2.9 percent (a rate at which the population doubles every 24 years).

2 Carr-Saunders differs from Willcox chiefly in placing the 1650 world population total at 545 million; Willcox places it at 470 million. Clark's 1650 estimate is 516 million (1967).

TABLE 1.2

Estimates of World Population by Regions, A.D. 14 to 1971 (in millions)

	World Total	Africa	Northern America	Latin America	Asia[a]	Europe[a]	Oceania
A.D. 14	256	23		3	184	44.5	1
350	254	30		5	185	32.6	1
600	237	37		7	168	24.3	1
800	261	43		10	173	34.2	1
1000	280	50		13	172	44.2	1
1200	384	61		23	242	57.5	1
1340	378	70		29	186	90.5	2
1500	427	85	1	40	225	73.8	2
1600	498	95	1	14	305	95	2
1650	470	100	1	7	257	103	2
1750	694	100	1	10	437	144	2
1800	919	100	6	23	595	193	2
1850	1,091	100	26	33	656	274	2
1900	1,571	141	81	63	857	423	6
1920	1,811	141	117	91	966	487	9
1930	2,070	164	134	108	1,120	534	10
1940	2,295	191	144	130	1,244	575	11
1960	3,005	278	199	213	1,660	639	16
1970	3,632	344	228	283	2,056	705	19
1971	3,706	354	229	291	2,104	711	20

SOURCES: Figures for 1400 to 1600 A.D. are from C. Clark (1967, table III); for 1650 to 1910 from the United Nations Department of Economic and Social Affairs, Population Division (1953, chapt. II, table 2); for 1920, from the U.N. *Demographic Yearbook 1962* (1963, table 2); and for 1930 to 1969 from the U.N. *Demographic Yearbook 1969* (1970, table 1).

[a]Estimates for Asia exclude Asiatic USSR. Estimates for Europe include Asiatic USSR.

Changing Patterns of Births and Deaths

Both the phenomenal growth of the world's population in the modern period and the differences between patterns of growth in the several continents are accounted for mainly by changing patterns of births and deaths. The two components of population growth are natural increase, which is the difference between the numbers of births and deaths, and net migration, which is the difference between the number of immigrants and emigrants. In the case of the total population of the world, of course, only natural increase need be considered. And in the case of the separate continents, it is only in certain periods in North and South America and Oceania that net migration has accounted for a substantial part of population growth.

Systematic data on population size, numbers of births and deaths, and migratory movements are simply nonexistent for most countries for most years. However, long statistical series available for a number of countries, notably those of Scandinavia, permit us to reconstruct the fer-

tility and mortality pattern that characterized Europe at about the time
of the Industrial Revolution. In addition, the census-taking and statistical
activities now conducted throughout the world offer much data concerning most recent trends, although they hardly present a complete body of
information.

On the basis of historical data from European countries and data
collected more recently in countries of every location and type, it appears
that preindustrial populations are characterized by both very high mortality and very high fertility rates. A crude birth rate [3] of between 30 and
40 per thousand of population may have characterized the European
countries in preindustrial periods, and even higher rates—between 40 and
50 per thousand—characterize unindustrialized countries today. The
crude death rate [4] in preindustrial Europe would fluctuate very widely
from year to year in accordance with climate, wars, famines, pestilence,
disease, epidemics, etc., but over the years it averaged around 30 to 35
deaths per thousand. Even higher crude death rates may have characterized non-European preindustrial countries until fairly recently, but so
much improvement has since taken place that current national crude
death rates nowhere exceed 32 per thousand. Under past high-fertility—
high-mortality conditions, preindustrial populations could grow only
very slowly and, indeed, in many periods they actually declined in size.

French demographers have used the term "demographic crises"
(Meuvret 1965) to denote periods of natural *decrease* (periods of at least
several months in which there is an excess of deaths over births). They
note that these periods are typically sudden, intense, and of short duration, and that they are a recurring feature of premodern demographic
history. P. Guillaume and J. P. Poussou indicate that there were five
serious *national* demographic crises in France at the close of the premodern period: in 1630-1631, 1649-1652, 1661-1662, 1693-1694, and 1709-
1710; they also suggest innumerable regional demographic crises. But,
the eighteenth century witnessed a marked decline in the frequency,
length, and gravity of "demographic crises" in France (Guillaume and
Poussou 1970).

Much the same preindustrial-postindustrial picture is reflected in
data from England. The numbers of burials, marriages, and baptisms in

---

3 The Crude Birth Rate is the annual number of births per thousand of population, computed as:

$$\frac{\text{total number of births in a given year}}{\text{average total population during the year}} \times 1{,}000$$

4 The Crude Death Rate is the annual number of deaths per thousand of population, computed as:

$$\frac{\text{total number of deaths in a given year}}{\text{average total population alive during the year}} \times 1{,}000$$

The Crude Rate of Natural Increase is simply the (Crude Birth Rate) minus (Crude
Death Rate).

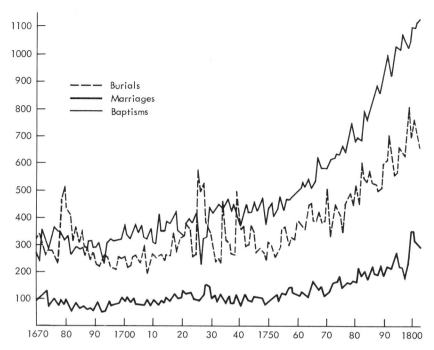

FIGURE 1.2. Burials, marriages, and baptisms in Vale of Trent, England, 1670–1800. Source: Guillaume and Poussou 1970, p. 156.

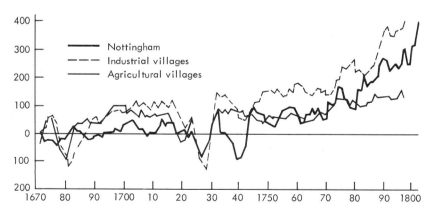

FIGURE 1.3. Population growth in the town of Nottingham, in "industrial" villages, and in "agricultural" villages in the Vale of Trent, 1670–1800. Source: Guillaume and Poussou 1970, p. 156.

the Vale of Trent, England, from 1670 to 1800, are shown in figure 1.2. From 1680 to 1690, and from 1728 to 1732, and again in 1736 and 1744, the number of burials exceeds the numbers of baptisms. Figure 1.3 shows population increase and decrease in the town of Nottingham, in "industrial" villages, and in "agricultural" villages in the Vale of Trent for the same period. Prior to 1750, the growth is very slow, and sometimes declines in population occur. After 1750, the growth accelerates, especially in the "industrial villages" and in the town of Nottingham.

Demographic Transitions

Technological changes in the production of food, and technological, social, economic, and political changes resulting in improvements in the distribution and availability of food, are believed to have effected a downward inflection and decline in death rates. In food production, a variety of biological and mechanical improvements greatly increased agricultural yields and the certainty of a harvest and also made it possible to cultivate previously barren ground. No less important was the change in patterns of communication, exchange, and trade connected with the emergence of broader regional, and even national, food markets. While increased yields operated to make food cheaper and more readily accessible to all income levels, the improved communications and expanded market reduced isolation, abolished local subsistence economies, and greatly reduced the vulnerability to crop failure and famine.[5]

But whatever the causes, a decline in death rates did take place in Northern and Western Europe beginning in about the second half of the eighteenth century and continuing until the first half of the twentieth. In the same period birth rates remained high, and the increasing gap between birth and death rates generated rates of population growth unprecedented in human history. Beginning in the second half of the nineteenth century, birth rates also began to decline in Northern and Western Europe, narrowing the gap between birth and death rates and diminishing the rate of population growth.

This process, represented in data for Sweden in figure 1.4, was repeated in other European countries, though not at identical times. In general, the beginning of the decline in mortality was associated in time with the beginning of industrialization, greatly improved agrculture, the consolidation of nation-states, and the improvement of transportation and communication. The entire process described above has been called the "demographic transition," and the general model of the process is typically viewed as having three stages:

1. the stage of high fertility and high mortality
2. the stage of declining mortality and high or medium fertility
3. the stage of low fertility and low mortality

5 Eversley offers a relevant discussion of problems confronting research on historical relationships between population and economic growth (see Eversley 1965a, pp. 23–69; and Eversley 1965b).

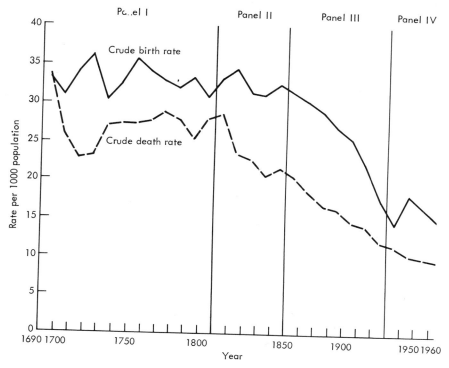

FIGURE 1.4. Sweden: Crude birth rate and crude death rate, 1691–1963.
Source: Table 1.3.

The first stage, characterized by both high fertility and high mortality, has been called the "high growth potential" stage, because a decline in mortality, in the absence of other changes, would imply very high rates of population growth. Panel I in figure 1.4 shows that Sweden was characterized by this "high growth potential" in the period prior to 1810.

The second stage (panels II and III in figure 1.4), which may be called the stage of "transitional growth," is characterized by continued high fertility but low or declining mortality. Figure 1.4 shows that Sweden enjoyed such a "transitional growth" from about 1810 to 1930, a period in which her population increased from 2.4 to 6.1 million. In this second stage of demographic transition, not only does the population grow very rapidly, but it also undergoes changes in age composition that are associated with increased longevity and especially with much greater infant and child survival. Thus, there is typically a slightly increased proportion of elderly persons (aged, say, 60 and over), which may be imputed in a general way to increased longevity, and a rather more marked increase in the proportion of young persons (under about 20 years) which derives from a great reduction in infant and child mortality. Conversely, there is a contraction of the proportion of persons aged, say, 20 to 59.[6] The stage of "transitional growth" is often partitioned into two sub-stages—one in which high fertility is maintained while mortality declines, one in which *both* fertility and mortality decline. In the case of Sweden, the first sub-stage would be from about 1810 through 1860 (panel II in fig. 1.4), and the second from 1860 to 1930 (panel III, fig. 1.4).

The third stage, characterized by both low mortality and low fertility, has been called the stage of "incipient decline." Fertility in this stage is presumably subjected to a considerable measure of deliberate control. The term "incipient decline" is used because populations experiencing this stage are capable of depressing fertility to levels so low as to produce negative natural increase (an excess of deaths over births) and hence a decline in population size. France experienced negative natural increase in the period from 1937 through 1945, and Belgium did so from 1940 through 1944.

No population has been characterized by the low fertility rates of the third stage without recourse to one or another mode of intervention, whether this be the prevention or postponement of marriage and mating itself or of pregnancies or births within marriage. Thus, populations with such low fertility rates are assumed to have access to customs and techniques of deliberately depressing fertility to the conceivable extent (probably under extreme economic or political conditions) of making the annual number of deaths exceed the number of births. Figure 1.4 shows that Sweden has been in the third stage since about 1930.

The most recent expositions of the theory of "demographic transition" have made the third stage more elaborate. The major addition has been the hypothesis of unstable fertility rates—i.e., fertility rates in accordance with economic, social, and political trends and cycles while mortality rates remain low.

In its general outlines, this model does *describe* the course of population trends in many European countries, even if some modifications are required in certain individual cases. Its operation has been thought to be related to, and in part caused by, industrialization, urbanization, and the spread of literacy and education, trends with which it has certainly been associated in the European case. But a major issue confronting demographers, and indeed a wide range of scientists and administrators, is whether or not the model of the "demographic transition" is applicable to newly developing countries, and whether declining birth rates will in fact follow the already spectacularly declining mortality rates and phenomenal growth of the populations of the underdeveloped world. (For

6 Relationships between a population's fertility, mortality, and age composition are discussed later in this volume. For a precise and detailed analysis of these relationships, see Pressat 1972.

TABLE 1.3

Recent Trends in Crude Rates of Birth, Death, and Natural Increase: Selected Countries, 1940–1967

	Crude Death Rates			Crude Birth Rates			Crude Rates of Natural Increase		
	1940	1960	1967	1940	1960	1967	1940	1960	1967
Mexico	23.2	11.4	8.9	44.3	45.0	42.7	21.1	33.6	33.8
Costa Rica	17.3	8.6	6.9	44.6	42.9	39.2	27.3	34.3	32.3
Chile	21.6	11.9	10.4[a]	33.4	35.4	30.6[a]	11.8	23.5	20.2[a]
Venezuela	16.6	8.0	6.7	36.0	49.6	41.3	19.4	41.6	34.6
Ceylon	20.6	9.1	8.2	35.8	37.0	31.5	15.2	27.9	23.3
Malaya	20.1	9.5	7.6[a]	40.7	37.7	37.3[a]	20.6	28.2	29.7[a]
Singapore	20.9	6.3	5.4	45.0	38.7	25.8	24.1	32.4	20.4
Japan	16.8	7.6	6.7	29.4	17.2	19.3	12.6	9.6	12.6

SOURCE: Dorn 1963, pp. 7–29.

[a]1966

a recent summary of the current debate, see Drake 1969, pp. 1-13.) The data in table 1.3 are relevant to this question.

The eight countries represented in table 1.3 were all characterized by fairly high crude death rates until 1940, and in all cases the death rate fell very steeply thereafter. In Japan the crude birth rate has also fallen sharply since 1940, and the crude rate of natural increase has not exceeded 12.6 per thousand in the years shown. But all the other countries have been characterized by sustained high fertility—even after mortality declined—and hence by high, and *increasing* crude rates of natural increase. Thus for Mexico, the crude rate of natural increase rose from 21.1 per thousand in 1940 (roughly corresponding to a doubling time of 33 years) to 33.8 per thousand (doubling time of 21 years) in the face of continued high birth rates and lowered death rates.

We shall find it useful in the rest of this book to refer to demographic *transitions* rather than to *the* demographic transition. Similarly, we shall refer to population transformations. This is because we view demographic transitions and population transformations as recurring phenomena. Some major objectives of the study of populations are to describe and analyze the variations in such transitions and transformations and to investigate their correlates, causes, and consequences. Or, put in terms of how we view such diagrams as figure 1.4, we are interested, both explicitly and implicitly, in a variety of their aspects: in the inflections of their death rate curves, the inflections in their birth rate curves, the spread between the curves, the time intervals and time lags between the curves, the movements of these intervals and lags, and in general in what we see as a *class* of sociohistorical phenomena—the nature, varieties, causes, and consequences of the zigs, zags, wigs, and wags of such diagrams. Our interest, then, extends beyond the question of whether "the demographic transition" is a general pattern or strictly a European one. It extends to the range of variations in such patterns and to their causes and consequences.

4. POPULATION HISTORIES AND HISTORICAL DEMOGRAPHY

It should be clear by now that the poverty of relevant data makes it extremely difficult to describe and analyze world population history. However, there are many individual populations for which fairly long statistical series are available (e.g., Finland, Sweden and Massachusetts), others for which studies and estimates permitting fairly detailed portrayal and analysis have been carried out (e.g., France, Japan and Italy).

Techniques and Data

Techniques in the study of population history include various types of population counts, counts of family units, measures of land area, and the use of information about cities or specific places of settlement (Hollingsworth 1969). Counts of individuals may include counts of entire populations or of individuals in given categories (for example, soldiers or taxpayers). In many cases, estimates of the total population of an area must be made on the basis of some theory or item of knowledge that relates the population of given categories to the total population. Often, where no counts of individuals are available, some count of families, households, or other units may be. In such cases, estimates of total populations must be made by applying some factor to inflate the units which are in fact counted. Thus, if the number of families is known, multiplying the average number of persons per family to that number will yield an estimate of the total number of persons in the population.

Estimates of city populations have sometimes been based on knowledge of the land area of the city. More specifically, the total number of areal units in the city is multiplied by the known or assumed density per land unit to arrive at an estimate of the city's population. In the case of countries, regions, or states for which there is no evidence of total population size, estimates may sometimes be based on the known size of cities. Such estimates use some city-hinterland ratio—or city-surrounding region relationship—to arrive at the size of the population surrounding the city.

A large variety of censuses, registers, or other counts may be available in more or less detail. Church and parish registers have been a particularly important source of local population data. They sometimes give not only the total population but also many details of age, sex, and even occupations, or population groups.

Two very promising approaches to the use of parish registers for historical demographic studies have been initiated and greatly developed in recent years. The first is called *aggregative analysis;* and the second, *family reconstitution.* Aggregative analysis uses parish registers to count the incidences of various phenomena—baptisms, burials, marriages, etc.,— with the amount of detail depending upon both what is available in the register and what the requirements and resources of the study are. Family reconstitution—a very much more laborious technique—brings together the parish register's scattered information about members of each family (or each of a sample of families) to arrive at as detailed a description as possible of the parish's chief demographic characteristics. Aggregative analysis enables the researcher to discover and describe quantitatively such phenomena as birth trends in a parish, while family reconstitution permits him to analyze the causal relationships between phenomena, e.g., the relationship of changing number of births to age at marriages (Wrigley 1966).

From the point of view of the portrayal of world population in any point in history, or of the growth of world population or individual populations, the sort of data described above may be quite inadequate. Again, our knowledge of actual populations prior to very recent decades is scanty indeed, and we can only guess or make indirect estimates with regard to populations in most areas of the world at most times in history. However, from the point of view of scientific interest and generalization, virtually any fact, estimate, or reconstruction about population is of some interest and value, the more so insofar as it may be related to historical, social, economic, or political conditions characterizing the time and places involved.

There are a number of countries for which modern census-type population statistics exist with reasonable completeness and comparability. Indeed, the statistics for some start as early as two centuries ago. For example, information on Sweden's population size, births, and deaths dates from 1750, and data from Swedish censuses and population registers permit a detailed study of migration since 1895. The United States census of population, which is constitutionally prescribed, has been carried out decennially since 1790, and over the years it has been expanding consistently to include more and more geographic, social, economic, and cultural information about the population and its aggregates. Thus, the U.S. series on total population, geographic distribution, and urban-rural populations start with 1790, while data on such details as age, sex, marital status, occupation, country of birth, and immigrant status begin at later dates. Other countries with relatively long histories of census-type data collection include Canada, Norway, England, Italy, and France.

Rather long, and sometimes fairly detailed, series of population enumerations or estimates are available for a number of national and subnational populations. Often these are neither standardized in their methods for deriving estimates nor comparable over time with respect to the bounds of the populations estimated. For example, one estimate in a series may be based upon a count of households, the next estimate may be based upon a complete count of adult males, a succeeding one upon tax records, etc. Nevertheless, there has been considerable interest in such series for their portrayal, at least, of the general direction and pace of various population developments. Among the examples that come to mind are a series of estimates of the population of China, by provinces, dating from 500 B.C., estimates of the population of Japan for the eighth century A.D. and subsequent periods, and estimates of the population of the Indian subcontinent (today, India and Pakistan) dating from the early seventeenth century. Similarly, series of population enumerations and estimates exist for Medieval Russia, Ancient Greece, and Ancient Rome, and for certain towns in England, France and Italy. Such series are originated, for example, in tax records, other administrative records, and parish registers, and often offer comparable data on population distribution, with regard to mortality, marriage, and fertility.

Some Representative Studies

There are a large number of historical studies which focus on the structure, changes, and other characteristics of populations with regard to some specific historical interval. For example, there are historical studies of births, deaths, and changing population distribution in Europe prior to the period of modern censuses. P. Deprez has summarized studies of population size, marriages, births, and deaths in eighteenth-century Flanders, paying special attention to regional differences (Deprez 1965). Similarly, there are historical studies of marriage, family size, and birth control. In a classic study, L. Henry found evidence of fertility control among sixteenth and seventeenth-century Genevan bourgeoisie (Henry 1956); and E. A. Wrigley studied birth control in Colyton, England, in the seventeenth century (Wrigley 1966). Finally, a number of investigators have been concerned with population policy in specific historical settings. Thus, E. P. Hutchinson traced the background of Swedish population policy and thought—largely pro-natalist—in the eighteenth century (Hutchinson 1959) and F. H. A. Micklewright studied the evolution of English neo-Malthusianism in the nineteenth century (Micklewright 1961).

Historical demographers have often limited their efforts to the specification, description, and analysis of some given population at some given time—in other words, to the first kind of issue in the study of population history. They have sought to establish the facts concerning some historical population or its changes and have often concerned themselves with the historical causes or effects of the changes and developments so established. Thus, J. C. Russell's important reconstructions of British medieval population size and change (Clark 1967), J. Beloch's studies of the populations of ancient Greece and Rome (Beloch 1886), and Reinhard's studies (Reinhard and Armengaud 1961) of world population history are primarily intended as descriptions of the demographic settings surrounding the events and histories of the places and periods involved. Only recently have historical demographers addressed themselves to the more general problems of population studies. And only recently have other demographers begun to draw upon the investigations of historical demography: now, finally, they are using historical data to formulate, document, and test generalizations about populations and about the cultural, social, economic, and political phenomena that result from, or attend population trends, changes, and transformations. The studies cited below, some discussed more fully in later chapters, illustrate the fruitful use of historical data.

FRIEDLANDER'S COMPARATIVE STUDY OF DEMOGRAPHIC TRANSITIONS. In his recent comparative study of population growth and redistribution in European countries (Friedlander 1969), D. Friedlander re-examines the relevance of the theory of demographic transition (see Section 3, above) to the great changes which took place in population growth during certain periods of the eighteenth, nineteenth, and early twentieth centuries. Drawing upon historical series for England, Wales, Sweden, France, Germany, Japan, and the United States, he is able to show the usefulness and theoretical power of introducing the urban-rural residence distinction, urban-rural fertility and population growth differentials, and rural-to-urban migration into the analysis of demographic transitions. He demonstrates that in countries where it could take place, rural-to-urban migration or overseas emigration absorbed excess rural population growth and provided an alternative to rural fertility decline. But where rural-to-urban migration or overseas emigration was not possible on a large scale, rural fertility declined early in the process of the demographic transition.

THE COALE STUDY OF MARRIAGE AND FERTILITY PATTERNS. Concerned with the problem of variation and change in patterns of marriage, age at marrige, and family formation, A. J. Coale and his colleagues have studied series of statistical data that give the composition by age, sex, and marital status of populations of a great many European countries, provinces, and smaller geographic or administrative units, all in preindustrial or early industrial periods (Coale 1969). While no persuasive, highly general, formulation of causes of shifting marriage patterns has yet emerged from it, the study does produce clear support for the hypothesis that widespread and successful control of marital fertility encourages early marriage. Even more important, it disproves a number of previous hypotheses concerning marriage and fertility and shows others to be highly inadequate.

MORONI'S STUDIES OF MARRIAGES BETWEEN BLOOD RELATIVES.   In a series of studies conducted by A. Moroni, records of ecclesiastical dispensations for consanguineous marriages were used to plot relative frequencies of such marriages in Italy, Sicily, and Sardinia from the sixteenth century onward (Moroni 1969). These studies show that after very low proportions of consanguinity in the seventeenth and eighteenth centuries, there was a sharp increase through the nineteenth century and a rapid decrease prior to World War II. Moroni suggests that the increase in consanguinity at the beginning of the nineteenth century was caused by both demographic and socioeconomic factors. In about 1800, rural society in Italy began to assign great value to the possession of land, and Moroni connects this to the increase in marriages between cousins. By marrying relatives rather than nonrelatives, people could combine their landholdings rather than further divide them. The subsequent disappearance of cousin-marriages was coincident with industrial development in Italy. Large landholdings were no longer profitable. More generally, Moroni advances the hypothesis that in rural societies, marriages between first cousins represent a societal defense against the division of the land property on which the stability of the familial economy is founded.

VARIATIONS IN POPULATION PATTERNS: CLARK'S STUDY OF GROWTH RATES AND THOMAS'S WORK ON MIGRATION.   The mobilization of demographic histories for the scientific study of populations and their relation to social structure requires, first, recognition of the *variation* in historical patterns, and in sequences, of growth, changing density, migration, and changing population structure. Two remarkable tables prepared and published by Colin Clark (1967) summarize sequences of decadal growth rates for national populations before and after 1800 (see table 1.4).

These tables show examples of—

1. virtually no change in population size (less than a two percent increase or decrease over the decade). Among the countries to which this applies are England and Wales, 1710–1740; Sweden, 1700–1721; Iceland, 1750–1800; Mauritius, 1800–1910; India, 1890–1900 and 1910–1920; France, 1880–1910 and 1930–1950; and others.
2. great increases in population size (20 percent or more during a decade)—e.g., the United States, 1620–1910; Puerto Rico, 1765–1812 and 1930–1940; Brazil since 1870; Egypt, 1880–1900 and since 1940; Argentina, 1800–1820, 1850–1930, and 1940–1950;

Venezuela since 1920; Hong Kong since 1910; the Philippines since 1930; Thailand since 1920; New Zealand since 1920.

3. substantial decreases in population size (five percent or more during a decade)—e.g., Ireland, 1840–1870, 1880–1900, 1920–1930, and 1950–1960; USSR, 1940–1950; Martinique, 1900–1910; and France, 1910–1920.

In addition, the tables indicate examples of different kinds of growth sequences:

4. declines followed by substantial growth—e.g., Iceland, 1700–1750; Rumania, 1880–1910; USSR, 1940–1960; Hawaii, 1850–1910.
5. increases followed by substantial declines—e.g., Mexico, 1890–1920; Ireland, 1800–1860.
6. various combinations of alternating rates of growth.

Obviously the consideration of regional, provincial, or other more localized populations would greatly multiply the numbers of examples of all types. In all cases, what is in question is not only the "cause" of the "effects" of a particular population increase, decrease, or growth sequence, but, especially, the common features of population changes and sequences of given types. The causes and consequences associated with given *types* of population growth patterns have yet to be investigated systematically.

In Dorothy S. Thomas's classic study of Swedish population movements (Thomas 1941), detailed rates of in-migration, out-migration, and net internal migration were presented for Swedish community-type groups from 1895 through 1933 (see table 1.5). Rates of in-migration per 1,000 of average population varied from 12.5 in 1895 in heavily forested communities to 118.0 in the same year in the large industrial towns (where "average population" refers to the average during the year for which the rate is given. A more detailed explanation is given in chapter 5). Rates of out-migration varied from 18.1 per 1,000 in the "wooded communities" in 1895, to 83.5 in nonindustrial small towns in 1904–1906, to 58.0 in 1933 in rural industrial places that had become towns in the period between 1915 and 1924. Rates of net internal migration varied from −10.3 per 1,000 for agricultural communities in 1895 to +30.8 for large industrial towns in 1895. Here, too, many variations in sequences of migration rates can be found.

Thomas classifies community types as follows:

1. Agricultural
2. Rural mixed
3. Rural industrial
4. Large industrial towns

TABLE 1.4
*Decadal Percentage Rates of Population Growth
Before and After 1800*

America:		1735–50	11
		1750–60	18
Puerto Rico		1760–70	15
		1770–80	14
1765–1812	34	1780–90	12
		1790–1800	14
United States			
		France	
1620–30	128		
1630–40	390	1700–55	2
1640–50	86	1755–62	4
1650–60	63	1762–76	6
1660–70	35	1776–1800	4
1670–80	36		
1680–90	36	*Iceland*	
1690–1700	29		
1700–10	32	1700–35	–4
1710–20	41	1735–50	7
1720–30	35	1750–75	0
1730–40	44	1775–1800	–1
1740–50	29		
1750–60	36	*Ireland*	
1760–70	35		
1770–80	29	1687–1712	11
1780–90	41	1712–18	6
1790–1800	35	1718–32	3
		1732–54	3
Asia:		1754–67	7
		1767–72	6
China		1772–81	15
Early periods of growth		1781–90	17
	4–12	1790–1821	17
Korea		*Italy*	
		1700–70	4
1700–1800	8	1770–1820	4
1648–1807	10		
		Norway	
Europe:		1700–35	2
		1735–50	2
Czechoslovakia		1750–75	8
		1775–1800	9
1700–50	5		
1750–1800	8	*Russia*	
		1722–62	8
Denmark		1762–96	13
1700–25	2		
1725–50	2	*Scotland*	
1750–75	2	1700–50	4
1775–1800	4	1750–90	5
		1790–1800	7
England and Wales			
1700–10	2	*Spain*	
1710–20	0		
1720–30	–1	1700–54	7
1730–40	0	1754–69	8
1740–50	3	1769–87	7
1750–60	7	1787–97	2
1760–70	7		
1770–80	7	*Sweden*	
1780–90	10	1635–1700	7
1790–1800	11	1700–21	–1
		1721–35	13
Finland		1735–50	4
		1750–75	6
1700–21	14	1775–1800	6
1721–35	17		

TABLE 1.4 con't.

	1800–10	1810–20	1820–30	1830–40	1840–50	1850–60	1860–70	1870–80	1880–90	1890–1900	1900–10	1910–20	1920–30	1930–40	1940–50	1950–60
Africa																
Algeria							12 →			14 →	17	4	13	18	16	23
Egypt											17	13	12	14	21	27
Mauritius							2		26 →		−1	2	9	3	11	37
Tunis								14 →	3	0		8	15	20	25	18
Union of S. Africa (whites)													20	20	21	18
Union of S. Africa total population											22	16	25	21	20	27
America																
Argentine	24 →			19 →		45 →		46	49	35	34	21	34	19	21	19
Bahamas						29	10		9	12	4	−5	13	15	13	33
Bermuda										17	8	6	38	0	15	19
Brazil	14	15	13	17	16	17	15	21	21	17	25	22	22	22	26	36
British Guiana						16	31	30	10	27	25	22	4	11	23	34
British Honduras									12	6 →		12	13	20	18	30
Canada						33		17	12	11	8	12	13	11	17	30
Chile						23	14	17	14	10	17	22	19	16	22	25
Colombia													22	22	25	25
Costa Rica									8				18	24	29	46
Cuba										−3	39	24	18	17	20	23
Ecuador													26	27	30	35
Greenland									2 →		13	7	20	19	21	43
Guadeloupe						11		17 →			17	7	16	29	22	31
Guatemala												8	16	25	27	34
Martinique								8	7	12		7	11	11	16	25
Mexico								8	7	12	−15	29	19	19	30	35
Nicaragua						5 →		8	15	19	11	−5	16	27	28	39
Panama												37	22	21	33	40
Peru						5 →		20 →/14 →				16	15	17	21	27
Puerto Rico									9	16	16	16	19	21	18	7
Surinam													26	14	22	47
United States	36	33	35	33	36	35	27	30	26	21	21	16	16	7	15	18
Uruguay									40	32	21	30	27	15	12	17
Venezuela								22	12	18	21		28	20	34	48
West Indies total	6 →						14	15	10	14 →	22		16	18	18	18
incl. Jamaica											3		18	20	16	14
incl. Trinidad											10		4	18	33	30
Asia																
Brunei												10	20	20	18	83
Burma											15		11	15	15	12
Cambodia															22 →	33
Ceylon									9	18	15	9	17	14	28	29
China (Taiwan)													24	30	27	39

TABLE 1.4 con't.

	1800–10	1810–20	1820–30	1830–40	1840–50	1850–60	1860–70	1870–80	1880–90	1890–1900	1900–10	1910–20	1920–30	1930–40	1940–50	1950–60
Cyprus											15	13	12	16	21	16
Federation of Malaya											41	24	30	25	16	33
Hongkong											18	37	27	117	27	32
India								23 ↔			7	1	11	14	13	20
Pakistan									11				9	19	10	23
Indonesia (Java)		15 ↔						19 ↔			13 ↔			16 ↔	45	34
Iraq											18 ↔					68
Israel													42	54		12
Japan											12 ↔			15 ↔		34
Jordan																20
Korea						13 ↔							14	22	25	36
Laos							6 ↔									
Philippines														26	21	60
Singapore													52	26	36	42
Syria															24	43
Thailand													25	29	21	32
Turkey														19	18	34
Vietnam													14 ↔			
Europe																
Albania										9	9	−2	2	9	12	32
Austria								8	8	10	11	0	7	0	3	2
Belgium						8		9	10	13	16		19	4	3	6
Bulgaria									6	8	7		7	11	14	9
Czechoslovakia											12	0	7	5		10
Denmark	18	10		11	10	13	11	10	10	12	12	12	9	8	12	11
Finland		19	13	11	10	8	6	11	15	13	26	8	10	7	8	7
France	4	6	6	4	4	4	3	3	1	1	1	−5	6	1	1	9
Germany			12 ↔			7 ↔		11 ↔	15 ↔							11
East Germany																−6
Greece		4 ↔				7	13 ↔	17	15	15	9	5	27	15	3	10
Hungary								1	11	10	8		9	7	1	7
Iceland				5		13		3	−1	10	9	12	15	13	18	23
Ireland	14	14 ↔			−20	−11		−4	−9	−5	−3	0	−6	1	0	−5
Italy		7 ↔		10 ↔		8		6	6	7	7	7	9	9	6	6
Netherlands		7 ↔			7	8		12	12	13	15	16	16	13	14	14
Norway		13 ↔		10	8			10	4	11	6	12	7	6	10	10
Poland													18	13		20
Portugal		6 ↔			4			9	11	7	10	1	13	13		20
Rumania								9	−7	18	22	9	14	12		9
Spain		12 ↔	12					2	6	6	7	7	11	10	8	13
Sweden	5 ↔			9		10	8	10	5	8	8	7	4	4	10	8
Switzerland		12			11	5	6	6	3	14	13	3	5	5	11	7
U.K. (England and Wales)	14	18	16	14	13	12	13	14	12	12	11	5	6	4	5	15
Scotland	12	16	13	11	10	10	10	12	7	11	6	8	−1	10	2	6
U.S.S.R.	9	11	12	8	10	10	12	13	14	14	18	8	14	10	−5	16
Yugoslavia								7	15	15	17	3	16	15	3	14
Oceania																
Australia												22	21	9	16	26
Fiji								40	41	19	18		12	20	33	36
Hawaii										23	30	21	20	16	16	24
New Zealand						−17 ↔				71	24	33	28	35	30	35
Western Samoa						−18 ↔			44				44	15	18	

SOURCE: Clark 1967, pp. 99–103.

5. Other large towns
6. Small industrial towns
7. Other small towns
8. Changing between 1905 and 1914
   a. from 1 to 2 (from agricultural to rural mixed)
   b. from 2 to 3 (from rural mixed to rural industrial)
   c. from 3 to 4, 5, 6, or 7
9. Changing between 1915 and 1924
   a. from 1 to 2
   b. from 2 to 3
   c. from 3 to 4, 5, 6, or 7

These types themselves suggest explanations for the variations in migration rates and sequences of rates. Note particularly that there was positive net internal migration throughout the period for two community types, towns and rural industrial communities. Thomas considers this indicative of a great capacity to absorb surplus agricultural population into industry in this period as compared to an earlier period when Sweden's surplus agricultural population emigrated to America. Further analysis by Thomas confirms a complicated relationship between internal migration patterns and business cycles. High levels of business activity are associated with net out-migration from agricultural communities and with in-migration to towns.

Additional questions may be raised concerning first, the causes and additional correlates of migration, and second, the consequences for individuals and communities of the sequences of migratory movement. These will be discussed in chapter 9, which deals specifically with migration. What is important here is that opportunities to address such questions often arise with regard to historical population materials, and that these opportunities should not be overlooked.

STUDIES USING PARISH RECORDS. As a final illustration of the importance of historical materials to demographic research, we cite examples of the use of parish records. An important objective in family reconstitution based on parish registers has been to investigate the characteristics of "natural fertility," i.e., the fertility of women in the *absence* of any intervention or practice to limit family size. One important consideration in the study of natural fertility is the length of intervals between births.[7] This length varies by birth order: the average "natural" interval between marriage and the first birth is shorter than

---

7 It is worth noting that aside from its intrinsic interest, knowing the length of birth intervals under conditions of "natural fertility" allows the researcher to evaluate the effectiveness of family limitation in observed populations by comparing these populations with a "natural fertility" one.

TABLE 1.5

In-Migration, Out-Migration, and Net Internal Migration per 1,000 Average Population (Trend Values) by Rural Community Types, 1895–1933

Year	Agricultural In-migration	Agricultural Out-migration	Agricultural Net internal migration	Rural Mixed In-migration	Rural Mixed Out-migration	Rural Mixed Net internal migration	Changing 1905–14 In-migration	Changing 1905–14 Out-migration	Changing 1905–14 Net internal migration	Changing 1915–24 In-migration	Changing 1915–24 Out-migration	Changing 1915–24 Net internal migration	Rural Industrial In-migration	Rural Industrial Out-migration	Rural Industrial Net internal migration
1895	46.5	56.8	-10.3	42.6	47.2	-4.6	50.8	54.4	-3.6	55.2	60.2	-5.0	62.4	55.6	6.8
1896	47.2	57.2	-10.0	43.1	47.8	-4.7	53.4	56.1	-2.7	56.5	61.3	-4.8	63.5	56.9	6.6
1897	47.9	57.7	-9.8	43.6	48.4	-4.8	55.9	57.8	-1.9	57.8	62.3	-4.5	64.5	58.1	6.4
1898	48.5	58.1	-9.6	44.1	48.9	-4.8	58.2	59.3	-1.1	59.0	63.2	-4.2	65.3	59.1	6.2
1899	49.2	58.6	-9.4	44.6	49.4	-4.8	60.3	60.6	-.3	60.2	64.1	-3.9	66.0	60.0	6.0
1900	49.8	59.0	-9.2	45.0	49.9	-4.9	62.2	61.8	.4	61.3	65.0	-3.7	66.7	60.8	5.9
1901	50.4	59.4	-9.0	45.4	50.4	-5.0	64.0	63.0	1.0	62.3	65.8	-3.5	67.2	61.4	5.8
1902	51.0	59.8	-8.8	45.8	50.8	-5.0	65.6	63.9	1.7	63.4	66.6	-3.2	67.6	62.0	5.6
1903	51.6	60.1	-8.5	46.1	51.2	-5.1	67.0	64.8	2.2	64.3	67.3	-3.0	67.9	62.5	5.4
1904	52.1	60.5	-8.4	46.4	51.5	-5.1	68.2	65.5	2.7	65.2	68.0	-2.8	68.1	62.9	5.2
1905	52.6	60.8	-8.2	46.8	51.9	-5.1	69.3	66.3	3.0	66.0	68.6	-2.6	68.3	63.2	5.1
1906	53.1	61.2	-8.1	47.1	52.2	-5.1	70.3	66.8	3.5	66.7	69.1	-2.4	68.4	63.5	4.9
1907	53.5	61.5	-8.0	47.3	52.5	-5.2	71.1	67.4	3.7	67.4	69.7	-2.3	68.4	63.7	4.7
1908	54.0	61.8	-7.8	47.6	52.8	-5.2	71.8	67.8	4.0	68.1	70.2	-2.1	68.4	63.9	4.5
1909	54.4	62.1	-7.7	47.8	53.1	-5.3	72.4	68.2	4.2	68.7	70.7	-2.0	68.4	63.9	4.5
1910	54.8	62.3	-7.5	48.0	53.3	-5.3	72.8	68.4	4.4	69.2	71.1	-1.9	68.3	64.0	4.3
1911	55.1	62.6	-7.5	48.2	53.6	-5.4	73.2	68.6	4.6	69.8	71.5	-1.7	68.1	64.0	4.1
1912	55.4	62.8	-7.4	48.4	53.8	-5.4	73.4	68.8	4.6	70.2	71.8	-1.6	67.9	64.0	3.9
1913	55.7	63.0	-7.3	48.6	53.9	-5.3	73.6	69.0	4.6	70.6	72.2	-1.6	67.7	63.9	3.8
1914	56.0	63.2	-7.2	48.7	54.1	-5.4	73.7	69.0	4.7	71.0	72.4	-1.4	67.4	63.8	3.6
1915	56.2	63.3	-7.1	48.8	54.2	-5.4	73.6	69.0	4.6	71.1	72.4	-1.3	67.2	63.7	3.5
1916	56.2	63.3	-7.1	48.8	54.2	-5.4	73.5	68.9	4.6	70.8	72.1	-1.3	67.0	63.6	3.4
1917	56.2	63.2	-7.0	48.7	54.2	-5.5	73.3	68.8	4.5	70.5	71.8	-1.3	66.7	63.5	3.2
1918	56.2	63.2	-7.0	48.7	54.1	-5.4	73.0	68.6	4.4	70.2	71.4	-1.2	66.4	63.3	3.1
1919	56.2	63.1	-6.9	48.6	54.0	-5.4	72.6	68.5	4.1	69.9	71.0	-1.1	66.1	63.1	3.0
1920	56.2	63.0	-6.8	48.5	53.9	-5.4	72.3	68.3	4.0	69.5	70.6	-1.1	65.7	62.8	2.9
1921	56.2	63.0	-6.8	48.4	53.8	-5.4	71.9	68.2	3.7	69.4	70.5	-1.1	65.2	62.5	2.7
1922	56.2	63.1	-6.9	48.4	53.8	-5.4	71.5	68.0	3.5	69.5	70.6	-1.1	64.8	62.2	2.6
1923	56.2	63.2	-7.0	48.4	53.8	-5.4	71.2	67.9	3.3	69.6	70.8	-1.2	64.3	61.9	2.4
1924	56.2	63.2	-7.0	48.3	53.7	-5.4	70.7	67.8	2.9	69.7	70.8	-1.1	63.9	61.6	2.3
1925	56.2	63.2	-7.0	48.3	53.7	-5.4	70.3	67.7	2.6	69.7	70.9	-1.2	63.4	61.2	2.2
1926	56.2	63.3	-7.1	48.2	53.6	-5.4	69.9	67.7	2.2	69.7	71.0	-1.3	62.9	60.8	2.1
1927	56.2	63.3	-7.1	48.1	53.5	-5.4	69.4	67.6	1.8	69.8	71.1	-1.3	62.4	60.5	1.9
1928	56.1	63.4	-7.3	48.0	53.3	-5.3	69.0	67.5	1.5	69.8	71.2	-1.4	61.8	60.1	1.7
1929	56.1	63.4	-7.3	47.8	53.2	-5.4	68.6	67.5	1.1	69.8	71.3	-1.5	61.3	59.7	1.6
1930	56.0	63.5	-7.5	47.7	53.1	-5.4	68.1	67.5	.6	69.8	71.4	-1.6	60.8	59.3	1.5
1931	55.9	63.5	-7.6	47.6	52.9	-5.3	67.7	67.6	.1	69.8	71.5	-1.7	60.2	58.9	1.3
1932	55.8	63.6	-7.8	47.4	52.8	-5.4	67.2	67.6	-.4	69.8	71.6	-1.8	59.7	58.5	1.2
1933	55.7	63.7	-8.0	47.2	52.6	-5.4	66.8	67.7	-.9	69.9	71.7	-1.8	59.1	58.0	1.1

SOURCE: D. S. Thomas 1941, p. 299.

TABLE 1.6

In-Migration, Out-Migration, and Net Internal Migration per 1,000 Average Population (Trend Values) by Town Types, 1895-1933[a]

Year	Large Industrial Towns			Other Large Towns			Small Industrial Towns			Other Small Towns		
	In-migration	Out-migration	Net internal migration	In-migration	Out-migration	Net internal migration	In-migration	Out-migration	Net internal migration	In-migration	Out-migration	Net internal migration
1895	118.0	87.2	30.8	83.8	69.3	14.5	88.0	68.0	20.0	88.9	74.9	14.0
1896	114.2	86.5	27.7	84.6	70.6	14.0	88.3	69.2	19.1	89.9	76.4	13.5
1897	110.8	85.9	24.9	85.2	71.8	13.4	88.3	70.2	18.1	90.8	77.7	13.1
1898	107.8	85.5	22.3	85.8	72.9	12.9	88.2	71.0	17.2	91.5	78.8	12.7
1899	105.2	85.1	20.1	86.1	73.8	12.3	88.0	71.6	16.4	92.1	79.8	12.3
1900	102.8	84.9	17.9	86.4	74.6	11.8	87.7	72.1	15.6	92.7	80.8	11.9
1901	100.7	84.6	16.1	86.7	75.2	11.5	87.2	72.5	14.7	92.9	81.5	11.4
1902	98.9	84.4	14.5	86.7	75.8	10.9	86.7	72.6	14.1	93.2	82.1	11.1
1903	97.2	84.2	13.0	86.8	76.2	10.6	86.0	72.7	13.3	93.4	82.6	10.8
1904	95.8	84.1	11.7	86.7	76.6	10.1	85.3	72.7	12.6	93.5	83.0	10.5
1905	94.4	84.0	10.4	86.7	76.9	9.8	84.6	72.6	12.0	93.5	83.3	10.2
1906	93.2	83.9	9.3	86.5	77.1	9.4	83.9	72.5	11.4	93.5	83.7	9.8
1907	92.2	83.8	8.4	86.3	77.3	9.0	83.0	72.2	10.8	93.4	83.7	9.7
1908	91.2	83.7	7.5	86.1	77.4	8.7	82.2	72.0	10.2	93.2	83.8	9.4
1909	90.4	83.7	6.7	85.8	77.4	8.4	81.3	71.6	9.7	93.1	83.9	9.2
1910	89.7	83.6	6.1	85.5	77.4	8.1	80.4	71.1	9.3	92.8	83.8	9.0
1911	89.2	83.6	5.6	85.2	77.3	7.9	79.4	70.7	8.7	92.4	83.7	8.7
1912	88.7	83.7	5.0	84.7	77.2	7.5	78.4	70.2	8.2	92.0	83.5	8.5
1913	88.3	83.7	4.6	84.3	77.0	7.3	77.5	69.7	7.8	91.6	83.3	8.3
1914	88.0	84.0	4.3	83.8	76.7	7.1	76.5	69.1	7.4	91.1	82.9	8.2
1915	88.0	84.5	4.0	83.6	76.7	6.9	75.4	68.4	7.0	90.6	82.5	8.1
1916	88.2	84.9	3.7	83.6	76.9	6.7	74.2	67.7	6.5	89.9	82.0	7.9
1917	88.5	85.2	3.6	83.5	77.0	6.5	73.0	66.9	6.1	89.1	81.3	7.8
1918	88.8	85.5	3.6	83.4	77.0	6.4	71.7	66.0	5.7	88.4	80.8	7.6
1919	89.1	85.8	3.6	83.2	77.0	6.2	70.4	65.0	5.4	87.5	80.0	7.5
1920	89.5	85.8	3.7	83.0	76.9	6.1	69.0	64.0	5.0	86.6	79.2	7.4
1921	89.7	86.0	3.7	82.5	76.6	5.9	67.8	63.1	4.7	85.8	78.5	7.3
1922	89.9	86.0	3.9	81.7	76.0	5.7	66.6	62.3	4.3	85.1	77.9	7.2
1923	90.1	86.0	4.1	80.9	75.3	5.6	65.5	61.5	4.0	84.4	77.2	7.2
1924	90.4	86.0	4.4	80.1	74.6	5.5	64.4	60.7	3.7	83.6	76.5	7.1
1925	90.7	86.0	4.7	79.3	73.9	5.4	63.3	59.8	3.5	82.9	75.9	7.0
1926	91.0	85.9	5.1	78.5	73.2	5.3	62.1	59.0	3.1	82.1	75.1	7.0
1927	91.3	85.8	5.5	77.6	72.5	5.1	60.9	58.0	2.9	81.3	74.3	7.0
1928	91.7	85.7	6.0	76.8	71.8	5.0	59.8	57.1	2.7	80.4	73.5	6.9
1929	92.0	85.5	6.5	75.9	71.0	4.9	58.5	56.2	2.3	79.6	72.6	7.0
1930	92.4	85.3	7.1	75.0	70.2	4.8	57.3	55.2	2.1	78.7	71.8	6.9
1931	92.8	85.1	7.7	74.1	69.4	4.7	56.0	54.2	1.8	77.8	70.8	7.0
1932	93.1	84.8	8.3	73.2	68.5	4.7	54.7	53.1	1.6	76.9	69.9	7.0
1933	93.5	84.4	9.1	72.2	67.7	4.5	53.4	52.1	1.3	75.8	68.9	6.9

SOURCE: D. S. Thomas 1941, p. 300.

[a]Data not presented for Stockholm or Gothenburg and Malmö.

the average interval between the first and second births; and both are much shorter than the average interval between the next-to-last and last births.

M. Frézel-Lozey has summarized data on birth intervals for Bilhères-d'Ossau, France, the parish which he studied, as well as for comparative parish-register findings from six other studies; these summaries are shown in table 1.7.

A recurring relationship in the table is the progressive increase in mean length of birth intervals over successive birth orders. On the other hand, there are some interesting dissimilarities—for example, between the Canadian and French parishes, and, indeed, between the Southwestern French (Bilhères and Thézel) parishes as compared to the other French parishes (Henry 1965).

An important finding of parish-register studies has been that at least some groups in some preindustrial populations systematically practiced some form of family limitation prior to the development and distribution of modern methods of contraception. Thus, in one of the first such studies, L. Henry found that the Genevese bourgeoisie began systematic control of fertility at the beginning of the eighteenth century, the average completed family size declining from 5.9 children at the end of the seventeenth century to 3.5 children in the first half of the eighteenth (Henry 1956). In a study reconstructing the births and fertility rates of Colyton, East Devon (England), E. A. Wrigley found evidence of rigid birth control between 1560 and 1790 (Wrigley 1966). Other historical evidence bearing upon family limitation in preindustrial populations is reported in the study by Coale, cited above (Coale 1969).

The importance of these findings lies in what they may suggest about the reasons for, and conditions of, the institutionalization of fertility control. As we have already indicated briefly and will discuss later in more detail, an important task in population studies is to discover the nature of the variations that take place in demographic transitions, in inflections in mortality and fertility rates, and in the conditions under which such inflections occur. Historical materials showing the origins of the adoption of fertility control promise to add to our understanding of this important sociodemographic process.

5. POPULATION VARIATION: CONTEMPORARY VIEWS

Some elementary and often personal acquaintance with differences between the populations of various communities, states, regions, or countries is extremely common in this era of widespread literacy, long-distance travel, and highly developed information and communications media. The populations of, say, India, the United States, Australia, Israel, and

TABLE 1.7
Mean Length of Intervals Between Births, by Birth Order: Selected Parish Record Data for Couples Married 1674–1799

Parishes	Number of families studied	Mean number of births	Marriage to first birth interval	Mean Length of Birth Intervals (in months)					
				1st to 2nd birth interval	2nd to 3rd birth interval	3rd to 4th birth interval	Anti-penultimate interval	Penultimate interval	Last interval
Bilhères[a] (marriages of 1740–1779)	54	7.31	20.2	23.7	27.2	30.0	31.1	31.5	38.1
Thézel-Saint-Sernin[b] (marriages of 1700–1792)	90	x	x	25.4	30.0	32.2	32.6	33.7	38.3
Crulai[c] (marriages of 1674–1742)	106	7.6	16.6	22.4	25.3	27.2	28.7	30.9	33.0
Three Ile-de-France Villages (marriages of 1740–1799)[d]	82	8.8	x	19.8	23.4	23.3	27.0	29.1	35.2
Sainghin-en-Mélantois[e] (marriages before 1770)	39	8.75	x	21.1	21.8	25.0	26.8	30.0	38.0
Sotteville-lès-Rouen[f] (marriages of 1760–1792)	x	7	x	19.2	21.9	x	23.7	27.3	30.0
Canada[g] (marriages of 1700–1730)	x	x	22.5	21.0	22.6	22.9	x	x	x

[a] Frézel-Lozey 1969. All families studied.
[b] P. Valmary 1965.
[c] Gauthier and Henry 1958. All families studied.
[d] Ganiage 1963. Completed families only.
[e] Deniel and Henry 1965. Completed families only.
[f] Girard 1959, pp. 485–508. All families with five or more children.
[g] Henripin 1954.
x indicates that data are not available.

Ghana differ from one another in many ways, and at least some of these kinds of differences or "axes of variation" are so widely recognized as to make self-evident the idea that there are in the world, at any moment in time, a large number of delineable populations which differ from one another with respect to various dimensions and characteristics. It is the observable variations in population size, structure, and other characteristics, and the determinants and consequences of these variations, that comprise the subject matter of scientific population studies. In dealing with variations among populations in this book, we shall be particularly concerned with their social-structural causes, effects, and correlates.

THE DELINEATION OF POPULATIONS.   Populations can be delineated or circumscribed on the basis of a number of different criteria. The most common of these is political integration. Thus, persons belonging to the political unit in question—be it a nation, tribe, township, municipality, kinship network, or whatever—as well as people living in the area delineated as belonging to that political unit, are "in" the population of the unit. Everyone else is considered to be "outside" it.

Populations are also often delineated in terms of "natural" geographic criteria. Thus, we have the populations of the earth's continents and the populations of some naturally bordered regions or distinct geomorphological units (e.g., Appalachia, the Low Countries of Northwest Europe, the Gulf Coast of the U.S.A.). Similarly, populations are often defined and bounded in accordance with a recognized range of economic integration—for example, "Metropolitan New York" or the Cotton Belt. Finally, cultural criteria (such as language, religion, or ethnic origin) and other bases for social integration or solidarity (such as race, occupational attachments, previous military service, physical ability or disabilities) are often invoked.

National Populations

Probably the most frequently encountered classification of populations is that of the nation-state, or national population. A national population is circumscribed either (a) territorially and politically, or (b) administratively. Typically, some information as to its size and major characteristics is available. In the past, national or imperial regimes took censuses of the populations under their political jurisdiction for purposes of tax collection or for the mobilization of manpower for armies and other kinds of public service. In modern times, it is usually the national government which collects the most detailed information concerning populations—still primarily for administrative purposes. As a consequence of all this data collection, most of the demographic information available has bearing on such nationally delineated populations.

National populations are conveniently classified according to such characteristics as (1) size, (2) areas in which they live, (3) population density in these areas, (4) composition in terms of sizes of places of settlement or in terms of urban or rural settlement, (5) age structure and growth characteristics, and (6) social, cultural, and economic characteristics. At this point our interest is in indicating briefly the range of variation among populations. Later we shall show how such variations have social, economic, and political consequences, and, in particular, how *change* in population size, density, composition, and structure affects political, economic, and social structure.

Table 1.8 shows the distribution of 151 sovereign nations by continents and by population-size class, area-size class, and density class. The data are based on United Nations estimates for 1968, which are in turn based on reports by the 151 countries themselves.

VARIATIONS IN POPULATION SIZE. All but 20 of the populations covered by table 1.8 consist of 30 million people or less. The twenty-nine countries reporting populations of one million or less are largely the so-called Arab sheikdoms of the Near East—for example, Kuwait, Qatar, Oman, and Bahrein—and certain tiny principalities in Europe, such as Andorra, Liechtenstein, Luxembourg, Monaco, and San Marino.

The largest group consists of populations in the one million but less than five million class, and all continents are represented here. Included are all the Central American republics and about half of the independent states of Africa, but relatively few nations from the other continents. Twenty-four nations have populations of between five and ten million, and 29 have populations of between 10 and 30 million. There are 12 large populations numbering between 30 and 75 million. These include Nigeria and Egypt on the African continent; Mexico on the North American continent; Turkey, the Philippines, and Thailand in the two extremes of Asia; and France, West Germany, Italy, Poland, Spain and the United Kingdom in Europe. In the category of giant populations—those with 75 million persons or more—there are only eight countries. The United States, of course, is one—and the only one in North America. Similarly, Brazil is the only one in South America, and the Soviet Union is the only one in Europe. By contrast, Asia has five such countries: Mainland China, India, Indonesia, Japan, and Pakistan.

VARIATIONS IN AREA SIZE. The same 151 populations are classified in table 1.8 by area size. Only 40 independent countries are in the smallest class (under 50 thousand square kilometers), and a mere seven are in the largest class (three million square kilometers or more). Over a third of the countries are in the 100,000 to 500,000 square kilometer class.

TABLE 1.8
*Number of Sovereign Nations by Continent and by Population-Size Class, Area-Size Class,
and Population Density Class, 1968*

Continent	Total: All Population Sizes	Population Size					
		Under 1,000,000	*1,000,000 to 4,999,999*	*5,000,000 to 9,999,999*	*10,000,000 to 29,999,999*	*30,000,000 to 74,999,999*	*75,000,000 and over*
World Total	151	29	49	24	29	12	8
Africa	45	8	20	7	8	2	0
North America	16	1	11	1	1	1	1
South America	11	1	3	3	3	0	1
Asia	41	9	8	6	10	3	5
Europe	33	8	5	7	6	6	1
Oceania	5	2	2	0	1	0	0

Continent	Total: All Area Sizes	Area Size					
		Under 50,000 sq. km.	*50,000 to 99,999 sq. km.*	*100,000 to 499,999 sq. km.*	*500,000 to 999,999 sq. km.*	*1,000,000 to 2,999,999 sq. km.*	*3,000,000 or more sq. km.*
World Total	151	40	12	53	18	21	7
Africa	45	7	2	15	9	12	0
North America	16	7	2	4	0	1	2
South America	11	0	0	4	2	4	1
Asia	41	12	4	14	5	4	2
Europe	33	12	4	14	2	0	1
Oceania	5	2	0	2	0	0	1

Continent	Total: All Density Classes	Population Density					
		Less than 10 per sq. km.	*10–24 per sq. km.*	*25–49 per sq. km.*	*50–99 per sq. km.*	*100–199 per sq. km.*	*200 or over per sq. km.*
World Total	151	30	39	22	19	23	18
Africa	45	16	15	10	1	2	1
North America	16	1	6	2	2	4	1
South America	11	4	7	0	0	0	0
Asia	41	6	6	7	7	7	8
Europe	33	1	4	2	8	10	8
Oceania	5	2	1	1	1	0	0

SOURCE: All data are from U.N., *Demographic Yearbook 1969* (1970, table 1).
Note: The table includes seven nonindependent territories with estimated populations of over one million: Angola, Mozambique, Southern Rhodesia, Puerto Rico, South Arabia Protectorate, Hong Kong, and New Guinea.

Europe and Asia are each represented in the smallest class by 12 populations—for Europe: Albania, Andorra, Belgium, Denmark, the Vatican, Liechtenstein, Luxembourg, 'Malta, Monaco, the Netherlands, San Marino, and Switzerland; and for Asia: Bahrein, Bhutan, Taiwan,

Israel, Kuwait, Lebanon, the Maldive Islands, Qatar, Sikkim, Cyprus, Singapore, and Hong Kong. North America is represented by seven countries—the small Central American and Caribbean Republics of El Salvador, the Dominican Republic, Haiti, Bahamas, Jamaica, Trinidad and Tobago, and Puerto Rico. There are seven such countries in Africa as well: Zambia, Mauritius, Lesotho, Swaziland, Equatorial Guinea, Burundi, and Rwanda. Finally, there are New Zealand and the Fiji Islands in Oceania. In South America there are no populations occupying such small areas.

Of the seven really enormous countries, two are in North America (Canada and the United States) and two in Asia (Mainland China and India). South America, Oceania, and Europe each only have one country in this category of three million square kilometers or more. These giants are Brazil, Australia, and, of course, the Soviet Union.

The 100,000 to 500,000 square kilometer category includes a large number of nations in Africa, Asia, and Europe, but relatively few in North and South America. Among the Africa populations, to name only some, are Ghana, Guinea, the Ivory Coast, Morocco, Tunisia, and Dahomey; and a sample of the European countries includes Bulgaria, Czechoslovakia, East Germany, West Germany, Greece, Norway, Poland, Rumania, and the United Kingdom. The Asian countries in this category include Iraq, Japan, Malaysia, Nepal, the Philippines, Syria, both North and South Vietnam, and Yemen.

VARIATIONS IN POPULATION DENSITY. The relationship between population and area is typically expressed in terms of population density, the number of persons per areal unit. In this case we are concerned with the number of persons per square kilometer. It should be clear that because of the innumerable possible combinations of population size, singularly different types of populations can have the same population density. For example, a population of 1,000 persons living in an area of 100 square kilometers will have a density of ten persons per square kilometer—but so also will a population of 10,000 persons living in an area of 1,000 square kilometers.

The density classes in table 1.8 range from less than 10 persons per square kilometer to over 200. Africa, South America, and Oceania have largely low-density nations, North America and Asia have a broad range of density patterns, and the nations of Europe are predominantly of high density. Of the thirty nations with low densities of less than ten persons per square kilometer, more than half are in Africa (e.g., Algeria, Chad, both Congos, Liberia, Libya, Mali, Somalia and Sudan), four are in South America (Argentina, Bolivia, Guiana, and Paraguay), one is in North America (Canada), and one is in Europe (Iceland).

No fewer than eight European populations have densities of 200 persons per square kilometer or more. These are Belgium, West Germany, the Vatican, Malta, Monaco, the Netherlands, San Marino, and the United Kingdom. European populations in the next highest category (100 to 200 persons per square kilometer) include Czechoslovakia, Denmark, East Germany, Hungary, Italy, Liechtenstein, Luxembourg, Poland, Portugal, and Switzerland. Asian countries in the highest density class include Taiwan, Japan, South Korea, and Lebanon, and those in the next highest include India, Pakistan, Israel, the Philippines, and Ceylon. Five North American populations are in the two highest classes (El Salvador, Haiti, Jamaica, Trinidad and Tobago, and Puerto Rico), as are three African countries (Rwanda, Burundi, and Mauritius). No South American or Oceanic country has such a densely packed population.

Note, again, that very different types of populations can have the same density. Thus, high density characterizes some countries because of their very small territories and fairly substantial populations (e.g., Burundi, Rwanda, Ceylon, Hong Kong, Taiwan, Singapore, South Korea, and the Netherlands), and others because of their mildly large territories but huge populations (e.g., Japan, Pakistan, the Philippines, Turkey, West Germany, and the United Kingdom). Conversely, countries may have very low densities by virtue of their small populations living in large areas (Sarawak, Gabon, Iceland), or by virtue of their moderately sized populations living in enormous areas (Libya, Mali, Canada, Bolivia, Saudi Arabia).

Populations Classified by Patterns of Settlement

A very important manner of classifying populations is in terms of the types or size of the place or agglomeration involved. Thus, we have categories like urban, rural, metropolitan, rural-farm, and rural nonfarm. Not only are there significant differences between, say, towns and villages with respect to work, residence, family, government, religion, recreation, education, voluntary organizations, social stratification, norms and values, and interpersonal relations, but the urban proportion in a population influences the social structure and relationships in both the urban and in rural sectors of the society. (See, for example, Sjoberg 1964; Gibbs and Schnore 1960; and Hauser and Schnore 1965.)

This sort of classification poses certain technical problems concerning the definition of the concepts involved. In certain countries, a place of settlement is considered urban if it is of a certain size—if it has, say, 2,000 persons, or 10,000, or more. In other countries, a certain kind of political administration is taken as the relevant criterion. And in still others, urbanity is measured in terms of such characteristics as the economy or the degree of population density.

TABLE 1.9

Urban Population and Population Living in Agglomerations of Different Sizes:
Selected Countries, circa 1950 and 1970 (in percentages)

	1950							1970	
	Percent urban	2,000+	5,000+	10,000+	20,000+	50,000+	100,000+	Percent urban	100,000+
Australia, 1943	68.9	74.2	66.4	61.6	57.3	52.4	51.4	88.5	64.7
India, 1951	17.3	37.7	21.1	15.3	12.0	8.7	6.6	18.8	10.0
Israel, 1950	71.3	73.6	66.2	61.9	51.3	45.6	45.6	81.3	55.1
United States, 1950	64.0	65.1	60.5	56.2	52.0	46.8	43.9	75.2	58.4
Thailand, 1947[a]	9.9	9.9	9.8	8.9	6.7	4.5	4.5	13.0	7.8
United Kingdom, 1951[a]	80.3	79.7	77.6	74.0	66.9	50.8	36.1	79.1	71.8

SOURCES: 1950 — Gibbs and Davis 1958, pp. 422–24; 1970 — Davis 1969.
[a]Cities and towns defined administratively.

    In the United States, a place is considered urban if it is incorporated and includes 2,500 or more inhabitants, or if it is contiguous to an urban place and densely settled. In Honduras, places of 1,000 or more inhabitants are considered urban, while in Yugoslavia the criterion is 15,000 or else a sufficiently large proportion of the labor force engaged in nonagricultural occupations. In Denmark, places are urban if they have 200 residents or more, but in Czechoslovakia at least 5,000 persons and a density level of 100 or more persons per square kilometer is required. In Italy, places are urban if no more than 50 percent of their inhabitants are engaged in agriculture, while Great Britain's country boroughs and districts are urban regardless of population size or occupational composition (Hauser 1965a). Thus, there is a real problem of noncomparability with regard to the "urban" sectors of various national populations.

    Nevertheless, all "urban" populations have a common note of high density, fairly large agglomerations of populations and generally nonagricultural occupation, and this makes it possible to at least compare countries in terms of their urban *proportions*. Table 1.9 shows the urban proportions of selected countries at around the midpoint of the twentieth century and in 1970. It may be seen in the first column that the 1950 figures range from 9.9 percent in Thailand in 1947 to 71.3 in Israel in 1949 and 80.3 in the United Kingdom in 1951. The left panel of table 1.9 also shows what proportions of the populations of these countries reside in localities of 2,000 persons or more, 10,000 or more, 20,000 or more persons, and so on. Not all these localities are necessarily considered urban, for while one country may designate a place of 2,000 persons as urban, another may not. However, nearly all countries consider places of 20,000 or more to be urban and the total population living in such places to be the urban population. In any event, size designations are not dependent upon definitions peculiar to any country or group of countries. They are merely descriptive of the localities in question. Table 1.9 shows that the occurrence of populations living in localities of 2,000 or over is smallest for Thailand (9.9 percent) and the largest for the United Kingdom (79.7 percent).

Most countries have at least one city whose population numbers 100,000 persons or more. In Australia in 1947 more than half the population lived in places of 100,000 or more, and at about the same period almost half the populations of Israel and the United States did so. In contrast, in 1951 only five percent of the Pakistani population, and seven percent of the Indian population, lived in places of this size.

By 1970, the proportion of the population in urban areas had increased in all countries (table 1.9) except the United Kingdom where it remained nearly stable. In every case the percent living in cities of 100,000 or more increased. This change is the result of rural migration to the cities stimulated by continuing industrialization and development of urban areas. Nonetheless, the range of urbanization remains great with Thailand having only 13 percent in urban areas by 1970, while 88.5 percent of Australia's population are in cities.

The process of urbanization varies over space and time. Australia and Israel are examples of countries in which initial modern settlement took place largely in the cities. Early immigrants to colonial America, by contrast, settled in rural places. The United States, initially a largely rural society, underwent a process of urbanization that began with its independence, accelerated after the Civil War, and is only now nearing completion. India and Pakistan, despite their very ancient and large cities and their recent upsurge in urbanization, are still at the very beginning of a process of rural-to-urban migration and population redistribution.

Classification by Age Structure and Growth Characteristics

Populations are very often characterized and classified in terms of their age structures *and* in terms of their growth characteristics. However, it is not always recognized that age structure and growth characteristics—primarily fertility—are very intimately related. To say that a population is a "young population" is to indicate that it has a relatively high proportion of children, adolescents, and young adults, and a relatively low proportion of middle-aged and aged persons. To say that a population is an "old population" implies the opposite. Figure 1.5 shows young and old populations graphically in the form of population pyramids for the United States in 1870, 1940, and 1970. Populations experiencing both high mortality and high fertility—the United States in 1870 had medium mortality and high fertility—tend to be quite young populations. Popu-

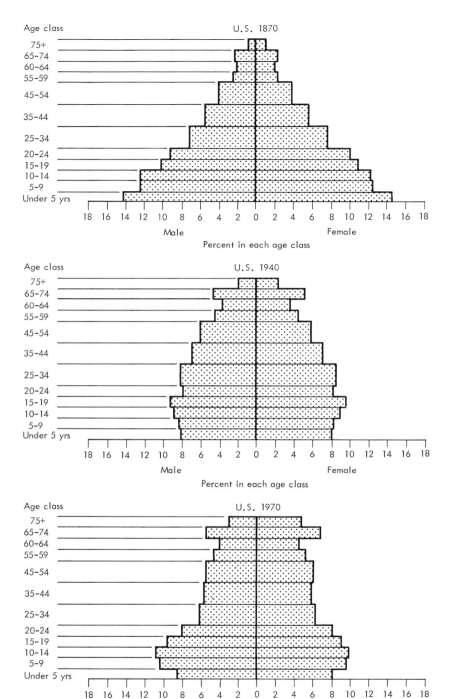

FIGURE 1.5. Population pyramids for the United States: 1870, 1940, and 1970. Source: U.S. Bureau of the Census, U.S. Census of the Population 1870, 1940, and 1970, *Characteristics of the Population.*

TABLE 1.10

Age Composition of Selected Countries, 1969 and 1970
(in percentages)

	<15	15–64	65+	<15 and 65+ / 15–64
U.S.A., 1970	28.5	61.6	9.9	62
Dominican Republic, 1969	47.3	49.7	3.0	101
Paraguay, 1969	45.9	50.2	3.9	99
Egypt, 1969	42.7	53.8	3.5	86
Denmark, 1969	23.8	64.8	11.4	54
United Kingdom, 1969	23.5	63.7	12.8	57
Austria, 1969	24.1	62.1	13.8	61

SOURCE: U.N. *Demographic Yearbook 1969* (1970).

lations characterized by both low mortality and quite low fertility—such as the United States in 1940—tend to be old populations, that is they have high proportions in middle ages and in more advanced ages. The pyramid for 1970 reflects both the low fertility prior to World War II, the high fertility of the extended postwar "baby boom," and the tapering off of fertility in the 1960s.

Thus, the population pyramid shown in Figure 1.5 for 1870 is broadest at the base, i.e., at ages under five years, and narrower at each higher age group, reflecting continued high fertility prior to 1870—each cohort or aggregate of new babies larger than the cohort of the previous year. After World War I, the annual number of births in the United States declined in absolute terms as well as relative to past rates and did not begin to recover until 1940. This trend is reflected in the population pyramid for 1940, in which the base is narrower than the middle. The number of births increased annually after World War II, reaching a peak in 1959–1961 and declining sharply thereafter. In the population pyramid for 1970 this is reflected in the breadth of the base corresponding to the 5–9 and 10–14 year age groups, with the youngest age group notably smaller.

We have already noted that countries and continents differ from one another with respect to their patterns of population growth. Table 1.10 indicates some of the variations that obtained among selected populations in 1969. The proportion under 15 years of age ranged from only about 24 percent in Austria to about 47 percent in the Dominican Republic. The proportion aged 15 to 64 ranged from about 50 percent in the Dominican Republic to nearly 64 percent in the United Kingdom. For ages 65 and over, the range was from three percent in the Dominican Republic to nearly 14 percent in Austria.

The last column of Table 1.10 shows ratios of the population under 15 and 65 and over to the population aged 15–64. This ratio is called the "dependency ratio" and is so named because it measures the ratio of the population in ages too young or too old to work—but consumers, just the same—to the population of working age. In the table it is seen that the Dominican Republic, Paraguay, and Egypt had very high dependency ratios because of the large percentages under 15 years of age.

The dependency ratio of Denmark is lowest, Austria's is higher than Denmark's because of a larger percentage of elderly persons, while that of the United States is higher because of higher percentages in both "under 15" and "65 and over" age categories.

Similar variations could be sketched for the fifty U.S. states, for the country's major racial and religious populations, for each of the "community areas" of the city of Chicago, for the population employed in, or dependent upon, each of the various economic sectors, or more generally for all populations, whatever the bases on which they are defined.

Preliterate and Small-Scale Societies

In principle, the kinds of variations described above can be studied for populations of nonliterate tribes or communities, for nomadic groupings, and for isolated village populations of every type. In practice, however, data for such populations are extremely difficult to obtain. For example, very little is known about the size, sex composition, age structure, or growth characteristics of American Indian tribes in the nineteenth century, even though ethnographers and historians had begun at that time to study the languages, customs, and economies of these tribes in some detail. Only vaguely do we know the demographic characteristics of the Eskimos, the African pygmies, or the Arapesh made famous by the publications of Margaret Mead. Probably the main reason for the absence of this information is simply the lack of interest, appropriate training, or both among those carrying out the field studies.

However, there is increasing interest among demographers in the populations of preliterate and small-scale societies; and there is increasing interest among anthropologists and ethnographers in the demographic characteristics of the societies they study. The recently published *Cross Cultural Summary* (Textor 1967), an extensive work which includes a number of demographic variables, is likely to stimulate research and analysis in this area.

The absence of data for preliterate and small-scale societies should by no means prohibit us from raising questions about such populations or from taking seriously the hypotheses and generalizations which might emerge from their study and analysis. Indeed, we shall have occasion later in this book to raise questions about variations in relationships between population and social structure in just such small-scale settings.

Two general conclusions have been derived from surveying what

TABLE 1.11
Cross-Cultural Survey: Mean Size of Local Communities

Mean Size of Local Communities	Number of Cultures
1. Fewer than 50 persons	46 cultures
2. From 50 to 99 persons	43 cultures
3. From 100–199 persons	46 cultures
4. From 200–399 persons	21 cultures
5. From 400–1,000 persons	24 cultures
6. More than 1,000 persons; no indigenous urban aggregation of more than 5,000 persons	5 cultures
7. One or more indigenous towns of more than 5,000 inhabitants but none of more than 50,000 persons	16 cultures
8. One or more indigenous cities with more than 50,000 inhabitants	23 cultures

SOURCE: Textor 1967.

materials we have on the populations of primitive societies. First, these populations are characterized by very considerable variation in size, density, structure, growth rate, and composition.[8] For example, the *Cross Cultural Summary* records 222 cultures characterized by patterns of fixed settlement, among them the Ashanti, Pawnee, Swazi, Tikopia, Yoruba, and Zuñi. The 110 cultures recorded as having nomadic or nonfixed patterns of settlement include the Andamanese, Bemba, Cheyenne, Navaho, Nuer, and Wichita. An example of the latter are the Shoshonean Indian tribes: they foraged and gathered vegetable foods and small game in family bands in spring and summer, but clustered in multifamily encampments through the winter months. Among the Carrier Indians in British Columbia, the population remained in permanent villages near lake or river fishing areas in the summer; in the winter families traveled alone in small bands to hunt and trap meat- and fur-bearing animals (Steward 1955).

Similarly, the summary presents a classification of size of local communities which includes 224 of the 400 cultures in the cross-cultural sample (see table 1.11). Approximately 46 cultures are characterized by communities of fewer than 50 persons (for example, the Andamanese, Lapps, Semang, and Yoruk), 45 are characterized by communities of 200 to 1,000 persons (the Cherokee, Creek, Kikuyu, Tallensi, and Tikopia), and in 44 cultures either the average communtiy size is 1,000 or greater

8 For a pioneer work on the demography of primitive societies, see Krzywicki 1934.

or there is a town or city of at least 5,000 (the Ashanti, Aztec, Kerola, Yoruba, and Zuñi).

The second general conclusion derived from our knowledge of primitive societies is that, despite frequent supposition to the contrary, they are often very unstable populations. Fluctuations in size due to changes in mortality levels and migrations are commonly recorded, and primitive populations are known to be characterized by fluctuating marriage and fertility rates, although these are less frequently studied. For an example of changing mortality levels, Petersen cites the Polynesians, American Indians, the Hispaniola Indians (in Haiti), and the Omagua (in the Caribbean) as cases of extreme reduction in population size following contact with Europeans. On the other hand, the Cocama—Caribbean neighbors of the Omagua—have retained their initial population size, more or less, while some of the New Hebrides Island populations and the Angmagssalik Eskimos on the east coast of Greenland increased markedly in size following contact with Europeans. Petersen concludes that the factor most responsible for population decimations—where they occurred—was the new diseases introduced by Europeans, but that the extent of such depopulation has probably been exaggerated. Armed conflict and the slave trade probably caused more depopulation indirectly—through disease and by prevention of marriage and reproduction—than by direct casualties (Petersen 1969).

In general, changes *within* populations of primitive societies are much less well known, and still less understood, than the variations *among* these societies.

CLASSIFICATION BY TECHNOLOGY. Primitive or nonliterate societies have been classified according to various criteria—by geographic location, such as continent or region (e.g., the Pacific Islands, Great Plains North America, East Africa); by type of environment (mountain, seacoast, forest, plains, etc.); or by racial stock (American Indians, Asiatic Mongoloids, Polynesians, Indo-Australians, and so on). Most frequently, however, they are classified in terms of their technologies and sustenance-producing arrangements, that is, according to whether the dominant feature of their material adaptation is hunting or gathering, pastoral nomadism, some form of horticulture or agriculture, or industry, and according to whether their residence is nomadic or settled. The different categories in such a classification are typically associated with diverse forms of social differentiation,[9] diversity of social roles and social division of labor, and with various political, religious, educational, and family institutions. Moreover, there are assorted population densities and population size group-

---

9 For a discussion of social differentiation and social structure, see especially chapter 4, Section 2.

ings typically associated with the different "technological" classifications. Thus, Hawley, citing data given by the anthropologist and geographer Weichel, presents the following population density ranges associated with different types of technologies and economies (Hawley 1950).

Type of Culture	Persons/sq. mile
Hunting and Fishing	1–8
Pastoral and Forestry	8–26
Beginnings of Agriculture	26–64
Agriculture	64–192
Beginnings of Industry and Trade	192–256
Agriculture and Industry	256–381
Industry Predominates	381 and over

Similarly, Murdock, Petersen, and others, and most recently the *Cross Cultural Summary,* have indicated that different technologies are also associated with differences in the sizes of population groupings (Petersen 1961; Murdock 1949; Ottenberg and Ottenberg 1960; and Forde 1964). Thus, for example, groupings characterized by hunting and gathering are said to number typically around 25 to 30 persons, and agricultural village societies are said to number between 500 and 1,000 persons.

MALTHUSIAN BRINKMANSHIP? A classic view of nonliterate societies is that they increase in size to the limits of subsistence, after which mortality operates to stabilize them or worse. This view imputes to these societies a kind of Malthusian brinkmanship, a chronic skirting of the edges of catastrophe. Now, there are indeed many instances of decimating decreases and even of the extinction of primitive populations (Krzywicki 1934; Petersen 1961), but a large share of these are associated, not with indigenous causes, but with contacts with European elements introducing previously unknown pathologies, epidemic diseases, social disorganization, and sometimes large-scale violence. An increasing body of evidence points to the conclusion that nonliterate populations and societies—far from existing on the brink of Malthusian catastrophe—frequently exercise deliberate or unconscious means of controlling population size, the better to assure not merely their physical survival but their survival either at some higher-than-minimum level, or their survival with a minimum of sustenance-producing work, or some intermediate arrangement (Lee and De Vore 1968; Borrie et al. 1957; Himes 1963). Thus, the Bushmen of the Kalahari desert who control their population size by practice of infanticide (Thomas 1959), have been described as enjoying "a kind of material plenty."

One of the best documented examples of population control in primitive societies is that of the Tikopia, a Pacific island people. In his field studies in Tikopia in 1929 and again in 1952, the anthropologist Raymond Firth carried out fairly elaborate population censuses. In addition two population enumerations were carried out on the island, in 1933 and 1944, yielding jointly a unique documentation of population change in a primitive society.

The data for Tikopia suggest that Tikopians have deliberately controlled population size: the means alleged by various observers to have been practiced for this purpose include infanticide, celibacy or delayed marriage, *coitus interruptus* by married and by unmarried people, induced abortions, and "overseas voyages" of young adult males from which quite frequently they did not return.

In a detailed analysis of the available data for the 1929 to 1952 period, Borrie, Firth, and Spillus conclude that mortality—and not birth control within marriage—was the major factor limiting population growth in the period. However, this mortality could include both infanticide and the high-casualty "overseas voyages" so that the analysis does not preclude or contradict the assertion of deliberate population control (Borrie, Firth, and Spillus 1957).

To conclude this brief discussion of nonliterate societies, it should be emphasized that increasing knowledge of the variations in population size and in population-control arrangements of nonliterate societies will open up an important frontier in the study of populations and societies.

6. POPULATIONS AND SOCIETIES IN TIME AND SPACE

An outline of historical developments in social structure and social relations, and an overview of geographical variation in social structure at any single moment in time, might conceivably be entitled "World Social Order and Societies of the World." We cannot undertake here even the outlines of such an outline, though there exists a tradition of distinguished sociological and historical investigations whose results would surely form the major part of such a work.

The origins of sociology, and to some extent of social anthropology, were dominated by attempts to weave rather ambitious accounts and explanations of societal developments, changes, and variations. In the early decades of the present century, such ambitions were disavowed and earlier work of this kind discredited. But more recently—probably in part as a consequence of the "discovery" of underdeveloped nations and societies around, and subsequent to, World War II—there has been a revival in the social sciences generally, and in sociology in particular, of discussion and analysis of societal development, evolution, change or transformation as observable recurring phenomena. In other words, these phenomena are now taken as bona fide subjects for scientific investigation (as distinguished from the speculation that characterized previous social thinkers and the fathers of sociology).

It should be clear by now that we heartily agree to the fact of historical transformations of social structure and to the fact of cross-sectional variation in social structure. Having already shown briefly some lines of change within, and variations among, populations, we shall conclude this chapter by exploring, but very tentatively, the proposition that societies and social structure vary in time and space concomitantly with populations.

Again, we may draw upon familiar contrasts, to illustrate concomitant variations of population and social structure. If we consider the family, the educational and religious institutions, and the economic and political organization and institutions of colonial America or in the original thirteen United States, with its small, low-density, and essentially rural population, these contrast sharply with their counterparts in the contemporary United States, with its enormous high-density and largely urban population. Within contemporary American society, the social life and institutions of the very densely populated communities—for example on the Eastern seaboard—are notably different from those of the sparsely populated areas—the Great Plains or Rocky Mountains. Similar contrasts between the England of Shakespeare and the England of the Beatles, or between contemporary England and contemporary Ireland, are familiar: again, both the population differences and social institutional differences are sharp. Finally, there are very broad international contrasts—from tiny, isolated, nomadic bands or settled tribal populations, through the smallest of national populations, to the largest and most densely packed populations among the nation-states. These contrasts typically correspond in at least some measure to variations in the role that family and kinship play in social structure, to variations in the extent of individual social differentiation and in extent of institutional differentiation and specialization, and to variations in the content and forms of relationships between individuals and between institutions.

Again, we may draw upon the *Cross Cultural Summary* for an initial systematic expression of relationships between population and social structure. Over the sample of 400 cultures, it is shown that whether or not settlements are fixed, whether or not there are urban agglomerations, the size of community, age at marriage, rules of mate selection, patterns of divorce, and level of fertility are related to a broad range of technological and social-structural variables, including societal complexity, community and political organization, stratification, work organization, occupational specialization, kinship, family organizations, and socialization.

Our central concern is how and why populations and societies are related, how such relationships vary, and how they change over time. We begin a more detailed consideration in chapter 2.

2

Population and
Societal Strategies
of Survival and Adaptation:
The Size-Density Model
and the Urban Revolution

1. SOCIETAL TAXONOMIES AND THE SIZE-DENSITY MODEL

In the previous chapter we were concerned with ways in which populations vary or change over time, and we indicated that societies and their
social structures vary concomitantly with variations in population. In
this chapter we try to show more explicitly how population on the one
hand, and societal structure and patterns on the other, are mutually dependent and, more particularly, how changes in population size and
structure are fundamental factors, indeed causes, of societal change. In
Parts II and III we shall document this analysis more fully.

A DEFINITION OF SOCIETY AND ITS RELEVANT CHARACTERISTICS. As
a working definition, we may say that a *society* is a human population
organized, or characterized, by patterns of social relationships for the
purpose of collective survival in, and adaptation to, its environment.
Thus, recalling our earlier discussion of the delineation of population,
this definition demands that the members of a society co-occupy a given
area or category. It also demands that they be associated in patterns of
social interaction and that the society (but not necessarily all the social
relationships in it) have at least the implicit *purpose* of promoting the
survival and adaptation of its members in the environment in which it

is found. Thus, tribal, regional, or national societies may be identified and distinguished by reference to the bounds of the geophysical environments in which their populations are located and according to which their social organization evolves.

A widely cited and accepted definition (Boulding 1953) holds that "A *population* may be defined as an aggregate of disparate items, or individuals, each one of which conforms to a given definition, retains its identity with the passage of time, and exists only during a finite interval. An individual enters a population, or is 'born,' when it first conforms to the definition which identifies the population; it leaves the population or 'dies' when it ceases to conform with its definition." But a *society* is an organization of men—a small organization or a large one, a simple organization or a complex one—and it consists of functioning groups and on-going relations among individuals who view themselves as belonging to such an entity.

The characteristics of societies which are of scientific interest include types of social roles, systems of institutionalized social relationships; the morphology of social systems, subsystems, and collectivities; modes of economic adaptation; political organization; and patterns of settlement and community organization. Societies, and the structure of societies and of social relationships, may be viewed in the abstract, and the formal relationships between components of social structure may in some instances be stated in the form of a sociological algebra. However, our interest here will be in identifying, specifying, and describing real societies and in examining variations in societies and social structures.

Following our definition of "society," it seems reasonable to hypothesize that societies vary in accordance with *how* they pursue collective survival and adaptation. A number of authors have taken note of the differences in social structure and social relationships associated with different modes of assuring sustenance and physical adaptation; and indeed, some have sought to base societal taxonomies upon distinctions between various survival and sustenance technologies.

Two Recent Taxonomies

FORDE'S TAXONOMY.   The classic study by C. Daryll Forde, *Habitat, Economy and Society* (1964), classifies a number of nonEuropean societies in terms of food-production technologies and economies. The relationships between these and the elements of social organization are examined in some detail for three types of societies—for hunting and gathering societies such as the Semang and Sakai of Malaya, the Bushmen of the Kalahari desert in Africa, and the North American Paiute Indians; for agricultural and animal husbanding societies such as the Yoruba in the

Congo Basin of Africa, the Hopi Indians of Arizona, and the Cochin of southwest India; and for nomadic pastoral societies such as the Masai of East Africa and the Kazaks and Kirghiz of Central Asia.

Societies characterized by food-gathering and hunting economies, Forde points out, tend to be composed of relatively small groupings which are sparsely settled or which migrate within specified territories. The populations are concentrated in small areas and are typically very small (not more than two or three persons per square mile), which limits the scope of political institutions and, indeed, of social differentiation and organization generally.

The Australian aborigines, for example, were a hunting society grouped in small bands of between 20 and 50 individuals. According to estimates of A. R. Radcliffe-Brown (cited by Steward 1955) each band owned roughly 100 to 150 square miles of territory and over the whole of the Australian continent the population averaged about one person per twelve square miles. The bands were autonomous, but typically the "chief" was not a strong role, and there was little in the way of "government" or authority institutions. Similarly, there was but little "religious" activity or worship organized on a group basis, although there were rites associated with individual crisis situations—births, puberty, sickness, or death.

Societies characterized by food cultivation economies and technologies, whether they use digging stick, hoe, or plough cultivation, are almost uniformly composed of larger and more densely located population groupings than are hunting and gathering societies. For some, such as the Boro in the Western Amazon Basin, the food cultivation is also migratory, but for others, such as the Polynesians of Hawaii or the Cochin in India, it is settled. Increasingly elaborate and efficient methods of cultivation apparently result in a production of food surpluses that releases some members of the population to spend part or all of their working time in other occupations. Accordingly, societies of this type are characterized by a differentiation of economic roles, by the presence of social, religious, and political roles, and hence by a very much more elaborate range of social, economic, and political organization.

Ancient Egypt was one of the earliest agricultural societies. Wheat and barley were cultivated—eventually under irrigation—and cattle, pigs, sheep, and goats were domesticated. There were elaborate metallurgy and ceramics technologies, food storage was facilitated by advanced pottery and basket-making, and trade and distribution of food and other goods were promoted by the design and construction of balsa or papyrus bundle boats. Food production was on a subsistence basis but sufficed for provision of sustenance for a ruling class and ultimately for priesthood, warrior, and artisan classes. The basic socio-political unit was initially the village or local community, with eventual appearance of centralized state, urban centers, and large scale warfare as well as a system of social classes.

Pastoral societies are typically nomadic, roam within well-defined areas, may combine animal husbandry and herding with some food cultivation, and generally maintain some contact with more sedentary food-cultivating societies. The size of population groupings and the nature of social and political organization also vary among pastoral societies. More than other types of economy and technology, pastoralism appears to be related to geographical characteristics. It is associated with latitudes, altitudes, and climates in which systematic crop cultivation is difficult, and it is rarely found in forested areas. Forde shows that there are some instances of pastoral societies, e.g., the Kirghiz, which are, in fact, dispossessed or otherwise uprooted food cultivating societies.[1]

The Arab Bedouins of Jordan, Southern Israel, and the Sinai desert live in groups varying from compact families of a dozen or so to entire tribes numbering in the hundreds. Their seasonal movements follow both availability of grazing areas for the flocks—sheep, goats, and, more recently, cattle—*and* planting and harvesting cycles. Jerusalem, Beersheba, Amman, Jericho, and other towns have long been centers of trade and communication for the Bedouins of the area. Social relationships focus around elaborate kinship or family organization and relationships, marriage rules and marriage transactions, and around the role of the Sheikh. Aside from his authority and importance within each Bedouin tribe, the Sheikh's importance and the importance of his close circle have been enhanced in recent decades by their role as inter-tribal and inter-cultural contacts and mediators.

THE DUNCAN-GOLDSCHMIDT TAXONOMY AND THE PRINCIPLE OF "ECOLOGICAL EXPANSION." A recent societal taxonomy presented by O. D. Duncan (1964) is based upon a combination of the society's sub-

---

[1] Another classic, but much more elaborate and systematic, study of the social–organizational and institutional variations associated with different economies and technologies is that of Hobhouse, Wheeler, and Gonsberg (1965), first published in 1915. In this work, societies are also classified according to whether they are Hunters, Agriculturalists, or Pastoralists. However, these classifications are elaborated and subdivided as follows:

Lower Hunters	Agriculture II
Higher Hunters	Agriculture III
Dependent Hunters	Pastoral I
Agriculture I	Pastoral II

Relationships between these classifications and the institutions of government, justice, the family, war ranks, cannibalism, infanticide, human sacrifice, and property are analyzed quantitatively for some 640 societies.

More recent work suggests that Australian hunter societies, which possess a number of special characteristics, are greatly overrepresented in the sample chosen by these authors (Murdock and Whiting 1968).

sistence technology (hunting and gathering, horticulture, agriculture, herding, or industry) and the nature and scope of the local territorial unit (nomadic band, nomadic tribal band, sedentary tribal village, peasant village, or urban community).[2] The taxonomy includes the following types of societies:

1. Nomadic food-hunting and gathering bands
2. Nomadic food-hunting and gathering tribal societies
3. Settled hunting and food-gathering tribal societies
4. Horticultural village and tribal societies
5. Nomadic herding tribal societies
6. Agricultural-state societies, including both peasant villages *and* urban communities
7. Industrial, urban-dominated, state societies

These societal categories, which represent a sequence of stages in the evolution of society, comprehend or are related to a number of key structural variables. The latter include political organization (whether it is local or interlocal), type of territorial occupation (nomadic or sedentary), method of obtaining food (collection or production), the economic pattern (self-sufficiency or exchange), and the utilization of energy (preindustrial or industrial) (*ibid.* 1964, pp. 53–54). The categories are also meant to comprise a typology of "basic ecological forms" based upon the distinction between different exploitative technologies.

Figure 2.1 depicts Duncan's taxonomy and shows the directions of the evolutionary stages suggested by Goldschmidt and Duncan: the hunting and gathering tribal village society (3) evolves from the hunting and gathering band society (1, 2); the horticultural village society (4) evolves from the hunting and gathering village society (3) and from it, in turn, evolves the agricultural state society (6), comprising peasant villages *and* urban communities. Nomadic herding societies (5) evolve from, or together with, agricultural state societies (6). Finally, the industrial urban society (7) evolves from the agricultural state society, (6), with the urban communities retained and peasant villages characteristic of the agricultural state society ultimately disappearing.

To Duncan's taxonomy of societies, we may add the category of "metropolitan-megalopolitan societies," and in later sections of this chapter we shall indicate in some detail the characteristics of this category and the justification for its addition. In general, we would expect to be able to view most real—historical or contemporary—societies as belonging to, or else comprising some combination of societies formerly belonging to, one of the categories of this expanded taxonomy.

---

[2] Duncan notes that the taxonomy was originally proposed by W. Goldschmidt (1959).

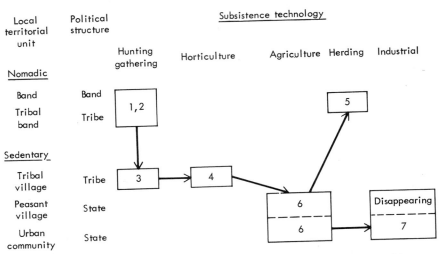

FIGURE 2.1. Taxonomy of societies according to Duncan, after Goldschmidt. Source: Duncan 1964.

Duncan raises the problem of accounting for evolutionary transitions—transitions from one societal "level" to the next—and he suggests "ecological expansion" as an explanatory principle. Ecological expansion is defined as: (1) an increase in numbers sustained by (2) increasing human resourcefulness in extracting the requisite supplies of energy and material from the environment and (3) an elaboration of the patterns of organization of the human collective efforts involved in this activity (*ibid.*, p. 40).

Clearly the Duncan-Goldschmidt societal types and structures are strongly related to the major facets of population, size, and density of settlement. Moreover, as shown in table 2.1, evolutionary transitions virtually always entail an increase either in population size, population density, or both. Finally, the explanatory principle of "ecological expansion" can be simplified somewhat by redefining it as "the population growth and economic, technological, and social-organizational changes mutually required to sustain one another." Thus the Duncan-Goldschmidt taxonomy, to which we add the metropolitan-megalopolitan category, may be viewed in terms of population size and density.

The Size-Density Model

We may extend the above line of approach somewhat by considering the classification of societies by population size and by the size of the territory to which the society has access or which it may exploit to

TABLE 2.1

*Modified Duncan-Goldschmidt Taxonomy, Showing
Typical Associated Population Size and Density*

Societal Type	Population Size	Population Density
1. Nomadic food-gathering and hunting bands	very small	low
2. Nomadic food-gathering and hunting tribal societies	small	low
3. Settled food-gathering and hunting tribal societies	small	medium
4. Horticultural village and tribal societies	medium	medium
5. Nomadic herding tribal societies	medium	low
6. Agricultural-state societies including both peasant villages and urban communities	large	medium
7. Industrial, urban-dominated, state societies	large	high
8. Metropolitan-megalopolitan societies	very large	very high

SOURCE: See text.

assure its survival and sustenance. Aside from its correspondence to the taxonomies based upon technologies and modes of assuring sustenance, such a classification has its own advantages and justification:

1. The *absolute population size* of a society bounds, or sets limits upon, the range of possible social and economic differentiation and division of labor possible in that society. Japan, Indonesia, and the United States, with populations in 1971 reaching 105 millions, 125 millions, and 207 millions respectively, have more alternatives than Canada, Australia, or Libya, with 1971 populations of 22 millions, 13 millions, and 2 millions respectively, with respect to social differentiation.

2. The *territorial scope* of a society bounds, or sets limits upon, the variety of environmental conditions and resources which can be exploited by the population in its search for sustenance. Brazil, with a 1971 population of 96 millions but with a territory totaling 8,500,000 square kilometers has more opportunities in this respect than does Indonesia, with a 1971 population of 125 millions but with only 1,500,000 square kilometers of area. Similarly, Canada's 1971 population of 22 millions have access to the resources of an area totaling 10 million square kilometers compared to North Vietnam, with 22 millions in the population but with an area of only 159,000 square kilometers.

3. Finally, the *density of population settlement* bounds, or sets limits upon, the number, frequency, or variety of human contacts and social and economic relationships possible in day-to-day

affairs. Ireland, with a population of about 3 millions and a density of about 43 persons per square kilometer has residential patterns, an economy, and a social structure quite different from that of Israel, whose 1971 population also numbered about 3 millions, but with a density of about 145 persons per square kilometer. A more extreme example is the comparison between Afghanistan, with 17 millions in 1971, and Taiwan, with 14 millions. Population density in Afghanistan amounts to about 26 persons per square kilometer, compared to 390 per square kilometer in Taiwan with corresponding extreme differences in social, economic, and political structure, in technology and levels of living, and in virtually all aspects of individual and community life.

The possible extremes in such a classification are given in the following four-fold scheme.

Population size	Territorial Scope	
	Small area	*Large area*
Small society	Small society Small area	Small society Large area
Large society	Large society Small area	Large society Large area

By way of drawing the most extreme contrasts possible, we may indicate some differences in physiographic environment and cultural adaptation between isolated nomadic food-gathering groups—those located at the smallest-size-lowest-density extreme—and the large, urban-industrial societies—located at the largest-size-highest-density extreme. The isolated nomadic group is at the mercy of its environment; life and death themselves depend on how successfully the population withstands daily environmental perils. By contrast, the mass urban-industrial society literally transforms its environment, virtually creates its own geography, and manipulates and exploits the geophysical features of the earth to its own benefit.

There is, of course, no necessary relationship between the areal and population sizes of societies and the level of their technology or social, political, and economic development. Thus, though they are areally large, with very large populations and very high population densities, we would not necessarily expect India and China to be the world's most advanced societies. However, their large areas, tremendous population sizes, and high densities do present certain basic social and economic *possibilities* and certain social, political, and economic imperatives.

Among the pioneers of sociological investigation and theory, it was Emile Durkheim who drew attention to the way in which population size, distribution, density and composition affect society and social structure. In his classic *The Division of Labor in Society* (1933), the French sociologist Durkheim proposes that the development of social differentiation is a universal phenomenon and contrasts relatively undifferentiated societies with highly differentiated ones in terms of the nature and basis of their social solidarity. He distinguishes between "mechanical solidarity" of the undifferentiated societies and an "organic solidarity" of the differentiated ones. We shall explain these concepts in the following section, but for the present, suffice it to say that organic solidarity is seen as resulting from the division of labor. In considering the causes of the division of labor, Durkheim poses this central proposition:

> The division of labor varies in direct ratio with volume and density of societies, and, if it progresses in a continuous manner in the course of social development, it is because societies become regularly denser and generally more voluminous. [Durkheim 1933, p. 262]

Durkheim initiated, and his students continued, a subfield of sociology called "social morphology," which is concerned with the study of social, economic, political, and other characteristics of human communities as related to population size, composition, and geographic distribution (Duncan and Pfautz 1960).

Although, among the earlier sociologists, only Durkheim and his students were concerned with the size-density basis of societal variation, the relationship was widely studied in related disciplines. Thus, the geographer and anthropologist Weichel classified density ranges for different types of economies, and Hawley, citing this classification, worked out an analysis of "population balance," i.e., the adjustment of numbers to the opportunities for living, involving (1) population size, (2) resource abundance, and (3) organization of the population (Hawley 1950, chap. 9). Hawley determined that societies which are small, isolated, and self-sufficient are characterized by constant social organizational forms, e.g., the family, church, or political institutions. Since resource materials are highly variable in time, the populations of these societies must vary in size in accordance with fluctuations in the habitat. Conversely, the extensive interdependence that obtains among large spatially dispersed population aggregates allows for a stabilization of resources by means of exchange, and the social organizational factor may be variable. Under such circumstances, adjustment and balance are effected by mobility of population and of all agents of production, rather than by mortality (*ibid.;* see also Schnore 1958 and Duncan 1959).

Among contemporary sociologists, it is P. M. Hauser who has most vividly portrayed the social interactional and organizational implications of variation in population densities:

> . . . let us consider the differences in potential social interaction in a community with a fixed land area but varying population density.

Let the land area be that which lies within a circle with a 10-mile radius, namely, 314 square miles. In such an area the size of the population under different density conditions is shown below.

Population Density (Population per Square Mile)	Number of Persons Circle of 10-mile Radius
1	314
50	15,700
8,000	2,512,000
17,000	5,338,000
25,000	7,850,000

The density of one person per square mile is not too far from the density of the United States when occupied by the Indians. The density of 50 is approximately that of the United States today, and also of the world as a whole. The density of 8,000, in round numbers, was that of central cities in metropolitan areas in 1950, the density figure of 17,000 was that of Chicago in 1950, and the 25,000 density figure that of New York.

Thus, in aboriginal America the person moving about within a circle of 10-mile radius could potentially make only 313 different contacts. In contrast, the density of the U.S. as a whole today would make possible well over 15,000 contacts in the same land area; the density of central cities in the U.S., in 1950, would permit over 2.5 million contacts; the density of Chicago over 5.3 million contacts; and the density of New York City about 7.9 million contacts. These differences in density and therefore in potential social interaction necessarily affect the nature of collective activity and social organization. [Hauser 1963, p. 4]

We discuss the size-density issue again in more detail in chapter 11.

2. SOCIETAL STRATEGIES OF SURVIVAL AND ADAPTATION: CHANGES IN TIME

An explanation of the social, economic, and technological variation associated with societal population size, areal scope, and density is presented here in terms of what we call the "societal strategy of survival and adaptation." This point of view assumes that populations must organize to effect their collective survival—and that in so doing they define other collective "interests" in addition to survival itself—and that populations disperse and settle themselves over the available territory and organize themselves socially and economically so as to assure their collective survival and promote what they view or accept as their key interests.

Our remarks pertain to populations of any size, located in bounded areas of any size. Thus, they might apply to colonial America, or to the

Eskimos, or to whatever society you choose. As noted above, both the absolute number of persons in the population and the size of the area available to it bound or limit the possible arrangements for adaptation and the derivation of sustenance. We may assume that whatever its size, area, and level of technology, a population tends to settle—or to choose a migratory pattern—and to arrange and organize itself otherwise so as to try to assure its physical and biological survival and promote its hierarchy of goals and values.[3]

Of course, any of a large variety of values or goals may be viewed or accepted by a population as constituting its vital interests, and any of a number of institutions or persons may articulate, define, or determine the population's vital interests and how these may change. A population could conceivably view high per capita income or per capita consumption as its most desirable goal. Other goals might be total national income, national power or prestige, leisure, knowledge, beauty or art, security or social welfare, individual freedom, love, the glory of God, longevity and health—the list is endless. In addition, a population's vital interests may be articulated or defined by some democratic political process, or by oligarchical, autocratic or aristocratic regimes, or by some other method or entity.

It is also worth remarking that a high level of technology is not equivalent to, nor even necessarily dependent upon, a high level of scientific knowledge. Technology has reference to processes and procedures actually employed in production, rather than to a knowledge of principles governing relationships in the physical, biological, or social spheres. For example, the United States in the nineteenth century, and Japan in the twentieth, became technologically very advanced by adopting the results of advanced scientific knowledge developed abroad.

Finally, even though populations are characterized by a rationality or purposiveness in organizing themselves to promote their own survival and other interests—thereby becoming societies—all individuals in these populations do not necessarily share this trait.

The Pressures of Population Growth

The social, economic, and technological arrangements which a population has for assuring its sustenance and survival are always subject to a certain amount of tension and threat of disruption. This tension or threat could be due to natural or climatic disaster, crop failure, epidemic, war, or any other exogenous disturbance; and the smaller and more iso-

---

[3] Presumably there could be exceptions. That is, it is conceivable that there are societies which deliberately adopt arrangements operating to diminish their chances of survival. But the very nature of such societies would seem to make obtaining information or observations extremely difficult, and we would have to exclude such societies from the analysis.

lated the society, the greater the susceptibility to it. But in addition to
exogenous sources of tension and pressure, there is universally an endog-
enous source as well. Every population is continually subject to the
pressures of its own tendency to increase in numbers, a tendency which
spells opportunity for some societies and disaster for others. It is under
the pressures of population growth that changes in the settlement, social
organizational, and economic and technological arrangements of a population are effected—or, alternatively, that institutionalized constraints
upon mating or procreation are evolved.

Thus, J. G. D. Clark, in his *Prehistoric Europe: The Economic
Basis* (1952), has viewed population pressure and growth as a central
factor in the transformations from "prehistory" to "history" in Europe:

> The main factors involved in the economic changes whereby Euro-
> pean peoples were ultimately able reach the state of recording their
> own history may be grouped under three heads. First, one should
> reckon with alterations in the natural environment brought about
> by processes external to man, changes which were inherent in the
> natural order of events, but which enlarged or contracted the range
> of opportunity open to human societies. The most widespread and
> dramatic of these were the climatic changes . . .
>
> Next, and more positively, may be cited changes in the needs
> and requirements of human societies brought about by a wide range
> of factors. Some of these, for example the pressure of population on
> food supply, were of a purely economic order. Others were primarily
> cultural, among the most important being the effects of contact be-
> tween the barbarians of prehistoric Europe and the civilized peoples
> of the East Mediterranean area . . .
>
> Lastly there are the changes in the external environment
> brought about directly or indirectly by human activities. As a domi-
> nant species man must always have affected the balance of nature
> to some degree, but his importance as an ecological factor grew as he
> increased in numbers and extended his control over external forces,
> until he became a principal agent of botanical and zoological change.
> Each advance in culture increased the ecological dominance of man:
> the more effectively he was able to intervene in natural processes,
> the more frequently he must have disturbed by his own activities the
> adjustment with external nature of his own culture, and the more
> often in consequence he had to modify his economy to meet the new
> conditions created by his own exertions. [Clark 1952, pp. 8–9]

Greek migration and colonization extending over the Mediterranean coastline and islands between 800 and 600 B.C. have been attributed
to overpopulation at home. The Greek word *stenochoria*—a combination
of *steno* (narrowness, tightness) and *choria* (place, soil area)—was used to
describe this ancient response to population pressure (Bérard 1960, cited
in Guillaume and Poussou 1970).

Another response to population pressure, the practice of contraception and abortion, is as old as society itself. In the introduction to his *Medical History of Contraception* (1963), N. E. Himes writes:

> . . . contraception, as only one form of population control, is a social practice of much greater historical antiquity, greater cultural and geographical universality than commonly supposed even by medical and social historians. Contraception has existed in some form throughout the entire range of social evolution, that is, for at least several thousand years. The *desire for,* as distinct from the *achievement of,* reliable contraception has been characteristic of many societies widely removed in time and place. Moreover, this desire for controlled reproduction characterizes even those societies dominated by mores and religious codes demanding that people "increase and multiply." [Himes 1963]

Himes goes on to describe contraceptive techniques in preliterate societies, in the ancient Western and Oriental civilizations, in the Middle Ages, and in modern folk practices, in addition to discussing the more recent (nineteenth century and later) popularization of birth control.

Thus, in studying any society, we are confronted with an ongoing interaction between population and its social organization, technology, and environment. A society characterized by a fixed technology and social organization must, when confronted by substantial growth in its own numbers, expand its environment by settlement, cultivation, or exploitation of new areas, or suffer a decline in the per capita level of subsistence. On the other hand, a society with a fixed area alone can increase its production and look after its growing numbers by effecting changes either in social organization or technology.

The alternative strategies of adaptation are neatly illustrated by R. L. Carneiro in his comparison of the Kuikuru Indians and other horticultural tribes of the Amazon Basin with horticultural societies of the Circum-Caribbean and Andean seas. The population of the Amazon Basin grew and expanded throughout the area with no notable dense concentrations of population, and no notable technological or social organizational innovations. However, the Circum-Caribbean and Andean areas are essentially circumscribed with regard to cultivable land. Such land is limited to the mountain valleys of Colombia, the coastal strips of Venezuela, the islands of the Greater Antilles, and the Peruvian coastal valleys. In these areas, population growth resulted in competition, warfare, elaboration of political organization, stratification and division of labor and intensification of agricultural activity (Carneiro 1968).

The society unable to alter its social or technological patterns and unable to expand its physical environment must institutionalize patterns of controlling population growth, or suffer substantial decreases in its levels of living, or lose all of its potential growth through high mortality.

HISTORY OF ADAPTATION ON THE DIYALA RIVER PLAINS. In his monumental study of the history of over 6,000 years of settlement on the Diyala River plains of Iraq, Robert McC. Adams has estimated population size and changes and traced the patterns of settlement, technology of food production, and broad lines of political, social, and economic organization (Adams 1965). The Diyala River plains are close to what is believed to be the locus of the beginnings of agriculture. Using modern methods of archaeological survey and analysis as well as historical and modern agricultural, hydrological, and geological methods, Adams is able to show *both* the physical expansion of settlement *and* some social organizational and technological changes in the lower Diyala region from 4000 B.C. to 1957 A.D., the date of the most recent census of Iraq available to him.

The population of the area increased from under 10,000 to over 90,000 between 4000 and 2000 B.C., with a corresponding increase in number of settlements (from 23 to 97) and some size differentiation and possible political differentiation among them. In the period from 2000 to 1000 B.C., the population declined to under 10,000 with a large number of sites abandoned. In the first millennium B.C., the population again began to rise, this time much more rapidly, especially under the Seleucid and Parthian regimes. The latter initiated the establishment of sizable cities, improvements in communications and commerce, and stable and peaceful conditions. In this period, the settlement of the lower Diyala region expanded to the banks of the Tigris and, with the construction of the cities of Seleucia and Ctesiphon, the area assumed a new status as a populous and vital region of a great empire. Irrigation development was made possible on a new scale, mobilizing the waters of the Tigris with the introduction of pulleys and animal traction. Increasingly, food production was connected to the development and use of complex and lengthy lateral canals conducting water from the major natural watercourses to the peripheries of cultivation. Thus, three new developments occurred in the period: unprecedented population growth (to roughly 300,000 persons), extensive urbanization, and the transformation of the irrigation system into an intensive, large-scale, artificially maintained, regionally interdependent enterprise.

Further population growth, urban and agricultural development, and political elaboration took place during the Sassanian period (266 A.D.–637 A.D.), and at its peak the population approached an estimated 825,000, which is somewhat higher than the 1957 population of the area. The number of urban centers and their sizes increased dramatically, and water and irrigation works were enlarged and elaborated to an unprecedented extent. The area above the Jebel Hamrin, which had previously been only very sparsely settled—perhaps with some dry farming or herding —was now densely settled with an elaborately irrigated agriculture. This enterprise, Adams concludes, could only have been undertaken under state initiative and control and must have reflected land shortages in the areas of traditional settlement.

The end of the Sassanian period and the onset of the Early Islamic period (ca. 637 A.D.) heralded a rapid deterioration of central authority— ten kings reigned in a period of nine years—and, according to Adams, real rule was increasingly an object of contention among the nobility, with many districts becoming entirely autonomous. In the social and political upheaval, the irrigation and agricultural system on which the wealth of the area had been based collapsed and disintegrated. In a short time, the area was depopulated and scores of settlement sites were entirely abandoned. Subsequently, Arab successors of the Sassanian rulers repaired and renewed the irrigation system, population increased, and Baghdad was established as a great metropolis—though not to the levels attained at the peak of the Sassanian regime. However, by the middle of the tenth century A.D., with the deterioration of the Abbasid caliphate, a decline in population and settlement had begun. This decline was accentuated by the Mongol invasions in the twelfth century, and it did not end until the present century. The population of the Lower Diyala region fell to around 50,000, with town life—except for Baghdad—virtually disappearing. Only in the present century has the population increased dramatically again, but urban development has been largely confined to the Baghdad area. Figures 2.2 and 2.3 graphically illustrate this six-thousand-year history.

We may recapitulate the points bearing on the societal strategy of survival and adaptation as follows:

1. In any given period of time, a society's strategy of survival and adaptation is bounded by and limited by the size of its population, the area and the nature of the territory in which it resides, and, derivatively, the population density of the area in question; and

2. Every society must confront the pressure of fertility and potentially expanding populations which, in general, operates to generate changes in the societal strategy of survival and adaptation. Only in special cases, such as the case of societies characterized by very high mortality or by deliberate control of population growth, does fertility not necessarily exert any special pressure toward change.[4]

4 It could prove to be the case, historically, that most societies have in fact been characterized for most of their histories either by very high mortality or by deliberate control of population growth. Nevertheless, in the analytical middle the more general case would be that of fertility implying the possibility of population growth.

Alternative Strategies of Adaptation

Armed with the foregoing material, let us consider in some depth a society with a given population size, a given territory, and a given strategy of survival and adaptation—that is, a society that falls into one of the categories, of, say, the taxonomy proposed by Duncan.

As we indicated earlier, we assume in any society a natural tendency toward population growth—a tendency which generates tension or pressure on the society and on its strategy of survival and adaptation. Under the pressure of population growth, the society must change its mode of adaptation and expand its effective environment, either extensively or intensively. A number of alternative strategies are open to such a society.

THE FIRST ALTERNATIVE: AREAL EXPANSION. In the first place, the society can expand its area of settlement. Two related possibilities for such expansion are, first, the division of the society or, second, the development of a second group within the society which simply migrates, leaves the original society, and forms its own settlement in another place.

(text continues on page 79)

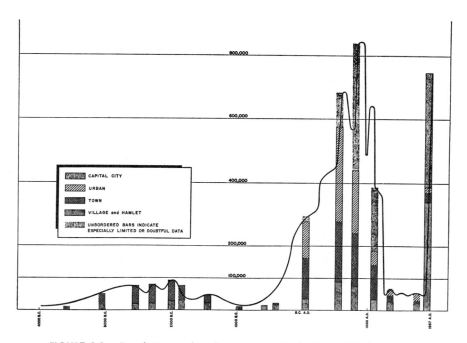

FIGURE 2.2. Population and settlement types in the lower Diyala region, by periods. Source: Adams 1965, table 25.

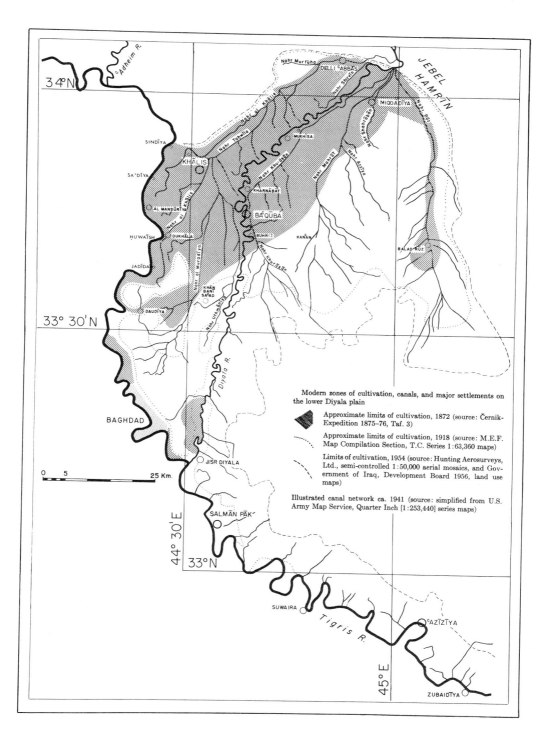

34°N

'Adhem R.

JEBEL HAMRIN

Nahr Murfūha
DELLI 'ABBĀS

MIQDĀDĪYA

Nahr Ruz

Nahr al Khāliṣ

Nahr Shahrabān

Nahr Tahmiz

SINDĪYA

MUKHĪSA

KHĀLIS

Nahr Khurasān

Nahr 'Azīzīya

Nahr Mahrūt

SA'DĪYA

Nahr ul Kharābla

KHARNĀBAT

AL MANSŪRĪYA

BA'QŪBA

HUWATSH

DUKHĀLA

BUHRIZ

KANĀN

Nahr ul Muqdādīya

Nahr Khurasān

BALAD RŪZ

JADĪDA

KHĀN BANI SA'AD

Nahr Uthmānīya

DAUDĪYA

Diyala R.

33° 30'N

BAGHDAD

Modern zones of cultivation, canals, and major settlements on the lower Diyala plain

Approximate limits of cultivation, 1872 (source: Černik-Expedition 1875–76, Taf. 3)

Approximate limits of cultivation, 1918 (source: M.E.F. Map Compilation Section, T.C. Series 1:63,360 maps)

Limits of cultivation, 1954 (source: Hunting Aerosurveys, Ltd., semi-controlled 1:50,000 aerial mosaics, and Government of Iraq, Development Board 1956, land use maps)

Illustrated canal network ca. 1941 (source: simplified from U.S. Army Map Service, Quarter Inch [1:253,440] series maps)

JISR DIYALA

0   5   25 Km.

44° 30' E

SALMĀN PĀK

33°N

SUWAIRA

Tigris R.

'AZĪZĪYA

45° E

ZUBAIDĪYA

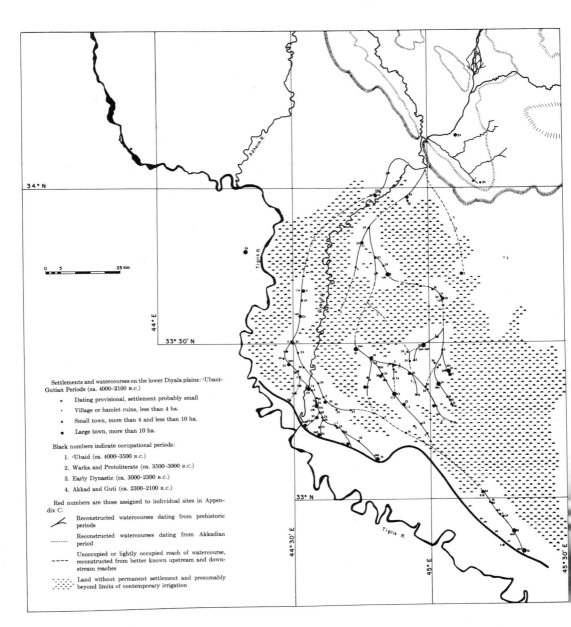

Settlements and watercourses on the lower Diyala plains: ʿUbaid-
Gutian Periods (ca. 4000–2100 B.C.)

  ○   Dating provisional, settlement probably small

  ·   Village or hamlet ruins, less than 4 ha.

  •   Small town, more than 4 and less than 10 ha.

  ●   Large town, more than 10 ha.

Black numbers indicate occupational periods:

  1. ʿUbaid (ca. 4000–3500 B.C.)

  2. Warka and Protoliterate (ca. 3500–3000 B.C.)

  3. Early Dynastic (ca. 3000–2300 B.C.)

  4. Akkad and Guti (ca. 2300–2100 B.C.)

Red numbers are those assigned to individual sites in Appendix C.

  ⟋ Reconstructed watercourses dating from prehistoric
     periods

  ········· Reconstructed watercourses dating from Akkadian
     period

  - - - Unoccupied or lightly occupied reach of watercourse,
     reconstructed from better known upstream and down-
     stream reaches

  ∴∴∴ Land without permanent settlement and presumably
  ∴∴∴ beyond limits of contemporary irrigation

FIGURE 2.3B

74

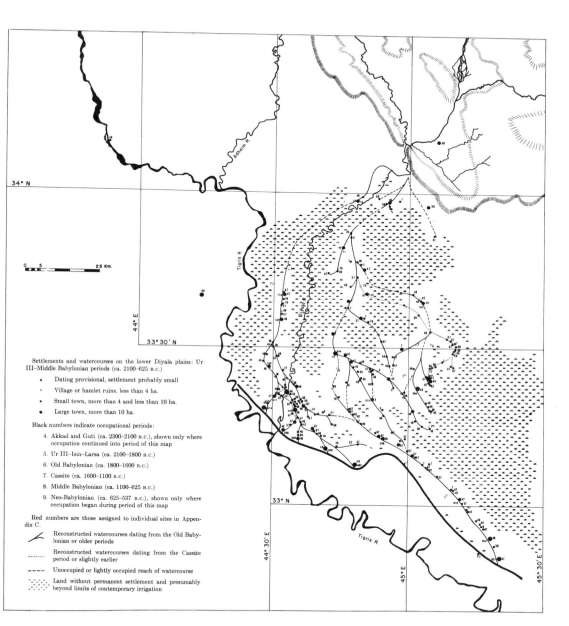

Settlements and watercourses on the lower Diyala plains: Ur III–Middle Babylonian periods (ca. 2100–625 B.C.)

- •   Dating provisional, settlement probably small
- ·   Village or hamlet ruins, less than 4 ha.
- •   Small town, more than 4 and less than 10 ha.
- ●   Large town, more than 10 ha.

Black numbers indicate occupational periods:

4. Akkad and Guti (ca. 2300–2100 B.C.), shown only where occupation continued into period of this map

5. Ur III–Isin–Larsa (ca. 2100–1800 B.C.)

6. Old Babylonian (ca. 1800–1600 B.C.)

7. Cassite (ca. 1600–1100 B.C.)

8. Middle Babylonian (ca. 1100–625 B.C.)

9. Neo-Babylonian (ca. 625–537 B.C.), shown only where occupation began during period of this map

Red numbers are those assigned to individual sites in Appendix C.

⟋   Reconstructed watercourses dating from the Old Babylonian or older periods

··········   Reconstructed watercourses dating from the Cassite period or slightly earlier

- - - -   Unoccupied or lightly occupied reach of watercourse

⸬⸬⸬   Land without permanent settlement and presumably beyond limits of contemporary irrigation

FIGURE 2.3C

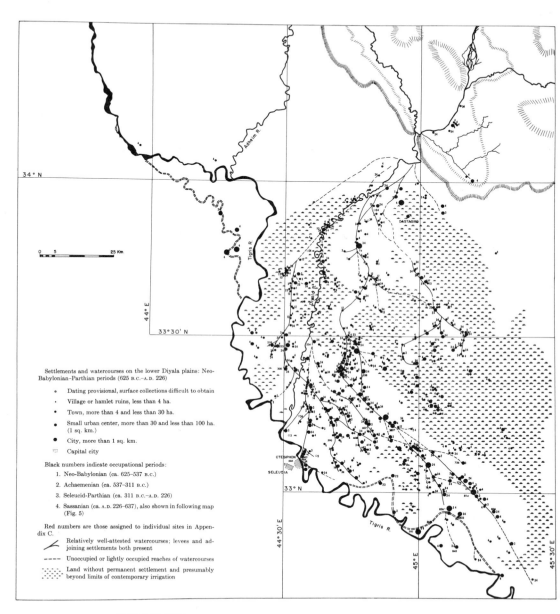

Settlements and watercourses on the lower Diyala plains: Neo-Babylonian–Parthian periods (625 B.C.–A.D. 226)

- • Dating provisional, surface collections difficult to obtain
- · Village or hamlet ruins, less than 4 ha.
- • Town, more than 4 and less than 30 ha.
- ● Small urban center, more than 30 and less than 100 ha. (1 sq. km.)
- ● City, more than 1 sq. km.
- ▭ Capital city

Black numbers indicate occupational periods:

1. Neo-Babylonian (ca. 625–537 B.C.)
2. Achaemenian (ca. 537–311 B.C.)
3. Seleucid-Parthian (ca. 311 B.C.–A.D. 226)
4. Sassanian (ca. A.D. 226–637), also shown in following map (Fig. 5)

Red numbers are those assigned to individual sites in Appendix C.

⟋ Relatively well-attested watercourses; levees and adjoining settlements both present

- - - - Unoccupied or lightly occupied reaches of watercourses

∴ Land without permanent settlement and presumably beyond limits of contemporary irrigation

FIGURE 2.3D

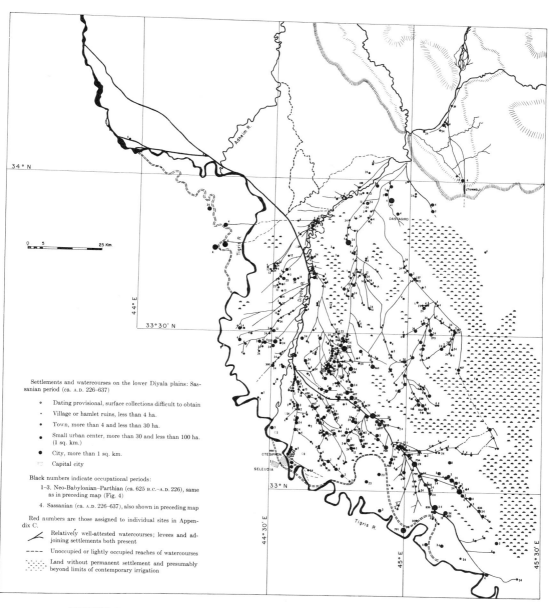

Settlements and watercourses on the lower Diyala plains: Sassanian period (ca. A.D. 226–637)

- ° Dating provisional, surface collections difficult to obtain
- · Village or hamlet ruins, less than 4 ha.
- • Town, more than 4 and less than 30 ha.
- ● Small urban center, more than 30 and less than 100 ha. (1 sq. km.)
- ● City, more than 1 sq. km.
- ⬚ Capital city

Black numbers indicate occupational periods:

    1–3. Neo-Babylonian–Parthian (ca. 625 B.C.–A.D. 226), same as in preceding map (Fig. 4)

    4. Sassanian (ca. A.D. 226–637), also shown in preceding map

Red numbers are those assigned to individual sites in Appendix C.

⊱ Relatively well-attested watercourses; levees and adjoining settlements both present

---- Unoccupied or lightly occupied reaches of watercourses

⋮⋮ Land without permanent settlement and presumably beyond limits of contemporary irrigation

FIGURE 2.3E

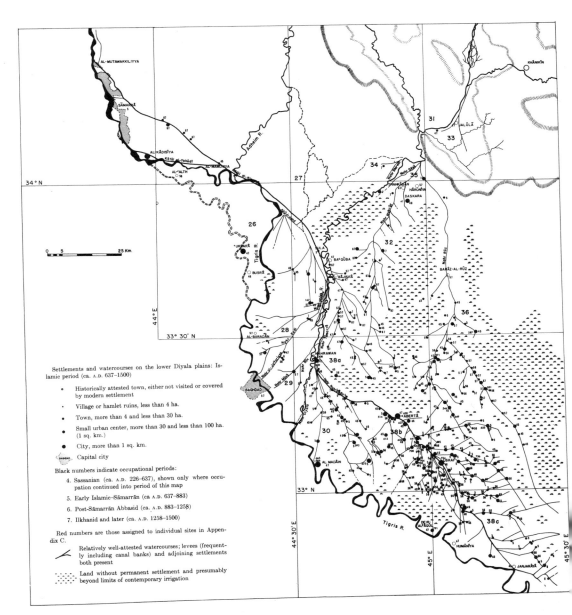

Settlements and watercourses on the lower Diyala plains: Islamic period (ca. A.D. 637–1500)

- Historically attested town, either not visited or covered by modern settlement

· Village or hamlet ruins, less than 4 ha.

• Town, more than 4 and less than 30 ha.

■ Small urban center, more than 30 and less than 100 ha. (1 sq. km.)

● City, more than 1 sq. km.

BAGHDAD Capital city

Black numbers indicate occupational periods:

4. Sassanian (ca. A.D. 226–637), shown only where occupation continued into period of this map

5. Early Islamic–Sāmarrān (ca A.D. 637–883)

6. Post-Sāmarrān Abbasid (ca. A.D. 883–1258)

7. Ilkhanid and later (ca. A.D. 1258–1500)

Red numbers are those assigned to individual sites in Appendix C.

Relatively well-attested watercourses; levees (frequently including canal banks) and adjoining settlements both present

Land without permanent settlement and presumably beyond limits of contemporary irrigation

FIGURE 2.3F

Two cases in point are the Greek colonization in the Mediterranean and the Roman conquests. Two other related possibilities are the movement of some, or many, or even all members of the society to peripheral areas, or the expansion of areas in which food is collected, grown, or produced. An example of *both* is the westward expansion of the United States.

However, any number of factors may operate to prevent a society from expanding its area of settlement. In the first place, neighboring societies may not permit such expansion. They may have territorial rights which are accepted by custom or defended by force. The Italian city-states of the late Middle Ages or the primitive Circum-Caribbean societies come to mind. In the second place, the society may not have the means of transport and communication to cover a wider area of settlement; thus, the expansion of physical settlement might necessitate breaking up the group or having part of the group remain incommunicado with the main body of the society. Some of the strains in maintaining the Roman Empire were of this nature. Finally the neighboring areas may not lend themselves to any reasonable sustenance-producing activities. That is, they may consist of sea, desert, or some other terrain which is not exploitable for the production or collection of food, or at least not exploitable by that particular society. This was the case in Ancient Egypt, where the population settled primarily along the banks of the Nile River, leaving the rest of the country unpopulated.

THE SECOND ALTERNATIVE: ADOPTION OF TECHNOLOGICAL AND SOCIAL INNOVATIONS. The second way in which societies may deal with the pressures of population increase is to intensify their expoitation of the territories which they have. This intensification may be effected in two general ways. First, the society may adopt improvements in technology which very substantially raise the sustenance yield per unit of area, and indeed per unit of labor, and thus permit the society to absorb and maintain a significant population increase. The adoption of cultivation or the change from digging-stick cultivation to hoe-cultivation, or from hoe-agriculture to plow-agriculture, significantly increases the amount of food which may be produced in any given area of land. The adoption of hybrid corn in North America and the "Green Revolution" in Asia are more recent examples. Similarly, the domestication of animals and the development of new forms of power and energy conversion, transportation, communication, and storage all operate to increase very substantially either the yield of sustenance per unit of land or the possibility of distributing such sustenance among a larger number of persons. The adoption of new technologies of extracting and processing resources and fabricating manufactured products also enhances the sustenance-producing ability of a society in a fixed area and allows for much higher population sizes and densities.

The second mode of intensifying the exploitation of a given territory involves changes in social organization. These changes—and particularly specialization and the division of labor—generally operate to increase very significantly the yield per unit of land and thus provide an alternative mode of coping with the pressure of population increase.

In his *Division of Labor in Society* (1933), Durkheim proposed as the key to the evolution of societies a process involving population growth, increased physical and social density, social and occupational differentiation, and the division of labor. In this process, according to Durkheim, the very basis of a society and of the social relationships in it change from one of "mechanical solidarity" to "organic solidarity." Mechanical solidarity denotes the interdependence, consensus, and cohesiveness attributable to similarities of social role, activity, background, outlook, and immediate activities and interests. Organic solidarity, on the other hand, is the dependence, cooperation, consensus, and cohesiveness born of differences and specializations of role, activity, mode of life, and outlook.

The transformation from mechanical to organic solidarity is, in Durkheim's analysis, associated with the differentiation and division of labor occasioned by population growth, increasing physical and social density, and competition for sustenance and status. Increasing social and economic differentiation and division of labor resolve the problem of competition in growing populations, and they resolve it productively by enhancing both the productive capacities and organic solidarity of the societies in question.

THE THIRD ALTERNATIVE: POPULATION CONTROL. What if a society of given size and territorial scope cannot expand its area of settlement or intensify its exploitation of this area? In such a case, the growing population exerts pressure on the society's limited resources, and the society suffers lower levels of living. The latter, in turn, entail high levels of mortality, typically sufficiently high to neutralize the pressure of population growth. Indeed, this describes the pattern of population growth throughout most of human history.

But there is another possibility. The society in question may, more or less self-consciously, institutionalize modes of controlling its population growth; that is, it may diminish directly the pressure of its growing population by either promoting mortality or dampening fertility. Celibacy, delayed marriage, and birth control and abortion within marriage are the most familiar modes of controlling population growth in modern Western societies. However, some societies have been known to engage in considerably more drastic means of population control — the abandonment of elderly and deformed persons, infanticide, human sacrifice, cannibalism, and slave-trading. The Aztecs practiced human sacrifice on a large scale; the ancient Greeks killed disabled infants; the Tikopia practiced infanticide. Hobhouse, Wheeler, and Ginsberg (1965) note ten societies which practice cannibalism,[5] 42 which practice human sacrifice, and 45 which practice infanticide.

SOME EXAMPLES OVER TIME. A few familiar examples of interaction between population, social organization, technology, and environment may be cited very briefly. The United States in the nineteenth century was characterized by high rates of population growth. These were due both to high rates of natural increase and to great waves of immigration. The well-known westward expansion of the frontier, which took place throughout most of the century, slackened not when the frontier became "closed," but when industrialization and changing technology produced new patterns of settlement—urbanization and concentration—that rendered such geographical expansion relatively obsolete or, at least, less advantageous as a social strategy. We return to this example in chapter 13.

Ireland and Spain, both Catholic and both characterized by low levels of urbanization and industrialization, are also characterized by fairly low mortality. Yet these populations have experienced very little growth in numbers for generations. In these cases, very late marriage and high proportions remaining single, rather than control of marital fertility, are usually viewed as the main reasons for the absence of population growth.

Newly developing countries in Asia have recently enjoyed spectacular declines in mortality and are now experiencing correspondingly spectacular increases in population. With available land already intensively settled, cultivated, and exploited, these populations are seeking to preserve and even improve their levels of living by introducing new technologies, on the one hand, and by promoting fertility-control practices, on the other. The deliberate, conscious, planned attempt to revise social strategies of adaptation in Asia and other areas undergoing rapid population growth has rendered more urgent an understanding of such processes generally and of the historical shifts in societal strategies of adaptation which accompanied the demographic transition in Europe.

In the case of Europe, it seems clear not only that great population growth was successfully sustained, but also that levels of living and the "quality of life" in general enjoyed great improvement. The spectacular population growth going on in the newly developing countries today is *itself* evidence that these countries have been successful in altering their strategies of survival and adaptation—otherwise, their high fertility would

---

5 But they do not distinguish between those practicing it on enemies or strangers and those practicing it on members of their own society.

be neutralized by high mortality, as indeed it was in the past. What is in question is whether or not—under conditions of rapid population growth—the already low levels of living in these countries can be prevented from falling further or whether they can be raised, as was the case historically for Europe. Because of the widespread political commitment of national elites to raising levels of living, and because of the increasing visibility—due to education, improved information, and communication—of the extreme differences between levels of living in the developed and underdeveloped countries, the possible *failure* to improve conditions in the rapidly growing countries is cast as a threat to local and world political stability. It is in this context that the social scientific questions of how population size, structure, and change are related to production, distribution, and levels of living take on their current urgency.

EASTERLIN'S ANALYSIS OF THE EFFECTS OF POPULATION GROWTH ON ECONOMIC DEVELOPMENT. We shall return to relationships between population and economy in Parts II and III. Before concluding this setting, let us review R. A. Easterlin's summary analysis of the effects of population growth on economic development historically and for presently developing countries (Easterlin 1967).

As Easterlin indicates, the viewpoint usually expressed in connection with the increasing concern over the dangers of population growth is that population growth has unfavorable effects upon economic development for two main reasons: (a) the fixity of natural resources, especially land, from which it is inferred that agricultural productivity and per capita food resources must decline; [6] and the consequent high dependency ratio, which, it is reasoned, causes the household to spend rather than save and depresses the rate of investment in the economy.[7]

It has also been urged that population growth enhances the prospects for economic development. Two basic reasons are cited: (a) that economies of scale are made possible by larger markets and a larger, more specialized, labor force, and (b) that the pressure of increased family size or community size causes individuals to work harder and both individuals and organizations to develop or adopt improved methods and processes of production. A further argument connecting population growth and development holds that the health improvements responsible for reduction in mortality are also responsible for increased productivity.

---

6 As Easterlin points out, this is essentially the Malthusian argument. See our discussion in chapter 1 of Malthus's formulation of the population-resources problem.

7 The current outstanding formulation of this argument is given by Coale and Hoover (1958).

TABLE 2.2

Frequency Distribution of Developing Nations by Growth Rate of Real Per Capita Income Cross-Classified by Growth Rate of Population, 1957–1958 to 1963–1964

Rate of Population Growth (percent per year)	Total	Rate of Growth of Real Per Capita Income (percent per year)						
		Less than zero	*0 to 0.9*	*1.0 to 1.9*	*2.0 to 2.9*	*3.0 to 3.9*	*4.0 to 4.9*	*5.0 and over*
Total	*37*	*3*	*4*	*12*	*12*	*2*	*2*	*2*
3.5 and over	2	1	0	0	0	0	1	0
3.0–3.4	10	0	2	3	4	0	1	0
2.5–2.9	11	1	2	5	1	1	0	1
2.0–2.4	8	0	0	3	5	0	0	0
1.5–1.9	4	1	0	0	2	1	0	0
Less than 1.5	2	0	0	1	0	0	0	1

SOURCE: Easterlin 1967, p. 106.

Easterlin has examined the available data on population growth and economic development for the period from 1957–1958 to 1963–1964 for all but three of the 37 noncommunist nations of Africa, Asia, and Latin America with populations of two million or more. (Japan, Israel, and the Union of South Africa are excluded because they fall outside the category of newly developing nations.) Easterlin finds that per capita income generally—though not uniformly—increased during this period of rapid population growth (see table 2.2). In the case of India, for example, the rate of economic growth was even higher than earlier in the century when population growth was not so rapid. "Thus," Easterlin concludes, "accelerating population growth in recent years has not precluded positive per capita income growth, and has perhaps even been accompanied by accelerated income growth." However, there appears to be no systematic statistical relationship for these countries between rate of population growth and rate of growth of real per capita income.

As far as the already-developed nations are concerned, the historical evidence indicates that virtually every one of them (other than those undergoing new settlement) went through a phase in which population growth rate was high in relation to both previous and present levels and also through a phase of declining mortality and still-high fertility. For the most part, the rapid-growth phase came early in the period of modern economic development and perhaps in some cases even before it began (Easterlin 1970). Thus the relationship between population growth and economic development, historically and currently, is complex, remains unresolved by the data so far analyzed, and continues as a topic of lively controversy.

3. THE URBAN-METROPOLITAN REVOLUTION: THE MODERN SOCIETAL STRATEGY OF SURVIVAL AND ADAPTATION

That there is a major revolution occurring in society is indicated by the principal population trends found throughout the world today: increasing population size, increasing density, increasing concentration and agglomeration, and the political organization and integration of large geographic areas. Virtually every facet of social life—from politics, to economics, to religion, to education—and many facets of private life, too, have been affected by this urban-metropolitan revolution. The societal strategy of adaptation is changing in the direction of increasing differentiation, but at the same time there is a greatly increasing interdependence among individuals, groups, and societies located at great distances from one another.

Although there has been a considerable amount of investigation done on the histories of individual cities, estimates of the urban population of the world are available only for about the last 150 years. In 1800, an estimated three percent of the population of the world lived in cities or urban places of 5,000 inhabitants or more; of this proportion, only about 2.4 percent lived in cities of 20,000 or more, and a mere 1.7 percent lived in cities of 100,000 or more. However, between 1800 and 1970, a period during which the population of the world increased four-fold, the population in urban places of 5,000 or more increased eleven-fold, and the population in cities of 100,000 or more increased almost fourteen-fold. Thus, by 1970 a third (33 percent) of the world's population lived in urban settlements of 5,000 persons or more, and 23 percent lived in cities of 100,000 or more. (See table 2.3)

In the United States, urbanization has by far exceeded the world trend. In 1790 some five percent of the population of the U.S. lived in "urban places" (places of 2,500 or more inhabitants), and there were only 24 such urban places in the nation. By 1970, however, there were 6,435 urban places in the United States, and these contained about 70 percent of the total population. Some other countries—for example, Great Britain and Israel—have even larger urban percentages in their populations, but most have considerably smaller ones.

We have already talked about prehistoric and ancient urban settlement, and it is clear that cities and urban living are older than recorded history itself. However, it should be clear that ancient and preindustrial urban residence cannot be viewed as a societal strategy of adaptation. While urban agglomerations were, and are, an integral part of state societies, nonagricultural production remained throughout most of human

TABLE 2.3

Percentage of World Population in Cities of 5,000+ and 100,000+ by Region, 1800–1970

	Total World Population (millions)	Percent in Cities 5,000+	Percent in Cities 100,000+							
			World total	*Europe*[a]	*Asia*[a]	*Russia-USSR*	*North[b] America*	*Latin[c] America*	*Africa*	*Australia-New Zealand*
1800	906	3.0	1.7	3.0	1.6	1.4	—	0.4	0.3	—
1850	1171	6.4	2.3	5.8	1.7	1.8	5.5	1.5	0.2	—
1900	1608	13.6	5.5	14.5	2.1	4.2	18.5	5.7	1.1	21.7
1950	2400	29.8	13.1	21.1	7.5	18.5	29.0	16.5	5.2	39.2
1960	2995	31.6	20.1	33 0	12.3	23.9	60.2	24.1	8.1	60.2
1970	3632	33.0[d]	23.3	39.0	20.2	31.5	57.6	33.4	11.5	61.1

SOURCE: 1800–1960 — E. E. Lampard 1965; 1970 — Davis 1969, and "1970 World Population Data Sheet," Population Reference Bureau, Washington, D.C.
[a]Excluding Russia/USSR
[b]U.S.A. and Canada
[c]Western Hemisphere, excluding U.S.A. and Canada
[d]Rough estimate

prehistory and history only a minute part of the population's total means of gaining sustenance. Indeed, nonagricultural production plays a relatively small part in many national economies even today.

Prehistoric, ancient, medieval, and even modern cities can be described in a variety of ways: as market centers; as fortresses, garrison cities, or points of political control; as centers of worship or ecclesiastical control; as loci of culture and the arts; or as combinations of any or all of these (Weber 1968). But historically, urban populations served—or exploited, as the case may have been—the mass of surrounding country folk engaged in agriculture and basic extractive occupations. The modern urban revolution—and it is not yet universal, for urban growth does not everywhere and inevitably have these characteristics—consists not merely in the increase in number and size of urban agglomerations, but in urban economic activity becoming the *major* part of national economies and in the urban sector playing a progressively greater part in absorbing and providing sustenance to the new population increments.

As Friedlander (1970) shows in his study of migration and demographic transitions, England's industrial revolution was accompanied by an urban revolution in this very sense: the enormous population growth of the period was absorbed mainly by the urban centers and employed mainly in urban industrial and service sectors. Similarly, as we show in more detail in chapter 13, after 1860 the bulk of U.S. population growth was absorbed in urban places and occupations. Thus, although American cities are of much more recent origin than their European or Asiatic counterparts, they participated much earlier in a nationwide "urban revolution" of the modern sort indicated here.

The Urban Community: Differentiated, Complex, and Largely Migrant

Urban communities differ from rural communities, not only with respect to population size and density, but with respect to virtually all other facets of social structure.[8] It is clear that the recognized social roles of cities differ from those of rural places. The city is the locus of both a large number and a great variety of different social and economic roles. The psychiatrist, the hippie, the artist, the chorus girl, the corporation lawyer—these are typically found in the city and only very infrequently in the village. And while there are merchants, school teachers, ministers, divorcees, and teenagers in rural places, it is in the city where there are both large numbers and many different subtypes of merchants, school teachers, ministers, divorcees, and teenagers.

The nature of the urban revolution and of urban growth is such that urban residents are sharply differentiated according to whether they are recent arrivals, residents of long duration, born and brought up in the city, and so on. Urban populations are typically migrant populations in considerable measure, and the absorption and integration of successive waves of new residents—often initially strange to the city altogether—is a central and recurring process of urban society.

In a 1958 survey taken in the United States, only a minority of white respondents, 18 years of age or older, reported having lived in the same place since birth. Percentages reporting different durations of residence varied by size of place, with those in the largest cities and in farm communities (43 percent and 40 percent respectively) most likely to report living in the same place since birth, and those in small cities in metropolitan areas reporting the shortest durations of residence (Taeuber, Chiazze, and Haenszel 1968, pp. 19–20). Table 2.4 shows the results of this survey in detail.

This typically migrant nature of urban populations is found everywhere. In a 1950 survey of Auxerre, a French provincial city of 30,000, C. Bettleheim and S. Frére found that three-fourths of the population were not native to the town and that 92 percent of all married couples included at least one nonnative partner (Bettleheim and Frére 1950). And again, of the African population of Cap-Vert, Dakar (in Senegal) in 1961, some 41 percent were born outside the area, and this number included the overwhelming majority of the adult population (see table 2.5).

A variety of urban social forms, institutions, and commercial services originate in the very "strangeness" of the population to the city and the urban setting. Thus, in response to the needs of population groups

8 For a classic statement on this, see Wirth (1938); and for a more recent one, see Hauser (1965b).

TABLE 2.4

Duration of Continuous Residence of White Population in Current Place, by Size of Place

Size of Place	Total	Duration (years)				
		Entire life	40 or more	10–39	1–9	Less than 1
500,000 or more	100.0	42.7	9.9	28.5	16.7	2.2
50,000–499,999	100.0	25.1	8.7	36.1	25.2	4.9
Metropolitan, 10,000–49,999	100.0	14.7	5.0	32.5	40.0	7.8
Metropolitan, 2,500–9,999	100.0	10.6	2.8	28.2	51.0	7.4
Metropolitan, rural nonfarm	100.0	17.8	3.7	29.8	42.3	6.4
Nonmetropolitan, 10,000–49,999	100.0	19.4	6.3	36.6	31.2	6.5
Nonmetropolitan, 2,500–9,999	100.0	16.2	7.5	38.7	31.9	5.7
Nonmetropolitan, rural nonfarm	100.0	22.1	5.0	32.7	32.7	7.5
Farm	100.0	40.1	7.2	31.1	31.1	3.5

SOURCE: Taeuber, Chiazze, and Haenszel 1968, pp. 19–20, table 7.

not native to the area, the city often spawns ethnically segregated communities and their institutions and formal and informal organizations—kinship and neighborhood groups, churches and social clubs (landsmannschaften), gangs and taxi-dance halls, settlement houses, lonely hearts clubs, and bars and red-light districts.

"Time in the system" or length of residence in the city is evidently a major factor in the adjustment of individuals and groups to the urban setting. A variety of indicators of socioeconomic status are characteristically found to be positively associated with duration of residence in the city. For example, Taeuber, Chiazze, and Haenszel, (1968) found that few

TABLE 2.5

Cap-Vert, Dakar: African Population by Age and Place of Birth, 1961

Age	Place of Birth		
	Cap-Vert	Other regions	Total
Under 1 year	16,100	680	16,780
1–4	58,800	6,580	65,380
5–9	52,540	9,340	61,880
10–14	27,300	8,080	35,380
15–19	14,800	14,240	29,040
20–29	22,200	48,980	71,180
30–39	17,000	39,680	56,680
40–49	11,340	19,560	30,900
50–59	6,760	10,640	17,400
60–69	3,440	4,720	8,160
70 years and over	3,000	2,280	5,280
Total	233,280	164,780	398,060

SOURCE: Dia 1967.

persons 18-24 years old have been able to stay 10 years or more in the same place; they compose the age group with the highest risk of migration. As time passes, however, those 45 and over reach the 10 year mark. They are shown as making up 66 percent of those with 10 years or more at the same residence. Other variables that affect duration of residence are region, foreign birth, and occupation. Similarly, indicators of social participation, such as membership in organizations and voter registration, are also found to be related positively to length of residence (Shannon and Shannon 1967).

A second factor crucial to the newcomer's adjustment to the city is his level of social and economic resources upon arrival. Level of education and occupational skill are particularly important. The ability of the newcomer to compete for access to urban social and economic roles, desirable urban space, and favorable urban associations is closely connected with the cultural, social, and economic resources represented by his occupational skills and education. Of Jewish immigrants to New York City in the nineteenth and early twentieth century, those from Germany were greatly advantaged by comparison with those from Eastern Europe—both by virtue of their earlier arrival and by virtue of the average levels of their educational achievement and occupational skills. Among current urban migrants, the professional and experienced skilled workers find adjustment to new surroundings much easier than do "off-the-farm" migrants. Similarly, the capacity of migrating population *groups* to be absorbed into the city depends in complex ways upon their educational, occupational, and cultural levels. But it *also* depends upon the nature of the receiving urban society and its own patterns of change and transformation (Shannon and Shannon 1967; Eisenstadt 1954). The subject of absorption, acculturation, and integration of migrant populations represents one of the great research frontiers in sociology and population studies. We shall discuss some of the problems in this area in chapter 9.

Just as roles in the urban environment are more numerous and complex, so the urban institutional network is far more complex than its rural counterpart. A simple computation of the number of possible *combinations* of institutionalized role relations indicates the institutional complexity made possible simply by the size and density of the urban populaton. The institutions of economic production are much more varied, just as the personal, business, public, and institutional services are. Educational, religious, and cultural institutions are more varied and complex, and voluntary organizations vie with one another for membership and the participation of mutually shared members.

The rural community has its local school, church, bar, newspaper, civic club, and political organization; and it has its stores and service station, its lawyer and its doctor. But the urban community may have whole *systems* of schools and educational institutions—kindergartens, universities, libraries, specialized academies, vocational and professional schools, etc.—and these may be interrelated in a variety of ways and degrees. The city or metropolitan area also has systems of churches—indeed, often organizations and hierarchies of churches, church institutions, and clergy. And it has systems, too, of bars, lounges, and nightclubs.

Similarly the metropolis has its many professional offices and organizations, its wholesale and retail businesses, and its processing, manufacturing, and fabricating industries. The city's recreational facilities and services, be they free or commercial, are many and diverse; and its clubs and voluntary organizations range from neighborhood sewing circles, to juvenile gangs, to business associations and political organizations.

Any given role in the city entails a much more complicated set of relationships with the multifarious other social roles and institutions surrounding it than is the case for social roles in rural places. In addition, the density of settlement and relative convenience of communication and transport within the city imply a *potentially* greater intensity and variety of social contacts and relationships.

Spatial Patterns and Their Social Effects

Given the extraordinary diversity and complexity described above, a crucial task in urban sociology and ecology is the classification of social roles, groups, and institutions in the urban community and the plotting and analysis of *actual* patterns of social contact and relationships among them.

The physical layout, land-use, and transport and communication arrangements and technology of the city are of concern to sociologists and human ecologists in just this respect. The social structure and the physical or spatial structure of a city are closely related; indeed they reflect one another. Accordingly, a city's social structure may often be studied or inferred with the aid of data bearing upon its physical structure (cf. Hawley 1950). For social relationships are mediated by physical proximity and accessibility, and the latter are in large measure a function of spatial patterns of settlement and the location of individual and clustered social roles, institutions, and social systems. By the same token, social proximity and accessibility may be the key factors in the competition among the various social and economic units for space or locations in the urban area. For this reason, patterns of settlement and institutional location in the urban area are widely viewed as representations of the urban social structure; and a long tradition of the study of spatial relationships obtaining in cities has shed considerable light upon the characteristics of urban social structure in America.

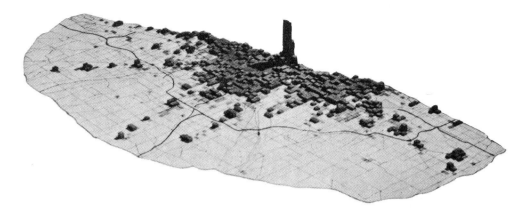

FIGURE 2.4. Total person-trip destinations, Chicago. The destinations of 10,212,000 person trips, on the average weekday, are distributed throughout the study area as shown in this model. The highest blocks represent 144,000 trip destinations per quarter square mile grid, the lowest blocks, 5,000. The flat shaded areas represent less than 5,000 but more than 2,500. Source: Schnore 1967, p. 165.

In figure 2.4 it is possible to compare the volume of local travel, cast in terms of "person trips" in an average weekday, to each point in Chicago. The greatest volume of "person trips" is to the very center of the city, of course, with a gradient approximately proportional to the distance from the center apparent. From the illustration it is clear that not only are certain locations *themselves* points of very high volumes of person trips, but some locations are more favorably located than others with respect to *access* to such points.

A major facet of the urban social structure, as of social structure generally, is the size of the population and its composition by key social roles, combinations of social roles, and institutional association. Cities differ, of course, with respect to population size, varying from a few thousand to several million. And, obviously, cities of several million are very different in every respect from those of a few thousand.

Thus, in a study involving U.S. metropolitan areas in 1960, M. G. Powers found that socioeconomic status indicators were highest for all ethnic subgroups the larger the category of metropolitan area. For all groups except Negroes, socioeconomic status was higher in the urban than in the rural parts of metropolitan areas, and almost always higher in the urban parts *outside* the central cities—i.e., in the suburbs—than in the central cities. For Negroes, median socioeconomic status scores were higher in central cities than in the suburban parts of metropolitan areas, but, in common with whites, lower in the rural parts of metropolitan areas (Powers 1968). These findings are detailed in table 2.6.

In addition, the population composition in the different neighborhoods and sub-areas of cities may vary with respect to place-of-birth (in the city itself, in different urban areas, in rural areas, abroad), with respect to age and sex, and with respect to major ethnic, linguistic, cultural, economic, and other social characteristics.

Thus, in their classic study of occupational stratification and mobility, Duncan and Duncan found that a "close relationship between spatial and social distances in a metropolitan community" was reflected in patterns of residential concentration and segregation of occupational groups in Chicago and adjacent areas in 1950. (Their focus of study was that area denoted as the "Chicago Metropolitan District" in the 1940 census.) The residential segregation of the occupational groups formed a U-shaped pattern, with the highest indexes of segregation found for the professional and laborer groups, at both extremes of the occupational scale, and the lowest values for the clerical workers in the middle of the scale, suggesting that urban residential segregation is greater for those occupation groups with clearly defined status than for those whose status is ambiguous (Duncan and Duncan 1955). Similar patterns have been found in later studies, most recently in Puerto Rico (Schwirian and Rico-Velasco 1971).

TABLE 2.6

Median SES (Socioeconomic Status) Scores of Selected Nativity and Ethnic Groups, and of the Negro Population in SMSAs (Standard Metropolitan Statistical Areas) by Size of SMSA, 1960

Residence in SMSA, by Size of SMSA	White Native Parentage	Native-European Parentage			Foreign-born (European)			Negro
		North and Western Europe	Central and Eastern Europe	Southern Europe	North and Western Europe	Central and Eastern Europe	Southern Europe	
In all SMSAs	60.1	60.3	62.8	56.1	52.6	46.7	42.2	33.9
Central cities	58.4	58.3	61.9	54.3	59.7	46.9	50.7	34.9
Urban part of ring	64.6	64.1	65.5	58.7	56.7	50.6	44.8	33.5
Rural part of ring	52.5	53.4	53.3	54.0	48.0	35.3	38.8	21.1
In SMSAs of 1,000,000 and over	62.7	61.9	64.3	56.8	53.8	47.9	43.1	37.7
Central cities	58.6	59.0	62.8	54.6	51.4	46.5	41.7	38.0
Urban part of ring	66.7	65.5	67.4	59.7	58.3	52.8	46.0	37.9
Rural part of ring	56.4	56.4	55.0	55.0	50.9	37.5	41.0	26.8
In SMSAs of 250,000 to 1,000,000	58.1	57.7	59.1	54.9	49.9	42.8	40.4	29.7
Central cities	58.1	57.3	59.5	53.8	48.8	43.4	39.5	30.8
Urban part of ring	61.7	60.3	60.6	56.6	52.4	44.6	41.8	27.8
Rural part of ring	51.3	52.5	52.9	54.1	46.8	33.5	39.7	22.3
In SMSAs of less than 250,000	56.4	55.7	57.2	53.1	48.9	41.6	38.6	26.0
Central cities	58.5	56.9	59.1	53.2	49.2	43.2	38.5	28.3
Urban part of ring	58.0	58.2	56.8	53.8	51.4	40.6	41.2	25.3
Rural part of ring	50.3	49.3	50.7	51.0	44.3	35.7	32.8	17.9

SOURCE: Powers 1968, table 2, p. 447.

The study of ethnic urban residential patterns, frequently carried out in connection with studies of ethnic assimilation, has a long tradition in sociology and human ecology. As Lieberson points out:

> . . . during the heyday of European immigration to the United States, the propensity of immigrants to first locate in ghettoes and their later movements out of these areas of first settlement were frequently utilized as a measure or index of an ethnic group's assimilation. Studies of such diverse urban centers as Chicago, Durban, Montreal, Paris, and the major cities of Australia attest to the widespread existence of residential segregation and its usefulness as an indicator of ethnic assimilation. Indeed, during the twenties and thirties, ethnic residential patterns were a major research interest of sociologists and others. [Lieberson 1961, p. 1]

Lieberson himself found that the extent of ethnic segregation influences citizenship status, ethnic endogamy and inter-marriage, the ability to speak English, and intergenerational occupational mobility (Lieberson 1961).

The maps of figure 2.5 (pp. 94-97) show the distribution of homes, by rental groups, and the distributions of immigrant ethnic groups and of Negroes in the city of Chicago in 1930. Inspection and comparison of the maps reveal the closeness or distance of the ethnic groups relative to one another, as well as indicating their locations in terms of high or low rental areas. Thus, for example the Negro population was, already in 1930, very highly segregated in a "Black Belt" inhabited almost exclusively by Negroes. Among the foreign-born, those from Italy, from Russia, and from Poland appeared most highly concentrated, while the immigrants from Germany appear very broadly dispersed throughout the city.

Areas of Negro residence were largely low and lowest rent areas, but there were also a number of high-rent areas with very high percentages of Negro residents. Some of the Russian-born immigrants and some of the German-born immigrants were concentrated in medium and high-rent areas. But for the most part areas of ethnic concentration in Chicago in 1930 tended to be also low or lowest-rent areas.

In their study of Negro residential patterns in American cities, Taeuber and Taeuber found that in virtually all large U.S. cities, North and South, the Negro population has always been highly segregated, is more segregated than are white ethnic groups, and that from the Civil War until World War II there was a general tendency for residential segregation to increase with the growth of Negro populations (Taeuber and Taeuber 1965). This tendency is shown clearly in table 2.7.

It is clear that variation of population in one respect is typically not unconnected with variation in some other respect. Thus, for example,

TABLE 2.7
*Indexes of Residential Segregation Between
Negroes and Native Whites in Ten Northern
Cities, 1910, 1920, 1930, and 1950*

City	1910	1920	1930	1950
Boston	64.1	65.3	77.9	80.1
Buffalo	62.6	71.5	80.5	82.5
Chicago	66.8	75.7	85.2	79.7
Cincinnati	47.3	57.2	72.8	80.6
Cleveland	60.6	70.1	85.0	86.6
Columbus	31.6	43.8	62.8	70.3
Philadelphia	46.0	47.9	63.4	74.0
Pittsburgh	44.1	43.3	61.4	68.5
St. Louis	54.3	62.1	82.1	85.4
Syracuse	64.0	65.2	86.7	85.8

SOURCE: Taeuber and Taeuber 1965, table 10, p. 54.

cities with large proportions of the population employed in manufacturing industries and small proportions in services tend to have smaller proportions with secondary or higher educations, and tend to have earlier marriages and higher fertility, than cities with large proportions employed in services. Thus, economic differentiation *among* cities tends to entail other social structural differences.[9]

Historically, the urban community's greater variety of jobs, living styles, contacts, amusements, social relationships, and general opportunities in life has been accompanied by higher per capita income and by a much larger variety of comforts and consumption opportunities than is the case for small or more isolated rural communities. Thus, with few exceptions, the majority of rural and urban migratory movements have historically been from rural to urban places and from smaller to larger urban places. Even the recent "suburbanization" trends—from New York City to Scarsdale, or from Chicago to Barrington—are properly viewed as the redistribution of population *within* large agglomerations rather than as movements "from larger to smaller" places.

4. CITIES AND HINTERLANDS: THE METROPOLITAN COMMUNITY

Typically, the "hinterland" of a city is considered to be the area surrounding and including the city, with better or more ready access to that city, its institutions, and services than to any other city or urban center.

9 For a detailed analysis of this tendency, see Duncan and Reiss (1956).

(text continues on page 98)

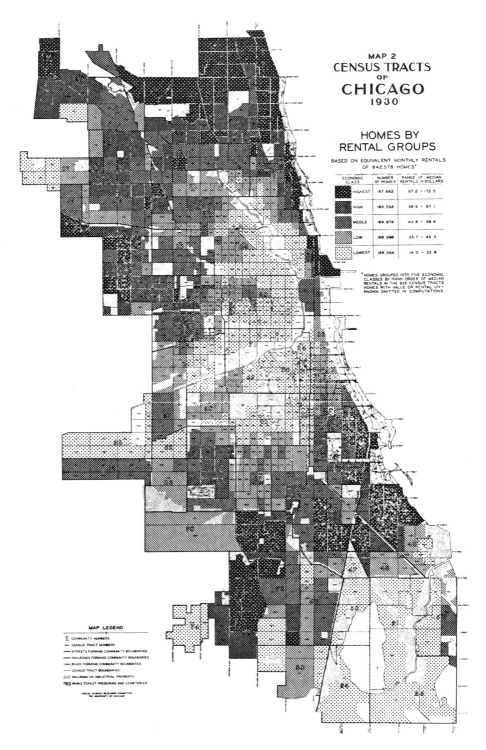

FIGURE 2.5. Census tracts of Chicago, according to selected characteristics. Source: Burgess and Newcomb, 1930.

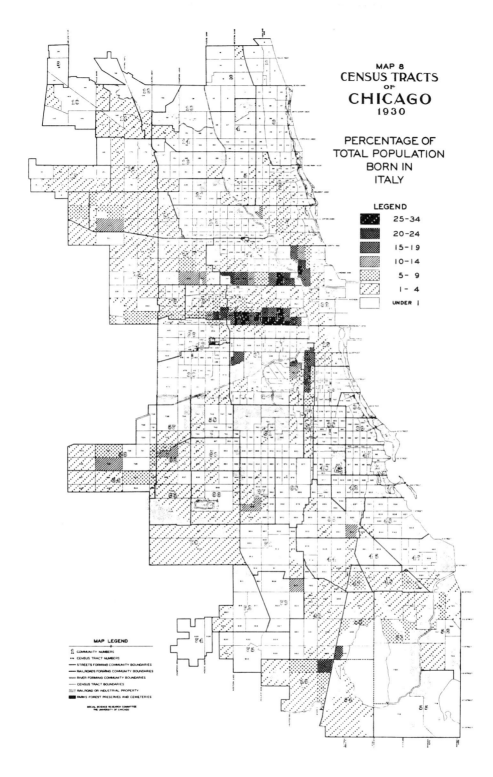

MAP 8
CENSUS TRACTS
OF
CHICAGO
1930

PERCENTAGE OF
TOTAL POPULATION
BORN IN
ITALY

LEGEND

▨	25-34
▨	20-24
▨	15-19
▨	10-14
▨	5- 9
▨	1- 4
☐	UNDER 1

MAP LEGEND

1   COMMUNITY NUMBERS
•••   CENSUS TRACT NUMBERS
——   STREETS FORMING COMMUNITY BOUNDARIES
——   RAILROADS FORMING COMMUNITY BOUNDARIES
≈≈≈   RIVER FORMING COMMUNITY BOUNDARIES
——   CENSUS TRACT BOUNDARIES
▨   RAILROAD OR INDUSTRIAL PROPERTY
■   PARKS FOREST PRESERVES AND CEMETERIES

SOCIAL SCIENCE RESEARCH COMMITTEE
THE UNIVERSITY OF CHICAGO

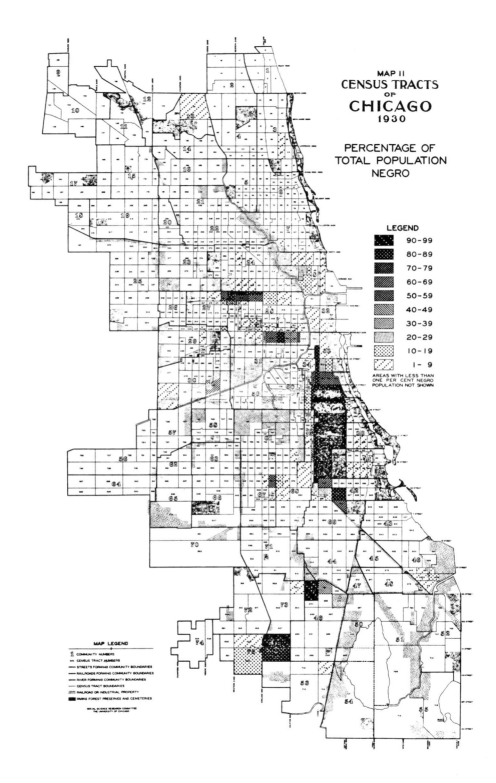

MAP II
CENSUS TRACTS
OF
CHICAGO
1930

PERCENTAGE OF
TOTAL POPULATION
NEGRO

LEGEND

	90-99
	80-89
	70-79
	60-69
	50-59
	40-49
	30-39
	20-29
	10-19
	1-9

AREAS WITH LESS THAN
ONE PER CENT NEGRO
POPULATION NOT SHOWN

MAP LEGEND

1 COMMUNITY NUMBERS
CENSUS TRACT NUMBERS
STREETS FORMING COMMUNITY BOUNDARIES
RAILROADS FORMING COMMUNITY BOUNDARIES
RIVER FORMING COMMUNITY BOUNDARIES
CENSUS TRACT BOUNDARIES
RAILROAD OR INDUSTRIAL PROPERTY
PARKS FOREST PRESERVES AND CEMETERIES

SOCIAL SCIENCE RESEARCH COMMITTEE
THE UNIVERSITY OF CHICAGO

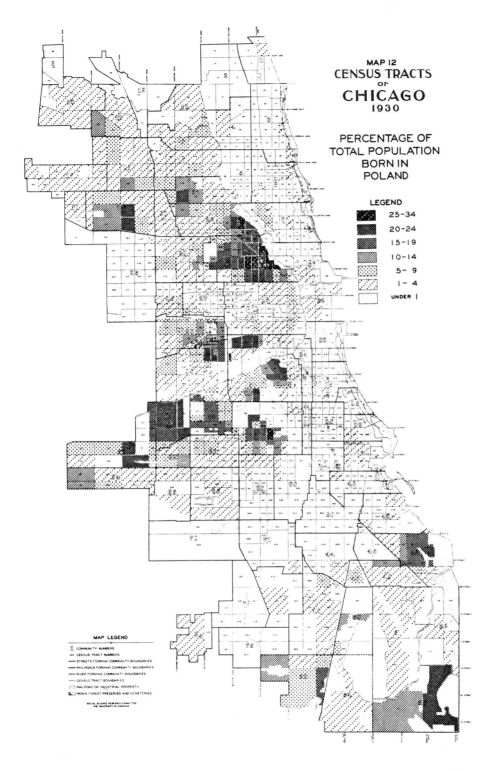

MAP 12
CENSUS TRACTS
OF
CHICAGO
1930

PERCENTAGE OF
TOTAL POPULATION
BORN IN
POLAND

LEGEND
25-34
20-24
15-19
10-14
5- 9
1- 4
UNDER 1

MAP LEGEND
1   COMMUNITY NUMBERS
··· CENSUS TRACT NUMBERS
—— STREETS FORMING COMMUNITY BOUNDARIES
—— RAILROADS FORMING COMMUNITY BOUNDARIES
—— RIVER FORMING COMMUNITY BOUNDARIES
—— CENSUS TRACT BOUNDARIES
▨▨ RAILROAD OR INDUSTRIAL PROPERTY
▨▨ PARKS, FOREST PRESERVES AND CEMETERIES

SOCIAL SCIENCE RESEARCH COMMITTEE
THE UNIVERSITY OF CHICAGO

The concept of "hinterland" may refer to general access to a city, or it may be more specialized and refer to access to specific services of a city. Thus, the entertainment, cultural, and banking services of a large city typically have greater "hinterlands" than do the bakery or grocery services. (People will travel farther to see a play or transact a loan than they will to buy a loaf of bread or a quart of milk.) Similarly, a given rural area may be in the "wholesaling hinterland" of one city but in the "educational hinterland" of another.

Figure 2.6 illustrates alternative schemes for determining boundaries of the New York and Boston hinterlands respectively. The heavy line in Figure I, which is marked 50%, is drawn through the points on the map from which the amount of railroad coach passenger flow to and from Boston is equal to that to and from New York. The light line in the New York (south-southwest) side of the 50% line is drawn through points from which passenger traffic to and from New York is nine times as heavy as that to and from Boston; and the light curved line in the Boston (north-northeast) side of the 50% line passes through points from which 90% of the total (Boston + New York) traffic is to and from Boston.

Figure II is prepared in the same manner, but with reference to circulation of daily metropolitan newspapers: the heavy, 50% line is drawn through the points in which the total New York and Boston paper circulation is divided exactly in half; and the New York side and Boston side 90% lines represent the points at which Boston and New York newspaper circulation is divided with 90% oriented to New York's or to Boston's newspapers respectively. Figure III is drawn on the same principles, but with reference to the total of New York and Boston long distance telephone calls; and Figure IV shows hinterland boundary lines drawn on the basis of location of the metropolitan headquarters of factories located in the Boston and New York hinterlands. The line passes through the points in which half the firms have an office in New York, half in Boston. A majority of the hinterland firms in the area south of the line have headquarters in New York; and the majority of the hinterland factories north-northeast of the line have headquarters in Boston.

In general, however, "hinterland" is used in reference to the area served by the various commercial, cultural, communication, and other services of the urban center.

The Evolvement of Cities and Their Hinterlands

The concept of hinterland has been of great value in accounting for the origins and evolvement of cities and for analyzing the social and economic relationships between cities and the total societies in which they are found. For example, here is a more or less "classical" account of the origin of cities.

Consider a society of food growers, hunters, collectors, or other primary producers with individual families, extended families, or tribes settled over a fairly extensive area. The production of food is such that each family is able to produce some surplus product, i.e., rice, in addition to its own immediate requirements. Suppose, now, that it occurs to one individual that by performing some service—say, shoeing horses—for many primary producers in exchange for surplus food, he can both eat well and work less hard.

Accordingly, the blacksmith, who perhaps has created a new role in the society, sets out wandering from place to place, shoeing horses in exchange for food. Suppose, however, that it occurs to him that he can shoe many more horses if he spends his time doing only that rather than wandering around the countryside, that is, if the horses come to him rather than he to them; besides, he reasons, there is much to be said in favor of a more permanent home and place of work. In such a contingency, the blacksmith should, if he is rational, try to choose a place of work accessible to a maximum number of potential clients. Such a place may be central to the entire area of the society's settlement, located on some path or crossroad, or otherwise conveniently situated with respect to the society's territorial distribution.

Suppose, further, that other individuals in the society decide to produce and exchange shoes, weapons, or tools for surplus food produced by the agriculturists, fishermen, hunters, or collectors; and that they, too, elect to establish permanent workplaces rather than peddle their wares in the countryside. If they are as rational as the blacksmith, they will, for exactly the same reasons of accessibility, establish their places of work and exchange in the same place as his or in very close proximity to it.

The blacksmith, shoemaker, toolmaker, and other tradesmen, then, have established a point of exchange. The agriculturists no longer shoe their own horses, make their own boots, or fashion their own tools, but, rather, are dependent upon the craftsmen at the exchange center for these goods and services. The craftsmen and manufacturers, in turn, are dependent for sustenance upon the agriculturists in their "hinterland," i.e., upon those to whom their services are accessible. Thus a simple reciprocal dependence has been established between two places of settlement—the nonprimary production or service area and its hinterland.

Metropolitan Dominance

As agricultural and extractive activities become specialized, more exchange services are needed for marketing of surplus produce and the purchase of primary products. In other words, when Farmer Brown stops growing everything his family needs and raises only corn, he must depend on others to buy his surplus corn and sell him milk and eggs. In addition,

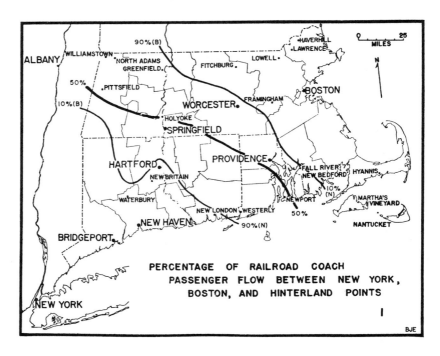

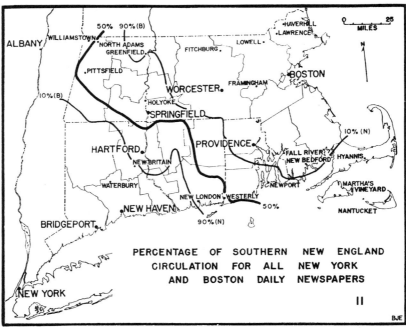

FIGURE 2.6. Alternative hinterland boundaries for Boston and New York. Source: H. L. Green, "Hinterland Boundaries of N.Y.C. and Boston in Southern New England," in J. P. Gibbs, *Urban Research Methods* (New York: Van Nostrand Co., Inc., 1961), pp. 286–309.

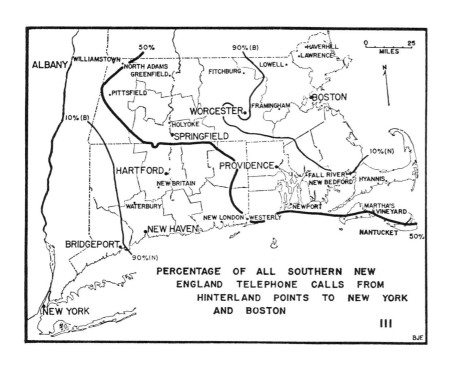

PERCENTAGE OF ALL SOUTHERN NEW
ENGLAND TELEPHONE CALLS FROM
HINTERLAND POINTS TO NEW YORK
AND BOSTON

III

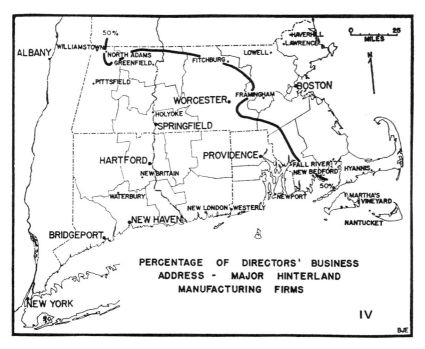

PERCENTAGE OF DIRECTORS' BUSINESS
ADDRESS - MAJOR HINTERLAND
MANUFACTURING FIRMS

IV

as relatively more surpluses become available for exchange, manufactured and fabricated products are demanded in greater quantity and variety. Thus, new, nonprimary, economic roles and activities emerge. These, like the initial ones, tend to locate at points of maximum accessibility and, if the process continues, eventually develop into "metropolitan" agglomerations that grow, become further differentiated, and achieve an increasing "metropolitan dominance" over their rural and smaller urban hinterlands (Bogue 1949).

The hypothesis of metropolitan dominance formulated by D. J. Bogue in 1949 must be cited at length:

> . . . Out of the attempts to understand cities and their place in the modern world has grown a generalization which may be called the "dominant city" hypothesis or the "hypothesis of metropolitan dominance." This hypothesis seeks to escape part of the difficulties of understanding "urbanism" as a single characteristic, and attempts to solve the problem of intercity interdependence. It classifies cities on the basis of the functions which they perform and their relative ability to "dominate" other cities and the surrounding countryside. The classification made in formulating this hypothesis is a dichotomous one; cities are divided into "metropolitan centers" and "hinterland cities." The metropolis is usually the largest and most complex (the farthest removed from the "average" city) of all of the cities in the territory. Because it is able to assemble cheaply a varied array of raw materials and products from all parts of the world; because a large number of specialized components and skills are required in the production of the goods required to sustain human beings at their present level of living; because up to a certain point machine production increases in efficiency with an increased scale of operations; and because certain mutual benefits appear to accrue to business enterprises, from their location in proximity to each other, the large city is able to produce and distribute more varied goods and services than is a smaller city. The more specialized the goods, and the more the goods are amenable to mass production, the greater these industrial and commercial advantages of large cities seem to become. From these facts it has been concluded that the metropolis, or modern large and complex city, exercises an organizing and integrative influence on the social and economic life of a broad expanse of territory far beyond the civil boundaries, and thereby dominates all other communities within this area. The hypothesis of metropolitan dominance assumes that there is a system of interdependency among cities, and that there are considerable differences between the activities of individual cities. It maintains that the organizing agent, and one of the forces making for intercity differentiation, is the metropolis. [Bogue 1949, pp. 5–6]

Bogue studied the relationships between metropolis and hinterland for 67 U.S. metropolitan communities. He found—

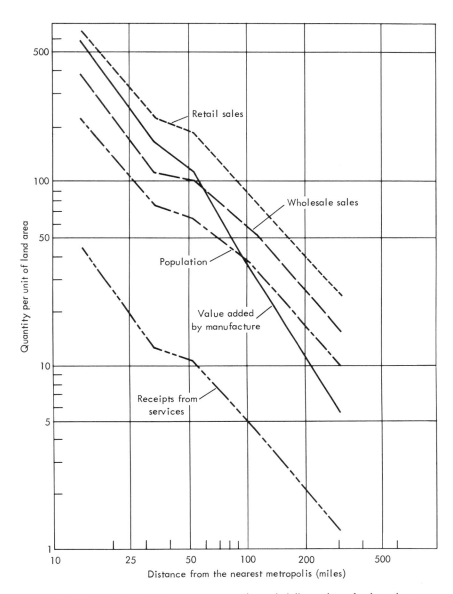

FIGURE 2.7. Population per square mile and dollar value of selected sustenance activities per 1/100 square mile of hinterland area, by distance outward from the nearest metropolis for 67 U.S. metropolitan communities, 1939–1940. Source: Bogue 1949, chart 3.1.

1. that density of population and volume of retail sales, wholesale sales, value added by manufacture, and receipts from services decrease as the distance from the metropolis increases (see figure 2.7);

2. that the size of the metropolis, the central city of the metropolitan community, is related to the intensity with which the entire hinterland is occupied;

3. that the urban, rural-nonfarm, and rural-farm populations of the hinterland are each located according to characteristic patterns of distance from the metropolis, but all tend to cluster toward the metropolis. Because of the different distance patterns, the urban-rural composition of the hinterland changes as distance from the metropolis increases (figure 2.8);

4. that there are specialized economic functions evident in the different sectors and distance zones of the hinterlands. Within the hinterland, there are subdominant cities with their own patterns of population and economic activity.

5. THE MEGALOPOLITAN NETWORK

Under conditions of general population growth and improved technology, cities grow and absorb a large portion of the population's increase by virtue of both centripetal and centrifugal population movements. A centripetal movement is from the periphery to the center; a centrifugal one, from the center to the periphery. As agricultural techniques improve, rendering more and more rural workers superfluous, the rural population is attracted to city employment and urban styles of life. Conversely, as cities grow in size and density, the urban population moves outward from the city center. New areas are then annexed to the city, or independent suburbs and populations are established beyond it. Thus, the urban area is no longer limited to the political boundaries of one or several cities. Rather, it may comprise a number of different *types* of urban areas.

Various concepts have been introduced to represent and analyze such urban areas. Thus, we have "metropolitan areas," "urbanized areas," "conurbation," "central cities," and "suburban rings." Concepts such as these and their statistical representations reflect the fact that a great many persons, institutions, and activities are urban in character, have close spatial and social relationships with cities and urban centers, but are themselves located outside cities or outside the dominant city of the area.

When the outlying areas of two cities undergo continued suburbanization in the direction of each other, the process evolves along the major transport routes and leads eventually to dense settlement of the entire ribbon of land between the cities. Such urbanized ribbons have sometimes been called "strip cities," and in some areas *networks* of interrelated and interconnected strip cities have emerged. For example, there

14 metropolitan communities with central cities of 500,000 or more inhabitants

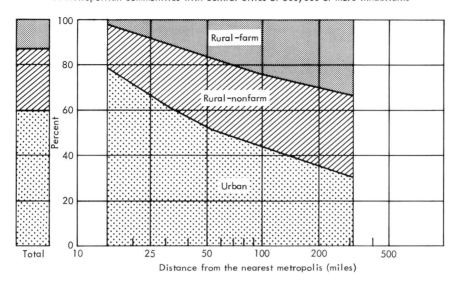

53 metropolitan communities with central cities of less than 500,000 inhabitants

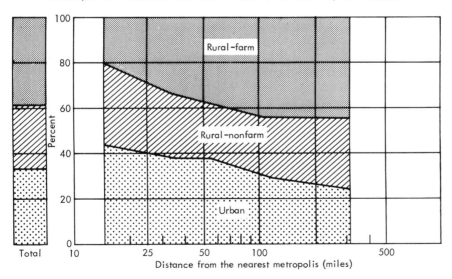

FIGURE 2.8. Urban-rural composition of the hinterland population by distance from the nearest metropolis and size class of the metropolis, United States, 1940. Source: Bogue 1949, chart 3.3.

is now a huge network of large cities connected by contiguous bands of urban settlement on the eastern seaboard of the United States. This network stretching from around Boston in the north to the Washington-Norfolk area in the south, has been called "megalopolis" (Gottman 1961). The term "megalopolis" has lately been used to denote an interconnected group of cities and connecting urbanized bands, and henceforth we shall call a network of such cities and bands a "megalopolitan network."

The most important characteristic of the megalopolitan network is the kind of specialization and interdependence that obtains among its cities. Whereas the key interdependence in a regional economy is between the city and its rural hinterland, or between the metropolitan center and its smaller urban satellites and rural hinterland, the interdependence characterizing the megalopolitan network is between cities of different types, different functional specialization, and different economic bases (Duncan et al. 1960). The megalopolitan network includes agricultural and other primary-production hinterlands, which send their products into the urban areas for processing, manufacturing, fabrication, and distribution. But mainly the megalopolitan network comprises urban populations living in cities, in suburbs of cities, or in or near urban bands connecting cities.

A careful inspection of maps and an analysis of the population, labor force, and economy of geographic units suggest that a number of megalopolitan networks may be identified in the United States. There is the eastern seaboard network mentioned above, but three others as well: a ring of cities and urban settlements stretching westward from the Boston-Albany region to the Great Lakes, eastward through the Cleveland-Youngstown-Pittsburg-Washington area, and northward to Boston; an urban line extending from Cleveland, to the Toledo-Detroit area, to Chicago, and finally to St. Louis; and a California megalopolitan line starting in the Sacramento-San Francisco region and moving through to San Diego. And the United States is by no means unique. Megalopolitan networks or lines can be identified in Great Britain, from the Liverpool-Manchester area to London-Dover, and in Western Europe, from Amsterdam to Milan, the latter crossing *national* boundaries. In Japan, such a network extends from the Tokyo-Yokohama area to Osaka (see figure 2.9). However, we still lack criteria for delineating megalopolitan networks and methods for describing, comparing and analyzing their geographic, demographic, social, and economic features.

Thus, population growth and agglomeration have been associated with the differentiation and mutual dependence attending the most recent societal strategy of survival and adaptation: megalopolitanization and the extension of megalopolitan networks across vast areas and some-

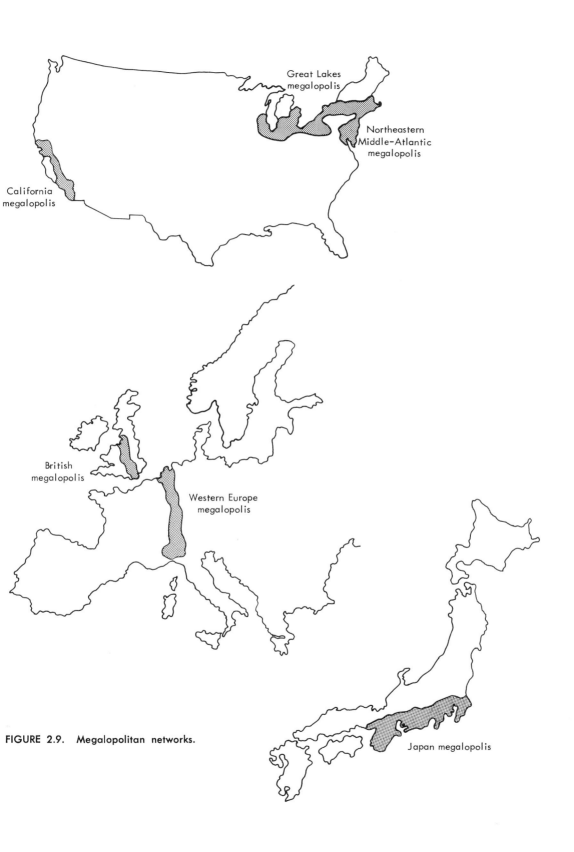

FIGURE 2.9. Megalopolitan networks.

times across national boundaries. While a few of the social and political problems associated with this type of development have been recognized, we are still far from understanding correlates and consequences of the process, be they demographic, social structural, political, psychological, or economic.

We shall return to the demographic and social structural consequences of population processes in Part III. In the rest of Part I, we turn to the data and procedures used in the study of populations and societies.

3

Data:
The Facts of
Populations and Societies

1. TYPES OF DATA

The crucial link between an actual phenomenon and the scientific analysis, description, or theory concerning it consists of data. A *datum,* according to the *Oxford Shorter Dictionary,* is something given, granted, known, or assumed as fact *and* made the basis of reasoning, calculation, or inference. The collection, processing, evaluation, and analysis of data are, accordingly, central concerns in every scientific discipline.

Any record, descriptive account, or symbolic representation of a phenomenon, event, relationship, or process may constitute a datum. Certain types of phenomena and events are routinely recorded, and it is often possible to exploit such records for purposes of scientific investigation. Other types are virtually never recorded, and for these, the researcher must devise ways and means of recording their occurrence and, hence, of generating his own data. Thus, election results, marriages, transfers of property, and the I.Q.'s of elementary school pupils are routinely recorded, and the records may be abstracted, collected, and analyzed for study in one or another area of inquiry. However, the television-viewing habits or courtship behavior of people, the weight of rabbits at birth, and the learning capacity of rats are not routinely recorded; whoever seeks to study these phenomena must devise ways of observing and describing them in some more or less standardized way.

Similarly, some types of phenomena are easily measured on interval or numerical scales, while others must, with considerable difficulty, be differentiated and counted on ordinal (rank) or nominal (classificatory) scales. Age, weight, population density, and income are examples of the first group; social status, occupational prestige, and academic diplomas and degrees may be measured on ordinal (rank) scales; and political identification, rural or urban residence, race, and marital status are examples of phenomena measurable on nominal (classificatory) scales only.

Thus, data can generally be classified in two different ways:

1. according to whether they are (a) routinely generated in the course of administrative, legal, commercial, or other, not specifically scientific, operations, or (b) deliberately produced by investigators and students for the specific purpose of scientific inquiry;
2. according to whether they consist of (a) *descriptions* of single events, phenomena or processes, or (b) *counts* of one or more categories of events or phenomena, or (c) *measurements* of one or more events or phenomena in one or more categories (see table 3.1).

The Convergence of Data and Studies on Populations and Societies

The origins of modern demography and population studies are very closely connected with the collection, analysis, and interpretation of data concerning numbers of deaths and numbers of births, and with the discovery of regularities in these numbers over time and in relation to the numbers of total populations. The earliest problems posed were couched in questions concerning regularities of fluctuations in the numbers of population, births, deaths, marriages, and migratory movements (cf. Lorimer 1959). Demography and population studies have since developed hand in hand, with ever more sophisticated and elaborate operations—usually administrative or legal in origin—for accumulating large and detailed amounts of data concerning the size of populations, their characteristics, and their vital events.

Demographic population data are commonly thought to be routinely collectable. After all, the reasoning goes, population studies typically use censuses, vital statistics, and survey materials obtained most often by governmental bureaus and other agencies in the course of their routine operations. Similarly, population data are thought to be readily quantifiable—always countable and very often measurable on interval scales. Thus, it is pointed out, we can count numbers of population and

TABLE 3.1
Types of Population and Societal Data

	Routinely Obtained		Special Inquiries		
	Census	*Vital statistics*	*School data*	*Family planning survey*	*Occupational mobility study*
Classification and Counting only	Sex Marital status Place of residence Own ethnic origin and ethnic origin of spouse	Sex Cause of death Place of marriage Race Marital status	Place of birth Race Ethnic origin Type of school authority	Knowledge of, attitude toward family planning Practice of contraception Authority structure in family Wife's employment status	Union membership Rural or urban origin Home ownership Family planning practices
Readily Measured or Ranked	Age Educational achievement Density Size of Places Own education and education of spouse	Birth weight Age at death Age of spouse	I.Q. Grades Size of class Ethnic composition of school	Number of births Number of children desired Own and spouse's education	Education Size of family of orientation Father's income Age at marriage Size of place of residence

numbers of births, deaths, marriages, and migratory movements, and we can measure on interval scales such things as ages and age distributions, distances of migratory movements, and population densities.

Sociological and anthropological data, on the other hand, are commonly seen as neither routinely collectable nor readily quantifiable. For example, data on kinship relationships, institutions insuring conformity, or socialization processes must typically be obtained specifically for the purposes of the investigation at hand; and often the data can take the form only of descriptive accounts or case studies, there being no axes of measurement, counting, or even comparison.

However, this mapping—population data routinely collected and quantifiable, societal and social structural data specially produced and nonquantifiable—does not really hold, not even approximately. Studies of population composition and of social structure clearly converge (and we discuss the convergence in some detail in chapter 4). For example, the total number of persons in a group is a fundamental aspect of the group's social structure. So is the sex and age composition—that is, the group's composition by sex role and age role—the socially-accepted behavior patterns associated with being male or female, or with being a given age —and the relationships between the numbers having the various types of roles. Similarly, the size and density of residential units are fundamental parts of social structure. It follows, then, that the types of data used in population studies are central to sociological and anthropological investigations of social structure: studies of social structure obviously need the descriptions, hypotheses, and verifications that population studies provide on population and societal composition by social role, whether the data be census-type or survey data, counts and measurements of migratory movements, measurements of status change, or whatever (see, for example, Glick 1962). In addition, data routinely collected by government agencies, voluntary organizations, business establishments, and other such bodies are exploited in sociological investigations of every type. Some examples are school data, labor force data, police data, license and permit data, welfare data, business sales and operations data, and local and super-local governmental data of all types.[1]

A classic example is Durkheim's (1951) use of suicide rates in his analysis of social integration and *anomie*. And Natalie Rogoff used marriage certificate data collected in Indianapolis in 1910 and 1940 to study changing patterns of intergenerational occupational mobility (Rogoff 1953). A long tradition of studies has used data on voting and population composition in many electoral districts at various times to investigate the social bases of political party support. (For a recent example, see O'Lessker 1968.)

[1] For a concise statement on the sources and types of sociological data, see Riley 1964, especially pp. 1010–1014, and Young 1949.

As for the data used in population studies, these are often *not* available in the routine collections made by legal, political, or administrative agencies. And they are often *not* amenable to quantitative presentation and analysis. Rather, many problems in population studies require the production of entirely original data, and these most often concern phenomena and events that are not readily quantifiable. Thus, investigations of the social structural and social psychological causes and correlates of variations in patterns of courtship, matchmaking and marriage, family planning and fertility, and mobility and migration frequently must generate their own data; and these data will often be contained in historical accounts, case studies, or other forms not easily amenable to classification and counting, much less to actual measurement.[2]

In the "Indianapolis Study," a pioneer study of family planning among 1,444 white couples sampled in Indianapolis in 1941, C. V. Kiser, P. K. Whelpton, and their associates (1958) investigated the extent of contraceptive practices, their effectiveness, and the size of planned families as affected by a series of social and psychological factors. To carry out this series of studies, it was necessary to devise ways of observing and analyzing various social and psychological factors on the basis of a survey questionnaire. These factors, to name only some, were socioeconomic status, economic insecurity and tension, family and childhood situations, liking for children, various personality characteristics, marital adjustment and marital dominance relationships, interest in religion, conformity, adherence to traditions, and tendency to plan.

For another example, R. Freedman and his associates have carried out a series of studies on the conditions under which Taiwanese couples adopt birth control practices and on the extent and correlates of successful fertility control in Taiwan (Freedman 1964; Freedman and Takeshita 1965). Among the variety of social variables studied and incorporated into the analysis were wife's and husband's frequency of newspaper reading, number of modern objects owned, wife's attitude toward traditional family values, and farm background. Table 3.2 shows the importance of the education, reading, and "ownership of modern objects" factors as compared to the husband's occupation, wife's attitude, farm background, and husband's cash income factors. The extent of practice of family planning *varies* among women and among categories of women. So do education, reading, attitudes, income and the like. Statistical analysis of *concomitant variation* of family planning and each of the factors

2 Hauser and Duncan offer the name "micro-demography" to kinds of small-scale studies in which both census-type and other factors bearing on population characteristics are studied. They suggest that such "micro-demographic" studies are able to focus upon new finds of problems and go beyond simply providing additional data bearing upon the traditional problems of demography. See Hauser and Duncan 1959, p. 52.

TABLE 3.2

Percent of the Total Variance in Use of Family Planning Associated with Different Social Variables, for Wives Aged 30–39

Social Variables	Percent of Variance in Family Limitation Use Explained
Variables considered singly	
Wife's education	13.1
Husband's education	11.3
Wife's frequency of newspaper reading	12.9
Husband's frequency of newspaper reading	10.7
Number of modern objects owned	14.8
Husband's work classification	4.4
Wife's attitude toward traditional family values	6.4
Couple's farm background	3.2
Husband's annual cash income	3.2
Variables considered in clusters	
Husband and wife's education	13.7
Husband and wife's education and newspaper reading by husband and wife (education-reading variables)	16.1
Education-reading variables and number of modern objects owned	18.7
Education-reading variables, number of modern objects owned, and husband's work status	18.8
Education-reading variables, number of modern objects owned, husband's work status and wife's attitudes toward traditional family values	19.2
Education-reading variables and couples' farm background	16.2
Wife-husband's education and husband's income	16.5

SOURCE: Freedman and Takeshita 1965, table 3, p. 182.

singly and in combination—education, reading, and so forth—yields measures of the part of the variation in extent of family planning practice, or "percent of variance," which can be accounted for in terms of each of the factors. This, then, measures the relative importance of each factor or combinations of factors associated with the practice of family planning.

In a study of family structure and change in 300 pre-World War II Yugoslav villages, Vera St. Erlich (1966) presents case studies and statistical materials showing characteristic relationships between members of traditional patriarchal families, on the one hand, and more modern, nucleated family units, on the other. Patterns and consequences of the transition are analyzed. In addition, changing patterns of marriage and childbearing are related to changes in family roles and power relationships, all set against the background of major educational, community, and economic trends in the different regions of Yugoslavia.

2. SPECIALIZED SOURCES OF POPULATION DATA

The usual sources of data for population studies are censuses, sample surveys, vital registration systems, and population registers. In addition, the records of various public or private agencies—school systems, social security administrations, hospitals, insurance companies, etc.—sometimes serve as important sources of data.

Censuses

A population census is primarily a count of the number of inhabitants of a given area, but usually it also includes the numbers of inhabitants in different population categories. Thus, most modern population censuses not only enumerate the total population but categorize it as well, by sex, age, and marital status, by place of residence, by administrative area, by economic activity, and by various other characteristics. An example of a tabulation of population by marital status, household relationship, sex, and race for selected counties in Michigan from the 1970 U.S. census is illustrated in table 3.3.

A population census yields data on the size of the total population at the time of the census, on the composition of the population by major biological, ethnic, social, or economic characteristics, on the territorial distribution of the population, and on the distribution of the population with respect to key social or economic attributes. In principle, there is no limit to the variety and detail of information obtainable in a census. In practice, however, the scope is always limited by considerations of cost, the availabiltiy of resources, difficulties in developing valid and reliable measuring instruments, and values dictating what information is appropriate to obtain and in what format it should be published. A sample census schedule is presented in Appendix A (page 509). The kinds of information obtained in the census is best learned by careful inspection of the census schedule.

So great are the human and material resources required for carrying out a full-scale census enumeration that even by 1954, well into the post-World War II period of unprecedented worldwide census activity and international cooperation, an estimated 20 percent of the world population had not been counted (Linder 1959). And census coverage today is still far from universal. There are areas of the world for which the most elementary population data are lacking, and others for which only the barest of demographic details have been obtained. Sample survey tech-

TABLE 3.3
Marital Status and Household Relationship by Race, for Counties: 1970

							Counties					Kala-			Ke-
	Gratiot	Hillsdale	Houghton	Huron	Ingham	Ionia	Iosco	Iron	Isabella	Jackson	mazoo	Kalkaska	Kent	weenow
Marital Status														
Total male, 14 years old and over	13 176	13 041	14 673	11 967	94 484	16 747	9 234	5 357	16 029	51 586	70 486	1 788	137 406	982
Single	3 559	3 335	6 518	3 547	34 882	5 472	2 713	1 548	7 353	14 049	22 593	434	37 783	355
Married	9 026	9 024	7 301	7 866	55 641	10 373	6 115	3 440	8 209	34 020	44 604	1 229	92 069	543
Separated	95	108	56	42	968	234	81	32	70	937	786	9	1 344	7
Widowed	366	364	589	355	1 565	419	215	260	257	1 351	1 522	78	3 749	45
Divorced	225	318	265	199	2 396	483	191	109	210	2 166	1 767	47	3 805	39
Total female, 14 years old and over	14 509	13 857	12 451	12 450	99 713	15 650	8 411	5 625	17 507	51 836	78 073	1 974	155 377	821
Single	3 166	2 831	2 848	2 561	30 046	3 094	1 335	1 068	7 520	10 527	22 121	263	38 301	150
Married	9 143	9 068	7 379	7 965	56 452	10 132	6 087	3 460	8 361	32 983	45 523	1 246	93 528	540
Separated	138	126	96	82	1 560	193	88	46	142	761	1 215	28	2 234	1
Widowed	1 827	1 547	1 949	1 691	8 744	1 916	790	972	1 295	6 114	7 220	356	17 098	115
Divorced	373	411	275	233	4 471	508	199	125	331	2 212	3 209	109	6 450	16
White male, 14 years old and over	13 124	12 975	14 554	11 933	88 967	15 647	8 823	5 335	15 650	47 336	67 202	1 783	130 264	969
Single	3 534	3 294	6 430	3 530	32 527	4 633	2 523	1 537	7 118	12 157	21 332	432	35 361	350
Married	9 000	9 001	7 271	7 850	52 778	10 173	5 907	3 429	8 082	32 104	42 791	1 227	87 997	536
Separated	94	108	55	41	785	192	73	28	66	549	658	9	1 004	7
Widowed	365	364	589	355	1 476	397	211	260	246	1 231	1 431	77	3 533	45
Divorced	225	316	264	198	2 186	444	182	109	204	1 844	1 648	47	3 373	38
White female, 14 years old and over	14 449	13 805	12 404	12 429	94 159	15 572	8 170	5 604	17 195	49 416	74 437	1 967	147 139	815
Single	3 140	2 808	2 831	2 555	28 118	3 070	1 306	1 065	7 370	9 920	20 942	262	36 083	149
Married	9 115	9 044	7 351	7 952	53 564	10 088	5 883	3 445	8 233	31 704	43 583	1 241	89 138	535
Separated	137	125	96	82	1 236	185	86	46	128	561	930	28	1 572	1
Widowed	1 822	1 544	1 948	1 690	8 389	1 908	785	970	1 268	5 777	6 943	355	16 319	115
Divorced	372	409	274	232	4 088	506	196	124	324	2 015	2 969	109	5 599	16
Negro male, 14 years old and over	21	34	22	15	4 617	1 041	335	...	160	4 032	2 954	—	6 552	11
Single	16	23	17	6	1 961	806	146	...	124	1 804	1 132	—	2 212	4
Married	5	10	5	8	2 379	179	180	...	31	1 820	1 626	—	3 736	6
Separated	1	—	—	—	170	41	6	...	1	383	122	—	318	—
Widowed	—	—	—	—	80	18	—	...	1	103	87	—	197	—
Divorced	—	1	—	1	197	38	9	...	4	305	109	—	407	1
Negro female, 14 years old and over	21	23	12	1	4 788	35	150	...	105	2 182	3 242	—	7 513	4
Single	14	13	7	—	1 685	9	20	...	69	560	1 042	—	2 033	—
Married	5	9	5	1	2 413	21	126	...	28	1 167	1 721	—	3 951	4
Separated	—	1	—	—	307	6	—	...	—	194	279	—	621	—
Widowed	2	—	—	—	331	5	2	...	6	268	253	—	717	—
Divorced	—	—	—	—	359	—	2	...	2	187	226	—	812	—
Relationship to Head of Household for Selected Age Groups														
Total persons, under 18 years old	14 770	13 302	9 853	12 850	85 138	17 305	9 150	4 134	14 288	51 450	68 463	1 938	153 163	594
Head or wife of head	25	42	27	21	275	56	25	5	35	121	122	14	348	—

Own child of head	14 080	12 562	9 501	12 342	80 384	16 445	8 747	3 982	13 123	48 747	64 557	1 831	146 895	564
In husband-wife households	13 031	11 645	8 667	11 480	71 211	15 175	8 040	3 662	12 144	44 243	58 365	1 648	131 693	499
In household with female head	899	752	739	736	8 316	1 085	618	269	839	4 014	5 599	167	13 822	58
Other relative of head	544	507	265	374	3 087	577	304	136	443	2 132	2 482	63	4 616	58
Other	121	191	60	113	1 392	227	74	11	687	450	1 302	30	1 304	25
White persons, under 18 years old	14 729	13 251	9 814	12 816	78 188	17 188	8 786	4 119	13 923	48 417	63 826	1 936	141 221	587
Head or wife of head	25	42	27	21	259	56	24	5	33	111	112	14	296	—
Own child of head	14 044	12 519	9 467	12 308	74 220	16 366	8 396	3 967	12 908	46 081	60 493	1 829	136 121	557
In husband-wife households	12 998	11 608	8 635	11 452	66 907	15 103	7 720	3 649	11 963	42 508	55 668	1 646	125 026	492
In household with female head	896	746	737	734	6 558	1 083	596	267	806	3 119	4 323	167	9 937	58
Other relative of head	541	504	262	374	2 602	572	293	136	418	1 824	2 070	63	3 682	25
Other	119	186	58	113	1 107	194	73	11	564	401	1 151	30	1 122	5
Negro persons, under 18 years old	6	19	13	14	6 179	56	313	...	95	2 872	4 249	2	11 111	5
Head or wife of head	—	—	—	—	14	—	—	...	1	10	9	—	45	—
Own child of head	4	12	6	9	5 452	45	280	...	42	2 526	3 710	2	10 016	5
In husband-wife households	2	8	6	8	3 675	45	255	...	33	1 622	2 389	—	6 052	5
In household with female head	2	4	—	1	1 692	—	16	...	9	870	1 230	—	3 756	—
Other relative of head	1	3	3	2	453	4	4	...	3	294	392	—	893	—
Other	1	4	4	3	260	7	29	...	49	42	138	—	157	—
Total persons, 65 years old and over	3 975	4 202	4 744	4 349	17 726	4 439	2 425	2 288	2 862	13 115	15 590	770	38 248	334
Head of family: Male	1 176	1 440	1 431	1 487	5 317	1 338	935	676	948	3 835	4 420	254	11 023	119
Female	140	158	298	205	734	187	61	109	130	567	625	25	1 689	21
Wife of head	767	979	829	961	3 564	896	577	400	603	2 611	2 980	166	7 592	55
Other family member	303	334	539	368	1 814	419	206	153	268	1 308	1 505	42	3 493	34
Not related to head	61	102	90	88	326	111	52	28	52	249	323	25	630	9
Primary individual: Male	201	278	445	309	971	264	189	225	158	754	885	69	2 233	46
Female	821	773	843	783	4 108	967	361	471	551	2 785	3 419	185	8 070	45
Inmate of institution	482	124	180	137	848	250	44	223	132	834	1 255	4	3 106	5
Other, in group quarters	24	14	89	11	44	7	—	3	20	172	178	—	412	—
White persons, 65 years old and over	3 968	4 194	4 740	4 344	17 189	4 410	2 413	2 285	2 810	12 495	15 130	768	37 164	334
Head of family: Male	1 173	1 438	1 430	1 486	5 152	1 336	933	676	933	3 716	4 305	253	10 741	119
Female	140	157	298	205	706	187	59	108	125	532	587	25	1 598	21
Wife of head	765	978	829	960	3 475	893	575	400	594	2 533	2 914	166	7 453	55
Other family member	303	330	539	368	1 719	416	204	153	259	1 239	1 421	41	3 322	34
Not related to head	61	102	90	87	291	111	52	28	51	229	305	25	581	9
Primary individual: Male	201	278	444	308	934	263	186	224	153	729	857	69	2 138	46
Female	820	773	842	782	4 042	962	360	471	549	2 698	3 349	185	7 876	45
Inmate of institution	481	124	179	137	827	235	44	222	130	652	1 219	4	3 046	5
Other, in group quarters	24	14	89	11	43	7	—	3	16	167	173	—	409	—
Negro persons, 65 years old and over	6	6	4	5	484	22	...	...	10	476	416	2	976	—
Head of family: Male	2	2	1	1	151	7	...	...	4	115	108	—	260	—
Female	—	—	—	—	27	1	...	...	2	35	35	—	83	—
Wife of head	1	—	—	1	80	3	...	...	2	72	62	—	128	—
Other family member	—	1	1	—	85	1	...	...	1	64	77	—	154	—
Not related to head	—	—	—	—	33	—	...	...	—	20	24	—	43	—
Primary individual: Male	—	—	—	—	33	1	...	...	—	17	15	—	83	—
Female	1	—	1	2	54	8	...	...	1	80	28	2	163	—
Inmate of institution	1	2	1	1	21	1	...	...	—	57	57	—	59	—
Other, in group quarters	—	1	—	—	—	—	...	...	—	16	4	—	3	—

SOURCE: Population Characteristics, U.S. Bureau of the Census, Final Report PC (1)-B24 Michigan.

niques are, to be sure, contributing partial solutions to this problem, but great gaps in census or equivalent population data are likely to remain for a long time to come.

Another problem is that of priorities. What questions should be asked in censuses? And if they are asked, how will they be received? Will they even be answered? In Israel or in Mexico, the inclusion of a question on the "race" of respondents might well generate serious political crises or, at the very least, great objection and considerable conflict; questions on the "religion" of the respondent, however, are routinely asked and draw no great objections. In the United States, by contrast, a question on the "race" of respondents is regularly asked, and no constitutional question seems to have been raised about it—but proposals to introduce a question on "religion" in the U.S. Census have stimulated powerful, highly organized, and articulate objections based on constitutional grounds.

Some census questions may be excluded, or withdrawn after previous inclusion, on grounds of insufficient importance or priority. Because it is extremely expensive to include a question and to process, analyze, and publish the responses to it, the use of one question generally requires the exclusion of another. Some questions, such as those on sex, age, marital status, place of residence, relationship to head of household, and economic activity are included in virtually all censuses. Questions on health, past military service, fertility of women, literacy or level of education, employment and income, migration, ethnic characteristics, or household equipment appear in some censuses but not in others. Each census has its own procedures and institutions for assigning priorities and balancing the demands and resources for meeting them.

Priorities with respect to the tabulation and publication of data must also be worked out. Typically, when a national government agency conducts a census, other national agencies, local government agencies, private business, and research institutions all seek to assure that the data will be tabulated in forms and combinations congenial to their respective needs. Census bureaus generally seek to publish the most widely demanded kinds of tabulation and are able to make unpublished tabulations available to individuals and agencies requiring them. In addition, census bureaus are often able to prepare special tabulations as needed. However, all these capabilities are limited, and many requests and requirements for tabulations of census data cannot be met.

An important development in recent years has been the recording of entire censuses, or samples from censuses, on magnetic tapes or punch cards. These tapes or cards can be tabulated by the *user* in accordance with his own requirements. As this development matures, users of census data will have an unlimited range of tabulations, and census agencies will be able to reduce significantly their own tabulations and publications of data. Thus far it has been restricted largely to the United States census.

Sample Surveys

A sample survey is ordinarily used to estimate the compositional and distributional characteristics of a population on the basis of information on only a part—a sample—of that population. Recently, however, sample surveys have also been designed to estimate the number of inhabitants of a given area. Because of the costs saved in enumerating only a fraction of the total population, the shorter time required to process the data, and the better quality of data made possible by the increased expenditure allotted to each respondent, sample surveys have become increasingly important in data collection. Indeed, sampling has recently been done in conjunction with population censuses, and in reducing the number of questions asked in the complete enumeration by including many of the detailed questions in the sample survey only, the costs of enumeration and processing have been sharply reduced and the quality of the data improved.[3] Appendix B (page 519) shows a sample Current Population Survey (CPS) schedule.

The Current Population Survey is conducted on an ongoing basis by the Bureau of the Census primarily to obtain up-to-date information on the number of persons "in the labor force" (employed or not employed but seeking work), the numbers employed and unemployed respectively, and the characteristics—sex, age, race, occupation, etc.—of those employed and unemployed. In addition to employment information, the Current Population Survey is used as a vehicle for obtaining other current information about the population. Thus, in the example shown of a CPS schedule, questions concerning living quarters and recent voting in Congressional elections were asked.

Vital Registration Systems

In areas in which it is carried out at all, the registration of births, deaths, marriages, divorces, and related vital events ordinarily has some legal or administrative purpose. However, when information based upon vital records is used in conjunction with census or sample survey data, basic data can be derived on the components of population change, fertility, and mortality and on the components of family formation, marriage, and divorce.

The nationwide registration of vital events requires a permanent and comprehensive system of local registration offices and elaborate procedures for ensuring the cooperation of government officials, of medical

---

3 For a more extensive and detailed discussion of the use of sampling in censuses and population studies, see C. Taeuber (1964). See also U.S. Bureau of the Census, *Procedural Report on the 1960 Censuses of Population and Housing* (1963); Taeuber and Hansen (1964); and Alterman (1969).

personnel and others concerned with vital events, and of the population as a whole. Understandably, the procedure is carried out only in those countries able to allocate the necessary human and economic resources, and even then the records are not always complete. Nevertheless, data based upon vital records, even if incomplete, are often adequate for research purposes and represent the most direct information obtainable on the components of population change. Examples of birth and death certificates are shown in figures 3.1 and 3.2.

Population Registers

A number of countries—for example, Denmark, Sweden, and Israel —maintain continuous population registers for various legal and administrative purposes. These registers are essentially *lists* of names, with each name accompanied by a number of personal characteristics. The

FIGURE 3.1. Certificate of Live Birth. Source: Vital Statistics of the United States, 1967, Vol. LL, Mortality, U.S. Dept. of Health, Education, and Welfare.

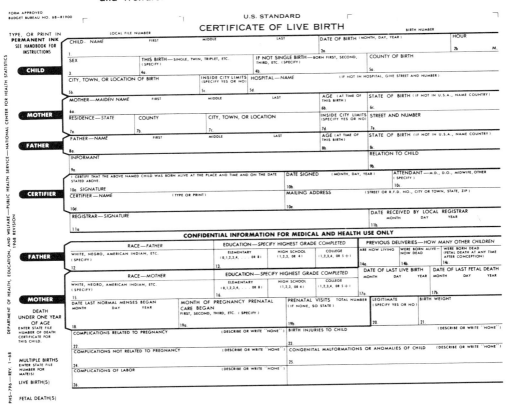

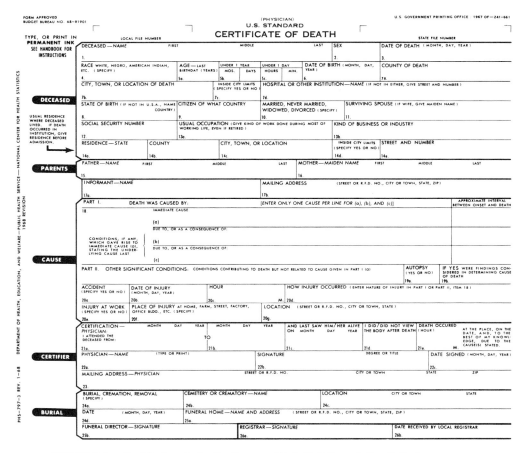

FIGURE 3.2. Certificate of Death. Source: Vital Statistics of the United States, 1967, Vol. LL, Mortality, U.S. Dept. of Health, Education, and Welfare.

population register in Israel lists every person in the population, giving his or her identity number, citizenship, nationality, religion, sex, date of birth, place of birth, date of immigration to Israel if born abroad, current marital status, and current address. The original purpose of the register was for the preparation of lists of eligible voters in the national and local elections and, during the 1948 conflict, for the administration of food rationing. The register has also been used in connection with military conscription, school enrollment, the issuance of passports, the carrying out of surveys and a population census, and for current estimates of the population.

A newborn child or a new immigrant to the country is issued a birth or immigration certificate and an identity number and at the same time is entered into the population register. If the individual changes his marital status, he is required by law to "inform" the population register, a procedure actually done automatically through the register's connection to registrations for marriage and divorce. Similarly, the register is automatically "informed" of deaths through the required death registration and burial permits (which also "inform" the register of the change in marital status of the decedent's surviving spouse). In much the same way, emigrants are removed from the register either by declaring their intention to emigrate upon leaving the country, or after failure to return to the country after a specified time abroad.

In principle, persons changing their place of residence are also required by law to inform the population register. But in practice, changes of address in Israel's population register are typically effected only after some time. Characteristically, the register is "brought up to date" by large numbers of change-of-address notifications in preparation for some special undertaking—for example, a forthcoming election, a census, or a change in eligibility for some welfare provision.

Critical Aspects of Data Collection Systems

The critical aspects of data collection systems are the *coverage, comparability,* and *quality* of the data produced. *Coverage* refers to the completeness with which the population or events being studied are in fact enumerated and the range of information obtained about the unit of observation. In addition, the time reference of the observation— whether it is an instant or an interval in time—may be considered under this heading as well.

Studies and analyses drawing upon data collected in different places, at different times, or by different data collection systems are beset by questions of *comparability.* Lack of comparability results most often from dissimilarities of definition; a case in point would be the definitions of "urban" cited earlier. But it may also arise from dissimilarity of coverage, differential quality, validity, and reliability, and of the data-collecting instruments such as census and survey questionnaires.

Quality refers primarily to the accuracy of the data—the extent to which the recorded observation corresponds to the characteristic or attribute of the unit observed—but also to the validity and reliability of the recording or data-collecting instrument or technique. *Validity* is the extent to which the data-collecting instrument records a datum by referring to the characteristic being studied rather than to some alternative, perhaps closely related, characteristic of the unit of observation. For example, if a questionnaire and interviewing routine elicit and record responses such as "textile worker," "government employee," or "in business," in a study of *occupations,* then the data-collecting procedure may be said to lack validity on that particular item. *Reliability* is the extent to which the particular datum obtained for the unit of observation is independent of the person or agency obtaining it. In some studies the same respondents may be interviewed two or more times in order to ascertain changes—for example, change in address, in occupation, in opinions, in political orientations, or in family size—such studies are called "panel studies." Typically included also are certain items of basic information, such as date and place of birth, or details of educational background. If the same individual is recorded once as "completed 12 years of schooling" and subsequently as "completed M.A. degree," then the data-collecting procedure may be said to lack reliability on that particular item.

The Evaluation of Data Collection Systems

Some techniques for measuring the extent of coverage of a census or a vital registration system are still in the developmental stage, and those that already exist are too complicated to be treated here.[4] As a rule, censuses and vital registration systems are subject to underenumeration and underregistration, respectively, rather than overenumeration or overregistration. Fortunately, census or registration agencies are often able to estimate what proportion of the total number of relevant persons or events has in fact been enumerated or registered.

Table 3.4 summarizes estimates of population coverage errors in the 1950 and 1960 United States censuses. The estimates of enumeration errors are based upon Census Bureau re-enumeration procedures developed specifically for purposes of evaluating coverage. The estimates of net census undercount of children are based on comparison with numbers of births reported in the Vital Statistics for the period preceding the census.

Agencies producing population data on a recurrent basis—e.g., those producing decennial censuses or annual surveys—are faced with a chronic conflict between the desire to assure comparability of data over time and the need to change definitions and procedures to meet changing requirements for current data. This conflict is never fully resolved: even the most minute change in definitions and procedures affects comparability over time. Moreover, there is always a lag between the time at which a new requirement emerges and the time at which the appriate change can finally be put into effect.

The most effective compromise is to tabulate the data according to both the old and new procedures and definitions, at least at the time

4 Such procedures are introduced and discussed at length in Hansen, Hurwitz, and Pritzker, 1953; and Shapiro, 1954. More recent work in evaluation of census data is summarized and cited in Taeuber and Hansen, 1964.

TABLE 3.4
Estimates of Population Coverage Errors in
U.S. Censuses of Population, 1950 and 1960
(by percent of census total)

Enumeration errors	1960	1950
Omissions of persons	3.0	2.3
In missed living quarters	1.6	1.6
In enumerated living quarters	1.4	0.6
Erroneous inclusions of persons	1.3	0.9
Net undercoverage of persons	1.7	1.4
Net census undercount of children		
Under five years old	2.6	4.7
5–9 years old	2.4	3.6
10–14 years old	1.9	1.8

SOURCE: C. Taeuber and Hansen 1964, table 2 and table 3, pp. 4–5.

of the change-over. However, since even this type of compromise is ordinarily too costly to be applied to all the data in a census or survey, such double presentations are usually limited to only a portion of the total data presented. An example is shown in table 3.5.

A full discussion of techniques for measuring the accuracy, validity, and reliability of data would go far beyond the scope of this volume. It is necessary here to note only that data referring to population growth and its components have an internal consistency embodied in the following relationship:

$$\begin{pmatrix} \text{Population} \\ \text{size at end} \\ \text{of period} \end{pmatrix} = \begin{pmatrix} \text{Population size} \\ \text{at beginning} \\ \text{of period} \end{pmatrix} + \begin{pmatrix} \text{No. of} \\ \text{births in} \\ \text{period} \end{pmatrix} -$$

$$\begin{pmatrix} \text{No. of} \\ \text{deaths in} \\ \text{period} \end{pmatrix} + \begin{pmatrix} \text{No. of} \\ \text{inmigrants} \\ \text{in period} \end{pmatrix} - \begin{pmatrix} \text{No. of} \\ \text{outmigrants} \\ \text{in period} \end{pmatrix}$$

To evaluate the accuracy of data on population size or on one or more of the components of growth, one might check the consistency of the data in question against the components of this relationship. In fact, this is a common procedure. Thus, for the U.S. intercensal period from 1 April, 1950 to 1 April, 1960, the components of the balancing equation are:

1.	Population, 1 April, 1960	179,323,000
2.	Population, 1 April, 1950	151,326,000
3.	Net Increase: (1) − (2)	27,997,000

Components of Change:

4.	Births (corrected for underregistration)	40,963,000
5.	Deaths	15,608,000
6.	Net movement of aliens and citizens	+ 2,695,000
7.	Net movement of armed forces abroad	− 330,000
8.	Expected Net Increase: (4) − (5) + ((6) + (7))	27,720,000
9.	Difference: (3) − (8)	277,000

TABLE 3.5

Urban and Rural Population of the United States 1790–1960

Census Date	Total Population Number	Urban		Rural	
		Number	Percent	Number	Percent
United States					
Current urban definition:					
1960	179,323,175	125,268,750	69.9	54,054,425	30.1
1950	151,325,798	96,846,817	64.0	54,478,981	36.0
Previous urban definition:					
1960	179,323,175	113,056,353	63.0	66,266,822	37.0
1950	151,325,798	90,128,194	59.6	61,197,604	40.4
1940	132,164,569	74,705,338	56.5	57,459,231	43.5
1930	123,202,624	69,160,599	56.1	54,042,025	43.9
Conterminous United States					
Current urban definition:					
1960	178,464,236	124,699,022	69.9	53,765,214	30.1
1950	150,697,361	96,467,686	64.0	54,229,675	36.0
Previous urban definition:					
1960	178,464,236	112,531,941	63.1	65,932,295	36.9
1950	150,697,361	89,749,063	59.6	60,948,298	40.4
1940	131,669,275	74,423,702	56.5	57,245,573	43.5
1930	122,775,046	68,954,823	56.2	53,820,223	43.8
1920	105,710,620	54,157,973	51.2	51,552,647	48.8
1910	91,972,266	41,998,932	45.7	49,973,334	54.3
1900	75,994,575	30,159,921	39.7	45,834,654	60.3
1890	62,947,714	22,106,265	35.1	40,841,449	64.9
1880	50,155,783	14,129,735	28.2	36,026,048	71.8
1870	38,558,371	9,902,361	25.7	28,656,010	74.3
1860	31,443,321	6,216,518	19.8	25,226,803	80.2
1850	23,191,876	3,543,716	15.3	19,648,160	84.7
1840	17,069,453	1,845,055	10.8	15,224,398	89.2
1830	12,866,020	1,127,247	8.8	11,738,773	91.2
1820	9,638,453	693,255	7.2	8,945,198	92.8
1810	7,239,881	525,459	7.3	6,714,422	92.7
1800	5,308,483	322,371	6.1	4,986,112	93.9
1790	3,929,214	201,655	5.1	3,727,559	94.9

SOURCE: U.S. Bureau of the Census 1960.

An analysis of the difference, 277,000, is then carried out in terms of possible sources of error in the components.

Finally, certain kinds of errors are known to recur in population data, and demographers have developed techniques for "correcting" the data to take account of them. For example, there is a common tendency to misreport ages, giving a number divisible by five; thus, someone will report his age as 40 or 45 instead of 42 or 43. Mathematical techniques of "smoothing" are often employed to adjust age-distribution data to eliminate this "heaping" of ages ending in zero or five.

3. ANALYTICAL UNITS FOR POPULATION STUDIES

In our reference to "population" in the first chapter, we indicated that a population may be defined in terms of co-occupation of a given areal unit (e.g., all persons living within the city limits of Rockford, Illinois) or in terms of similarity with respect to a specified characteristic (e.g., all males over the age of 40). Censuses, vital statistics, and population surveys can circumscribe populations on both these bases. Thus, they can identify separate population groupings on the basis of areal units—the populations of the fifty United States, of the 6,435 urban places in the U.S. 1970 Census of Population, of the separate counties of Nebraska, of the conurbations of Great Britain, of the provinces of Canada, etc. Similarly, they can identify populations on the basis of specified characteristics— the population of rural Kentucky, the French-speaking population of Canada, the Jewish population of Israel, the Croatian population of Yugoslavia, the miners of Colorado, the families dependent upon agriculture in Mexico, the clerical and sales workers of New York City, and so on. In addition, censuses, surveys, and vital statistics can be used in a variety of ways by manipulating sets of *primary analytical areal units*.

Primary Analytical Areal Units

Cities, other urban areas, or rural areas are very often characterized by distinct sections, quarters, neighborhoods, or other smaller subareas, each having its own peculiar history, land use, population density, population composition, and social and economic activities. It is often of great interest to study such areal units separately. And when data can be obtained on the population and physical characteristics of small areas within areas (e.g., blocks, enumeration districts, tracts, or neighborhoods), it is possible to describe and analyze intra-areal differentiation at any moment in time and to analyze changes occurring over time but differently in the separate small areas. For example, it is known, on the basis of such data, not only that different areas within cities are inhabited by different ethnic, racial, occupational, or age groups, but also that the various neighborhoods and subareas may be characterized by different rates of fertility, mortality, delinquency, and morbidity, and by different patterns of consumption, school attendance, or voting.

For purposes of analyzing differentiation within areas, it is useful to employ some set of small areal units as primary analytical units (cf. Hauser and Matras 1965). In countries which have more or less permanent census-taking or population-survey arrangements, it may be most convenient to use enumeration districts or census tracts, typically the smallest geographic units assigned a single census enumerator or a single team of enumerators as the primary areal units of analysis. Such units should be more or less permanent or at least fixed over several censuses or other investigations; and they should be relatively homogeneous with respect to the characteristics of the population residing in them at any moment in time. It is usually useful to delineate such areas in terms of physical characteristics or distinguishing aspects of land utilization—e.g., natural boundaries, such as rivers and streams, or relatively permanent manmade boundaries, such as railroads or major traffic arteries.

In their Introduction to the *1960 Local Community Fact Book: Chicago Metropolitan Area*, E. M. Kitagawa and K. E. Taeuber (1963) describe the community areas of Chicago:

> The 75 community areas within the City of Chicago were first delineated more than 30 years ago, through the work of the Social Science Research Committee of the University of Chicago, building upon the years of research activity of its predecessor, the Local Community Research Committee, with the cooperation and concerted effort of many local agencies and the United States Bureau of the Census. The boundaries of the 75 community areas were originally drawn on the basis of several considerations, chief among which were: (1) the settlement, growth, and history of the area; (2) local identification with the area; (3) the local trade area; (4) distribution of membership of local institutions; and (5) natural and artificial barriers such as the Chicago River and its branches, railroad lines, local transportation systems, and parks and boulevards. The actual boundaries drawn were necessarily a compromise, involving in addition to these factors the tabulation requirements of the U.S. Bureau of the census. Community areas comprise complete census tracts, so that the regularly published census data for hundreds of tracts can be compiled into more convenient form for studying the characteristics and changes in the characteristics of local communities.
>
> Community areas at the present time are best regarded as statistical units for the analysis of varying conditions within the City of Chicago at a given time, and for studying changes over time in conditions within local communities. When community area boundaries were delineated more than 30 years ago, the objective was to define a set of subareas of the city each of which could be regarded as having a history of its own as a community, a name, an awareness

on the part of its inhabitants of common interests, and a set of local businesses and organizations oriented to the local community. As initially designated, community areas measured up to these criteria in varying degree. Over time, there have been major changes in distribution of people and in specific patterns of land use. Rather than revising the boundaries of community areas at each census in an attempt to take account of these changes, there has been a deliberate effort to maintain a constant set of subareas within the city in order to analyze changes in the social, economic and residential structure of the city during the past 30 years. Redefining boundaries every ten years would destroy the usefulness of the grid for studying change, and would not greatly increase the utility of community areas for the study of a wide range of characteristics at one point in time. The initial set of community area boundaries represented a compromise, and no single set of boundaries then or now could satisfy everyone interested in studying local communities. For particular analyses, researchers may find other groupings of census tracts more useful, for example, to pinpoint areas of dilapidated housing or areas of high income at a given point in time, but a fixed set of communities with some historical basis—such as that provided by the 75 community areas—are generally most useful for the analysis of changing composition and structure over time. The 75 community areas, for which Chicago statistics have been compiled since 1930, not only serve this purpose admirably, but they remain, in many cases, meaningful local communities. [Kitagawa and Taeuber 1963, pp. xiii–xiv]

The community areas discussed by Kitagawa and Taeuber are shown in figure 3.3. Street names are given on the periphery of the map.

Coding and Use of Primary Analytical Areal Units

If the same primary areal analytical units used locally are to be used in national censuses or surveys, it is essential that national and local authorities and agencies cooperate in delineating the areas to be employed. The purpose of this is to ensure the most advantageous use of the units at both local and national levels.

Once a network of such primary analytical units is established and delineated, provision must be made for carrying out subsequent analyses or investigations. In other words, it is necessary to make some more or less permanent arrangement for relating new data and information to the system of primary areal analytical units. This can usually be achieved by identifying the primary analytical unit associated with each datum, i.e., by assigning each datum a coordinate or location in terms of the network of primary analytical units, using maps or coding guides. Figure 3.4 presents a sample coding guide for a group of streets in Chicago.

The primary analytical units can be indicated by number or by some other identification on a map of the area being studied. Data referring to persons residing in a given unit, or working in a unit, or to

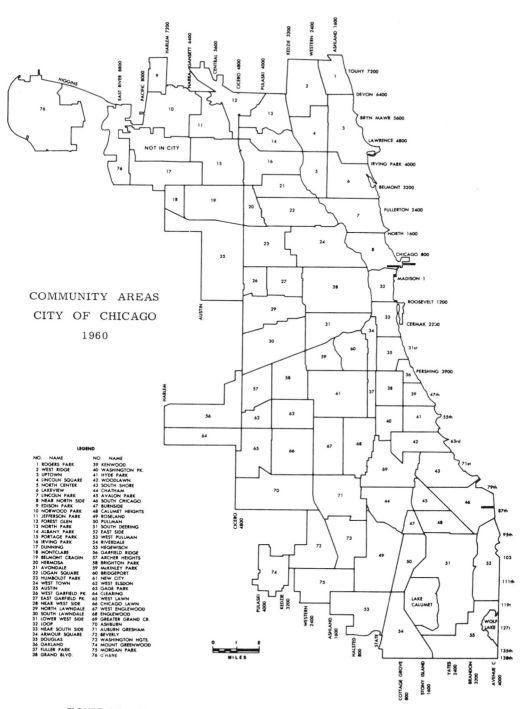

FIGURE 3.3. Community areas, city of Chicago, 1960. Source: Kitagawa and Taeuber 1963, p. ix.

BERENICE Av. W.
  1800 - 1999 5-55
  2400 - 2599 5-58
  4600 - 4799 15-176
  4800 - 5199 15-173
  5200 - 5599 15-172
  5600 - 5999 15-171
  6000 - 6399 17-200

BERKELEY Av. S.
  3920 - 4299 36-562
  4300 - 4699 39-594
  5200 - 5499 41-615

BERNARD St. N.
  2400 - 2799 22-238
  2800 - 3199 21-232
  3600 - 3999 16-186
  4000 - 4399 16-189
  4400 - 4799 14-163
  4800 - 4999 14-166
  5000 - 5599 13-157
  5600 - 5999 ....13-159b
  6000 - 6399 ....13-159a

BERTEAU Av. W.
  1400 - 1599 6-66
  1600 - 1799 6-67
  1800 - 1999 5-52
  2000 - 2399 5-53
  2400 - 2599 5-51
  2600 - 3199 16-190
  3200 - 3599 16-189
  3600 - 3999 16-188
  4000 - 4231 16-183
  4232 - 4635 16-180
  4636 - 4799 15-175
  4800 - 5199 15-174
  5200 - 5599 15-170
  5600 - 5999 15-169
  6000 - 6399 15-168
  8200 - 8399 ....17-193z

BERWYN Av. W.
  800 - 1199 3-35
  1200 - 1499 3-34
  1500 - 1799 3-31
  1800 - 2399 ....4-49z
  2400 - 2799 4-47
  2800 - 3199 4-48
  3200 - 3999 13-157
  4800 - 5099 12-153
  5100 - 5599 11-150
  5900 - 5999 11-149
  6000 - 6399 11-147
  6400 - 7199 ....10-145y
  7200 - 8299 ....10-142z

BESLY Ct. N.
  1600 - 1799 24-308
  1800 - 1899 22-264

BEVERLY Av. S.
  8700 - 8999 71-914
  9000 - 9499 73-922
  9500 - 9899 ....73-923a
  9900 -10299 ....73-923b
  10700 -11099 75-934

BEVERLY GLEN Parkway W.
  1500 - 1999 72-917

BICKERDIKE Square W.
  1400 - 1599 24-316

BINGHAM St. N.
  2000 - 2149 22-245

BIRCHWOOD Av. W.
  1300 - 1559 1-7
  1560 - 2133 1-6
  2134 - 2399 2-17
  2400 - 3199 2-16
  7200 - 7761 9-138

BIRKHOFF Av. S.
  8300 - 8499 71-909

BISHOP St. N.
  0 - 399 28-415
  400 - 799 24-316
  800 - 1199 24-313

BISHOP St. S.
  800 - 1199 28-428
  1600 - 2199 31-496
  4600 - 4699 61-787
  4700 - 5099 61-792
  5100 - 5499 ....61-809z
  5500 - 5899 67-857
  5900 - 6299 67-858
  6300 - 6599 67-859
  6600 - 7099 ....67-867z
  7100 - 7499 67-869
  7500 - 7899 71-907
  7900 - 8199 71-906
  8200 - 8299 ....71-912a
  8300 - 8699 ....71-912d
  8700 - 8899 71-911
  8900 - 9499 73-926
  9500 - 9899 ....73-923a
  10700 -11099 75-934
  11100 -11499 75-935
  11500 -12299 53-711

BISSELL St. N.
  1600 - 1999 7-115
  2000 - 2399 7-106

BITTERSWEET Pl. W.
  400 - 799 ....3-21z

BLACKHAWK St. W.
  400 - 599 8-122
  600 - 799 8-121
  800 - 1199 8-120
  1200 - 1399 24-312
  1400 - 1599 24-311
  1600 - 1699 24-310

BLACKSTONE Av. S.
  4700 - 5099 39-599
  5100 - 5199 41-611
  5200 - 5511 ....41-613z
  5512 - 5999 ....41-620z
  6000 - 6198 even...42-630
  6001 - 6199 odd....42-632
  6200 - 6299 42-632
  6300 - 6699 42-633
  6700 - 7099 43-645
  7100 - 7499 43-646
  7500 - 7749 43-647
  7900 - 8699 45-661
  8700 - 8899 48-676
  8900 - 9299 48-677

BLAKE St. S.
  3600 - 3699 ....59-756z

BLANCHARD Ct. S.
  2200 - 2599 33-520

BLISS St. W.
  600 - 999 8-126

BLOOMINGDALE Av. W.
  1400 - 1598 even...22-264
  1401 - 1599 odd....24-308
  1600 - 1798 even...22-264
  1601 - 1799 odd....24-307
  1800 - 1998 even...22-263
  1801 - 1999 odd....24-306
  2200 - 2398 even...22-260
  2201 - 2399 odd....24-296
  2400 - 2598 even...22-259
  2401 - 2599 odd....24-295
  2600 - 2798 even...22-258
  2601 - 2799 odd....24-284
  2800 - 2998 even...22-257
  2801 - 2999 odd....24-283
  3000 - 3198 even...22-256
  3001 - 3199 odd....23-273
  3200 - 3498 even...22-255
  3201 - 3499 odd....23-272
  3500 - 3598 even...22-252
  3501 - 3599 odd....23-267
  4800 - 5199 25-324
  5200 - 5599 25-323
  5600 - 6399 25-322
  6400 - 7199 25-321

BLUE ISLAND Av. S.
  600 - 999 28-422
  1000 - 1199 28-435
  1200 - 1399 28-440
  1400 - 1599 ....28-434z
  1600 - 1999 31-496
  2000 - 2199 31-495
  2200 - 2461 31-510
  2462 - 2599 31-506

BOARD OF TRADE Ct. W.
  0 - 299 32-514

BONAPARTE St. S.
  2900 - 3099 60-769

BOND Av. S.
  8300 - 8699 46-666

BONFIELD St. S.
  2600 - 3099 60-768

BOONE St. W.
  (see DeKalb St. W.)

BOSWORTH Av. N.
  1200 - 1599 24-311
  1600 - 1799 24-308
  2300 - 2399 7-103
  2400 - 2799 7-101
  3400 - 3599 6-70
  3600 - 3999 6-69
  6400 - 6699 1-2
  6700 - 7199 1-3
  7600 - 7799 1-8

BOULEVARD WAY S.
  2400 - 2599 30-489

BOWEN Av. E.
  400 - 499 38-576
  500 - 799 38-575
  800 - 999 36-561

FIGURE 3.4.   Sample coding guide. Source: Guide for Coding Street Address to Community Area and Census Tract, Chicago, 1960 (Chicago: Chicago Community Inventory, University of Chicago, May 1961).

businesses, schools, institutions, factories, or other entities contained in a unit can be located on the map and grouped according to the number or other identifying symbol of that unit. In larger or more complex urban areas, coding guides relating street addresses to primary analytical unit numbers or other identifying symbols may be employed to relate new data to the network of primary areal units. The coding guide in figure 3.4, for instance, presents a primary analytical areal unit code number for each possible street address in the area. Thus, someone living at 500 Bittersweet Place West is quickly identified as belonging to Community Area 3, Tract 212. As new data attached to particular addresses are accumulated, they can quickly be compared to previous data on the same addresses. Classification by individual primary areal analytical units, or by groups or classes of such units, allows for the comparison of all sorts of data—data on population characteristics, social and economic institutions, land use and values, transportation, recreational facilities, etc.

While primary analytical areal units are readily employed for analyses dealing with a wide variety of research problems, their uses may be limited by problems of comparability. In particular, variations in the number of units delineated for a given area affect the results of analyses concerning the distribution of population and activities within that area. For example, if a given area is divided into two primary analytical units, it may be found that land in both units is devoted to both business and residential use. If, however, the same area is divided into four primary analytical units, it may be found, just as correctly, that two of the units contain only residential land, and the other two only business property. The latter finding is not necessarily inconsistent with the former, but in the latter it might well be concluded that the urban area being studied is characterized by a concentration of business and residential land use in distinctly separate parts of the area.

Community Area 41 in Chicago (Hyde Park, which includes a substantial part of the University of Chicago campus) is fairly unique among Chicago community areas in that its population is neither entirely white nor entirely Negro: of the total community area population, 37.7 percent are Negro, 2.6 percent other nonwhites, and 27.0 percent white foreign stock (foreign-born or native-born of foreign or mixed parentage). In other words, it seems to be an "integrated" community. However, an inspection of data on the 14 census tracts of the area shows that three are almost entirely Negro (87 percent or more Negro), that six contain almost no Negroes (less than five percent), that one is only 8.6 percent Negro, and that only four are actually "integrated" (56.5, 36.5, 57.4, and 62.1 percent Negro respectively).[5] Figure 3.5 breaks down the figures for Hyde Park by census tracts.

5 For a detailed discussion of the measurement of residential segregation and related problems, see Taeuber and Taeuber (1965, appendix A) and Duncan, Cuzzort, and Duncan (1961).

POPULATION BY RACE, AGE; HOUSING BY TENURE: 1930-60

SUBJECT	NUMBER				PERCENT DISTRIBUTION			
	1960	1950	1940	1930	1960	1950	1940	1930
Total Population	45,577	55,206	50,550	48,017	100.0	100.0	100.0	100.0
White	27,214	52,375	49,750		59.7	94.9	98.5	
Negro	17,163	1,757	573	521	37.7	3.2	1.1	1.1
Other races	1,200	1,074	227		2.6	1.9	0.4	
Under 5 years old	4,302	3,802	2,441	2,285	9.4	6.9	4.8	4.8
5-19 years old	7,553	7,284	7,441	7,380	16.6	13.2	14.7	15.4
20-44 years old	18,520	23,473	23,832	23,863	40.6	42.5	47.2	49.6
45-64 years old	9,931	14,571	12,446	11,270	21.8	26.4	24.6	23.5
65 years & older	5,271	6,076	4,390	3,219	11.6	11.0	8.7	6.7
Total Housing Units	19,621	19,928	17,013		100.0	100.0	100.0	
Owner occupied	1,861	1,800	978		9.5	9.0	5.7	
Nonwhite owners	541	127	76		2.8	0.6	0.4	
Renter occupied	15,889	17,433	14,773		81.0	87.5	86.9	
Nonwhite renters	4,953	594	304		25.2	3.0	1.8	
Other	1,871	695	1,262		9.5	3.5	7.4	

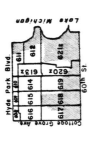

CA 41 — HYDE PARK

SELECTED CHARACTERISTICS OF CENSUS TRACTS: 1960

SUBJECT	CA TOTAL	608	609	610	611	612	613-Z	614	615	616	617	618	619	620-Z	621-Z
Total Population	45,577	1,118	1,517	1,880	2,412	4,430	3,552	4,839	5,166	6,524	3,974	1,192	2,965	2,727	3,281
% Negro	37.7	95.9	87.0	56.5	4.7	3.1	8.6	36.5	57.4	89.9	62.1	1.9	0.9	1.1	0.3
% other nonwhite races	0.5	...	0.2	1.3	1.2	1.0	3.0	6.1	3.1	0.5	5.0	4.1	2.8	5.4	0.9
% Puerto Ricans	...	...	...	...	0.3	0.6	0.6	...	...	1.6	0.7	0.3	0.1	0.1	...
% foreign stock	27.0	4.0	7.1	11.9	43.4	44.8	40.4	29.5	18.7	5.2	15.1	31.5	32.1	40.0	51.6
% living in group quarters	5.5	...	1.0	...	0.8	1.8	0.3	1.2	4.6	4.6	1.4	0.3	18.5	17.5	...
% under 18 years old	23.4	28.6	27.5	20.4	11.4	16.8	19.2	29.0	31.1	31.2	34.3	72.6	20.5	16.6	10.0
% 65 years & older	11.6	6.4	5.2	10.5	11.4	19.7	15.1	9.7	6.1	5.5	3.4	4.4	9.1	11.4	27.9
% in different house, 1955	68.0	68.3	75.9	76.1	64.0	57.2	66.2	70.6	74.7	74.5	76.5	77.8	71.0	63.1	44.2
Median school years completed	12.5	10.3	12.4	12.3	12.4	12.6	12.4	12.4	12.4	10.8	12.0	16+	16+	16+	12.9
Median family income in 1959...$	6,772	5,870	6,189	5,327	5,907	8,589	5,891	6,205	5,977	5,690	5,644	...	9,851	9,472	10,224
% with income under $3,000	13.5	13.6	17.0	24.3	14.8	7.2	15.5	17.8	12.0	13.8	14.9	...	8.6	5.9	9.2
% with income of $10,000+	26.3	3.6	12.1	12.1	22.6	41.5	20.1	15.6	20.0	17.1	20.0	...	49.1	44.9	50.6
% white-collar workers: males	62.3	38.8	43.9	21.4	59.2	79.8	65.1	57.2	55.5	31.7	50.2	87.9	81.8	88.6	85.0
% riding to work by auto	35.2	46.3	34.4	38.0	25.1	40.6	33.4	32.2	43.1	35.2	35.0	17.3	28.9	24.0	47.4
% unemployed: male labor force	5.1	3.2	7.2	2.2	4.9	4.1	4.5	5.2	5.0	8.7	8.6	...	3.1	4.7	1.5
Population per household	2.43	3.06	3.10	2.25	1.73	2.02	1.92	2.62	2.97	3.25	3.21	2.12	2.32	2.30	1.79
Total Housing Units	19,621	379	495	1,018	1,711	2,423	2,087	1,937	1,781	1,965	1,328	169	1,083	1,101	2,144
% owner occupied	9.5	10.6	8.1	3.9	2.5	3.7	5.7	8.4	13.1	2.1	9.0	34.3	17.4	17.2	16.8
% built 1950 or later	2.7	4.7	0.8	...	0.4	0.8	2.9	0.8	0.7	19.7	5.3	...	14.0	0.7	4.7
% in substandard condition	13.9	13.5	4.6	6.6	21.1	14.4	33.9	14.7	3.0	20.0	10.8	1.2	11.4	7.4	4.0
% with 1+ persons per room	9.6	12.3	10.9	13.1	7.2	6.2	6.5	10.6	14.2	10.6	19.0	1.3	3.6	2.4	1.7
Median value: owner u's $	18,800	...	...	...	...	25,000+	17,200	16,200	16,900	18,900	17,200	16,600	25,000+	23,000	15,000
Median gross rent: renter u's $	100	111	100	101	95	115	83	94	97	102	98	...	...	108	118
Median number rooms: all units	3.2	4.2	4.2	2.2	2.0	2.5	2.3	3.4	4.0	3.9	4.1	4.3	4.2	3.9	3.0

[Measures not shown when base is insufficient; see text. Plus (+) after number indicates median above that number.]

FIGURE 3.5. A sample community area of Chicago metropolitan area.
Source: E. H. Kitagawa and K. E. Taeuber 1963, pp. 39, 65, 87, 91, and 97.

Primary analytical areal units have been used extensively in social scientific research for many decades. Early examples of such research include the comparative studies of living conditions in the various sections of London, studies of differential mortality and infant mortality in the Paris *arrondissements* grouped by relative affluence, and studies of delinquency and mental illness in American cities. More recently, the use of primary analytical units has expanded to a much wider range of subjects. The general approach of these analyses usually calls for grouping the primary analytical units within an area in terms of some shared characteristic, e.g., distance from center, median income of families, average age of residential structures, percentage of land devoted to manufacturing, proportion of adult population foreign-born, etc. Characteristics of the population or activities in the respective groups of primary analytical units are then measured and compared. The advantages of grouping primary analytical units will become clear below.

4. FUNCTIONAL COMBINATIONS OF PRIMARY ANALYTICAL UNITS

Data on primary analytical units lend themselves to a wide variety of uses in social research, particularly when the units have been grouped into meaningful categories.

Grouping by Contiguity or Shared Characteristic

One method of combining primary analytical units is to group adjacent ones into larger areal units when the larger units have some special historical, political, economic, administrative or social significance (and, of course, when data are available on a primary analytical unit basis). For example, the primary analytical units of historically delineated quarters or boroughs of a city, or of a waterfront or manufacturing subarea, or of an administrative ward or school district, can be combined for investigation or for comparison with areal units of larger size. In Chicago, community areas 35-40, 42, and 69 (see figure 3.2) comprise a belt of contiguous areas whose populations were 85 percent or more Negro in 1960. This larger unit has been called the Chicago "Black Belt."

A second type of grouping of primary analytical units ignores contiguity entirely and considers only the characteristics of the primary areal unit or its population. Thus, units characterized by high socioeconomic status levels and by low socioeconomic status levels have been grouped accordingly and compared with respect to such characteristics as fertility, mortality, health, educational level, labor force participation, type of housing, etc. Such groupings are based not upon areal contiguity but upon homogeneity with respect to some specified characteristic.[6] In order to form combinations of this sort, it is necessary first to have basic data on the characteristics in question for each primary unit. For example, a researcher grouping units in Chicago by recent economic status would have to know that in Chicago in 1959, community areas 2, 9, 10, 12, 13, 45, 48, and 72 (see figure 3.2) were characterized by median family incomes of $8,500 or more. Or, if he were grouping by occupational distribution, he would have to know that areas 1, 2, 12, 13, 41, 43, and 72 had 60 percent or more of their male workers employed in white-collar jobs.

While maps and coding guides are particularly useful in delineating combinations based upon areal contiguity and physiographic considerations, they do not ordinarily suffice for grouping primary units on the basis of homogeneity of characteristics. The statistical (and other) data on primary analytical units most helpful for this sort of grouping are often found in censuses, publications of governmental agencies, and city or administrative-unit fact books and directories. Using such aids, it is usually possible to establish categories of primary analytical units in terms of a given variable (e.g., percentage of housing units valued over a specified amount, or percentage of adult females gainfully occupied) and then to array all the primary analytical units in terms of that variable.

An Example

An example of use of functional combinations of primary analytical units is the analysis by B. Duncan and P. M. Hauser (1960) of areal variation in housing. This analysis is part of the authors' broader study of Chicago housing conditions and their changes from 1950 through 1956. The 935 census tracts making up the City of Chicago were grouped into five areas referring specifically to housing inventory, housing characteristics, and occupancy:

Area 1:   Deteriorated Central Nonwhite Residential Area (91 tracts)
Area 2:   Deteriorated Central White Residential Area (197 tracts)
Area 3:   Mixed Residential Area (221 tracts)
Area 4a: Outer Residential Area, North
Area 4b: Outer Residential Area, South

Figure 3.6 depicts these groupings, and table 3.6 presents the data on them.

6 For a discussion of relationships between alternative principles for combining primary analytical units, see Form et al. (1954), reprinted Gibbs (1961).

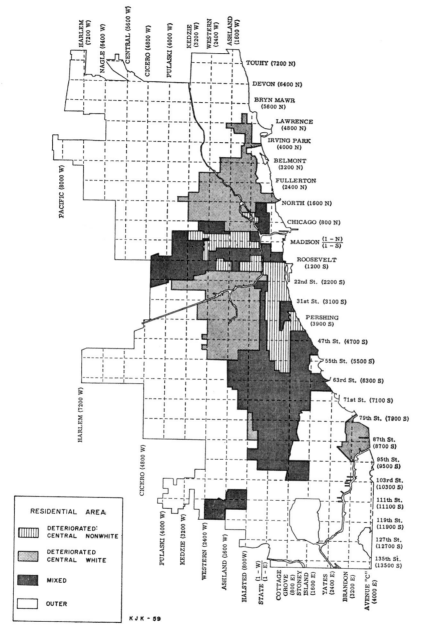

FIGURE 3.6. Subareas of the city delineated for the Chicago Supplement to the National Housing Inventory, 1956. Source: B. Duncan and Hauser 1960, table 6–4, p. 214.

TABLE 3.6
Housing and Occupancy Characteristics: Five Areas of the City of Chicago, 1950 and 1956

Change in the Housing Inventory, by Occupancy Status and Color of Occupant, 1950-56: Five Areas of the City of Chicago

Item	City of Chicago	Deteriorated Central Area		Mixed Area	Outer Area	
		Nonwhite	White		North	South
Number of dwelling units, 1956 (in thousands)	1,165	94	213	241	398	219
With white occupants	919	12	199	110	388	210
With nonwhite occupants	214	77	7	123	3	4
Vacant	32	5	7	8	8	5
Number of dwelling units, 1950	1,106	97	216	237	367	189
With white occupants	956	19	209	183	361	184
With nonwhite occupants	131	76	3	50	1	2
Vacant	19	2	4	4	6	3
Change, 1950 to 1956						
All dwelling units	59	-3	-3	4	31	30
With white occupants	-37	-7	-10	-72	27	26
With nonwhite occupants	83	2	4	73	2	2
Vacant	13	3	3	3	2	3

Total Housing Inventory, Housing Quality, and Color Composition: Five Areas of the City of Chicago, 1956 and 1950

Item	City of Chicago	Deteriorated Central Area		Mixed Area	Outer Area	
		Nonwhite	White		North	South
Number of dwelling units (in thousands)						
1956	1,165	94	213	241	398	219
1950	1,106	97	216	237	367	189
Substandard housing (per cent of units substandard)						
1956	15	53	28	20	4	1
1950	23	67	42	26	7	7
Nonwhite occupancy (per cent nonwhite)						
1956	19	87	3	53	1	2
1950	12	80	1	22	. . .	1
Change in number of dwelling units, 1950-56 (in thousands)	59	-3	-3	4	31	30
Units added by new construction, 1950-56 (in thousands)*	78	5	<1	8	32	34

. . . 0.5 per cent or less.
*Occupied units only.

136

TABLE 3.6 con't.

Selected Characteristics of Occupied Dwelling Units: Five Areas of the City of Chicago, 1956

| Characteristic | City of Chicago (1) | Deteriorated Central Area | | Mixed Area | | Outer Area | |
		White (2)	Nonwhite (3)	Nonwhite occupants (4)	White occupants (5)	North (6)	South (7)
Number of occupied units (in thousands)	1,133	206	89	123	110	390	214
Home ownership (per cent owner-occupied)	34	23	8	22	20	39	60
Substandard housing (per cent substandard)	15	27	52	21	17	4	1
Owner	3	4	13	12	3	2	...
Renter	21	34	56	24	21	6	2
No central heating (per cent with no central heating)	19	44	17	11	19	9	16
Owner	16	38	15	14	21	7	16
Renter	20	45	17	11	18	11	16
Older structures (per cent in structures built before 1920)	60	87	89	71	68	47	36
Owner	46	87	92	58	62	39	31
Renter	68	87	88	75	70	52	44

SOURCE: B. Duncan and P. Hauser 1960, tables 6–22, 6–23, and 6–26, pp. 218, 220, and 224.
... 0.5 per cent or less.

housing—most prevalent in the Deteriorated Central Areas and least prevalent in the Outer Areas—was reduced in all areas between 1950 and 1956. Nonwhite occupancy increased in each area in that period, but the increase was most marked in the Mixed Area. The Deteriorated Central White Area was occupied almost exclusively by whites in both 1950 and 1956.

The second panel of table 3.6 indicates that nonwhites obtained additional housing largely by moving into dwellings formerly occupied by whites rather than by gaining access to new housing. In the Mixed Residential Area, the housing inventory grew very little, but the proportion of nonwhites increased sharply. The data show that the number of dwellings in this area occupied by whites decreased by 72,000, while the number of dwellings occupied by nonwhites increased by 73,000. The bottom panel of the table portrays characteristics of dwelling units. The data show that in the deteriorated central area, the percent classified substandard housing among the nonwhite areas is almost twice that among the white areas; but in the mixed area the difference between percent substandard housing among nonwhite residents and that among

From the data on these areal groupings (table 3.6), Duncan and Hauser found that although housing conditions and racial composition varied within each grouping, the areas were nevertheless distinct in their overall characteristics. The first panel of the table shows that substandard white residents was relatively small overall and in renter-occupied dwellings. But dwellings occupied by nonwhite owners in the mixed area were four times as likely to be substandard as were those occupied by white owners.

Particular care must be taken in relating the results of one study based upon combinations of primary analytical units to the results of other studies based upon them, for often the combinations are not identically defined or delineated. For example, two studies might both group primary analytical units into "high" and "low" income categories, but each might use a different cut-off point in distinguishing "high" from "low." Accordingly, when conducting and using analyses based upon functional combinations of primary analytical units, it is extremely important to ascertain precisely the grouping method used.

4

Quantitative Representation
and Analysis of
Population Composition
and Social Structure

1. INTRODUCTION

In this chapter and the chapter which follows we present some techniques of quantitative description, measurement, and analysis of populations and societies and their changes. The basic elements of modern demographic analysis are presented in these two chapters. Study of these should provide the reader with concepts and tools sufficient for reading and mastering the descriptions and analyses of the great majority of modern demographic studies, articles, monographs, and texts.

Readers with different purposes and interests will wish to use these materials in different ways. For some it will suffice to skim the various sections to obtain an overview of the methods and issues of demographic and quantitative social structural analysis, returning to review and master individual methods as required. Others will wish to master in detail some, though not necessarily all, of the approaches and techniques presented. Still others will find it useful to study all of the methods, or indeed to apply them in exercises and actual research projects. For some readers the handling of quantitative data or mathematical symbols will be entirely familiar while others may have less experience. Finally, some will find it of interest and use to delve further into the more technical and advanced literature on theory and methods of population description and analysis. For these a bibliography is provided at the close of chapter 5.

Scientific discipline requires that assertions and propositions concerning any phenomena be based upon, and verifiable against, observations of the same phenomena in the real world. Any description of an observed society and its social structure must, in order to be amenable to scientific classification, comparison, and analysis, be cast in terms of objective and parsimonious—usually symbolic—representations. Thus, in the taxonomy presented earlier, we referred to "hunting and gathering" as contrasted with "urban-industrial" societies. Some sociologists frequently distinguish between "particularistic" and "universalistic" social relationships, or between "ascriptive" and "achieved" bases of social status. There are symbolic representations of societies and aspects of social structure. Traditionally, scientific analysis has been based primarily upon various types of classification and measurement; and physical, biological, and social processes have been represented symbolically *either* as patterns (or operators) which bring some *order* to a set of measurements, classification of phenomena, or set of coordinates, or as patterns (or operators) which effect some *change* in these measurements, classifications, or coordinates.

Relationships between two variables are inferred, in scientific analysis, basically by plotting the covariation of their respective measurements, i.e., by studying the manner in which the differences in the measurements of one variable are associated with differences in the measurements of the other. For example, in figure 4.1 the three variables are marital status and fertility for white and black women. This diagram shows that white and black women who were separated, widowed, or divorced at the time of the 1960 census, had substantially fewer children than the general population during the five years that preceded the census. Such covariation between the measurements of two or more variables can be described in varying degrees of detail and complexity, but the description has traditionally been cast in quantitative terms. Thus, mathematics is often called "the language of science."

Quantitative representations of populations and population composition have already appeared in our brief description of world population history, in our discussion of variations in size and structure among different populations. In this chapter, we shall describe more explicitly and systematically some of the conventional ways of representing population size and composition quantitatively and of relating population composition to social structure. We shall begin with a review of the elements of social structure and population composition.

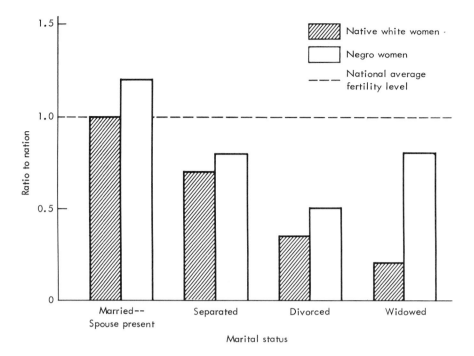

FIGURE 4.1. Depressive impact of broken marriage upon fertility during five years preceding census: ratio to national average fertility level, for native white and Negro women, standardized for age: 1955–60. Source: Cho, Grabill, and Bogue 1970, figure 4–1.

2. ELEMENTS OF SOCIAL STRUCTURE

Social Roles

The basic and most elementary concept in the analysis of social structure, and in sociological analysis generally, is that of *social role*. A great deal has been written about the concept of social role, both by way of definition and elaboration and for the purpose of incorporating the concept into theories of varying complexity. We shall say here simply that a social role is a set of socially prescribed behaviors and relationships; and that an individual occupies that role if his social behavior toward others and their behavior toward him *both* satisfy the prescriptions of the role. Some examples of social roles include the President of the United States, the hobo, the hippie, the schoolteacher, the ward politician, the mother, the bus driver, the child, the playmate, the bank clerk, the bricklayer, the uncle, or the steady girlfriend. Each role is characterized by a socially prescribed set of behaviors on the part of the incumbent and on the part of others in relationship to him.

A social role which recurs in a society, is recognized in the society, and whose set of behaviors is *normatively* prescribed in the society, is said to be *institutionalized* in that society. Such a role, the behaviors it prescribes for the incumbent and for others toward the incumbent, and the norms or rules governing these behaviors together comprise one of the society's *institutions*. Thus, we say that the mother-in-law is an "institution" in American society, that the matchmaker was an "institution" in agrarian European societies, and that the Emperor is an "institution" in Japanese society.

Social Systems

A second facet of social structure comprises the recurring patterned relationships between recognized or institutionalized social roles. This facet of social structure has received by far the most attention in sociological research and analysis. Relationships between incumbents of different social roles, far from being spontaneous and random, typically conform to socially prescribed patterns. Take, for example, some common two-person relationships: mother-child, husband-wife, employer-employee, or leader-follower. In any given society, these tend to conform to expected, socially prescribed, boundaries. On the other hand, the nature of the mother-child and other relationships may well vary from society to society.

Similarly, in any given society distinctive patterns characterize relationships within groups, whether these be small groups (family, friendship club, work group) or larger ones (churches, businesses, factories, political parties). When a number of social roles are gathered into such *systems* of patterned relationships, the larger units are called *social systems,* or sometimes *subsystems,* of the society. The socially prescribed relationships between incumbents of a system's component social roles are said to be institutionalized relationships. Thus, a society's social systems may include any recognized system of social roles, e.g., the family, the church, voluntary organizations, businesses, neighborhood groups, the government, and political parties. Finally, the entire society is itself a social system.

A social system which is recognized in the society and for which a set of relationships between role incumbents is prescribed in the society is said to be *institutionalized* in that society. The system of roles, the prescribed relationships between role incumbents within the system, and the norms or rules governing these relationships together comprise one of the society's institutions. Thus the family, the school, the church, and the political party are all "institutions" in American society, and they may be institutions in other societies as well.

A social system typically includes subsystems which are less complex but also characterized by institutionalized role relationships. Thus, for example, the family includes the mother-father subsystem, the brother-sister subsystem, the father-daughter subsystem, etc., all characterized by socially prescribed and recurring relationships. The factory includes work-group subsystems, the board-of-directors subsystem, the office-staff subsystem, the maintenance-staff subsystem, and so on.

Similarly, any two or more social systems may be related to one another in a *system of social systems,* with stable or recurring relationships prescribed and recognized among them. Thus, the family, the school, and the police department comprise a system of social systems; the federal government, the United States Chamber of Commerce, and the American Federation of Labor comprise a system of social systems. A municipal administration, too, is a system of social systems.

Composition of the Population by Social Roles

The last major facet of social structure is the composition of the society's population with respect to recognized social roles and key combinations of social roles. This has received much attention by some students of social structure (e.g., those in the American rural sociology tradition) and has been virtually ignored by others (e.g., most American social anthropologists). The composition of a population by social role and by combinations of social roles indicates (a) the relative frequency in the society of given social roles or types of roles and (b) the relative frequency of characteristic combinations of roles, i.e., the relationships between social roles as reflected by joint incumbency. Thus, in the first case, the roles of unskilled laborer and professional worker may both be recognized in two different societies, but the relative number of laborers in one society may be considerably different from that in the other. Similarly, rural occupancy may be a recognized role in many societies, but the relative number of rural folk may be greater in one society than in another. As for the relationships between social roles, being an unskilled laborer in one society may be related to rural residence, while being a laborer or a professional worker in another society may have nothing whatsoever to do with the urban or rural role.

In one society there may be many educated women, but in another relatively few. Many women in society A, but not society B, have occupational roles outside the home; and in society C, but not society D, employment of women outside the home may be related to women's levels of education.

The Three General Facets of Social Structure

Proceeding from the elements discussed above, the social structure of a society can be described as that society's particular combination of—

1. all its recognized social roles;
2. the patterned relationships and systems of patterned relationships between recognized social roles and between systems of social roles;
3. the composition of the population with respect to recognized social roles and key combinations of social roles.

SOCIETAL VARIATIONS.   It would appear obvious that societies may vary with respect to all three facets of social structure. We may illustrate variations in the first facet, recognized social roles, simply by pointing out that there are societies with and without engineers, with and without telephone operators, with and without shamans and sorcerers. And we may illustrate variations in the *content* of social roles by contrasting the role of grandfather in, say, biblical society, with that in our own, or by contrasting the role of the English monarch a century ago and today.

As for the second facet, certain *kinds* of social systems obviously exist in many societies; thus, nearly all societies have a family system, an economic system, a political system, a religious system, and so on. At the same time, however, these systems may vary both within and among societies. And, some types of social systems—baseball teams, armies, lonely hearts clubs—may be found in some societies but not in others.

Finally, societies sharing roles and social systems may vary with respect to the way in which their members are distributed among them. Thus, relative to the total populations, there are fewer married persons in Ireland than in the United States, and relatively more in India. Relatively more teenaged girls are married in India, the Arab countries, the United States, and Canada than in England, the Scandinavian countries, or Israel. There are relatively more farmers in Thailand and in Turkey than in Belgium and in Holland, and more in North Dakota and Vermont than in Nevada and Rhode Island. Similarly, there are relatively more members of labor unions in Israel than in the United States; and in the United States, there are more in Ohio than New Mexico. On the other hand, there are relatively more stockholders in large corporations in the United States than in Israel or most other countries of the world.

EMPHASES IN SOCIAL STRUCTURAL RESEARCH.   Sociological and social anthropological investigations of social structure have covered a variety of topics. With regard to roles, they have been concerned with the content and purpose of roles, the form and extent of role differentiation, and the relative ease of access to different social roles. The investigation of social systems has included studies of their size, content, and purpose, as well as studies of role relationships within social systems and subsystems; in the latter case, considerable attention has been given to differential prestige, power, rank, and other hierarchical facets of role relationships. Studies of networks of social systems have analyzed the differentiation within systems, the differential prestige and power among them, and the relative size and complexity of systems of social systems. Finally, a major topic of investigation has been the nature, direction, magnitude, and correlates of *change* in these facets of social structure.

3. ELEMENTS OF POPULATION COMPOSITION

Any human population may be viewed as an aggregate of individuals of different types and characteristics. It is these types, and their absolute or relative numbers in the population, that are the subject of concern in the analysis of population composition.

As Hawley has observed (1959), such an analysis constitutes a quantitative description of a society's human resources; and, historically, as in the case of census population counts, the delineation of human resources has been the major purpose of analyses of population composition. Demographers, however, have always accorded first priority in their studies of population composition to the age-sex factor. This is because they have recognized that a population's age-sex characteristics are intimately related to its rate and pattern of growth and also to those facets of its composition subsumed under the rubric of human resources.

Thus, in population studies, the composition of a population is seen as particularly relevant to actual or potential population growth and to the society's stock of human resources. Techniques of demographic analysis have, in turn, been involved in the study of changes in human resources, for a population's changing size and its changing composition by sex, age, and geographic distribution are certainly the fundamental factors in changes in its human resources.

Composition by Sex

The very earliest demographers took note of the fact that the number of male births in a population always exceeds the number of female births, and that, at virtually all ages, the number of male deaths exceeds the number of female deaths. Typically, the number of males in a pop-

ulation exceeds the number of females at the very earliest ages; at subsequent ages this male excess is reduced by an excess of male mortality,
and at the most advanced ages the number of females exceeds the number
of males.

The exact ratio of total number of males to females in a population
may vary in accordance with patterns of mortality (including foetal
mortality, which affects the sex ratio at birth), and it may also vary with
the age composition of the population and with patterns of migration.
Thus, other things being equal, populations with low general mortality
or large proportions of younger persons have higher proportions of males
than do populations with high general mortality or large proportions of
older persons, respectively. Countries attracting overseas migrants have
high proportions of males, cities attracting rural-to-urban migrants have
high proportions of females, and industrial communities have high proportions of males, other things being equal.

Composition by Age

Populations are sometimes considered "young" or "old," depending
upon whether they have high proportions of young or old persons. Populations with large proportions of adults and relatively small proportions
in both the younger and older ages of dependency are generally believed
to be in a favorable position with regard to levels of living, investment,
and development. Age divides a population into groups of potential
producers and consumers: the independent adults in the population are
both producers and consumers, while the dependent children and the
retired or infirm are consumers only. (The reader may wish to refer to
table 1.10, which shows the age composition of selected countries.)

The age composition of a population also affects the number and
scope of social and economic arrangements and institutions, from maternity wards, kindergartens, and schools, to entertainment, transportation,
religion, and homes for the aged. Moreover, central social and economic
processes such as family formation and homes purchase, job-seeking, retirement and savings, and migration and mobility are closely related to
the age composition of a population.

A population's age composition depends first and foremost upon
its level of fertility and only secondarily upon its level of mortality. However, migratory movements are of great significance in determining age
composition, especially in the case of relatively small or localized populations. Changes in age composition over time wherein the proportions of
adults and elderly persons increase and the proportions of children and
adolescents decrease is called the "aging of populations" and is always a
consequence of low or declining fertility.

Composition by Marital Status

Next to sex and age, the most familiar compositional characteristic of the population is marital status, which categorizes persons according to whether they are single, married, widowed, or divorced. Obviously, marital status varies sharply with age and sex, and it is closely connected with fertility and population growth. In addition, the composition of the population by marital status is indicative of the number of nuclear family units, the potential number of marriages, the composition of the "marriage market," and other factors affected by marital status or concerning marriage and the family.

The household status, or an individual's relationship to the head of the household, is a characteristic by which population composition is often plotted. Thus, the number of persons in and not in households, the number of persons bearing each of the different possible kinship and non-kinship relationships to the head of the household, and the number of family and nonfamily household groupings may be described for a population. Often studied, too, are a population's marital characteristics (e.g., year of present or first marriage, age at marriage, number of marriages) and its fertility characteristics (e.g., total number of liveborn children, number of liveborn children surviving beyond a given age).

Composition by Origin

After sex, age, and marital status, the most important theme in analyzing population composition concerns the origins of the population: place of birth, citizenship, race, religion, language, ethnic characteristics, and migrant or refugee status. In the United States, census and vital statistics operations avoid ascertaining or publishing data concerning the composition of the population's religion.[1] Nevertheless, there is much interest in this topic, and many students of American population and society have sought ways of studying the religious composition of the population in the absence of census data.

Data on composition by origins serve both to classify population groupings by origin and to provide a basis for the study of population movements. Thus, when birthplaces are tabulated, a population can be classified by geographic origins and by the distinction between persons still residing in their place of birth or not; in addition, this tabulation makes it possible to study the volume of migration.

---

[1] An important exception was the Current Populations Survey conducted in March 1957 by the Bureau of the Census, in which religious preference was asked. Results of this survey are still the most important source available on the religious composition of the U.S. population.

Composition by Economic Activity

Another key element of population composition is that of economic activity or participation in the labor force. Individuals in a population are often classified by the extent of their participation in the labor force, by their occupation or industry group, by employment or unemployment, by their employment status (employees, self-employed, employer, etc.), and sometimes by the amount of time they have worked, their secondary occupations, and their annual, monthly, or other incomes.

Composition by Literacy and Education

We are also concerned with the literacy, educational achievement, and school attendance of the population. There has traditionally been great interest in the relative numbers of a population able or not able to read and write. More recently, however, in countries where literacy is virtually universal, composition by literacy is no longer investigated. On the other hand, composition by educational achievement may be studied in great detail, with attention given to both the number of school years completed and the types of education completed.

Composition by Place of Residence

Finally, mention must be made of the frequent study of the composition of the population by geographic location or by type of place or residence. Such studies typically distinguish rural from urban residence, residence in places of different size classes, and residence in places of different types such as "metropolitan" and "non-metropolitan" places.

Population Composition as Role Distribution

It should be obvious from the foregoing discussion that the compositional characteristics of populations, as conventionally studied by demographers and other students of population, are social roles or categories of social roles. The fact that *all* social roles are not seen as "compositional characteristics" is due primarily to the difficulty, or lack of interest, in enumerating them in censuses, surveys, and records of vital statistics (Hawley 1959). We shall explore this convergence of a population's composition and its social roles in somewhat more detail.

The set of all the roles occupied by a given individual is called that individual's *role profile*. Any role in an individual's role profile may or may not be independent of one or more of his other roles. Characteristic or recurring combinations of roles in role profiles constitute what A. L. Stinchcombe (1968, pp. 209-214) has called "the demography of opportunity."[2]

Now, an individual's role profile may be specified in more or less detail. Obviously, if individual role profiles are specified in the greatest possible detail, there will be as many different role profiles in a society as there are persons in the population. But there is always a point beyond which further detail in specifying a role profile is neither of social relevance for the individual or society nor of sociological interest. Thus, when role profiles are specified with sufficient generality to make them of sociological interest, it is assumed that there are fewer distinct role profiles than persons in the population. This being the case, there is a distribution of the population over the set of distinct role profiles in the society, and this is called the *role distribution.*[3]

With role distribution defined in terms of the population's composition by categories (role profiles), *change* in a role distribution may be studied in a manner analogous to the demographic study of change in population composition.[4] Changes in role distribution may be thought to originate, fundamentally, in two ways—

1. as the net result of differential rates of increment to the population (i.e., entrance into the population by birth or in-migration, and exit from the population by death or out-migration). Thus, higher-than-average birth rates among lower socioeconomic level population groups imply a changing role distribution for the society as a whole.
2. as the net result of the aggregate of individual changes in role profiles. Net rural-to-urban migration implies a changing role distribution.

Considerable success in specifying and analyzing role distributions and time changes in them is possible using data bearing upon population composition. Moreover, the analysis of population composition and of changes in it is much more powerful a tool for analyzing social structure than is ordinarily supposed. Thus, the study of population composition and distribution converges naturally with the study of social roles and social systems.

2 Moreover, Stinchcombe's important incorporation of population composition into what he calls "demographic explanations of social phenomena" (1968, pp. 60–79) is most akin to what we shall be describing—in the next and subsequent chapters—under the rubric of "population transformations."

3 Compare the use of the concept "role distribution" in Nadel (1957) and Eisenstadt (1954).

4 We shall discuss approaches and methods of studying population change in chapter 6, below.

4. COUNTS, RATIOS, AND FREQUENCY DISTRIBUTIONS

The most elementary quantitative representation of a population is simply the total *number* of persons in that population; and, obviously, the most elementary quantitative representation of a society is the count of the number of persons in its population. We have already pointed to variations in population size; and we have mentioned some reasons why societies with small populations necessarily differ from societies with large populations, and why societies necessarily undergo changes as their populations grow in numbers.

The composition of a population with respect to two or more categories of some variable, e.g., sex, place of residence, age, etc., can be represented by *counts* of the number of persons belonging to each category. The set of such counts over all the exhaustive and mutually exclusive categories of a variable is usually called a *frequency distribution*. Frequency distributions and the measures derived from them yield much more detailed quantitative representations of population than do total counts. Finally, *ratios* involving population in their numerators, denominators, or both are very often used in describing and comparing populations.

We may illustrate counts, ratios, and frequency distributions by referring to table 4.1, which presents the size and some selected characteristics of the populations of Ohio and South Carolina.

TABLE 4.1
Size and Selected Characteristics of the Populations of Ohio and South Carolina, 1960

	Ohio	S.C.
Area (sq. miles)	40,975	30,272
Total population	9,707,136	2,382,594
Pop. density/sq. mile	236.9	78.7
Males	4,763,795	1,175,672
Females	4,943,341	1,206,922
Sex ratios	96.4	97.4
Urban	7,123,901	981,386
Rural	2,063,722	1,050,054
% Distribution		
Total — All places	100.0	100.0
Urban	73.4	41.2
Rural nonfarm	21.3	44.1
Rural farm	5.3	14.7

SOURCE: U.S. Bureau of the Census 1960.

A glance at the *total population* of each state gives us our first basis for comparison: with 9.7 million in Ohio and 2.4 million in South Carolina, the population of Ohio is about four times larger than that of South Carolina. On the other hand, comparing the areas of the two states—about 41,000 square miles for Ohio and about 30,000 square miles for South Carolina—we find that Ohio is just over a third larger than South Carolina. The relationships between population and area are represented by population density ratios—the number of persons in the population divided by the number of areal units—and these are usually expressed as "population per square mile" or "population per square kilometer." Thus, in our data:

$$\frac{\text{Ohio}}{\text{population}} = \frac{9,707,136 = \text{total pop. of Ohio}}{40,972 = \text{total no. of square miles in Ohio}} = 236.9 \text{ persons per square mile}$$

This is compared to:

$$\frac{\text{South Carolina}}{\text{population}} = \frac{2,382,594 = \text{total pop. of S. C.}}{30,272 = \text{total no. of square miles in S. C.}} = 78.7 \text{ persons per square mile}$$

It is clear that the population density of Ohio is about three times that of South Carolina.

The next figures, which classify and count the populations by sex, indicate that females are only slightly more numerous than males in both Ohio and South Carolina; both states come close to having populations that are half male and half female. A somewhat more precise comparison between the two states is afforded by the sex ratio, computed as the ratio of males to females times some constant number, conventionally 100 or 1,000. In the present case:

$$\frac{\text{Ohio}}{\text{sex ratio}} = \frac{4,763,795 = \text{total males in Ohio}}{4,943,341 = \text{total females in Ohio}} \times 100 = 96.4 \text{ males per 100 females}$$

$$\frac{\text{S. C.}}{\text{sex ratio}} = \frac{1,175,672 = \text{total males in S. C.}}{1,206,922 = \text{total females in S. C.}} \times 100 = 97.4 \text{ males per 100 females}$$

Alternatively, a computation of the percentages of males and females in each of the respective states would provide another mode of description and comparison. From the data in table 4.1, we can compute the percentages of males in Ohio and South Carolina as 49.1 percent and 49.3

percent respectively; their complements, of course, are the percentages of females—50.9 percent in Ohio and 50.7 percent in South Carolina.

The table classifies places of residence according to three categories —urban, rural nonfarm, and rural farm—and gives the frequency distribution of the two populations by these categories. Thus, it is clear that some 7.1 million of Ohio's population were urban residents in 1960, and, adding the counts of rural nonfarm and rural farm residents, that about 2.6 million lived in rural places. In South Carolina, just under one million were urban and some 1.4 million were rural.

The rural population of Ohio exceeds that of South Carolina in absolute numbers. Yet, looking at the percentage distribution of the populations of the two states by type of residence, it is clear that Ohio is primarily urban (with some 73 percent of the population residing in urban places), while South Carolina is substantially rural (nearly 59 percent in rural places). Altogether, the percentage distributions by place of residence show that Ohio's population is about 73 percent urban, 21 percent rural nonfarm, and five percent rural farm, while South Carolina's is about 41 percent urban, 44 percent rural nonfarm, and 15 percent rural farm. Such percentage distributions computed according to frequency distributions over sets of exhaustive and mutually exclusive population categories are probably the most widely used quantitative representations in analytical studies of population.

In the chapters which follow, we shall continue to see numerous examples of counts, ratios, absolute number distributions, and percent distributions as quantitative presentations of population size, structure, and composition. We proceed now to somewhat more specialized, but still quite simple, quantitative representations.

5. COMPARISON OF DISTRIBUTIONS

For small-scale comparisons of frequency distributions or percentage distributions, it is possible and practical to make detailed component-by-component comparisons as we did in the place-of-residence distribution in the section above. However, for more extensive comparisons—for example, those involving a large number of populations or distributions over large numbers of categories—component-by-component comparisons quickly become unwieldy.

We shall describe two very different approaches to the summary comparison of distributions. The first uses measures of central tendency to summarize or characterize an entire frequency distribution. The second computes indexes that measure differences between pairs of distributions.

Measures of Central Tendency

The use and computation of measures of central tendency for comparing frequency distribution are discussed in most elementary statistics texts, and we will not repeat the material here. However, recalling the distinction we have already made between measurement on *nominal, ordinal,* and *interval* scales (chapter 3, section 1), we may note that each of the respective scales has its own type of measure of central tendency.

Nominal scales are those which allow classification, counts of frequencies, and frequency distributions only. There is no possibility of indicating either order or distance between the different classes. Thus persons can be *classified* by race, by sex, by marital status, by color of hair and complexion—all measurable on nominal scales only.

Ordinal scales are those which allow classification *and* indication of rank order, but not measurement nor precise comparison of distances between categories. Thus upper class is higher than middle class; and middle class is higher than lower class. But it is not possible to determine whether the distance between upper and middle classes is the same, greater than, or less than the distance between middle and lower classes.

Interval scales are those allowing classification, rank ordering, *and* measurement of distance between objects measured. Thus the difference between a community with 50,000 persons and one with 30,000 persons can be measured precisely and compared to the difference between communities of 100,000 and 150,000 persons respectively. Annual income of $15,000 can be compared precisely to annual income of $10,000.

NOMINAL SCALES: THE MODE. The appropriate indicator of central tendency for frequency distributions of variables measured on nominal scales (e.g., the variables of sex, race, region, and place of birth) is the *mode* defined as the most frequent value.[5] Thus "urban" is the modal type of residence in Ohio, while "rural nonfarm" is the modal residence category in South Carolina.

ORDINAL SCALES: THE MEDIAN. For frequency distributions of variables measured on ordinal scales (e.g., size of place, socioeconomic status, educational achievement, and occupational class) the most refined measure of central tendency available is the *median,* that value that divides a frequency distribution exactly in half. Thus, in table 4.1 it is seen that the median age in 1960 was 28.7 years in Ohio and 23.4 years in South Carolina. Similarly, the median number of school years com-

---

[5] These and other measures of central tendency and dispersion, as well as statistical tests of hypotheses concerning such measures, are described in Freeman (1965).

TABLE 4.2
*Selected Characteristics of the Populations of Ohio and
South Carolina, 1960*

	Ohio	S.C.
Median age	28.7	23.4
Median number of school years completed	10.9	8.7
Women aged 15–44		
Total	1,973,674	495,670
Ever-married	1,512,166	363,116
% ever-married	76.6	73.3
Number of live-born children	3,476,150	946,629
Per woman	1.761	1.910
Per ever-married woman	2.299	2.607

SOURCE: U.S. Bureau of the Census 1960.

pleted among persons 25 years of age or older was 10.9 years in Ohio and 8.7 years in South Carolina. Frequency distributions for variables measured on ordinal scales may also be summarized using the same measure used for variables measured on nominal scales, i.e., mode, but this is a more refined measure.

INTERVAL SCALES: THE MEAN.   Frequency distributions for variables measured on interval scales (e.g., age, income, number of hours worked, number of liveborn children, etc.) are typically summarized and characterized using the average or the arithmetic *mean* as the measure of central tendency. Both "nominal variable" and "ordinal variable" measures of central tendency (mode, median) can also be used to summarize the distributions, but they are less refined than the mean. Table 4.2 shows that the mean number of liveborn children for ever-married women age 15–44 was 2.3 in Ohio and 2.6 in South Carolina.[6]

SAMPLING VARIATION.   We mention, finally, that measures of central tendency computed on the basis of sample data are subject to sampling variation, the deviations of values computed from sample results from the true value in the parent population. The extent to which an observed difference between two quantitative summary representations can be accounted for by reference to sampling variation alone

6 Note that this mean number of liveborn children is equivalent to the ratio of liveborn children per ever-married woman aged 15–44 in 1960:

$$\frac{\text{children per}}{\text{woman ratio}} = \frac{\text{total no. liveborn children for women 15–44}}{\text{total no. ever-married women 15–44}}$$

(rather than, or in addition to, true differences between parent populations) is conventionally determined on the basis of *statisical tests*. But a discussion of statistical tests is beyond the scope of this work, and the reader may refer to one of the many excellent texts on the subject.

The Index of Dissimilarity

The comparison of distributions on the basis of measures of central tendency suffers from the discarding of information which is in the very nature of measures of central tendency. Thus, two very different frequency distributions with similar average, central, or modal values may be represented as essentially similar, as in the example of table 4.3. Use of medians or means to describe and compare the frequency distributions by educational achievement—in table 4.3—would obscure the differences between the three hypothetical populations. For this reason, indexes of differences between entire distributions, such as indexes of concentration, indexes of segregation, and indexes of dissimilarity, are very often used to characterize and measure differences between distributions. Such indexes enjoy certain basic conceptual and computational similarities, and

TABLE 4.3

Hypothetical Examples of Three Populations: Percent Distributions by Number of School Years Completed

School Years Completed	Population A	Population B	Population C
Total	100	100	100
0	20	10	30
1–4	20	20	15
5–8	20	40	10
9–12	20	20	15
13+	20	10	30
Median	6.5	6.5	6.5

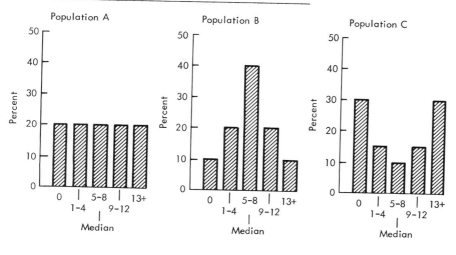

WORKSHEET A
Computation of Index of Dissimilarity

Total	Category Code a_i	Ohio % dist.	Category Code b_i	S.C. % dist.	Absolute Value of Difference $\|a_i - b_i\|$
Urban	a_1	73.4	b_1	41.2	32.2
Rural nonfarm	a_2	21.3	b_2	44.1	22.8
Rural farm	a_3	5.3	b_3	14.7	9.4

$$\sum_{i=1}^{3} |a_i - b_i| \qquad 64.4$$

Index of Dissimilarity $= \Delta a, b = \frac{1}{2} \sum_{i=1}^{3} |a_i - b_i| = \frac{1}{2} (64.4) = 32.2\%$

SOURCE: Figures for Ohio and South Carolina are from table 4.1
Note: Vertical lines enclose absolute values

we shall confine the discussion here to what is currently the most widely used index of this form, the Index of Dissimilarity.

The Index of Dissimilarity measures the differences between two relative (proportional or percentage) distributions over a given set of categories by (a) summing over all categories the absolute values of the differences between the relative frequencies in each category, and (b) then halving that sum, so that the index will take a value between 0 and 1 or between 0 and 100 percent. Thus, comparing the urban-rural distributions of Ohio and South Carolina given in figure 4.1, the computation of the Index of Dissimilarity is carried out as shown in worksheet A.

The Summation sign $\sum_{i=1}^{3}$ indicates that the absolute values of the differences $|a_i - b_i|$ are to be summed over all values of the subscript i beginning with $i = 1$ and through $i = 3$ inclusive:

$$\sum_{i=1}^{3} |a_i - b_i| = |a_1 - b_1| + |a_2 - b_2| + |a_3 - b_3| = 64.4$$
$$= \quad 32.2 \quad + \quad 22.8 \quad + \quad 9.4$$

Since the Index of Dissimilarity denoted $\Delta a,b$ (read: "Delta of a, b") is equal to one-half this summation, its value is

$$\Delta a,b = \frac{1}{2} \sum_{i=1}^{3} |a_i - b_i| = (\frac{1}{2}) \, 64.4 = 32.2$$

Put as simply as possible, the Index of Dissimilarity indicates the minimum proportion in one or the other population which would have to change categories in order for the two distributions to be identical. Thus, in the case at hand, the value of the Index of Dissimilarity between the urban-rural distributions of Ohio and South Carolina is 32.2 percent (see bottom of worksheet), interpreted as indicating that a minimum of 32.2 percent of *one* of the populations would have to move to a different type of residence in order for the two distributions to be identical.

Indexes of Dissimilarity find their most extensive use in situations where large numbers of distributions must be compared either to one another or to some single standard distribution, or where large numbers of comparisons between pairs of distributions are in order.

O. D. Duncan and his students have made extensive use of these indexes in analyses of ethnic segregation and assimilation, occupational and residential structure, and race relations. Table 4.4 presents a set of Indexes of Dissimilarity which were computed by Duncan to show patterns of residential distribution among racial and ethnic groups in the 75 "community areas" of Chicago in 1950. Analyzing these data, Duncan concludes that—

TABLE 4.4

Indexes of Dissimilarity in Residential Distribution among Selected Race-Nativity Groups, Chicago, 1950

Race or Nativity	Dissimilarity to Native White	Average Index of Dissimilarity with Respect to:		Dissimilarity to Negro
		"Old" immigrants	*"New" immigrants*	
Native White	—	26	46	80
Foreign-Born White				
"Old" immigrants:				
Austria	18	31*	48	82
England & Wales	19	28*	51	78
Germany	27	38*	52	85
Ireland (Eire)	32	38*	59	81
Sweden	33	41*	63	86
"New" immigrants:				
Italy	40	52	57*	70
U.S.S.R.	44	48	61*	87
Poland	45	59	51*	91
Czechoslovakia	49	56	53*	89
Lithuania	52	58	58*	85
Negro	80	82	84	—

SOURCE: O. D. Duncan 1957.

*Average index of dissimilarity with respect to the other countries in this group.

1. "New" immigrant groups (those who arrived in the U.S. mainly between 1890 and World War I) are separated residentially from the native-white population to a much greater extent than "old" immigrant groups (arriving prior to 1896); values of the indexes in the bottom half of the table are consistently higher than the corresponding values in the top half;

2. the greatest degree of residential separation is observed for the Negro population. The highest values of the index appear in the last column of the table;

3. each immigrant group is separated more from the remaining immigrant group (total immigrants less the group in question) than from the native white population, a tendency more apparent among "new" than among "old" immigrant groups (Duncan 1957). The lowest values of the index appear in the first column of the table.

6. POPULATION COMPOSITION AND OTHER CORRELATES OF VARIATION IN INDIVIDUAL TRAITS: "EXPECTED CASE" ANALYSIS

The analysis of relationships between individual traits and characteristics is not, of course, limited to population studies nor indeed even to the social sciences; and it is a subject which has been treated extensively in works on statistical description and inference. We shall merely note here some of the relationships between individual characteristics in population studies and mention very briefly the approaches used in their description and analysis.

The relationships between age and marital status, between educational achievement and fertility, between type of residence and participation in the labor force, between income and morbidity and mortality, or between religion and social status or class are all examples of relationships between individual characteristics which might be of interest to population studies.

Three Approaches to the Analysis of Relationships

There are three conventional approaches to the quantitative description and analysis of relationships between individual characteristics: (1) the comparison of ratios or of frequency distributions in absolute or relative numbers, (2) the computation of measures of association, and (3) tests of the statistical "significance" of observed differences or relationships between individual characteristics. Thus, using the first approach, since the percentage in the labor force among males exceeds that among females, we may infer that being male is positively related to labor-force participation. In other words, we may infer that males are more likely than females to be in the labor force, and we may specify "by how much" as well. Using the second approach, we can compute the characteristic degree of association between attributes of two variables measured on the same or different scales.[7] Finally, there are statistical tests for assessing the likelihood or possibility that a given observed relationship stems from sampling variation rather than from a systematic and recurring relationship between the characteristics in question; these tests are also treated fully in statistical texts.

An "Expected Case" Analysis

Characteristics such as age, sex, marital status, and educational achievement are widely recognized to be intimately related to other individual characteristics. For example, close relationships are found between age and marital status, between marital status and fertility, between educational achievement and occupational status, and between occupation and income. But it is often recognized that an apparent relationship between variables may in fact be due to factors of population composition. Thus, an apparent tendency for smaller towns to have relatively fewer married persons than larger towns might be accounted for by differences in age distribution: if the smaller towns have relatively more teenaged or elderly persons, their total proportion of married persons is likely to be low, even if the proportions married or unmarried at each individual age level do not differ from those in larger towns.

A procedure called "method of expected cases" is used to neutralize the effects of compositional differences in the populations of the groups, places, or categories being compared. This procedure involves computing the "expected" incidence of some trait or characteristic on the assumption of a fixed rate or frequency per component and taking into account only the variation in population composition. Subsequently, a comparison of the "actual" incidence of the trait with the "expected" or "calculated" incidence measures the effect of the second variable *exclusive* of the effects of population composition.[8]

As an example, we may consider the study of patterns of Negro

---

7 Thus, we can determine the coefficient of correlation between two interval-scale variables, the "correlation ratio" between one interval-scale and one nominal-scale variable, the "coefficient of ordinal association" between two ordinal-scale variables, etc. For a full discussion and historical account of measures of association, see the important series of papers by Goodman and Kruskal (1954), Goodman and Kruskal (1959); see also Freeman (1965).

8 For an analysis of the relationship between this approach and the statistical techniques of the analysis of covariance, see Duncan, Cuzzort, and Duncan (1961); Fennessey (1968); and Schuessler (1969).

TABLE 4.5

Total and Negro Employment (Males) in
Selected Industry Groups, 1960

	Total	Negro	% Negro
Aircraft construction	542,492	16,805	3.1
Wholesale trade	1,762,082	110,758	6.3
Hotel	276,184	45,318	16.4
Total — all industries	43,466,955	3,640,851	8.4

SOURCE: Computations by Karl and Alma Taeuber, Department of Sociology, and Institute for Poverty Research, University of Wisconsin.

employment in different U.S. industry groups.[9] Table 4.5 shows that while Negroes comprised 8.4 percent of the total number of persons employed in 1960, they comprised only 3.1 percent in the aircraft manufacturing industries and only 6.3 percent in the wholesale trade industries, but 16.4 percent in the hotel sector of the personal service industries. A number of hypotheses may be advanced to account for these differences in the employment of Negroes.

Differences between Negroes and whites with respect to regions, places of residence, educational achievement, occupational achievement, marital status, and other factors in addition to direct racial discrimination may be related to the differences in the percent of Negroes among the employed in the various industry groups. To assess the effect of Negro-white *occupational* differences on employment in the different industries, we may compute the number of Negroes in each of the industry groups "expected" on the assumption that the proportion of Negroes in each *occupation* group employed is the same in the industry group in question as it is in the entire country. This computation is shown in worksheet B.

In the worksheet, the proportion of Negroes in each major occupation group is shown in column (2). Multiplying the total number employed in each occupation group in the aircraft construction industries [column (3)] by the nationwide proportion of Negroes in the respective occupation groups [column (2)] yields an "expected" number of Negroes in each occupation group in the aircraft manufacturing industries [column (4) = Column (2) × Column (3)]. Summing over the entire column yields an "expected number" of Negroes in the aircraft industry. The same procedure is employed to arrive at "expected numbers" of Negroes in the wholesale trade and hotel industries. An "expected percent Negro" for each industry can be computed, and the differences between these "expected percents" reflects differences in the occupational composition of

9 Such a study is now being carried out by Karl and Alma Taeuber. We are indebted to them for making some of their computations available for use in this example.

WORKSHEET B

Computation of "Expected Numbers" of Negroes in Aircraft Construction, Wholesale Trade, and Hotel Industries, 1960, Assuming Fixed Proportions Negro in Each Major Occupation Group

Major Occupation Groups	All Industries		Aircraft Construction		Wholesale Trade		Personal Service Hotels	
	Total: All persons employed (1)	Proportion Negro (2)	Total: All persons employed (3)	Expected Negroes (4)	Total: All persons employed (5)	Expected Negroes (6)	Total: All persons employed (7)	Expected Negroes (8) (7) x (2)
Professional, technical, and kindred workers	4,479,358	.02520	137,168	3,457	57,184	1,441	7,863	198
Managers, officials, and proprietors, excluding farm	7,017,426	.03115	18,163	566	395,963	12,334	65,078	2,027
Clerical and kindred workers	3,015,476	.06094	48,648	2,965	178,313	10,866	25,689	1,565
Sales workers	2,977,872	.01628	2,992	49	479,131	7,800	1,022	17
Craftsmen, foremen, and kindred workers	8,488,777	.04206	161,657	6,799	147,228	6,192	27,488	1,156
Operatives and kindred workers	8,641,692	.10291	149,801	15,416	340,867	35,079	8,024	826
Service workers, except household	2,659,736	.20121	9,069	1,825	15,196	3,058	129,299	26,016
Laborers	4,199,711	.23596	5,817	1,373	122,279	28,853	7,594	1,792
Not Reported	1,986,907	.15336	9,177	1,407	25,921	3,975	4,127	633
Total: All Occupation Groups	43,466,955		542,492	33,857	1,762,082	109,598	276,184	34,230
Expected Percent		8.4		6.2		6.2		12.4
Actual No. of Negroes Employed				16,805		110,758		45,318
Ratio: Actual/Expected				0.49635		1.01058		1.32392

SOURCE: Computations by Karl E. and Alma F. Taeuber, Department of Sociology and Institute for Research on Poverty, University of Wisconsin.

employment among the respective industries. Thus, we learn that the occupational distribution in the hotel industry leads to an "expected percent Negro" exceeding by about one-half the general percentage of Negroes among employed U.S. males (12.4 percent in the hotel industry, compared to 8.4 percent for the total); the opposite obtains for the aircraft and wholesale trade industries.

Comparing now the actual with the "expected" numbers of Negroes employed in the several industry groups, we find that considerably fewer Negroes are employed in the aircraft industries than is "expected" on the basis of the occupational distribution: 16,805 (3.1 percent) "actual," compared to 33,857 (6.2 percent) "expected." The ratio of "actual" to "expected" numbers is .49635. Conversely, in the hotel industry, the ratio of "actual" to "expected" numbers exceeds unity by close to one-third (1.32392); the "actual" number employed is 45,318, whereas a total of 34,230 is "expected." Finally, the worksheet shows that the number and percentage of Negroes employed in the wholesale trade industries are remarkably close to those "expected" on the basis of occupational distribution alone. The method of "expected cases" is closely related to the procedure of "standardization" commonly used in demography and described in chapter 5.

7. GROUP CHARACTERISTICS AND INDIVIDUAL TRAITS: CONTEXTUAL, STRUCTURAL, AND COMPOSITIONAL EFFECTS AND ECOLOGICAL CORRELATION ANALYSIS

We turn finally to a type of analysis which is still novel enough in studies of populations and societies to render any exposition necessarily tentative. Yet it represents so significant a frontier of social scientific theory and method that some introduction, however hesitant and reserved, is justified. We refer to the description and analysis of the effects of alternative combinations and configurations of individual traits upon group structure and group attributes. We may illustrate the type of problem involved and the terminological conventions adopted thus far by referring to the relationship between group productivity and education of the individual members.

An Example: Individual and Aggregate Effects of Education on Productivity

Assuming, for purposes of illustration, that a positive correlation between education and productivity exists, we can conceive of a number of forms which this relationship might take. The most obvious one might be that persons with more education are more productive than those with less education. This correlation by itself could suffice to render work groups with relatively more educated members more productive than work groups with relatively fewer educated members; following from this, *groups, collectivities,* or *societies* characterized by "higher educational achievement" might be said to be more productive than similar bodies characterized by "lower educational achievement." Here, the characterization of the unit in terms of its "educational level" is based strictly on the number of its members with individually high or low levels of educational achievement.

Consider, however, the productivity of persons with low educational achievement. Might it not be possible that their productivity, far from being fixed, varies depending upon whether the work groups to which they belong have larger or smaller numbers of educated persons? That is in fact the case; uneducated persons may be more productive if their work organizations include many highly educated persons rather than few or none at all. More generally, uneducated and unskilled persons in a highly organized, rationalized, and "educated" economy are more productive than their counterparts in an "uneducated" economy. Conversely, it is probably the case that rather highly educated persons are less productive in an economy whose majority is mostly uneducated than in one whose majority is highly educated. In other words, the fact of a high or low percentage of educated persons may affect the productivity of educated and uneducated alike in the same kinds of work groups, organizations, or economies. If this is the case, we may say that *compositional* or *structural effects* attend the individual trait of "educational achievement." A large number of distinctions among correlations between individual traits and structural effects could be cited (Blau 1960 and 1957; Kendall and Lazarsfeld 1955; Davis, Spaeth, and Huson 1961; Warren 1965; and references cited therein).

Analyzing Education and Productivity of Individuals and Groups: Structural Effects and Ecological Correlation

Two kinds of problems arise in such situations. The first concerns the analytical criteria of "structural effects": under what circumstances are relations between, say, education and productivity imputable only to a correlation between the two traits in individuals, and under what circumstances are they imputable to structural effects? In other words, when can "educational level" be considered a bona fide structural property of the collectivity with—as in the example above—the group's high education able to raise the poorly educated individual's productivity, or vice-versa?

The opposite problem arises when the data that are available give distributions or measures of central tendency on educational achievement and productivity separately for each aggregate but not jointly for individuals. We often wish to determine from these data whether *individual* education and productivity are correlated. The attempt to infer individual relationships on the basis of relationships observed for aggregates has been called *ecological correlation* (Robinson 1950) or "ecological regression." These terms, which are probably misnomers, derive from the fact that early "human ecologists" sought to relate data on two dimensions—ethnic composition and distribution of the vote—for small areal units such as polling districts, census tracts, etc.

Analysis of Structural Effects in Durkheim's Study of Suicide

Perhaps the first formal attempt to impute "structural effects" to aggregates of individual attributes was made by Durkheim. In his classic study *Suicide* (1951), Durkheim shows: (1) that Protestants are characterized by higher suicide rates than Catholics, but that (2) Protestants residing in Catholic areas have lower suicide rates than do those residing in Protestant areas; while Catholics living in Protestant areas have higher suicide rates than do those living in Catholic areas. Durkheim's structural-effect or *contextual-analysis* strategy is summarized very neatly by Warren:

> In *Suicide* Durkheim seeks to demonstrate the role of social structure by comparing the rates of suicides for individuals with the same status characteristics, e.g., Catholic and Protestant, in different social settings. Although Durkheim wants to generalize to all variations in suicide via the framework of "social integration," the state of integration is operationally measured by the summation of the individual status attributes of populations. Thus in areas where Protestants are the majority group, Catholics commit more suicides than their counterparts in predominantly Catholic areas. The assumption underlying this type of analysis seems to be that Protestants, in a Catholic region, are exposed to the constraints of Catholic normative integration; whereas Catholics in predominantly Protestant areas are exposed to the individual norms of Protestants. What is implied in the kind of approach Durkheim uses is that by controlling for the individual's orientation, and showing his behavior in various social settings, one has demonstrated the constraints of societal and group norms as imposed on individuals even if they are predisposed against such constraints. Fundamentally, this is the strategy of contextual analysis. [Warren 1965, p. 2]

Summarizing Durkheim's analysis and illustrating with reference to the elements of table 4.6, we may say that Durkheim found that suicide rates were higher for Protestants than for Catholics generally, and that within all areas, Catholic areas or Protestant areas, respectively, the same comparison holds. Referring to the symbols of table 4.6, this says

TABLE 4.6
Suicide Rates for Catholics and Protestants in Catholic Areas and in Protestant Areas

Individual Traits	Aggregate Traits		Total — All Areas
	Catholic areas (majority of population Catholic)	Protestant areas (majority of population Protestant)	
Catholics	S_{cc}	S_{cp}	$S_{c.}$
Protestants	S_{pc}	S_{pp}	$S_{p.}$
Total — both faiths	$S_{.c}$	$S_{.p}$	$S_{..}$

Note: S = suicide rate;
$\quad S_{cc}$ = suicide rate of Catholics in Catholic areas;
$\quad S_{pc}$ = suicide rate of Protestants in Catholic areas;
$\quad S_{cp}$ = suicide rate of Catholics in Protestant areas;
$\quad S_{pp}$ = suicide rate of Protestants in Protestant areas.
$\quad S_{c.}$ = suicide rate of Catholics in all areas;
$\quad S_{p.}$ = suicide rate of Protestants in all areas;
$\quad S_{.c}$ = suicide rate of both faiths in Catholic areas;
$\quad S_{.p}$ = suicide rate of both faiths in Protestant areas;
$\quad S_{..}$ = suicide rate of both faiths in all areas.

that, overall $S_p. > S_c.$ (where $>$ means "greater than"); that within Catholic areas $S_{pc} > S_{cc}$; and within Protestant areas $S_{pp} > S_{cp}$. However, Durkheim found also that the suicide rate of Catholics living in Protestant areas exceeds that of Catholics living in Catholic areas, i.e., $S_{cp} > S_{cc}$, and that the suicide rate of Protestants living in Protestant areas exceeds that of Protestants living in Catholic areas, i.e., $S_{pp} > S_{pc}$. Durkheim inferred from these findings there is a systematic difference between Catholic and Protestant "countries," "areas," and "settings" which affects both Catholics and Protestants irrespective of their individual religious traits. It is just such systematic differences which have been called "structural effects," "compositional effects," or "contextual effects" by various authors, and it is just such quantitative relationships (i.e., not only $S_p. > S_c.$, but also $S_{cp} > S_{cc}$ and/or $S_{pp} > S_{pc}$) which have been adopted as their empirical criteria.

An Example of Structural Effects Analysis

As a concrete example of how researchers determine structural effects, we shall consider first the U.S. Census Bureau's summary of distributions of the number of school years completed in 1960 by selected craftsmen, foremen, and men in kindred occupational groups (see table

4.7). The summary measures are "median numbers of school years completed," and it will be recalled that the median is that value that divides a frequency distribution (on an ordinal or interval scale) exactly in half. Table 4.7 shows that half the brick masons, stone masons, and tile setters in the U.S. in 1960 had completed 9.7 years of school or less, and that half had completed 9.7 years or more. Or, for another median, half the telegraph, telephone, and power linemen and servicemen had completed 12.3 years of school or less, just as half had completed 12.3 years or more.

Drawing upon the information in table 4.7, we can construct two composite occupational groups, one characterized by a "low" median number of school years and the other by a "high" median number. ("Under ten years is taken as 'low,' and '12 or more years' is taken as high.") Using these two groups and data published in the census volume, it is possible to compute each group's mean 1959 annual income for white employees with no education beyond the elementary level (eight years or less) and for those with some college education (12 years or more). These computations are shown in table 4.8.

It is evident from table 4.8 that individuals with low educational achievement (elementary only) had substantially higher incomes if they were employed in "high educational-level occupations" rather than "low educational-level" ones. Conversely, individuals with high educational

TABLE 4.7

Median School Years Completed by Experienced Male Labor Force of Selected Craftsmen, Foremen, and Kindred Occupational Groups, 1960

Occupation Group	Median School Years Completed
Craftsmen, Foremen, and Kindred Workers, Total	10.5
Brick masons, stone masons, & tile setters	9.7
Carpenters	9.3
Cement and concrete finishers	8.6
Compositors and typesetters	12.1
Electricians	11.8
Foremen (not elsewhere classified)	11.5
Linemen and servicemen, telegraph, telephone and power	12.3
Locomotive engineers	9.8
Machinists	10.8
Airplane mechanics and repairmen	12.2
Automobile mechanics and repairmen	9.9
Radio and television mechanics and repairmen	12.2
Painters, construction and maintenance	9.1
Plasterers	9.0
Toolmakers, and diemakers and setters	11.7
Craftsmen and kindred workers (not elsewhere classified)	10.5

SOURCE: U.S. Bureau of the Census, *1960 Subject Reports* PC(2)-7A (1963), table 9.

TABLE 4.8

Mean Annual Income by Number of School Years
Completed for White Craftsmen, Foremen, and Kindred
Workers of "Low" and "High" Educational Level

Occupational Groups	Educational Achievement of Employees	
	Elementary (8 yrs. or below)	*College* (over 12 years)
"Low" median educational level[a]	$ 4,279	$ 5,430
"High" median educational level[b]	$ 5,437	$ 6,272

SOURCE: Table 4.7 and U.S. Bureau of the Census, *1960 Subject Reports,* PC(2)–78 (1963), table 1.

[a]Median school years completed: less than ten years. Includes: brick masons, stone masons, tile setters, carpenters, cement and concrete finishers, locomotive engineers, automobile mechanics and repairmen, painters, and plasterers.

[b]Median school years completed: twelve years or over. Includes: compositors and typesetters, linemen and servicemen, airplane mechanics and repairmen, and radio and television mechanics and repairmen.

achievement (some college or more) had notably lower annual incomes if they were employed in "low educational-level occupations" rather than "high educational-level" ones. By the criteria indicated above, these data imply that these "structural effects" follow from the educational-achievement composition of occupational groups. That such a finding leaves open the precise nature and causes of such effects seems obvious, and we shall mention this problem again briefly at the close of this chapter.

Ecological Correlation Analysis

It often happens that comparisons of $S_c.$ to $S_p.$ type, i.e., comparisons between different categories of individuals, are possible when only area totals are known. For example, although we cannot know how individuals of different ages, ethnic groups, races, or occupational statuses voted in a given election, we can often compare the distributions of voting rates in different ethnic, racial, occupational, or industrial *areas*. Sociological, political, and demographic analyses have long used such areal or aggregate comparisons in order to infer individual relationships (Robinson 1950; Goodman 1959; Fennessey 1968). In terms of the elements in table 4.6, this is equivalent to using the known relationships between the overall suicide rates of Catholic and Protestant *areas,* respectively, $S_{.c}$ and $S_{.p}$, to make inferences about the unknown relationships between suicide rates of Catholics and Protestants, respectively $S_c.$ and $S_p.$, a procedure equivalent to "ecological correlation."

Careful consideration of table 4.6 should suggest that the link between the relationship between suicide rates of Catholic and Protestant areas, $S_{\cdot c}$ and $S_{\cdot p}$, and the relationship between suicide rates of Catholics and of Protestants, $S_{c \cdot}$ and $S_{p \cdot}$ is not uniform and straightforward. Rather, it depends (1) upon the magnitude of the differences between suicide rates of Catholics and of Protestants, $S_{c \cdot}$ compared to $S_{p \cdot}$, and on (2) the relative sizes and (3) homogeneity of the Catholic areas and Protestant areas respectively. This is so even if we assume that there are no "structural effects" within the religious groupings and between the different "area" types, i.e. that $S_{cc} = S_{cp}$ and that $S_{pc} = S_{pp}$.[10] Structural effects, if they exist, further complicate the connection between the relationship between the areal rates, $S_{\cdot c}$ and $S_{\cdot p}$ and between the "individual" Catholic and Protestant rates, $S_{c \cdot}$ and $S_{p \cdot}$.

More generally it has been shown that "ecological correlations" are poor (and sometimes very misleading) estimates of individual correlations, except under some fairly specific sets of conditions (Robinson 1950). However, in all but very unusual situations, "ecological correlations" and other comparisons based on aggregates generally do preserve both the *direction* of individual relationships and the *relative magnitudes* of such relationships over sets of comparisons.[11] For this reason, the approach is widely used in sociological, demographic, and ecological studies. Moreover, not only is there great intrinsic interest in areal and aggregate comparisons per se, but areal and aggregate comparisons represent the only empirical approach to the analysis of certain types of relationships, e.g., social status and actual vote, housing conditions and morbidity and mortality, unemployment and delinquency. These two facts suggest that more, rather than less, interest in the methods, techniques, and limitations of this sort of approach are likely to be forthcoming. In particular, two processes of both compositional effects and ecological correlations which have been considered as possible *causes* of the observed relationships, *viz.* selection and socialization (see Warren 1965), are likely to be examined in more detail, and additional processes may be identified and studied as well.

10 Indeed, it is easier to see under that assumption. For, then, the suicide rates for Catholic and Protestant areas respectively would be simply weighted averages of the Catholic and Protestant rates, with the weights being the corresponding numbers of population by religion and type of area, N_{cc}, N_{cp}, N_{pc}, and N_{pp}, and

$$S_{\cdot c} = \frac{N_{cc}\, S_{c \cdot} + N_{pc}\, S_{p \cdot}}{N_{cc} + N_{pc}} \text{ and } S_{\cdot p} = \frac{N_{cp}\, S_{c \cdot} + N_{pp}\, S_{p \cdot}}{N_{cp} + N_{pp}}$$

11 The direction would not be preserved in instances where "reverse structural effects" obtain. An example of "reverse structural effects" would be a situation in which those individuals with high educational achievement exhibit higher productivity the lower the average level of education in the group; or those with low educational achievement have lower productivity the higher the educational level of the group as a whole. See Blau (1960) for examples, criteria, and interpretations of "reverse structural effects."

5

Quantitative Representation
and Measurement of
Population Movements
and Transformations

1. INTRODUCTORY REMARKS

This chapter continues the review and presentation of techniques of measurement and analysis in population studies. It deals particularly with description and analysis of population *changes*. It does not, however, assume previous study or mastery of the materials of the preceding chapter; rather, it is entirely self-contained and can be studied or used independently of the previous chapter or of other parts of the book.

As was the case of chapter 4, different individuals will use the materials in different ways and with different purposes. For some it will suffice to skim the sections of this chapter and to obtain an overview of measurement and analysis of mortality, fertility, migration and mobility, coming back to the specific concepts and techniques as necessary. Others will wish to achieve a full understanding of quantitative representation and measurement of population movements and transformations. For those who wish to go beyond the materials offered in this and the preceding chapters a bibliography is offered at the end of this chapter.

Measuring Growth

The growth of a population is always measured with reference to the size of that population at some initial point in time. The basic relationship is of the form:

$$\begin{pmatrix} \text{Size of population} \\ \text{at terminal point} \end{pmatrix} = \begin{pmatrix} \text{Size of population} \\ \text{at initial point} \end{pmatrix} + \begin{pmatrix} \text{Growth in the} \\ \text{interval of time} \end{pmatrix}.$$

Two measures of population growth are conventionally employed. The first measure, the percentage change in the size of the population during the interval, is obtained by calculating the ratio of the growth in the interval of time to the initial population size and then multiplying by 100:

$$\text{Percentage change} = \frac{\text{growth in the interval}}{\text{initial population size}} \times 100.$$

Thus, drawing upon the data in table 5.1, we can determine the percentage change in the size of the U.S. population in the intercensal period from 1 April 1960, to 1 April 1970:

$$\text{Percentage change} = \frac{(1970 \text{ Total Pop.})-(1960 \text{ Total Pop.})}{(1960 \text{ Total Pop.})} \times (100)$$

$$= \frac{203,184,772-179,323,175}{179,323,175} \times (100)$$

$$= 13.3 \text{ percent.}$$

The corresponding change in the intercensal period from 1 April 1950 to 1 April 1960, was:

$$\frac{179,323,175-151,325,798}{151,325,798} \times (100) = 18.5 \text{ percent}$$

TABLE 5.1
Estimates of Total Resident U.S. Population and Components of Change, 1950-1971 (in thousands)

	April 1, 1970[a] to Jan. 1, 1971	April 1, 1960 to April 1, 1970	April 1, 1950 to April 1, 1960
Population at beginning of period	203,185	179,323	151,326
Births in period	2,866	39,033	40,963
Deaths in period	1,413	18,192	15,608
Net migration in period[b]	437	3,020	2,642
Population at end of period	206,488	203,185	179,323
Net change	3,303	23,862	27,997

SOURCE: U.S. Bureau of the Census, *Current Population Reports, Population Estimates,* Series P-25, No. 460, June 7, 1971 and No. 465, Sept. 8, 1971.
[a]Preliminary estimates
[b]Includes net civilian migration less movement of armed forces overseas and error of closure.

The second measure, the average annual rate of change in the size of the population during the interval, is obtained by calculating the ratio of the growth in the interval to the initial population size and dividing that ratio by the number of years in the interval:

$$\begin{array}{c} \text{Average} \\ \text{annual rate} \\ \text{of change} \end{array} = \frac{\left(\begin{array}{c}\text{Growth in}\\ \text{the interval}\end{array}\right) \Big/ \left(\begin{array}{c}\text{Initial population}\\ \text{size}\end{array}\right)}{\text{Number of years in the interval}}.$$

For the U.S. in the 1960–1970 period, the average annual rate of change was 1.33 percent. This represents a sharp decline from the average annual rate of change of 1.85 percent in the 1950–1960 period. Other, somewhat more elaborate, measures of population growth are sometimes employed, and these are given in the more technical texts.

Components of Population Growth

The growth of a population during a given interval of time may be divided into four major components as follows:

$$\left(\begin{array}{c}\text{Growth}\\ \text{in the}\\ \text{interval}\end{array}\right) = \left(\begin{array}{c}\text{Births}\\ \text{in the}\\ \text{interval}\end{array}\right) - \left(\begin{array}{c}\text{Deaths}\\ \text{in the}\\ \text{interval}\end{array}\right) + \left(\begin{array}{c}\text{No. of}\\ \text{in-migrants}\end{array}\right) - \left(\begin{array}{c}\text{No. of}\\ \text{out-migrants}\end{array}\right).$$

Combining the birth and death components yields

$$\left(\begin{array}{c}\text{Growth due to}\\ \text{natural increase}\end{array}\right) = \left(\begin{array}{c}\text{Number of births}\\ \text{in the interval}\end{array}\right) - \left(\begin{array}{c}\text{Number of deaths}\\ \text{in the interval}\end{array}\right),$$

and combining the in-migration and out-migration components yields

$$\left(\begin{array}{c}\text{Growth}\\ \text{due to net}\\ \text{migration}\end{array}\right) = \left(\begin{array}{c}\text{Number of}\\ \text{in-migrants in}\\ \text{the interval}\end{array}\right) - \left(\begin{array}{c}\text{Number of}\\ \text{out-migrants}\\ \text{in the interval}\end{array}\right).$$

Measurements of population growth due to natural increase and of growth due to net migration are analogous to the measurement of total population growth. Thus, percentage change due to natural increase

$$= \frac{\text{Growth due to natural increase}}{\text{Initial population size}} \times 100,$$

and average annual rate of growth due to national increase

$$= \frac{(\text{Growth due to natural increase}) \ / \ (\text{Initial population})}{\text{Number of years in the interval}}.$$

Similarly, percentage change due to net migration

$$= \frac{\text{Growth due to net migration}}{\text{Initial population size}} \times 100,$$

and average annual rate of growth due to net migration

$$= \frac{(\text{Growth due to net migration}) \ / \ (\text{Initial population})}{\text{Number of years in the interval}}.$$

From table 5.1, we have for the United States in the 1960–1970 period:

$$\begin{matrix} \text{Percentage change due} \\ \text{to natural increase} \end{matrix} = \frac{20,841,000}{179,323,175} \times 100 = 11.6 \text{ percent.}$$

Thus, the average annual rate of growth due to natural increase was 1.16 percent. The table also shows that:

$$\begin{matrix} \text{Percent change due to} \\ \text{net international} \\ \text{migration} \end{matrix} = \frac{3,020,000}{179,323} \times 100 = 1.7 \text{ percent.}$$

Thus, the average annual change due to net migration was 0.17 percent.

It is very often the case that data for calculating total population growth and natural increase components are available for a given urban or other areally delineated population, but that there are no data relating to the net migration component. The volume of net migration to (or from) the area in question may be inferred by subtracting the increment due to natural increase from total population growth:

$$\begin{pmatrix} \text{Growth due to} \\ \text{net migration} \end{pmatrix} = \begin{pmatrix} \text{Total population} \\ \text{growth} \end{pmatrix} - \begin{pmatrix} \text{Growth due to} \\ \text{natural increase} \end{pmatrix}.$$

which follows from the relationships outlined above.

2. MORTALITY ANALYSIS

The analysis of mortality requires a measure of the frequency of deaths relative to the number of persons in the population exposed to the risk of death. In a given interval of time, the number of persons exposed to the risk of death includes: (a) those persons initially in the population and remaining in the population throughout the interval; (b) those persons initially in the population but leaving it during the interval (through death or out-migration); and (c) those persons initially not in the population but entering it during the interval (through birth or in-migration). Only persons in the first category are exposed to the risk of death throughout the entire interval; those in the second and third categories are exposed during only part of the interval.

Crude Death Rate

The actual number of deaths in a given time interval pertains to persons in all three of the above categories. The simplest measure of the frequency of deaths in a population in a given time interval is the crude death rate, which is the ratio of the number of deaths in the population during the interval to the average population exposed to risk of death in that interval, multiplied by 1,000. The rate is conventionally computed with reference to single-year intervals, and the number of persons exposed to death is calculated by taking the average of that interval's fluctuating numbers. Thus:

$$\text{Crude death rate} = \frac{\text{Deaths in the population during the year}}{\text{Average population size during the year}} \times 1{,}000$$

or, alternatively:

$$\text{Crude death rate} = \frac{\text{Deaths in the population during the year}}{\text{Midyear population size}} \times 1{,}000.$$

The alternative is generally used because the midyear population is easier to obtain than the average population and is accepted as a good enough approximation of the average population. The crude death rate measures the number of deaths in a year per 1,000 persons in the population being studied.

Using the data in table 5.2, we can compute crude death rates in the United States for the years 1915, 1935, 1955, 1968, and 1969. These are as follows:

$$1915: \frac{1{,}327{,}000}{100{,}549{,}000} \times 1{,}000 = 13.2 \text{ per } 1{,}000,$$

$$1935: \frac{1{,}393{,}000}{127{,}250{,}000} \times 1{,}000 = 10.9 \text{ per } 1{,}000,$$

TABLE 5.2
*Estimated Midyear Population and Total Marriages, Births, Deaths,
and Infant Deaths for the U.S. 1915, 1935, 1955, 1968, and 1969*

	Estimated July 1 Population[a]	Marriages	Births	Deaths	Infant Deaths
1915	100,549,000	1,008,000	2,965,000	1,327,000[b]	296,000[b]
1935	127,250,000	1,327,000	2,377,000	1,393,000	120,000
1955	165,069,000	1,531,000	4,104,000	1,529,000	107,000
1968	199,870,000	2,059,000	3,502,000	1,923,000	75,000
1969	201,921,000	2,146,000	3,571,000	1,916,000	74,000

SOURCE: U.S. Bureau of the Census (1970), tables 2 and 53.
[a]Total resident population.
[b]Estimates

$$1955: \frac{1,529,000}{165,069,000} \times 1,000 = 9.3 \text{ per } 1,000,$$

$$1968: \frac{1,923,000}{199,870,000} \times 1,000 = 9.6 \text{ per } 1,000,$$

$$1969: \frac{1,916,000}{201,921,000} \times 1,000 = 9.5 \text{ per } 1,000.$$

It is obvious that crude death rates may vary considerably over different populations or in the same population in different years. Indeed, they may also vary among different subgroups or categories within a single population. We can always compute category-specific death rates as we do the crude death rate, using the ratio of the number of deaths in the category to the average number of persons in that category during the year. Thus:

$$\frac{\text{Category-specific}}{\text{death rate}} = \frac{\text{Deaths of persons in the given category}}{\substack{\text{Average or midyear population} \\ \text{in the given category}}} \times 1,000.$$

Age-Specific Death Rates

Age-specific death rates are almost always computed separately for males and females. The set of age-specific death rates—i.e., the male and female age-specific death rates for ages 0, 1, 2, . . . , etc., or for age intervals 0–4, 5–9, 10–14, . . . , etc.—observed in a population for a given year is called the *schedule* of age-specific death rates or the *mortality schedule*. This schedule is the most commonly used detailed representation of mortality conditions obtaining in given populations in given years.

Estimates of the midyear population of the United States by sex and age for 1967 are given in table 5.3. These are the denominators for

TABLE 5.3
Estimates of Total Resident Population of U.S. by Age, Color, and Sex: 1 July 1967

Age	Total			White			Nonwhite		
	Both sexes	Male	Female	Both sexes	Male	Female	Both sexes	Male	Female
Total: All ages	197,863,000	96,694,000	101,169,000	173,920,000	85,127,000	88,793,000	23,942,000	11,567,000	12,376,000
0-1	3,539,000	1,806,000	1,733,000	2,933,000	1,501,000	1,432,000	607,000	306,000	301,000
1-4	15,652,000	7,989,000	7,664,000	13,084,000	6,695,000	6,390,000	2,567,000	1,293,000	1,274,000
5-9	20,910,000	10,642,000	10,268,000	17,771,000	9,071,000	8,700,000	3,139,000	1,571,000	1,568,000
10-14	19,885,000	10,101,000	9,784,000	17,074,000	8,696,000	8,378,000	2,811,000	1,405,000	1,406,000
15-19	17,693,000	8,909,000	8,784,000	15,325,000	7,732,000	7,592,000	2,368,000	1,176,000	1,192,000
20-24	14,572,000	7,042,000	7,530,000	12,817,000	6,202,000	6,616,000	1,754,000	840,000	914,000
25-29	11,958,000	5,875,000	6,083,000	10,531,000	5,202,000	5,329,000	1,427,000	673,000	753,000
30-34	10,860,000	5,323,000	5,538,000	9,561,000	4,721,000	4,839,000	1,300,000	601,000	699,000
35-39	11,506,000	5,609,000	5,897,000	10,173,000	5,002,000	5,172,000	1,333,000	607,000	725,000
40-44	12,332,000	5,992,000	6,340,000	11,005,000	5,378,000	5,627,000	1,327,000	614,000	713,000
45-49	11,816,000	5,719,000	6,096,000	10,625,000	5,161,000	5,464,000	1,190,000	558,000	633,000
50-54	10,772,000	5,217,000	5,556,000	9,724,000	4,723,000	5,001,000	1,049,000	494,000	555,000
55-59	9,524,000	4,572,000	4,951,000	8,642,000	4,153,000	4,484,000	881,000	419,000	462,000
60-64	8,048,000	3,798,000	4,250,000	7,327,000	3,452,000	3,875,000	721,000	346,000	374,000
65-69	6,501,000	2,958,000	3,543,000	5,983,000	2,714,000	3,269,000	518,000	245,000	274,000
70-74	5,177,000	2,236,000	2,941,000	4,793,000	2,067,000	2,726,000	384,000	169,000	214,000
75-79	3,785,000	1,587,000	2,198,000	3,500,000	1,462,000	2,038,000	285,000	125,000	160,000
80-84	2,160,000	874,000	1,286,000	1,995,000	800,000	1,195,000	165,000	74,000	91,000
85 & over	1,174,000	446,000	727,000	1,057,000	396,000	661,000	116,000	50,000	66,000

SOURCE: Vital Statistics of the U.S. 1967, Vol. I, Natality Table 3-2.

computation of age-specific death rates. Numbers of deaths to white and nonwhite males in each age group in 1967—the numerators for computation of white and nonwhite male age-specific death rates—are shown in table 5.4.

Age-specific death rates in 1967 for U.S. males by color are given in table 5.4, and the pattern of age and color differences is shown in figure 5.1. The death rate drops sharply after the first year of age and begins to climb again between ages 15 and 19. Death rates of nonwhites are consistently higher than those of whites until ages 70 to 74. From ages 75 to 79 and over, death rates of white males exceed those of nonwhite males substantially.

INFANT MORTALITY RATE. A special age-specific death rate is the infant mortality rate, which commands particular interest both because of its magnitude relative to other age-specific death rates and because of its great sensitivity to socioeconomic conditions obtaining in the community. Since infant deaths tend to be highly concentrated in the interval just after birth, the denominator of the infant mortality rate is con-

TABLE 5.4

U.S. Male Deaths and Death Rates by Age and Color, 1967

Age	Total		White		Nonwhite	
	No.	*Rate*	*No.*	*Rate*	*No.*	*Rate*
Total	1,045,945	.010817	919,514	.010802	126,431	.010930
0–1	45,442	.025162	33,565	.022362	11,877	.038814
1–4	7,651	.000958	5,687	.000849	1,964	.001519
5–9	5,191	.000488	4,158	.000458	1,033	.000658
10–14	5,170	.000512	4,243	.000488	927	.000660
15–19	13,047	.001464	10,839	.001402	2,208	.001878
20–24	14,138	.002008	11,348	.001830	2,790	.003321
25–29	11,217	.001909	8,376	.001610	2,841	.004221
30–34	11,701	.002198	8,449	.001790	3,252	.005411
35–39	17,472	.003115	13,179	.002635	4,293	.007072
40–44	28,273	.004718	22,171	.004123	6,102	.009938
45–49	42,771	.007478	35,368	.006853	7,403	.013267
50–54	62,592	.011998	53,106	.011244	9,486	.019202
55–59	85,994	.018809	74,608	.017965	11,386	.027174
60–64	106,492	.028039	94,252	.027304	12,240	.035376
65–69	122,632	.041458	108,534	.039990	14,098	.057543
70–74	138,250	.061829	125,434	.060684	12,816	.075834
75–79	132,744	.083645	123,104	.084202	9,640	.077120
80–84	103,919	.118900	97,690	.122113	6,229	.084176
85+	90,906	.203825	85,191	.215129	5,715	.114300
Age Unknown	343	—	212	—	131	—

SOURCE: U.S. Bureau of the Census, *Vital Statistics,* 1967, Vol. II, Part A, tables 1–8 and 1–25.

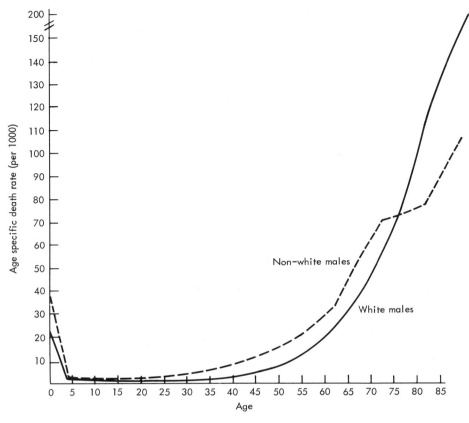

FIGURE 5.1. Age-specific death rates: males, white and nonwhite, U.S., 1967. Source: Table 5.4.

ventionally taken as the number of births during the year. The numerator, which corresponds to those of other age-specific death rates, is restricted to the first year of life, since in this case the category of "infant" is defined as including all ages below the age of one year. Thus:

$$\text{Infant mortality rate} = \frac{\begin{array}{c}\text{Number of deaths of infants}\\ \text{under one year of age in the year}\end{array}}{\text{Number of births in the year}} \times 1,000.$$

Table 5.2 provides us with the data we need for computing U.S. infant mortality rates for 1915, 1935, 1955, 1968, and 1969:

$$1915: \frac{296,000}{2,965,000} \times 1,000 = 99.8 \text{ per thousand,}$$

$$1935: \frac{120,000}{2,377,000} \times 1,000 = 50.5 \text{ per thousand,}$$

$$1955: \frac{107,000}{4,104,000} \times 1,000 = 26.1 \text{ per thousand,}$$

$$1968: \frac{75,000}{3,467,000} \times 1,000 = 21.6 \text{ per thousand,}$$

$$1969: \frac{74,000}{3,571,000} \times 1,000 = 20.7 \text{ per thousand.}$$

3. STANDARDIZATION

It is very often desirable to compare mortality conditions in two different populations or in the same population at two different times. If the schedule of age-specific death rates is known for each of the communities, it is possible to compare the communities by comparing their age-specific death rates for each age-sex category. But the comparison of complete mortality schedules tends to be very detailed and awkward, and it is preferable instead to compare summary measures of mortality conditions.

The crude death rate is an overall summary measure of mortality in a community, and comparison of crude death rates for two communities does enable the researcher to make some inferences about comparative mortality conditions in the respective communities. However, careful analysis of the relationship between the schedule of age-specific death rates and the crude death rate indicates that while the crude death rate is, in fact, an average of the various age-specific death rates, it weights each age-specific death rate by the proportion of the total population in that age-sex category. Thus, the crude death rate measures the overall death rate as it is affected jointly by the age distribution of the population and the mortality schedule. As a consequence, the difference between the crude death rates of two communities may be due either to differences in the schedules of age-specific death rates, or to differences in the age composition of the two populations, or to both.

Consider, for example, a hypothetical population of hypothetical creatures—which we shall name "luvmees." Suppose that, unlike humans, luvmees are quite short-lived; but that, like humans, they have high mortality rates at very youngest ages, low mortality rates midway through life, and high mortality at oldest—for luvmees—ages:

TABLE 5.5

Midyear Population, Deaths, and Death Rates by Age for First Luvmee Population

Age (x)	Midyear Population	Deaths	Age-specific Death Rates
0	2,000	200	.100 (100 per thousand)
1	1,000	25	.025 (25 per thousand)
2	500	200	.400 (400 per thousand)

Consider now a second population of luvmees with different size, age structure, and pattern of deaths:

TABLE 5.6

Midyear Population, Deaths, and Death Rates by Age for Second Luvmee Population

Age (x)	Midyear Population	Deaths	Age-specific Death Rates
0	4,000	300	.075 (75 per thousand)
1	1,000	25	.025 (25 per thousand)
2	2,000	6,000	.300 (30 per thousand)

The age-specific death rates in the second luvmee population are the same or lower than those of the first population—i.e., mortality at each age is the same or higher in the first luvmee population. However, comparisons of mortality in the two populations using the crude death rates computed for each would yield the following results:

TABLE 5.7

	First Luvmee Population	Second Luvmee Population
Total deaths	425	925
Total midyear population	3,500	7,000
Crude death rate	$\frac{425}{3,500} \times 1,000 = 12.14$ per thousand	$\frac{925}{7,000} \times 1,000 = 13.21$ per thousand

The crude death rate in the second luvmee population exceeds that of the first, although mortality rates at each age are the same or lower than those of the first luvmee population. Closer inspection of the computation reveals that this result is due to the fact that the second population has a large proportion of "old"—high mortality risk—luvmees among the total, and a small proportion of "middle-aged"—low mortality risk—luvmees. This difference in age composition is reflected in the composition of the two crude death rates.

This problem of confounding the effects of age composition, sex composition, or other characteristics of a population with those of the mortality schedule may be overcome in large measure by using a procedure called "standardization." Standardization, which is employed quite extensively in demographic studies, controls the effects of composition by applying a schedule of specific rates to a corresponding schedule of population characteristics that has been adopted as the standard for a particular comparison. For example, if the mortality schedules for the U.S. urban and rural populations were applied to the age distribution of the total population of the United States (the latter having been adopted as the standard population), standardized death rates could be determined for the urban and rural populations respectively. An explanation of this procedure follows.

The researcher must first compute and sum over all ages the "expected number of deaths" which *would* occur at each age in the standard population if the standard population were subject to the age-specific death rates of the given population. This computation and summation is done in the following way:

$$
\begin{pmatrix} \text{Expected number of} \\ \text{deaths at ages 0–4} \\ \text{in standard population} \end{pmatrix} = \begin{pmatrix} \text{Number of persons} \\ \text{aged 0–4 in} \\ \text{standard population} \end{pmatrix} \times \begin{pmatrix} \text{Death rate at} \\ \text{ages 0–4 in} \\ \text{given population} \end{pmatrix}
$$

$$
\begin{matrix} \cdot & = & \cdot & \times & \cdot \\ \cdot & = & \cdot & \times & \cdot \\ \cdot & = & \cdot & \times & \cdot \\ \cdot & = & \cdot & \times & \cdot \end{matrix}
$$

$$
\begin{pmatrix} \text{Expected number of} \\ \text{deaths at ages 85 and over,} \\ \text{in standard population} \end{pmatrix} = \begin{pmatrix} \text{Number of persons} \\ \text{aged 85 and over in} \\ \text{standard population} \end{pmatrix} \times \begin{pmatrix} \text{Death rate at ages} \\ \text{85 and over in} \\ \text{given population} \end{pmatrix}
$$

Total expected number of deaths at all ages in standard population if subject to the schedule of age-specific death rates in the given population

The researcher can now determine the "age-standardized" death rate of the given population. The death rate is the product of the crude death rate of the standard population times an adjustment factor consisting of the ratio of (a) the total expected number of deaths in the standard population if subject to the age-specific death rates of the given population and (b) the total actual number of deaths in the standard population.

Returning to the hypothetical populations of "luvmees," we may take the total of the two populations as the Standard Luvmee Population. Adding the midyear populations at each age yields the following age distribution for the Standard Luvmee Population:

TABLE 5.8

Age (x)	Midyear Standard Luvmee Population
0	4,000 + 2,000 = 6,000
1	1,000 + 1,000 = 2,000
2	2,000 + 500 = 2,500
Total	7,000 + 3,500 = 10,500

The number of deaths in the Standard Luvmee Population would be $425 + 925 = 1350$, and the crude death rate of the Standard Luvmee Population would be $\dfrac{1,350}{10,500} \times 1,000 = 12.85$ per thousand. The computation of the standardized death rate for the first and second luvmee populations is shown below:

TABLE 5.9

	First Luvmee Population			Second Luvmee Population	
	Col. (1)	Col. (2)	Col. (3)	Col. (4)	Col. (5)
Age	Standard Luvmee population	Age-specific death rates of first Luvmee population	Expected deaths in standard Luvmee population with rate of first population: Col. (1) x Col. (2)	Age-specific death rates of second Luvmee population	Expected deaths in standard Luvmee population with rate of second population: Col. (1) x Col. (4)
0	6,000	.100	600	.075	450
1	2,000	.025	50	.025	50
2	2,500	.400	1,000	.300	750
Total	10,500		1,650		1,250
Standardized death rate:		$12.85 \times \dfrac{1,650}{1,350} = 15.71$		$12.85 \times \dfrac{1,250}{1,350} = 11.90$	

Thus the standardized death rate for the first luvmee population is 15.71 per thousand, compared to a standardized death rate of 11.90 per thousand for the second luvmee population. This comparison no longer confounds the effects of age differences with those of mortality differences.

Reviewing and generalizing the procedure, we have:

$$\begin{pmatrix}\text{Age-standardized} \\ \text{death rate for} \\ \text{given population}\end{pmatrix} = \begin{pmatrix}\text{Crude death rate} \\ \text{of standard} \\ \text{population}\end{pmatrix} \times \dfrac{\begin{pmatrix}\text{Total expected number} \\ \text{of deaths in standard} \\ \text{population if subject} \\ \text{to the schedule of} \\ \text{age-specific death rates} \\ \text{of given population}\end{pmatrix}}{\begin{pmatrix}\text{Total actual number of} \\ \text{deaths in standard} \\ \text{population}\end{pmatrix}}$$

The comparison of two age-standardized death rates entails the following computations:

$$\begin{pmatrix}\text{Age-standardized} \\ \text{death rate for first} \\ \text{given population}\end{pmatrix} = \begin{pmatrix}\text{Crude death rate} \\ \text{of standard} \\ \text{population}\end{pmatrix} \times \dfrac{\begin{pmatrix}\text{Total expected deaths in} \\ \text{standard population if} \\ \text{subject to age-specific} \\ \text{death rates of first} \\ \text{given population}\end{pmatrix}}{\begin{pmatrix}\text{Total actual number of} \\ \text{deaths in standard} \\ \text{population}\end{pmatrix}}$$

and

$$\begin{pmatrix}\text{Age-standardized} \\ \text{death rate for second} \\ \text{given population}\end{pmatrix} = \begin{pmatrix}\text{Crude death rate} \\ \text{of standard} \\ \text{population}\end{pmatrix} \times \dfrac{\begin{pmatrix}\text{Total expected deaths in} \\ \text{standard population if} \\ \text{subject to age-specific} \\ \text{death rates of second} \\ \text{given population}\end{pmatrix}}{\begin{pmatrix}\text{Total actual number of} \\ \text{deaths in standard} \\ \text{population}\end{pmatrix}}$$

Since (Crude death rate of standard population) has in its denominator (Total actual number of deaths in standard population), it is equivalent and simpler to write the equation as follows:

$$\begin{pmatrix}\text{Age-standardized} \\ \text{death rate for} \\ \text{given population}\end{pmatrix} = \dfrac{\begin{pmatrix}\text{Total expected deaths in standard} \\ \text{population if subject to age-specific} \\ \text{death rates of given population}\end{pmatrix}}{(\text{Total standard population})}$$

This is done in the computation of table 5.10, which uses age-standardized death rates to compare white and nonwhite male mortality in the United States in 1967. Taking the total U.S. male population of 1967 as the standard population, the standardized death rates for white and nonwhite males are 10.5 per thousand and 13.6 per thousand respectively.

TABLE 5.10
Computation of Standardized Death Rates for U.S. White and Nonwhite Males, 1967

Age (1)	Standard Population = Total U.S. Males, 1 July 1967 (2)	White Male Age-Specific Death Rates, 1967 (3)	[Col. (2)] x [Col. (3)] Expected Deaths in Std. Pop. on Basis of White Male Rates (4)	Nonwhite Male Age- Specific Death Rates, 1967 (5)	[Col. (2)] x [Col. (5)] Expected Deaths in Std. Pop. on Basis of Nonwhite Male Rates (6)
0–1	1,806,000	.022362	40,386	.038814	70,098
1–4	7,988,000	.000849	6,783	.001519	12,135
5–9	10,642,000	.000548	4,874	.000658	7,002
10–14	10,101,000	.000488	4,929	.000660	6,667
15–19	8,909,000	.001402	12,490	.001878	16,731
20–24	7,042,000	.001830	12,887	.003321	23,386
25–29	5,875,000	.001610	9,459	.004221	24,798
30–34	5,323,000	.001790	9,528	.005411	28,803
35–39	5,609,000	.002635	14,780	.007072	39,667
40–44	5,992,000	.004123	24,705	.009938	59,548
45–49	5,719,000	.006853	39,192	.013267	75,874
50–54	5,217,000	.011244	58,660	.019202	100,177
55–59	4,572,000	.017965	82,136	.027174	124,240
60–64	3,798,000	.027304	103,701	.035376	134,358
65–69	2,958,000	.039990	118,290	.057543	170,212
70–74	2,236,000	.060684	135,689	.075834	169,565
75–79	1,587,000	.084202	133,629	.077120	122,389
80–84	874,000	.122113	106,726	.084176	73,570
85 and over	446,000	.215129	95,948	.114300	50,978
Total – all ages	96,695,000		1,014,793		1,310,198

$$\frac{\text{White Male}}{\text{Standardized Death Rate}} = \frac{\Sigma\,[\text{Column (4)}]}{\Sigma\,[\text{Column (2)}]} \times 1{,}000 = \frac{1{,}014{,}793}{96{,}695{,}000} \times 1{,}000 = 10.495$$

$$\frac{\text{Nonwhite Male}}{\text{Standardized Death Rate}} = \frac{\Sigma\,[\text{Column (6)}]}{\Sigma\,[\text{Column (2)}]} \times 1{,}000 = \frac{1{,}310{,}198}{96{,}695{,}000} \times 1{,}000 = 13.558$$

SOURCE: Figures in column (2) from table 5.3; figures in columns (3) and (5) from table 5.4.

The symbols at the bottom of table 5.10 of the form

$$\frac{\Sigma\,[\text{column (4)}]}{\Sigma\,[\text{column (2)}]}$$

mean:

$$\frac{\text{Summation of all the values in column (4)}}{\text{Summation of all the values in column (2)}}$$

which equals:

$$\frac{40,386 + 6,783 + \cdots + 133,629 + 106,726 + 95,948}{1,806,000 + 7,988,000 + \cdots + 1,587,000 + 874,000 + 446,000}$$

but these sums are themselves given at the bottoms of the respective columns:

$$\Sigma \text{ [column (4)]} = 1,014,793$$

and

$$\Sigma \text{ [column (2)]} = 96,695,000$$

4. LIFE EXPECTANCY AND THE LIFE TABLE

By using a mathematical model called a life table (sometimes called a mortality table), it can be shown that with any given schedule of age-specific death rates there is associated an average number of years of life remaining to persons born and similarly an average number of years remaining to persons of each subsequent age. The average number of years of life remaining to persons born into the population is conventionally called the "expectation of life at birth" or "life expectancy at birth."

We return again to the hypothetical creatures, our friends, the luvmees. Consider now the lives, times, and deaths of one thousand luvmees born at exactly the same moment, and suppose that of the total born:

200 die in the first year of life, i.e., before reaching their first birthday.

100 die in the second year of life, i.e., they survive the first year, reach their first birthday, but die before reaching their second birthday.

350 die in the third year of life, i.e., they survive the first two years, reach their second birthday, but die before reaching their third birthday.

350, i.e., all the rest, die in the fourth year of life, before reaching their fourth birthday.

The pattern of survival to each age, and of mortality, at each age until the entire luvmee group—or birth cohort—dies can be summarized in table 5.11.

By relating the number dying at each age to the number surviving to the beginning of the age interval—i.e., for each age dividing the entry of col. (2) by the entry of col. (1), we can compute the proportion dying

TABLE 5.11

*Survivors and Deaths, by Age, in a Cohort of
1,000 Luvmees Born at the Same Time*

Exact Age in Years	Number of Luvmees Surviving to Exact Age (x) (1)	Number of Luvmees Dying at Age (x)* (2)
0	1,000	200
1	800	100
2	700	350
3	350	350
4	0	

*I.e., after reaching exact age (x) and before reaching exact age (x + 1)

at each age, or the "probability of dying" at each age for persons surviving to the beginning of the age interval:

TABLE 5.12

Exact Age in Years (x)	Survivors to Age (x) (1) l_x	Number Dying at Age (x) (2) d_x	For Persons Surviving to Age (x): The Probability of Dying Before Reaching Age (x+1) = Col. (2) ÷ Col. (1) (3) q_x
0	1,000	200	.200
1	800	100	.125
2	700	350	.500
3	350	350	1.000
4	0		

The number of survivors to exact age x is conventionally denoted l_x. The number dying at age x is denoted d_x; and the probability of dying at age x is conventionally denoted q_x.

Consider, now, the number of life-years lived by the entire luvmee cohort at exact age 0 years (i.e., before the first birthday). Those surviving the first year and reaching their first birthday each live a full life-year at age 0 years, i.e., 800 life years in all. In addition, those dying in the first year of life (before reaching their first birthday) also live partial life-years at age 0 years. If the 200 deaths in the first year of life are spread evenly throughout the year, we might assume that luvmees dying in the first year of life live on the average one-half year each. Then, altogether 100 additional life-years at age 0 are lived by those dying before their first birthday. For the total cohort, then, the total number of life-years at age 0 is 800 + 100 = 900 life-years. (See Table 5.13.)

By similar reasoning, the total number of life-years lived by the cohort of luvmees in the second year, i.e., at age 1 year, totals 750 life years (700 for those surviving to exact age 2 years + 50 for those dying at age 1 year). The number of life-years at age 2 years is 525 years and at age 3 years the total life-years lived is 175 years. The number of life-years lived by the total birth cohort at age x is conventionally denoted L_x.

The number of life-years lived by the cohort of luvmees at age 3 years is also the number of life-years lived by the cohort between the time it reaches age 3 years and the time that the entire cohort dies out. The number of life-years lived by the luvmee cohort between the time it reaches age 2 years and the time that the entire cohort dies out is, then, (525 years at age 2 years + 175 years at age 3 years) = 700 years. Similarly the number of life-years lived by the cohort at age 1 year and all subsequent ages is (750 + 525 + 175) = 1450 years; and the total number of life-years lived by the luvmee cohort at all ages—i.e., from birth until all have died, is simply the summation of the L_x or life years column for all ages: (900 + 750 + 525 + 175) = 2350 years. The computation of life years left to the cohort of luvmees from a given age, x, until all die, is conventionally denoted T_x.

Consider, finally, the group of luvmees surviving to exact age 3 years. Recalling (1) that there are 350 survivors to age 3 years, and (2) that the total number of life years remaining to the cohort at age 3 and all subsequent ages—until all are dead—is 175 years, it is easy to calculate the *average remaining years of life* per luvmee surviving to age 3 years:

$$\frac{175}{350} = \frac{1}{2} \text{ year.}$$

TABLE 5.13

Exact Age in Years (x)	Survivors to Age (x)	Number Dying at Age (x)	Probability of Dying at Age (x)	Life-Years Lived by Cohort At Age (x)	At Age (x) and All Subsequent Ages
	(1)	(2)	(3)	(4)	(5)
	l_x	d_x	q_x	L_x	T_x
0	1,000	200	.200	900	2,350
1	800	100	.125	750	1,450
2	700	350	.500	525	700
3	350	350	1.000	175	175
4	0				

Similarly, for 700 luvmees surviving to exact age 2 years (read from the l_x column) there are 700 life-years remaining at age 2 and all subsequent ages (read from the T_x column), or an average remaining life-time of 1 year. The number of life years remaining to the survivors of the cohort at age 1 year and thereafter is 1450 years, with the survivors numbering 800 luvmees. Thus the average remaining lifetime for luvmees reaching 1 year of age is:

$$\frac{1450}{800} = 1.81 \text{ years approximately.}$$

Finally, for luvmees reaching age 0, i.e., for the initial cohort at birth numbering 1000 luvmees, the total number of life years remaining to be lived by the cohort at age 0 years and at all subsequent ages until the entire cohort dies out is 2,350 years. Thus the average remaining lifetime for a luvmee *at birth* is:

$$\frac{2350}{1000} \text{ years, or 2.35 years.}$$

This number is called the "expectation of life at birth" or "life expectancy" for luvmees.

The "average remaining lifetime" at age 1 year, 2 years, and so forth is similarly called "expectation of future life" at age 1 year, at age 2 years, and so on. The expectation of future life at a given age, x, or the average number of years of life remaining to those surviving to a given age, x, and calculated in this way, is conventionally denoted e_x. Thus the "life table" describing the pattern of attrition of the hypothetical cohort of hypothetical luvmees shows, at each age, the number of survivors; the number dying; the probability of dying; the number of life-years lived by the cohort; the number of life-years lived by the cohort at this and at all subsequent ages—including the *total* life-years for the cohort at all ages; and the average number of life-years remaining to survivors. (See Table 5.14.)

We turn now briefly to the use of "life expectation" in mortality analysis and return later to the construction and interpretation of life tables.

Comparison of Life Expectancy

The expectation of life at birth is dependent upon the entire schedule of age-specific death rates, but it is entirely *independent* of the age structure of the population in which these death rates are observed.

TABLE 5.14
Life Table for Hypothetical Luvmee Population

| | | | | Life-Years Lived by Cohort | | Average Life- |
| | Survivors | Number Dying | Probability of Dying | At Age (x) | At Age (x) and All Subsequent Ages | Years Remaining to Survivors |
Age x	l_x	d_x	q_x	L_x	T_x	e_x
0	1,000	200	.200	900	2,350	2.35
1	800	100	.125	750	1,450	1.81
2	700	350	.500	525	700	1.00
3	350	350	1.000	175	175	0.50

Hence, expectation of life at birth is frequently employed as a summary measure of mortality conditions prevailing in a community, and it is often used in conjunction with the same measure for a different community so that mortality conditions in the two communities can be compared.

Comparisons of the future life expectancy of males and females of selected ages in the United States and Togo are shown in table 5.15. The table shows not only that expectation of life is higher among women than among men in both countries, but that the mortality differences between a "developed" population are smaller among women (see bottom panel). It is in infant mortality that the patterns of the two countries differ most.

In addition to the uses described above, computations of life expectancy at birth and at subsequent ages as implied by a given schedule of age-specific death rates are widely employed by insurance companies, social security administrations, and other agencies concerned with longevity and its measurement.

Life Table Functions

Our discussion of the computation of life tables and their functions will be brief. To begin with, the functions conventionally computed are—

q_x: for persons reaching exact age x, the probability of dying before reaching exact age $x + 1$;

l_x: in a "life table population," the number of survivors reaching exact age x. In such a population, l_0 is the number of persons born, and this number is conventionally taken as 100,000 or 1,000,000;

d_x: the number of persons dying between exact ages x and $x + 1$ (equal to $q_x \times l_x$);

L_x: in a "life table population," the number alive in the age group x to $x + 1$, conventionally called the "stationary population" aged x.

T_x: in a life table population, the number alive in the age group x to $x + 1$ *and* in all older age groups. The computation for this is:

$$T_x = \sum_{a = x}^{\infty} L_a.$$

This is the summation, Σ, of all values, L_a of the stationary population beginning with the x-th age group symbolized by

TABLE 5.15
Expectation of Future Life at Selected Ages,
by Sex: U.S., 1967, Togo, 1961

Age	United States, 1967		Togo, 1961	
	Males	*Females*	*Males*	*Females*
0	67.0	74.2	31.6	38.5
1	67.7	74.6	36.4	42.9
5	63.9	70.9	40.1	47.2
10	59.1	66.0	37.4	44.3
15	54.2	61.1	33.8	40.4
20	49.6	56.3	30.3	37.8
25	45.1	51.5	28.4	34.1
30	40.5	46.7	25.5	31.3
35	35.9	41.9	22.5	28.1
40	31.4	37.3	19.7	24.7
45	27.1	32.8	17.1	21.4
50	23.1	28.4	14.2	18.5
55	19.3	24.2	11.6	15.4
60	16.0	20.2	8.5	11.9
65	13.0	16.4	6.6	10.1
70	10.4	13.0	6.7	7.2
75	8.3	10.0	5.0	5.0
80	6.4	7.3	—	—
85	4.7	5.0	—	—

Expectation of Life of Togo Population as
Percentage of U.S. Expectation of Life,
Selected Ages

Age	Males	Females
0	47.2	51.9
10	63.3	67.1
20	61.1	67.1
30	63.0	67.0
40	62.7	66.2
50	61.5	65.1
60	53.1	58.9
70	64.4	55.4

SOURCE: U.N. *Demographic Yearbook 1969* (1970), table 46.

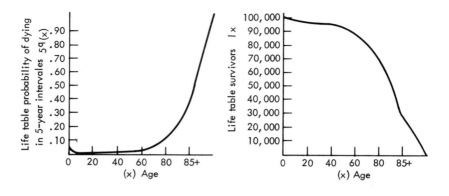

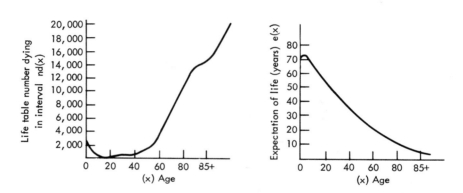

FIGURE 5.2.   Life table functions by age, U.S., 1966.

$(a = x)$ and continuing through all higher age groups until none remain alive, symbolized by $(a = \infty)$. In particular, T_0, the number in the entire life table population, is computed as:

$$T_o = \sum_{a = 0}^{\infty} L_a.$$

e_x: the average number of years of life remaining to persons surviving to exact age x. (The computation for this is:

$$e(x) = \frac{T_x}{l_x}.$$

In particular, e_o, computed as:

$$e_o = \frac{T_o}{l_o},$$

is the expectation of future life at *birth,* a very important and widely used summary index of mortality.)

In addition to these functions, rates of survival are often computed as probabilities of the form

$$\frac{L_{x+k}}{L_x} \quad \text{or} \quad \frac{l_{x+j}}{l_x}.$$

The first ratio gives the probability that persons in the *age group x* to *x + 1* will survive an additional *k* years to reach *age group x + k* to *x + k + 1*. The second ratio gives the probability that persons *surviving to exact age x* will live an additional *j* years and *survive to exact age x + j.*

More specialized texts show that *all* the values of the different life table functions are uniquely associated with the schedule of age-specific death rates. Thus, a given set of age-specific death rates uniquely determines the expectation of life at birth, e_o; the size, T_o, and age distribution of the stationary population, L_x; the various survival and mortality probabilities, and so on. Table 5.16 shows an example of a recent United States life table.

5. THE ABRIDGED LIFE TABLE

In contrast to a "complete life table," an abridged life table contains all the usual functions for *age groups* rather than for single years of age. Conventionally, the first age group is much narrower than the others; thus, an abridged life table for five-year age groups would probably include age groups 0–1, 1–4, 5–9, 10–14, and so on. For most purposes of demographic analysis, abridged life tables are sufficiently detailed. The functions in such a table are—

$_nq_x$: for persons reaching exact age *x*, the probability of dying before reaching age *x + n;*

l_x: the number of survivors reaching exact age *x*, as in the complete life table;

$_nd_x$: the number of persons dying between exact ages x and (*x + n*). This is computed by multiplying $_nq_x$ by l_x.

$_nL_x$: in a life table population, the number alive in the age group *x* to (*x + n*), called the "stationary population" in the age group *x* to (*x + n*) ;

TABLE 5.16

Life Table for White Males: United States, 1959-61

Age Interval	Proportion Dying	Of 100,000 Born Alive		Stationary Population		Average Remaining Lifetime
	Proportion of persons alive at beginning of age interval dying during interval	Number living at beginning of age interval	Number dying during age interval	In the age interval	In this and all subsequent age intervals	Average number of years of life remaining at beginning of age interval
Period of life between two ages (1)	(2)	(3)	(4)	(5)	(6)	(7)
x to $x + t$	$_tq_x$	l_x	$_td_x$	$_tL_x$	T_x	S_x
Days						
0-1	0.01079	100,000	1,079	272	6,754,846	67.55
1-3	.00509	98,921	503	540	6,754,574	68.28
3-28	.00392	98,418	386	6,722	6,754,034	68.63
28-365	.00636	98,032	624	90,230	6,747,312	68.83
Years						
0-1	.02592	100,000	2,592	97,764	6,754,846	67.55
1-2	.00153	97,408	149	97,334	6,657,082	68.34
2-3	.00101	97,259	99	97,210	6,559,748	67.45
3-4	.00081	97,160	78	97,121	6,462,538	66.51
4-5	.00069	97,082	67	97,048	6,365,417	65.57
5-6	.00062	97,015	60	96,985	6,268,369	64.61
6-7	.00057	96,955	55	96,927	6,171,384	63.65
7-8	.00053	96,900	52	96,874	6,074,457	62.69
8-9	.00049	96,848	47	96,825	5,977,583	61.72
9-10	.00045	96,801	43	96,779	5,880,758	60.75
10-11	.00042	96,758	40	96,738	5,783,979	59.78
11-12	.00042	96,718	40	96,698	4,687,241	58.80
12-13	.00047	96,678	46	96,655	5,590,543	57.83
13-14	.00059	96,632	56	96,604	5,493,888	56.85
14-15	.00075	96,576	73	96,539	5,397,284	55.89
15-16	.00093	96,503	90	96,458	5,300,745	54.93
16-17	.00111	96,413	107	96,359	5,204,287	53.98
17-18	.00126	96,306	121	96,246	5,107,928	53.04
18-19	.00139	96,185	134	96,118	5,011,682	52.10
19-20	.00149	96,051	143	95,979	4,915,564	51.18
20-21	.00159	95,908	153	95,831	4,819,585	50.25
21-22	.00169	95,755	162	95,674	4,723,754	49.33
22-23	.00174	95,593	167	95,509	4,628,080	48.41
23-24	.00172	95,426	163	95,345	4,532,571	47.50
24-25	.00165	95,263	157	95,184	4,437,226	46.58
25-26	.00156	95,106	149	95,032	4,342,042	45.65
26-27	.00149	94,957	141	94,887	4,247,010	44.73
27-28	.00145	94,816	137	94,747	4,152,123	43.79
28-29	.00145	94,679	137	94,611	4,057,376	42.85
29-30	.00149	94,542	141	94,471	3,962,765	41.92
30-31	.00156	94,401	147	94,327	3,868,294	40.98
31-32	.00163	94,254	154	94,177	3,773,967	40.04
32-33	.00171	94,100	161	94,020	3,679,790	39.10
33-34	.00181	93,939	170	93,855	3,585,770	38.17
34-35	.00193	93,769	180	93,679	3,491,915	37.24
35-36	.00207	93,589	194	93,491	3,398,236	36.31
36-37	.00225	93,395	210	93,290	3,304,745	35.38
37-38	.00246	93,185	229	93,070	3,211,455	34.46
38-39	.00270	92,956	251	92,830	3,118,385	33.55
39-40	.00299	92,705	278	92,566	3,025,555	32.64

TABLE 5.16
Life Table for White Males: United States, 1959-61 (continued)

Age Interval	Proportion Dying	Of 100,000 Born Alive		Stationary Population		Average Remaining Lifetime
Period of life between two ages	Proportion of persons alive at beginning of age interval dying during interval	Number living at beginning of age interval	Number dying during age interval	In the age interval	In this and all subsequent age intervals	Average number of years of life remaining at beginning of age interval
(1)	(2)	(3)	(4)	(5)	(6)	(7)
x to $x + t$	$_tq_x$	l_x	$_td_x$	$_tL_x$	T_x	S_x
Years						
40–41	.00332	92,427	306	92,274	2,932,989	31.73
41–42	.00368	92,121	339	91,952	2,840,715	30.84
42–43	.00409	91,782	376	91,594	2,748,763	29.95
43–44	.00454	91,406	415	91,198	2,657,169	29.07
44–45	.00504	90,991	458	90,762	2,565,971	28.20
45–46	.00558	90,533	505	90,280	2,475,209	27.34
46–47	.00617	90,028	556	89,751	2,384,929	26.49
47–48	.00686	89,472	613	89,165	2,295,178	25.65
48–49	.00766	88,859	681	88,519	2,206,013	24.83
49–50	.00856	88,178	754	87,801	2,117,494	24.01
50–51	.00955	87,424	835	87,007	2,029,693	23.22
51–52	.01058	86,589	916	86,131	1,942,686	22.44
52–53	.01162	85,673	995	85,176	1,856,555	21.67
53–54	.01264	84,678	1,071	84,142	1,771,379	20.92
54–55	.01368	83,607	1,144	83,035	1,687,237	20.18
55–56	.01475	82,463	1,216	81,855	1,604,202	19.45
56–57	.01593	81,247	1,295	80,599	1,522,347	18.74
57–58	.01730	79,952	1,383	79,261	1,441,748	18.03
58–59	.01891	78,569	1,486	77,826	1,362,487	17.34
59–60	.02074	77,083	1,598	76,284	1,284,661	16.67
60–61	.02271	75,485	1,714	74,628	1,208,377	16.01
61–62	.02476	73,771	1,827	72,858	1,133,749	15.37
62–63	.02690	71,944	1,935	70,976	1,060,891	14.75
63–64	.02912	70,009	2,039	68,990	989,915	14.14
64–65	.03143	67,970	2,136	66,902	920,925	13.55
65–66	.03389	65,834	2,231	64,718	854,023	12.97
66–67	.03652	63,603	2,323	62,441	789,305	12.41
67–68	.03930	61,280	2,409	60,076	726,864	11.86
68–69	.04225	58,871	2,487	57,627	666,788	11.33
69–70	.04538	56,384	2,559	55,105	609,161	10.80
70–71	.04871	53,825	2,621	52,514	554,056	10.29
71–72	.05230	51,204	2,678	49,865	501,542	9.80
72–73	.05623	48,526	2,729	47,161	451,677	9.31
73–74	.06060	45,797	2,775	44,410	404,516	8.83
74–75	.06542	43,022	2,815	41,615	360,106	8.37
75–76	.07066	40,207	2,841	38,786	318,491	7.92
76–77	.07636	37,366	2,853	35,940	279,705	7.49
77–78	.08271	34,513	2,855	33,086	243,765	7.06
78–79	.08986	31,658	2,844	30,236	210,679	6.65
79–80	.09788	28,814	2,821	27,403	180,443	6.26
80–81	.10732	25,993	2,789	24,599	153,040	5.89
81–82	.11799	23,204	2,738	21,835	128,441	5.54
82–83	.12895	20,466	2,639	19,146	106,606	5.21
83–84	.13920	17,827	2,482	16,586	87,460	4.91
84–85	.14861	15,345	2,280	14,205	70,874	4.62
85–86	.16039	13,065	2,096	12,017	56,669	4.34
86–87	.17303	10,969	1,898	10,020	44,652	4.07

TABLE 5.16
Life Table for White Males: United States, 1959–61 (continued)

Age Interval	Proportion Dying	Of 100,000 Born Alive		Stationary Population		Average Remaining Lifetime
Period of life between two ages	Proportion of persons alive at beginning of age interval dying during interval	Number living at beginning of age interval	Number dying during age interval	In the age interval	In this and all subsequent age intervals	Average number of years of life remaining at beginning of age interval
(1)	(2)	(3)	(4)	(5)	(6)	(7)
x to $x + t$	$_t q_x$	l_x	$_t d_x$	$_t L_x$	T_x	S_x

Years						
87–88	.18665	9,071	1,693	8,225	34,632	3.82
88–89	.20194	7,378	1,490	6,633	26,407	3.58
89–90	.21877	5,888	1,288	5,244	19,774	3.36
90–91	.23601	4,600	1,086	4,058	14,530	3.16
91–92	.25289	3,514	888	3,070	10,472	2.98
92–93	.26973	2,626	709	2,271	7,402	2.82
93–94	.28612	1,917	548	1,643	5,131	2.68
94–95	.30128	1,369	413	1,163	3,488	2.55
95–96	.31416	956	300	806	2,325	2.43
96–97	.32915	656	216	548	1,519	2.32
97–98	.34450	440	152	364	971	2.21
98–99	.36018	288	103	237	607	2.10
99–100	.37616	185	70	150	370	2.01
100–101	.39242	115	45	92	220	1.91
101–102	.40891	70	29	56	128	1.83
102–103	.42562	41	17	32	72	1.75
103–104	.44250	24	11	19	40	1.67
104–105	.45951	13	6	10	21	1.60
105–106	.47662	7	3	6	11	1.53
106–107	.49378	4	2	2	5	1.46
107–108	.51095	2	1	2	3	1.40
108–109	.52810	1	1	0	1	1.35
109–110	.54519·	0	0	1	1	1.29

T_x: in a life table population, the number alive at ages x and over, as in the complete life table;

e_x: the expectation of life remaining to persons surviving to exact age x, as in the complete life table.

Using the data in tables 5.3 and 5.4, we have constructed an abridged life table for the total male population of the United States in 1967 (see worksheet C). Such a table is computed as follows.

1. The symbol x refers to exact age. Some of the functions in the table refer to these exact ages, while others refer to the interval between an exact age and the exact starting age of the next age group. The number of ages in an age group is denoted by the subscript n, which is placed in front of the symbol for the function being considered, e.g., $_n q_x$, $_n d_x$, $_n L_x$.

WORKSHEET C
Abridged Life Table for Total U.S. Male Population, 1967

(x)	n	$_nm_{(x)}$	$_nq_{(x)}$	$l_{(x)}$	$_nd_{(x)}$	$_nL_{(x)}$	$T_{(x)}$	$e_{(x)}$
0	1	.025162	.024849	100,000	2,485	98,261	6,890,920	68.91
1	4	.000958	.003825	97,515	373	389,314	6,792,659	69.66
5	5	.000488	.002434	97,142	236	485,120	6,403,345	65.92
10	5	.000512	.002557	96,906	248	483,910	5,918,225	61.07
15	5	.001464	.006648	96,658	643	481,683	5,434,315	56.22
20	5	.002008	.009990	96,015	959	477,678	4,952,632	51.58
25	5	.001909	.009500	95,056	903	473,023	4,474,954	47.08
30	5	.002198	.010930	94,153	1,029	468,193	4,001,931	42.50
35	5	.003115	.015455	93,124	1,439	462,023	3,533,738	37.95
40	5	.004718	.023315	91,685	2,138	453,080	3,071,715	33.50
45	5	.007478	.036693	89,547	3,286	439,520	2,618,635	29.24
50	5	.011998	.058243	86,261	5,024	418,745	2,179,115	26.49
55	5	.018809	.089821	81,237	7,297	412,943	1,760,370	21.67
60	5	.028039	.131011	83,940	10,997	392,208	1,347,427	16.05
65	5	.041458	.187823	72,943	13,700	330,465	955,219	13.10
70	5	.061829	.261521	59,243	15,493	257,483	624,754	10.55
75	5	.083645	.345894	43,750	15,133	180,918	367,271	8.39
80	5	.118900	.458277	28,617	13,115	110,298	186,353	6.51
85	?	.203825	1.000000	15,502	15,502	76,055	76,055	4.91

SOURCE: Tables 5.3 and 5.4.

2. Attention must be paid to the size of each age interval, that is, to the number of ages n included in each age group. This number need not be the same for all age groups, and it appears in some of the formulae used to compute certain functions. The number of n is unspecified in the last line of the table.

3. Detailed data on age-specific mortality are necessary for the computation of a life table. If a schedule of age-specific death rates, $_nm_x$, is not available, rates must be computed by dividing, at each age, the number of deaths in a given period by the mean population in the same period, as indicated above in section 2. Thus:

$$_nm_x = \frac{_nD_x}{_nP_x}.$$

Referring to tables 5.3 and 5.4 for number of deaths and mean population respectively, we compute the death rate for ages 25–29 as follows:

$$_5m_{25-29} = \frac{11,217}{5,875,000} = .001909.$$

4. The age-specific death rates must now be transformed into probabilities of dying within a given age interval, $_nq_x$. There are several, more or less accurate, formulae for computing the probability of dying on the basis of age-specific death rates. The one suggested here is:

$$_nq_x = \frac{n_n m_x}{1 + \dfrac{n}{2} n_n m_x}.$$

Thus, in our worksheet, the probability that persons reaching age 1 will die before reaching age 5 is computed as follows:

$$_4q_1 = \frac{4 \times .000958}{1 + \dfrac{4}{2} \times .000958} = \frac{.003832}{1.001916} = .003825$$

It is assumed that the probability of dying after the last age listed in the table is 1, i.e., that death is certain in the interval following that age.

5. The initial life table population, l_0, is conventionally taken as some power of 10, i.e., 10,000 or 100,000 or 1,000,000. The number of deaths in the first interval, usually the first year, $_1d_0$, between exact age 0 and prior to reaching exact age 1, is obtained by multiplying the initial life table population, l_0, by the probability of dying before reaching the next age, $_1q_0$:

$$_1d_0 = l_0 \, _1q_0 = 100,000 \times .024849 = 2485 \text{ in our worksheet}$$

$$\cdot$$
$$\cdot$$
$$\cdot$$

$$_nd_x = l_x \, _nq_x$$

6. The number of survivors to a given age, l_x, is obtained by subtracting the number dying in the age interval prior to (x) from the number surviving to the previous age:

$$l_1 = l_0 - _1d_0 = l_0 - l_0 \, _1q_0$$
$$l_5 = l_1 - _4d_1 = l_1 - l_1 \, _4q_1$$
$$l_{10} = l_5 - _5d_5 = l_5 - l_5 \, _5q_5$$
$$\cdot$$
$$\cdot$$
$$\cdot$$
$$l_{x+n} = l_x - _nd_x = l_x - l_x \, _nq_x$$

Thus, substituting in the above equations, we have in our worksheet:

$$l_1 = 100,000 - 2485 = 97,515;$$
$$l_5 = 97,515 - 373 = 97,142;$$
etc.

The last computation indicates that by five years of age, 97,142 out of an original cohort of 100,000 will have survived. Note that at the beginning of the highest age listed in the table, there are still survivors, so that, in our example, $l_{85} > 0$.

7. The number of deaths in each age interval, $_nd_x$, is obtained by multiplying the number surviving to the beginning of the age interval l_x, by the probability, $_nq_x$, of dying before reaching the end of the interval. In our worksheet, these are computed:

$$_1d_0 = l_0 \ _1q_0 = (100{,}000) \ (.024849) = 2485$$
$$_4d_1 = l_1 \ _4q_1 = (\ 97{,}515) \ (.003825) = \ 373$$

.

.

.

$$_nd_x = l_x \ _nq_x$$

8. The number of years spent between two consecutive ages listed in the table (the life table population in the corresponding age groups), denoted $_n L_x$, can be computed as an average of the survivors at the beginning and at the end of the period, multiplied by the number of years in the age group.

$$_n L_x = \frac{n}{2} \ (l_x + l_{x+n})$$

For example:

$$_4 L_1 = \frac{4}{2} \ (97{,}515 + 97{,}142) = 389{,}314$$

The computation shows 389,314 persons in the stationary population at ages 1 to 4. This procedure assumes a linearity in the mortality function that is not always realistic, especially at the lowest and highest age groups. Accordingly, for these groups different procedures are used. L_0 can be computed as a weighted average between l_0 and l_1 ensuring that the decrease in the initial life table population is rapid at the beginning rather than at the end of the first year of life. The following weights are suggested on the basis of empirical experience:

$$L_0 = .3 \times l_0 + .71_1$$

In worksheet C:

$$L_0 = .3 \times 100{,}000 + .7 \times 97{,}515 = 30{,}000 + 68{,}261 = 98{,}261.$$

For the last line in the table, where the number of years in the age group is unknown, there are different possible solutions. T. N. Greville's (1943) method, which we shall adopt, is to compute

$$\infty L_x = \frac{l_x}{\infty m_x} = T_x$$

for the last age group, where the symbol ∞ indicates that the last groups are open-ended age categories.

9. The number of persons living after a given age—i.e., the life table population older than that given age—is represented by T_x. It is computed by summing the consecutive values of $_n L_x$. Summation starts from the bottom line of the table, at the terminal age group, where at other ages,

$$T_x = {}_n L_x.$$

$$T_x = \sum_{a=x}^{\infty} {}_n L_a.$$

Thus, in worksheet C, the life table population older than 75 is computed as follows:

$$T_{75} = 76{,}055 + 110{,}298 + 180{,}918 = 367{,}271.$$

10. The average expectation of future life for those surviving to exact age x, denoted as e_x, is obtained by dividing the number of persons living after that age, T_x, by the number of survivors at that age. The computation for e_x is:

$$e_x = \frac{T_x}{l_x}.$$

In worksheet C:

$$e_{50} = \frac{2{,}179{,}115}{86{,}261} = 26.49$$

This indicates that those in the life table population who have survived to age 50 have an average expectation of 26.49 more years of life.

Theoretical Significance of the Life Table

Aside from its practical importance for the analysis of mortality rates and life expectancy, the life table is of considerable theoretical significance in the study of population dynamics and in the analysis of relationships between the synchronic (current, or momentary) and dia-chronic (dynamic, or processual) dimensions of populations and societies. With the help of the life table, it is readily seen that, for a fixed regime of annual fertility, the fixed operation over some minimal period of time of a given schedule of mortality rates generates an associated size and age structure of the population. Thus, under the assumptions of—

a. a given annual number of births in the population, fixed over an indefinite period of time, and

b. a given schedule of age-specific death rates, fixed over an indefinite period of time,

the population so generated has a specified and unchanging total size and a specified and unchanging age distribution. Accordingly, this population which is theoretically generated by the operation of (a) and (b) in association with an observed schedule of age-specific death rates is called the "stationary population" associated with the schedule of death rates. The *differences* in the size and age structure of the population implied by differences in mortality conditions may be studied by referring to the columns of the respective life tables (one table being based on the first schedule of death rates, and the other on a different schedule of rates). Similarly, the temporal *changes* in size and age structure implied by changing mortality conditions may also be studied via the comparison of life tables.

6. FERTILITY ANALYSIS

As in the measurement of mortality, the chief focus in the measurement of fertility is the frequency of incidence of a vital event—in this case births—among the population exposed to the risk of that event. Certain analogies to the measurement of mortality will be immediately evident in the measurement of fertility.

Crude Birth Rate and Crude Rate of Natural Increase

The simplest measure of fertility is the crude birth rate, which is thoroughly analogous to the crude death rate. Thus:

$$\text{Crude birth rate} = \frac{\text{Number of births during the year}}{\text{Average or midyear population}} \times 1{,}000$$

Using data from table 5.2, we can compute crude birth rates for the United States for 1915, 1935, 1955, 1968, and 1969:

$$1915: \frac{2,965,000}{100,549,000} \times 1,000 = 29.5 \text{ per thousand}$$

$$1935: \frac{2,377,000}{127,250,000} \times 1,000 = 18.7 \text{ per thousand}$$

$$1955: \frac{4,104,000}{165,069,000} \times 1,000 = 24.9 \text{ per thousand}$$

$$1968: \frac{3,502,000}{199,870,000} \times 1,000 = 17.5 \text{ per thousand}$$

$$1969: \frac{3,571,000}{201,921,000} \times 1,000 = 17.7 \text{ per thousand}$$

The difference between the crude birth rate and the crude death rate is called the *crude rate of natural increase* and is a widely used measure of population growth. In the second section of this chapter we calculated the crude death rates in the U.S. for the same years as above, also using data from table 5.2. With these two sets of data—crude birth and crude death rates—we can compute crude rates of natural increase for the corresponding years:

1915: 16.3 per thousand
1935: 7.8 per thousand
1955: 15.6 per thousand
1968: 7.9 per thousand
1969: 8.2 per thousand

Figure 5.3 shows recent trends in crude rates of natural increase for selected countries. Note that rate of natural increases for Ceylon, Mauritius, Singapore, and Mexico were initially—in 1959—very much higher than those of the United States and of the European countries shown. But only the rate for Mexico has remained at its initial high level, with that for the other non-European populations shown moving in a downward direction in the period shown. We return to more detailed discussion of components of population growth in Part II.

General Fertility Rate

It is obvious, of course, that the entire population is not exposed to the "risk" of births. For example, a theoretical population composed entirely of males, very young girls, and very old women would be exposed to no risk at all, and a population including a large proportion of women of childbearing age would be exposed to substantially greater

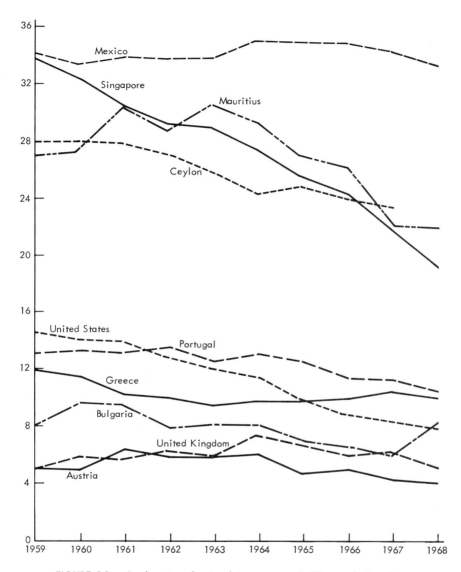

FIGURE 5.3. Crude rates of natural increase per 1,000 population. Source: Population Index, July–September 1969.

"risk" than one with a smaller proportion. This being the case, the measurement of fertility can be refined considerably by limiting the denominator to the population more directly "exposed to risk," namely, the female population in the reproductive ages. Thus, we have a second sim-

TABLE 5.17
Births by Age and Color of Mother, U.S., 1967

Age of Mother	Total	White	Nonwhite
Total: all ages	3,520,959	2,922,502	598,547
Under 15	8,593	2,761	5,832
15–19	596,445	435,239	161,206
20–24	1,310,588	1,116,686	193,902
25–29	867,426	749,997	117,429
30–34	439,373	370,069	69,304
35–39	227,323	189,322	38,001
40–44	67,053	55,045	12,008
45–49	4,158	3,383	775

SOURCE: U.S., *Vital Statistics, 1967* (1969a: Vol. I Natality).

ple rate, the general fertility rate:

$$\begin{array}{c} \text{General} \\ \text{fertility} \\ \text{rate} \end{array} = \frac{\text{Number of births during the year}}{\begin{array}{c}\text{Midyear or average number of} \\ \text{women in reproductive ages} \\ \text{(usually 15–44 or 15–49)}\end{array}} \times 1{,}000$$

In 1967, this rate for American women aged 15 to 44 was 87.6 per thousand. (The number of women in the age group was determined from table 5.3; the number of births, from table 5.17.) Figure 5.4 shows the trend of the U.S. General Fertility Rate and Crude Birth Rate in the period 1935 to 1970. Note that the movements and changes are virtually parallel throughout the 35-year period.

Category-Specific Birth Rates

Although recent years have witnessed a certain amount of interest in male fertility rates, category-specific birth rates ordinarily refer only to the women in the categories in question. In other words, their denominators indicate only the number of women in the category.

Age-specific birth rates are the ones most commonly used. For example, the age-specific birth rate for women aged 20–24 would be:

$$\frac{\text{Births during the year to women aged 20–24}}{\begin{array}{c}\text{Average or midyear number of women aged} \\ \text{20–24 in the population}\end{array}} \times 1{,}000.$$

Using data from tables 5.3 and 5.17, we can determine age-specific fertility rates for all U.S. women in 1967:

Age	Rate per 1,000
10–14	0.9
15–19	67.9
20–24	174.0
25–29	142.6
30–34	79.3
35–39	38.5
40–44	10.6
45–49	0.7

A second common measure is the *duration-of-marriage-specific birth rate*. This is defined analogously to the age-specific rate but refers instead to women married for specified periods of time. Finally, an index now receiving increased attention is the *parity-specific birth rate,* often called "parity-progression rates." Parity determines the total number of children a woman has borne by denoting the birth order of her most recently delivered child (if the second child, she has borne two children; if the third, three children; etc.). A duration-specific birth rate for women married 5 to 9 years would be:

FIGURE 5.4. U.S. annual birth rate and general fertility rate, 1935–1970. Source: U.S. Bureau of the Census, *Current Population Reports. Population Estimates and Projections*, Series P–25, No. 465, Sept. 8, 1971, figure 2.

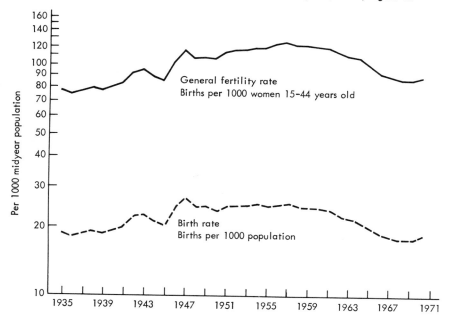

$$\frac{\text{Births during the year to mothers married 5 to 9 years}}{\substack{\text{Average or midyear number of women married 5 to 9} \\ \text{years in the population}}} \times 1{,}000.$$

A parity-specific birth rate, or parity progression rate for women with three previous live births (or, for "parity-three" women) would be:

$$\frac{\text{Fourth-order births during the year}}{\substack{\text{Average or midyear number of "parity-three"} \\ \text{women, i.e., women with three live births,} \\ \text{in the population}}} \times 1{,}000.$$

Ordinarily, duration-of-marriage and parity-specific birth rates may be computed only in connection with a census enumeration. This is because estimates of the female population by duration of marriage and by parity (the denominators of the two rates) are extremely difficult to obtain except in years of census enumerations or in surveys specifically designed to yield such information. Thus, age-specific birth rates are the most regularly computed detailed measures of fertility. All of the birth rates presented so far depend upon availability of annual vital statistics, so that their use is necessarily restricted to those countries that maintain a vital registration system.

A further refinement obviously is to compute age-specific birth rates for married women only. These "marital fertility rates" (or "legitimate fertility rates") are calculated by dividing the number of children born to married women in each age group by the number of married women in each age group. Such rates are in fact routinely computed and used in fertility analyses in countries maintaining detailed estimates of the population by marital status (e.g., France). Corresponding "illegitimate fertility rates"—number of children born to unmarried women in each age group divided by number of unmarried women in each age group—are also often computed. In the United States, the use of marital fertility rates has been severely restricted by the absence of appropriate statistics on marriage and marital status.

Age-specific birth rates and age-specific marital fertility rates for Poland around 1960 are portrayed in figure 5.5. Marital fertility rates are, of course, higher than the age-specific birth rates at all ages. For married women, the rate of fertility *declines* consistently with advancing age. Clearly the reason for the sharp climb in age-specific birth rates between ages 15 and 20 or 24 is that the *proportion married* among the total females increases sharply in this age range. Thus, comparison of curves of age-specific birth rates for two populations confounds the

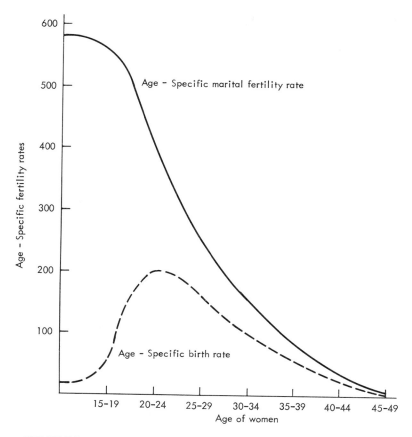

FIGURE 5.5. Age-specific marital fertility rates (live births per 1,000 married women) and age-specific birth rates (births per 1,000 women in each age group), Poland, c. 1960. Source: U.N. 1963b, p. 103; Berent 1970a, p. 253.

effects of differences in proportions married at each age with differences in levels of fertility at each age.

Comparison of patterns of age-specific *marital* fertility rates may confound the effects of marriage with those of fertility levels only at the youngest ages—since large proportions of girls marrying at earliest ages are already pregnant at marriage, and, presumably, might well have remained single but for the fact of being pregnant. However, at most ages comparison of marital fertility rates is free of effects other than actual marital fertility levels and hence is most satisfactory for fertility analysis where available.

TABLE 5.18
Reproduction Rates for U.S. Women by Color, 1967

	Total	White	Nonwhite
Gross reproduction rate	1,255	1,193	1,676
Net reproduction rate	1,213	1,158	1,582

SOURCE: U.S. Bureau of the Census, *Statistical Abstract of the United States* 1968.

Comparison of Fertility: Standardized Birth Rates and Reproduction Rates

The comparison of fertility conditions obtaining in two communities presents the same kinds of problems encountered in comparing mortality conditions. In particular, the comparison of crude birth rates presents the danger of confounding the effects of age-sex-distribution with those of the schedule of age-specific birth rates precisely to the pitfall inherent in comparing crude death rates. However, in a manner entirely analogous to the procedure described for age-standardized death rates, age-standardized birth rates can be computed and compared for two populations.

Two commonly employed summary measures of fertility are the gross reproduction rate and net reproduction rate. The gross reproduction rate, on which we shall concentrate here, is often interpreted as the ratio of mothers to daughters implied by the observed schedule of age-specific birth rates. The net reproduction rate is interpreted as the same ratio but takes into account the mortality conditions to which females in the population are subject up to and including their reproductive ages (see table 5.18).

The computations in table 5.18 adhere strictly to the definition of gross reproduction rate as the sum of the age-specific *female* birth rates (i.e., rate of births of daughters) over all childbearing ages. However, since the proportion of females among all births tends to be quite stable over time and with respect to the age of the mothers—about 0.485 of all children born are female, no matter what maternal age group is considered—the gross reproduction rate is usually computed as:

(Proportion female among births) × (Sum of age-specific birth rates over all ages).

When computing the gross reproduction rate, age-specific birth rates given for five-year age groups (15–19, 20–24, etc.), are each assumed to be the same for each single age in every age group. The computation is:

(.485) × (5) × Σ (five-year-age-group, age-specific birth rates)
where the symbol Σ means "summation"

The gross reproduction rate for all U.S. women in 1967 is computed in the following way.

Age	Age-Specific Birth Rate per Woman
10–14	.0009
15–19	.0679
20–24	.1740
25–29	.1426
30–34	.0793
35–39	.0385
40–44	.0106
45–49	.0007
Summation	0.5145

(5) × (Summation) = 2.5725
G.R.R. = (.485) × (5) × (Summation) = 1.248 (which is
very slightly under the 1.255 rate given in table 5.18).

A measure called the *total fertility rate* is often used as a summary gauge of age-specific fertility rates. This rate is simply the summation of fertility rates (male and female births together) over all ages: (5) × (Summation of five-year-age-group fertility rates). It can readily be seen that we have already computed the U.S. *total fertility rate* for 1967 in the above example:

TFR = (5) × (Summation) = 2.5725.

Procedures for deriving the net reproduction rate and other refined measures of fertility, reproduction, and replacement of generations are given in more specialized texts and manuals.

Measures Based on Census or Survey Data Alone

The measures of fertility described so far are all based upon the numbers of registered births and cannot be used where births are not registered. There are, however, important measures of fertility which can be derived from census or population survey data and do not presuppose an effective system of birth registration. Of these, the simplest and most widely used is the child-woman ratio, a measure requiring only a detailed enumeration or estimate of the population by age and sex. It is defined in the following way:

$$\text{Child-Woman ratio} = \frac{\text{Number of children under 5 years of age in population}}{\text{Number of women in reproductive ages (usually 15–44 or 15–49) in population}} \times 1,000$$

Using data in table 5.3, we can compute the child-woman ratio for the U.S. in 1967 as follows:

	Children Under 5 Years (1)	Women 15–44 (2)	Child-Women Ratio (per 1000 women) (3)
Total	19,191,000	40,172,000	477.7
White	16,017,000	35,175,000	455.4
Non-white	3,174,000	4,996,000	635.3

When available census or survey data give the relationships of persons enumerated to household heads, the correct relationship between the children and wives of household heads, or between children and female heads of households can generally be inferred. This makes it possible to compute the fertility ratio—the ratio of the number of "own children" under five years of age to number of women of childbearing age. Age-specific fertility ratios, restricting the numerators to "own children" of women of a specified age and the denominators to the number of women of that age, may also be computed. Thus, the fertility ratio for women aged 20–24 would be:

$$\frac{\text{Number of "own children" of women aged 20–24}}{\text{Total women in the population aged 20–24}} \times 1,000.$$

Finally, when census or survey data give numbers of children ever born to the women enumerated, the researcher can analyze the distribution of women by number of children ever born, both for women with completed fertility and for women with incomplete fertility (usually by age). Derivative measures, such as the proportion of childless women or the mean and median numbers of children ever born, can also be analyzed.

Cohort Fertility Analysis

Up to now, we have been discussing measures of fertility in terms of a given instant or interval in time. The various age-specific birth rates ordinarily have reference to different age groups of women all present in the population during the period in question. However, most of the measures can also be applied to the study of real cohorts of women—for example, women born in the same year or marrying in the same year. In cohort fertility analysis, the fertility of each cohort is measured in terms of successive ages or in terms of different durations of marriage, and the resulting analyses compares the fertility histories of women entering the "fertile population" at different times.

7. POPULATION PROJECTIONS: MORTALITY, FERTILITY, AND CHANGES IN THE SIZE AND COMPOSITION OF A POPULATION

Projections of future populations of nations, areas, and social categories are obviously important for all types of planning, decision making, and investment. But in addition to their practical value, they also summarize the relationships between population size and structure and the vital population processes, fertility and mortality. To simplify the analysis, we shall consider here only the projection of populations closed to migration, i.e., populations in which entry and exit are by birth and death only.

If we have an initial population—say 12,000 luvmees—whose numbers at each exact age are known, and if we know the mortality rates or probabilities affecting the population at each age, then we can derive survival rates and *compute* the numbers of luvmees from this population who will still be alive in exactly one year *provided* that the mortality probabilities do not change.

TABLE 5.20

Initial Age x (1)	Initial Population P_x (2)	One-Year Survival Rate $\dfrac{L_{x+1}}{L_x}$ (3)	Projected Population After One Year $P_x{}' = $ Col. (2) x Col. (3) (4)	Now Age x' (5)
0	4,000	$\dfrac{750}{900} = .833$	3,332	1
1	3,000	$\dfrac{525}{750} = .700$	2,100	2
2	3,000	$\dfrac{175}{525} = .333$	1,000	3
3	2,000	0	0	
Total	12,000		6,432	

Thus, the projected luvmee population includes a large number surviving from the initial population.

The Basic Ideas of Population Projection

Suppose that we are constructing a projection of some present population. The first point to consider, if our projection covers any reasonably short interval of time, is that the larger part of the future population has already been born and will comprise the survivors of the present population. Thus, the population that will be, say, 20–24 years old ten years from now consists of the *survivors* of the population currently aged 10–14. If we know how to compute a survival rate for persons aged 10–14 from a current life table, we can apply the ten-year survival rate to the total number of such persons in the present population and thus arrive at a number for the projected population aged 20–24 ten years hence. More generally, the population in ten years may be projected for all age groups of 10 years and over as follows:

$$\begin{pmatrix} \text{Projected population} \\ \text{aged 10–19 in ten} \\ \text{years} \end{pmatrix} = \begin{pmatrix} \text{Present} \\ \text{population} \\ \text{aged 0–9} \end{pmatrix} \times \begin{pmatrix} \text{Ten-year survival} \\ \text{rate for persons} \\ \text{aged 0–9} \end{pmatrix}$$

$$\begin{pmatrix} \text{Projected population} \\ \text{aged 20–29 in ten} \\ \text{years} \end{pmatrix} = \begin{pmatrix} \text{Present} \\ \text{population} \\ \text{aged 10–19} \end{pmatrix} \times \begin{pmatrix} \text{Ten-year survival} \\ \text{rate for persons} \\ \text{aged 10–19} \end{pmatrix}$$

Thus, by using a life table, we can establish a schedule of survival rates which, when applied to the present population projection by sex and age will yield a population projection by sex and age for the end of the interval in question.

Suppose that the age-specific birth rate of luvmees is 600 per thousand at age 1-year and 400 per thousand at age 2-years. A projected number of births can be computed:

TABLE 5.21

Age (1)	Initial Population (2)	Projected Population (3)	Average Population (4)	Age-Specific Birth Rate (5)	Projected Births (6)	Projected Population, Including Surviving Births (7)
0	4,000			0		2,628
1	3,000	3,332	3,116	.600	1,900	3,332
2	3,000	2,100	2,550	.400	1,020	2,100
3	2,000	1,000	1,500	0	0	1,000
Total	12,000				2,920	9,060

The projected luvmee population age 0-years is derived by applying the birth-to-first year survival rate, $\dfrac{L_0}{l_0} = \dfrac{900}{1000} = .900$ to the total number of births:

$$P_0 = (2920) \times (.900) = 2628$$

We generalize this procedure below.

The future population *under* ten years of age is calculated by projecting the number of births in the interval, by year, and the rates at which newborn children will survive to the date of the projection:

$$
\begin{pmatrix} \text{Projected population} \\ \text{aged 0–9 in ten} \\ \text{years} \end{pmatrix} = \begin{pmatrix} \text{Projected} \\ \text{births in the} \\ \text{first year} \end{pmatrix} \times \begin{pmatrix} \text{Nine-year survival} \\ \text{rate for persons} \\ \text{aged 0} \end{pmatrix}
$$

$$
+ \begin{pmatrix} \text{Projected} \\ \text{births in the} \\ \text{second year} \end{pmatrix} \times \begin{pmatrix} \text{Eight-year survival} \\ \text{rate for persons} \\ \text{aged 0} \end{pmatrix}
$$

$$
\vdots \qquad\qquad \vdots
$$

$$
+ \begin{pmatrix} \text{Projected} \\ \text{births in the} \\ \text{tenth year} \end{pmatrix} \times \begin{pmatrix} \text{One-year survival} \\ \text{rate for persons} \\ \text{aged 0} \end{pmatrix}
$$

The projected number of births, in turn, are computed by applying age-specific birth rates to the projected numbers of women in each age group in each year:

$$
\begin{pmatrix} \text{Projected number} \\ \text{of births in} \\ \text{first year} \end{pmatrix} = \begin{pmatrix} \text{Projected number} \\ \text{of women 15–19 in} \\ \text{first year} \end{pmatrix} \times \begin{pmatrix} \text{Age-specific} \\ \text{birth rate for} \\ \text{women aged 15–19} \end{pmatrix}
$$

$$
+ \begin{pmatrix} \text{Projected number} \\ \text{of women 20–24 in} \\ \text{first year} \end{pmatrix} \times \begin{pmatrix} \text{Age-specific} \\ \text{birth rate for} \\ \text{women aged 20–24} \end{pmatrix}
$$

$$
\vdots \qquad\qquad \vdots
$$

$$
+ \begin{pmatrix} \text{Projected number} \\ \text{of women 40–44 in} \\ \text{first year} \end{pmatrix} \times \begin{pmatrix} \text{Age-specific} \\ \text{birth rate for} \\ \text{women aged 40–44} \end{pmatrix}
$$

This whole set of fertility and mortality conditions (which we shall call M_1), transforms the size and composition of the initial population π_0 into that of the new population projected for the end of the interval π_1.

We denote this transformation symbolically as:

$$\pi_0 \, M_1 = \pi_1.$$

For our hypothetical luvmee population, we can denote, for the initial population by age:

$$\pi_0 = \begin{pmatrix} \text{Initial} & \text{Initial} & \text{Initial} & \text{Initial} \\ \text{population} & \text{population} & \text{population} & \text{population} \\ \text{0 years old} = P_0; & \text{1 year old} = P_1; & \text{2 years old} = P_2; & \text{3 years old} = P_3 \end{pmatrix}$$

$$= (4{,}000, \ 3{,}000, \ 3{,}000, \ 2{,}000)$$

A table showing the quantitative relationship—if any—between *each* age grouping in the projected population would contain elements representing the fertility and mortality conditions of the population during the time interval of the projection. We denote such a table M_1 which for our luvmee population projection would be:

TABLE 5.22

Initial Age	Final Age of Projected Population, After One Year			
	0	1	2	3
0	Per capita offspring of population, initially 0-years old, born during year, surviving, and aged 0-years at end of year = f_0	Proportion of initial 0-year old population surviving and 1-year old at the end of a year = S_0	No relationship	No relationship
1	Per capita offspring of population, initially 1-year old, born during year, surviving, and aged 0-years at end of year = f_1	No relationship	Proportion of initial 1-year old population surviving and 2-years old at the end of a year = S_1	No relationship
2	Per capita offspring of population, initially 2-years old, born during year, surviving and aged 0-years at end of year = f_2	No relationship	No relationship	Proportion of initial 2-year old population surviving and 3-years old at the end of a year = S_2
3	No relationship No offspring at this age for luvmees	No relationship	No relationship	No relationship

$M_1 =$

In our luvmee population, intially age 0-years (i.e., not yet reached first birthdays) almost half will have survived and reached their first birthdays and will have been 1-year old during the year of the projection. The survivors, .833 proportion of the initial group, are therefore exposed to an age-specific birth rate half the magnitude of the birth rate for one-year olds, i.e., 300 per thousand. (See the birthrate column of table 5.21). Of those born, the proportion surviving an average of $\frac{1}{2}$ year to remain in the 0-year age group at the close of the projection period is

$$\frac{L_0}{l_0} = .900 \text{ for the luvmees.}$$

Therefore, f_0, the per capita number of offspring of luvmees initially aged 0 years who are born and survive to be themselves 0-years old at the close of the projection period is:

$$f_1 = (.833) \times (.300) \times (.900) = .225$$

The luvmees initially aged 1 year old spend an average of half the year exposed to the 1-year old's luvmee birth rate, and those surviving, .700 of the initial group, spend an average of half the year exposed to the 2-year old's birth rate. Their per capita number of births during the year is, therefore, $\frac{1}{2}$ [.600 + (.700) .400]. Of this number of births, the proportion surviving to the end of the projection period is $\frac{L_0}{l_0} = .900$ for the luvmees. Accordingly f_1, the per capita number of offspring of the luvmees initially aged 1-year who are born and survive to be 0 years old at the close of the projection period is:

$$f_0 = \frac{1}{2} [.600 + (.700) (.400)](.900) = .396$$

Writing our previous result in the same format would give:

$$f_0 = \frac{1}{2} [0 + (.833) (.600)](.900) = .225$$

By the same reasoning and procedure, the per capita number of offspring of the luvmees initially age 2 years who are born and survive to be 0-years old at the close of the projection period is:

$$f_2 = \frac{1}{2} [.400 + (.333) (0)](.900) = .180$$

Since luvmees aged 3-years have no fertility, clearly $f_3 = 0$.
Thus the entries of the first column of our table 5.22 are:

$$f_0 = .225$$
$$f_1 = .396$$
$$f_2 = .180$$
$$f_3 = 0$$

We can see already that the sum of the products of the initial populations, P_x, at each age, and the first column entries per capita numbers of surviving offspring to persons of each age, f_x, is:

$$(P_0)(f_0) + (P_1)(f_1) + (P_2)(f_2) + (P_3)(f_3) \text{ denoted } \sum_x P_x f_x$$

and for our luvmee population this summation,

$$(4000)(.225) + (3000)(.396) + (3000)(.180) + (2000)(0) = 2{,}628$$

yields the number of the population aged 0-years at the end of the projection interval of one year. For our luvmee population the computation yields 2,628 for the projected population aged 0 years, as before.

The rest of the entries of the M_1 table may simply be taken from the survival rate column of table 5.20. The proportion of initial 0-year-olds surviving and aged 1-year at the end of a year is for the luvmees:

$$S_0 = \frac{L_1}{L_0} = \frac{750}{900} = .833$$

More generally, the one-year survival probability (or "survival rate," or "proportion surviving") for any age group, x (a population group which has passed the x-th birthday but not yet reached the (x + 1)st birthday) is

$$S_x = \frac{L_{x+1}}{L_x}$$

where L_{x+1} and L_x are taken from appropriate life tables. Thus for the luvmees:

$$S_0 = \frac{L_1}{L_0} = \frac{750}{900} = .833 \text{ as above}$$

$$S_1 = \frac{L_2}{L_1} = \frac{525}{750} = .700$$

$$S_2 = \frac{L_3}{L_2} = \frac{175}{525} = .333$$

$$S_3 = 0$$

Thus the table, M_1, can now be computed:

$$M_1 = \begin{pmatrix} f_0 = .225 & S_0 = .833 & 0 & 0 \\ f_1 = .396 & 0 & S_1 = .100 & 0 \\ f_2 = .180 & 0 & 0 & S_2 = .333 \\ f_3 = 0 & 0 & 0 & S_3 = 0 \end{pmatrix}$$

Recalling that the initial population was denoted:

$$\pi_0 = (P_0 = 4000, P_1 = 3000, P_2 = 3000, P_3 = 2000)$$

We note again the sum of the products of the entries of the initial population and the corresponding entries of the *first* column of the M_1 table

$$(P_0 f_0) + (P_1 f_1) + (P_2 f_2) + (P_3 f_3) =$$
$$(4000)(.225) + (3000)(.396) + (3000)(.180) + (2000)(0) = 2628$$

gives the number P'_0, of luvmees aged 0 years in the projected population: $P'_0 = 2628$.

The sum of the products of the entries of the initial population and the corresponding entries of the *second* column of the M_1 table:

$$(P_0)(S_0) + (P_1)(0) + (P_2)(0) + (P_3)(0) =$$
$$(4000)(.833) + 0 + 0 + 0 = 3332$$

gives the number, say P'_1, of the luvmees aged 1 year in the projected population: $P'_1 = 3332$. The sum of the products of the entries of the initial population and the corresponding entries of the *third* column of the M_1 table

$$(P_0)(0) + (P_1)(S_1) + (P_2)(0) + (P_3)(0) =$$
$$(0) + (3000)(.700) + 0 + 0 = 2100 = P'_2,$$

the projected population aged 2-years.

Finally, the sum of the products of the entries of the initial population and the corresponding entries of the fourth column of the M_1 table give the projected population, aged 3-years:

$$P'_3 = (P_0)(0) + (P_1)(0) + (P_2)(S_2) + (P_3)(0)$$
$$= 0 + 0 + (3000)(.333) + 0 = 1000$$

Denoting the projected population by π_1 as follows:

$$\pi_1 = \begin{pmatrix} \text{Projected} & \text{Projected} & \text{Projected} & \text{Projected} \\ \text{population} & \text{population} & \text{population} & \text{population} \\ \text{0 years} = P'_0; & \text{1 year} = P'_1; & \text{2 years} = P'_2; & \text{3 years} = P'_3 \end{pmatrix}$$

$$= (2628, 3332, 2100, 1000)$$

Now the symbolic representation,

$$\pi_0 \, M_1 = \pi_1$$

describes a set of changes for the luvmees whereby the population *is transformed* both in size and in age structure. Thus the set of fertility and mortality conditions operating upon a population—whether in a projection for the future, or in past history—may altogether be denoted a *population transformation*.

The symbolic representation of such a transformation,

$$\pi_0 \, M_1 = \pi_1$$

can be seen as a multiplication equation in which the rules for obtaining the elements of the product (projected) population are:

1.   The *first* element of the projected population, P'_1, is taken as the sum of the products of the elements of the initial population and the corresponding elements of the *first* column of the fertility-mortality table, M_1, conventionally called a "projection matrix."

2.   *Any* given element of the projected population, say, the j-th element, P'_j, is taken as the sum of the products of the elements of the initial population and the corresponding elements of the *j-th* column of the fertility-mortality table, M_1.

We now generalize this procedure for the ten-year population projection. The operations of the complete ten-year population projection can be summarized symbolically in the following way:

$$(P_{0-9} \; P_{10-19} \; P_{20-24} \cdots P_{70-79} \; P_{80+})
\begin{pmatrix}
0 & {}_{10}S_{0-9} & 0 & 0 & \cdots & 0 \\
{}_{10}f_{10-19} & 0 & {}_{10}S_{10-19} & 0 & \cdots & 0 \\
{}_{10}f_{20-29} & 0 & 0 & {}_{10}S_{20-29} & \cdots & 0 \\
\cdot & \cdot & \cdot & \cdot & & \cdot \\
\cdot & \cdot & \cdot & \cdot & \cdots & \cdot \\
0 & 0 & 0 & 0 & \cdots & {}_{10}S_{70-79} \\
0 & 0 & 0 & 0 & \cdots & {}_{10}S_{80+}
\end{pmatrix}$$

$$= (P'_{0-9} \; P'_{10-19} \; P'_{20-29} \cdots P'_{70-79} \; P'_{80+}),$$

where P_{x-x+9} = present population aged x to x + 9,

P'_{x-x+9} = projected population aged x to x + 9, in ten years

${}_{10}S_{x-x+9}$ = probability that persons aged x to x + 9 will survive ten years,

${}_{10}f_{x-x+9}$ = for persons aged x to x + 9, average number of children born in the next ten years and surviving to the end of the ten-year period.

The calculation for the projected population aged 0–9 in ten years is

$$P'_{0-9} = \sum_x P_{x-x+9}\, f_{x-x+9},$$

and the calculation for the projected population of all other ages is

$$x \neq 0 \;\; P'_{x-x+9} = \sum_x P_{x-x+9}\, {}_{10}S_{x-x+9}.\;{}^1$$

Projections Over Successive Intervals of Time

Table 5.23 shows some population projections adapted from the important work of N. Keyfitz (1968, chap. 2). The material is handled in five-year intervals. Mortality and fertility elements of the population transformation are represented in the matrix, T, and the initial 1964 female population is represented by the row vector, π_0. The projected 1969 population, π_1, is derived from the operation of the mortality and fertility regime, T, upon the initial population, π_0, and the entire transformation in the five-year period is represented by the equation:

$$\pi_1 = \pi_0 T$$

The same schedule of five-year survival and fertility rates is applied to the newly projected population to yield a projection for the end of the following five-year period. The same procedure could be applied indefinitely to yield population projections over any interval of time. For example, the projected population for 1989 is

$$\pi_5 = \pi_4 T = [\pi_3 T] T = \cdots = \pi_0 TTTTT,$$

or, simply,

$$\pi_5 = \pi_0 T^5.$$

1 Those familiar with matrix algebra will recognize that by denoting the elements of the initial population P_i, the elements of the matrix m_{ij}, and the elements of the projected population P'_j, the computations can clearly be generalized as:

$$P'_j = \Sigma_i P_i m_{ij}.$$

But this is identical to the rules of matrix multiplication in linear algebra. Thus, what we have called a "population transformation" is directly analogous to the "linear transformation" in algebra; the equation $\pi_0 M_1 = \pi_1$ is identical to postmultiplication of the n-dimensional vector, π_0, by the n × n matrix M_1, yielding a new n-dimensional vector, π_1. Indeed, much of the theory of linear alegbra may be invoked in the study and analysis of population transformations.

A more detailed development of this point is presented in Matras and Winsborough, 1969.

TABLE 5.23
Projection Matrix Representing Fertility and Mortality Regime for U.S. Females, 1964

Projection Matrix = T

Age														
0–4	0	.99661	0	0	0	0	0	0	0	0	0	0	0	0
5–9	.00103	0	.99834	0	0	0	0	0	0	0	0	0	0	0
10–14	.08779	0	0	.99791	0	0	0	0	0	0	0	0	0	0
15–19	.34873	0	0	0	.99682	0	0	0	0	0	0	0	0	0
20–24	.47607	0	0	0	0	.99605	0	0	0	0	0	0	0	0
25–29	.33769	0	0	0	0	0	.99472	0	0	0	0	0	0	0
30–34	.18333	0	0	0	0	0	0	.99229	0	0	0	0	0	0
35–39	.07605	0	0	0	0	0	0	0	.98866	0	0	0	0	0
40–44	.01744	0	0	0	0	0	0	0	0	.98304	0	0	0	0
45–49	.00096	0	0	0	0	0	0	0	0	0	.97416	0	0	0
50–54	.0	0	0	0	0	0	0	0	0	0	0	.96222	0	0
55–59	.0	0	0	0	0	0	0	0	0	0	0	0	.94430	0
60–64	.0	0	0	0	0	0	0	0	0	0	0	0	0	.91410
65 and over	.0	0	0	0	0	0	0	0	0	0	0	0	0	.86938

SOURCE: Adapted from Keyfitz 1968, table 2.

TABLE 5.23B

Projected Female Population, 1964–1999

Age	Female Population = π_t (thousands)							
	$\pi_0 = 1964$	$\pi_1 = 1969$	$\pi_2 = 1974$	$\pi_3 = 1979$	$\pi_4 = 1984$	$\pi_5 = 1989$	$\pi_6 = 1994$	$\pi_7 = 1999$
0–4	10,136	10,244	11,623	13,075	14,227	15,047	16,003	17,397
5–9	10,006	10,102	10,209	11,584	13,030	14,178	14,996	15,949
10–14	9,065	9,989	10,085	10,192	11,564	13,009	14,155	14,971
15–19	8,045	9,046	9,968	10,064	10,170	11,540	12,981	14,125
20–24	6,546	8,019	9,017	9,937	10,032	10,138	11,504	12,940
25–29	5,614	6,520	7,988	8,982	9,898	9,992	10,098	11,458
30–34	5,632	5,584	6,486	7,946	8,934	9,845	9,939	10,045
35–39	6,193	5,589	5,541	6,436	7,884	8,865	9,769	9,863
40–44	6,345	6,123	5,525	5,478	6,363	7,795	8,765	9,659
45–49	5,796	6,237	6,019	5,432	5,386	6,255	7,663	8,616
50–54	5,336	5,646	6,076	5,863	5,291	5,246	6,093	7,465
55–59	4,642	5,134	5,433	5,847	5,642	5,091	5,048	5,863
60 and over	14,023	15,532	17,042	18,443	19,862	20,809	20,927	20,784
Total — all ages	97,379	103,765	111,013	119,277	128,284	137,812	147,942	159,137

SOURCE: Adapted from Keyfitz 1968, table 2.3.

In practice, of course, projections over increasing time intervals steadily diminish in value, since the assumptions of fixed fertility and mortality conditions become progressively less realistic as the time intervals increase.

There is, however, an important theoretical value to the repeated projection over an indefinite number of intervals: it can be shown that a fixed schedule of death rates combined with a fixed schedule of birth rates (*not* a fixed annual *number* of births) generates a population with a stable, unchanging, age-sex composition and a fixed annual rate of growth. Both the fixed annual ("true" or "intrinsic") rate of growth and the fixed age-sex composition can be derived for any given schedule of birth and death rates, and these serve as additional dimensions for the analysis and comparison of fertility and mortality conditions in different populations.

8. MIGRATION AND CHANGES IN THE GEOGRAPHICAL DISTRIBUTION OF A POPULATION

It seems self-evident that migratory movements within a population operate to alter or transform the geographical distribution and rural-urban composition of that population. Thus, the very considerable trans-continental migratory movements that have occurred in the United States have changed the population distribution among the country's major regions, and the rural-to-urban population movements in the United States and elsewhere have been accompanied by urbanization trends.

Two aspects of migration complicate its analysis. In the first place, migration can be studied either from the point of view of the populations of origin or from the point of view of the populations of destination. In the second place, migration between any two places, or between any two categories of places, typically occurs in both directions, thus making it necessary to distinguish between gross and net migration between any two points. These considerations are illustrated in our following references to table 5.24, which shows the U.S. population's geographic distribution in 1935, its migratory movements from 1935 to 1940, and its subsequent distribution at the end of the interval.

Rates of In-Migration

Using the data in table 5.24, rates of in-migration to each destination may be computed as follows:

$$\text{In-migration rate} = \frac{\substack{\text{Number of In-migrants} \\ \text{in interval}}}{\substack{\text{Initial population at} \\ \text{beginning of interval}}} \times 1,000.$$

Thus the rate for the New England division was

$$\frac{\left(\substack{1940 \text{ total} \\ \text{population} \\ \text{of New England}}\right) - \left(\substack{\text{Total population of New England} \\ \text{in both 1935 and 1950} \\ \text{(diagonal cell entry)}}\right)}{\substack{1935 \text{ total population} \\ \text{of New England}}} \times 1,000$$

$$= \frac{154,880}{7,761,647} \times 1,000 = 20.0 \text{ per } 1,000 \text{ initial population.}$$

By contrast, the 1935–1940 in-migration rate for the Pacific division was

$$\frac{9,742,046 - 8,694,450}{8,919,384} \times 1,000 = \frac{1,047,596}{8,919,384} \times 1,000$$

$$= 117.5 \text{ per } 1,000.$$

THE INFLOW PROPORTION. An alternative expression of the volume of in-migration is the proportion of recent migrants in the final population of the place of destination. (The migrants are classified by place of origin.) This measure, conventionally called the "inflow" proportion, is computed in the following way:

TABLE 5.24

U.S. Migration and Population Redistribution 1935–1940: Census Division of Residence in 1935 by Division of Residence in 1940

Census Division of Residence in 1935	Total,* All Divisions in 1940	Census Division of Residence in 1940								
		New England	Middle Atlantic	East North Central	West North Central	South Atlantic	East South Central	West South Central	Mountain	Pacific
New England	7,761,647	7,591,581	85,941	17,849	3,600	35,010	2,521	3,402	2,905	18,838
Middle Atlantic	25,364,757	98,817	24,814,459	124,100	15,546	193,952	12,295	17,254	11,522	76,812
East North Central	24,381,033	17,623	109,269	23,753,142	121,334	107,569	59,237	39,963	31,929	140,967
West North Central	12,297,182	5,271	23,047	193,505	11,453,287	30,863	17,346	97,151	143,762	332,950
South Atlantic	15,925,618	17,872	136,869	79,649	10,752	15,535,919	78,991	24,448	7,926	33,187
East South Central	9,575,044	3,032	17,502	138,005	22,933	150,962	9,144,298	70,369	7,706	20,237
West South Central	11,710,519	2,512	14,089	64,005	91,752	31,158	56,495	11,119,721	109,925	220,862
Mountain	3,696,386	1,788	7,268	20,230	40,593	8,477	3,710	40,997	3,369,580	203,743
Pacific	8,919,384	7,965	24,871	32,254	27,678	25,218	5,180	26,359	75,409	8,694,450
Total,* All Divisions in 1935	119,631,570	7,746,461	25,233,315	24,422,739	11,787,475	16,119,128	9,380,073	11,439,669	3,760,664	9,742,046

SOURCE: *1940 Census:* Age of Migrants, table 13.

*Excludes unreported migrant status and overseas immigrants.

221

$$\text{Inflow proportion} = \frac{\text{Number of in-migrants in interval}}{\text{Final population at end of interval}}.$$

Thus, again for New England, the inflow proportion is

$$\frac{154{,}880}{7{,}746{,}461} = 0.0200,$$

which is virtually identical to the in-migration rate. But for the Pacific division, the inflow proportion is

$$\frac{1{,}047{,}596}{9{,}742{,}046} = .1075$$

In the case of the Pacific division, the two rates differ substantially because of the difference between their denominators—the total population in 1935 and the total population in 1940. This difference, in turn, is due to the volume of in-migration itself. A complete, detailed set of inflow proportions is called an "inflow" table. For table 5.24, such a table would consist simply of percentage distributions computed for each 1940 divisional population, i.e., for each *column* in table 5.24.

Rates of Out-Migration

Rates of out-migration may be computed as follows:

$$\text{Out-migration rate} = \frac{\text{Number of out-migrants in interval}}{\text{population at beginning of interval}} \times 1{,}000.$$

Thus, for New England, the computation of the out-migration rate is:

$$\frac{\left(\begin{array}{c}\text{1935 total}\\\text{population of}\\\text{New England}\end{array}\right) - \left(\begin{array}{c}\text{Total population of New England}\\\text{in both 1935 and 1940}\\\text{(diagonal cell entry)}\end{array}\right)}{\text{(1935 total population of New England)}} \times 1{,}000 =$$

$$\frac{(7{,}761{,}647) - (7{,}591{,}581)}{(7{,}761{,}647)} \times 1{,}000 = \frac{170{,}066}{7{,}761{,}647} \times 1{,}000 = 21.9 \text{ per } 1{,}000.$$

For the Mountain division, the calculation is:

$$\frac{3{,}696{,}386 - 3{,}369{,}580}{3{,}696{,}386} = \frac{326{,}806}{3{,}696{,}386} \times 1{,}000 = 88.4 \text{ per } 1{,}000.$$

Since the net migration rate is merely the difference between the in-migration and out-migration rates, we can use the calculations described above and the data from table 5.24 to determine 1935–1940 rates of interdivisional in-migration, out-migration, and net migration for the nine geographic divisions of the United States:

Geographic Division	1935–1940 In-Migration Rate	1935–1940 Out-Migration Rate	1935–1940 Net Migration Rate
New England	20.0	21.9	- 1.9
Middle Atlantic	16.5	21.7	- 5.2
East North Central	27.5	25.8	1.7
West North Central	27.2	68.6	-41.4
South Atlantic	36.6	24.5	12.1
East South Central	24.6	45.0	-20.4
West South Central	27.3	50.4	-23.1
Mountain	105.8	88.4	17.4
Pacific	117.5	25.2	92.3

OUTFLOW RATES. When rendered as percentages or proportions of the initial populations, rates of out-migration are also called outflow rates. A complete, detailed set of outflow proportions or percentages is called an "outflow table." Referring to a given interval of time, the outflow table shows the probability of persons in any category of origin (a) remaining in the initial category, or (b) moving to any of the specific alternative categories. The categories may be residential, geographic, or of some other designation such as metropolitan or non-metropolitan; or industrial, commercial, or political. Table 5.26, an outflow table, is based upon the data in table 5.24.

If we apply the outflow rates in table 5.26 to each of the original populations—the 1935 population by divisions—and combine the numbers of migrants to each of the destinations, we emerge with a new distribution of the population—the 1940 population by divisions:

$$
\begin{pmatrix} \text{End-of-interval} \\ \text{population in} \\ \text{first category} \end{pmatrix} = \begin{pmatrix} \text{Beginning-of-interval} \\ \text{population in first} \\ \text{category} \end{pmatrix} \times \begin{pmatrix} \text{First category} \\ \text{to first category} \\ \text{outflow rate} \end{pmatrix}
$$

$$
+ \begin{pmatrix} \text{Beginning-of-interval} \\ \text{population in second} \\ \text{category} \end{pmatrix} \times \begin{pmatrix} \text{Second category} \\ \text{to first category} \\ \text{outflow rate} \end{pmatrix}
$$

$$
\vdots
$$

TABLE 5.26
Destination-Specific Out-Migration Proportions by Division of Residence in 1935, for U.S. Population, 1935–1940

Division of Residence in 1935	Proportions Remaining in, or Moving to, Divisions of Residence in 1940									
	N.E.	*M.A.*	*E.N.C.*	*W.N.C.*	*S.A.*	*E.S.C.*	*W.S.C.*	*Mtn.*	*Pac.*	*Total*
New England	.9781	.0111	.0023	.0004	.0046	.0003	.0004	.0003	.0025	1.0000
Middle Atlantic	.0038	.9783	.0050	.0006	.0078	.0005	.0006	.0004	.0030	1.0000
East North Central	.0007	.0045	.9742	.0050	.0045	.0024	.0015	.0012	.0058	1.0000
West North Central	.0004	.0019	.0157	.9314	.0025	.0014	.0078	.0118	.0271	1.0000
South Atlantic	.0011	.0087	.0050	.0007	.9755	.0050	.0015	.0005	.0020	1.0000
East South Central	.0003	.0018	.0145	.0024	.0157	.9550	.0074	.0007	.0022	1.0000
West South Central	.0002	.0012	.0055	.0079	.0027	.0048	.9496	.0094	.0187	1.0000
Mountain	.0005	.0020	.0054	.0110	.0023	.0010	.0111	.9116	.0551	1.0000
Pacific	.0009	.0028	.0038	.0033	.0029	.0006	.0031	.0088	.9748	1.0000

SOURCE: Table 5.11.

$$+ \begin{pmatrix} \text{Beginning-of-interval} \\ \text{population in last} \\ \text{category} \end{pmatrix} \times \begin{pmatrix} \text{Last category} \\ \text{to first category} \\ \text{outflow rate} \end{pmatrix}$$

Thus, the rates in the outflow table operate to transform the population from its initial distribution at the beginning of the interval to its subsequent distribution at the end. The procedure can be represented as:

$$\pi_0 \, M_1 = \pi_{1_1},$$

where π_0 is the initial 1935 population, M_1 the outflow-table matrix, and π_1 the subsequent 1940 population.

The notion of studying the composition, distribution, or structure of a population implied by, or associated with, the operation of a set of rates will be considered again later with regard to other aspects of population composition and social structure. We shall examine a number of social processes wherein schedules of rates operating upon some initial population or social structure can be shown to transform the initial structure over time. Such processes are equivalent to what A. L. Stinchcombe (1968, pp. 60–80) has called "complete or closed demographic explanations" of social phenomena; we shall refer to them hereafter as *population transformations*.

Distributions Compared via the Index of Dissimilarity

The change resulting from this migration-redistribution transformation may be measured by comparing the new geographic distribution with the original one via the Index of Dissimilarity presented in chapter 4. By calculating the 1935 and 1940 percentage distributions by geographic division (using data from table 5.24), and then computing their absolute differences, we obtain the following results:

TABLE 5.27

Geographic Division	Percent Distributions		Absolute Differences
	1935	*1940*	
N.E.	6.49	6.47	0.02
M.A.	21.21	21.20	0.11
E.N.C.	20.38	20.42	0.04
W.N.C.	10.28	9.85	0.43
S.A.	13.31	13.48	0.17
E.S.C.	8.00	7.84	0.16
W.S.C.	9.79	9.56	0.23
Mtn.	3.09	3.14	0.05
Pac.	7.45	8.14	0.69
		Sum =	1.90

The Index of Dissimilarity, denoted Δ, is:

$$\Delta = \tfrac{1}{2}(1.90) = 0.95 \text{ percent}$$

Recalling our earlier interpretation of the Index of Dissimilarity, we may say that interdivisional migration on the part of only 0.95 percent of the total population would be the minimum movement required to effect the shift in percentage distribution which occurred. In fact, the actual percentage of the population reporting interdivisional migration from 1935 to 1940 can be computed from table 5.24 as follows:

$$\begin{array}{c} \text{Percent} \\ \text{interdivisional} \\ \text{migrants} \end{array} = \frac{\left(\begin{array}{c}\text{U.S.}\\ \text{total population}\end{array}\right) - \left(\begin{array}{c}\text{Total population in same}\\ \text{division in 1935 and 1940}\\ \text{(sum of diagonal entries)}\end{array}\right)}{\text{(Total population)}} \times 100$$

$$= \frac{4,155,133}{119,631,570} \times 100 = 3.47 \text{ percent.}$$

EXCHANGE MIGRATION. The ratio between the percentage actually moving interdivisionally and the minimum percentage represented by the Index of Dissimilarity has been used as a measure of the volume of "exchange" migration, i.e., of that migration in excess of the migration associated with population redistribution. Thus, using the figures in our example:

$$\text{``Exchange'' Migration Index} = \frac{\text{Percent Interdivisional Migrants}}{\text{Index of Dissimilarity}}$$

$$= \frac{3.47 \text{ percent}}{0.95 \text{ percent}} = 3.65.$$

This index may be interpreted as indicating that the total volume of interdivisional migration in the 1935 to 1940 period was 3.65 times as great as the volume which can be directly accounted for by the changing distribution.

All the measures covered in this section can also be used, of course, to compare migration processes and changes in migration among different populations or in the same population during different time periods.

TECHNICAL BIBLIOGRAPHY

BARCLAY, G. W. *Techniques of Population Analysis* (New York: John Wiley & Sons, 1958).

BLUMEN, I., KOGAN, M. and McCARTHY, P. J. *The Industrial Mobility of Labor as a Probability Process* (Ithaca, N.Y.: Cornell University Press, 1955).

BOGUE, D. J. *An Exploratory Study of Migration and Labor Mobility Using Social Security Data* (Oxford, Ohio: Scripps Foundation, 1950).

———— and KITAGAWA, E. M. *Manual of Demographic Research*, in preparation.

COX, P. R. *Demography*. 4th Ed. (Cambridge, England: Cambridge University Press, 1970).

DUNCAN, O. D., CUZZORT, R. and DUNCAN, B. *Statistical Geography: Problems in Analyzing Areal Data* (Glencoe, Ill.: Free Press, 1961).

KEYFITZ, N. "Matrix Multiplication as a Technique of Population Analysis," *Milbank Memorial Fund Quarterly*, Vol. 42. No. 4 Pt. 1, October 1964, 68–84.

————. *Introduction to the Mathematics of Population* (Reading, Mass.: Addison-Wesley, 1968).

———— and MURPHY, E. M. *Comparative Demographic Computations Based on Official (Unadjusted) Data for 69 Selected Countries and Regions* (Chicago: University of Chicago, Population Research and Training Center, 1964).

———— and FLIEGER, W. *Population Facts and Methods of Demography* (San Francisco: W. H. Freeman and Co., 1971).

KITAGAWA, E. M. "Standardized Comparisons in Population Research," *Demography*, Vol. 1, No. 1, 1964, 294–315.

McFarland, D. D. "On the Theory of Stable Populations: A New and Elementary Proof of the Theorems Under Weaker Assumptions," *Demography*, Vol. 6, 1969, 301–322.

Milbank Memorial Fund, *Emerging Techniques in Population Research* (New York: Milbank Memorial Fund, 1963).

Newcombe, H. B., et al. "Automatic Linkage of Vital Records," *Science*, Vol. 130, October 1959, 954–959.

Pressat, R. *Demographic Analysis Methods, Results, Applications*, trans. by J. Matras (Chicago: Aldine Publishing Co., 1972).

Rogers, A. *Matrix Analysis of Interregional Population Growth and Distribution* (Berkeley: University of California Press, 1968).

Shryock, H. S. and Siegal, J. S. *The Materials of Demography*. 2 vols. (Washington: Government Printing Office, 1971).

Spiegelman, M. *Introduction to Demography*, rev. ed. (Cambridge: Harvard University Press, 1968).

United Nations, *Manual IV Methods of Estimating Basic Demographic Measures from Incomplete Data*, Population Studies No. 42 (New York: United Nations, 1967).

———, *The Concept of a Stable Population Application to the Study of Populations of Countries With Incomplete Demographic Statistics*, Population Studies No. 39 (New York: United Nations, 1968).

———, *Methods of Analyzing Census Data on Economic Activities of the Population*, Population Studies No. 43 (New York: United Nations, 1968).

two

COMPONENTS OF POPULATION GROWTH AND CHANGING COMPOSITION

6

Trends and Variations
in Mortality
and the Social Structure
of Mortality Control

1. INTRODUCTORY REMARKS

The universality and inevitability of human death have long made mortality a subject of reflection, speculation, and discourse. Throughout history, poets and philosophers, generals and chiefs of state, priests and medicine men have all articulated their thoughts about death. But it was John Graunt's systematic study of the number of deaths in relation to the total populations in London that launched modern demography and population studies in 1662. Today, the study of mortality and its relationship to population size, composition, and change retains a central position in population research.

The most important result of Graunt's observations was the recognition that relative frequencies and patterns of mortality are recurrent and stable over time. Graunt's contemporaries and later investigators confirmed and elaborated on his contributions, and subsequently, in the eighteenth and nineteenth centuries, there was an outpouring of investigations of mortality, fertility, and population size in Europe. This deluge coincided with the increasing availability of data concerning populations and vital events and with the emergence of far-reaching population trends associated with the pervasive transformation of European societies and culture. Among the most important of the European trends were declining mortality and rural-to-urban, as well as overseas, migration. In the same period, social reformers as well as their opponents were increasingly concerned with conditions of life and health among the various population groupings, and this interest generated more and increasingly detailed studies of morbidity and mortality.

Contemporary concern with health conditions has centered upon questions of (a) the availability, (b) the costs, and (c) the equality of access to medical and health services. Though many countries in the West have long had universal—or, at least, very broad—health protection and sickness insurance programs, the United States has lagged far behind in all three aspects—equality of access, costs, and availability—of health care. Just as mortality studies served to highlight the desperate straits of the nineteenth century industrial and rural poor in Europe, so can analyses of mortality be mobilized today to document one of America's gravest social problems in the twentieth century: the persistence, and inadequacy, of archaic institutions and systems for provision of medical care.

Measures of Mortality

We have already discussed the major indexes and measurements of mortality (chapter 5). In our presentation of the basic mortality rate for age-sex categories, we described the universal age variation in mortality rates: a fairly high rate immediately following birth (around 20 to 30 deaths per 1,000 births in Western Europe, North America, and Oceania, but reaching 200 to 300 deaths per thousand births in underdeveloped countries); a diminishing rate throughout the ages of childhood, reaching a minimum at around the ages of 10 to 14 (about 0.5 to 1.0 death per 1,000 in Western populations); and, finally, an increasing rate at subsequent ages (reaching about 30 to 50 deaths per 1,000 close to age 65 in Western populations and rising very sharply thereafter). Figure 6.1 depicts this age variation in mortality rates with regard to the male and female populations of Italy in the mid-1950s.

We have also indicated that male mortality is usually higher than female mortality at all ages of life.[1] For example, the infant mortality rate in the United States in 1950 was 34.0 per 1,000 for white males but only 25.7 per 1,000 for white females;[2] and the death rate at ages 75–84 in the

1 For a recent analysis of some South Asian exceptions, see El-Badry (1969).

2 It might be noted here that the U.S. infant mortality rate has been consistently higher in the past several decades than the rates of a number of other Western countries, among them the Netherlands, Sweden, Norway, Australia, and New Zealand. Moreover, the U.S. rate has been declining at a slower pace than the rates of other Western countries, so that countries with previously higher levels of infant mortality, e.g., England and Wales, Denmark, and Scotland, have rates below that of the United States. See table 6.8 and, for much more detail, H. C. Chase (1967) and H. C. Chase (1969).

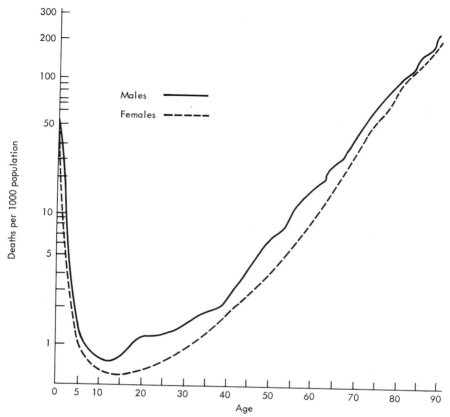

FIGURE 6.1. Male and female mortality by age, Italy, 1954–57. Source: Federici 1968.

same year was 105.3 per 1,000, for white males but only 84.8 per 1,000 for white females. Thus, the pattern of mortality for any population is described by a *set* of mortality rates by age and sex. As stated in the previous chapter, such a set of age-sex-specific mortality rates is conventionally called the *mortality schedule* of a population; and it is the variations and changes in *mortality schedules* which are the focus of this chapter.

Among the measures we gave for summarizing the mortality schedule, i.e., the overall pattern of mortality in a population, were the crude death rate, the standardized death rate, and the expectation of life at birth. These summary measures may differ for, say, two populations if mortality rates in the two populations differ either at *every* age or at only *some* ages. We indicated also that in the case of crude death rates, differences can occur between the rates of two populations if the age compositions differ, even when the mortality schedules are identical.

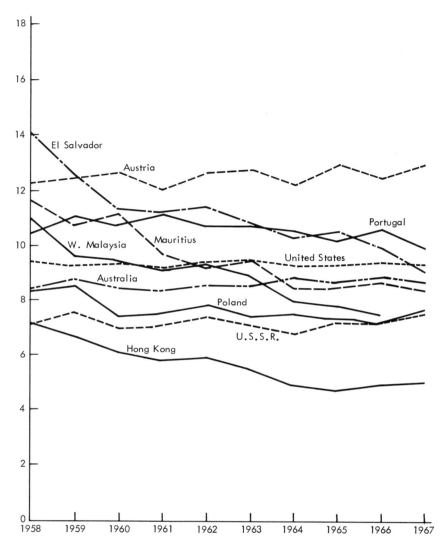

FIGURE 6.2. Deaths per 1,000 population. Source: Population Index, January–March 1969.

Historical Trends in Mortality

It is generally assumed that mortality was once universally very high—although not necessarily uniformly so in time and space—reaching as many as 40 to 50 deaths annually per 1,000 population. It is *known* that mortality rates in countries now characterized by low mortality have declined historically from much higher levels, and it is *known* that mortality rates in countries now characterized by fairly high mortality have only recently declined from higher levels. These declines are closely connected with declining morbidity (incidence of disease) and with increasingly effective treatment of disease. Neither the decline in morbidity nor

FIGURE 6.3. Infant deaths per 1,000 live births. Source: Population Index, April–June 1969.

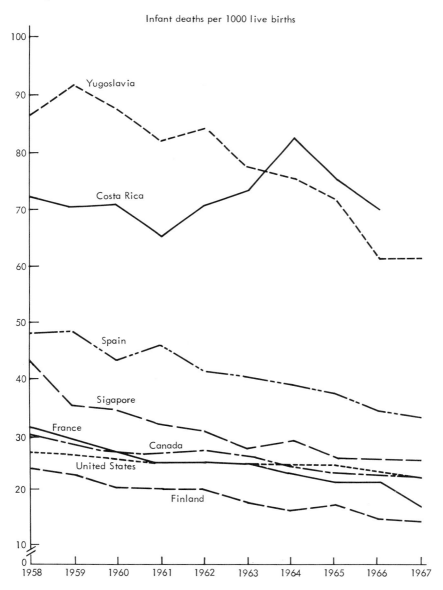

the increasing effectiveness of treatment have occurred uniformly for all diseases, in all places, or in all populations. (In the next section we shall review briefly the major modern trends in overall levels of mortality and the hypotheses concerning the causes of reduced mortality.)

Differential Mortality

It should be clear by now that mortality varies in different countries and in different areas of the world. In general terms, a crude distinction may be made between the mortality of developed countries and that of underdeveloped ones: the Western countries are characterized by crude death rates of about 10–20 per 1,000, while the least developed countries have rates of about 20–30 per 1,000.

Within any one country, too, mortality rates often differ by type of settlement. Thus, mortality in the United States has long been higher in the South and in the mountain states than in the Northeast or Pacific Coast states. And in Europe, until well into the present century, urban mortality was notably higher than rural mortality.

Mortality within countries also differs by socioeconomic status and by occupation. In general, groups with low socioeconomic status have higher mortality rates and lower life expectancies than do groups with higher socioeconomic status. However, mortality differences do not uniformly favor the higher socioeconomic groups, since certain causes of mortality are more prevalent among them. Similarly, mortality differences among occupational groups are not uniform in direction.

Finally, mortality varies by race, by religion, and by marital status. It is commonly hypothesized that mortality differences among racial and religious groups are rooted in differences of socioeconomic level, occupation, geographic location, or type of residence. However, it is not easy to document this hypothesis convincingly. An even more obscure area is that of marital status. Among adult males and females alike, mortality is substantially higher among single persons than among ever-married ones, and it is lower among married persons than among widowed or divorced ones. These differences obtain in virtually every population, but their causes are not entirely clear.

Mortality variations among different countries and among the different subpopulations of any one country are undoubtedly related to group variations in morbidity, on the one hand, and in access to, and effectiveness of, treatment, on the other. But the direct study of differential morbidity and of differential access to treatment presents many problems, and indeed, is so difficult that, until very recently, the study of differential mortality has had to substitute for it. (Fortunately, the recent development of the National Health Survey has opened up new opportunities for investigation in this area.) Some of the findings and problems of research on differential mortality will be discussed in more detail in the third section of this chapter.

DIFFERENTIAL CONTROL OF MORTALITY. It is often stated that the desire to reduce mortality and increase longevity is universal. This may be so, but it is nevertheless a fact that different societies, and different social groupings within any given society, are differently organized to combat mortality. Societies and social collectivities differ in the means they adopt to prevent, avoid, or delay morbidity, and in the protection against mortality afforded to persons variously located in their social structures.

Thus, countries and communities differ sharply in the number of physicians and numbers of other medically trained personnel per 1,000 of population. Communities and societies differ in absolute numbers of hospitals and physical facilities for treatment, as well as in the availability of specialists.[3] (Table 6.1 presents some pertinent data on the availability of medical care at around the middle of this century in selected states of the U.S. and in selected countries; also indicated is the availability of physicians in the U.S. from 1886 to 1963.) The various population groups within a society differ in the amounts and proportions of total income allocated to medical care. And, finally, countries may differ in the extent to which their various social classes are similar or dissimilar with respect to mortality and, presumably, with respect to exposure to risk and access to treatment.[4] In the last section of this chapter we consider the social structure of mortality control in more detail.

2. THE MODERN DECLINE OF MORTALITY

A spectacular decline in mortality took place during the modern period in Europe and in countries of European settlement. The following discussion sketches very briefly the facts of this decline.

The Extent of the Fall in Death Rates

Until the end of the seventeenth century, and even through the first decades of the eighteenth century, European populations were characterized not only by generally high mortality but by periodic population

3 For example, Duncan shows that health services and facilities in the United States are clearly more accessible to residents of large, rather than small, cities. Infant mortality varies inversely with city size, and these differentials have increased over time as infant mortality rates have declined (Duncan 1956).

4 Thus, a comparison of mortality rates for males classified by occupational level reveals much greater mortality differences between U.S. groups at the lowest and highest levels than between similar groups in England and Wales (see Moriyama and Guralnick 1956).

TABLE 6.1

Medical Care Facilities: Health Services in the U.S. by State, 1940 and 1946; Population per Physician in the U.S., 1886– 1963, and in Selected Countries, 1940-1964

State	General Hospital Beds per 1,000 Population 1946	Population per Physician 1940	Population per Dentist 1940
New York	4.8	496	1,314
California	3.6	580	1,268
New Jersey	3.9	716	1,547
Massachusetts	5.1	547	1,530
Washington	3.9	790	1,376
Indiana	2.8	830	1,890
Texas	2.5	930	3,179
West Virginia	3.3	1,037	3,186
Tennessee	2.3	1,003	3,455
Alabama	2.2	1,365	4,683
Mississippi	1.9	1,459	5,212

Year	Number of Physicians in the U.S., 1886-1950	Population per Physician
1886	87,521	662
1900	119,749	637
1912	137,199	694
1925	147,010	787
1940	175,163	775
1950	209,040	730
1963	—	690

Selected Countries in Americas, Europe, and Asia	Population per Physician		
	1940	1950	1964
U.S.	775	741	690[a]
Canada	1,515	901	890[b]
Mexico	8,333	7,142	1,800[b]
Guatemala	9,091	9,091	4,000
Puerto Rico	—	2,941	1,300
Brazil	4,762	2,500[c]	2,100[b]
Chile	1,493	1,900[c]	1,800[b]
Argentina	870	800[c]	670[b]
U.K.	943	1,200[c]	830
France	1,587	1,100[c]	910
Norway	1,235	1,099	830[a]
Sweden	2,128	1,613	960[a]
Poland	2,564	3,030	830
Switzerland	588	800	760
Japan	1,111	1,205	920[a]
Turkey	12,500	7,692	3,200
Lebanon	—	1,493	1,300[a]
Israel	—	430[c]	420
Union of South Afr.	2,326	2,500	1,900[a]
Egypt	—	4,167	2,400
Kenya	—	20,000	9,700[a]
Angola	—	33,333	13,000[a]
Mozambique	—	50,000	18,000
Australia	1,087	1,613	740
New Zealand	885	800	670
New Guinea	—	50,000	17,000

SOURCE: Woytinsky and Woytinsky 1953, tables 118 and 124; U.N., *Compendium of Social Statistics, 1967* (1968), p. 206-13.

[a]1963.
[b]1962.
[c]1952.

TABLE 6.2

Age-Specific Mortality Rates per 1,000 by Sex and Period of Birth: European Nobility

Age	Males Born in:			Females Born in:		
	1480–1679	*1680–1779*	*1780–1789*	*1480–1679*	*1680–1779*	*1780–1789*
15–19	64	43	29.5	43	39	42
20–24	102.5	92.5	47	55	59	42
25–29	104	67	44.5	79.5	67	44
30–34	95	74	61.5	86.5	71	51
35–39	100	81.5	24	94.5	67	42
40–44	105	82	41	116.5	70	38
45–49	158	104	62	136.5	77	42

SOURCE: Peller 1965.

catastrophes, including famines, epidemics, and wars. Systematic data bearing upon this period are, of course, scanty. However, genealogical records of certain European ruling families exist, and, since we assume that mortality in the general population must have greatly exceeded that of the aristocracy, their mortality patterns may be taken as lower bounds for the periods in question. Death rates among members of the European nobility born in the period between 1480 and 1789 have been computed by S. Peller (1965) and are shown in table 6.2. It is clear from this table that mortality was initially very high but began to fall in almost all age groups long before the development of modern medicine. However, maternal mortality declined very little in the period. Mortality conditions among the European nobility since 1500 are summarized in table 6.3 in terms of expectation of life at birth.

A. M. Carr-Saunders estimated that the average annual crude death rate in the first half of the eighteenth century reached 30.4 per thousand in Sweden and between 28 and 36 per thousand in England and Wales (see fig. 6.4). But from about 1750 onward, both countries enjoyed a virtually uninterrupted decline in crude death rates, and by about 1920 the rates in both had diminished to less than 15 per 1,000 (Carr-Saunders 1936b; chap. V).

TABLE 6.3

Expectation of Life at Birth (e_o) of European Nobility by Sex and by Period of Birth

Sex	Period of Birth			
	1500–1599	*1600–1699*	*1700–1799*	*1800–1885*
Males	32.2	28.1	36.1	45.8
Females	35.9	33.7	37.4	48.0

SOURCE: Peller 1965, table 5.

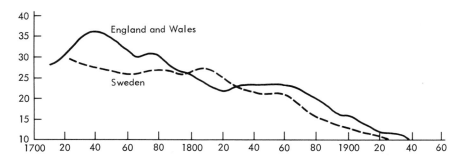

FIGURE 6.4. Crude death rates in England, Wales, and Sweden, 1700–1930. Source: Carr-Saunders 1936b.

Stabilization of Annual Mortality

However, even the high average rates of mortality at the beginning of the eighteenth century obscure the violent fluctuations in numbers and rates of deaths still characteristic of Northwestern Europe. Such fluctuations occurred even later in countries of Eastern and Southern Europe, and they had been characteristic of all of Europe up to the close of the seventeenth century (summary based on Helleiner 1957). European famines and crop failures known to have taken enormous tolls of human life are recorded variously for Finland in 1696–1697, for Sweden in 1698, for France in 1693–1694, for Britain between 1693 and 1699, and for Britain and France in 1708–1709. The War of the Spanish Succession (1701–1714) and the Great Northern War (1699–1721) both took high tolls among the combatants but inflicted even greater losses by instigating the spread of typhus and the plague. Between 1708 and 1711, the plague reportedly killed tens of thousands of persons, including between one-third to one-half of the total population of Danzig, a third of the inhabitants of Copenhagen, and large numbers in Königsberg, Riga, Stockholm, Helsinki, and Uppsala. The populations of Prussia, Lithuania, Germany, Austria, Bohemia, and Bavaria were also hit hard by the plague. The last incidence of the plague in western Europe was in 1720–1721, in the area of Marseilles and the region of Provence in France. In Marseilles, some 40,000 out of a total of 90,000 inhabitants lost their lives; and the epidemic killed about three-fourths of the population of the Provençal towns of Arles and La Valette, half the population each of Toulon and Berre, and one-third the population each of Aix-en-Provence, Martigues, and St. Rémy.

Many subsequent crop failures, famines, wars, and epidemics are reported for Europe in the rest of the eighteenth century and in the nineteenth century as well. However, they are much more sporadic and

TABLE 6.4

Crude Death Rates in Europe, by Areas and Selected Periods

Area	1900–1910	1935–1938	1945–1948	1955–1958	1971
Britain, Netherlands, Scandinavia	14.1	10.7	10.3	9.7	9.8
Other countries in Western Europe	17.7	13.3	13.0	11.3	11.8
Southern Europe	21.7	15.6	12.7	9.4	9.0
Eastern Europe, excluding USSR	24.5	15.7	10.0	10.0	10.0

SOURCE: U.N., *Population Bulletin,* No. 6, 1962; and *1971 World Population Data Sheet,* Population Reference Bureau, Washington, D.C.

much less catastrophic than their predecessors, and the overall picture of mortality in that period matches the decline of mortality in Sweden and in England and Wales, but generally with a lag of at least several decades. At the end of the nineteenth century, mortality was still substantially higher in southern and eastern Europe than in western and northwestern Europe. In the present century, mortality rates have continued to decline and life expectancy has increased substantially (see tables 6.4 and 6.5 and figure 6.5).

TABLE 6.5

Gains in Expectation of Life at Birth in the Twentieth Century

		Males	Females
United States (Whites)	1900–1902	48.23	51.08
	1955	67.30	73.69
	1967	67.80	75.10
Sweden	1901–1910	54.53	56.98
	1951–1958	70.48	73.43
	1967	71.85	76.54
Netherlands	1900–1909	51.00	53.40
	1953–1955	71.00	73.90
	1967	71.00	76.50
France	1898–1903	45.74	49.03
	1950–1951	63.60	69.30
	1966	68.20	75.40
England and Wales	1901–1910	48.53	52.38
	1953–1955	67.52	72.99
	1965–1967	68.70	74.90

SOURCE: 1900–1958 — U.N., *Population Bulletin,* No. 6, (1962); 1965–1967 — U.N., *Demographic Yearbook 1969,* No. 21 (1970).

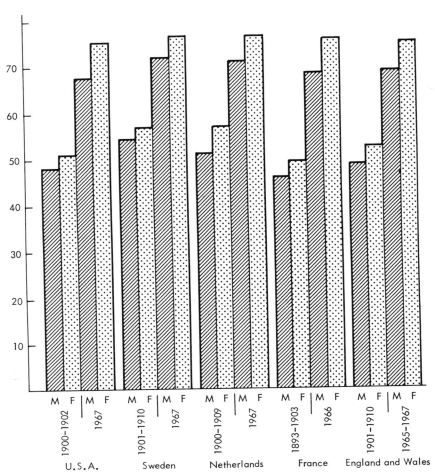

FIGURE 6.5. Twentieth-century gains in expectation of life at birth. Source:
Table 6.5.

Differential Declines by Time, Age Groups, and Geographic Area

Expectation of life in western Europe and the United States increased by some 20 years in the first half of the twentieth century.[5] Judging
from life tables for France (1817–1831) and Sweden (1816–1840), the
average life expectancy at birth in western Europe at the end of the first
quarter of the nineteenth century was around 40 years. The data of table
6.5 suggest that, at the turn of the century, Swedish life expectancy was
just over 50 years and French life expectancy about 47 years, on the aver-

5 For a recent study on changes in the United States, see Spiegelman (1968).

age. Thus, expectation of life increased by only about seven to ten years from the first quarter until the close of the nineteenth century—about half the increase experienced in the following 50 years.

It should also be noted that improvements in mortality conditions have been far from uniform for all ages of life. The decrease in mortality rates has been most spectacular for ages 1–4 and 5–14 and for the one-year period following birth.[6] Improvements have been substantial at adult ages, though less impressive after the age of 65 (for data on Sweden, see table 6.6).

The decline in mortality between 1750 and 1900 was, with the notable exception of Japan, confined largely to Europe and to areas of European settlement. As late as 1947, the crude death rates of Africa and south central Asia were estimated to average about 25–30 per 1,000 of population, and for the Near East and Far East (excluding Japan, whose crude death rate, just over 25 per thousand in 1920, had already declined to 16.5 per thousand by 1940 and to 7.6 per thousand by 1960), crude death rates averaged around 30–35 per thousand (U.N. 1953). Of course, these averages obscure crude death rates which reached or surpassed 40 per thousand in certain countries.

However, since the end of World War II spectacular declines in mortality have been recorded for countries of Asia, Africa, and Latin America. For example, comparing crude death rates in 1935–1939 with those of 1955–1959, Ceylon's rate declined from 24.5 to 9.9, Hong Kong's from 29.1 to 7.6, Chile's from 23.7 to 12.5, Mexico's from 23.3 to 12.5, and Mauritius's from 27.3 to 12.0 (Stolnitz 1965). Similarly, expectation of life at birth increased for Egypt from 38.0 years in 1947 to 50.0 years in 1961; for females in India from 31.7 years in 1941–1950 to 42.1 years in

6 For a detailed discussion of this, see Peller 1948, pp. 405–56.

TABLE 6.6
Decrease of Mortality Rates in Sweden by Age Groups, 1751–1800 to 1901–1945

Age	Percent increase (+) or decrease (–) of death rate			
	1751–1800 to 1801–1850	1801–1850 to 1851–1900	1851–1900 to 1900–1945	1751–1800 to 1901–1945
Under 1	–14.6	–27.9	–53.8	–71.6
1–4	–27.5	–15.6	–74.5	–84.4
5–14	–29.1	–10.1	–65.6	–78.1
15–24	–11.5	–17.9	–26.5	–46.6
25–44	– 5.5	–29.4	–39.7	–59.7
45–64	+ 5.9	–31.9	–35.2	–53.3
65 and over	+ 7.1	–21.5	–19.0	–31.9

SOURCE: U.N. Department of Economic and Social Affairs 1953.

1956–1961; and for females in Puerto Rico from 46.9 years in 1939–1941 to 71.9 years in 1959–1961 (Stolnitz 1965).

Causes of Declining Mortality

The causes of the decline in mortality are of historical—and very practical—significance: since it is the search for collective and individual survival that impels societies to pursue mortality control, any knowledge of the means by which such control is achieved is of primary importance. The factors conventionally set forth as causes or conditions of declining mortality include—

1. political circumstances, e.g., internal order, absence of wars and strife;
2. social and educational factors, e.g., knowledge concerning the production and exploitation of food, clothing, and shelter;
3. sanitary factors, e.g., water supply, drainage;
4. medical factors, including knowledge about the prevention, diagnosis, and cure of disease;
5. economic development and rising income levels, e.g., the replacement of subsistence food production and distribution with market mechanisms, investment in roads and communication;
6. social reforms, e.g., control of working conditions, establishment of minimum wages, and provision of accessible services (Carr-Saunders 1936; U.N. 1953).

However, there is considerable obscurity and controversy surrounding the question of the relative importance of these factors in the historical declines of mortality. Pioneer students of European mortality trends frequently held that social conditions, sanitary improvements, and scientific and medical advances were the primary causes of mortality decline. In part this hypothesis was based upon analyses of mortality by cause of death and upon the knowledge that mortality due to infectious and epidemic diseases declined spectacularly during a period experiencing reforms in housing and working conditions, improvements in sanitation, discoveries in medicine, and the development of hospital and other treatment facilities. More recently, however, it has become clear that the general declines in mortality in Western countries began and took place during the eighteenth and first part of the nineteenth centuries, substantially *before* the development of scientific methods of controlling individual diseases. Evidently, the major influences responsible for the decline in mortality were (a) rising levels of living, which included improved diet (fundamental to the declining incidence of tuberculosis and the decrease in infant mortality); (b) hygienic changes introduced by sanitary reforms (basic to the reduced incidence of the typhus-typhoid and cholera diseases); and possibly (c) favorable genetic developments (connected with the declining incidence of scarlet fever and perhaps with the decrease in tuberculosis, typhus, and cholera). Thus, the declines in mortality were due mainly to the *declining incidence of diseases* rather than to improvement in therapy. The effects of treatment, therapy, medical discoveries, and the like seem to have been restricted to smallpox, with the effect of this on the total reduction of death rates a matter of some dispute (cf. U.N. 1953, p. 60; and especially McKeown and Record 1962; McKeown and Brown 1955; Helleiner 1957; and McKeown 1965).

On the other hand, twentieth-century declines in mortality, especially the spectacular ones achieved in countries outside Europe or European settlement, may much more reasonably be imputed to the deliberate introduction of measures of public health and preventive medicine. These include, for example, immunization programs, the use of DDT against malaria-carrying mosquitos, and improved standards of sanitation in food and water distribution and sewage disposal. The "underdeveloped countries" have been able to import and apply directly the knowledge and techniques which accumulated only very slowly in the European countries, where mortality declines had to await economic, social, educational, and scientific developments. The rapid reductions in mortality in the underdeveloped countries have, moreover, been obtained at relatively low cost, often with the help and direct subsidy of other, more developed, nations. Thus, one student of mortality in the underdeveloped countries has concluded that low per capita income is no longer an insurmountable barrier to increasing longevity and lower mortality; however, he adds, relatively higher income is always associated with greater longevity (Vallin 1968). But, of course, these same improvements in mortality, longevity, and population growth—unaccompanied as they are by the economic, social, and educational advances that characterized Europe—may portend new and menacing problems for the underdeveloped countries and for the world as a whole.

3. DIFFERENTIAL MORTALITY

Historically, mortality studies have developed concurrently with life insurance and public health programs in addition to their connection with studies of population growth and dynamics. The originators of official mortality statistics envisaged them as major tools for improving the living conditions of the population, and, indeed, they have played this very role in the past two centuries in the West and in the twentieth century throughout the world. One of their major uses in this connection has been in the comparative analysis of living and mortality conditions in different countries and in different populations within any given country.

The study of differential mortality has played a key role in the discovery of correlates and causes of morbidity and mortality in general, and of the incidence of specified diseases and maladies in particular. For the knowledge that a particular disease is more prevalent or more fatal in one population category than another is generally suggestive of the reasons for, or factors in, the observed differences. A case in point is the study of perinatal mortality (infant deaths in the first week of life, which, in populations with relatively low infant mortality, may constitute more than half the total number of infant deaths). When it was discovered that perinatal mortality was strikingly lower among infants born to mothers living in maternity homes prior to the delivery of the child—and inversely related to the amount of time before birth spent in such maternity homes—the new information received widespread attention and led to greater developments in obstetrics and prenatal care and nutrition.[7] Similarly, the discovery of great differences between smokers and nonsmokers in rates of mortality due to lung cancer has stimulated the search for how smoke, smoking, and air-pollution cause, or are correlated with, lung cancer, and a long list of other diseases as well.[8]

Types of Differential Mortality

As indicated earlier in this chapter, there are a number of types of differential mortality. Variations in mortality by geographic location, socioeconomic level, occupation, place of residence, and ethnic, racial, and religious characteristics have all been studied in the past and remain topics of current investigation. Each type of study presents certain methodological problems, and a few of these will be mentioned briefly along with examples of research results.

DIFFERENTIAL MORTALITY AMONG NATIONS. We have already referred to the great gaps between mortality rates of "developed" and "underdeveloped" countries. But in addition, within each of the two great "categories" there is very considerable variation. Table 6.7 presents crude death rates, infant mortality rates, and expectation-of-life-at-birth figures for selected "developed" and "underdeveloped" countries around the period from 1960 to 1969, and figures 6.2 and 6.3 portray recent trends in crude death rates and infant mortality rates in selected industrialized and less-developed countries.

There are many limitations to the comparison of data such as those in table 6.7. In the first place, the several countries have different regis-

7 For a detailed discussion of this, see Peller 1948, pp. 405–56.
8 The major publications on this subject include Doll and Hill 1956, pp. 1071–81; Dorn 1959, pp. 581–93; Hammond 1966; and U.S. Department of Health, Education, and Welfare, PHS–1103, 1964.

TABLE 6.7

Mortality Indexes for Selected "Developed" and "Underdeveloped" Countries

	Crude Death Rate	Infant Mortality Rate	Expectation of Life at Birth (e_0)		
			Year	Males	Females
Developed Countries					
United States, 1969	9.6	22.1	1967	67.0	74.2
Canada, 1969	7.3	23.1	1960–62	68.4	74.2
France, 1969	10.9	20.6	1967	68.1	75.4
Netherlands, 1969	7.9	13.4	1967	71.0	76.5
England and Wales, 1969	11.2	18.8	1966–68	68.7	74.9
Sweden, 1969	10.1	12.6	1967	71.9	76.5
USSR, 1969	8	26	1965–66	66.0	74.0
Underdeveloped Countries					
Chile, 1969	10.0	108.0	1952	49.8	53.9
India, 1969	18.0	139	1951–60	41.9	40.6
Ceylon, 1969	8.0	56	1962	61.9	61.4
Egypt, 1969	15	120	1960	51.6	53.8
Mauritius, 1969	9	65	1961–63	58.7	61.9
Upper Volta			1960–61	32.1	31.1

SOURCE: *Population Index* (October–December 1969) and our Figure 1.2.

tration practices and definitions. Second, they perform their enumerations and registrations with different degrees of completeness. And finally, they may compute nominally identical indexes in different ways. Thus, definitions of "live birth," "stillbirth," and "infant death" differ among the different countries. Deaths are recorded in some countries with reference to time of occurrence but in others with reference to time of registration. In some countries, the registration of death is voluntary, in others it is obligatory but incomplete, and in still others it is obligatory and virtually complete. Where registration is incomplete, statistics and indexes may or may not be corrected for underregistration of deaths or for underenumeration of the base populations. Finally, the different techniques of computation affect the calculation of mortality rates, life tables, and the life expectation at birth derived from life tables (Spiegelman 1968; Jaffe 1951; and Wolfenden 1954).

GEOGRAPHIC VARIATION WITHIN NATIONS. Geographic variations in mortality within a given nation are fairly clearly portrayed in a country's official statistics and present fewer problems of comparability than do international variations. However, only in the study of regional, urban-rural, size-of-place, or other geographic variations in infant mortality are the comparisons easily interpreted. In all other instances—and often even in the case of infant mortality rates—the comparisons must be interpreted with great caution.

In the first place, the various regional populations of a country often differ in age composition, a factor which renders the comparison of crude death rates hazardous. And, the urban-rural or size-of-place compositions of regional populations are even more likely to vary. Similarly, in regions or other types of places, ethnic, occupational, industrial, or educational compositions may differ, and each of these variables may generate differences in mortality. Thus, differences in the composition of populations may affect regional, urban-rural, size-of-place, and other geographic comparisons of mortality. Finally, and perhaps most difficult to manage analytically, the population of any region, area, or place may include migrants, and it may include relatively many or relatively few of them, and they may have arrived recently or long ago. Thus, the question arises of the legitimacy of associating the mortality characteristics of a geographically circumscribed subpopulation with the area or place in question and with its special geographic, social, and economic characteristics or institutions.

VARIATIONS AMONG NATIONAL, ETHNIC, RELIGIOUS, AND RACIAL GROUPS. In many countries, national, ethnic, religious, or racial population groupings are distinguished in official and other statistics, and there is often great interest in the mortality differences among them. In the United States, the mortality of Negroes and other nonwhites is consistently higher than that of whites, and in Israel, the mortality of non-Jews exceeds that of Jews at most ages (table 6.8).

VARIATIONS BY SOCIOECONOMIC STATUS. Perhaps the most difficult approach to differential mortality is that which seeks to relate different mortality rates to different levels of socioeconomic status. Both the col-

TABLE 6.8
Racial and Religious Mortality Differentials in the United States and Israel, 1968

	Crude Death Rate	Infant Mortality Rate	Expectation of Life at Birth (e_0)	
			Males	*Females*
United States, 1968	11.1	21.9	67.5	74.9
Whites	11.1	21.9	67.5	74.9
Nonwhites	11.6	37.8	60.1	67.5
Israel, 1968				
Jews	6.9	20.3	69.8	73.4
Non-Jews	6.1	42.4	68.4	70.9

SOURCE: Population Index 34, No. 3 (1968), and 31, No. 4 (1965); *Israel Statistical Abstract,* No. 20, 1969.

lection and the interpretation of data representing the mortality of different socioeconomic groupings in a population present many difficulties. In the first place, it is not always easy to classify a population in terms of socioeconomic status; thus, the specification of a base population relative to which rates can be computed is the first difficulty. In the second place, the classification of numbers of deaths by the socioeconomic status of decedents is even more difficult: in particular, the classification of decedents whose socioeconomic status is determined by other related persons, e.g., wives, children, or other dependents, must be determined on the basis of information other than that normally recorded in death certificates and other vital records. In all cases, there arises the problem of what status to impute to decedents who are known to have *changed* their socioeconomic level; this difficulty would apply, for example, to retired persons and recently-married persons.

We shall describe three separate approaches to the collection and use of data bearing on socioeconomic differences in mortality.

THE AREAL UNIT APPROACH. The first approach, an indirect one, involves computing mortality rates for areas or combinations of small areas determined to be characterized by different socioeconomic levels. (The combinations of small areas might be census tracts or wards in a city, townships, or other well-defined areas for which both base population data and death statistics can be obtained.) The bases for classifying census tracts or other areal units in terms of socioeconomic categories have included such characteristics as median income, median rental paid, median educational achievement, and percentage of the population in white-collar occupations.[9]

An example of such an approach is Sauvy's study of Paris for the years 1891, 1936, and 1946 (Sauvy 1954). The Parisian areal units, *arrondissements,* are classified according to whether they are "well off," "middle class," or "poor," and mortality rates are computed for each category of *arrondissement* (table 6.9).

Table 6.9 shows that mortality is substantially lower in the "well-off" *arrondissements* than in the "middle-class" or "poor" ones, but that the differences have been diminishing slightly since 1891. The socioeconomic gradient seems much steeper in the case of infant mortality than general mortality: Between 1891 and 1936, infant mortality diminished spectacularly in Paris as a whole and in all three socioeconomic categories as well; moreover, the ratio between the infant mortality rates of the "poor" and "well off" diminished. However, in the period just after World War II, infant mortality *increased* in the "middle class" and "poor" areas but remained stable in the "well-off" ones; and the ratio between the

9 See our earlier section on functional combinations of primary areal units, chapter 3, section 3.

TABLE 6.9

Mortality by Socioeconomic Areas of Paris

Areal Categories	Standardized Death Rates			Infant Mortality Rate			
	1891	*1936*	*1946*	*1891*	*1936*	*1946*	*1951*
Well off	16.8	9.6	9.5	91.9	47.2	47.1	24.1
Middle class	22.6	12.5	11.3	135.3	61.7	75.0	36.5
Poor	23.9	13.7	12.0	157.2	72.2	81.2	37.2
Total Paris	22.5	12.2	11.2	136.3	63.5	71.7	34.4
Ratio: $\frac{\text{Poor}}{\text{Well off}}$	1.42	1.43	1.26	1.71	1.53	1.72	1.54

SOURCE: Sauvy 1954.

infant mortality rates of the "poor" to "well off" increased. In the following postwar period, infant mortality in all socioeconomic categories declined very considerably and the differences again diminished.

In a study based on Chicago census-tract data on population and on mortality by age and color, A. J. Mayer and P. M. Hauser (1953) were able to compute life tables and expectations of life for white and nonwhite males by economic status. In this study, census tracts were classified on the basis of median rentals.

In table 6.10, the mortality differences between white and nonwhite males are clearly reflected, as are differences in mortality among white "high" and "low" rental-tract categories. In the case of nonwhite males,

TABLE 6.10

Expectation of Life at Birth (e_0) by Color and Economic Status: Chicago, 1920, 1930, 1940

Color and Economic Status	1920 e_0	1930 e_0	1940 e_0
White			
High-rental census tracts	61.8	65.0	67.8
Low-rental census tracts	51.8	53.7	60.2
Total	57.7	59.7	64.9
Nonwhite			
High-rental census tracts	—	45.4	55.9
Low-rental census tracts	—	40.0	49.9
Total	42.3	44.5	53.6
Total U.S.A.	54.1	56.7	59.0

SOURCE: Mayer and Hauser 1953.

the meaning of the difference between "high" and "low" rental-tract categories is often obscure and in any case not identical to that for whites. The reason for this is that, other things being equal, nonwhites have always been obliged to pay higher rents than whites for equivalent or less-than-equivalent housing; thus, areal delineation on the basis of median rentals may involve a "double standard" insofar as reflection of socioeconomic status is concerned. In other words, to the extent that "poor" or "low socioeconomic status" persons are concentrated in "low-rental census tracts" and "rich" or "high socioeconomic status" persons are concentrated in "high-rental census tracts," the area-type differences do in fact reflect mortality differences between the "poor" and the "rich," or between "low" and "high-socioeconomic status" persons. But if poor or low socioeconomic status nonwhites are forced—by the nature of the housing market and patterns of racial segregation—to pay exorbitant rentals, this alone would cause many nonwhite neighborhoods to be characterized by high rentals, i.e., to be "high rental census tracts" even if the people living there and forced to pay such high rents are actually quite "poor" or of low socioeconomic status.

THE OCCUPATIONAL MORTALITY APPROACH. A second approach to the analysis of mortality differences by socioeconomic status deals with "occupational mortality." The study of "occupational mortality" is of considerable interest in its own right in that it reflects the different mortality and morbidity hazards associated with different occupations. Unfortunately, however, it is usually impossible to distinguish between the mortality connected with strictly occupational hazards and that connected with the level or style of life, i.e., the socioeconomic status, associated with the various occupations.

Studies of occupational mortality generally seek to compute occupation-specific mortality rates, that is, to relate the mortality of persons having a given occupation at, or prior to, death with the base population in that specific occupation. In addition, attempts are made to compute occupation-specific mortality rates for persons dependent upon, or otherwise attached to, the respective occupations and the socioeconomic categories associated with them; thus, mortality rates are computed for women and children in terms of the occupations of their husbands and fathers.

There is a long tradition of studies of this type in England and Wales. In table 6.11, whose figures for England and Wales are based on occupation by socioeconomic class, it can be seen that general mortality is highest in the lower "social classes" but that mortality from certain causes rises the higher the social class. Standardized mortality ratios for each social class are calculated with reference to the corresponding cause-specific death rate for all social classes together, e.g.,

TABLE 6.11
Standardized Mortality Ratios by Cause and Social Class for Men and Married Women Aged 20–64: England and Wales, for Specified Time Periods

Cause of Death and Year	Men Social class I	II	III	IV	V	Married Women Social class I	II	III	IV	V
All Causes										
1921–1923	82	94	95	101	125	[1]	[1]	[1]	[1]	[1]
1930–1932	90	94	97	102	111	81	89	99	103	113
1950	97	86	102	94	118	96	84	101	104	117
Respiratory Tuberculosis										
1921–1923	49	81	95	97	137	[1]	[1]	[1]	[1]	[1]
1930–1932	61	70	100	104	125	52	67	99	106	132
1950	64	62	103	95	149	<u>43</u>	52	104	107	166
Cancer of Stomach										
1921–1923	60	82	100	106	130	[1]	[1]	[1]	[1]	[1]
1930–1932[2]	59[3]	84[3]	98[3]	108[3]	124[3]	54	78	104	104	121
1950	57	67	100	114	132	<u>57</u>	72	101	106	138
Cancer of Lung										
1921–1923	100	109	97	79	124	[1]	[1]	[1]	[1]	[1]
1930–1932	107	95	100	92	114	<u>95</u>	100	108	81	94
1950	80	79	108	89	116	<u>120</u>	94	104	96	91
Cancer of Breast										
1930–1932	[4]	[4]	[4]	[4]	[4]	136	116	103	84	82
1950	[4]	[4]	[4]	[4]	[4]	144	100	106	76	97
Cancer of Cervix Uteri										
1950	[4]	[4]	[4]	[4]	[4]	<u>61</u>	69	98	109	150
Leukemia										
1930–1932	153	125	96	94	85	<u>167</u>	118	107	76	76
1950	<u>153</u>	101	107	81	88	<u>145</u>	<u>73</u>	110	<u>91</u>	<u>95</u>
Coronary Heart Disease										
1930–1932	237[3]	148[3]	95[3]	66[3]	67[3]	157	126	93	85	88
1950	150	110	104	79	89	92	93	101	100	108
Myocardial Degeneration										
1930–1932	77[3]	92[3]	94[3]	105[3]	122[3]	54	75	99	110	129
1950	67	82	97	98	137	<u>66</u>	67	98	120	134
Bronchitis										
1921–1923	26	55	94	121	177	[1]	[1]	[1]	[1]	[1]
1930–1932	31	57	91	124	156	<u>27</u>	56	99	119	155
1950	33	53	97	103	172	<u>33</u>	48	100	130	152
Diabetes Mellitus										
1921–1923	125	145	92	75	66	[1]	[1]	[1]	[1]	[1]
1930–1932	122	155	95	82	69	56	89	104	108	106
1950	<u>167</u>	97	97	91	<u>108</u>	<u>86</u>	88	98	109	117

SOURCE: Great Britain, Registrar General, 1954.

[1] Data not available.   [3] Ages 35–64 years only.

[2] Includes esophagus.   [4] Data not applicable.

NOTES: All social classes = 100 in each specified group (see text). Social class of married women grouped according to husband's occupation. Ratios based on less than 50 deaths are underlined. Social class groupings: I – professional, II – intermediate, III – skilled, IV – semiskilled, V – unskilled.

$$\text{1950 Standardized mortality ratio for males of social class I from cancer of stomach} = \frac{\text{1950 male death rate from cancer of stomach in social class I}}{\text{1950 male death rate from cancer of stomach in all social classes}} \times 100 = 57$$

Similarly,

$$\text{1950 Standardized mortality ratio for males of social class V from cancer of stomach} = \frac{\text{1950 male death rate from cancer of stomach in social class V}}{\text{1950 male death rate from cancer of stomach in all social classes}} \times 100 = 132$$

The standardized mortality ratios for "all social classes" would equal 100 in each specified group. Thus, the higher the social class, the greater the frequency of coronary heart disease for both sexes, cancer of the breast for women, and leukemia for both sexes.

Attempts have been made to carry out studies of occupational mortality differentials in the United States and in France as well. However, these have been much less detailed than the British studies and their interpretation much more problematic. For the United States it was possible to classify 1950 male decedents aged 10–64 by occupation or previous work experience. Relating the number of deaths in 1950 for the following groups to the corresponding groups, as recorded in the 1950 census, it was possible to compute mortality rates:

    I. Professional workers
    II. Technical, administrative, and managerial workers
    III. Proprietors; clerical, sales and skilled workers
    IV. Semiskilled workers
    V. Laborers, except mine and agricultural workers
    VI. Agricultural workers

These were compared by Moriyama and Guralnick within each age group, using ratios of mortality in each occupation level group to the mortality of the total age group. These indexes, in turn, were compared to those of males in the respective socioeconomic groups in Britain in 1950. The results are shown in table 6.12.

Table 6.12 reveals that in the United States in 1950, the mortality of professionals (level I) was lower than the mean, regardless of age, and that the mortality of laborers (level V) was higher than the mean. In England and Wales, the departures from the average were smaller at all ages (as mentioned earlier in this chapter), and in both countries the

TABLE 6.12
Ratios of Death Rates by Occupation Level to Total Death Rates, by Age, for Men Aged 20–64, United States and England and Wales, 1950

Occupation Level	20–24 Years	25–34 Years	35–44 Years	45–54 Years	55–59 Years	60–64 Years
All Occupations						
United States	100	100	100	100	100	100
England and Wales	100	100	100	100	100	100
Occupation Level I						
United States	49	53	66	87	94	97
England and Wales	102	90	83	98	99	100
Occupation Levels II, III, and IV						
United States	80	84	91	96	99	101
England and Wales	94	95	96	97	99	101
Occupation Level V						
United States	190	232	219	178	146	128
England and Wales	122	138	143	129	115	106
Agricultural Workers						
United States	132	125	92	84	84	85
England and Wales	139	104	87	75	75	72

SOURCE: Moriyama and Guralnick 1956.

occupational-level differences in mortality were less at advanced ages (about 45 and over) than at younger ages (around 25 to 44).

THE RECORD LINKAGE APPROACH. The last approach to the study of mortality differences by socioeconomic status involves a technique known as "record linkage," which entails the matching of vital statistics death reports for individuals with population census returns of the same individuals. The census information is then added to the information on the death certificates so that mortality rates may be computed for every population category identifiable in the census (Kitagawa and Hauser, 1963 and 1968).

In a large-scale record linkage study of white mortality in the United States from May through August 1960, E. M. Kitagawa and P. M. Hauser (1968) were able to establish a strong inverse relationship between mortality and level of educational attainment. This education differential obtained for virtually all causes of death and was much greater for women than for men, especially above the age of 65. Table 6.13 shows the extent to which mortality differentials were associated with level of educational attainment. Again, the indexes for each education-level group are ratios of the mortality rate in that sex-age-education group to the mortality rate for the total in the sex-age group.

As the authors of this study point out, education cannot be considered the sole factor accounting for the variation in causes of death and in levels of mortality. However important it may be, the educational factor in such studies also reflects the socioeconomic variables with which education is closely associated—e.g., income, level of occupation, working conditions, style of life, diet and nutrition, quality of housing, and type of residence (Kitagawa and Hauser 1968, p. 353).

4. THE SOCIAL STRUCTURE OF MORTALITY CONTROL

The previous two sections left implicit a point which, although fairly well understood, deserves to be made explicit because of its implications for the analysis of the social structure of mortality control. Variations among population groups as well as changes over time in mortality are due to variations and changes in two distinct factors: in the *exposure* to the hazards that lead to mortality—malnutrition, disease, and injury—and in the quality and *accessibility* to the treatment of malnutrition, disease, and injury.

Differential Mortality Control among Societies

If we consider that the reduction of mortality must entail the reduction of exposure to hazards leading to mortality and/or the improvement or expanded accessibility of what we may generally describe as "medical technology," it becomes clear that human societies do not uni-

TABLE 6.13
Education Differentials in Mortality (All Causes) by Sex and Age — White Population of U.S., 1960 (Age-Sex total = 1.00)

Number of School Years Completed	White Males			White Females		
	Total 25 years and over	25–64 years	65 years and over	Total 25 years and over	25–64 years	65 years and over
Total	1.00	1.00	1.00	1.00	1.00	1.00
Less than 8 years	1.03	1.15	1.01	1.16	1.30	1.09
Elementary, 8 years	1.01	1.06	1.00	1.05	1.08	1.03
High school 1–4 years	1.00	.97	.98	.90	.89	.94
College, 1 or more years	.89	.77	1.00	.73	.81	.70

SOURCE: Kitagawa and Hauser 1968, table 8.

versally take measures to reduce mortality. The practice of putting to death certain types of persons, or of systematically permitting them to die, is well documented for certain primitive societies and for a number of ancient civilizations. Societies are often slow or entirely unable to discard practices or institutions demonstrably associated with excessive mortality or to adopt practices or institutions demonstrably capable of reducing mortality or exposure to disease and injury (cf. Wellin 1955). Thus, even in the United States today it seems clear that neither alcoholic consumption nor cigarette smoking are likely to be discarded soon despite their association with excessive mortality; or consider nationalized medical insurance plans or less powerful automobiles: both are capable of reducing mortality and exposure to disease and injury, yet neither is likely to be adopted soon in the United States.

Differential Mortality Control within Societies

Even among societies which systematically seek and adopt means of controlling exposure to disease and injury, there are great variations in the nature, scope, and structure of the institutions and practices for medical treatment and cure. Within any society—regardless of its overall mortality, its exposure to hazard, or the overall quality and scope of its medical technology—there is both a social structure of exposure to hazards of various types and a social structure of access to medical treatment and cure.

Unfortunately, differential mortality studies and their data do not, and generally cannot, distinguish between differential exposure to disease and injury and differential access to medical technology. Nevertheless, there can be no doubt that there are two *separate* social processes operating here: the first distributes individuals in the society in a manner that exposes them differentially to the risks of disease and injury; and the second institutionalizes treatment and care facilities and medical technologies in such a way that they are differentially accessible to different population subgroups. Thus, farmers, farm workers, and their families may be considerably less exposed than others to diseases of the lungs or to infectious diseases associated with urban life; but, on the other hand, they may have much less access than others to medical services, both because of their geographic isolation and because of their inability to afford expensive care. Military pilots are exposed to extraordinary daily hazards but at the same time may have unusually great access to medical services.

In the United States, for example, mortality rates are closely associated with income. This is because persons with higher incomes tend to be relatively less exposed than others to the hazards of undernutrition, disease, injury, and violent death, *and* because medical facilities and treatment are available primarily in a *market,* with persons able or willing to pay more being able to command more and better services. On the other hand, persons in certain subgroups in the population, e.g., members of the armed forces or of certain labor unions, have access to medical treatment and care by virtue of their organizational associations, whereas others with the same income or socioeconomic status but without membership in comparable organizations have less access to such care.

The Institutionalization of Mortality Control

From the foregoing discussion, it should be clear that not all societies seek to control mortality completely, and that those which institutionalize their attempts to control mortality do so selectively rather than uniformly for all members of the society. As a tentative general hypothesis, we may suggest that the extent of institutionalized efforts to control mortality is inversely related to the ease with which role incumbents are replaced. Thus, *individuals* having more strategic or more prestigious roles—i.e., those who are less easily replaced—are less exposed to the hazards of illness or injury in their occupations, diet, shelter, style of life, and routine activities *and* have greater access to institutionalized means of treating illness or injury, should it occur. *Societies* institutionalize means of controlling mortality to the extent that role differentiation and specialization put a premium upon role incumbents: the replacement of role incumbents becomes more difficult as roles become more differentiated and specialized. Conversely, to the extent that roles are not elaborately differentiated and the replacement of role incumbents is trivial, societies do not institutionalize means of mortality control.

Our hypotheses and analyses of differential mortality and the differential control of mortality must be far more detailed than they are at present if we are to understand, predict, and combat mortality. In addition, we need more hypotheses and more detailed data bearing upon morbidity. The use of health surveys and detailed, large-scale, analyses of insurance and health plan records are among the pursuits that seem to promise considerable progress in the analytical separation and better understanding of morbidity and mortality.

7

Matchmaking,
Marriage, and
Family Formation

1. INTRODUCTION

Marriage and divorce have been of long concern in population studies because of their recognized relationship to population composition, on the one hand, and to fertility, on the other. Next to age and sex, no characteristic is more basic to a population than its composition by marital status: its absolute and relative numbers of single, married, widowed, and divorced persons of each sex and at each age. Although children may be born outside of marriage, in every society childbearing is intimately associated with marriage and generally is viewed both as the object and as a more or less immediate consequence of marriage and conjugal relations.

With their focus on population composition and fertility, demographers and other students of population have been much less aware of, or interested in, the relationships of patterns of marriage to family structure, kinship structure and social stratification. While there have been a number of important and distinguished exceptions among demographers, by and large it has been the sociologists and social anthropologists who have studied marriage and divorce with these relationships in mind. But the sociologists and anthropologists, for their part, have generally ignored the implications of marital patterns for population composition and fertility.

Historically, marriage has been virtually universal and, especially in the case of the female, has taken place at early ages. The two reasons generally advanced for this are: (1) that under the conditions of high mortality characterizing most populations and societies throughout most of human history, universal or near-universal early marriage has been absolutely essential to assure the levels of fertility required for sheer survival and demographic viability; and (2) that marriage is central both to the maintenance of the kinship structure (the fundamental axis of social organization in most societies) and to the social integration and control of individuals within the environs of the kinship structure.

A large array of demographic and social structural questions may be posed concerning marriage and divorce. In this work, we shall be concerned primarily with two kinds of demographic and social structural problems:

1. What are the variations and deviations from the pattern of universal, early marriage? Under what conditions can societies allow, or even promote, bachelorhood and spinsterhood? What are the demographic and social structural implications and consequences of such variations and deviations? We shall examine below some variations and try to draw some inferences concerning their origins and consequences.

2. How is universal marriage—or for that matter, less-than-universal marriage—managed and sustained in populations and societies in which there are *changing numbers of marriageable males and females* of different ages, different personal characteristics, and often different social categories? What rules govern "marriage markets"? How do such rules change under changing populations and changing social structural characteristics and conditions? We shall indicate below that "marriage regimes," i.e., systems of marriage rates and patterns of mate-selection, *cannot* in general *remain stable* very long over time, and we shall present some illustrations of changing marriage regimes.

In this chapter we shall consider variations and changes in patterns of (a) frequency of marriage—and of nonmarriage, or celibacy, (b) age at marriage, and (c) mate selection and its related transactions and arrangements. We shall also try to show that there is an important convergence of the research interests and approaches to population composition and fertility, on the one hand, and to social stratification and family and kinship structure, on the other. Thus, the demographic analysis of marriage has much to contribute to sociological and social anthropological studies of interrelationships between marriage, family and kinship, and social stratification. Conversely, analyses of population composition and fertility are incomplete to the extent that they ignore these aspects of marriage and family formation rooted in family and kinship structure and in social stratification.

We begin with a review of the concepts and definitions used in the study of family, kinship, and marriage, and with an overview of the interrelationships between marriage, family and kinship, and social structure.

SOME BASIC DEFINITIONS: FAMILY, MARRIAGE, AND KINSHIP. The family has been widely recognized as the universal social institution par excellence. Every known society has recognized the family as a key social unit, and certain activities, functions, and human relationships occur almost universally within the framework of family units.

Basically, a *family* consists of an adult male and female living in a common residence, maintaining a socially approved sexual relationship, and sharing the residence with their offspring and sometimes with other persons united with them in some biologically based relationship. *Marriage* is the establishment of this residence and socially approved sexual relationship between the adult male and female. *Kinship* relationships are all interpersonal relationships based upon a recognized biological connection arising out of common ancestry or marriage.

Patterns of Courtship, Marriage, and Family Formation

The manner in which marriages are contracted and families formed varies considerably among societies and among subunits within societies. Indeed, the very extent of marriage and family living, as opposed to celibacy and nonfamily residential arrangements, also varies widely. While all societies require the formation of families or some other framework of reproduction for their survival, some societies, and especially some subgroups within societies, have placed considerable emphasis and value upon social life and living arrangements outside the structure of the family. Societies with institutionalized monastic orders are a case in point.

SOCIAL RELATIONSHIPS BETWEEN THE SEXES. Patterns of courtship, marriage, and family formation are influenced by the nature of social relationships between the sexes from the earliest ages. The manner in which children are socialized and educated, and the extent and nature of social interaction between boys and girls at every age, are connected with the eventual courtship styles and marriage partners chosen. In some societies, boys and girls are segregated from each other in infancy and remain segregated until marriage; this occurs, for example, among the ultra-orthodox Jews in Jerusalem. In other societies, boys and girls may be brought up together at first but then segregated—in early childhood, like the Arapesh of New Guinea and the Teton Dakota of the American Great Plains, or at adolescence, like the Masai and Tallensi of Africa. In some societies, relationships between children or adolescents of opposite sex are characterized by shyness or shame, as in Victorian England, while in others they are casual and matter-of-fact, as with the Samoans and the Trobriand Islanders of Melanesia.

In some societies premarital social relationships between adolescents of opposite sex are permitted only persons already betrothed, while in others a large variety of institutionalized relationships between the sexes may precede actual betrothal. Thus, while betrothal of children is very common in some societies, in others "dating" and other premarital social and sexual relationships of varying extent begin at different ages and continue into early adulthood, preceding actual betrothal and marriage.

Age at First Marriage. The range of ages at which marriages are contracted is relatively narrow in some societies and quite wide in others. However, in every society the great majority of first marriages tend to be concentrated within a relatively narrow age span. This is particularly true for the ages at which females marry for the first time. Thus, while some females in a given society may marry for the first time at, say, 12 or 13 years of age, and others not until 29 or 30, the great majority are likely to enter into their first marriage at one of a much narrower band of ages, perhaps between 18 and 20. Finally, the modal (most frequent) age at first marriage varies substantially among societies and between subgroups within societies: it is early in the United States and Canada, late in Eastern Europe, and later in the Northeastern part of the United States than in the South.

Choice of Marital Partner. The choice of marital partner is most often in the hands of one or both parents of the young marriageable male or female. This is the case, for example, in traditional Islamic societies. However, in many societies, the marriage choice and arrangements are made by some other kinsman or by the head of the extended family, lineage, or clan. The prospective bride or groom may or may not be consulted, may or may not know anything about the chosen spouse, and may or may not be allowed any say or veto rights over the choice. In some societies, however, the initiative, courtship, and choice all rest primarily with the young marriageable man or woman; the parents or other kin may or may not enjoy some initiative or power of veto in the matter.

The choice of marital partner, is, in every society, subject to some set of restrictions. In general, marriages tend to be contracted among persons of similar social characteristics or background. In other words, they tend to be *homogamous*. Restrictions upon choice of partner may be more or less formalized and rigid. They may be institutionalized in laws prohibiting marriages of certain types or in customs prescribing who is eligible to marry whom. Alternatively, restrictions may arise simply out of the opportunity, or lack of it, for social contact and interaction between the marriageable male and female or their families: for example, the opportunities for a coal miner's son to meet and interact with a banker's daughter are limited.

The restriction of marital partners to someone of the *same* group, clan, lineage, village, ethnic category, etc., is called *endogamy*. Conversely, the restriction of the partner to one or several *different* groups, clans, lineages, ethnic categories, etc., is called *exogamy*. Both endogamy and exogamy occur as a consequence of formalized or rigidly institutionalized rules and customs or as a consequence of less formal patterns of social contact and interaction. Thus, homogamous, endogamous, or exogamous restrictions may vary with respect to their content, range, and rigidity.

MARRIAGE TRANSACTIONS.   Marriages in most societies entail some kind of material transaction between the families or kin groups or the bride and groom. Such transactions may be more or less important in determining the choice of partner. They may take the form of bride-price —as in Albania, Cambodia, and among Arabs, and as obtained historically in ancient Israel and among Yemenite Jews before the creation of modern Israel. Or they may be in the form of dowry (Burma, Ireland, Ancient Rome, Serbia), or service obligations (the Bemba in Africa, the Haida of the American Northwest coast, the Zuñi of the Southwest), or simply gifts (the Samoans, the Kwakiutl of the American Northwest coast, the Tikopia of Polynesia). On the other hand, they may involve only "paper transactions" or exchanges of equivalent items. Table 7.1 shows the distribution of 400 societies by type of marriage transaction.

A bride-price is a gift or sum paid by a groom or his family to the family of the bride, compensating the family for the loss of the bride's services. The bride's family may keep the bride-price, give it to the bride herself, or use it in contracting a marriage for a son, i.e., as a bride-price to be paid to the family of *their* son's bride. In table 7.1 we see that marriage in 163 (41 percent of the 400) of the societies in the cross-cultural survey involves payment of a bride-price. Of course the whole process may be considerably simplified if two families are able to exchange daughter-brides as is the case for 16 of the societies in the cross-culture summary sample. In such a case, no actual transfer may take place, but it is recognized that equivalent bride-prices have been paid; this obtains among the Bemba and among the Kariera in Australia.

A dowry is a gift or sum paid by the family of the bride to the

TABLE 7.1
Distribution of Societies in Cross-Cultural
Summary Sample by Type of Marriage
Transaction

Type of Transaction	Number	Percent
Bride-price	163	40.8
Dowry	15	3.7
Gift exchange	26	6.5
Bride-service	54	13.5
Exchange of sister, other female relative of groom	16	4.0
Token bride-price	31	7.8
No significant consideration	90	22.5
Unknown	5	1.2
Total	400	100.0

SOURCE: Textor 1967.

groom. The groom may be permitted to use the gift or sum as he pleases, or he may be obligated to leave all or part of it untouched. The latter assures the bride and her family that she will be treated well and adequately provided for: if the marriage is dissolved, the groom may be obliged to return all or part of the dowry to the bride or to her family. Marriage in fifteen of the societies included in the cross cultural summary sample involves payment of dowries (table 7.1).

Figure 7.1 shows a marriage contract of a Jewish bride and groom, Columbina daughter of Yehuda Badir, and Hezkiah, son of Moshe Levi, of Turin, Italy, in 1691. To this union the bride brings a dowry of 666 lire, 13 soldi, and 4 dinars plus her own clothing valued at 333 lire, 6 soldi, and 8 dinars. The groom puts up the sum of 222 lire, 4 soldi, and 4 dinars as a gift to the bride, so that the bride's total dowry is 888 lire, 17 soldi, and 8 dinars:

> ". . . and this is the contract which the groom undertakes for her life and death, and for his heirs himafter."

2. THE FREQUENCY OF MARRIAGE AND NONMARRIAGE

The Historical Universality of Marriage

There seems to be no dispute among modern sociologists or social anthropologists about Ralph Linton's assertion that "practically all societies consider married life the most normal and desirable type of existence for adults" (Linton 1936, p. 174; and Head 1950, p. 70). Indeed, so common is the assumption that marriage is universal or nearly universal

FIGURE 7.1. Jewish marriage contract from Turin, Italy, 1691. The contract is in the form of a building with a cupola. Hebrew inscriptions and incantations appear in the surrounding decorations. Source: Shahar, 1971, No. 62.

in primitive societies that actual documentation is extremely rare.[1] True, in some ancient civilizations there were apparently high incidences of celibacy or prohibition of marriage among certain population subgroupings (Reinhard and Armengaud 1961; chaps. 3 and 4), especially among

---

[1] But see Krzywicki 1934, (pp. 221–22 and 260) for some documentation of his assertion that "every woman in primitive society is a wife."

slaves and certain upper-class groups, and there was institutionalization of celibacy among the medieval Roman Catholic priesthood. Nevertheless, marriage—or widowhood, for survivors of marital unions—seem historically to have been the dominant and almost universal pattern of existence for human adults.

The "European Marriage Pattern"

A major and extended deviation from the pattern of universal marriage occurred—and, to a considerable extent, continues—in Western Europe and in countries of Western European settlement beginning in about the sixteenth century. Not only have Western European marriages typically been delayed to more advanced ages than in the rest of the world, but bachelorhood and spinsterhood have been an accepted, and statistically not infrequent pattern of life.[2]

Table 7.2 shows the percentage of single men and women aged 45–49 in selected countries of Western Europe, Eastern Europe, Asia, and Africa. The data, which cover various years between 1891 and 1952, show that the countries of Western Europe in that period were characterized by substantial percentages of unmarried adults. In Asia and Africa, on the other hand—barring some exceptions—marriage was virtually universal. Some countries of Eastern Europe also had nearly universal marriage, while in others the percentages remaining single were significant (but hardly ever as high as in Western Europe). The United States has also been characterized by substantial percentages of single adults, but never to the degree reached in Western Europe (see table 7.3).

In Europe, the United States, and other countries of European settlement, the period during and immediately following World War II witnessed a sharp increase in the annual numbers of marriages and in the annual marriage rates at all ages (Hajnal 1953a). Because the great bulk of these marriages took place between persons under 40 years of age, the effect of the increase is not yet fully reflected in data on the marital status (percent single or percent ever married) of persons aged 45 or over. However, declines in the percentages of single persons are already apparent and will become even more so in these countries that experienced the "marriage boom."

Characteristics Associated with Likelihood of Marriage

Data for the United States (Taeuber and Taeuber 1958; Bogue 1959) suggest some of the personal characteristics associated with likelihood of marriage.

---

2 The research and writings of John Hajnal are the major sources for this review. See Hajnal (especially 1965; but also 1953a and 1953b).

TABLE 7.2
Percent Single at Ages 45–49, by Sex, Selected Countries in Western Europe, Eastern Europe, Asia, and Africa

Country and Date		Percent Single	
		Males	Females
Western Europe			
Austria	1900–1901	11	13
	1939	10	18
Belgium	1900–1901	16	17
Denmark	1900–1901	9	13
Finland	1900–1901	14	15
France	1900–1901	11	12
Germany	1900–1901	9	10
	1939	7[a]	15[a]
Great Britain	1900–1901	12	15
Holland	1900–1901	13	14
Iceland	1900–1901	19	29
Ireland	1891	20	17
Italy	1911	11	11
	1936	10	14
Norway	1900	11	18
Portugal	1900–1901	13	20
Spain	1940	9	18
	1900–1901	6[b]	10[b]
	1940	9	19
Sweden	1900–1901	13	19
Switzerland	1900–1901	16	17
Eastern Europe			
Greece	1907	9	4
	1928	7	4
Hungary	1900	5	4
	1941	6	9

Country and Date		Percent Single	
		Males	Females
Eastern Europe (cont.)			
Poland	1931	4	7
Romania	1899	5	3
Bosnia	1910	6[c]	2[c]
Bulgaria	1900	3	1
	1934	3	1
USSR	1897[d]	4	5
	1926	3[a]	4[a]
Serbia	1900	3	1
Yugoslavia	1931	5	5
Asia and Africa			
Morocco	1952 (Moslems)	2	2
Algeria	1948 (Moslems)	5	2
Tunisia	1946 (Indigenous population)	6	4
Egypt	1947	2	1
Mozambique	1950	4	3
Mauritius	1952	5	5
Turkey	1935	3	3
India	1931 (Including Pakistan)	4	1
Ceylon	1946	8	3
Thailand	1947	4	3
Malaya	1947	2	1
Formosa	1930	4	0
Korea	1930	1	0
Japan	1920	2	2
	1951	2	2

SOURCE: Hajnal 1965 and 1953a.
[a] Ages 40–49.
[b] Ages 46–50.
[c] Ages 41–50.
[d] European Russia.

TABLE 7.3

Percent Single at Ages 45–54,
by Sex, United States,
1890–1969

Year	Males	Females
1890	10.1	7.1
1900	10.3	7.8
1910	11.1	8.5
1920	12.0	9.6
1930	11.4	9.1
1940	11.1	8.7
1950	10.1	7.8
1955	8.5	6.8
1960	8.7	7.2
1969	7.1	4.9

SOURCE: Bogue 1959a, p. 219, and U.S. Bureau of the Census, Statistical Abstract of the United States, 1961, 1970, tables 27 and 36, respectively.

LIKELIHOOD BY RACE AND TYPE OF RESIDENCE. White persons of both sexes are more likely to remain single than are Negroes. Among white females, those in urban places are most likely to be single—*either* because urban women are more likely to remain single than are non-urban women, *or* because unmarried nonurban women tend to migrate to cities and urban places. Both urban and rural nonfarm women are more likely to be single than are rural farm women. Among white males, the urban-rural differences in percent single (or in percent ever married) are small and not consistent in direction. Among nonwhite females and males alike, the highest percentage remaining single is found among the rural nonfarm population and the lowest among the rural farm population (with the "urban" population intermediate); however, the rural-urban differences are much more pronounced among males than among females.

LIKELIHOOD BY NATIVITY. Viewing the U.S. white population from 1890 by sex and nativity (table 7.4), the native-born males of native parentage were least likely to remain single to ages 45–54. Native-born males of foreign-born parentage were most likely to remain single, and foreign-born males were intermediate. Among white females, the foreign-born were consistently less likely to remain single than the native-born of native parentage. But native-born women of foreign parentage were the most likely to remain single.

TABLE 7.4
Percent Single at Ages 45–54 in the U.S. White Population, by Sex and Nativity, 1890–1920

Year	White Males			White Females		
	Native born with native parentage	*Native born with foreign-born parentage*	*Foreign born*	*Native born with native parentage*	*Native born with foreign-born parentage*	*Foreign born*
1890	8.0	11.8	10.7	8.1	8.7	5.3
1900	9.0	14.8	11.5	8.5	10.7	6.0
1910	9.8	15.8	11.6	8.5	13.2	11.1
1920	10.6	17.1	12.2	9.2	15.3	6.8

SOURCE: Adapted from table 49 in C. Taeuber and Taeuber 1958.

LIKELIHOOD BY EDUCATIONAL ACHIEVEMENT. Among U.S. males aged 45–54 in 1950, the percentage remaining single varied inversely with level of educational achievement; some 16 percent of those with no schooling were single, compared to less than seven percent of those with four years of college or more. However, among females of the same age group in the same year, the reverse obtained: some 24 percent of the women with four or more years of college remained single, compared to just under nine percent of those with no education at all, 4.5 percent of those with one to four years of elementary school, and five percent of those with five to eight years of elementary school (Taeuber and Taeuber 1958, table 51; Bogue 1959, table 10–37).

LIKELIHOOD BY OCCUPATION AND NONFARM INCOME. Among employed males aged 45–64 in 1957, some 6.4 percent were single. However, there were great variations among employment categories: The designation "single" applied to some 22 percent of those employed as "farm laborers and foremen" and to some 20 percent of those employed as "private household workers," but to only 2.5 percent of the "sales workers" and less than four percent of the "managers, officials, and proprietors" as well as the "craftsmen, foremen, and kindred workers." Among employed women of the same ages and in the same year, some 13 percent were single. This proportion included 27 percent of those defined as "professional, technical, and kindred workers" and 19 percent of those defined as "clerical and kindred workers" (Bogue 1959, table 10–37). Finally, among U.S. urban and rural nonfarm males aged 45–64 in 1957, the percent single varied inversely and sharply by amount of income in 1956. Among those with incomes of under $2,000, some 23 percent were single; conversely, the figure was only 1.7 percent for those earning $6,000 or more (*ibid.,* table 10–38).

3. AGE AT MARRIAGE

From the point of view of its relationship to, and impact upon, population growth and composition, the age at which marriage takes place—especially among females—is only slightly less important than the fact of marriage itself. Yet anthropological and sociological studies of marriage mention age at marriage only in passing, if at all, and demographic studies of age at marriage have been severely limited in the range and scope of the societies and populations investigated.

MALTHUS: DELAYED MARRIAGE AS PREVENTIVE CHECK. In modern population studies, the question of age at marriage was most forcefully raised by Malthus in the early nineteenth century, in the second and later editions of his famous *Essay on the Principle of Population* (see Malthus 1958). In the first edition of his work, Malthus had concluded that vice, misery, famine, and war were the inevitable outcomes of the tendency for populations to grow beyond their means of sustenance, and, indeed that it was these factors that checked further population growth. But in his second and later editions, Malthus introduced "another check to population which does not come under the heading of either vice or misery." The newly recognized check was "moral restraint," by which Malthus meant primarily delayed marriage.[3] Yet, despite the controversy generated by these doctrines, and despite the studies and writings which they stimulated, even demographers have been slow to analyze patterns of age at marriage. More research on the subject has recently been undertaken, however, largely because of the concern over rapid population growth and because of the interest in means and prospects of controlling it.

The Universality of Early Marriage

There are good reasons to suppose that in most societies in most places and at most times, marriage has been not only virtually universal but universally undertaken at very young ages—among girls, probably at, or very close to, puberty. The overwhelming picture from observations of travelers, administrators, missionaries, and anthropologists is that girls marry early in primitive or preliterate societies and are often betrothed before puberty (see, for example, Krzywicki 1934, p. 221; Wilson 1950;

---

3 For a discussion of the development of Malthus's ideas, see Petersen (1971).

Fortes 1950; and Nadel 1950). For ancient societies, there is literary and documentary evidence of similarly early betrothal and marriage (Reinhard and Armengaud 1961, Part I; Hopkins 1965). This evidence takes the form of actual accounts of early marriages, as in the Old Testament, or of enjoinments upon parents concerning the obligation or advisability of arranging marriages for their daughters and sons at an early age.

In addition, we do know that high mortality and low modal and average expectations of life previously characterized most populations in most places at most times, suggesting that societies in which marriage and childbearing did not take place at early ages *could not have survived* over successive generations. The late French demographer Jean Fourastie (1959) showed that under conditions of high mortality, even with high and uncontrolled fertility, population growth and replacement are heavily dependent upon age at marriage. Thus, under mortality conditions characterized by life expectancies of no more than 25 years (which was the case in France from 1680 to 1725), a mean age of 25 years at first marriage for females would result in a population decline of about ten percent per generation, even taking into account remarriages after widowhood. Under the same mortality conditions, a mean age at first marriage of 22.5 years would result in a population increase of about six percent per generation. Improved mortality conditions (with life expectancies at birth reaching 30 years) would result in a growth rate of nine percent per generation if the average age at first marriage were 25 years, and in a growth rate of 34 percent per generation if the average age were 22.5 years.

The Modern European Deviation from Early Marriage

Just as there is a modern European deviation from the near universality of marriage, so there is a clearly discernible European pattern of relatively late marriage which deviates sharply from the early marriages so common outside of modern Europe, especially among females. Table 7.5, which covers selected years between 1891 and 1952, shows that in most countries of Western Europe only about one-third of the women aged 20–24 were married—and this despite the fact that marriage before the age of 25 was substantially more frequent among females than males. In all the countries except Sweden, Iceland, and Ireland, the majority of women aged 25–29 were already married, but very large minorities— from about 26 percent in Spain to about 45 percent in Switzerland—were still single. At around the turn of the century in Western Europe, the marriage of males before the age of 25 was infrequent. The percentages single among males between 20 and 24 years of age varied from just over 80 percent to more than 95 percent; and in most countries not more than half the males aged 25–29 were already married.

TABLE 7.5

Percent Single at Ages 20-24 and 25-29, by Sex, in Selected Countries of Western Europe, Eastern Europe, Asia, and Africa

		Percent Single			
		Males		Females	
Country and Date		20-24	25-29	20-24	25-29
Western Europe					
Austria	1900-1901	93	51	66	38
	1939	89	60	68	42
Belgium	1900-1901	85	50	71	41
Denmark	1900-1901	88	50	75	42
Finland	1900-1901	84	51	68	40
France	1900-1901	90	48	58	30
Germany	1900-1901	91	48	71	34
	1939	91	51	64	31
Great Britain	1900-1901	83	47	73	42
Holland	1900-1901	89	53	79	44
Iceland	1900-1901	92	66	81	56
Ireland	1891	96	78	86	59
Italy	1911	86	46	60	30
	1936	91	54	69	39
Norway	1900-1901	86	54	77	48
Portugal	1900-1901	84	48	69	41
	1940	85	48	69	40
Spain	1900-1901	81[a]	34[b]	55[a]	26[b]
	1940	94	63	79	44
Sweden	1900-1901	92	61	80	52
Switzerland	1900-1901	91	58	78	45
Eastern Europe					
Greece	1907	82	47	44	13
	1928	83	52	56	26
Hungary	1900	81	31	36	15
	1941	88	46	53	24
Poland	1931	83	41	61	30
Romania	1899	67	21	20	8
Bosnia	1910	63[c]	31[d]	23[c]	6[d]
Bulgaria	1900	58	23	24	3
	1934	56	20	35	11
USSR	1897[e]	42		23	
	1926	51	18	28	9
Serbia	1900	50	18	16	2
Yugoslavia	1931	60	27	35	15
Asia and Africa					
Morocco (Moslems)	1952	59	28	8	3
Algeria (Moslems)	1948	68	37	23	10
Tunisia (Indigenous population)	1946	73	46	29	13
Egypt	1947	69	35	20	6
Mozambique	1950	54	23	17	7
Mauritius	1952	72	33	24	12
Turkey	1935	49	24	18	6
India (Including Pakistan)	1931	35	14	5	2
Ceylon	1946	80	43	29	12
Thailand	1947	61	24	30	11
Malaya	1947	54	17	7	2
Formosa	1930	52	19	15	4
Korea	1930	33	10	2	1
Japan	1920	71	26	2	1
	1951	83	34	55	15

SOURCE: Hajnal 1965 and 1953a.
[a]Ages 21-25.   [d]Ages 25-30.
[b]Ages 26-30.   [e]European Russia.
[e]Ages 21-24.

In the Eastern European countries, a substantial majority of the women aged 20–24 were already married, as were all but a small minority of those aged 25–29. The Eastern European countries in which women of these age groups were relatively more likely to be single included Poland, Hungary, and Greece. Among the men, much larger minorities than in Western Europe were married by the ages of 20–24, as were quite substantial majorities of those aged 25–29.

Finally, the countries of Asia and Africa were characterized by somewhat earlier male marriages than in Eastern Europe, but by universally earlier marriages for females. In all of the countries shown except Japan, less than 30 percent of the women aged 20–24 were still unmarried, and in Japan there has evidently been a drastic change in the pattern of age at marriage since 1920. In all countries of Asia and Africa, the overwhelming majority (85 percent or more) of the women aged 25–29 were already married.

The data in tables 7.5 and 7.2 are largely consistent with the hypotheses cited at the beginning of the chapter in explanation of the universality and early age of female marriage. The first hypothesis, very briefly, was that conditions of high mortality make universal and early marriage mandatory for a society's survival. The countries of Asia and Africa have certainly been characterized by much higher mortality rates in this century than the countries of Western Europe, and it can clearly be reasoned that their extent of marriage and age at marriage have had immediate bearing not only upon their population growth but upon their survival as well. Conversely, mortality in Western European countries has long been low enough to assure quite considerable population growth even without universal or early marriage. As for Eastern Europe, its mortality and marital patterns have held an intermediate position between the Western European and Asian and African extremes.

The second hypothesis, again very briefly, held in part that marriage is central to the maintenance of kinship structure, around which the social organization of most societies revolves. Although it is difficult to measure and compare the importance—and relative exclusiveness—of kinship on the basis of social organization, the foregoing data make it not so surprising that the place of kinship in social structure is widely believed to have remained stronger and more central in Eastern Europe than in Western Europe, and stronger and even more totalistic in Asia and Africa. It is important, however, to recognize that the data may be equally consistent and equally well explained by alternative hypotheses, some of which we shall discuss below.

The Postwar "Marriage Boom" in Western Europe and the United States: Some Facts and Some Hypotheses

A comparison of the data in table 7.6 with those in table 7.5 indicates that age of marriage for both men and women in the United States

TABLE 7.6

*Percent Single, at Ages 20–24 and 25–29
by Sex: United States, 1890–1969*

	Males		Females	
	20–24	25–29	20–24	25–29
1890	80.7	46.0	51.8	25.4
1900	77.6	45.8	51.0	27.5
1910	74.9	42.8	48.3	24.9
1920	70.7	39.4	45.6	23.0
1930	70.8	36.7	46.0	21.7
1940	72.2	36.0	47.2	22.8
1950	59.1	23.8	32.3	13.3
1960	54.7	23.0	28.9	9.5
1969	54.6	18.0	35.4	11.0

SOURCE: Bogue 1959*a*, and U.S. Bureau of
the Census, *Statistical Abstract of the United
States* 1961, 1970, tables 27 and 36,
respectively.

has been substantially earlier than in Western Europe but somewhat later than in most countries of Eastern Europe (cf. Hajnal 1953a; Matras 1965a and 1965b).

However, Western Europe, the United States, and other countries of European settlement share one very important trend: Comparing the last three lines of table 7.6 with the rest of the table, it is clear that the post-World-War-II years were characterized by a sharp drop in the proportions of single persons of both sexes at ages 20–24 and 25–29 (Rele 1965). Similar sharp declines in proportions of single persons occurred at about the same period in virtually every country of Western Europe except France and Ireland, heralding a greatly increased tendency to marry and to marry at early ages (Hajnal 1953a, especially table 3).

Very little is known about the reasons for this decline in age at marriage. However, one hypothesis (Davis 1956) holds that the decline is associated with the popularization of contraceptive techniques. According to this line of reasoning, individuals previously wishing to keep their number of births in check did so by postponing marriage; similarly, societies wishing to do so institutionalized the delay of marriage until relatively advanced ages, very much as Malthus argued. However, the reasoning continues, the development of contraceptive measures have rendered the postponement of marriage unnecessary. Coale (1969), in his historical study of fertility and marriage in Europe, finds support for this thesis. Nevertheless, far more research must be done if the reasons for this very important trend are to be fully understood. We shall return to this point in chapter 8 below.

For the United States, a number of factors and characteristics have been found to be related to variations in age at marriage.[4] Both males

4 The following summary draws upon the materials presented in Taeuber and

and females have tended to marry earlier in the South, and later in the Northeast, than in other areas of the United States. Marriage is earlier among rural nonfarm than rural farm females, later among urban residents, and later the larger the urban place. Marriage is later, too, among rural farm males than among urban males.

Nonwhites in the United States have tended to marry at younger ages than whites, the difference being considerably more pronounced for females than for males. Native-born whites of native parents marry earlier than foreign-born whites, but native-born whites of foreign parents marry latest of all.

Among both males and females, persons with some education marry earlier than persons with none or very little. But persons with college educations marry latest of all. Among males, those employed as managers, officials, proprietors, craftsmen, foremen, or operatives (semi-skilled machine operators) tend to marry relatively early, while those in sales occupations tend to marry late. Among employed females, those in managerial, sales, operative, or service occupations tend to marry early, while those in professional, clerical, craft, or foreman occupations tend to marry late. Among males, high income is associated with early marriage and low income with later marriage.

Recalling the discussion in the previous section of factors associated with variations in frequencies of marriage and nonmarriage, it is evident, by and large, that the characteristics associated with nonmarriage are also associated with later or delayed marriage. However, there are some interesting and important exceptions; for example, professional and highly educated males delay marriage to relatively late ages but ultimately are characterized by low percentages remaining single. Nevertheless, it is still appropriate to see late or delayed marriage and nonmarriage as similar or, indeed, as two facets of the same phenomenon: deviation from the pattern of universal and early marriage.

Finally, it is important to note that the post-World-War-II "marriage boom" in Western Europe, the United States, and countries of Western European settlement took place especially among those population groups which had previously been characterized by the most consistent nonmarriage or postponement of marriage. Thus, the marriage boom both lowered the average age at marriage and increased the percentages ever marrying in these groups, thus *reducing* the overall differentials among regional, urban-rural, racial, nativity, and socioeconomic groups with regard to age at marriage and incidence of marriage.

Taeuber (1958, chap. 8); Bogue (1959, chap. 10); and Rele (1965). By comparing distributions by age at marriage among female once-married-husband-present cohorts, we are able to provide an alternative approach to the analysis of differentials in age at marriage. See Matras (1966) and other "social strategy" papers cited therein.

For societies in which marriage is voluntary—i.e., for those in which nonmarriage is a recognized, acceptable, and realistic alternative—and for societies in which age at marriage is variable rather than strictly prescribed, the social psychological factors associated with an individual's marriage or nonmarriage and age at marriage are of great interest. But, as we have already indicated, our concern here is not primarily with individuals. Rather, it is with variations and changes over time in the extent to which societies or social collectivities tend to institutionalize universal and early marriage or, alternatively, nonmarriage or the postponement of marriage. Thus, we are concerned (a) with the problem of why European societies (and those of European origin) differ from non-European societies in their patterns of frequency of marriage and age at marriage; (b) with the reasons for variations among the European societies; and (c) with the reasons for changes over time in the marital patterns of both European and non-European societies.

Hajnal's Analysis of the Modern European Marriage Pattern

The British demographer John Hajnal, a leader among contemporary students of marital frequency and age at marriage, has already been cited in this and previous chapters. In his paper, "European Marriage Patterns in Perspective," Hajnal concludes—

1. that the distinctively European pattern of late marriage and of high proportions remaining unmarried can be traced in the general population as far back as the seventeenth century;
2. that the origins of this European pattern can, in the case of several aristocratic or upper-class groups, be found somewhere in the sixteenth century but never earlier;
3. that such data as exist for Europe in the Middle Ages and for the ancient world suggest the prevalence of the non-European pattern of marriage, i.e., of virtually universal and early marriage (Hajnal 1965, p. 134)

By way of explaining this pattern peculiar to modern Europe, Hajnal mentions some reasons already advanced by others: (1) some peculiarly European difficulties in matchmaking, such as the widespread conviction that marriage should be decided upon only after the prospective spouses are well acquainted with one another; and (2) the surpluses of marriageable women in modern Europe (as opposed to the apparent shortages of such women outside Europe and in premodern Europe) combined with declining rates of marriage for males. However, Hajnal himself hypothesizes that the unique European marriage pattern is closely connected to the economic independence of the European stem-family.[5] In Hajnal's words:

> It is tempting to see in this feature a key to the uniqueness of the European marriage pattern. In Europe it has been necessary for a man to defer marriage until he could establish an independent liveli-hood adequate to support a family; in other societies the young couple could be incorporated in a larger economic unit, such as a joint family. This, presumably, is more easily achieved and does not require such a long postponement of marriage. This line of argu-ment seems especially convincing if the larger economic unit is such that extra labour is often felt to be an economic asset. A system of large estates with large households as in Eastern Europe might thus be conducive to a non-European marriage pattern, while small hold-ings occupied by a single family and passed on to a single heir would result in a European pattern. [*Ibid.*, p. 133]

Hajnal argues further that the modern pattern may well have been closely connected to the uniquely European "take-off" into modern eco-nomic growth (*Ibid.*, p. 132).[6]

Hajnal observes, quite correctly, that if the connection between European marriage patterns and the European stem-family system ob-tained, it must have led to a fundamental social and economic trans-formation of the society and to certain problems thereof; in other words, it must have led to what Max Weber has called the "dissolution of the manorial system" (Weber 1961, pp. 81–99).

The details of such a transformation are far beyond the scope and competence of this book. However, we may apply to Hajnal's analysis the idea that the change in Europe to nonuniversal and late patterns of marriage involved the institutionalization of these patterns as part of a new societal strategy of survival and adaptation. Perhaps the main fea-ture of the new societal strategy was the shift from a localized subsistence pattern of agricultural production and distribution to a more differen-tiated regional market pattern; incorporated in the shift was a greater differentiation of tasks, an expansion of services and industries, and an accompanying demand for free labor, that is, for labor neither inden-tured nor otherwise connected to land (Weber 1961; see also Hobhouse 1966, pp. 281–92, and Bottomore 1962, pp. 133–43). Apparently, these very changes in societal strategies of survival and adaptation generated the great decline in mortality that began in the eighteenth century (Eversley 1965a). Both this decline in mortality *and* rising standards of

---

5 A stem family consists of parents and the adult child who is to inherit the family property (in Europe, typically the family farm); if the inheritor is married, the stem family also includes his (or her) spouse and children.

6 The term "take-off" has reference to an acceleration of economic growth as formulated by Rostow (1956 and 1960).

living may have been connected either to widespread individual attempts to control fertility through postponement of marriage, or to institutionalized patterns of late marriage or nonmarriage (Hajnal 1965; Eversley 1965a). Much remains to be learned about these transformations, and we shall have occasion to mention them again in Part III.

4. MATE SELECTION

The Variability of Rules and Patterns of Mate Selection

We can conceive readily enough of a mate-selection and marriage situation wherein any eligible male is as likely to marry any one of the eligible females in his society as he is to marry any other; and, conversely, wherein any eligible female is equally likely to marry any one of the eligible males. Thus, if there are M eligible males and F eligible females in the society, there will be M x F possible and equally likely matches. In fact, however, such a situation hardly ever exists: there are always some constraints upon reciprocal mate selection that absolutely prohibit certain kinds of matches, make others so infrequent as to be virtually nonexistent, and render still others more or less frequent.

In the United States (and elsewhere too) marriage between brothers and sisters is prohibited; marriages between 80-year-old women and 17-year-old boys, and between female college professors and male waiters, are rare enough to be virtually nonexistent; marriages in which both partners are Protestant or both Catholic are considerably more common than those involving one Protestant and one Catholic, or one Christian and one Jew; and marriages in which both partners are white or both partners Negro are far more frequent than racially mixed marriages. In many states of the Union, eligible first cousins are *prohibited* from marrying one another—but in many societies it is understood that they *ought* to marry one another, and in some they *must* marry one another. French-speaking Swiss are more likely to marry other French-speaking Swiss than they are to marry Swiss who speak German, Italian, or Romansch; and French-speaking Canadians are more likely to marry French-speaking than English-speaking Canadians.

Thus age, race, religion, ethnic origin, place of residence, educational level, social status, kinship, language, and other social, economic, and cultural factors may intervene in the process of mate selection, either singly or in combination. Such intervention almost always operates to restrict and reduce the choice and number of potential mates, regardless of the total number and variety of eligible males and females in the marriage market at any moment in time. However, some factors do operate to enhance the range of possible marital partners—for example, travel, going to college, commercial marriage brokerages, and lonelyhearts clubs.

The rules and patterns of mate selection in any society have far-reaching demographic and social structural implications. However, it is not always possible to plot these implications in exact detail, and they vary over societies and among different subgroups within societies. Similarly, the institutions affecting the processes of matchmaking and mate selection vary in different societies. In this section, we shall be able to touch only briefly on the subject of variation and change in patterns of mate selection, and we shall discuss only a few of the issues and problems that occupy research in this area.

Norms, rules, and customs governing choice of marriage partners may be more or less rigid, and they may be more or less explicit in different groups within societies. The study of patterns of mate selection is carried out typically through one or both of the following approaches:

1. the direct study of marriage rules, customs, and norms through observation, analysis of laws and literary sources, and use of informants or interview material. This approach has typically—although not exclusively—characterized anthropological and sociological studies of preliterate or primitive societies, historical studies, and field studies of single communities;

2. the quantitative analysis of different types of matches; that is, the study of differential frequencies or couples, C_{ij}, comprising husbands from each group, M_i, and wives from each group, F_j. The following discussion makes use of both approaches.

Some Broad Generalizations on Age Patterns in First-Marriage Mate Selection

Let us classify eligible bachelors and spinsters into the following broad age categories: (a) "Young"—under about 20 years of age; (b) "middle-aged"—say, over 20 but under 30; (c) "old"—about 30 years of age or over. Given these categories, and reasoning on the basis of a variety of findings from many simple and complex societies, it is possible to arrive at some broad generalizations concerning age patterns in mate selection when both bride and groom are marrying for the first time. Grooms are generally more likely to be older than their brides than to be either the same age or younger, a phenomenon which is more pronounced the younger the bride or the older the groom. "Acceptable" or relatively frequent matches are those involving:

a. "young" (< 20) grooms and "young" (< 20) brides
b. "middle-aged" (20–29) grooms and "young" (< 20) brides
c. "middle-aged" (20–29) grooms and "middle-aged" (20–29) brides

    d. "middle-aged" (20–29) grooms and "old" (30+) brides

    e. "old" (30+) grooms and "old" (30+) brides

    f. "old" (30+) grooms and "middle-aged" (20–29) brides.

Less acceptable, unconventional, or relatively infrequent matches are those involving:

    g. "young" (< 20) grooms and "middle-aged" (20–29) brides

    h. "young" (< 20) grooms and "old" (30+) brides

    i. "old" (30+) grooms and "young" (< 20) brides.[7]

Of course there are variations in the extent to which each type of match is acceptable, but variations and changes over time in the relative frequencies of the types often derive simply from variations in the population composition of the groups or societies in question. In other words, the relative frequencies of the matches are often dictated by the number of eligible males and females in each of the society's different age groups, this number in turn varying in accordance with the society's past patterns of fertility, infant and child mortality, and migration. However, demographically based variations probably affect first marriages much less than remarriages. In the case of remarriages—marriages involving widowed or divorced persons—and polygamous marriages, there is greater variability in the acceptance and frequency of a type of match connected both to population composition and to its related patterns of fertility, mortality, marriage and divorce, migration, and other social structural factors.

    Conventions about age-selection of mates tend to be more rigid for marriages of single, never-before-married brides and grooms than is the case for marriages involving previously-married persons. Thus the imbalances due to past demographic and social structural factors are more likely to be resolved by flexibility in the patterns of age-choices characteristic of remarriages rather than in those of first marriages.

Marriage and Marital Status: An Example

    Let us return now to our hypothetical population of "luvmees" and suppose now that there are boy luvmees and girl luvmees who may marry at age 1 year or at age 2 years. To simplify the example, let us suppose that all luvmees die at exactly 3 years of age—not before and not after. Suppose our population of luvmees is composed as follows:

S_0: male luvmees aged 0 years, and too young to marry

S_1: male luvmees aged 1 years, unmarried but old enough and eligible for marriage

---

7 Cf. Bogue (1959, pp. 249–50) for U.S. data on age patterns in mate selection.

S_2: male luvmees aged 2 years, unmarried but eligible
M_{11}: male luvmees aged 1 year, married to female luvmees aged 1 year
M_{12}: male luvmees aged 1 year, married to female luvmees aged 2 years
M_{21}: male luvmees aged 2 years, married to female luvmees aged 1 year
M_{22}: male luvmees aged 2 years, married to female luvmees aged 2 years
F_0: female luvmees aged 0 years, and too young to marry
F_1: female luvmees aged 1 years, unmarried, but eligible for marriage
F_2: female luvmees aged 2 years, unmarried, but eligible
N_{11}: female luvmees aged 1 year, married to male luvmees aged 1 year
N_{12}: female luvmees aged 1 year, married to male luvmees aged 2 years
N_{21}: female luvmees aged 2 years, married to male luvmees aged 1 year
N_{22}: female luvmees aged 2 years, married to male luvmees aged 2 years.

Let us suppose that, initially, our population includes:

S_0:	200	F_0:	200
S_1:	100	F_1:	150
S_2:	50	F_2:	50
M_{11}:	50	N_{11}:	50
M_{12}:	50	N_{12}:	100
M_{21}:	100	N_{21}:	50
M_{22}:	50	N_{22}:	50

Clearly we must have

$$M_{11} = N_{11}$$
$$M_{12} = N_{21}$$
$$M_{21} = N_{12}$$
$$M_{22} = N_{22}$$

i.e., the numbers of couples involving males and females of *given* age combination must be the same whether we look at them from the point of view of the males (M_{ij}) or from the point of view of the females (N_{ji}). And in our example this is the case.

Consider now the changes of status possible in the course of a single year. In the first place, everybody in the initial population of luvmees either ages by one year (those initially aged 0 years or 1 year) or dies (those initially aged 2 years). In the second place, eligible unmarried persons may either remain unmarried or may marry—and if they marry, they may choose partners of any age. Consider, for example, the initial group of luvmees aged 0 years: suppose half of them remain unmarried and, hence, belong, at the end of the year, to the S'_1 category—where the prime (') indicates the category as of the end of the period. This is represented in the entry, (.5) in the cell corresponding to the S_0 row and the S'_1 column in table 7.7. The other half—those marrying, may choose females either the same age—entering the M'_{11} category—or else females one year older than themselves—entering the M'_{12} category. These possibilities are shown as marriage rates or probabilities, .25 and .25 in the (S_0, M'_{11}) and (S_0, M'_{12}) cells respectively.

Married persons may stay married, divorce, or be widowed. Persons aged one year and married to partners aged two years (M_{12} or N_{12} in the initial population) must, by our rules and assumptions, become widowed during the year in question: for they live and their partners reach age 3 years and die. Accordingly, they return to the "unmarried, aged 2 years," categories.

Finally, married female luvmees give birth to little luvmees, male or female, and the rates of birth are represented in the entries of the S'_0 column and F'_0 column respectively in table 7.7. For it is these births that become the new population of male and female luvmees aged 0.

The rates of marriage mate selection, and births of the luvmee population are shown in table 7.7. We can use these data to make a one-year projection of the luvmee population by sex, age, and marital status, as follows:

For the new male luvmee population:

$$
\begin{aligned}
S'_0 &= N_{11} (.4) + N_{12} (.6) + N_{21} (.8) + N_{22} (.6) \\
&= 50 (.4) + 100 (.6) + 50 (.8) \, 50 (.6) = 150 \\
S'_1 &= S_0 (.5) = 200 (.5) = 100 \\
S'_2 &= S_1 (.1) + M_{11} (.20) + M_{12} = 100 (.1) + 50 (.2) + 50 = 80 \\
M'_{11} &= S_0 (.25) = 200 (.25) = 50 \\
M'_{12} &= S_0 (.25) = 200 (.25) = 50 \\
M'_{21} &= S_1 (.5) = 100 (.5) = 50 \\
M'_{22} &= S_1 (.4) + M_{11} (.8) = 100 (.4) + 50 (.8) = 80
\end{aligned}
$$

For the new female luvmee population:

$$
\begin{aligned}
F'_0 &= N_{11} (.4) + N_{12} (.6) + N_{21} (.8) + N_{22} (.6) = 150 \\
F'_1 &= F_0 (.5) = 200 (.5) = 100 \\
F'_2 &= F_1 (.6/15) + N_{11} (.2) + N_{12} = 150 (6/15) + 50 (.2) + 100 = 170 \\
N'_{11} &= F_0 (.25) = 200 (.25) = 50 \\
N'_{12} &= F_0 (.25) = 200 (.25) = 50 \\
N'_{21} &= F_1 (.333) = 150 (.333) = 50 \\
N'_{22} &= F_1 (4/15) + N_{11} (.8) = 150 (4/15) + 50 (.8) = 80
\end{aligned}
$$

In the new luvmee population it turns out, as previously, that the numbers of couples in each age combination are the same, whether we compute them for male or for female luvmees, i.e.,

$$
\begin{aligned}
M'_{11} &= N'_{11} \\
M'_{12} &= N'_{21} \\
M'_{21} &= N'_{12} \\
M'_{22} &= N'_{22}
\end{aligned}
$$

Marital Status at Beginning of Year	Marital Status at End of Year													
	S'_0	S'_1	S'_2	M'_{11}	M'_{12}	M'_{21}	M'_{22}	F'_0	F'_1	F'_2	N'_{11}	N'_{12}	N'_{21}	N'_{22}
S_0	0	1/2	0	1/4	1/4	0	0							
S_1	0	0	1/10	0	0	1/2	2/5							
S_2	0	0	0	0	0	0	0							
M_{11}	0	0	1/5	0	0	0	4/5							
M_{12}	0	0	1	0	0	0	0							
M_{21}	0	0	0	0	0	0	0							
M_{22}	0	0	0	0	0	0	0							
F_0								0	1/2	0	1/4	1/4	0	0
F_1								0	0	6/15	0	0	1/3	4/15
F_2								0	0	0	0	0	0	0
N_{11}	4/10							4/10	0	1/5	0	0	0	4/5
N_{12}	6/10							6/10	0	1	0	0	0	0
N_{21}	8/10							8/10	0	0	0	0	0	0
N_{22}	6/10							6/10	0	0	0	0	0	0

The entire luvmee marriage regime consisting of rates of marriage and mate selection may be viewed as a population transformation, in which a set of rates of marriage and of "un-marriage" transforms the population from an initial size and marital-status composition to a new size and composition.

The Mate-Selection and Marriage Regime as a Population Transformation

One type of population transformation involves fertility, mortality, and changing marital status (marriage, divorce, and widowhood). We can represent such a transformation by incorporating the variables of age, sex, and marital status into a matrix equation similar to those previously used for population transformations. Such an equation might be of the form

$$\gamma_0 \, T = \gamma_1,$$

where γ_0 and γ_1 represent the initial and subsequent populations classified by sex, age, marital status, and—for married persons—age of spouse. Elements of the initial population would be:

S_x = the number of unmarried males aged x
F_y = the number of unmarried females aged y
M_{xy} = the number of males aged x and married to wives aged y
N_{yx} = the number of females aged y and married to husbands aged x

In the subsequent population, the corresponding elements would be S'_x, F'_y, M'_{xy}, and N'_{yx}.

The marriage regime transformation, T, would include elements representing not only rates of survival (the complement of probabilities of dying in the interval) and rates of fertility, but also rates of marriage of the form

r_{xy} = probability that an unmarried male aged x
survives and marries an unmarried female aged y, and
s_{yx} = probability that an unmarried female aged y
survives and marries an unmarried male aged x.

T would also include rates of remaining unmarried and of *becoming* unmarried (through divorce or widowhood).

It is clear that an important requirement of the transformation is that the number of males in *xy* couples must be identical to the number of females in *yx* couples, i.e., that initially (in γ_0) we must have $M_{xy} = N_{yx}$.

This identity must also hold in γ_1. Thus in the subsequent population we must have

$$M'_{xy} = N'_{yx}.$$

It follows that we must require in the marriage-population transformation, $\gamma_0 T = \gamma_1$, that

$$M'_{xy} = N'_{yx}.$$

If this condition holds for the first interval, $\gamma_0 T = \gamma_1$, it cannot, in general, hold for the second interval, $\gamma_1 T \neq \gamma_2$. In other words, a marriage transformation cannot in general be repeated over two time intervals and a marriage regime, or set of rates of marriage and of age-assortative mating, cannot in general be stable (Matras, *in press*).

Returning briefly to our hypothetical population of luvmees, we can see this clearly by trying to carry out a second projection by age and marital status using the *same* luvmee marriage regime. The luvmee population at the end of the *first* projection comprised:

$$
\begin{array}{ll}
S'_0 = 150 & F'_0 = 150 \\
S'_1 = 100 & F'_1 = 100 \\
S'_2 = 80 & F'_2 = 170 \\
M'_{11} = 50 & N'_{11} = 50 \\
M'_{12} = 50 & N'_{12} = 50 \\
M'_{21} = 50 & N'_{21} = 50 \\
M'_{22} = 80 & N'_{22} = 80
\end{array}
$$

Using the same procedure and the same rates of marriage, un-marriage, and birth as previously, the luvmee population at the end of the *second* projection would comprise:

Males:

$$
\begin{aligned}
S''_0 &= N'_{11} (.4) + N'_{12} (.6) + N'_{21} (.8) + N'_{22} (.6) \\
      &= 50 (.4) + 50 (.6) + 50 (.8) + 80 (.6) = 138 \\
S''_1 &= S'_0 (.5) = 150 (.5) = 75 \\
S''_2 &= S'_1 (.1) + M'_{11} (.2) + M'_{12} = 100 (.1) + 50 (.2) + 50 = 80 \\
M''_{11} &= S'_0 (.25) = 150 (.25) = 38 \\
M''_{12} &= S'_0 (.25) = 150 (.25) = 37 \\
M''_{21} &= S'_1 (.5) = 100 (.5) = 50 \\
M''_{22} &= S'_1 (.4) + M'_{11} (.8) = 100 (.4) + 50 (.8) = 80
\end{aligned}
$$

Females:

$$
\begin{aligned}
F''_0 &= N'_{11} (.4) + N'_{12} (.6) + N'_{21} (.8) + N'_{22} (.6) = 138 \\
F''_1 &= F'_0 (.5) = 150 (.5) = 75 \\
F''_2 &= F'_1 (6/15) + N'_{11} (.2) + N'_{12} = 100 (6/15) + 50 (.2) + 50 = 100
\end{aligned}
$$

$$N''_{11} = F'_0 (.25) = 150 (.25) = 38$$
$$N''_{12} = F'_0 (.25) = 150 (.25) = 37$$
$$N''_{21} = F'_1 (.333) = 100 (.333) = 33$$
$$N''_{22} = F'_1 (4/15) + N'_{11} (.8) = 100 (4/15) + 50 (.8) = 37$$

But in this example it is obvious that the numbers of male luvmees and female luvmees in couples involving two-year-old males and one-year-old females, one-year-old males and two-year-old females, and two-year-old males and two-year-old females do not correspond, i.e., although $M''_{11} = N'_{11}$, it turns out that

$$M''_{12} \neq N''_{21}$$
$$M''_{21} \neq N''_{12}$$
$$M''_{22} \neq N''_{22}$$

which cannot be allowed. Thus it is clear that the marriage regime itself must change over the successive time intervals.

Thus, in countries which sustained great losses in wars—for example, France in World War I or Germany and the Soviet Union in World War II—frequencies of marriage, age at marriage, and age of marriage partner were subsequently affected (Henry 1969). Populations experiencing drastic changes in fertility levels are also confronted with "marriage squeezes" years later when those born in the periods of inflection are old enough to marry. Thus, American males born in the 1930s, a period of sharply declining fertility, were generally more numerous than the females whom they would normally have married—those born two to five years later. Conversely, American females born in the 1946–1955 "baby boom" have had to seek husbands among the smaller number of males born two to five years earlier (Hirchman and Matras 1971).

The "marriage squeezes" generated by such inflections in fertility may in principle be resolved in a number of ways. Some of those adversely affected can conceivably (1) stay single—and marry later or not at all, or (2) choose a partner from some other, previously less conventional, age group—for example, males in the worsening "market" of the 1950s chose younger brides (Hirschman and Matras 1971) and females in the worsening market of the 1970s will probably be found to have chosen younger grooms than has previously been conventional. In addition, persons who otherwise (in the absence of a marriage squeeze) might have remained single (or divorced or widowed) may marry and "take up the slack." Recent theoretical work by L. Henry (1969) has shown that perturbations in age composition always are resolved (i.e., do not necessarily result in *anyone* being forced to remain unmarried) by variations in age-assortive mating, *provided* that all candidates for marriage are not obliged to marry within any specified time interval.

Social and Cultural Factors in Mate Selection

FREE OR "NON-ARRANGED" MARRIAGES. The effects of cultural and social factors on patterns and practices of mate selection differ in accordance with whether or not, or within what more or less formalized limits, eligible males and females reciprocally choose their own marriage partners. Insofar as individual reciprocal choice determines mate selection, marriage tends to be: (1) homogamous—i.e., to take place primarily between persons with similar social, economic, cultural, and other such characteristics; and (2) endogamous—i.e., to take place primarily between members of the same or similar ascriptive social subgroups or collectivities.[8] The acceptability or relative frequencies of deviations from homogamous and endogamous marriage vary over societies and collectivities and change over time. These variations have both demographic and other social structural origins and correlates.

One factor in the extent of homogamous and endogamous mate selection appears to be that of sheer physical or geographic access to eligible partners: patterns of mobility notwithstanding, there is a strong tendency for persons to choose their partners from among eligibles living in close geographic proximity to their own and their parents' homes— even among young persons temporarily away from home. Thus, homogamous and endogamous marriage follows, to a considerable extent, from the fact of residential segregation alone. However, as we shall demonstrate below, other factors also operate to promote homogamy and diminish heterogamy. Among nonhomogamous marriages, hypergamous marriages (in which females of lower rank or social status marry males of higher rank or status) are much more frequent than hypogamous marriages (in which the rank or status of the male is lower than that of the female).

In many primitive societies, the choice of marriage partners may be made by the partners themselves, with the restriction that the marriage be exogamous, i.e., that they take place between members of explicitly different ascriptive groups. Exogamous institutions may involve simply a prohibition upon marriage between members of the same group, lineage, clan, village, or other social unit; or they may prescribe, or stipulate as preferential, marriages between members of two or more specified groups or social units (Murdock 1949). Exogamous marriages tend to be homogamous; that is, the bride and groom typically share a number of important social characteristics other than membership in their respective ascriptive groups.

8 For a summary and discussion of some findings on the tendency toward homogamous and endogamous marriages in the United States, see Zelditch, Jr. (1964) and Hertzler (1961, pp. 240–45).

All marriages implicitly entail mutual undertakings on the part of bride and groom with respect to joint residence, sexual rights, and economic cooperation. But arranged marriages (as distinct from marriages in which only the partners themselves are involved in the choices) ordinarily also represent transactions between the groom's family, lineage, or other group and that of the bride (see our discussion of marriage transactions in section 1). These transactions, in addition to involving joint residence, sexual rights, and economic cooperation, may also be specific with regard to money, children, services, property, status, political power, inheritance or other rights, and anything which might conceivably be exchanged between the groups. Thus, in principle any of these exchangeable things can be bartered for social status or rank, and indeed many instances of such exchanges have been recorded (Barber 1955). Nevertheless, arranged marriages tend also to be homogamous.

Both arranged and nonarranged marriages may be governed or influenced by rules or customs of preferential mating with regard to either first marriages or remarriages. The most common type of preferred first marriage is cross-cousin marriage, i.e., the mating of the male with father's sister's daughter or with mother's brother's daughter. Another common preference is parallel-cousin marriage, which involves the male's mating with father's brother's daughter or with mother's sister's daughter. Regulations or customs governing first marriages may define certain relatives as preferred mates or exclude others as too closely akin (Murdock 1949, pp. 28–30). The most common customs governing secondary marriages are the levirate and sororate—the former prescribing that a widow preferably marry the brother of her deceased husband, and the latter that a widower preferably marry the sister of his deceased wife (Murdock 1949). Systems of ascriptive (based on ascribed, rather than achieved, characteristics) social groupings or classes are generated and perpetuated by homogamy, by certain patterns of preferential-marriage customs and norms, and by practices associating the offspring of different types of marriage to particular population groupings or categories. We shall return to this briefly in our discussion of changing elements of the marriage regime.

MATCHMAKING INSTITUTIONS AND ARRANGED MARRIAGES. The social institutions that directly affect matchmaking and mate selection in collectivities where people choose their own marriage partners are basically different from those in collectivities in which marriages are arranged. In the first category are all those institutions operating to structure and bound, or to catalyze, the random meetings and interaction of eligible males and females. As Zelditch has noted:

> Even where mate selection is free, and instrumental calculations are unconscious if they operate at all, some mechanisms of mate selection

tend to ensure that mates are at least of similar social rank. The control mechanisms are to some extent managed by parents, to some extent the result of the way in which a society's system of stratification affects interaction, and to some extent the result of peer group control over the dating process. [Zelditch, Jr. 1964, p. 688]

Thus, colleges and beaches, churches and nightclubs, offices and assembly lines, street corners and parlors are all places at which eligible males and females can meet and court, and at the same time they tend to encourage the matching of likes and to discourage the matching of unlikes. Conversely, institutions such as hospitals, political parties, conventions, and ocean cruises may provide arenas for the meeting of eligible unlikes.

Where marriages are typically arranged by persons other than the marital partners themselves, the circumstances and agencies of matchmaking may vary widely. In many societies, either fathers, or both parents, or uncles, or sometimes other relatives may be assigned the duty of arranging marriages. Alternatively, matchmaking may be included in the duties of political, religious, or other functionaries, and matchmaking may be a recognized occupation in its own right.

Obviously, in societies in which marriages are arranged, the range and efficiency of matchmaking institutions affect not only mate selection but also people's chances of eventual marriage and their patterns of age at marriage. Indeed, the arrangement of marriages may in many situations overcome possible geographic and social-class barriers to mating, thus expanding very considerably the range and variety of the marriage market. Exogamous arrangements, transactions between families of different rank, and marriage among the European nobility are cases in point. The institutions and mechanisms of mate selection in societies in which eligibles choose their own partners also affect—although perhaps not so obviously —the chances of eventual marriage and patterns of age at marriage, and these, in turn, affect patterns of fertility and population growth (Hajnal 1965).

Changing Dimensions of the Marriage Regime

There are two dimensions to the marriage regime: (1) patterns of frequency of marriage and age at marriage, and (2) patterns of matchmaking and mate selection. An analysis similar to that used in representing marriage and age-assortative mating as a population transformation can be invoked to show that the first dimension generally cannot be compatible with the second over any extended period of time. That is, the patterns of frequency and age at marriage prevailing at any one time in a society will eventually be influenced by changing demographic and social conditions to such an extent as to be rendered incompatible with the prevailing patterns of matchmaking and mate selection (Matras, *in press*). A fundamental problem is: which elements and dimensions of the "marriage regime" change, and by how much and in what directions, under different conditions of demographic and social change? This problem is basic both to the study of population composition and growth and to the study of social structure and stratification. Before pursuing it further, a few words on the relationship between mate selection and social organization are in order.

In all societies mate-selection patterns, norms, and practices have far-reaching consequences for social structure and social stratification. In societies in which kinship or descent groupings constitute the main axes of social organization and stratification, rules of matchmaking, mate selection, and preferential marriage obviously define and systematize the relationships within and between such groupings. The nature of the kinship relationships generated by marriages of the different types penetrates literally every facet of the society's social life.

In such societies both endogamous groupings and closed systems of exogamous groupings generate social strata or population subgroups which, in principle, are demographically bounded and self-sufficient. Such groupings can continue as endogamous or closed exogamous systems only to the extent that they remain demographically self-sufficient, i.e., that they continue to provide marital partners for all eligible persons. In practice, it may occur that such a system becomes demographically nonviable, or, alternatively, that the institutionalized patterns of matchmaking and mate selection become incompatible with demographic viability.[9]

In societies in which other ascriptive groupings or nonascriptive groupings constitute the major axes of social organization and stratification, mate-selection norms and practices are less explicit but still remain major factors in determining the strictness of closure among classes or strata and the extent to which relationships within them are based upon kinship. Again, residential, ethnic, religious, racial, or educational endogamy or homogamy generate classes and operate to convert originally nonascriptive groupings into ascriptive ones. These groupings, in turn, are viable only insofar as they are demographically self-sufficient.

Keeping in mind (1) that mate-selection processes strongly affect social structure and social stratification, and (2) that their own viability depends heavily on the society's demographic conditions of fertility and population growth, and (3) that fertility and population growth are strongly affected by frequency of marriage and age at marriage, we return to the issue posed earlier: the not infrequent incompatibility between a

---

9 For an example of a mathematical representation of this phenomenon, see Goldberg (1958, pp. 238–41). For a much more elaborate mathematical presentation, see White (1963).

society's matchmaking and mate-selection pattern, on the one hand, and its pattern of age at marriage and frequency of marriage on the other. The fundamental question raised by this incompatibility is, as we suggested earlier: which of these two dimensions of the marriage regime changes under different conditions of social and demographic change, and by how much and in what direction? The recurrence of the incompatibility suggests that either or both of the dimensions are much more frequently in the process of change and mutual adjustment than has been recognized.

We may illustrate this by referring to recent trends in marriage and mate selection in the Jewish population of Israel. The dominant feature of marriage in this population is that—in contrast to the considerable proportions remaining single in Jewish populations in Europe and North America—marriage is nearly universal (but not early) in all subgroups and sectors. By 1970, the near universality of marriage had been a characteristic of this population for at least two decades and possibly longer (Gabriel 1960; Israel C.B.S. 1969, No. 20). A second feature of Israeli marriage has been country-of-origin homogamy and—at least in the population of European or Israeli birth—educational-level homogamy (Matras 1968, chap. 3).

At least three types of "marriage squeezes" have characterized the marriageable Israeli Jewish population over the past few decades. First, with a steady annual increase in the absolute numbers of Jewish births in pre-independence Palestine and in Israel, and with grooms normally somewhat older than their brides, Israeli-born females have always been affected by shortages of Israeli-born males of marriageable age. A substantial proportion of Israeli-born females marry foreign-born males. Marriage between Israelis and foreign-born persons have very frequently been homogamous with respect to ethnic or geocultural origin; that is, the foreign-born partner is very likely to choose an Israeli-born spouse whose *parents* were born in the country of his or her own birth. Similarly, marriages involving two Israeli-born partners are also frequently homogamous with respect to country-of-birth of the couple's parents (Israel C.B.S., 1968, table 35).

Second, immigrants from the different countries have arrived in Israel in *waves* of immigration, rather than steadily over an extended period. Each wave and age group of marriageable immigrants to Israel has found the population of marriageables somewhat differently composed. Thus, while the *random* chance of marrying a partner born in Israel has increased steadily over time, the random chance of marrying a foreign-born partner of any given country of birth has increased and decreased over time in accordance with the size, age, and marital-status composition of the waves of immigration from each country of origin.

Finally, the average level of educational attainment in the population generally, and among the immigrant populations from Asia and

Africa in particular, has been increasing steadily during recent decades. Thus, successive age groups are characterized by a progressively higher average level of education. In particular, successive cohorts of marriageable females are faced with shortages of older males of comparable or superior levels of educational achievement. Conversely, the least well-educated marriageable males are faced with shortages of younger, even less well-educated, marriageable females.[10]

In view of the patterns of ethnic and educational homogamy, on the one hand, and these three types of "marriage squeeze" on the other, it is remarkable that marriage in the Jewish population has remained very nearly universal. The exact manner in which these patterns of high marriage frequencies are sustained has not yet been studied in sufficient detail, but at least two factors are pertinent: (1) marriage is not necessarily early, and any given age group may "marry itself out" over an extended period of time, allowing enough leeway to achieve universal marriage despite the "marriage squeezes" affecting the group, and (2) marriages may be homogamous with respect to ethnic origin or with respect to educational level, but *not necessarily with respect to both*. A certain trade-off of ethnic status for educational status occurs, with low-ethnic-status marriageables of high educational achievement more likely to marry cross-ethnically than those of low educational achievement, and with high-ethnic-status marriageables more likely to marry cross-ethnically the lower their educational achievement (Matras 1968). Thus the Kurdish or Moroccan immigrant male—who shares the low-ethnic status of his origin group—is far more likely to marry the daughter of English or of Hungarian parents if he has a college degree than if he has only elementary or secondary education; and the daughter of English or of Hungarian parents is more likely to marry cross-ethnically if she has only elementary or secondary education. Thus, the universal marriage pattern in Israel is sustained in part by the diminishing rigidity of the patterns of ethnic and educational homogamy.

10 For details, see the 1961 census publications of Israel dealing with educational achievement (Publication Nos. 15, 29 and 30).

8

Patterns
of Childbearing

1. GENERAL REMARKS

Human fertility—the direct antecedent of population growth and composition—has been the primary focus of population studies and speculations since Malthus. Now, moreover, particularly with the recent world-wide trend toward lower levels of mortality and the widespread concern over rapid population growth, the analysis of fertility and the attendant childbearing and family-building have become more dominant in population studies than ever before.

Practical Concerns in the Study of Fertility

There are, of course, a host of very practical purposes to be served by the recording and analysis of fertility: babies and their mothers need hospital facilities, diapers, formulas, cribs, new homes, and, eventually, teething cookies and playpens—the list is endless—and all of these require counts and projections of numbers of births. Moreover, today's babies are tomorrow's toddlers, school children, soldiers, labor force, and, ultimately, the parents of the next generation of babies. Anyone dealing with future school children, soldiers, consumers, brides, or bridegrooms is well advised to keep abreast of the volume and composition of fertility and their variations and changes.

Regardless of the method by which it is measured, fertility exhibits broad variations over societies and social groups and distinct changes over time. Thus, beyond the immediate practical objectives noted above, numerous studies have sought to discover the causes, correlates, and consequences of variations and changes in fertility. The recent rediscovery and increasing acknowledgement of the likelihood of a close relationship between population growth and levels of living, social welfare, and economic development—the rekindling of the Malthusian debate—have lent greater impetus and, indeed, considerable urgency to these investigations. The recognition of these relationships has been acompanied in many instances by a widespread and relatively new willingness, if not determination, to seek means of intervening in societal policies and in group and individual behavior in order to promote enhanced levels of social and economic well-being.[1]

In the 1930s, a variety of pro-natal measures were introduced in Europe, ranging from taxes on bachelors in Italy to the very strongly enforced suppression of contraception and abortion in Germany. Similarly, there were restrictions on abortion in the Soviet Union and a variety of monetary inducements to procreation in Sweden and, especially, in France. Many such measures have recently been rescinded, however. For example, the French law prohibiting both abortion and all publicity and promotion of contraception was abolished in 1968.

In 1948 Japan adopted its Eugenic Protection Law, which relaxed some of the previous restrictions on abortions, and in 1952 this law was amended to legalize abortion and free it from virtually all restrictions. At the same time, the government of Japan introduced a program to promote family planning. The first *government-sponsored* birth control clinic in the world was opened in Mysore, India, in 1930, and the government of independent India has had an official family planning program since 1951. The progressively increased expenditures on this program are shown in figure 8.1.

There are government-sponsored family planning programs in an increasing number of Asian and African countries—for example, South Korea, Taiwan, Pakistan, Tunisia, and Egypt—and "nonofficial" programs run by voluntary organizations in a number of Latin American countries (e.g., Chile, Argentina, Brazil, and Mexico). "Nonofficial" programs also exist in North America, and in the United States the privately sponsored activities of Planned Parenthood-World Population and its affiliates are complemented in some areas by family planning services

---

1 Eversley has pointed out that previously, especially before Malthus, the impetus behind studies and speculations about fertility and population was much more often philosophical, historical, theological, or political (Eversley 1959, pp. 7–11).

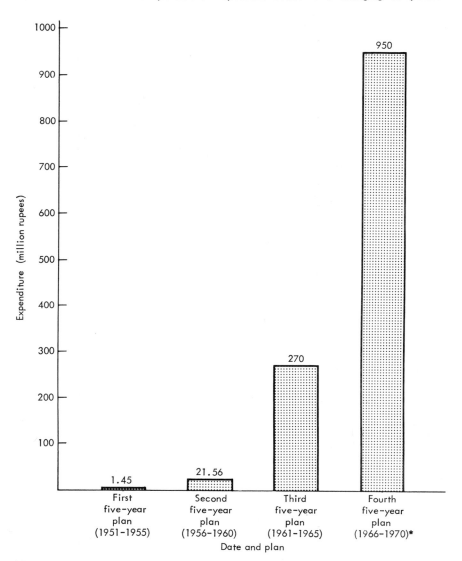

FIGURE 8.1. India: expenditures on family planning program. Source: Raina 1961.

provided by local public health units and planned parenthood organizations operating without affiliation (see figure 8.2).

Fertility studies in the twentieth century have echoed the thrust of the programs described above: in the first half of the century, they were closely connected to the attempt in Europe and the West to introduce national policies designed to combat aging, stagnation, or depopulation. Since the end of World War II, however, they have been just as closely associated with attempts to deal with the threat of overpopulation outside Europe and the West (Glass 1965).

Individual and Group Variations

It is of fundamental importance to distinguish between variations among individual women or couples in patterns and practices of childbearing and variations among groups. In any group of women there are individual variations in age patterns of childbearing, in the timing of childbearing, in the time elapsed between marriage or previous births and childbearing, in the total number of children ultimately borne, and in the size of completed individual families. Individual women or couples also vary in the extent, means, and success of intervention, planning, and control of pregnancy and childbearing.

Between any set of groups there may be variations in the *distribution* of births by mother's age or by duration of mother's marriage, or in the distribution of births of each of the different birth orders (first child, second child, etc.), again by mother's age or duration of marriage. Simi-

FIGURE 8.2. Family planning services in health departments, by county, and Planned Parenthood-World Population affiliates, by city, 1965. Source: Corsa 1966, p. 264.

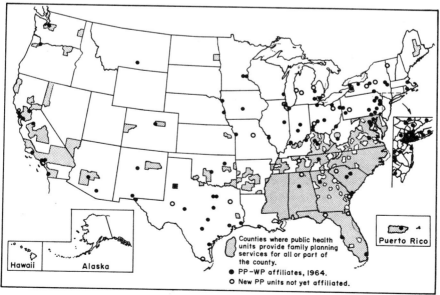

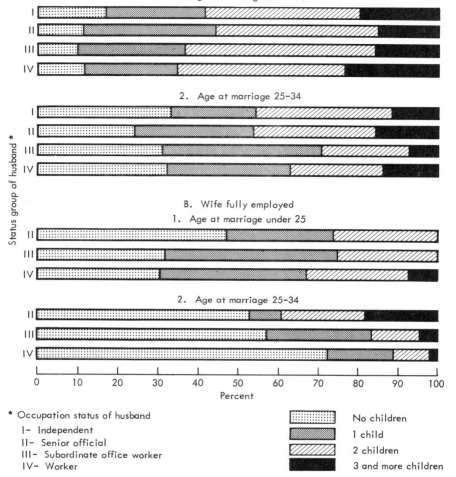

FIGURE 8.3. Distribution of couples married in Copenhagen in 1939 by number of children, occupational status of husband, employment status of wife, and age of wife at marriage, 31 December, 1948. Source: Johnson 1960, p. 62.

larly, patterns of spacing births vary among different groups; and distributions of women or couples by total number of children ever born to them or by completed family size may also vary among separately identified groups. Group or societal differences in patterns of childbearing generally reflect differences in the composition of the respective groups by individual characteristics.

But there are basic group differences in patterns of fertility which supersede those implied by compositional differences alone. As we shall see below, different norms and patterns of fertility are institutionalized in different societies and social groupings. Figure 8.3 shows how groups of Danish women differ in their distributions by number of children borne. Employment of the women, occupational status of the husbands, and the ages at which the women married all have bearing on these differences. The group and societal variations in institutions of fertility, the changes in these institutions, and relationships of the changes to societal strategies of survival and adaptation are of particular interest in the context of this volume.

In the next section we shall review briefly the main trends in fertility that have characterized the modern period in the several continents of the world and the major axes of differentiation in levels of fertility and patterns of childbearing. Then, in the following sections, we shall review some findings and hypotheses concerning factors related to variations and changes in patterns of childbearing.

2. TRENDS AND VARIATIONS IN FERTILITY

We have already indicated (chap. 5, section 6 and 7) some alternative methods of measuring fertility, and we shall employ a number of different measures in the discussion of fertility differentials. However, in discussing historical trends in fertility, we shall confine ourselves to the crude birth rate only, that is, to the number of annual live births per thousand persons in the mean (average) population. An extensive comparative analysis of world fertility trends since 1900 has been prepared by the United Nations Population Branch, and we shall draw upon this work. However, for data concerning previous trends in fertility, it will be necessary to turn to a number of separate sources.

Trends and Variations Before 1900

A compact summary of fertility trends for Sweden from 1701 to 1900, and for all of Europe from 1801 to 1900, is presented in table 8.1. As the table shows, approximate levels of Swedish natality are known for periods as early as the first half of the eighteenth century, at which time crude birth rates fluctuated around a level of about 34 per 1,000 (Carr-Saunders 1936, chap. 5; Gille 1949). In about 1760, however, Swedish fertility rates began to decline, and they continued to do so until the present century. According to Carr-Saunders (1936), fertility in England and Wales in the first half of the eighteenth century approximated that of Sweden, but the decline in English fertility began only around 1880.

TABLE 8.1
Crude Birth Rates for Sweden, 1701–1900, and for Europe, 1801–1900

Period	Sweden: Crude Birth Rate per 1,000	Period	Europe: Crude Birth Rate per 1,000	
			Total Europe	*Western Europe*
1701–1750	34.2	1801–1820	38.5	34.4
1751–1775	34.4	1821–1830	39.8	36.0
1776–1800	33.1	1831–1840	38.6	34.6
1801–1825	32.9	1841–1850	37.9	33.7
1826–1850	31.6	1851–1860	37.9	33.4
1851–1875	31.7	1861–1870	38.6	34.1
1876–1900	28.5	1871–1880	38.9	34.3
		1881–1890	38.1	32.8
		1891–1900	37.0	31.4

SOURCE: Federici 1968.

Beginning with the first decade of the nineteenth century, data became available for a much larger proportion of European countries. The crude birth rate in northwest Europe, excepting France, fluctuated at around 35 per 1,000 throughout most of the nineteenth century and began to decline to lower levels only as the century ended. The rate for eastern Europe fluctuated at around 45 per 1,000 throughout the nineteenth century, but at around the turn of the century declined to levels slightly below 40 per thousand (Carr-Saunders 1936).

This sketch necessarily obscures variations among the different countries in Europe, but for these we have only fragmentary data. It is hazardous to assume that the eighteenth-century Swedish birth rates are representative of those in all of Europe, of northwestern Europe, or even Scandinavia. We know, for example, that crude birth rates in Finland in the second quarter of the eighteenth century were consistently higher than those in Sweden (Jutikkala 1965). Similarly, a study by Eversley of parish registers from 1660 to 1860 in Worcestershire, England, shows that the rates of *baptism* per 1,000 population increased from 36 per 1,000 in 1705–1714 to about 44 per 1,000 in 1730–1744. Birth rates in Italy and southern Europe in the eighteenth and nineteenth centuries were evidently somewhat higher than those of northwestern Europe (Carr-Saunders 1936; Cipolla 1965; Frederici 1968, fig. x.1), and the birth rate in France began to decline even before the close of the eighteenth century, remaining substantially lower than that of the rest of western Europe throughout the nineteenth century (Bourgeois-Pichat 1965).

Estimates of the crude birth rate in North America suggest levels of fertility unknown elsewhere. In the Catholic population of Quebec, French Canada, the crude birth rate is estimated to have reached about

60 per 1,000 in 1670, declining to about 45 per 1,000 in 1690 but recovering again to over 55 per 1,000 between 1710 and 1750 and to over 60 per 1,000 between 1770 and 1780. The rates declined thereafter, more closely resembling those of Europe (Carr-Saunders 1936).

The crude birth rate for the white population of the United States is estimated to have been as high as 55 per 1,000 in 1780, to have remained above 50 per 1,000 until after 1830, and to have declined thereafter to levels characteristic of late nineteenth-century Europe (Thompson and Whelpton 1933).

The pattern for Europe is one of high birth rates until the nineteenth century—around 35 per 1,000 in western Europe and 40–45 per thousand in eastern and southern Europe—with steep declines occurring earlier or later in the nineteenth century; the exception is France, where the decline began in the second half of the eighteenth century. Sauvy (1967, p. 178) summarizes beginning dates of the fertility decline as follows:

France	1760	England	1875
Sweden	1820	Germany	1880
Belgium	1840	United States	1885
Switzerland	1860	Italy	1885
Netherlands	1875	Hungary	1890

However, the date cited for the onset in the United States does not agree with other sources.

For other areas of the world, we have almost no data on numbers of births before the last quarter of the nineteenth century and hence no direct way of computing early fertility rates. However, data exist for Australia and New Zealand indicating that fertility rates there were higher than those of Europe in the nineteenth century, declining sharply beginning in the second half of the century. The Australian crude birth rate reached 43 per 1,000 in 1860–1862, declining thereafter and falling to 27 per 1,000 in 1900–1902. In New Zealand, the birth rate reached a peak of 43 per 1,000 around 1870 but had declined to 28 per 1,000 by the turn of the century (Reinhard and Armengaud 1961, pp. 339–43). The crude birth rate for Hindus in India was estimated at 49 per 1,000 between 1881 and 1891, changing only a little toward the turn of the century (*ibid.,* p. 375). Finally, the birth rate for Japan increased from about 25 per 1,000 in 1875 to about 32 per 1,000 in 1900 and further to 36 per 1,000 in 1920 (*ibid.,* pp. 394–99; see also Carr-Saunders 1936, chap. 18). For pre-twentieth century periods in other non-European countries there are substantial data on *total* population growth, and there is some information on family size, but for the most part no systematic account of fertility trends prior to the present century can be put together.

Fertility Trends in the Twentieth Century

As indicated above, the United Nations Populations Branch has made a comparative analysis of fertility levels and trends throughout the world in the twentieth century (U.N. 1965). In summarizing the results of this analysis, the investigators have divided the countries of the world into "low fertility" and "high fertility" countries, the first having crude birth rates of under 30 per 1,000 and the second having rates of 30 per 1,000 or above. The distribution of countries by estimated crude birth rate in or around 1960 and by level of development of the region is shown in table 8.2.

In table 8.2 we note that, of 123 countries included, 39 were characterized by low fertility levels (less than 30 per 1,000) in 1960—of which all but six were in the more developed regions of the world. Of the 86 countries characterized by high fertility (30 per thousand or over) all but two were in the less developed regions.

"LOW-FERTILITY" COUNTRIES. The "low fertility" countries divide into three subgroups. In the first subgroup—which includes the majority of countries in northern, western, and central Europe, together with Argentina, Australia, Canada, Israel, New Zealand, and the United States

TABLE 8.2
*Distribution of Countries by Level of Crude
Birth Rate, 1960*

Crude Birth Rates per 1,000 Population	Total	Less Developed Regions	More Developed Regions
Total	123	88	35
Low Rates			
Under 15	3	—	3
15.0 – 19.9	18	1	17
20.0 – 24.9	14	4	10
25.0 – 29.9	4	1	3
High Rates			
30.0 – 34.9	3	3	—
35.0 – 39.9	11	11	—
40.0 – 44.9	22	21	1
45.0 – 49.9	29	28	1
50.0 – 54.9	12	12	—
55.0 – 59.0	5	5	—
60.0 and over	2	2	—

SOURCE: U.N., *Population Bulletin,* No. 7, 1963.

TABLE 8.3

Twentieth-Century Fertility Trends in France, Sweden, England and Wales, the United States, and Israel

Year	France	Sweden	England and Wales	United States	Israel
1900–1904	21.2	26.4	28.2		
1905–1909	20.1	25.6	26.7		
1910–1914	19.0	23.7	24.3		
1915–1919	11.4	20.8	20.9	24.1	
1920–1924	19.9	20.3	21.3	22.8	
1925–1929	18.5	16.3	17.1	20.1	
1930–1934	17.2	14.4	15.3	17.6	32.0[a]
1935–1939	15.1	14.5	14.9	17.2	24.7[b]
1940–1944	14.6	17.7	15.5	19.9	25.1
1945–1949	20.2	19.0	18.0	23.4	29.0
1950–1954	19.4	15.5	15.5	24.5	30.8
1955–1959	18.3	14.5	15.9	24.6	25.6
1960	17.9	13.7	17.2	23.7	23.9
1969	16.9	15.4	17.5	17.4	25.0

SOURCE: U.N., *Population Bulletin,* No. 7, 1963, table 6.2; fig. 1.2, p. 5.

[a] 1930–1933.

[b] 1938–1939.

—fertility declined in the twentieth century until the 1930s, turned upward at the close of the 1930s or early 1940s, developed into a "baby boom" in the late 1940s and early 1950s and then, with one exception, leveled off; the exception is the United States, where the "baby boom" extended through the 1950s and fertility leveled off only in the 1960s. Table 8.3 covers selected countries of the first subgroup.

The countries of the second "low fertility" subgroup—those of southern and southeastern Europe, except for Spain—are for the most part less industrialized than those of the first subgroup. These countries were characterized by a more or less consistent decline in fertility throughout the 1930s, 1940s, and 1950s. Their average levels of fertility were much lower at the close of the 1950s than at the beginning of the 1930s and, indeed, were very close to the low levels of the first subgroup (table 8.4). In 1967, Roumania adopted a policy severely restricting induced abortions, and a dramatic increase in the crude birth rate quickly ensued. However, the 1967 peak of almost 28 per 1,000 has since been followed by a declining crude birth rate.

The last subgroup of "low fertility" countries includes only Japan and the Ryukyu Islands, both characterized by high fertility until the end of World War II, very sharply declining fertility in the 1950s, and some recovery of fertility most recently (U.N., P.B., 1965, table 4.4). The crude birth rates for Japan are:

1920	36.2
1925	35.0
1930	32.5
1937–1940	28.7
1947–1949	33.7
1950–1954	23.7
1955–1959	18.2
1960	17.2
1969	19.0
1971	18.0

"HIGH-FERTILITY" COUNTRIES. Virtually all the countries in the "high fertility" category are in Africa, Asia, Middle America, and South America. In these areas, only Argentina, Cyprus, Israel, Japan, the Ryukyu Islands, Uruguay, and Zanzibar are in the "low fertility" category. Of the "high fertility" countries, only a few have reliable series of birth statistics extending back over a period of two decades or more. Thus, for the majority (including virtually all the countries of Africa), no historical series of birth data exist. The difficulty is compounded, moreover, by variations in the completeness of registration and of base population estimates.

In the face of this difficulty in establishing trends over time, we can say merely that although some fluctuation is evident in these countries of "high fertility," the overall picture is one of fairly stable birth rates at high levels. A number of countries, including Taiwan, Malaya, Singapore, Mauritius, and Réunion, appear to have been characterized by

TABLE 8.4

Twentieth-Century Fertility Trends in Italy, Romania, Bulgaria, and Yugoslavia

Year	Italy	Romania	Bulgaria	Yugoslavia
1900–1904	32.6	39.6	40.7	—
1905–1909	32.6	40.1	42.5	39.2
1910–1914	31.8	41.8	39.0	37.8
1915–1919	22.7	40.0	26.4	—
1920–1924	30.1	37.6	39.6	35.3
1925–1929	27.3	35.4	34.2	33.9
1930–1934	24.5	33.7	30.3	33.0
1935–1939	23.2	30.2	24.1	27.9
1940–1944	20.8	23.2	22.1	—
1945–1949	21.1	24.9	24.6	28.2
1950–1954	18.3	24.9	21.7	28.8
1955–1959	18.0	22.9	18.7	24.8
1960	18.3	19.1	17.8	23.5
1969	18.1	27.1	15.0	19.5

SOURCE: U.N., *Population Bulletin,* No. 7, 1963, fig. 1.2, p. 5.

declining fertility since World War II, whereas at least two countries in the Caribbean area, Jamaica and the dominion of Trinidad and Tobago, have experienced increasing fertility. Table 8.5 shows birth rates in selected "high fertility" countries of Asia.

Geographic Variations in National Fertility Levels

DIFFERENCES AMONG COUNTRIES. In discussing twentieth-century trends in fertility, we have already hinted at the range of variation in current fertility levels of different countries. This range, for 1960, is plotted in somewhat greater detail in table 8.6 which shows the number and continental distribution of countries characterized by crude birth rates ranging from less than 15 per 1,000 to above 60 per 1,000.

An important conclusion drawn by recent studies is that the birth rates of different *European* countries have lately been converging over time (Glass 1968). This is illustrated in different ways in figure 8.4 and in figure 8.5.

The twentieth century trends in the crude birth rate are summarized graphically in figure 8.4 for selected countries. The data—and hence the trend lines drawn—are not complete for all countries. However the trend toward convergence over time of the crude birth rates for all but two of the countries (Mexico and Union of South Africa, "colored population") is evident.

TABLE 8.5
Birth Rates in Selected Asian Countries, 1955–1966

	Taiwan	Hong Kong	Singapore	Malaya	Ceylon
1955	45.3	36.3	44.3	44.0	37.3
1956	44.8	37.0	44.4	46.7	36.4
1957	41.4	35.8	43.4	46.1	36.5
1958	41.7	37.4	42.0	43.3	35.8
1959	41.2	35.2	40.3	42.2	37.0
1960	39.5	36.0	38.7	40.9	36.6
1961	38.3	34.3	36.5	41.9	35.8
1962	37.4	33.3	35.1	40.4	35.5
1963	36.3	32.8	34.7	39.4	34.5
1964	34.5	30.1	33.2	39.1	33.1
1965	32.7	27.7	31.1	36.7	32.7
1966	32.5[a]	24.9	29.9	—	—
1969	29.0	23.0	27.0	—	32.2

SOURCE: Data for 1955 through 1966 from Kirk 1969, p. 80; fig. 1.2, p. 5; 1969 data from *Demographic Yearbook* 1969.

[a]Figure for 1966 is not comparable owing to more (i.e., earlier) registration of births in the latter part of the year in connection with the national census. This is reflected in very low birth rates reported for the first months of 1967.

TABLE 8.6

TABLE 8.6

Distribution of Countries by Continent and by Level of Crude Birth Rate, circa 1960

Crude Birth Rate per 1,000 Population	World Total	Africa	Asia (excluding USSR)	Middle and South America	Europe (excluding USSR)	Northern America	Oceania	USSR
Total	123	37	24	27	29	2	3	1
Under 15	3	—	—	—	3	—	—	—
15.0–19.9	18	—	1	—	17	—	—	—
20.0–24.9	14	—	2	2	7	1	1	1
25.0–29.9	4	—	1	—	1	1	1	—
30.0–34.9	3	—	1	2	—	—	—	—
35.0–39.9	11	3	4	4	—	—	—	—
40.0–44.9	22	9	3	9	1	—	—	—
45.0–49.9	29	13	7	8	—	—	1	—
50.0–54.9	12	5	5	2	—	—	—	—
55.0–59.9	5	5	—	—	—	—	—	—
60.0 and over	2	2	—	—	—	—	—	—

SOURCE: U.N., *Population Bulletin,* No. 7 — 1963 (1965).
Note: Excludes countries with fewer than 250,000 inhabitants in 1960 and those having no satisfactory data.

Inter-country variation in crude birth rates in 1963 is illustrated in the panels of maps of figure 8.5 (pp. 306–10). However, the European panel is unique for its relative homogeneity: all countries except Greece and Turkey had crude birth rates below 25 per thousand, and the majority had rates under 20 per thousand.

TABLE 8.7

Crude Birth Rates in Mauritius, Union of South Africa, Ceylon, India, and Mexico, 1900–1969

Year	Mauritius	Union of South Africa ("Colored")	Ceylon	India[b]	Mexico
1900–1904	36.9		38.6	48	
1905–1909	36.1		37.4		
1910–1914	38.4		37.5	49	
1915–1919	35.6		37.0		
1920–1924	37.3		38.5	46	
1925–1929	37.5		40.6		
1930–1934	30.9		37.8	45	43.4[c]
1935–1939	33.8		35.6		44.7[d]
1940–1944	34.0	43.7	36.6	40	
1945–1949	—	46.4[a]	38.2		
1950–1954	46.3	47.4	38.5		44.9
1955–1959	41.5	46.1	36.6		45.9
1960	39.6	47.8	36.6		46.0
1969	30.0	46.0	32.0	43	43.0

SOURCE: U.N., *Population Bulletin,* No. 7 — 1963, tables 4.4, 5.4.
[a]1946–1949.   [c]1931–1934.
[b]Estimated from Census data.   [d]1938–1942.

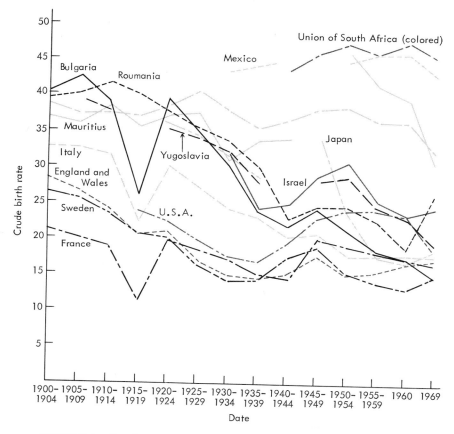

FIGURE 8.4. Trend in crude birth rate for selected countries, 1900–1969.
Source: Tables 8.3, 8.4, 8.7, and text.

In countries outside of Europe, however, birth rates are much less homogeneous. Moreover, there does not appear to be any readily identifiable set of factors with which to associate levels of crude birth rates in the "high fertility" countries of Asia, Africa, and Middle and South America. The United Nations Population Branch has attempted to identify such factors by measuring the correlation between levels of fertility, on the one hand, and social and economic indicators, on the other, using the Gross Reproduction Rate, an index of the *schedule* of age-specific fertility rates which is considerably more refined than the crude birth rate. The social and economic indicators have included per capita income, per capita energy consumption, proportion of the labor force employed in nonagricultural industries, degree of urbanization, female literacy rate, newspaper circulation, radio receivers per 1,000 population,

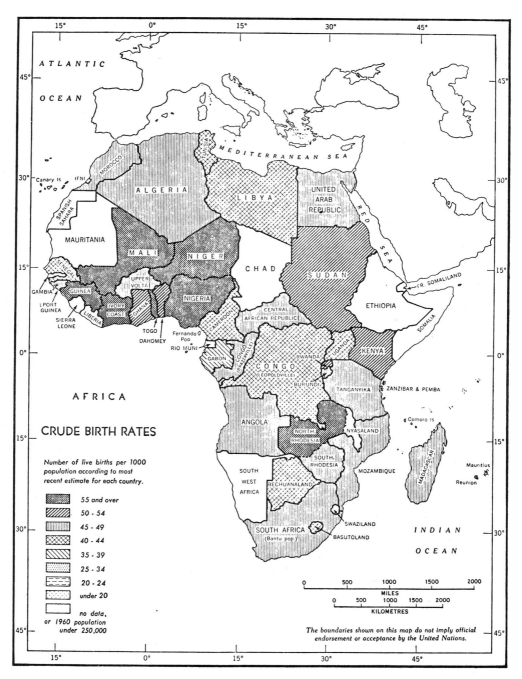

FIGURE 8.5. Panel of maps showing crude birth rate, selected countries, 1963. Source: U.N. 1963b, figures 3.1, 4.1, 5.1, 5.2, 5.3, and 6.1.

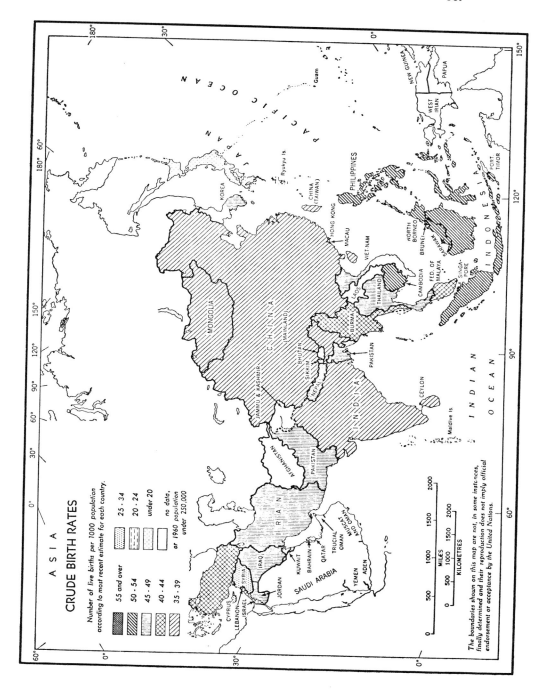

ASIA

CRUDE BIRTH RATES

Number of live births per 1000 population
according to most recent estimate for each country.

55 and over
50 - 54
45 - 49
40 - 44
35 - 39
25 - 34
20 - 24
under 20
no data,
or 1960 population
under 250,000

The boundaries shown on this map are not, in some instances,
finally determined and their reproduction does not imply official
endorsement or acceptance by the United Nations.

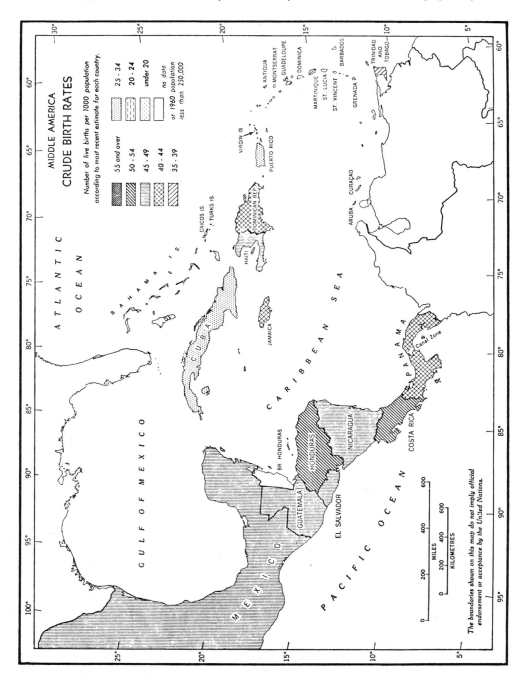

MIDDLE AMERICA
CRUDE BIRTH RATES

*Number of live births per 1000 population
according to most recent estimate for each country.*

55 and over
50 - 54
45 - 49
40 - 44
35 - 39
25 - 34
20 - 24
under 20
no data
or 1960 population
less than 250,000

*The boundaries shown on this map do not imply official
endorsement or acceptance by the United Nations.*

Number of live births per 1000
population according to most
recent estimate for each country

	55 and over
	50 - 54
	45 - 49
	40 - 44
	35 - 39
	25 - 34
	20 - 24
	under 20
	no data,
or 1960 population
less than 250,000

SOUTH AMERICA

CRUDE BIRTH RATES

The boundaries shown on this map do not imply official
endorsement or acceptance by the United Nations.

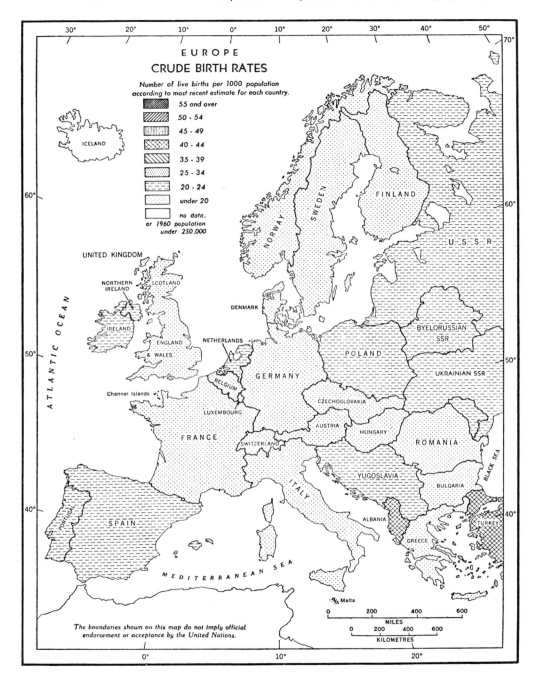

EUROPE
CRUDE BIRTH RATES

*Number of live births per 1000 population
according to most recent estimate for each country.*

55 and over
50 - 54
45 - 49
40 - 44
35 - 39
25 - 34
20 - 24
under 20
no data,
or 1960 population
under 250,000

*The boundaries shown on this map do not imply official
endorsement or acceptance by the United Nations.*

and measures of general and infant mortality. In all cases, very low coefficients of correlation have been achieved when the analysis has been limited to "high fertility" countries (U.N., P.B., No. 7– 1963, 1965, chaps. 1 and 9). On the other hand, there is some support for the hypothesis of an inverse relationship between a country's population density and its level of fertility, although the evidence is not conclusive (U.N., P.B., No. 7 – 1963, 1965; see also Grauman 1965). Summary and detailed fertility rates computed or estimated for 136 countries are given in figure 1.2.

Besides the national differences already noted, there are at least two other types of geographic variation in levels of fertility: (1) regional variations, and (2) variations by urban-rural designation or by size of place of residence.

REGIONAL DIFFERENCES. Regional variations in fertility derive principally from historical differences in patterns of settlement, economic and social development, and population composition, and there is some evidence relating them to climatological and topographical variations as well (see, for example, James 1966 and Heer 1967).

Regional and state differences in fertility have been apparent in the United States from the earliest censuses. Thus, looking at child-woman ratios—numbers of children under five years of age per 1,000 women of childbearing age—the rates in the U.S. Census of 1800 for rural white women aged 20 to 44 years were 1,319 for the entire country but 1,799 in the East South Central states and only 1,126 in the New England states. These regional differences were preserved throughout the ninetenth century and first decade of the twentieth, a period of sharply declining fertility in the United States. In the U.S. Census of 1940, when the national "child-woman ratio" (measured as above) had declined to its all-time low of 551 children per 1,000 rural white females, the rates in the New England and East South Central states were 443 and 648 respectively. With the rise in fertility in the 1940s, these differentials persisted. Thus, in 1950 the "child-woman ratio" for rural white women was 673 per 1,000 in the U.S. as a whole but 720 in the East South Central states and only 612 in the New England states. Regional variations have been much less pronounced, however, for the country's *urban* white women (Grabill 1959). Moreover, in more recent years, especially since 1960, overall regional differences in the U.S. have notably diminished (U.S. National Center for Health Statistics, 1967: Public Health Service Publication, No. 1,000, Series 21 – No. 11). Table 8.8 shows that between 1960 and 1969, crude birth rates declined at a rate directly related to their initial levels: the higher the initial birth rate, the greater the decline. The tendency, then, is toward an equalization of crude birth rates—a trend that is even more pronounced when more refined rates are analyzed.

TABLE 8.8

*Birth Rates and Percent Change in Each Geographic
Division and State of the United States, 1960 and 1969*

Division and State[1]	1960	1969	Percent Change
	Birth Rate per 1,000 population		
United States	23.7	17.7	−25.3
Geographic Division			
New England[2]	22.5	17.6	−21.8
Middle Atlantic	21.5	18.3	−14.9
East North Central	24.2	19.7	−18.6
West North Central	24.0	18.7	−22.1
South Atlantic	24.2	20.0	−17.4
East South Central	24.4	20.1	−17.6
West South Central	25.4	20.2	−20.5
Mountain	27.3	20.6	−24.5
Pacific	23.6	19.0	−19.5
New England			
Maine	24.0	17.9	−25.4
New Hampshire	22.8	17.3	−24.1
Vermont	24.1	17.8	−26.1
Massachusetts[2]	22.4	18.2	−18.8
Rhode Island	21.4	17.4	−18.7
Connecticut	22.4	16.4	−26.8
Middle Atlantic			
New York	21.4	18.6	−13.1
New Jersey	21.8	18.5	−15.1
Pennsylvania	21.3	17.8	−10.3
East North Central			
Ohio	23.8	19.1	−19.7
Indiana	24.2	20.0	−17.4
Illinois	23.7	19.6	−17.3
Michigan	25.0	20.1	−19.6
Wisconsin	25.2	20.0	−14.3
West North Central			
Minnesota	25.7	19.9	−22.6
Iowa	23.3	18.5	−20.6
Missouri	22.7	18.1	−20.3
North Dakota	26.3	20.2	−23.2
South Dakota	25.9	19.7	−23.9
Nebraska	24.3	18.8	−22.6
Kansas	23.3	17.6	−24.5
South Atlantic			
Delaware	25.9	21.2	−18.1
Maryland	24.9	21.0	−15.7
District of Columbia	26.0	22.5	−13.5
Virginia	24.1	20.0	−17.0
West Virginia	21.2	17.7	−16.5
North Carolina	24.1	19.9	−17.4

TABLE 8.8 (cont.)

Division and State[1]	1960	1969	Percent Change
	Birth Rate per 1,000 Population		
South Carolina	25.1	20.8	−17.1
Georgia	25.3	21.7	−14.2
Florida	23.3	18.4	−21.0
East South Central			
Kentucky	23.8	19.4	−18.5
Tennessee	23.0	19.0	−17.4
Alabama	24.7	20.4	−17.4
Mississippi	27.2	22.5	−17.2
West South Central			
Arkansas	22.7	18.7	−17.6
Louisiana	27.7	22.5	−18.8
Oklahoma	21.9	17.3	−21.0
Texas	26.0	20.4	−21.5
Mountain			
Montana	25.9	19.3	−25.5
Idaho	25.7	19.3	−24.9
Wyoming	25.8	19.3	−25.2
Colorado	24.5	18.7	−23.7
New Mexico	32.3	23.6	−26.9
Arizona	28.2	21.1	−25.2
Utah	29.5	22.5	−23.7
Nevada	25.5	21.5	−15.7
Pacific			
Washington	22.9	17.7	−22.7
Oregon	21.7	17.4	−19.8
California	23.7	19.1	−19.4
Alaska	33.4	27.9	−16.5
Hawaii	27.2	23.0	−15.4

SOURCE: U.S. National Center for Health Statistics, Publication No. 1,000, Series 21, No. 11, Public Health Service, 1967; and Bureau of the Census, *Statistical Abstract of the United States* 1970, table 5.

[1] By place of residence

[2] Figures for Massachusetts, 1964, exclude 1,800 live births.

RURAL-URBAN AND SIZE-OF-PLACE DIFFERENTIALS. One of the most widely recognized contrasts—especially in the United States—is that between high rural fertility and low urban fertility. This differential has been recorded in almost all the countries of Europe and North America, but its incidence has probably been most pronounced in the United

TABLE 8.9
U.S. Urban and Rural Child-Woman Ratio, 1800–1960

Children Under 5 Years per 1,000 Females 20–44			Rural to
Year	Total U.S.	Urban	Rural	Urban Ratio
1800	1,281	845	1,319	1.56
1810	1,290	900	1,329	1.48
1820	1,236	831	1,276	1.57
1830	1,134	708	1,189	1.68
1840	1,070	701	1,134	1.61
•	•	•	•	•
•	•	•	•	•
•	•	•	•	•
1910	609	469	782	1.67
1920	581	471	744	1.58
1930	485	388	658	1.70
1940	400	311	551	1.77
1950	551	479	673	1.41
1960	689	653	784	1.20

SOURCE: Grabill 1959, and U.S. Bureau of the Census, *Characteristics of the Population,* Vol. 1, 1960.

States and Canada. Table 8.9 shows the U.S. "child-woman" ratio by urban and rural residence for selected decades between 1800 and 1960.

With the United States and Canada there have been regional variations in the extent of urban-rural fertility differentials. Similarly, there are broad variations among the different countries of Europe (table 8.10).

TABLE 8.10
European Urban and Rural Child-Woman Ratios (children under five years of age per 1,000 women ages 15 to 49)

Country	Date	Total	Urban	Rural	Rural to Urban Ratio
Albania	1955	725	692	738	1.07
Bulgaria	1956	346	312	366	1.17
Czechoslovakia	1961	359	315	403	1.28
Denmark	1960	338	310	436	1.41
Finland	1960	382	348	435	1.25
France	1962	329	307	375	1.22
Greece	1961	362	287	442	1.54
Hungary	1960	332	263	382	1.45
Ireland	1961	503	474	535	1.13
Netherlands	1960	432	382	517	1.35
Norway	1960	378	327	438	1.34
Poland	1960	477	406	553	1.36
Portugal	1960	398	274	441	1.61
Romania	1956	392	303	437	1.44
Sweden	1960	286	279	310	1.11
Switzerland	1960	332	274	404	1.47
United Kingdom					
England and Wales	1961	336	329	361	1.10
Scotland	1961	385	380	398	1.05
Northern Ireland	1961	443	412	484	1.17
Yugoslavia	1961	415	323	456	1.41

SOURCE: Glass 1968, Appendix 3.

TABLE 8.11

Fertility by Size of Place, United States (1950) and West Germany (1958)

Size of Place (No. of Inhabitants)	Mean Number of Children Ever Born per Ever-Married Women Aged 45–49	
	United States, 1950	West Germany, 1958
Over 500,000	1.99	2.08
250,000–500,000	2.07	2.1
100,000–250,000	2.28	
25,000–100,000	2.36	2.4[a]
10,000–25,000	2.50	2.5[b]
5,000–10,000	2.64	
2,000–5,000	2.88[c]	2.6
Under 2,000	not available	2.7

SOURCE: U.N. Population Bulletin No. 7–1963 (1965).
[a]For places with 20,000–100,000 inhabitants
[b]For places with 5,000–20,000 inhabitants
[c]For places with 2,500–5,000 inhabitants

It is important to bear in mind that "urban" and "rural" are not the same things in all places and at all times. Places of very different size may be called "urban," just as very different places may be called "rural." Obviously, fertility must vary among different kinds of urban places and among different rural places as well. For urban populations, there is an inverse relationship between fertility and the size of the city. Thus, as table 8.11 demonstrates, the larger the city, the lower the fertility. Within rural populations, on the other hand, fertility is inversely related to geographic and socioeconomic proximity to urban areas. Thus, in the United States, rural fertility is higher outside standard metropolitan areas than within them; and a Canadian study has indicated that the greater the distance from the city, the higher the average number of children born per ever-married woman of completed fertility (Keyfitz 1952).

There is now considerable evidence that urban-rural fertility differentials exist in the high-fertility countries of Africa, Asia, and Latin America. However, the data are often poor. In order to avoid the bias introduced by using census results suffering from underenumeration of children under five, the U.N. Population Branch has computed child-woman ratios from numbers of children aged five to nine per 1,000 women aged 20–49 as reported in national censuses. Data for countries of Asia and Latin America are shown in table 8.12.

DISTORTIONS FROM MIGRATION. For all types of geographically based fertility differentials, it is important to bear in mind the distortions introduced by migration. Migration from rural to urban communities by childless couples and other persons without children (the unmarried, the

TABLE 8.12

Urban and Rural Child-Women Ratios for Selected Asian and Latin American Countries, 1946–1960 (number of children aged five to nine per 1,000 women aged 20–49)

Country	Date	Urban	Rural	Rural to Urban Ratio
Ceylon	1953	655	741	1.69
India	1951	600	629	1.05
Philippines	1957	809	943	1.16
Turkey	1950	504	695	1.37
Barbados	1946	384	403	1.05
Brazil	1950	486	1,038	2.12
Chile	1952	513	911	1.72
Costa Rica	1950	534	895	1.67
Cuba	1953	437	931	2.12
Dominican Republic	1950	491	919	1.89
Ecuador	1950	616	831	1.35
El Salvador	1950	531	805	1.52
Guatemala	1950	561	806	1.43
Jamaica	1960	547	873	1.59
Nicaragua	1950	580	890	1.54
Panama	1950	524	970	1.85
Paraguay	1950	751	917	1.22
Puerto Rico	1960	620	985	1.20
Trinidad and Tobago	1946	392	666	1.69

SOURCE: U.N., *Population Bulletin,* No. 7–1963 (1965).

aged, etc.) operates to introduce urban-rural differences into most measures of fertility, regardless of the similarity or dissimilarity of age-specific marital fertility rates in the respective communities. In particular, cities and urban communities in Africa, Asia, and Middle and South America tend to include large proportions of recent migrants, and the effect of compositional variations upon urban-rural fertility contrasts is elusive (cf. Beshers 1967, chaps. 2 and 4; Goldberg 1959, 1960; and especially Duncan 1965).

Fertility Differences among Primitive and Other Small-Scale Societies

Leaving the question of variations among national populations and turning now to local, regional, and other areally delineated societies, we are again confronted by the low quality, noncomparability, or sheer lack of data bearing upon fertility.

KRZYWICKI'S SURVEY OF PRIMITIVE "HUNTING" AND "SETTLED" SOCIETIES.   In his survey of population data for primitive societies, Krzywicki cites variations in numbers of children born to women both among the nomadic "hunting races" and among the cultivating "settled peoples," but does not indicate any systematic axis of differentiation (Krzywicki 1934: chaps. V and VI). That is, instead of concerning himself with the circumstances under which more or less children are born, he devotes far more interest to the question of the number of children surviving and reared. The number of children surviving indeed varies among different tribal societies, and Krzywicki finds that a systematic difference between the "hunting" societies and the "settled" societies is indicated. The former reduce their number of survivors by induced abortion and infanticide much more frequently and intensively than the latter. Among the "settled peoples," according to Krzywicki, induced abortion and infanticide are much more likely to be frowned upon and, in any event, are much less frequent and limited to relatively extreme exigencies. Indeed, such societies tend to develop positive fertility values, the view being that childlessness is a misfortune, and they tend to have behavioral norms conducive to higher fertility (*ibid.,* p. 197). The greater dependability of sustenance in such societies diminishes the tension between fertility and survival of adult members of the society and hence mitigates the use of drastic customs effecting control of numbers of survivors among births.

LORIMER'S ANALYSIS OF PREINDUSTRIAL SOCIETIES. One of the most ambitious surveys and analyses of data and accounts bearing upon the fertility of preindustrial societies is that carried out by F. Lorimer under the auspices of UNESCO, the United Nations Economic, Scientific, and Cultural Organization (Lorimer 1954). In this study, the author reviews evidence bearing upon the capacity for procreation or fecundity and analyzes the relationship between kinship systems and fertility, the factors associated with control and noncontrol of fertility in primitive societies, and the relationships between cultural conditions and fertility in stable agrarian civilizations. Lorimer comes to the following conclusions:

1. In highly organized societies, modes of behavior and values may tend either to sustain high fertility or to induce restriction of fertility. In disorganized societies, however, there may be little relationship between values and actual levels of fertility. Highly structured societies tend to enforce high fertility if: (a) there are sufficient resources to assure sustenance and (b) there is a supporting ideology—religious, cultural, political, or whatever—for high fertility. Otherwise, highly structured societies may tend to restrict fertility. Social disorganization may lead to sharp declines in fertility or to cultural and societal indifference to fertility— which can itself result in unrestricted fertility.
2. Primitive societies may have approved methods of restricting fertility when located in isolated or restricted areas, when forced by limited resources to move in small bands in constant search of sustenance, or when pushed by more powerful societies into un-

favorable locations. Even more commonly, such societies, lacking motives for high fertility, may be indifferent, ambivalent, or permissive with respect to restrictive or anti-natal practices.

3. Primitive societies with favorable situations for sustenance, with the strong social organization required to maintain such situations, and with unilineal descent and corporate kinship groups, tend to have strong cultural motives for high fertility.

4. Corporate kinship groupings, whether of matriarchal or patriarchal lineage, generate strong motivations for high fertility.

5. In agrarian societies, the "group-family" lends support for the universal and early marriage of its members and for their procreation. A group family is composed of kindred, closely associated, nuclear family units—units each composed of mother, father, and unmarried children—not necessarily characterized by membership in a common household or economy. Within societies characterized by relatively isolated nuclear family living, there are variations with respect to both age at marriage and numbers of children born per family (Lorimer 1954, pp. 198–203.)

Lorimer's conclusions recall our previous indication of the possibility of an inverse relationship between fertility and population density (p. 311). In addition, they also recall the idea (presented in section 1 of this chapter, and in chapter 2) that societal variations in fertility and fertility control may be responses to actual or potential pressures of population growth: stable and assured sustenance supports high fertility values and behavior, and unstable sustenance undermines them. However, the data on which Lorimer's conclusions are based are neither systematic nor particularly convincing. Finally, we shall recall and reconsider the relationship between "nuclear" or "group-family" societies and fertility in section 4 of this chapter.

NAG'S STUDY OF 61 PREINDUSTRIAL SOCIETIES. In a study of 61 preindustrial, mostly nonliterate, societies, M. Nag (1962) found that 35 could be characterized as having "high fertility," 16 as having "low fertility," and ten as having "very low fertility." [2] Nag studied the relationship between each level of fertility and a list of variables, the latter including factors related to frequency of coitus (e.g., various types of abstinence, age at marriage, and permanent or temporary termination of marriage); factors related to conception (e.g., diet, reproductive span, sterility, venereal disease, psychological considerations, and contraception); and factors related to fetal development and the survival of new-

---

2 The fertility characteristics summarized in the previously cited Cross-Cultural Summary material (Textor 1967) are taken from Nag's study.

born children. Nag was able to report some regional variations in fertility: low fertility in the Pacific societies and high fertility in societies of the Americas. However, he could report significant relationships between fertility and only three of the variables studied. All these relationships were *negative:* there was an inverse relationship between length of post-partum abstinence and degree of fertility (the shorter the sexual absti-nence after the birth of each child, the more children a woman was likely to have); (2) an inverse relationship between frequency of sterility and level of fertility (the lower the society's incidence of sterility, the higher its level of fertility); and (3) an inverse relationship between frequency of venereal disease and fertility (the lower the incidence of venereal disease, the higher the fertility). The latter two variables, steril-ity and venereal disease, are themselves strongly related. Nag found in his data no relationship between fertility and the extent of contraceptive practice or between fertility and abortion. Moreover, examining a num-ber of earlier findings and hypotheses regarding fertility levels of primi-tive or nonindustrial societies, Nag found no support for any but the postpartum-abstinence and venereal disease-sterility hypotheses.

The study of the fertility of primitive and other small-scale societies has been undertaken by only a few researchers, and most of the research questions in this area still await formulation. Hopefully, the future will bring many more comparative studies of actual fertility levels in these societies and of their practices of marriage and childbearing—or non-childbearing—for these promise to yield many insights into the relation-ships between fertility and societal strategies of survival and adaptation.

Fertility Differences Related to Socioeconomic, Religious, Racial, and Psychological Characteristics

We turn finally to a brief review of studies examining the relation-ships between fertility differentials and variations in the socioeconomic, religious and racial, and psychological characteristics of women or cou-ples. Such investigations probably had their beginning with the post-World War I publication of fertility and child mortality data obtained in the 1911 Census of England and Wales, and their number has been increasing steadily ever since. (Just as the 1911 British census returns suf-fered delayed publication, so the detailed data on the fertility of women collected in the 1910 U.S. Census of Population went untabulated and unpublished for three decades thereafter.) The main body of these studies has been concerned with the measurement and analysis of relationships between fertility and the components of socioeconomic status; however, a number of investigations have been concerned also with the influence on fertility of individual psychological traits and marital relationships, and there have been many studies of the influence of religion, race, and ethnicity.[3]

In this section we confine our review to summarizing of findings of such studies; but in section 4 of this chapter we shall see how some of these findings are incorporated into explanations and theories of individual fertility behavior and of the fertility institutions, practices, and patterns of societies.

A BRIEF REVIEW OF SOME FINDINGS ON FERTILITY AND SOCIOECONOMIC STATUS.   In the low-fertility countries of Europe, North America, and Oceania, there was for some time a marked inverse relationship between fertility and such components of socioeconomic status as income, education, occupational level, and upward social mobility. More recently, however, considerable evidence has pointed to a growing convergence of fertility rates, or at least to substantially diminishing differentials, among the different socioeconomic categories (especially when certain other characteristics, e.g., religion, rural-urban migration status, and background, have held constant); at the same time, in the upper socioeconomic-status arrays, there has been evidence of a *direct* relationship between fertility and income, educational level, occupational status, etc.

Trends in the fertility of marriage cohorts (women marrying for the first time in the same year or period) classified by husband's occupational category are portrayed in figure 8.6. Among the oldest group of women—those married in 1912 or earlier—fertility was highest for wives of small farmers and wives of farm workers: small farmers' wives had, on the average, more than six births per woman, and farm workers' wives had just under that number. The lowest fertility in that cohort was that of the wives of professional workers and executives—with about 3.5 births per woman on the average. For the cohorts married up to 1942—and reported in the 1960 census of Norway—fertility was lower for all categories of women. But the declines in fertility were steepest among those groups of women previously characterized by highest fertility: wives of farm workers, of small farmers, and factory workers. Thus there was a convergence in levels of fertility characterizing the different socio-occupational groupings, resulting especially from the steep declines of those with lowest socioeconomic status.

While the convergence of fertility patterns among socioeconomic groups is usually believed to take place as a result of the lower groups adopting the low fertility patterns characteristic of the middle or higher

3 Among the most important summaries of differential fertility findings are Ryder (1959); National Bureau of Economic Research (1960); U.N., "Recent Fertility Trends" (1958); U.N., Population Bulletin No. 7–1963 (1965); Goldberg (1965); Freedman (1962); and Goldscheider (1971). In addition, the summary in U.N., "Determinants and Consequences" (1953) remains a basic statement in this area.

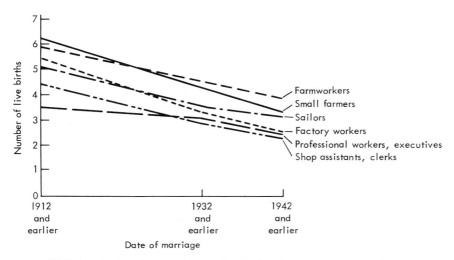

FIGURE 8.6. Fertility in Norway by husband's socio-occupational category, based on the population censuses of 1930, 1950, and 1960. Source: Pressat 1970, p. 71.

groups, the data in table 8.13 and figure 8.7 show that the opposite has been the case among fairly recent U.S. childbearing female cohorts. (The socioeconomic indicator in both the table and the figure is educational attainment: "cohort" refers to all women born in the same span of years.) The table shows that there was a decrease in fertility in the 1906–1910 cohort compared with the cohort born 1901–1905, but that from then on there were increases only. Among the least educated group, the decline continued through the 1911–1915 cohort, but among the next

TABLE 8.13

Estimated Number of Children Ever Born per 1,000 Women by end of Childbearing Period, for Ever-married White Women by Educational Attainment

Educational Attainment	Cohort Group							
	1901- 1905	1906- 1910	1911- 1915	1916- 1920	1921-1925 Low	High	1926-1930 Low	High
Total	2,456	2,329	2,354	2,515	2,706	2,786	2,867	3,170
Less than 8th grade	3,422	3,265	3,205	3,328	3,473	3,532	3,580	3,907
8th grade	2,643	2,589	2,601	2,769	2,957	3,022	3,118	3,407
High school 1-3	2,290	2,274	2,332	2,539	2,776	2,867	2,950	3,221
High school 4	1,818	1,829	2,013	2,275	2,557	2,664	2,758	3,081
College 1-3	1,698	1,813	1,970	2,279	2,550	2,649	2,802	3,200
College 4+	1,437	1,595	1,828	2,195	2,447	2,541	2,546	2,945

SOURCE: Campbell 1965, p. 202.

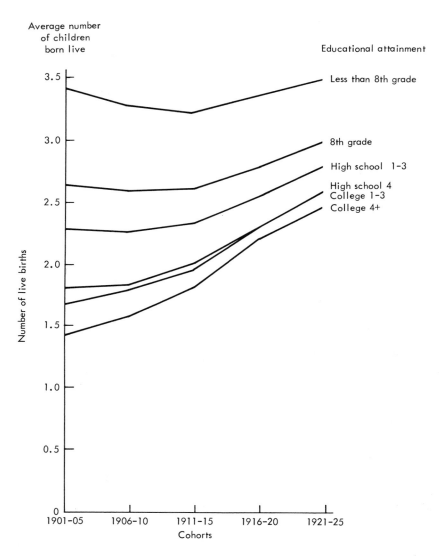

FIGURE 8.7.   United States: estimated number of live children ever born, per 1,000 women by end of childbearing period, for ever-married white women by educational attainment. Source: Pressat 1970, p. 74.

two groups it occurred only in the cohort of 1906–1910. Among the three better-educated groups, the increase in fertility started at the very beginning, among the cohorts born in 1906–1910, and is much more marked throughout than the increase among the less educated women. The increases are especially sharp among the college-educated groups. Thus, the convergence of fertility levels has come about because of a sharp rise in fertility among the higher socioeconomic groups rather than because of a decrease among the lower groups (Campbell 1965).

These trends notwithstanding, there remain substantial differences in fertility among white American women classified by socioeconomic status, and even sharper socioeconomic differences among Negro women. In the 1965 National Fertility Study (Ryder and Westoff 1971), it was found that the mean current parity (number of live-born children, up to the date of the investigation) of white American college-graduate women was 2.1, compared to 2.9 births to white women with 1–3 years of high school, and compared to 3.5 births to white women who went no further than grade school (table 8.14). Mean current parity for Negro college graduate women was only 1.4, compared to 3.5 births to Negro women with 1–3 years of high school and 4.8 births to Negro women who did not study beyond grade school. We shall have occasion to cite other findings of this study in the present chapter.

RELIGIOUS AND RACIAL DIFFERENTIALS. In the United States, Canada, Ireland, and the Netherlands, the fertility of Catholics has long been, and remains, higher than that of non-Catholics, while the fertility of Jews has generally been lower than that of Christians. In India, the Parsees have been characterized by much lower fertility than other religious groups, but the differences between those other groups are small. In Israel, the fertility of Christian Arabs is higher than that of Jews, and the fertility of Druze and Moslem Arabs is higher still.

A question frequently posed about religious differentials in fertility is: to what extent do such differences simply reflect the different socioeconomic status characteristic of the different religious groupings? Do Catholics have high fertility simply because their average educational attainment or occupational status is lower than that of Protestants? Do

TABLE 8.14

1965 National Fertility Study: Mean Current Parity Reported by U.S. White and Negro Women, by Education

Education	White Women		Negro Women	
	Number Reporting	*Mean Current Parity*	*Number Reporting*	*Mean Current Parity*
Total — All women	3,770	2.6	968	3.3
College 4+	277	2.1	38	1.4
College 1–3	457	2.2	74	2.3
High School 4	1,790	2.4	301	2.6
High School 1–3	850	2.9	343	3.5
Grade School	396	3.5	212	4.8

SOURCE: Ryder and Westoff 1971, table IV–1, p. 54.

Jews have lower fertility simply because of higher average educational attainment or occupational status?

Since there is no question on religion in United States censuses, it has not been possible to draw upon census fertility tabulations in studying religious differences. However, the findings of a sequence of nationwide fertility studies in the United States [4] indicate that these differences in fertility remain even when socioeconomic status is taken into account (and "controlled" or "held constant" in the analysis), i.e., that fertility of Catholic women is higher, and fertility of Jewish women lower, than would be "expected" simply on the basis of their respective compositions by education, by income, by place of residence, by husbands' occupation, or by other indicators of socioeconomic status. Indeed for Catholics, there is some evidence of a direct relationship between socioeconomic status and fertility. The relationship between social class and fertility appears to be U-shaped among Catholics: higher and lower socioeconomic categories both have and expect higher fertility than the middle categories.

The national surveys of fertility have included Jews as well as Protestants and Catholics, but the numbers of Jews in such sample surveys have typically been too small to allow analysis of socioeconomic differences within this religious population category. However, more specialized studies (Goldscheider 1965; Goldscheider 1967; Goldstein 1969; and Goldstein and Goldscheider 1968) indicate that Jewish couples of high socioeconomic status have somewhat higher fertility and larger families than those with lower status, though the trend over time is toward a leveling of these differences (Whelpton, Campbell, and Patterson 1966; tables 51–5–3).

Goldscheider (1971, pp. 280–81) views the relationship between socioeconomic status and fertility among Catholics, and the direct relationship between socioeconomic status and fertility among Jews, as examples of the direct relationship between fertility and income, occupation, education, etc., appearing in the upper parts of socioeconomic status arrays— presumably largely those couples with knowledge and motivation to plan their families rationally.

The differences in fertility between white and Negro women in the United States have been the subject of considerably diverse opinions. Current Negro fertility rates have clearly been much higher than white ones (see figure 8.8), but measures by cohort indicate that for some cohorts this relationship does not obtain. In particular, there has been some controversy concerning historical trends in Negro fertility in the United States (c.f. Grabill 1959; Farley 1965; Zelnik 1966; Lunde 1965).

4 For a careful review, critical discussion, and extensive bibliography see C. Goldscheider (1971), chap. 10, on "Religion, Minority Group Status, and Fertility." See also Ryder and Westoff (1971), pp. 66–86.

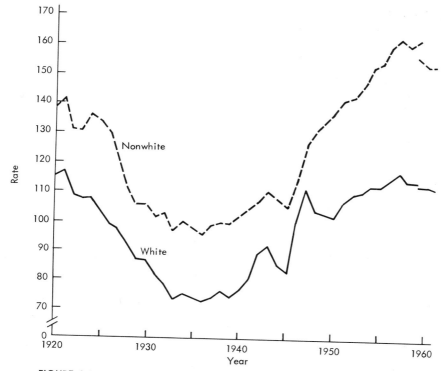

FIGURE 8.8. Births per 1,000 women 15–44 years of age, for whites and nonwhites, U.S., 1920–1961. Source: Whelpton, Campbell, and Patterson 1966, Figure 37.

Data comparing Negro and white fertility from the 1965 National Fertility Survey (Ryder and Westoff 1971) are shown in table 8.15. Negro women had an average of 3.3 births, compared to 2.6 births for white women in the same marital status and age group (married, living with husbands, and under 45 years old). The data show that the lower the educational achievement level the greater the difference between Negro and white fertility: among those with only grade school education, Negro women reported an average of 4.8 births compared to 3.5 births for white women. Fertility differences between Negro and white women who completed high school or attended college are very small, though Negro fertility remains measurably higher. But among those who graduated from college, the fertility of white women is substantially higher than that of Negro women! This finding reproduces findings of the earlier, 1960, national survey, the Growth of American Families (GAF) study (Whelpton, Campbell, and Patterson 1966) and also returns of the 1960 U.S. Census.

TABLE 8.15
*1965 National Fertility Survey: Negro
and White Women Under 45 Years Old,
Currently Married, and Living with
Husbands, by Education of Wives —
Mean Number of Children Born to 1965*

Wife's Education	Negro	White
Total	3.3	2.6
College 4+	1.4	2.1
College 1–3	2.3	2.2
High School 4	2.6	2.4
High School 1–3	3.5	2.9
Grade School	4.8	3.5

SOURCE: Ryder and Westoff 1971, table
IV–4.

In the 1960 data, the fertility of nonwhite women (primarily Negro, but including small proportions of other nonwhites which varied by region and types of communities) exceeded that of white women by 26 percent in the U.S. as a whole. However, this excess was very highly concentrated in the South, where nonwhite fertility exceeded white fertility by 42 percent (by 64 percent for the rural farm population, by 53 percent for the rural nonfarm category, and by 34 percent for the urban populations). Outside the South, nonwhite fertility was only moderately higher than white fertility: by 7 percent in the Northeast, by 12 percent in the North Central, and by 10 percent in the West (Whelpton, Campbell, and Patterson 1966; table 184).

Reporting the findings of the 1960 GAF study, Whelpton, Campbell, and Patterson explored data from that study, from the 1960 census, and from previous studies bearing upon white-nonwhite fertility differentials in the United States. Their analysis of color differences in actual fertility in 1960 and in expected future fertility reported by white and nonwhite respondents is more elaborate than any previously possible.

Examining these socioeconomic and regional variations in nonwhite-white fertility differentials, Whelpton, Campbell, and Patterson observed:

> When we come to nonwhite couples without any previous Southern farm residence, we find average past and expected numbers of births that do not differ significantly from those of . . . the white sample. In other words, by the time nonwhite couples are one generation or more removed from the rural South, their fertility is very much like that of the white population.

and they continue and conclude the analysis:

When we consider the white-nonwhite fertility differentials, we find that the largest differentials exist among couples who have relatively low educational attainment (grade-school or incomplete high school) and who have lived or are living on Southern farms. Among couples with no Southern farm background and among well-educated couples, white and nonwhite do not differ greatly in their fertility.

We can present these facts more clearly by dividing the nonwhite and white samples into three main groups:

I. Those who have completed high school or have had some college education and those with less education who have never lived on a Southern farm.

II. Those who have a grade school or incomplete high school education and who have previously lived on a Southern farm.

III. Those who have a grade school or incomplete high school education and who were living on a Southern farm when interviewed.

Within Group I, nonwhites have very nearly the same past and expected fertility as whites . . . inasmuch as this group contains 63 percent of the nonwhite sample, we can say that a majority of nonwhite couples have and expect about the same number of children as white couples in similarly defined socioeconomic groups. . . .

Within Group II, nonwhites have moderately higher past and expected fertility than whites. . . . This group contains 26 percent of the nonwhite sample.

Finally, within Group III, nonwhites have much higher fertility than whites. This group contains 11 percent of the nonwhite sample.

The most important facts brought out here are (a) that the fertility of a majority of nonwhites does not differ widely from that of whites in similar socioeconomic groups, and (b) that the differences that exist for the remainder of nonwhites are closely associated with characteristics that will have less influence in the future than they do now—previous and current Southern farm residence and low educational achievement. These findings give us reason to believe that fertility differences between whites and nonwhites will become narrower. [Whelpton, Campbell, and Patterson 1966; p. 342 and pp. 347–8]

These findings and conclusions are essentially supported and sustained in the 1965 sequel, the National Fertility Study. Indeed Ryder and Westoff, in reporting findings of this study, are able to assert that "with the ever-diminishing importance of rural life in this country, the rapid disappearance of racial differences in fertility seems imminent" (Ryder and Westoff 1971; p. 91).

This idea suggests that, as development, urbanization, and—especially—education of women proceed in less developed high fertility countries, changing patterns of marriage and adoption of family limitation practices among the higher social classes, modern sectors of the population, educated groups of women, or in the most developed geographic areas will result in distinct—lower—patterns of fertility. Insofar as such differentials are actually found, special importance is attached to them: for they are commonly viewed by demographers and other population-watchers as indicators of the beginnings of fertility control and heralding a downward inflection in the birth rate and in the rate of natural increase.

In an attempt to address the question of the influence of recent development and urbanization trends upon fertility in developing countries, M. B. Concepcion (1967) reviews a number of studies measuring and analyzing differential fertility.[5] She found pronounced educational differences, religious differences, and social class differences reported for a number of developing countries. Rural-urban fertility differences were also found, but are explained, in Concepcion's view, by the lower rates of marriage and lower infant mortality rates in the cities. (The connection between marriage and fertility is obvious; higher infant mortality may imply higher birth rates because mothers who lose their children in infancy are able to conceive again much more quickly than are those with surviving live babies—for the death of the infant implies termination of breast-feeding and high risk of a new conception.)

In the short run, modernization may cause "emerging differentials" in fertility by bringing about *increased* fertility in certain subgroups of the population. Finally, Concepcion's review suggests that improvements in education do not necessarily bring about reductions in fertility. Thus, despite the many examples of "emerging differentials" in fertility by socioeconomic status in the developing high fertility countries, it seems premature to interpret these in terms of fertility inflections or of a "demographic transition." Many of the "emerging differentials" are actually part of a *rise* in fertility in some areas—whether temporary or permanent is not always obvious, and others actually reverse the pattern of differentials familiar from European or North American fertility history—e.g., with urban exceeding rural fertility, or with wealthier or better educated groups having higher fertility than illiterates.

---

5 In his review of factors associated with fertility and fertility differentials, Clark cites and presents data in urban-rural, occupational, educational, and religious fertility differentials in developing countries as varied as Brazil, Guinea, India, Egypt, Cuba, Taiwan, Ceylon, Chile, and others. (Clark 1967, chap. VI.) However, he presents these comparative data by way of listing and examining factors which affect fertility and in search of clues and an explanation of the *reasons* for introduction and acceptance of family limitation. He attaches no special significance to differential fertility in developing countries and develops no model of a process of changing fertility patterns and their diffusion through a population. (But cf. Goldscheider 1971, chap. 6, for development of such a model.)

EMERGING DIFFERENTIALS IN THE HIGH FERTILITY COUNTRIES. In the high-fertility countries of Latin America, Asia, and Africa, an inverse relationship between components of socioeconomic status and fertility has been found, but it is much less consistent than in the low-fertility countries. A number of studies reveal only few signs of such fertility differentials, while others yield convincing evidence at least of differentials associated with the educational achievement of women and the occupational status of husbands (cf. summaries in Beshers 1967 and in U.N., P.B. No. 7–1963).

A recurrent notion in the literature on fertility in high–fertility underdeveloped nations is that of "emerging differentials" (see especially Abu-Lughod 1965 and Yaukey 1961).

PSYCHOLOGICALLY-BASED FERTILITY DIFFERENTIALS. The pioneer investigation of relationships between fertility and psychological variables was the famous Indianapolis study carried out in 1941 (Whelpton and Kiser 1946–58, Vols. I-V). This study was restricted to white Protestant couples judged "relatively fecund," i.e., with no biological fertility impairments, and in which both wife and husband had had at least eight years of school completed. The study was designed to (1) describe and measure the extent, nature, and effectiveness of practice of contraception; (2) measure, and investigate variations in, the size of "planned" families; and (3) "test," or at least investigate systematically, a set of 23 hypotheses concerning social and psychological factors affecting fertility. The hypotheses concerned the effects of (1) status and security, (2) community and family background, (3) interest in home and children, (4) personality characteristics, and (5) marital adjustment and husband-wife dominance upon family planning and fertility.

The "personality characteristics" measured and studied included:

1. feelings of personal adequacy
2. feeling that children interfere with personal freedom
3. ego-centered interest in children
4. fear of pregnancy
5. tendency to plan
6. interest in religion
7. adherence to tradition
8. conformity to group patterns

A total of 1,444 couples were interviewed, and it was found that good marital adjustment, interest in religion, adherence to traditions, and liking for children are positively associated with fertility, while feelings of personal inadequacy, ego-centered interest in children, fear of pregnancy, and tendency to plan are all negatively associated with fertility. Relationships between the other "personality characteristics" measured and fertility were not found to be "statistically significant" (i.e., with very low probability of occurring by chance—see the explanation of the concept of "statistical significance" in chapter 4, section 6). Moreover, even the associations found to be "significant" statistically were of a low order, so that students of demographic behavior have not been inclined to view these results as convincing evidence of these relationships.

An investigation widely considered to be a sequel to the Indianapolis study is the Family Growth in Metropolitan America Study, a longitudinal study of white couples in seven of the eight largest metropolitan areas of the United States and often denoted the "Princeton Study" (Westoff, et al., 1961). Interviews for this study were first carried out in 1957 among 1,165 such couples who had just had their second child; 905 of the same couples were re-interviewed three years later, in 1960; and 814 of the same couples were re-interviewed six to ten years later, upon reaching the close of their reproductive ages.

In this study—much more elaborate and more carefully designed than the Indianapolis study—an attempt was made to obtain further data on psychological factors of fertility as well as further data on socioeconomic factors. The main personality variables measured and investigated in the Princeton Study were:

1. generalized manifest anxiety
2. need for nurturance
3. compulsiveness
4. tolerance of ambiguity
5. cooperativeness
6. need for achievement

Although some low orders of relationships between these personality variables and the two aspects of fertility studied—number of children desired and fertility planning success—were found, the results were basically disappointing. The researchers ultimately concluded that—for all practical purposes—no significant relationships appeared in the analyses (Westoff, et al. 1963). Thus the search for psychological factors and bases of differential fertility in the large-scale fertility surveys has been disappointing and has fallen under some criticism (see, for example, Hauser and Duncan 1959b).

A somewhat more promising line of psychological—or, perhaps more correctly, of social psychological—inquiry is the study of the effect of variations in husband-wife relationships upon fertility (Hill, Stycos, and Back 1959; Rainwater 1960; Matras and Auerbach 1963; and Rainwater

1965). If couples are viewed as varying insofar as they have a more segregated or less segregated conjugal role-relationship (the degree to which their role activities and the values that go with them are handled separately by each spouse or jointly by the couple), then the central "finding" of these studies is that the less segregated the conjugal role-relationship, the lower the couple's fertility—or, at least, the more effective is family planning. *Use* of contraception among all couples, *effective use* among those using contraception, choice of *technically more effective* methods, and assumption by the wife—whose motivation to limit pregnancies is greater—of responsibility for contraception, are all associated with less segregated conjugal role-relationship—i.e., with *joint* handling of husband's and wife's role activities and values.

3. DIMENSIONS OF CHILDBEARING

Early discussion and speculation about the factors associated with variation and change in fertility levels bore little or no relationship to systematic factual knowledge of fertility trends or of differential fertility. Pre-Malthusian thought about population in general and fertility in particular was basically programmatic and oriented to promoting high fertility and population growth (Eversley 1959). But Malthus himself made extensive use of data assembled by contemporary scholars, and subsequent theorists and writers made progressively greater use of the increasing body of data available especially in northern and western Europe.

More recent writers on fertility have drawn upon empirically based studies of differential fertility and indeed have begun their inquiries with the results of such studies. Thus, theories of human reproduction have increasingly represented attempts to account for and explain documented trends in fertility and differential fertility.

FACTORS OF REPRODUCTION SUBJECT TO SOCIAL AND CULTURAL INFLUENCES: THE DAVIS-BLAKE MODEL. The steps in reproduction which are subject to the influence of social and cultural patterns have been listed by K. Davis and J. Blake (1956) as follows:

I. *Factors Affecting Exposure to Intercourse*
   A. Those governing the formation and dissolution of unions in the reproductive period.
      1. Age of entry into sexual unions
      2. Extent of permanent celibacy, proportion of women entering sexual unions
      3. Amount of reproductive period spent after or between unions

         a. when unions are broken by divorce, separation, or desertion
         b. when unions are broken by death of husband
     B. Those governing the exposure to intercourse within unions.
         4. Voluntary abstinence
         5. Involuntary abstinence (from impotence, illness, and unavoidable but temporary separations)
         6. Coital frequency (excluding periods of abstinence).
   II. *Factors Affecting Exposure to Conception*
         7. Fecundity or infecundity, as affected by involuntary causes
         8. Use or nonuse of contraception
           a. by mechanical and chemical means
           b. by other means
         9. Fecundity or infecundity, as affected by voluntary causes (sterilization, subincision, medical treatment, etc.)
 III. *Factors Affecting Gestation and Successful Parturition*
       10. Foetal mortality from involuntary causes
       11. Foetal mortality from voluntary causes (i.e., induced abortion)

The cross-cultural study by M. Nag (1962), cited earlier, draws heavily upon this framework and attempts to measure relationships between these factors and fertility. Aside from Nag's study, there has been little systematic research completed, and few theoretical statements formulated, on the patterns and correlates of variations in these factors of reproduction, except as regards age at marriage, extent of permanent celibacy, and the use or nonuse of contraception (and, to a certain extent, birth control by means of induced abortion). However, current research is dealing with most if not all of these factors, and theoretical developments on these fronts will probably be forthcoming in the near future (see Sheps and Ridley 1965).

We have already reviewed some of the findings in one of the two dimensions of existing research—marriage and nonmarriage—in our discussions of trends and variations in frequency of marriage and in age at marriage. For the other dimension—the deliberate intervention of couples to postpone or prevent births—we turn now to a brief review of findings concerning family limitation practices. Following this review, we shall examine a third dimension—values about family sizes—which, although not listed by Davis and Blake, has been credited with increasing importance by students of fertility.

Family Limitation Practices

The first question we must ask is: *to what extent* do couples intervene in the "natural" processes of reproduction in order to control the number or timing of births? While we may conceive theoretically of societies in which no intervention at all takes place, their actual existence is highly unlikely. Probably no society is completely free of practices inhibiting conception and birth. However, these practices may not be motivated by the desire to control the number and timing of births. On the contrary, intervention deliberately designed to limit and control fertility has been, and remains, exceptional among societies, and it is far from universal in those societies in which it is known and practiced.

Voluntary Birth Control in Various Countries: A Brief Review of Selected Studies

Unfortunately, it is not yet possible to present a cross-national table indicating the prevalence of voluntary birth control in different countries. The first studies bearing on the frequency of voluntary family limitation were undertaken in the United States in the 1930s, and these yielded data indicating that the explanation of fertility differentials—and probably of trends over time in fertility—lies in the *voluntary*, rather than biologically based, restraint of fertility (see the concise summary in Kiser 1967). Those studies were followed in the United States by the "Indianapolis Study," which began in 1938 (Whelpton and Kiser 1946–1958), and in England by a study sponsored by the United Kingdom Royal Commission on Population (Lewis-Fanning 1949), which was carried out in the early 1940s. However, although the Indianapolis Study showed widespread practice of family limitation, the samples on which it was based were such that no assessment could be made of the extent of family limitation in the population generally. In the Lewis-Fanning study in England, it was estimated that some type of contraception was practiced by about 66 percent of the women in England who had gotten married between 1935 and 1939, but by just 40 percent of those married in 1910–1919 and by only 15 percent of those married before 1910.

In the Growth of American Families (GAF) study, a 1955 investigation of family planning whose scope was comparable to that of a census, 2,700 white wives between 18 and 39 years of age were interviewed. Seventy percent reported having used some method of contraception specifically to avoid conception (these women were called "motive users") and an additional 11 percent reported "douching for cleanliness only." Eighty-one percent, then, were considered "action users" of contraception (Freedman, Whelpton, and Campbell 1959). Of the women aged 35–39 (those closest to "completed fertility" in this study), 65 percent were "motive users." They included 74 percent of all women residing in the suburbs of the largest cities, 69 percent of those residing in both small cities (2,500 to 50,000 inhabitants) and large cities (over 50,000 inhabitants), and 52 percent of the farm respondents.

In a sequel to this study (Whelpton, Campbell, and Patterson 1966),

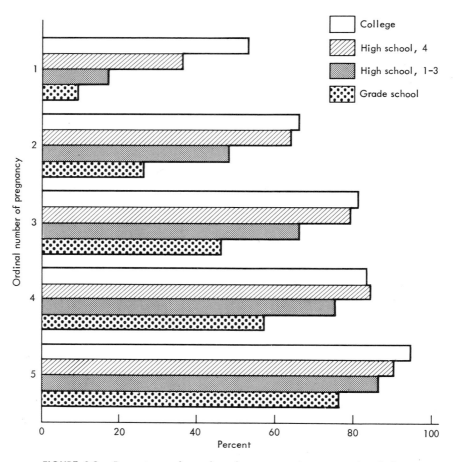

FIGURE 8.9. Percentage of couples who ever used contraception before specified pregnancy, for couples with four pregnancies, by wife's education. Source: Whelpton, Campbell, and Patterson 1966, Figure 27.

about eleven percent of the white couples were found to be sterile (mainly because of surgical sterilizations about half of which had been indicated by pathological disorders and half for contraceptive purposes). Some 81 percent reported having practiced contraception already, and another six percent reported plans to practice it in the future (these were primarily recently married couples wishing to have one or two children first). It was found that people of lower educational achievement—grade school only—were more likely to begin the practice of contraception only after several pregnancies and that Catholics were more likely than Protestants to delay the practice of contraception or never to use it. (Fig. 8.9.)

In a 1965 sequel, high proportions of married women again reported the use of contraception. However, a new and important finding was that a majority of those planning their families had failed either to achieve the number of births desired or to time the births according to plan. Among those who had intended to have no more children, only 26 percent were successful, the rest experiencing either "number failure" or "timing failure." Among those intending to have more children, the probability of a "timing failure" was estimated at 67 percent (Ryder and Westoff 1969). Reasons for these failures remain to be investigated.

Tables 8.16 and 8.17 show other results of the 1965 study. By 1965 some 90 percent of white couples reported either past, or expected future, use of contraception, up from the 87 percent in 1960 and 79 percent in 1955. In table 8.16 two kinds of convergences in extent of use of contraception are evident: between Catholics and Protestants, and between

TABLE 8.16

Percentage of White Couples Who Have Used or Expect to Use Contraception, By Wife's Education and Religion: 1955, 1960, and 1965

Education	Total[a]			Protestant			Catholic		
	1955	*1960*	*1965*	*1955*	*1960*	*1965*	*1955*	*1960*	*1965*
Percent Have Used									
Total	70	81	84	75	84	87	57	70	78
College	85	88	88	90	93	90	62	67	81
High school 4	74	83	86	80	86	88	61	73	82
High school 1-3	66	78	83	70	80	86	59	73	75
Grade school	49	66	65	53	73	72	41	54	55
Percent Have Used or Expect to Use									
Total	79	87	90	83	90	91	67	80	87
College	88	93	94	92	96	95	71	82	89
High school 4	83	90	92	88	92	92	71	83	90
High school 1-3	76	85	88	79	87	90	68	80	85
Grade school	59	72	75	63	77	79	49	64	72
Number of Couples									
Total	2713	2414	2912	1817	1596	1902	787	668	845
College	417	427	584	306	284	399	73	79	136
High school 4	1236	1153	1420	794	752	909	396	341	438
High school 1-3	681	579	641	457	392	434	208	168	177
Grade school	377	255	267	260	168	159	110	80	94

SOURCE: Westoff and Ryder 1969, table 12, p. 408.

[a]Includes women who are neither Catholic nor Protestant.

TABLE 8.17

Percentage of Nonwhite and White Couples Who Have Used or Expect to Use Contraception, By Region of Residence, Southern Farm Residence, Education of Wife, and Income of Husband, 1960 and 1965

| Characteristic | Percent Have Used | | | | Percent Have Used or Expect to Use | | | | Number of Non-whites | |
| | Nonwhite | | White | | Nonwhite | | White | | | |
	1960	1965	1960	1965	1960	1965	1960	1965	1960	1965
Total	59	77	81	84	76	86	87	90	270	837
Region										
Northeast	76	84	77	84	95	91	85	89	41	158
North Central	59	74	82	84	76	79	88	91	74	131
West	*	83	80	83	*	93	89	92	19	46
South	51	75	83	87	68	85	88	88	136	502
Southern Farm Residence										
On farm now	36	63	86	76	52	80	87	82	33	67
All other	62	78	81	84	79	86	87	90	237	770
Wife's Education										
College	86	85	88	88	95	88	93	94	37	106
High school 4	67	83	83	86	81	91	90	92	73	285
High school 1-3	56	79	78	83	79	87	85	88	86	290
Grade school	42	58	66	65	57	71	72	75	74	156
Husband's Income										
$6,000 or more	76	82	86	88	88	90	89	90	25	183
5,000–5,999	63	81	80	82	81	89	88	88	32	162
4,000–4,999	59	79	81	78	73	85	88	87	51	172
3,000–3,999	56	75	77	81	80	82	85	86	45	156
Under $3,000	56	68	70	70	71	81	82	80	117	155

SOURCE: Westoff and Ryder 1969, table 15, p. 411.
*Too few cases.

the education-category groups. In the 1955 survey 83 percent of Protestant couples, but only 67 percent of Catholic couples reported past or expected future use of contraceptives. But by 1965, these percentages were markedly closer: 91 percent of Protestant, and 87 percent of Catholic couples.

The 12-percentage point spread between the "college" and "high school 1–3" groups in 1955 (88 percent of the former and 75 percent of the latter reporting past or expected used of contraception in 1955) was reduced to a 6-percentage point difference, with increases for both categories, but a much steeper increase for the "high school 1–3" group. Similarly, the "grade school" group increased its percentage of expecting to practice contraception faster than any other category, similarly reducing the differences between the education category groups over the time period studied.

In table 8.17, a general convergence between 1960 and 1965 of percentages using or expecting to use contraception is evident for all categories of white couples for which husband's income is under $3000. For nonwhite couples a steep increase in the overall extent of use of contraception, convergence and diminishing of residence and socioeconomic differences within the nonwhite population, and a contraction of the differences between white and nonwhite practice of contraception are indicated for the 1960 to 1965 period. Thus the data from the sequence of national fertility surveys portrays a movement—on all color, religious, and social fronts—in the direction of near-universal practice of contraception among American couples.

A study of family limitation in Great Britain was carried out in 1959 and 1960 under the auspices of the Population Investigation Committee (Rowntree and Pierce 1961). In this study, about 73 percent of those marrying between 1940 and 1947, but only 54 percent of those marrying in 1929 or earlier, reported having practiced contraception. Of those marrying before 1920, some 64 percent in the non-manual labor group and only 40 percent in the unskilled manual labor group had practiced contraception, but of those married between 1940 and 1949, 74 percent in the non-manual labor group and 71 percent in the unskilled manual labor group had done so.

Among countries in which estimates of contraceptive use have been attempted, the percentages reporting family limitation practices are generally smaller than in the United States or in the United Kingdom. However, a pattern of association with socioeconomic status occurs in virtually every instance in which socioeconomic indicators are measured,[6] and in the United States and Canada—but not in the United Kingdom—there are clear urban-rural and size-of-city differentials. Nevertheless, these and the socioeconomic-status differential have been diminishing over time (see Matras 1965). A selection of findings on the extent of contraceptive practice around the world (table 8.18) shows variations ranging from six percent in rural Turkey to 96 percent within the top social group in Sweden. However, it is important to bear in mind that these estimates are of varying quality and reliability.

For the most part, studies of the extent of contraceptive practice have dealt separately, if at all, with induced abortion. However, it is necessary to recognize that in many societies induced abortion has been, and remains, the primary method used to limit fertility and control population growth. In Japan, Eastern Europe, and to a certain extent Scandinavia, abortion has been a major means of birth control (Tietze 1965).[7]

---

6 See, however, the analysis of Westoff, Potter, and Sagi (1964) emphasizing that rural-urban background and religious differences may account for the inverse socioeconomic differential.

7 For example, rates of abortion per 1,000 women in 1963 were 1,571 in Hungary, 570 in Japan, 423 in Czechoslovakia, 48 in Denmark, and 31 in Sweden.

TABLE 8.18

Percentage Practicing Contraception: Selected Countries and Areas circa 1965

Country and Area	Percentage Reporting Practice of Contraception
Turkey	
Rural Areas	6
Towns	18
Cities	21
Metropolitan areas	29
Dacca, Pakistan (Educated and Urban Group)	
Wives' reports	21
Husbands' reports	36
Lahore, Pakistan	
Wives' reports	8
Husbands' reports	18
Beirut, Lebanon: Women married 10+ years	
Uneducated	60
Educated	83
Bogota, Columbia	39.5
Buenos Aires, Argentina	77.6
Caracas, Venezuela	59.4
Mexico City, Mexico	37.5
Panama	59.7
Rio de Janeiro, Brazil	58.1
San Jose, Puerto Rico	65.0
Japan	51.9
South Korea	22.6
Urban	30.2
Rural	19.2
Genoble, France — Total	69
Women, 33–37	87
Sweden — Total	91.6
Top social group	96.3
Farmers	87.5
Netherlands	
Members of Netherlands Society for	
Sexual Reform	93
Nonmembers — Total	47
No religious affiliation	61
Upper social stratum	60
Hungary	20–30

SOURCE: Berelson et al. 1966.

However, in other countries, too, the number and proportion of women preventing births by means of induced abortion are probably fairly large.

IMPACT AND METHODS OF VOLUNTARY BIRTH CONTROL. In all cases, family limitation has been shown to have a substantial impact upon fertility. Although there are variations, of course, in the extent to which individuals are successful in their contraceptive efforts, individual women or couples practicing family limitation generally have fewer children than those not doing so, and population groups with large proportions practicing family limitation have lower levels of fertility than those with small proportions doing so.

Contraception may be practiced by any one or a combination of methods. One conventional distinction is that made between "natural" and "artificial" (mechanical or chemical) methods. One of the two primary methods in the first category is *coitus interruptus* (male withdrawal just before ejaculation). This is the method mentioned in the Old Testament. Apparently widely known and used throughout the Western world, it is probably largely responsible for the modern decline in European fertility. The second primary method in the "natural" category is the "safe period," or "rhythm" technique currently sanctioned by the Catholic Church, which prohibits the use of other methods. Artificial methods include the condom, diaphragm, and intra-uterine devices; spermicidal creams, jellies, douches, etc.; and oral contraceptive pills (for a concise summary, see Woutham 1966). The relative frequency of use of each of the respective methods varies over populations and over population subgroups. Similarly, the effectiveness with which any of the respective methods is used varies over different population groupings.

Finally, individuals and groups practicing family limitation vary in their pattern and timing of its use. Generally, we may distinguish initial undertakings of family limitation according to whether they occur before the first birth, or after the first birth but before completion of the family, or after completion of the desired family size.

Values of Family Size

With evidence that fertility in certain populations has been increasingly subject to the direct control and wishes of parents, demographers have become progressively more interested in values about family size, in variations among these values, and in the relationship of expressed ideals of family size to expected and actual fertility. Indeed, one argument holds that the key to the reduction of fertility in high-fertility countries lies not only in family planning programs and economic development but in the generation of a small-family ideal (Blake 1965).

This dimension of childbearing differs in an important way from the "marriage" and "intervention" dimensions and other factors listed by Davis and Blake (1956). The Davis and Blake factors all represent behavioral characteristics which can be observed and measured for individuals, groups, or social collectivities, whereas the dimension of preferred family size must be inferred indirectly. Nonetheless, it is of great impor-

TABLE 8.19
*Ideal Number of Children Reported in Selected Countries
of Europe and European Settlement*

Country	Date	Average Ideal Number Children	Percent Saying Four Children or More
Austria	1960	2.0	4.0
Belgium	1952	2.64	25.0
Finland	1953	2.84	22.0
France	1944	3.17	34.0
	1945	2.92	24.0
	1946	2.70	20.0
	1947	2.77	23.0
	1948	2.88	23.0
	1959–1960	2.77	16.9
Italy	1951	2.80	19.0
Netherlands	1947	3.66	46.0
	1960	3.3	38.7
Norway	1960	3.1	25.0
Switzerland	1960	2.9	22.4
Great Britain	1938	2.94	25.0
	1939	2.96	29.0
	1944	3.00	33.0
	1947	2.84	25.0
	1952	2.84	26.0
	1960	2.8	23.2
Sweden	1947	2.79	22.0
West Germany	1950	2.21	11.0
	1953	2.28	11.0
	1958	2.6	12.0
Australia	1947	3.79	64.0
Canada	1945	4.06	60.0
	1947	3.91	55.0
	1960	4.2	70.1
United States	1936	3.17	34.0
	1941	3.42	41.0
	1945	3.61	49.0
	1947	3.37	43.0
	1949	3.91	63.0
	1953	3.33	41.0
	1960	3.6	50.6

SOURCE: Blake 1965.

tance to consider values of family size and to review, however briefly, some of the research results in this area.

VALUES OF IDEAL FAMILY SIZE. Our information on family-size values comes almost exclusively from opinion and attitude surveys, some of whose data are summarized in table 8.19. The average ideal number of children varies from two children in Austria in 1960 to 4.2 children in Canada in the same year; for most countries the average lies between about 2.5 and 3.5. Thus, countries of Europe and European settlement are fairly homogeneous with respect to average ideal family size. An unexpected finding is that ideal family sizes reported in countries outside Europe *also* center in the range of two to four children.

Reports such as these and data on actual fertility performances in different population groupings represent the only obvious clues we have to institutionalized values and patterns of family size in different communities, collectivities, and socioeconomic categories. The data at hand, however, suggest but little differentiation—less than is the case for fertility itself—among socioeconomic categories or ascriptive groups.

SOME PRESSING QUESTIONS REGARDING VALUES OF FAMILY SIZE. An important kind of discrepancy has been recorded in some studies of family-size preferences between fertility ideals and expectations of own behavior. Examining such discrepancies, J. Blake (1965) finds that outside the higher social and economic classes, many people in Europe expect to have, and actually do have, considerably fewer children than they consider "ideal." Accordingly, she reasons, the fact that actual fertility is lower in the countries of Europe than in the "frontier" countries of European settlement represents a coming to terms, in the case of Europe, with harsh economic realities, for the family-size preferences in both cases are very similar—averaging at around three children. Further, given this similarity of family-size preference in the face of disparate economic conditions, Blake concludes that there is no a priori reason to expect "modernization" and "economic development" by themselves to generate small-family values. Only direct policies affecting family structure and fertility behavior are likely, in Blake's opinion, to influence family-size values and, ultimately, actual fertility.

There is some question about whether, in fact, the attitudes expressed in surveys actually reflect societal norms and values concerning fertility or family size, and we do not know what mechanism transmits and diffuses such societal norms. Clearly, if such opinions really do reflect societal values and norms, an explanation of the discrepancy between ideal, expected, and actual fertility is surely required and it is fitting to ask if the economic explanation proposed is the correct one.

The number of children reported as "ideal" or "preferred" is very closely related to the number of children actually already borne, except that women or couples with no children, or with one child, are very likely to indicate a desire for additional children (Bachi and Matras 1964). We know also that the "ideal" family size reported typically increases with increasing age—as do the numbers of children borne—and that over a large range of populations the "preferences" are very highly concentrated at around two to four children, regardless of the patterns of cumulative total fertility characterizing the population in question. This striking similarity of results may be a consequence of studying cross-sections of women or couples with all or almost all reporting exactly the number of children born as the "ideal" or "preferred" number. Thus, the exact meaning of the results of opinion surveys concerning preferred family size must be considered carefully, and alternative and additional representations of family-size values and ideals must be sought.

These considerations suggest that the concept of the "planned family," with both number of children and timing of their birth planned, and the idea of the newly-married couple sharing an image of the family-to-be may be artifacts of the researchers' vocabularies and descriptive realities. In the first large-scale American investigation of family planning, the Indianapolis study, couples were classified according to whether (1) both the number and timing of their children's births were achieved according to previous plan ("Number and Spacing Planned"), (2) the couple had achieved the desired number of children ("Number Planned"), or (3) the couple had had more births than they had wanted ("Excess Fertility"). Obviously the "Number and Spacing Planned" group represented the most effective fertility. This idea of the "planned family" was picked up and somewhat sloganized by the groups advocating and promoting birth control and "planned parenthood" in the United States and elsewhere; and it was also picked up as a standard of reference in subsequent demographic research and discussion. And it became reasonable to seek to explain the variations in actual fertility *within* the "Number and Spacing Planned"-type categories in terms of ideals, values, and desires.

It seems quite clear that there are societies and sub-cultural groups within societies in which the very concepts of "number of children *desired*" or "*ideal* number of children" are unknown (Bachi and Matras 1964). But even for those cultural settings in which the concept *is* meaningful a model more realistic than that of the couple's fixed image of its desired family would be one in which the *image* of the desired family *may change* in time and over the couple's marital life cycle.

A Word on the Relationship Between Marriage, Intervention, and Values of Family Size

The most important thing to say about these three dimensions of childbearing—marriage, intervention, and values of family size—is that they are very closely interwoven. The precise ways in which they are related, however, have not yet been established empirically. As we have already seen, it was Malthus who first raised the possibility of controlling population growth by postponing marriage,[8] and Hajnal has hypothe-

---

[8] That postponement of marriage does indeed have this result has been clearly shown by Leasure (1963).

sized that it was precisely the widespread desire to keep families small and assure their support which was responsible in large measure for the unique "European pattern" of delayed marriage and high proportions remaining single. Finally at least *two* of the three dimensions of child-bearing, patterns of marriage and patterns of intervention to limit family size within marriage, have been widely shown to vary directly and jointly with levels of fertility (see Matras 1965); the contraction over time of differentials in marriage and family limitation patterns corresponds to the contraction of fertility differentials among the various countries of Europe and among different subgroups in European national populations.

However, the exact role of family size values in the interaction between marriage, intervention, and fertility is yet to be assessed. Similarly, the effect on fertility of different patterns of family formation have yet to be studied. Finally, and perhaps most important, we must study and describe in detail the manner in which societal strategies of survival and adaptation, and of population growth or nongrowth, are translated and reflected in marriage and family formation.

4. MICROANALYTIC AND MACROANALYTIC THEORIES OF FERTILITY AND POPULATION GROWTH

A major issue in fertility research, as in other areas of social inquiry, turns upon the relative promise and importance of microanalytic versus macroanalytic levels of investigation and explanation. These have been contrasted by N. B. Ryder as follows:

> The macroanalytic level of inquiry consists of propositions or state-ments of relationships among the properties of the population as a unit of reference. The microanalytic level of inquiry consists of prop-ositions or statements of relationships among the properties of the individual as the unit of reference. *In general, it is invalid either to transform a proposition about populations into a proposition about individuals or to transform a proposition about individuals into a proposition about populations.* [Ryder 1959; my italics]

To render the issue more concrete, we may reconsider briefly the historical trends in fertility outlined in section 2 of this chapter (as rep-resented, for instance, in tables 8.1, 8.3, and 8.4, in the estimates of beginning dates of fertility decline, and in the data for Japan in the discussion of "low fertility" countries). The general form of these trends is that shown in the figure 8.10—initially high rates (A), a point or pe-riod of downward inflection (B), a period of declining fertility (C), a point or period ending the decline (D), and a leveling off of fertility at lower rates (E). The reader may recall mention of variations in initial levels (A) of fertility, in the time and circumstances under which the

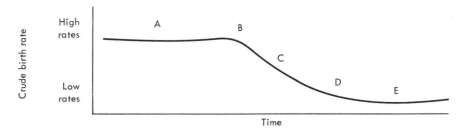

FIGURE 8.10.   General form of the historical trend in fertility.

downward inflection (B) occurs, and so on. Both microanalytic and macroanalytic theories of population growth bear upon the understanding of such variations.

The subject matter of a microanalytic theory of population growth consists of: (1) individual survival or life span, variations in individual survival or life span, and the causes and correlates of both; and (2) the fertility of individuals or couples, variations in number and spacing of births, and causes and correlates of such variations. In particular, such a theory must consider individual characteristics, decisions, or behavior at various stages of the life cycle in order to plot their relationships to survival, on the one hand, and fertility, on the other.

The subject matter of a macroanalytic theory of population growth consists of: (1) societal patterns of fertility and mortality; and (2) the structural and institutional features of societies bearing upon survival, mortality, and fertility. In particular, such a theory seeks to account for historical and cross-sectional *societal* variations in growth patterns in terms of structural attributes of entire societies or collectivities. We can review here only very briefly a few important examples of microanalytic and macroanalytic explanations of fertility and of attempts to reconcile them.

Microanalytic Theories: Three Examples

We shall present three examples of microanalytic theories of fertility. The first seeks to connect individual fertility decisions and behavior to declining mortality; the second seeks to connect them to the preservation or enhancement of social status; and the third to "utility-cost" considerations in the economic sense.

THE "DECLINING MORTALITY" THEORY. The "declining mortality" explanation of fertility holds that declining mortality—

1. implies a need for fewer children to be born to assure a desired family size, or to assure that a given number of children survive to look after the elderly parents, or to assure that a given number of children survive to "continue the family line," and

2. imposes objective hardship upon families having to support and educate ever-larger numbers of surviving offspring. Therefore, those people who

   a. are alert enough or educated enough to recognize the implications of declining mortality, and who

   b. have access to knowledge, means, and social support for controlling fertility,

—will in fact control their fertility.

Probably the most systematic formulation and exploration of this theory so far is contained in a series of papers by D. M. Heer, D. O. Smith, and D. A. May (Heer 1966; Heer and Smith 1967; May and Heer 1968; and Heer and Smith 1969). Suppose, say Heer and his colleagues, that couples want to be quite certain that one male child will survive to the couple's old age. As table 8.20 indicates, a computer simulation technique establishes the following relationships:

A. Conditions of rather high mortality (summarized by an expectation of life at birth of, say, no more than 20 years) require a very large number of births and very high age-specific birth rates (summarized by a gross reproduction rate of 5.2). Childbearing must continue throughout the reproductive age span, and the average age at motherhood is quite high, 28.7 years. Even so, under conditions of such high mortality a substantial fraction of the women (nearly 39 percent) never bear the number of sons needed to assure that at least one will survive to his parents' old

TABLE 8.20

Results of Computer Simulation: Fertility of Parents Assumed to Bear Children Until They Can be 95 Percent Certain That At Least One Son Will Survive to Father's 65th Birthday, by Life Expectancy

$e_{(0)}$ (Life expectancy, both sexes)	Percentage of Wives Who Never Bear Needed No. of Sons	GRR (gross reproduction rate)	NRR (net reproduction rate)	Average Age at Motherhood	Intrinsic Rate of Natural Increase
20.0	38.9	5.20	1.62	28.7	.017
30.0	9.1	4.11	1.99	27.3	.026
42.5	2.5	3.04	2.02	25.2	.028
55.0	0.9	2.21	1.79	23.8	.026
70.2	0.0	1.73	1.66	21.8	.023
73.0	0.0	0.97	0.95	20.4	-.003

SOURCE: Adapted from May and Heer 1968, table 1.

age. However, the rate of natural increase in such a population over a long period of time (the "intrinsic rate" of natural increase) is fairly high, 1.7 percent annually (41 years to double).

B. Under conditions of moderate mortality (say, $e_0 = 42.5$), substantially lower birth rates are required (GRR = 3.04) and all but 2.5 percent of the mothers are able to bear enough sons to assure that at least one will survive to his parents' old age. Childbearing may slow down or stop late in the reproductive age span, and the average age at motherhood is 25.2 years. But under such conditions, a population would experience natural increase at the phenomenal rate of 2.8 percent annually (25 years to double)!

C. Under conditions of rather low mortality (say, $e_0 = 73.0$), a single male birth is almost certain to promise a male survivor. Therefore, the achievement of the goal requires that childbearing be continued over only a short part of the reproductive span (the mean age at motherhood being 20.4 years). Fertility rates would probably assure no more than a *replacement* of the population and certainly no substantial increase (the GRR would be 0.97, and the intrinsic rate of natural increase only 0.3 percent annually—233 years to double!).

THE "SOCIAL STATUS" THEORY. The "social status" explanation of fertility, as originally formulated in 1890 by the French demographer Arsène Dumont, held that the ambition to rise from inferior to higher social positions is widespread, but that large families inhibit social mobility. Accordingly, those seeking to enhance their status will tend to control fertility and family size.

A modern formulation of the "social status" explanation by J. A. Banks (1954) attempts to account for the sharp decline in fertility in England between 1870 and 1900 by arguing that—

1. after a generation of prosperity, the British economy experienced a leveling off in the 1870s and 1880s;
2. to preserve their own newly acquired occupational and social status and assure its transmittal to their children—the latter entailing substantial investment in the education of the offspring— couples of the British salaried middle class restricted their births drastically;
3. the restriction of births became simpler and more acceptable socially during the period in question because of technological improvements in, and the promotion of, contraception;
4. as communication between the classes increased and as primary and post-primary education among the lower classes expanded the pattern of family limitation started gradually to be diffused;
5. the further expansion of interclass communication and lower-class education intensified personal contacts and the motivation to acquire new prestige to such an extent that the pattern of family limitation came to permeate the entire social structure.

Variations of this analysis are sometimes formulated as explanations of fertility differentials, between, for example, urban and rural populations, Jewish and Christian ones, and foreign-born and first-generation native ones. Lower urban, as compared to rural, fertility; lower Jewish, as compared to Christian, fertility; and lower first-generation native, as compared to foreign-born, fertility are thus all explained in terms of attempts of the respective former categories to improve or assure socioeconomic status.

THE "UTILITY-COST" THEORY. The "utility-cost" explanation of fertility has received much attention and has been elaborated considerably in recent years, but its basic ideas were set forth by H. Liebenstein in 1957:

> It is not going too far to say that the essential element to be explained is the incentive or rationale behind the desire to have larger or smaller families. We have to visualize various contraceptive techniques as merely facilitating factors the utilization of which involves an economic or emotional cost of some sort. But the major burden of any theory must be on the explanation of the forces that create the necessary motivations for the creation of smaller rather than larger families.
>
> A distinction has to be made between the knowledge of alternatives and the choice among known alternatives. It seems reasonable to suppose that as incomes increase, the knowledge of the alternatives pertinent to family limitation also increases. But we still have to explain what determines the choice from among a range of known alternatives. The basic idea behind our theory is that motivations with respect to family size are, to a considerable extent, rational; that, on the whole, parents will want an extra child if the satisfactions to be derived from that child are greater than the "costs" that are involved—where "costs" are to be interpreted rather broadly. [Liebenstein 1957, p. 159]

Thus, the "utility-cost" explanation of fertility assumes, first, that people behave rationally with respect to their own fertility, that is, that they behave as if they were applying rough calculations to the problem of determining the desirable number of births. Second, these calculations are assumed to be directed toward balancing the satisfaction or utility to be derived from an additional child against the "cost," both monetary and psychological, of having that child.

The theory distinguishes between three types of "utility" to be derived from an additional child:

1. The child's utility as a "consumption good," i.e., as a source of personal pleasure to the parents
2. The child's utility as a productive agent, i.e., as a person who

may be expected eventually to work and contribute to the family income

3. The child's utility as a potential source of security, e.g., in the parents' old age

The costs of having an additional child are both direct and indirect:

1. The direct costs are the usual expenses of maintaining the child until he is self-supporting.
2. Indirect costs are incurred when opportunities—for example, the wife's employment—are foregone because of the child's existence.

The "utility-cost" analysis offers an explanation of class differentials in fertility at any moment in time. In the first place, it holds, since income varies over the different socioeconomic groups, different groups can afford more or fewer children, or a "higher" or "lower" quality of children, if we assume a fixed pattern of utilities and costs (see Becker 1960).[9] In the second place, the pattern of utilities and costs varies among the different socioeconomic groups. For example, the utility of an additional child is different for the farmer than for the clerk, just as the direct cost is different for the professor than for the unskilled laborer. Similarly, the indirect cost is different for the college-educated career woman than for the housewife (Duesenberry 1960).

The "utility-cost" analysis also offers an explanation of changes in fertility over time. Economic development, it reasons, can alter the pattern of utility and cost. For example, both the direct and indirect costs of an additional child probably rise as per capita income increases, whereas the utility of the additional child as a source of security and as a contributor to family income probably diminish. On the other hand, the utility of the additional child as a "consumption item" is probably fixed (Liebenstein 1963, p. 162).[10]

Macroanalytic Theories: Three Examples

We shall briefly discuss three macroanalytic theories of fertility. The first is Malthus's classic analysis of the relationship between food production, per capita income, and preventive checks on population growth. The second is the macroanalytic analysis of changing family structure as expressed in the emergence of the conjugal family, the establishment of the nuclear family couple as a decision-making unit,

9 It is Becker's article that brought the "utility-cost" analysis of fertility to the attention of demographers.

10 F. Lorimer (1965) has carried out some hypothetical calculations showing variations in costs and utilities of children.

and the rationalization of family formation. The third, finally, is the theory of "population balance," in which changes in population size, distribution, and other characteristics are related to the availability of environmental resources, to technology, and to social organization.

Malthus's Theory. Diminished per capita income is, in Malthus's analysis, a structural attribute of a society which has theretofore experienced too rapid a population growth. The mortality and diminished fertility associated with the "positive checks" of "vice," "misery," "wars," and "famine" affect all people in such societies, not just those who marry too early, or who bear too many children, or who do not earn enough. Further, the delayed marriage, solvency, and continence associated with "preventive checks" are primarily institutionalized means of diminishing fertility rather than individual acts of wisdom and foresight (cf. Spengler 1971). In Malthus's analysis, the key societal variable is the survival or nonsurvival—or, perhaps more correctly, the survivability or nonsurvivability—of populations at subsistence levels. Malthus only implicitly took into account the possibility of survival at alternative levels of living. However, the more modern renditions of his theory have it that societies institutionalize preventive checks, not only upon threats to actual survival, but upon threats to survival at some acceptable minimum level.

The Theory of Changing Family Structure. The theory of changing family structure, formulated by W. J. Goode (1963) and others, holds that urbanization and industrialization are associated with the subversion and breakdown of the extended family system. In the extended family, the childbearing couple, or nuclear family couple, is not generally a decision-making unit. Arrangements and decisions regarding matchmaking and marriage, residence, work and economic relations, and even the care and socialization of the young are made, not by the couple affected, but by the head or senior couple of the extended family. Similarly, no childbearing or birth-spacing decisions are made by the fertile couple.

In the relatively independent or isolated nuclear family, however, decisions are made by the couple, both before and after marriage. Each partner may decide to marry or not marry, each may choose his or her own spouse, and jointly the couple may make residential, occupational, and child-bearing decisions. Such decisions may be determined entirely by tradition, or they may be entirely "rational," or they may comprise some combination depending upon the couple's individual characteristics— especially their literacy and socioeconomic status—and upon the nature of the various nuclear family institutions of the society in question.

According to Goode's formulation, it is industrialization that causes and sustains the institutionalization of the conjugal, relatively small, in-

dependent and mobile family. More precisely, industrialization undermines traditional family systems by rewarding mobility; by creating
class-differentiated mobility within kin groupings; by organizing extra-
kinship institutions for meeting needs and problems previously handled
by kinship institutions; by creating a value structure recognizing achievement; and by promoting specialization and differentiation, thereby
diminishing the opportunities for kin to aid one another in occupational
arrangements. It follows that industrialization promotes change in these
specific aspects of family formation that concern the independence and
mobility of newly formed families. Its effect is to enhance the independence and mobility of the newly formed family and to diminish the
control exerted over this family by the larger, extended one. For example,
industrialization works to place marriage decisions and choice of spouse
in the hands of the principal parties themselves, to diminish economic
entailments of marriage, to diminish the rigidity and frequency of endogamous and exogamous practices, to increase the frequency of neolocal
residence (wherein the home of the new couple is located fairly independently of the locations of either of their parents' homes), and to make
age at marriage, and variations of age, consistent with the increasing
independence and mobility of the younger generation. Similarly, industrialization promotes attempts to control fertility, even if this control is
not necessarily expressed in diminished fertility.

THE THEORY OF "POPULATION BALANCE." Elements of the "Population Balance" theory as formulated by human ecologists are found in
modern sociology in the writings of Durkheim, M. Halbwachs, W. F.
Ogburn, and, particularly, A. H. Hawley (1950, especially chap. 9) and
O. D. Duncan (1959). We have already reviewed some aspects of this
theory in chapter 2. To recapitulate briefly, all societies are confronted
with the pressures of their own tendencies to increase in number. Taking
it as axiomatic that males and females in any human population mate
and produce offspring, it follows that in the absence of social, institutional, physical, biological, or other inhibiting factors, populations tend
to increase in size.

The pressures of population increase spell opportunity for some
societies and disaster for others. It is under the pressure of population
growth that changes in the social organization and in the economic and
technological arrangements of a population are effected; or, alternatively,
that institutionalized constraints upon mating and procreation are
evolved. Thus, in any society there is an ongoing interaction between the
population, its social organization, its technology, and its environment.
A society characterized by fixed technology and social organization must,
when confronted by substantial growth in its own numbers, seek to expand its environment by settlement, cultivation, or exploitation of new

areas, or suffer a decline in its per capita level or subsistence. On the other hand, a society with a fixed area can increase its production and look after its growing numbers by effecting changes either in its social organization, or in its technology, or both. But the society unable to alter its social or technological patterns and unable also to expand its physical-geographical environment must either institutionalize patterns of controlling population growth, suffer substantial decreases in its levels of living, or—historically the most common case of all—lose all of its potential growth through high mortality.

This analysis differs from that of Malthus in that it explicitly incorporates the possibility that not just one technology and social organization, but various ones, affect the balance between population and resources and bear upon levels of subsistence and quality of life.

A Comparison of Microanalytic and Macroanalytic Approaches to Change in Levels and Patterns of Fertility

Any individual woman or couple must make a set of decisions bearing upon marriage and childbearing. These decisions are taken at different points of time in the life cycle of the marriage—e.g., before the birth of any children, after the first child is born, when children enter or complete school, etc.—and each is associated with that stage of the marital cycle currently in operation. A number of the decisions are cancellable or reversible, so that there is room in microanalytic studies for some analysis of individual "change" in decisions or behavior regarding fertility. However, in practice this analysis is very severely limited by difficulties in separating and distinguishing such changes from changes based on age or on stage of life cycle. Thus, an individual decision to have an additional child may reflect *either* continuation of the acceptable life cycle sequence of childbearing *or* a change in that sequence.

Fundamentally, microanalytical theories of change in fertility patterns assume static relationships between decisions and behavior regarding fertility and the population's various independent socioeconomic variables and characteristics. Any change in a population's level of fertility is generally viewed as taking place because of a *change in the socioeconomic or demographic composition* of the population, not because of a change in the relationship between fertility and socioeconomic characteristics. The problem of change in patterns of fertility for microanalytic theory thus becomes reduced to a problem of plotting in sufficient detail the relationship of and behavior regarding fertility decisions to age, life-cycle location, and socioeconomic characteristics.

It follows that the application of such theories to the *prediction of change* in patterns and levels of fertility rests upon the predictability of changes in the composition of the population over major demographic and socioeconomic variables. Thus, it is possible to predict that fertility will decline in Latin America as education is extended or as urbanization proceeds. However, where fertility differences by educational achievement or by urban-rural residence are less pronounced—as they are, for example, in the Middle East and in South Asia—microanalytic analyses do not provide such ready insights into future trends.

In macroanalytic theories of population growth, the levels and patterns of stability of a population's fertility are of *direct* interest; similarly, the change over time in these levels and patterns can be approached directly. Change in fertility occurs in different directions (toward increase or decrease), by different means (e.g. delayed marriage, family limitations), and with different origins and correlates (e.g., urbanization and social differentiation, population growth, settlement and colonization, wars). Macroanalytic theory examines these in terms of aggregate patterns rather than as sum totals of individual decisions.

The important differences between macroanalytic and microanalytic approaches to changing fertility are (1) that macroanalytic theory seeks to explain change in terms of changing features of characteristics of the population and in terms of relationships between structural changes in different populations, whereas microanalytic theory seeks to explain change in terms of *changing composition of decision-makers and behavers;* and (2) that macroanalytic theory arrives at its explanations on the basis of longitudinal investigations of society, whereas microanalytic theory does so by projecting static, cross-sectionally inferred, relationships. The application of macroanalytic theory to predictions of change in levels and patterns of fertility invokes direct relationships between change in fertility and family-formation institutions, on the one hand, and change in other structural and institutional features of populations on the other.

The microanalytic type of analysis cannot predict what shifts in patterns of fertility are likely to accompany economic development in underdeveloped countries or what shifts are likely to accompany economic recessions in developed countries. Nor can it predict the effect of expanding literacy or higher education, or of diminishing mortality, or of the increasing concentration of a population in large agglomerations, or of social differentiation and secularization and mass communication. The reason for this low order of generality and predictability is that microanalytical theories are "culture-bound." That is, they cannot "explain" associations between fertility and age, or between fertility and socioeconomic indicators, except in the context of some given socioeconomic-technological regime, or, as Duncan has put it, of some given "ecosystem." But it is precisely the variations and changes in fertility brought on by variations and changes in the ecosystem itself which are often of the most critical concern—and these, precisely, are the subject matter of macroanalytic theory.

Some Attempts to Reconcile Microanalytic and Macroanalytic Analyses

INSTITUTIONALIZATION OF NEW FERTILITY BEHAVIOR. A number of attempts have been made to reconcile microanalytic and macroanalytic analyses of fertility and population growth. R. Freedman (1963) argues that when large numbers of persons exhibit characteristic patterns of decision-making and behavior in response to changing typical exigencies—e.g., changing mortality levels or changing modal utility and cost patterns—then these behavioral patterns become institutionalized and normatively prescribed in the society. Thus, not only do diminishing mortality and increasing education have the effect, predicted by microanalytic analysis, of lowering the fertility of individuals, but these individual responses of lower fertility may be institutionalized and normatively supported in societies experiencing substantial decreases in mortality and increasing literacy and education. In terms of our discussion in chapter 4, there are "structural effects" of changes in the variables affecting individual decisions and behavior.

"TASTES" AS A SOCIOLOGICAL VARIABLE. Looking for ways to relate the microanalytic economic and macroanalytic sociological analyses of fertility, R. A. Easterlin focuses upon the concept of "tastes" as a bridge between the two (Easterlin 1969). Working with the utility-cost model of fertility behavior, he suggests viewing the formation of tastes—which determine utility and cost under a given pattern of income and prices —as a "sociological" as well as "economic" variable:

> To turn to the formation of tastes, it is here that many of the fertility variables emphasized by the sociologists come to the fore. While it is attitudes . . . , which together with resource and price constraints immediately determine fertility decisions, a host of other variables lie behind these attitudes. In general, one's preference system at any given time may be viewed as molded by heredity and past and current environment. The process starts with birth and continues through the life cycle. Religion, color, nativity, place of residence, and education enter into the shaping of tastes. So, too, does one's childhood and adolescent experience in one's own home with material affluence and family size. One reaches family-building age with preferences already molded by this heritage, but these preferences are subsequently modified by ongoing occupational, income, and family-building experiences, among others. Exposure to various information media influences tastes throughout the life cycle.
>
> Because of the important role of cumulative experience in the formation of tastes, it is probably correct that typically tastes change rather slowly over time. For some analytical purposes, this may justify the economist's usual assumption of constant tastes. But in

areas of time period where cross-section differences among classes are of interest, such an assumption seems dubious.

Nor can the economist dismiss taste phenomena as noneconomic in nature, for it is clear that economic variables enter into the shaping of tastes and affect behavior through this channel as well as via the resource and price constraints traditionally emphasized. Hence, an adequate framework for fertility analysis calls for explicit attention to preference phenomena and the factors entering into their formation. [*Ibid.*, p. 135]

In an important critical review of recent research on fertility, G. Hawthorn (1970) adopts the Easterlin scheme and begins a systematization and summary of the findings bearing upon variations in resources, costs, and tastes. These variations, in interaction with one another, are seen as determining fertility decisions and behavior. Religion, education, female employment, urbanization, race, and social mobility are all re-examined from the point of view of their influence on tastes in the utility-cost analysis. But the approach is still very novel and its concrete applications remain to be worked out and evaluated.

MULTI-PHASIC RESPONSE TO DEMOGRAPHIC AND ECONOMIC CHANGE. The well-known attempt by K. Davis to analyze fertility trends in modern demographic transitions in terms of a "theory of change and response" (Davis 1963) may also be viewed as an attempt to reconcile microanalytic and macroanalytic analyses. Davis points out that in countries experiencing a demographic transition there were typically more than a single means by which the birth rate was brought down following the lowered mortality and a period of sustained growth. These means generally included delayed marriage, international migration, sterilization, abortion, and the increasing use of contraception. Such "multiphasic responses," according to Davis, represented reactions to the decline in mortality and to the sustained natural increase which ensued, but *not* to poverty or to crises of subsistence. They were prompted by *personal,* rather than by societal or national, goals and considerations. The demographic transitions, on the other hand, took place only under conditions of economic expansion and growth.

Davis's theory seeks to explain and predict variations in individual strategies of marriage and family formation—concerns of the microanalytic analysis—in terms of the individual's location in the society's social and economic structure. And he argues that differential location gives rise to differential opportunities for exploiting—or for avoiding the negative effects of—changes in the scope or structure of the society's economic activity—macroanalytic variables. His theory presumes childbearing to be a normal activity and seeks to identify the circumstances under which childbearing is controlled or diminished. According to this analysis, location in the social and economic structure makes for differences in the advantages to be reaped from the control of fertility in any given economic circumstance. Those individuals who stand to gain most from adopting practices which diminish fertility do so, while those so located in the society and economy as to derive little or no reward from fertility control do not.

LINKAGES BETWEEN VARIABLES. We mention, finally, a recent attempt by B. C. Rosen and A. B. Simmons (1971) to discover and assess some linkages between macroanalytic variables, social-psychological variables, psychological variables, and fertility. Examining relationships between industrialization and social class, husband-wife decision-making processes, wives' attitudes, and fertility, Rosen and Simmons suggest that industrialization influences fertility through shifts in the status, role conceptions, and self-images of the women. Education and new employment opportunities promote respectively, "modern" conceptions of the role of women in society and egalitarian decision-making in the family. These, in turn, are related to preferences for smaller families and to lower fertility.

Figure 8.11 shows the directions of relationships between the structural-psychological factors and fertility in the industrial communities studied by Rosen and Simmons. Fertility—denoted "actual family size" in the diagram—was found to be *directly* influenced:

1. negatively by extent of "wife's participation in decisions" (i.e. wife's participation in family decisions is associated with low fertility; non-participation or low levels of participation with high fertility);
2. negatively by "wife's role attitudes" (i.e., the possession of strong attitude concerning independence of wife's role is associated with low fertility);
3. positively with "wife's preferred family size";
4. positively with wife's age: the older the wife, the more children;
5. negatively by wife's education: the higher the educational achievement, the lower the fertility;
6. negatively by husband's occupational status; and
7. negatively by wife's labor force status: wives who work tend to have fewer children.

In addition to the above, the fertility was found to be *indirectly* influenced:

1. by wife's role attitudes, since they affect wife's participation in decisions positively and wife's preferred family size negatively;
2. by wife's education, since it affects wife's role attitudes positively;

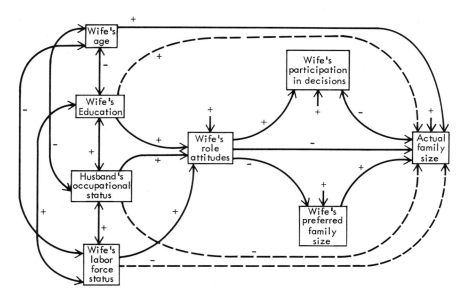

FIGURE 8.11. Causal diagram of structural-psychological factors related to fertility in industrial communities. Source: Rosen and Simmons 1971, p. 64.

3. by husband's occupational status, since it affects wife's role attitudes positively;
4. by wife's labor force status, since it affects wife's role attitudes positively.

The web of relationships between the structural-psychological factors and fertility in non-industrial communities differs significantly, particularly in that education and employment opportunities do not result in the same kinds of role attitudes or participation in decisions.

Problems of Macroanalytic Analysis

While the majority of recent fertility studies can contribute considerably to the microanalytic analysis of population growth, they have little relevance for macroanalytic theory. One result of this neglect is that recent fertility studies have added very little to our understanding of the relationship between sociohistorical trends and processes and population movements. Similarly, they have not rendered population processes any more predictable. Thus, although demographers were able to anticipate a recent decline in fertility in the United States on the basis of survey data (in much the same way as automobile sales or election votes are forecasted), this by no means indicates that they know why these changes have occurred or under what conditions new changes might take place.

Macroanalytic analyses of fertility and population change derive the greater part of their data from historical materials. Studies which are comparable and which represent sets of observations of fertility over a number of societies of "ecosystems" have tended to be very general in nature, concerning themselves with such factors as levels or patterns of fertility, or levels or patterns of marriage, alone rather than in relationship to the social, economic, or demographic features of the society or national population studied.

There are many bases for differentiating and classifying societies or complete ecosystems, and it is possible to use standardized measures for a wide range of societies, countries, and subpopulations. For example, societies can be measured or classified by size of population, size of territory, and population density; by urban-rural distribution, industrial composition, or economic structure; by total product, per capita income, and the structure of consumption; by religious organization, educational achievement, or type of political authority; by level and pattern of mortality; by extent of occupational or other social differentiation; by volume and direction of migration; and by social mobility. This list by no means exhausts the possibilities.[11] Moreover, societies can be characterized in terms of the direction and extent of *change* in these characteristics.

The study of levels and patterns of fertility, of patterns in marriage, and to some extent of patterns of family limitation, and also the study of changes therein, can—when related to the structural characteristics of societies—contribute much to the development, expansion, and verification of a genuine scientific and macroanalytic theory of fertility and population growth. However, some very basic problems confront empirical studies of relationships between social or economic structural variables and patterns and factors of fertility. These involve questions of

1. the accuracy, validity, reliability, and detail with which a society's structural attributes, including population growth, can be portrayed, measured, or characterized;
2. the accuracy and detail with which change in a society's structure, attributes, and patterns of population growth can be portrayed, measured, or characterized;
3. the establishment of rules for inferring relationships among various social-structural characteristics or changes therein or among various fertility patterns or changes therein.

There is no readily available, conventionally used, body of measures and techniques for carrying out such analyses. This absence of techniques

11 For an excellent example of the many measures that can be used, see United Nations, *Population Bulletin*, No. 7–1963 (1965).

for plotting and measuring associations and for testing the independence or nonindependence of structural attributes contrasts markedly with the availability and wide acceptance of methods of measuring and inferring relationships between variables relating to individuals. It is probably this contrast that accounts, at least in part, for the great difference in the relative attention paid to microanalytic and macroanalytic issues in American research on fertility.

Those who would consider macroanalytical issues must often be prepared, then, to make do with simpler, perhaps less sophisticated and less convincing, techniques of measurement and analysis. However, they must also seek to contribute to the improvement of techniques for dealing with structural attributes and variables and changes therein. The rewards would appear to be great.

9

Migratory
Movements

1. INTRODUCTORY REMARKS

Of all the components of population growth, migration may well be the most complex. In the first place, unlike the case for birth or death, the definitions themselves of migration and migrant are always problematic, and so is the counting of migratory movements. In the second place, because of the myriad alternative ways of grouping individuals, any one migratory move can be assigned a variety of origins and destinations. Also, in a different sense from that of births and deaths, the individual move is a voluntary action; thus, societal values and norms concerning movement, and the manner in which these are manifested in individual and collective behavior, must be studied in relation to both movement and nonmovement. Finally, migratory movements have consequences for the individual migrant, for the populations of origin and destination, and for the greater, more inclusive, societal unit within which the migration takes place, and all these consequences must be described and analyzed separately and in combination.

In the next section, we shall review problems of the definition and measurement of migration, extending the discussion beyond that of chapter 5. In section 3, we shall attempt to contrast patterns of migratory movements in and among societies to draw a contrast between one-time migrations and recurring migratory movements. The following sections will consider migration and population redistribution and differential migration from the point of view of movers and nonmovers within a population, communities of origin and destination, and societies within which population migration takes place. Our last section is devoted to a consideration of the individual, community, and societal consequences of migration.

2. THE DEFINITION AND MEASUREMENT OF MIGRATION

Definition and Measurement in Terms of the Population Balancing Equation

The concepts of "migrant" and "migration" seem clearest when considered in the light of the population balancing equation:

$$P_1 = P_0 + B - D + I - 0,$$

where

$P_0 =$ population at the beginning of an interval
$B\ \ =$ the number of births in the interval
$D\ \ =$ the number of deaths in the interval
$I\ \ =$ the number of in-migrants in the interval
$O\ \ =$ the number of out-migrants in the interval
$P_1 =$ population at the close of the interval

Obviously, following this equation, a "migrant" is a person entering (or added to), or leaving (or subtracted from), the population of a given place or category by means other than birth or death (or aging, if the population category is an age group); and the total gross and net increments caused by such entrances or departures comprise "migration."

Unfortunately, there are some serious practical obstacles to this approach. In contrast to the case of birth and death, phenomena which are widely recorded, it is only in very exceptional instances that entrance to, or departure from, a circumscribed population is recorded. Metaphorically, the borders and boundaries of life itself are presided over by various gatekeepers and recorders of vital statistics, but the borders and boundaries of communities and populations generally are not.

Of course, international frontiers are usually—although not always—exceptions to this rule; and, indeed, there are routine and recurrent counts of numbers of border crossings and of international migrants. But the great bulk of migratory movements take place unheralded, un-

remarked, and—worst of all for demographers and other social scientists
—uncounted and unclassified. Indirect estimates of the volume of net
migration are often obtainable by using the balancing equation and
assuming that population change unaccounted for by natural increase
may be imputed to net migration, i.e., that $(P_1 - P_0) - (B - D) = (I - O)$.
However, this method, while very useful, is severely restricted in the range
and scope of information it provides concerning correlates, causes, and
consequences of migration and concerning characteristics of migrants and
nonmigrants.

The Use of Population Registers

A second approach to the study of migration entails the use of
population registers. We have already noted (in chapter 3) that a number
of countries maintain continuous population registers and that in these
cases persons are generally required to report changes of address. When
maintained on a reasonably up-to-date basis, such registers and the related flow of change-of-residence reports comprise a very important source
of migration data.[1]

In many countries where registers do not cover the entire population, certain kinds of partial registers are maintained. These can often
be exploited for purposes of measuring and analyzing mobility. In the
United States, for example, the social security system constitutes a partial
population register; and it is this register, indeed, upon which several
studies of migration and labor mobility have been based (see Bogue 1952).
The main limitation of using population registers, where they exist,
is that the analysis is restricted to those characteristics recorded in the
register, generally only such basic demographic characteristics as sex,
place and date of birth, marital status, and previous place of residence.
However, as Goldstein has shown, combining such data with carefully
chosen place-of-origin and place-of-destination categories and groupings
can yield very important insights into variations in patterns of migration (Goldstein 1964, pp. 1121–32, and 1965, pp. 267–77). But even in the
absence of data on origin and destination, there remains much interest in
population registers, for they permit the direct comparison of migrants
with nonmigrants, and of migrants of different types.

The "Mobility Status" Approach via Censuses and Surveys

In this search for direct information, researchers have turned increasingly to the "migrant status," or "mobility status," approach, which
seeks to reconstruct past movements on the basis of information returned

---

1 For recent examples of the use of such data, see Goldstein 1963, 1964, and 1965.

by individuals in census or survey inquiries. Persons are asked either where they resided at some previous date or whether or not they changed residences within some interval preceding the date of the census or survey. Data so generated can yield information on both the volume and direction of migratory movements.

In variation of this approach, respondents are asked their place of birth, i.e., their state of birth, country of birth, etc. This information, together with data on present place of residence, also yields quantitative representations of migratory movements.

An example of how the "mobility status" approach can be used is provided by the way in which migration is studied in United States censuses and the Current Population Survey.[2] These studies classify the population by mobility status, determining this status by comparing the individual's current place of residence with his place of residence five years ago. The following classifications are used (Shryock 1964, p. 10):

Same house
Different house in same county (intracounty movers)
Migrants (intercounty movers)
    different county, same state (intrastate migrants)
Interstate migrants
    between contiguous states
    between noncontiguous states
Movers from abroad

This approach makes it possible not only to count numbers of migrants of the different types but to analyze differential frequencies of the various types of moves in relation to any one, or any combination, of the other characteristics investigated in the census or survey. The problem of specifying what kinds of moves actually constitute "migration," or who is and who is not a "migrant," is solved differently in different research settings. Thus, as the foregoing classifications indicate, the United States Census considers someone who moves to a new house a "migrant" only if he changes his county of residence; otherwise, he is merely a "mover." For the anthropologist, however, an entire society may be a "migrant" or "nomadic" society by virtue of moving over even shorter distances.

Measuring Migration as a Component of Change
or as a Representation of Interchange

We have already presented the basic general model for the quantitative representation and analysis of migratory movements (chapter 5, section 8). In addition, there are a number of detailed technical procedures

2 Shryock (1964) offers a detailed description and analysis of these migration studies.

for dealing with the measurement of geographic mobility (for example, Bogue 1959b and Shryock 1964). We limit the discussion here to a brief review of the distinction between measuring migration as a component of the change in size of a single population and measuring it as a representation of the interchange between a system of two or more populations.

In the first instance, we want to measure either the I component (in-migrants) or the O component (out-migrants) or the (I − O) component (net migration) in the balancing equation

$$P_1 = P_0 + B - D + I - O,$$

where, again, B denotes births, D denotes deaths, I denotes the number of in-migrants, and O denotes the number of out-migrants during the trial interval considered. Such measurement may entail either counts of I, O, or (I − O) or the computation of rates. In the latter case, the rates may be computed with respect to the initial population size, or the final population size, or, as is most frequently the case, the mean population during the period (see chapter 5). In all cases, the concern is with the relationship between migration and the change in a single population, no attention being paid to the question of the origins of the in-migrants or destinations of the out-migrants.

The second approach deals with at least two separately identified populations (one of which can be a residual "all other" population) and with the migratory movements between them. Assuming that two populations are being studied, let us call them P_a and P_b, and let us call the migratory movements in each of the two directions M_{ab} and M_{ba}. The rates of the form M_{ab}/P_a and M_{ba}/P_b correspond to the rates of the "outflow table" in chapter 5 (section 8), while the rates of the form M_{ab}/P_b and M_{ba}/P_a comprise the rates of an "inflow table." When considered in conjunction with the initial and final population sizes—say, the initial P_{ao} and P_{bo} and the final P_{a1} and P_{b1}—such rates provide a complete description of the migration streams in each direction, of the total gross mobility and net mobility between the two populations, and of the way in which the population distribution of the whole system $(P_a + P_b)$ is altered by the volume and directions of migratory movement.

3. MIGRATORY MOVEMENTS IN DIFFERENT KINDS OF SOCIETIES

In Part I we noted that prehistoric and primitive small-scale hunting and food-collecting societies are characterized by virtually continuous nomadic movement, and that in other societies, too, the migration of part or of all of the population is encountered as a societal strategy of

TABLE 9.1

Cross-Cultural Summary Sample: Prevailing Patterns of Settlement

Pattern of Settlement	Number of Cultures
Non-permanent Settlement	
Fully migratory or nomadic bands	36
Seminomadic communities: members wander in bands for at least half the year but occupy a fixed settlement during some season or seasons — for example, recurrently occupying the same winter quarters.	36
Semi-sedentary communities (1) whose members shift from one to another fixed settlement in different seasons, or (2) whose members occupy, more or less permanently, a single settlement — from which, however, a substantial proportion of the population departs seasonally to occupy shifting camps, e.g., during transhumance (the seasonal moving of livestock).	28
Compact but impermanent settlements, e.g., villages whose location is shifted every few years	10
Permanent Settlement	
Neighborhoods of dispersed family homesteads	40
Separated hamlets, several of which form a more or less permanent single community	33
Compact and relatively permanent settlements, e.g., nucleated villages or towns	140
Complex settlements consisting of a nucleated village or town with outlying homesteads or satellite hamlets (including urban aggregations)	9
Unascertained	68
Total Sample	400 cultures

SOURCE: Textor 1967.

survival. However, it is frequently asserted that in comparison to other types of societies, the modern urban-industrial society is characterized by extremely high rates of migration and by a high degree of geographic mobility. The discrepancy here suggests that there may be distinctive patterns of geographic mobility characteristic of different types of populations and societies. Table 9.1 taken from the Cross Cultural Survey (Textor 1967) illustrates how anthropologists have classified cultures by pattern of settlement. The table and descriptive category titles indicate the variety of settlement patterns found among the 332 cultures for which information was obtained. Moreover, each of the eight settlement pattern categories could be further subdivided into groupings even more specific and detailed in terms of settlement patterns. We present now the briefest sketch of these societal variations.

MIGRATORY MOVEMENTS IN SMALL-SCALE SOCIETIES. For small-scale, low-density populations, such as those of food-gathering and hunting bands, the primary fact of life is the inconsistent availability of food. Thus, the chief social economic, and demographic characteristic of these populations is their virtually constant physical movement in search of sustenance. On the basis of what has been observed for existing hunting bands (e.g., the Bushmen), it is generally assumed that such migratory movements involve the entire population simultaneously.[3]

Societies with some food-cultivating technology enjoy somewhat more stable food supplies and are generally only seminomadic. An example would be the Papago Indians of the American Southwest (Hackenberg 1962, pp. 186–95). In such populations there is typically some seasonal migration, but in many cases this is temporary; for example, there may be long food-gathering or hunting expeditions involving only part of the population.

Small-scale societies characterized by somewhat higher population density, e.g., village or tribal agricultural societies, are also typically characterized by temporary migrations. These may consist of seasonal movements or hunting expeditions involving all or large parts of the population. In addition, there are frequent migratory movements on the part of individuals in connection with marriage, feuds, or simply the search for a more congenial or more comfortable habitat.

MIGRATORY MOVEMENTS IN SOCIETIES OF PERMANENT SETTLEMENT. Larger agrarian societies face an important barrier to geographic mobility: institutions of property. Either ownership of land or the prospect of inheriting land may tie individuals to their places of residence. Alternatively, a wide variety of customs and roles binding individuals and families to land owned by someone else (e.g., the feudal lord) may similarly prevent migratory movement. On the other hand, agrarian societies have always been associated with centers of high-density settlement providing services of various types. Such urban centers have always attracted some countryside-to-town migrants, and in large, highly differentiated, agrarian societies the rural-to-urban movement has been of very great magnitude. At the same time, such societies are typically characterized by considerable return movement from town to countryside.

The Soviet Union was until recently a largely agrarian society, and indeed large parts of the Soviet Union consist of agrarian communities to this day. Table 9.2 and figure 9.1 indicate that in the period from 1926 to 1958, when the urban population grew by a spectacular 70 millions

---

[3] For a more detailed description and discussion, see Forde 1964, Part I; cf. also Lee and Devore 1968, "Problems in the Study of Hunters and Gatherers."

TABLE 9.2
Sources of Growth of Urban Population of the Soviet Union,
1926–1938 and 1939–1958

	1926–1938[a]	1939–1958[b]
Total Increase in the Urban Population of the Soviet Union (in millions)	29.8	39.6
Accounted for by:		
Migration from rural to urban areas	18.7	24.25
Transformation of villages into towns	5.8	7.0
Natural increase	5.3	8.0

SOURCE: Daragan 1967.
[a]Frontiers on 17 September 1939.
[b]1965 frontiers.

just over two-thirds of the urban growth can be imputed to migratory moves of population from rural to urban places. Thus the modernization of the Soviet Union in the present century has been closely connected to large scale migratory movements.[4]

Urban-industrial societies are not only characterized by large-scale, rural-to-urban, net migration, but over time they have also witnessed the increasing interchange of population, both *among* different urban places and centrifugally from the urban centers to their surrounding fringes. The urban interchange has generated a growing specialization among cities, so that large-scale urban-industrial societies increasingly comprise systems of differentiated cities and urban centers.

An important step in the derivation and formulation of generalizations concerning migration in different kinds of societies is found in the work of Goldscheider (1971, chapter 7), in which he analyzes the relationship between migration and socioeconomic modernization in Africa. According to Goldscheider, the extent of migration in traditional—including agrarian, but also "pre-agrarian,"—societies is quite low and involves almost exclusively moves which are at the same time short-distance moves and moves between homogeneous areas. Such moves tend either to involve whole populations—i.e., nomadic movement—or else are idiosyncratic—i.e., without pattern—in nature.

Migration in traditional societies, in Goldscheider's view, may be related to development of new territories or new sources of sustenance, to marriage—especially in exogamous networks of tribes, villages, or societies—or to warfare, conquest, or other political causes. Both because of their limited volume and because of their idiosyncratic nature, migration

4 For an extensive treatment of this and other facets of Soviet population trends, see Petersen 1969, pp. 648–65.

has relatively little impact or consequences either for origin communities or for destination communities. The amount of migration in traditional societies is, in turn, constrained by rigidity of status-reward systems, by high community loyalty and low status of moves, by physical barriers to movement, and by high levels of solidarity and integration in such societies.

These propositions formulated by Goldscheider are tentative and will need to be reexamined and elaborated as better data become available. However, Goldscheider is able to go on and contrast the migration characteristics outlined above with quite different patterns of migration associated with socioeconomic development and modernization—e.g. under colonialism or under emerging nationalism and the social, political, and economic trends attending them. Migration and population redistribution are integral parts of modernization processes: under the economic and political changes of modernization previous constraints on migration are reduced. In addition, economic changes generated expanded trade and production; taxation forced individuals to move from subsistence farming to wage employment; and new patterns of recruitment of workers evolved. And all these changes were accompanied by changing attitudes about migration (Goldscheider 1971, pp. 182–96).

FIGURE 9.1. Increase in urban population of the Soviet Union, 1926–1938 and 1939–1958: Source: Table 9.2.

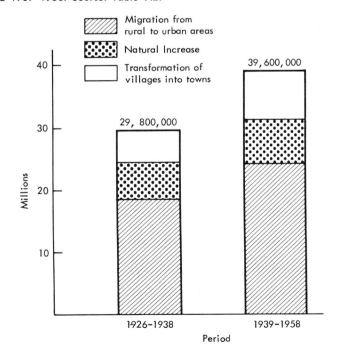

4. MIGRATION AND POPULATION REDISTRIBUTION

In chapter 5 (section 8) we represented the pattern of "regime" of migration rates among a *set* of places or areal categories as a *population transformation*. In our matrix and vector motation, we represented the initial population, classified by place of residence, as $\pi_0 = (P_1, P_2, \cdots P_i \cdots)$, the matrix of rates of mobility between the i-th and j-th places as

$$M_1 = \begin{pmatrix} m_{11} \, m_{12} \cdots m_{1j} \cdots \\ \cdot \quad \cdot \quad \cdot \\ \cdot \quad \cdot \quad \cdot \\ \cdot \quad \cdot \quad \cdot \\ m_{i1} \, m_{i2} \cdots m_{ij} \cdots \\ \cdot \quad \cdot \quad \cdot \\ \cdot \quad \cdot \quad \cdot \\ \cdot \quad \cdot \quad \cdot \end{pmatrix}$$

and the subsequent, redistributed, population as

$$\pi_1 = (P'_1, P'_2, \cdots P'_j).$$

In this representation

$\pi_0 = $ the initial population
$P_1 = $ the initial population in the first areal or residence category
$P_2 = $ the initial population in the second areal or residence category
$P_i = $ the initial population in the i-th areal or residence category
$M_1 = $ the matrix, set, system, or "regime" of migration rates in the first interval studied
$m_{ij} = $ of persons initially in area or residence category i: the proportion migrating to area or residence category j during the interval
$\pi_1 = $ the population at the end of the interval
$P'_i = $ the population in the first areal or residence category at the end of the interval
$P'_j = $ the population in the j-th areal or residence category at the end of the interval.

The population transformation, consisting of a process of migration redistributing the population, was represented by the equation:

$$\pi_0 M_1 = \pi_1.$$

More generally, populations are subjected to sequences of migration regimes, $M_1 M_2 M_3 \ldots M_k \ldots$, in the first, second, third ... k-th intervals, which continuously effect shifts in the distribution of the population, resulting in $\pi_1, \pi_2, \pi_3, \cdots \pi_k$, etc.

TABLE 9.3
Percent Distribution of U.S. Population by Regions, 1870 to 1950

	1870	1880	1890	1900	1910	1920	1930	1940	1950
Total U.S.	100.0	100.0	100.0	100.0	100.0	100.0	100.0	100.0	100.0
Northeast	34.6	31.4	29.9	29.9	30.1	30.1	30.0	29.4	28.5
South	29.2	30.4	29.5	30.1	30.0	29.3	28.9	29.6	29.0
North Central	33.7	34.6	35.6	34.7	32.5	32.2	31.4	30.5	29.5
West	2.6	3.5	4.9	5.4	7.4	8.4	9.7	10.5	13.0

SOURCE: Eldridge and Thomas 1964, table 1.6.

Changes in the Regional Distribution of the U.S. Population Between 1870 and 1950

A summary of changes in the regional distribution of the U.S. population between 1870 and 1950 is given in table 9.3. As the table shows, the proportion of the total population residing in the Northeast dropped from 34.6 to 28.5 percent between 1870 and 1950, while that of the North Central region dropped from 33.7 to 29.5 percent. In the same period, the proportion of the population residing in the West increased greatly, from 2.6 to 13.0 percent, while the proportion residing in the South changed hardly at all.

In a monumental study at the University of Pennsylvania, a team of demographers and economists analyzed this 1870–1950 population redistribution and the relationship between it and simultaneous trends in the volume and structure of economic activity (Lee et al. 1957; Kuznets, Miller and Easterin 1960; Eldridge and Thomas 1964). Population redistribution, viewed as differential regional population growth, was analyzed by natural increase (births minus deaths) and by net migration (total in-migrants minus total out-migrants) for each decade between 1870 and 1950. The data are shown in table 9.4 and 9.5.

With the exception of the Northeast from 1900 to 1910, the decade in which European immigration to the U.S. reached its peak, the main component of population growth in regions *other than the West* was natural increase. For the West, however, in every decade, net migration was much more important than natural increase.

The South shows negative net migration (i.e., net *out*-migration) in every decade after 1880, and the North Central Region exhibits net out-migration in the 1930–1940 and 1940–1950 decades. As for natural increase, the South has consistently higher rates, and the Northeast consistently lower ones than the rest of the country. The West has consistently been characterized by spectacularly high *rates* of net migration, reaching close to 400 net migrants per 1,000 average population in both the 1880–

TABLE 9.4

*Natural Increase, Net Migration, and Total Increase, by
Regions, 1870–1880 to 1940–1950 (in thousands)*

	Natural Increase	Net Migration	Total Increase	Average Population
Northeast				
1870–1880	2,091	339	2,430	14,551
1880–1890	1,633	1,443	3,076	17,305
1890–1900	1,985	1,871	3,856	20,771
1900–1910	2,272	2,728	5,000	25,173
1910–1920	2,613	1,461	4,074	29,710
1920–1930	3,457	1,543	5,000	34,246
1930–1940	1,563	376	1,939	37,716
1940–1950	3,786	253	4,039	40,704
South				
1870–1880	3,895	112	4,007	13,254
1880–1890	3,368	− 236	3,132	16,823
1890–1900	4,342	− 91	4,252	20,626
1900–1910	4,698	− 23	4,675	25,132
1910–1920	4,451	− 985	3,466	29,202
1920–1930	5,983	−1,540	4,443	33,157
1930–1940	4,527	−1,091	3,436	37,097
1940–1950	6,947	−2,241	4,705	41,167
North Central				
1870–1880	3,392	991	4,383	15,173
1880–1890	3,341	1,660	5,000	19,864
1890–1900	3,400	529	3,929	24,315
1900–1910	3,151	400	3,551	28,047
1910–1920	3,063	1,072	4,135	31,890
1920–1930	3,982	572	4,554	36,234
1930–1940	2,266	− 717	1,549	39,286
1940–1950	4,684	− 577	4,107	42,114
West				
1870–1880	268	434	702	1,261
1880–1890	369	891	1,260	2,242
1890–1900	423	579	1,001	3,373
1900–1910	608	2,083	2,691	5,249
1910–1920	710	1,340	2,050	7,620
1920–1930	1,029	1,867	2,897	10,093
1930–1940	668	1,310	1,978	12,531
1940–1950	2,035	3,539	5,573	16,307

SOURCE: Eldridge and Thomas 1964, Vol. III, table 1.13.

1890 and 1900–1910 decades, and surpassing 100 net migrants per 1,000
average population even in the decade of the Great Depression, 1930–1940.

TABLE 9.5

*Rates of Natural Increase and Net Migration per 1,000 Average Population, by Regions,
1870–1880 to 1940–1950*

	Northeast		South		North Central		West	
	Natural increase	Net migration	Natural increase	Net migration	Natural increase	Net migration	Natural increase	Net migration
1870–1880	144	23	294	8	224	65	213	344
1880–1890	94	83	200	−14	168	84	164	397
1890–1900	96	90	211	− 4	140	22	125	172
1900–1910	90	108	187	− 1	112	14	116	397
1910–1920	88	49	152	−34	96	34	93	176
1920–1930	101	45	180	−46	110	16	102	185
1930–1940	41	10	122	−29	58	−18	53	105
1940–1950	93	6	169	−54	111	−14	125	217

SOURCE: Eldridge and Thomas 1964, Vol. III, table 1.14.

In regions other than the West, foreign-born whites consistently represent the major component of white net in-migration. For the West, however, the migration of native-born whites is net *out-migration* from these regions in most decades, native white net in-migration comprises the bulk of the decadal increments (Eldridge and Thomas 1964, Vol. III, table 1.22).

Migration out of the South in all decades included large proportions of Negroes moving primarily to the Northeast and North Central regions. The North Central region was characterized by a net in-migration of Negroes in all decades, but particularly after 1920. In-migration to the West was largely by native whites, with substantial Negro in-migration beginning only in the 1940–1950 decade (*ibid.*, chap. IV).

The redistribution of the population of the United States has been reflected not only in regional shifts but in great increases in the number of urban places, in the size and density of urban places, and in the proportion of the population in urban places increased from 5.1 percent in 1790 to 25.7 percent in 1870, and to 59.0 percent in 1950. The percentage of the population in cities of 100,000 or more increased from 10.7 percent in 1870 to 29.4 percent in 1950.

The Pennsylvania group was able to study the relationship between migration and urbanization only indirectly, since they were not able to study *intrastate* migration. They were able to conclude only

> that migration is very likely a unified problem, that urbanization has been in large measure a migration phenomenon and that the two processes, interstate migration and urban growth, have tended to vary together because they have migration in common and because they have been associated with pervasive changes in social and economic organization. [Eldridge and Thomas 1964, p. 226]

TABLE 9.6

Percentage Distribution of U.S. Native-Born Population, Aged 18 and Over, by Size of Birthplace and Size of Current Residence, 1958

Size of Birthplace	Size of Current Residence							
	Total	(1)	(2)	(3)	(4)	(5)	(6)	(7)
Total native population 18 years and over	100.0	15.2	19.5	9.9	12.3	15.7	15.6	11.8
(1) 500,000 or more	15.6	8.8	1.3	2.1	1.9	.6	.7	.2
(2) 50,000–499,999	14.8	1.4	7.9	1.5	1.9	1.0	.8	.3
(3) Metropolitan, 2,500–49,999	5.2	.4	.7	2.5	.8	.4	.3	.1
(4) Metropolitan, rural nonfarm	5.4	.3	.6	.4	3.3	.3	.4	.1
(5) Nonmetropolitan, 2,500–49,999	15.1	1.6	2.8	1.1	1.2	6.1	1.7	.6
(6) Nonmetropolitan, rural nonfarm	16.6	1.1	2.5	1.0	1.3	2.8	7.0	.9
(7) Farm	27.3	1.6	3.7	1.3	1.9	4.5	4.7	9.6

SOURCE: K. E. Taeuber, Chiazze, Jr., and Haenszel 1968, table 51.

Redistribution of the U.S. Native-Born Population in 1958

Some data bearing directly upon the relationship between migration and population redistribution are available from a recent study by K. E. Taeuber and associates (Taeuber, Chiazze, Jr., and Haenzel 1968). In a national sample of the U.S. population in 1958, persons aged 18 and over reported their residence *histories.* Their histories yielded a large amount of data concerning migratory moves, migrants, and places of origin and destination.

Table 9.6 shows the percentage distribution of the native-born population by size of birthplace and size of current residence. The diagonal cells represent persons whose 1958 place of residence was the same size as that of their birthplace and include 45 percent of the total native-born population. This percentage includes 29 percent who have *always* lived in the same place and 16 percent who have lived in at least two places. About 37 percent of the population reported moving to places larger than their birthplaces (the cells below the diagonal) and 18 percent reported moving to places smaller than their birthplaces (cells above the diagonal). Of the farm-born population (some 17 percent of the total) only a little more than one-third (35 percent) were in places classified as "farm" in 1958, and only a fourth (24 percent) were in "rural nonfarm" places; the rest (41 percent) were in cities. Of the total adult population in cities of 500,000 or more, about two-fifths were born in smaller places; and of the total in cities of 50,000–499,999 inhabitants, more than half were born in smaller places. As table 9.6 shows, the migratory shifts favored the metropolitan towns of 2,500–49,999 and of 50,000–499,999 (with 29.4 percent of the population in such places in 1958, compared to 20.0 percent born there). The table also reveals a very sharp decline in the farm population (11.8 percent in 1958, compared to 27.3 percent born there).

Some Conclusions on Migration and Economic Differentials

The Pennsylvania research group, whose study we described earlier in this section, conducted a very intricate analysis of relationships between income, economic activity, and migration rates, again for the period between 1870 and 1950. They concluded: (1) that the volume of net migration "responded positively and significantly" to swings in economic activity, increasing during periods of prosperity and diminishing during periods of depression; (2) that all major color-nativity sectors of the population (i.e., native-born white, foreign-born white, and Negro) responded to temporal variations in economic activity; (3) that the directions of migration were related positively to income per worker in the different regions and subregions, with the overall pattern of migration operating in support of a convergence of income levels and a decline of regional differences; (4) that some streams of migration took place in directions not consistent with income differentials; (5) that nonwhites seemed in general to be more responsive than whites to subregional income differentials (Eldridge and Thomas 1964, Part II, chap. 4, Conclusions). In other words, the migratory patterns were closely connected with differentials in income and economic opportunity, but not uniformly so for all population categories or groups. We shall return to this point below and in the final chapter of the book.

5. DIFFERENTIAL MIGRATION

There are at least three different kinds of questions to be asked concerning differential migration in large-scale and relatively highly differentiated societies:

1. What kinds of persons, or groups, migrate with high and with low frequencies?
2. What kinds of communities attract large inflows of migrants, and what kinds of communities generate large outflows?
3. What kinds of societies sustain high volumes of migration and what kinds sustain low ones?

As we shall see, the search for generalizations has been somewhat disappointing.

Differential Migration Among Individuals and Groups

D. J. Bogue (1956b) has summarized research findings bearing on the first question as follows:

> Only one migration differential seems to have systematically withstood the test—that for age. The following generalization has been found to be valid in many places and for a long period of time. Persons in their late teens, twenties, and early thirties are much more mobile than younger or older persons. Migration is highly associated with the first commitments and acts of adjustment of adulthood that are made by adolescents as they mature [e.g. entrance into the labor force, marriage, family formation].

Support for this generalization is found in many empirical studies in different social settings rendering this one of the most accepted generalizations in the social sciences.

Other differentials holding for the United States are indicated by Bogue as follows:

1. Men are more migratory than women, especially over long distances and when conditions at the destination are insecure or difficult.
2. Persons with professional occupations are among the most migratory groups in the population, whereas laborers and operatives (semi-skilled workers) have below average mobility.
3. Unemployed persons are more migratory than employed persons.
4. Negroes are less migratory than whites (*ibid.*, p. 504).

With regard to the last differential, Shryock (1964, table 11.1) notes that nonwhites (comprising primarily Negroes) have higher intracounty mobility rates than whites; he agrees, however, that they have lower migration rates, and he supports the rest of Bogue's conclusions.

In a study of migration in Chile, Herrich concluded that migrants were very similar to nonmigrants with regard to personal characteristics, except that migrant women were much more frequently in the labor force than were nonmigrant women (Herrich 1965, chap. 6; see also Slizagu 1966). In his study of internal migration in India between 1901 and 1931, Zachariah (1964) concluded that the number of male migrants exceeded female migrants, especially in long-distance and rural-urban streams, but that short-distance migration in rural areas was dominated by female migrants.

Studying migration among professional workers on the basis of the U.S. 1960 Census of Population, Ladinsky (1967) concluded that age differences are largely responsible for migration differentials, but that income, education, regional location, sex, family size, and marital status are also factors. In particular, he found that low income and high education operate to stimulate migration, whereas increased family size and advanced age dampen migration. In a study of migration to Bombay, India, Zachariah found that the propensity to migrate was unusually high among minority religious groups (Zachariah 1966).

Types of Communities Stimulating In-Migration and Out-Migration

In comparison with the findings above, there have been even fewer conclusions made on the kinds of communities attracting in-migration or generating out-migration. Indeed, very little is known about this aspect of differential migration. In his summary, Bogue (1959b) indicates that rates of out-migration from an area vary inversely with the general level of educational attainment in the area, and that, in general, rates of out-migration are closely related to rates of in-migration. Geographic variations in rates of mobility in the United States are shown in some detail by Shryock (1964), but no association is proposed between these variations and any areal classification or population category. Similarly, rates of out-migration and in-migration have been shown to differ systematically by "type of residence"—e.g., urban, rural, metropolitan, nonmetropolitan—but no attempt has been made to classify cities or other communities on this basis.

In an investigation of gross and net migration in which in-migration, out-migration, and net migration were studied in relation to population composition, income levels, and the demand for labor, I. S. Lowry (1966) found no evidence that labor-market conditions influence the rate of out-migration. Rates of out-migration are determined primarily by the composition of the population. The highest propensities to migrate are found among young single adults and among young adult couples with small children and populations with high proportions in these categories tend to have high rates of out-migration.

However, the choice of alternative destination *is* influenced by both distance to the destination and labor-market conditions there. Thus, rates of in-migration are affected by employment and income.

Depressed communities and prosperous communities *both* experience out-migration, primarily in relation to their age composition. However, while prosperous communities attract in-migrants from the national pool of persons "on the move," and especially from nearby places, depressed communities do not attract enough in-migrants to replace their out-migrants; hence, depressed communities are frequently characterized by negative net migration, or net out-migration, as well as by a shift in the age distribution toward higher proportions in the less mobile ages. By contrast, prosperous communities attracting an excess of in-migrants over out-migrants also may experience a shift in their age distributions over time toward higher proportions in the mobile ages. It is thus that long-depressed communities eventually become characterized by low rates of out-migration, complementing their low rates of in-migration, and that long-prosperous communities become characterized by higher rates of out-migration along with their higher rates of in-migration, a conclusion consistent with that of Bogue, cited above (Lowry 1966, chap. 5).

Intersocietal Comparisons of Migration

Finally, we have virtually no basis for intersocietal comparisons of volume of patterns of migration. Curiously, although there has been very substantial interest in international comparisons of volume and direction of social mobility (as we shall see in chapter 10), there appears to have been little interest in such comparative analyses of internal migration.

Thus, other than the correspondence between modal ages of migrants and modal ages of entrance into the labor force, marriage and earliest family formation, there is little basis for a theory of differential migration. Only the finding that professional workers are characterized by unusually high migration rates, and the conclusion that migration among professionals is part of occupational career mobility on the one hand and of family life cycle on the other may be suggestive of a "change and response" theory reminiscent of Davis's theory of differential intervention in marriage and family formation (see chapter 8, above).

Ladinsky's finding was that professionals whose careers are not tied either to equipment whose location is geographically fixed nor to clientele in a fixed locale very often move their places of residence in connection with job advancements. These movements, in turn, are concentrated in the early stages of their family life cycles—typically before deep involvement of children in their own educational and social locales. Thus certain professionals, who may be so located in the social and occupational structure as to have access to special economic and occupational opportunities—provided they move—do in fact move at rates higher than those of other occupational categories and of other social locations.

The hypothesis of a relationship between volume of migration and "numbers of opportunities," formulated originally by Stouffer (1940), appears repeatedly in the modern sociological and demographic literature on migration and mobility. An hypothesis bearing upon *differential* migration patterns would hold that individuals differently located in the social structure (1) have different degrees of knowledge about, and (2) are able to benefit to differing extents from, opportunities at places other than those in which they currently reside.[5]

Another hypothesis concerning differential migration would focus upon the predicament-resolving properties of migration. For example, Bogue (1959b, p. 499) has listed as stimulants to migration such predicaments as lack of an offer of marriage; loss of farm; loss of nonfarm employment; prolonged receipt of low income; retirement; death of spouse, parent, or other relative; onset of poor health; political, racial, or religious oppression and discrimination; disaster in the community; and forced movement resulting from legal enactments. To the extent that there are differential frequencies of the various predicaments in different population groups, we would expect differential resort to migration as a predicament-resolving tactic.[6]

Both hypotheses seem to find some support in such meager empirical materials as are available. But they both leave open the question of community and societal determinants of differential migration.

6. INDIVIDUAL, COMMUNITY, AND SOCIETAL CONSEQUENCES OF MIGRATION

Analyses of the consequences of geographic mobility are among those pursuits of social research in which great emphasis is placed upon the contradictions of human social existence. For although few such studies result in conclusions denying the individual or societal benefits of migration, a large number stress the personal and community disorganization, the problems of adjustment and conflict, the *anomie* and alienation, associated with migration.

Individual Consequences of Migration

A literature so vast as to defy concise summary—beginning probably with the classic *Polish Peasant in Europe and America* by W. I. Thomas and F. Znaniecki (1918–1920)—has arisen to describe and analyze the processes of adjustment and acculturation undergone by migrants in their new social settings. This literature has stressed the role segregation of migrants, i.e., their exclusion from certain spheres of activity and social life and their performance of specialized migrant roles in other spheres; and it has stressed the difficulties in adjustments and acculturation as-

5 For a similar hypothesis cast in terms of a theory of decision-making, see Beshers and Nishiura 1960, and Beshers 1967, especially chapter 5.

6 For discussions of differential frequencies of predicaments, see Matras, Rosenfeld, and Salzberger 1969; see also Rossi 1955.

sociated with the differences in norms, values, and customs of migrants and nonmigrants. As Louis Wirth (1945) wrote:

> As newer immigrant groups followed older waves, the latest comers increasingly became the objects of prejudice and discrimination on the part of natives and older immigrants alike. Moreover, as the various ethnic groups concentrated in specific areas and in large urban colonies and thus conspicuously unfolded their Old World cultural heritages, their life became virtually autonomous and hence, by isolation, their contact with the broad stream of American culture was retarded. In addition, their very success in competing with native and older settlers in occupations, professions, and business provoked antipathies which found expression in intolerance movements and in the imposition of official and unofficial restrictions and handicaps.
>
> Although the ethnic minorities in the United States suffer mainly from private prejudices rather than restrictive public policies, their path of assimilation is not without its serious obstacles. The distinctive cultures of the various ethnic groups are not merely assemblages of separable traits but historically welded wholes. Each immigrant group not only has its own language or dialect which serves as a barrier to intergroup communication and to the sharing of common ideas and ideals, but also its own religious, social, and even political institutions which tend to perpetuate group solidarity and to inhibit social intercourse with members of the "out" group. Moreover, each ethnic group in the United States, especially in the early period after its arrival, tends to occupy a characteristic niche in the economy which generates certain definite similarities among its members in occupation, standard of living, place of residence, and mode of life. On the basis of such likenesses within the group and differences without, stereotypes are built up and fixed attitudes arise which inhibit contact and develop social distances and prejudices. Overanxiety about being accepted sometimes results in a pattern of conduct among minorities that provokes a defense reaction on the part of the dominant group; these defense reactions may take the form of rebuffs which are likely to accentuate minority consciousness and thus retard assimilation.

A very large number of studies deal with the relationships between migrants or migrant status and alienation, delinquency, family disorganization, mental illness, unemployment and poverty, promiscuity, and also marriage, intermarriage, and fertility. Generally the findings have been that migrants have higher frequencies or rates of all these phenomena than have nonmigrants, and there have been analyses in varying detail of intervening variables and circumstances.

In the classic sociological work, *The City,* published in 1925, R. E. Park wrote:

> The mere movement of the population from one part of the country to another—the present migration of the Negroes—is a dis-

turbing influence. Such a movement may assume, from the point of view of the migrants themselves, the character of an emancipation, opening to them new economic and cultural opportunities, but it is none the less disorganizing to the communities into which they are now moving. It is at the same time demoralizing to the migrating people themselves, and particularly, I might add, to the younger generation.

The enormous amount of delinquency, juvenile and adult, that exists today in the Negro communities in northern cities is due in part, though not entirely, to the fact that migrants are not able to accommodate themselves at once to a new and relatively strange environment. The same thing may be said of the immigrants from Europe, or of the younger generation of women who are just now entering in such large numbers into the new occupations and the freer life which the great cities offer them. [Park 1925]

Bonilla (1961) describes the *favelas* of Rio de Janeiro:

Recent estimates put as many as a third of Rio's three-million inhabitants within these jerry-built, vertical islands of squalor. Children and adolescents make up a large part of that population . . .

The growth of the *favela* is thus linked to the general flight from the countryside into the cities of Brazil, to a generally high rate of demographic growth, to the excessive concentration of industry and commerce in a few major cities, and finally to an almost absolute absence of serious concern with the process of urban expansion among city officials. The anarchic growth of the city marked by large-scale profiteering and speculation in real estate and construction simply took no account of the housing needs of the large number in the city automatically eliminated from the housing market by their low incomes.

. . . The *favelado* is plagued by all the ills that beset his kind everywhere. As a group, the *favela* population is on the wrong side of every standard index of social disorganization, whether it be illiteracy, malnutrition, disease, job instability, irregular sexual unions, alcoholism, criminal violence, or almost any other on the familiar list.

A closely related literature has sought to analyze the conditions under which adjustment and acculturation in varying forms and degrees takes place. Most authors dealing with this problem have treated it as a matter of individual learning, accommodation, or "resocialization" (see Germani 1965 and 1961), but more recently an increasing number, following S. N. Eisenstadt (1954), have viewed it as a problem of social change or of change in role distributions or systems of role allocation. We shall return to this approach shortly.

Curiously, there has been little research dealing with the actual economic advantages reaped by migrants. On the one hand, migration tends to take place in "streams," and presumably there is a sufficient feedback of information from migrants to would-be migrants to suggest that repeated failures to find opportunities would have some effect upon the stream. The fact that migration streams continue would seem to suggest that some benefits are indeed obtained. On the other hand, there *is* considerable return migration along the path of any migration stream, which suggests that there may be high, or variable, rates of failure. Although there are empirical materials relating the volume of return migration to the volume or velocity of migration streams, these do not bear specifically upon the question of the migrant's "success" in his new setting.

Similarly, though there has been much concern with new predicaments presumably generated by, or at least associated with, migratory moves, there have been virtually no studies of the extent to which migration-stimulating predicaments are in fact resolved by migration.

Community Consequences of Migration

The community consequences of migration which have been studied are confined mainly to the areas of population size and composition, size and structure of the labor force, residential patterns, voluntary organizations, and political structure. In his analysis of the absorption of immigrants, Eisenstadt (1954) presents the problem of absorption as one of change in the role-allocation structures of both the migrant groups and the absorbing societies. The absorption process thus generates *change,* both in the migrant groupings and in the absorbing communities, the variables in question being: (1) the types of pluralistic structures—i.e. systematically *different* allocation of social roles—arising from different types of migration; (2) the limits, in various kinds of absorbing communities, to which pluralistic structures may develop without undermining the social structure; and (3) the types of disintegrative behavior which may develop on the part of both migrants and non-migrants, and the possibility of institutional disorganization and change taking place in the absorbing community.

Thus, Eisenstadt, in dealing primarily with migrant *groups* rather than with individuals, anticipated the study of what has since been called "chain migration"—the sequential migration of connected individuals to the same destination.[7] In Eisenstadt's scheme, the formation on the one hand of *landsmannschaften* (groups sharing common geo-cultural origin) and specialized religious, educational, or other institutions serving migrants, and the existence on the other hand of community patterns of residential, occupational, or social segregation are both subsumed under the rubric of differences in roles allotted to, and performed by, migrants and nonmigrants respectively. The community change may

7 Cf. the extensive use of this concept in Price 1964; and MacDonald and Mac-Donald 1964.

tend either toward the convergence of role distributions or toward the stabilization and institutionalization of separate, pluralistic role structures.

Thus Southern European immigrants to the large cities of the United States were initially segregated from the native-born population, concentrated in ethnic ghettos and unskilled occupations, and organized in ethnic church and mutual aid associations. That is, they were initially allotted special "immigrant" roles in a pluralistic structure. Later, the immigrants or their offspring dispersed residentially, occupationally, and socially, although their role distributions may not yet have converged entirely with those of "old American" parts of the population.

In a somewhat similar manner, black, Puerto Rican, and Mexican immigrants to the large cities of the United States were initially segregated residentially, occupationally, and socially from the native white population. But far from undergoing a change in the direction of role distributions converging with those of native whites, the evidence indicates an institutionalization of separate, pluralistic black and white role structures. (See Taeuber and Taeuber. 1964.)

Societal Consequences of Migration

The chief societal consequences of migration lie in the redistribution of the population both areally and by type of community. Thus, Shryock summarizes the historical record of the United States as follows:

> The dominant trend in the geographic redistribution of the population was along the advancing frontier of settlement essentially in the Westward direction. . . . Beginning later than the Westward movement was the movement out of the South to the North, . . . involving both whites and Negroes. The out-migration of Negroes was particularly heavy during World War II. In recent years there have been counter-movements of whites from the Northwest to certain metropolitan and urban areas in the South.
>
> The current trend of geographic redistribution involves movement out of the heartland of the United States to the seacoasts and to the shores of the Great Lakes. There has apparently been a net migratory movement from rural to urban areas for a long time. Within metropolitan areas there is now a centrifugal movement of population, most large cities losing people in the interchange with their own suburbs. [Shryock 1964, pp. 63–64]

Similar accounts can be put together for other countries as well. However, these descriptions do not complete the picture of the social and economic organizational effects of migratory movements: typically, the migration streams tend to be selective—that is, they include certain types of people and exclude others—so that far from there being a simple redistribution of the total population, there is a changing distribution of

TABLE 9.7

Indexes of Disproportionate Change for Three Educational Classes in the Chicago Metropolitan Area, 1950-1960: A Methodological Illustration[1]

Population (aged 25 and over) by Years of School Completed[2]	Percent of City Population, 1950	Percent of Ring Population, 1950	City-Ring Difference, 1950	Percent of City Population 1960	Percent of Ring Population 1960	City-Ring Difference, 1960	Indexes of Disproportionate Change, 1950-60
	(1)	(2)	(3)	(4)	(5)	(6)	(7)
Total	100.00	100.00		100.00	100.00		Col. (6) – Col. (3)
Grade	46.80	40.35	–6.45	42.92	30.13	– 12.79	–6.34
High	39.99	41.41	+1.42	42.80	47.90	+ 5.10	+3.68
College	13.21	18.24	+5.03	14.28	21.97	+ 7.69	+2.66

SOURCE: Schore and Pinkerton 1966, p. 494.

[1] The 1950 Standard Metropolitan Area (and its equivalent, the 1960 Standard Consolidated Area) for Chicago and Northwestern Indiana.

[2] "Grade" = 0 through 8 years; "High" = 1 to 4 years of high school; "College" = 1 to 4 or more years of college.

given types of people in distinct ways. Thus, for example, the interchange within metropolitan areas does not merely send net increases to the suburbs or "metropolitan ring"; rather it sends persons of higher income and status to the suburbs and persons of lower income and status from the suburbs to the cities, a process operating to polarize cities and metropolitan ring with respect to income and socioeconomic level (Schnore and Pinkerton 1966). Similarly, there is some evidence that systems of migratory movements deepen racial segregation (Duncan and Hauser 1960; Taeuber and Taeuber 1965, chaps. 6 and 7; Hodge and Hauser 1968).

The manner in which suburbanization trends have operated to concentrate higher-status population in the metropolitan ring and low-status persons in the central city is illustrated and measured for the Chicago metropolitan area in table 9.7. The table shows the composition of the central city and metropolitan ring populations respectively by educational achievement categories in 1950 and in 1960, city-ring compositional differences in 1950 and 1960, and "indexes of disproportionate change" during the ten-year period. For the Chicago metropolitan area, the indexes of disproportionate change show that the suburbs or metropolitan ring enjoyed disproportionate increases in population with high school or college educational levels and a disproportionate decrease in population with grade school education only. In table 9.8 it is seen that the same pattern occurred in 216 of the 363 U.S. metropolitan areas studied, i.e. that suburbanization generally operates to shift the higher-education-level population outside the central cities of metropolitan

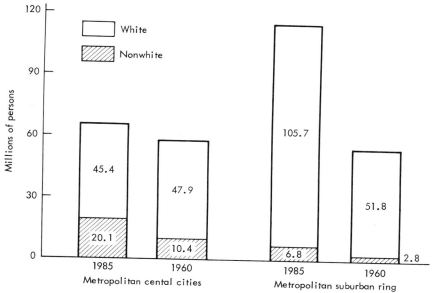

FIGURE 9.2. The prospect of further racial separation, showing growth of nonwhite proportion in central cities and of whites in suburbs. Source: Hodge and Hauser 1968, p. 54.

areas and to concentrate the lower-education-level population inside the central cities.

In-migration from overseas and rural-to-urban movements have been responsible historically for another major societal consequence: the

TABLE 9.8

Six Possible Patterns of Residential Redistribution of Three Educational Classes, Based on Indexes of Disproportionate Change for the Metropolitan Ring, 1950–1960

Type of Pattern:	"1"	"2"	"3"	"4"	"5"	"6"	Total
Grade	–	–	–	+	+	+	
High	+	+	–	+	–	–	
College	+	–	+	–	+	–	
Number of metropolitan areas by type	216	100	12	16	9	10	363
				13.0			
Percent of metropolitan areas by type	59.5	27.5	3.3	4.4	2.5	2.8	100.0

SOURCE: Schnore and Pinkerton 1966, p. 495.
A minus sign (–) indicates a disproportionate decline in the ring; a plus sign (+) indicates a disproportionate increase in the ring.

population of the great cities of America and the building of the industrial labor forces of the nineteenth and twentieth centuries in Europe and in the United States. Whether migratory movements in the Western world and in the underdeveloped countries today have the same relationship to industrialization, or whether they bear any relationship at all to changing economic organization, is a topic of fairly intensive current research.

10

Social and
Occupational Mobility

In social scientific investigations, the term "social mobility" has been used to describe two somewhat dissimilar, although not independent, kinds of phenomena. One is the change in the relative status, power, or prestige of different social groups, with consequent changes in social status for the individual members of these groups. Thus, the income or prestige of the individual clerk may rise over time if increasing importance, power, and control over resources accrues to clerical occupational groups. Similarly, as a family dynasty rises or falls, so may the fortunes, influence, style of life, and prestige of its individual members. A political group or party may be elected to power or seize power in a *coup*, increasing the responsibilities or benefits enjoyed by its members and supporters. In all such instances, the individual neither relinquishes a role nor acquires a new one; rather, the position or the role he *has* changes in its relationship to the total social structure.

This kind of "social mobility" has often been called "group mobility" or "class mobility." Basically, it involves a shift in role relationship between some group or category of roles and the rest of the social structure. It is the conscious attempt to initiate or promote such shifts, or conversely, the deliberate effort to frustrate, inhibit, or delay them, which is associated with the idea of group or class conflict.

In its second usage, "social mobility" refers to individual shifts among social roles.[1] Thus, just as individuals may change their place of residence, so may they change their other "social locations." They may change their occupations, employers, or branches of industry; their political associations, voluntary organizations, or religious affiliations; or the amount or intensity of their political, organizational, or religious activities.

In general such individual role changes do not affect the content or nature of the roles in question, and relationships of these roles to others and to the social structure remain unaffected. Usually it is only the individuals involved, and the aggregate distributions of individuals over roles, that are affected. However, we will qualify this later to indicate that patterns of individual role shifts do sometimes influence the relationships between roles.

This kind of mobility, which has often been called "individual mobility," is conceptually akin to migration; and, indeed, we shall try to show that it is usefully viewed as a process of population transformation that has much in common with the population transformations already discussed with regard to fertility and mortality, marriage and divorce, and migration. It is demographers and students of population who have been at the forefront of empirical research on patterns of "individual mobility," and it is this type of mobility with which we shall be concerned in this chapter, mentioning group or class mobility only tangentially. In the rest of the chapter we shall confine ourselves to an exploration of the problems formulated in the study of individual mobility and the approaches proposed for solving them, with particular attention given to occupational mobility.

2. OCCUPATIONAL MOBILITY: SOURCES OF DATA AND METHODS OF MEASUREMENT

INTRAGENERATIONAL AND INTERGENERATIONAL MOBILITY. The type of "individual social mobility" most extensively and intensively studied is occupational mobility. Persons are said to be occupationally mobile (1) if, in their working lives, they shift from one type of occupation to another, or (2) if their occupations are substantially different from those of their fathers. The first type of mobility, which is reckoned according to the individuals' own past occupations or occupational category or status,

---

1 For a penetrating discussion of the distinction between group mobility and individual mobility, see Ramsøy, in press.

is conventionally called *intragenerational mobility*. The second type, reckoned according to the parent's occupation or occupational category or status, is conventionally called *intergenerational mobility*.

Sources of Data

The measurement and portrayal of any type and of social mobility require that data on the social roles of interest be gathered by means of direct observation at two points in time, i.e., by means of direct observations of instances of change over an interval of time. Conventional sources of social or demographic data are usually of no help here, and the limited sources which do contain relevant information are often overlooked or ignored.

The most fruitful routine sources of data on individual changes are registers and listings which are maintained and updated over time. Thus, union membership records, tax and credit-rating files, selective service and social security records, insurance files, and the membership records of churches, political parties, and voluntary associations can all yield data on individual changes of occupation, residence, and other social roles.

Of course, some countries have full population registers which maintain current information on the population by sex, age, marital status, citizenship, and place of residence. However, while such registers are important sources of migration data, they generally do not include information on occupations.

As for population censuses and surveys, these are basically *counts* of population rather than registers, each count being carried out with regard to some *moment* in time. Every census count is, in principle, independent of the preceding one, so that individuals counted in two censuses are counted separately each time; thus, unless the census includes questions regarding previous status, no record is obtained of an individual's occupation or any other characteristic at the two points in time. However, it has become increasingly possible, technically, to link the records of an individual in two separate censuses or statistical investigations. Thus, through record linkage the researcher might relate an individual's occupation as reported in the 1960 U.S. population census to the same individual's occupation as reported in the 1970 U.S. population census. This could constitute data for the study of occupational shifts between 1960 and 1970.

Record linkage presents many technical problems for data processing. But even more important, it raises questions concerning the right and ability of an individual to protect his own privacy. Both beyond and within the ranks of data collectors, processors, and users, there has been a certain amount of wariness about—and, indeed, of opposition to—record linkage. However, it is important to recognize the technical feasibility of record linkage as well as its potential for generating the kinds of data required for the study of social mobility and social change generally.

Although censuses, surveys, and counts are not registers of population, they *are,* by the inclusion of certain information, able to count instances of change or nonchange among the populations investigated. Thus, as we saw in the previous chapter, it is possible in a single census to obtain the respondent's previous address—say of one year ago—as well as his current address; the two pieces of information together constitute a record of change or nonchange in residence over the one-year interval. In addition, we also indicated that entire residence histories can be obtained in a population survey by asking respondents where they resided at some previous date, or whether they changed residences within some specific interval, and that such data yield information on patterns of migration.

In the same way, censuses and surveys can yield retrospective data concerning occupations and other social roles. When their biases due to migration or mortality are taken into account,[2] census or survey data on the respondents' own past occupations or the occupations of their fathers yield revealing information on individual change or nonchange of occupation and represent a central source for the empirical investigation of social mobility.

Some Approaches to the Measurement of Occupational Mobility

We can portray an occupational mobility process and the manner by which it transforms the occupational structure by referring to a recent nationwide study of intergenerational and intragenerational occupational mobility in the United States (U.S. Bureau of the Census, *Current Population Reports,* Series p-23, No. 11, 1964; and Blau and Duncan 1967, chap. 1). In this study a large sample of males, aged 25 to 64, living in private households, were asked about their own and their father's occupations. The results are tabulated in table 10.1. The vertical totals in the table indicate the occupational distribution of the fathers of the respondents, while the horizontal totals show the occupational distribution of the respondents themselves. Similarly, the vertical and horizontal "no-answer" entries apply to the fathers and respondents respectively. The rest of the entries show the numbers of intergenerational occupational changes—or nonchanges in the cases of those in the main (top-left

---

2 Retrospective information concerning an individual's behavior during a time interval can be obtained only for those surviving and remaining in the population at the end of the period—a group generally *not* equivalent in number or in composition to the total number ever belonging to the population during the interval.

TABLE 10.1

Mobility from Father's Occupation to 1962 Occupation of Males, 25 to 64 Years of Age, in the Civilian Noninstitutional Population of the United States, March 1962 (frequencies in thousands)

Father's Occupation	Respondent's Occupation in March 1962																	No Answer	Total
	1	2	3	4	5	6	7	8	9	10	11	12	13	14	15	16	17		
Professionals																			
1. Self-Empl.	83	158	49	47	22	20	7	10	9	11	13	8	9	2	11	10	4	23	496
2. Salaried	40	388	157	72	58	93	21	46	54	12	84	63	41	12	7	10	2	58	1,218
3. Managers	50	320	275	88	111	108	16	77	75	44	57	36	21	15	12	7	2	100	1,414
4. Salesmen, other	32	137	165	101	72	41	27	22	42	15	20	29	13	—	6	8	2	46	778
5. Proprietors	106	390	522	165	455	175	94	100	148	112	146	102	80	14	35	32	11	155	2,842
6. Clerical workers	28	295	141	74	64	111	16	83	89	23	48	58	70	13	22	16	—	106	1,257
7. Salesmen, retail	5	92	95	59	77	43	18	39	23	21	59	34	31	1	21	15	—	39	672
Craftsmen																			
8. Mfg.	22	337	193	54	141	139	39	346	145	99	246	141	105	38	55	10	3	148	2,261
9. Other	23	286	236	99	167	195	38	200	313	114	211	236	118	32	71	24	8	199	2,570
10. Construction workers	17	130	138	51	161	153	16	200	158	268	145	119	100	22	84	16	12	142	1,932
Operatives																			
11. Mfg.	30	262	161	82	171	183	44	371	221	96	545	210	156	123	107	24	19	235	3,040
12. Other	16	304	134	67	174	165	37	186	246	130	273	330	155	55	110	25	30	198	2,635
13. Service workers	13	151	128	60	103	154	33	138	110	93	201	139	180	46	56	17	4	94	1,720
Laborers																			
14. Mfg.	6	42	37	5	23	31	5	75	42	20	127	66	66	50	41	12	6	55	703
15. Other	64	82	59	41	58	146	29	129	137	95	212	177	135	57	165	15	19	111	1,673
16. Farmers	2	439	421	126	677	447	109	580	696	595	1,056	890	499	251	557	1,696	405	826	10,334
17. Farm laborers	—	20	30	6	42	37	13	67	69	61	137	113	78	33	96	60	98	84	1,046
No answer	36	232	231	55	210	208	57	212	276	150	394	273	327	87	255	72	53	250	3,378
Total	573	4,065	3,172	1,252	2,786	2,449	619	2,881	2,853	1,959	3,974	3,024	2,184	851	1,711	2,069	678	2,869	39,969

SOURCE: Blau and Duncan 1967, Appendix J, table 2.1.

389

to bottom-right) diagonal cells—among this group of respondents vis-à-vis the occupational categories of their fathers. For example, the first horizontal row (under "I") shows that 83,000 of the 496,000 sons of self-employed professionals had become self-employed professionals themselves, but that only 4,100 had become farm laborers. Similarly, the first vertical column (under "1") shows that 83,000 of the 573,000 total respondents who became self-employed professionals were themselves sons of self-employed professionals; and 2,000 respondents who became self-employed professionals were sons of farm laborers.

There are many possible approaches to the measurement or summary of the mobility represented in table 10.1. Here are only a few examples:

1. The occupational distribution of the fathers and the sons may be compared, perhaps by using Δ, the Index of Dissimilarity (see chapter 4).

2. The number or percentage of mobile respondents, i.e., the sum of the nondiagonal (off the top-left to bottom-right diagonal) entries, or the number or percentage of nonmobile respondents, can easily be computed. Similarly, if the occupational groups are ranked in some way, then the numbers or percentages that are upwardly mobile (below the top-left to bottom-right diagonal) and downwardly mobile (above the diagonal) can easily be computed.

3. A measure of association may be used to calculate the relationship between fathers' and sons' occupations; and the statistical significance of such relationships can easily be tested. Measures of association are presented in most elementary statistics texts.

4. Rates of entrance into the different occupational groups can be computed for each group of sons classified by father's occupation (in other words, row-wise percentage distributions can be calculated). Such a table of rates or percentage distributions—a "standard outflow table"—allows the researcher to compare the differential opportunities attached to the sons' various occupational origins (see table 10.2).

Examining the horizontal entries of table 10.2, it can be seen that sons of professional fathers are themselves more likely to be professionals than anything else, while sons of retail salesmen are more likely to be *almost anything other* than salesmen. About 37 percent of the respondents who reported that their fathers' were retail salesmen were themselves professionals, about 19 percent were operatives (semi-skilled), but less than three percent were retail salesmen. All but about 20 percent of the sons of farmers, and all but about 15 percent of the sons of farm laborers, were themselves in nonagricultural occupations.

Leaving the row comparisons and comparing the sons' chances of moving into professional roles, i.e. entries in the first column, it is clear

TABLE 10.2

Mobility from Father's Occupation to 1962 Occupation of Males, 25 to 64 years of Age: Outflow Percentages

Father's Occupation	Respondent's Occupation in March 1962																	Total[a]
	1	2	3	4	5	6	7	8	9	10	11	12	13	14	15	16	17	
Professionals																		
1. Self-Empl.	16.7	31.9	9.9	9.5	4.4	4.0	1.4	2.0	1.8	2.2	2.6	1.6	1.8	.4	2.2	2.0	.8	100.0
2. Salaried	3.3	31.9	12.9	5.9	4.8	7.6	1.7	3.8	4.4	1.0	6.9	5.2	3.4	1.0	.6	.8	.2	100.0
3. Managers	3.5	22.6	19.4	6.2	7.9	7.6	1.1	5.4	5.3	3.1	4.0	2.5	1.5	1.1	.8	.5	.1	100.0
4. Salesmen, other	4.1	17.6	21.2	13.0	9.3	5.3	3.5	2.8	5.4	1.9	2.6	3.7	1.7	.0	.8	1.0	.3	100.0
5. Proprietors	3.7	13.7	18.4	5.8	16.0	6.2	3.3	3.5	5.2	3.9	5.1	3.6	2.8	.5	1.2	1.1	.4	100.0
6. Clerical workers	2.2	23.5	11.2	5.9	5.1	8.8	1.3	6.6	7.1	1.8	3.8	4.6	5.6	1.0	1.8	1.3	.0	100.0
7. Salesmen, retail	.7	13.7	14.1	8.8	11.5	6.4	2.7	5.8	3.4	3.1	8.8	5.1	4.6	.1	3.1	2.2	.0	100.0
Craftsmen																		
8. Mfg.	1.0	14.9	8.5	2.4	6.2	6.1	1.7	15.3	6.4	4.4	10.9	6.2	4.6	1.7	2.4	.4	.1	100.0
9. Other	.9	11.1	9.2	3.9	6.5	7.6	1.5	7.8	12.2	4.4	8.2	9.2	4.6	1.2	2.8	.9	.3	100.0
10. Construction workers	.9	6.7	7.1	2.6	8.3	7.9	.8	10.4	8.2	13.9	7.5	6.2	5.2	1.1	4.3	.8	.6	100.0
Operatives																		
11. Mfg.	1.0	8.6	5.3	2.7	5.6	6.0	1.4	12.2	7.3	3.2	17.9	6.9	5.1	4.0	3.5	.8	.6	100.0
12. Other	.6	11.5	5.1	2.5	6.6	6.3	1.4	7.1	9.3	4.9	10.4	12.5	5.9	2.1	4.2	.9	1.1	100.0
13. Service workers	.8	8.8	7.4	3.5	6.0	9.0	1.9	8.0	6.4	5.4	11.7	8.1	10.5	2.7	3.3	1.0	.2	100.0
Laborers																		
14. Mfg.	.0	6.0	5.3	.7	3.3	4.4	.7	10.7	6.0	2.8	18.1	9.4	9.4	7.1	5.8	1.7	.9	100.0
15. Other	.4	4.9	3.5	2.5	3.5	8.7	1.7	7.7	8.2	5.7	12.7	10.6	8.1	3.4	9.9	.9	1.1	100.0
16. Farmers	.6	4.2	4.1	1.2	6.0	4.3	1.1	5.6	6.7	5.8	10.2	8.6	4.8	2.4	5.4	16.4	3.9	100.0
17. Farm Laborers	.2	1.9	2.9	.6	4.0	3.5	1.2	6.4	6.6	5.8	13.1	10.8	7.5	3.2	9.2	5.7	9.4	100.0
Total[b]	.4	10.2	7.9	3.1	7.0	6.1	1.5	7.2	7.1	4.9	9.9	7.6	5.5	2.1	4.3	5.2	1.7	100.0

SOURCE: Blau and Duncan 1967, table 2.2.

[a]Rows as shown do not total 100.0, since men not previously employed are not shown separately.

[b]Includes men not reporting father's occupation.

that the sons of nonprofessional white-collar workers are much more likely to become professionals than are the sons of skilled and semi-skilled workers. The latter, in turn, are much more likely to become professionals than are the sons of laborers or farmers. We proceed now to two more approaches to the measurement of mobility.

> 5. For each occupational group of the sons, percentages originating in each of the fathers' groups may be computed (column-wise percentage distributions). Such a table of proportions or percentages —a "standard inflow table"—allows the researcher to compare the compositions of the sons' final occupational groups by sons' occupational origins (table 10.3).

Table 10.3 shows that self-recruitment is greatest among farmers, some 82 percent of the farmer respondents reporting that their fathers also were farmers. The professional groups, taken together, are also characterized by high self-recruitment. Some 36 percent of the self-employed professionals, 25 percent of the salaried ones, 20 percent of the managers, and 25 percent of the salesmen and other professionals were recruited from among sons of professional fathers. High percentages of professionals were recruited from among the sons of proprietors. Since a large number of the respondents were of farm origin, large percentages in every occupational group are drawn from the sons of farmers. But the percentages recruited from among the sons of farmers are systematically higher in the blue-collar than in the white-collar occupations. We shall now examine a final approach to the measurement of mobility.

> 6. Assuming that under strict equality of opportunity, equal percentages from each group of origin would enter each of the final groups (i.e., that the row-wise percentage distributions would be identical), we achieve a hypothetical mobility regime which can be called "perfect mobility." A measure of deviation can then be made by comparing the sons' actual occupational distribution —the actual mobility regime—with the "perfect mobility" regime. This measure, the "index of association," is simply the ratio of an actual percentage in a diagonal (i.e. sons in same category as fathers) cell to the expected percentage in the same cell under "perfect mobility." The index of association is a measure of "occupational inheritance," or the extent to which sons tend to enter their fathers' occupational categories beyond the degree implied under the "perfect mobility" of a completely egalitarian mobility regime (such computations are presented in Blau and Duncan 1967, table 2.5).

Data showing *intragenerational* mobility, from the sons' first jobs to their present occupations, are shown in tables 10.4 and 10.5. The standard inflow table as well as all the measures and indices mentioned

TABLE 10.3
Mobility from Father's Occupation to Occupation in 1962, for Males Ages 25 to 64: Inflow Percentages

Father's Occupation	Respondent's Occupation in March 1962																
	1	2	3	4	5	6	7	8	9	10	11	12	13	14	15	16	17
Professionals																	
1. Self-Empl.	14.5	3.9	1.5	3.8	.8	.8	1.1	.3	.3	.6	.3	.3	.4	.2	.6	.5	.6
2. Salaried	7.0	9.5	4.9	5.8	2.1	3.8	3.4	1.6	1.9	.6	2.1	2.1	1.9	1.4	.4	.5	.3
3. Managers	8.7	7.9	8.7	7.0	4.0	4.4	2.6	2.7	2.6	2.2	1.4	1.2	1.0	1.8	.7	.3	.3
4. Salesmen, other	5.6	3.4	5.2	8.1	2.6	1.7	4.4	.8	1.5	.8	.5	1.0	.6	.0	.4	.4	.3
5. Proprietors	18.5	9.6	16.5	13.2	16.3	7.1	15.2	3.5	5.2	5.7	3.7	3.4	3.7	1.6	2.0	1.5	1.6
6. Clerical workers	4.9	7.3	4.4	5.9	2.3	4.5	2.6	2.9	3.1	1.2	1.2	1.9	3.2	1.5	1.3	.8	.0
7. Salesmen, retail	.9	2.3	3.0	4.7	2.8	1.8	2.9	1.4	.8	1.1	1.5	1.1	1.4	.1	1.2	.7	.0
Craftsmen																	
8. Mfg.	3.8	8.3	6.1	4.3	5.1	5.7	6.3	12.0	5.1	5.1	6.2	4.7	4.8	4.5	3.2	.5	.4
9. Other	4.0	7.0	7.4	7.9	6.0	8.0	6.1	6.9	11.0	5.8	5.3	7.8	5.4	3.8	4.1	1.2	1.2
10. Construction workers	3.0	3.2	4.4	4.1	5.8	6.2	2.6	6.9	5.5	13.7	3.6	3.9	4.6	2.6	4.9	.8	1.8
Operatives																	
11. Mfg.	5.2	6.4	5.1	6.5	6.1	7.5	7.1	12.9	7.7	4.9	13.7	6.9	7.1	14.5	6.3	1.2	2.8
12. Other	2.8	7.5	4.2	5.4	6.2	6.7	6.0	6.5	8.6	6.6	6.9	10.9	7.1	6.5	6.4	1.2	4.4
13. Service workers	2.3	3.7	4.0	4.8	3.7	6.3	5.3	4.8	3.9	4.7	5.1	4.6	8.2	5.4	3.3	.8	.6
Laborers																	
14. Mfg.	.0	1.0	1.2	.4	.8	1.3	.8	2.6	1.5	1.0	3.2	2.2	3.0	5.9	2.4	.6	.9
15. Other	1.0	2.0	1.9	3.3	2.1	6.0	4.7	4.5	4.8	4.8	5.3	5.9	6.2	6.7	9.6	.7	2.8
16. Farmers	11.2	10.8	13.3	10.1	24.3	18.3	17.6	20.1	24.4	30.4	26.6	29.4	22.8	29.5	32.6	82.0	59.7
17. Farm Laborers	.3	.5	.9	.5	1.5	1.5	2.1	2.3	2.4	3.1	3.4	3.7	3.6	3.9	5.6	2.9	14.5
Total[a]	100.0	100.0	100.0	100.0	100.0	100.0	100.0	100.0	100.0	100.0	100.0	100.0	100.0	100.0	100.0	100.0	100.0

SOURCE: Blau and Duncan, 1967, table 2.8.
[a]Columns as shown do not total 100.0, since men not reporting father's occupation are not shown separately.

TABLE 10.4

Mobility from First Job to Present Occupation for Males, Ages 25 to 64, in the Civilian Noninstitutional Population of the United States, March 1962 (frequencies in thousands)

First Job	1	2	3	4	5	6	7	8	9	10	11	12	13	14	15	16	17	No Answer	Total
Professionals																			
1. Self-Empl.	147	70	5	13	7	4	–	4	2	–	2	–	–	–	7	–	2	12	275
2. Salaried	188	1,585	358	82	161	142	11	47	57	12	36	35	28	2	8	28	4	123	2,907
3. Managers	6	99	173	21	44	32	11	11	20	14	10	7	6	3	6	3	2	17	485
4. Salesmen, other	3	46	136	128	67	27	15	3	18	7	29	21	15	–	–	2	–	24	541
5. Proprietors	2	16	45	15	85	6	6	4	5	1	10	10	7	2	5	9	–	6	234
6. Clerical workers	68	551	733	307	327	744	77	194	182	109	237	177	187	41	78	50	9	258	4,229
7. Salesmen, retail	39	189	295	139	219	219	96	85	90	54	115	140	58	20	36	19	1	75	1,889
Craftsmen																			
8. Mfg.	11	112	101	32	157	53	9	290	96	55	117	45	48	10	51	29	–	72	1,288
9. Other	5	136	101	29	157	63	52	166	323	71	108	83	54	21	26	18	10	96	1,519
10. Construction workers	3	48	29	14	95	27	2	76	113	225	43	37	21	9	27	18	7	65	859
Operatives																			
11. Mfg.	24	366	317	119	416	367	104	801	400	277	1,124	456	280	189	206	122	35	364	5,967
12. Other	20	221	268	130	384	189	50	321	476	305	422	661	265	61	187	81	44	311	4,396
13. Service workers	7	108	74	21	95	76	19	52	97	95	202	117	302	38	88	6	7	119	1,523
Laborers																			
14. Mfg.	7	110	79	31	58	125	25	211	107	78	364	177	147	165	126	33	35	137	2,015
15. Other	8	176	175	78	216	133	41	196	310	220	339	346	201	78	371	69	30	229	3,216
16. Farmers	3	29	32	23	47	38	15	52	74	68	104	63	58	18	45	449	63	67	1,248
17. Farm laborers	12	99	135	43	268	156	60	302	362	313	595	529	328	160	382	1,101	398	461	5,704
No answer	20	104	116	27	83	48	26	66	121	55	117	120	179	34	62	32	31	433	1,674
Total	573	4,065	3,172	1,252	3,786	2,449	619	2,881	2,853	1,959	3,974	3,024	2,184	851	1,711	2,069	678	2,869	39,969

Occupation in March 1962

SOURCE: Blau and Duncan 1967, table 2.3.

TABLE 10.5

Mobility from First Job to 1962 Occupation for Males Aged 25 to 64: Outflow Percentages

First Job	Respondent's Occupation in March 1962																	Total[a]
	1	2	3	4	5	6	7	8	9	10	11	12	13	14	15	16	17	
Professionals																		
1. Self-Empl.	53.5	25.5	1.8	4.7	2.5	1.5	.0	1.5	.7	.0	.7	.0	.0	.0	2.5	.0	.7	100.0
2. Salaried	6.5	54.5	12.3	2.8	5.5	4.9	.4	1.6	2.0	.4	1.2	1.2	1.0	.0	.3	1.0	.1	100.0
3. Managers	1.2	20.4	35.7	4.3	9.1	6.6	2.3	2.3	4.1	2.9	2.1	1.4	1.2	.1	1.2	.6	.4	100.0
4. Salesmen, other	.6	8.5	25.1	23.7	12.4	5.0	2.8	.6	3.3	1.3	5.4	3.9	2.8	.6	.0	.4	.0	100.0
5. Proprietors	.9	6.8	19.2	6.4	36.3	2.6	2.6	1.7	2.1	.4	4.3	4.3	3.0	.0	2.1	3.8	.0	100.0
6. Clerical	1.6	13.0	17.3	7.3	5.4	17.6	1.8	4.6	4.3	2.6	5.6	4.2	4.4	.9	1.8	1.2	.2	100.0
7. Salesmen, retail	2.1	10.0	15.6	7.4	11.6	11.6	5.1	4.5	4.8	2.9	6.1	7.4	3.1	1.1	1.9	1.0	.1	100.0
Craftsmen																		
8. Mfg.	.9	8.7	7.8	2.5	12.2	4.1	.7	22.5	7.5	4.3	9.1	3.5	3.7	.8	4.0	2.3	.0	100.0
9. Other	.3	9.0	6.6	1.9	10.3	4.1	3.4	10.9	21.3	4.7	7.1	5.5	3.6	1.4	1.7	1.2	.7	100.0
10. Construction workers	.3	5.6	3.4	1.6	11.1	3.1	.2	8.8	13.2	26.2	5.0	4.3	2.4	1.0	3.1	2.1	.8	100.0
Operatives																		
11. Mfg.	.4	6.1	5.3	2.0	7.0	6.2	1.7	13.4	6.7	4.6	18.8	7.6	4.7	3.2	3.5	2.0	.6	100.0
12. Other	.5	5.0	6.1	3.0	8.7	4.3	1.1	7.3	10.8	6.9	9.6	15.0	6.0	1.4	4.3	1.8	1.0	100.0
13. Service workers	.5	7.1	4.9	1.4	6.2	5.0	1.2	3.4	6.4	6.2	13.3	7.7	19.8	2.5	5.8	.4	.5	100.0
Laborers																		
14. Mfg.	.3	5.5	3.9	1.5	2.9	6.2	1.2	10.5	5.3	3.9	18.1	8.8	7.3	8.2	6.3	1.6	1.7	100.0
15. Other	.2	5.5	5.4	2.4	6.7	4.1	1.3	6.1	9.6	6.8	10.5	10.8	6.3	2.4	11.5	2.1	.9	100.0
16. Farmers	.2	2.3	2.6	1.8	3.8	3.0	1.2	4.2	5.9	5.4	8.3	5.0	4.6	1.4	3.6	30.0	5.0	100.0
17. Farm laborers	.2	1.7	2.4	.8	4.7	2.7	1.1	5.3	6.3	5.5	10.4	9.3	5.8	2.8	6.7	19.3	7.0	100.0

SOURCE: Blau and Duncan 1967, table 2.4.

[a]Rows as shown to not total 100.0, since men not in the experienced civilian labor force are not shown separately.

in connection with the data on intergenerational mobility, are easily computed for the intragenerational data as well.

What is probably most remarkable about table 10.5 are the generally low entries in the cells, i.e., the smallness of the likelihood—other than for professionals—of remaining in the same kind of occupation as one had in one's first job. Within this general trend, there were some major differentials: those beginning their careers in white-collar occupations were more likely to move on to professional occupations than were those beginning in blue-collar jobs, and craftsmen and skilled workers were considerably more likely to continue in their initial occupational groups than were clerical workers. Those beginning as proprietors and farmers were more likely than everyone, except professionals, to remain in their initial categories.

3. THE OCCUPATIONAL MOBILITY REGIME

The pattern of individual occupational shifts discussed in the preceding section represents an occupational mobility *regime,* and it is important that we explore further the nature of such a regime as the social process directly transforming the population's occupational structure from what it is at some initial point in time to what it becomes at some subsequent time. Regardless of how mobility and change in the occupational structure are ultimately measured, a table of the form of table 10.2 represents one of the most detailed ways available for quantifying the occupational mobility regime.

A Representation of the Occupational Mobility Regime

We can denote the initial (or fathers') occupational distribution by a Greek letter and a subscript—say, π_0—and the subsequent (or sons') occupational distribution by the same letter but with a subscript greater by one to indicate the fact that one time interval has elapsed, that is, by π_1. Occupational distributions at subsequent points in time would then be π_2, π_3, π_4, etc. We can represent the *set* of mobility *rates* characterizing the process in the first interval by a Latin letter and a subscript, M_1; thus, the subsequent sets of mobility rates in the following intervals would be M_2, M_3, etc. The entire mobility regime taking place in the first interval would then be represented as

$$\pi_0 \, M_1 = \pi_1. \tag{1}$$

In English, this equation says: the mobility process (i.e., the set of mobility rates), M_1, operates upon the initial occupational distribution to effect a new occupational distribution, π_1.[3]

Similarly, the mobility process of the second interval can be denoted as

$$\pi_1 \, M_2 = \pi_2, \tag{2}$$

which means that the mobility process, M_2, of the second interval operates on the "time one" occupational structure, π_1, to effect a new, "time two," occupational structure, π_2.

It should be easy to see that the left side of equation (1) can be substituted for π_1, in equation (2), producing

$$\pi_0 \, M_1 \, M_2 = \pi_2, \tag{3}$$

which means that the *sequence* of mobility processes—M_1 in the first interval, then M_2 in the second—operates upon an initial ("time zero") occupational distribution, π_0, to effect a new occupational distribution, π_2. More generally, we can represent a sequence of mobility regimes either as

$$
\begin{aligned}
\pi_0 \, M_1 &= \pi_1 \\
\pi_1 \, M_2 &= \pi_2 \\
\pi_2 \, M_3 &= \pi_3 \\
\pi_3 \, M_4 &= \pi_4 \\
&\cdot \\
&\cdot \\
&\cdot \\
\pi_{n-1} \, M_n &= \pi_n
\end{aligned}
\tag{4a}
$$

where the n denotes the last time interval, and M_n the last mobility regime, considered, or as

$$\pi_0 \, M_1 \, M_2 \, M_3 \, M_4 \cdots M_{n-1} \, M_n = \pi_n \tag{4b}$$

This representation is similar to those sketched in earlier chapters to describe migration, marriage, and the process of population growth and compositional change. (Earlier formulations of this idea are found in Hauser and Duncan 1959; Schnore 1961; and Ryder 1964.)

3 Those familiar with elementary matrix algebra will recognize that if the fathers' occupational distribution in table 10.1 is taken as in initial *vector* π_0, and if the set of mobility rates from the standard outflow table is arranged as a square *matrix*, M_1, and if the sons' occupational distribution is represented by π_1, then equation (1) exactly describes the mobility regime represented by table 10.1, and equations (2), (3), (4a), and (4b) exactly describe the sequence of such transformations. Cf., also chapter 5, and discussion of population transformations there.

Questions in the Investigation of Occupational Mobility Regimes

Mobility regimes and sequences of mobility regimes provoke the following questions:

1. What are the factors affecting M, the pattern of mobility rates, and, in particular, what are the relationships between π_0 and M_1, between π_1 and M_1, and between π_0 and π_1 jointly and M_1? In other words, how do the initial and the subsequent occupational distributions separately and jointly affect the pattern of mobility rates?

2. What are the relationships between successive patterns of mobility rates or between sequences of such patterns? That is, what is the relationship between M_i and M_{i+1}, the sets of mobility rates in successive time intervals, or between pairs, triplets, or other clusters of mobility-rate patterns in the sequence $M_1 M_2 M_3 \cdots M_{n-1} M_n$? It is of particular interest to study the extent to which mobility-rate patterns or parts of them recur (i.e., are stable over time), both empirically and theoretically. The bounds upon variation in mobility-rate patterns in a sequence are also of great interest.

3. Finally, the new occupational distributions—the proportions in each of the various occupational categories—generated by the various mobility-rate patterns or by the various sequences of such patterns are of considerable interest and have great bearing on the analysis of changing social structure generally. In terms of our symbols, we refer here to the new occupational distributions, $\pi_1, \pi_2, \pi_3 \cdots \pi_n$, resulting from the mobility regimes,

$$\pi_0 \, M_1 = \pi_1$$
$$\pi_1 \, M_2 = \pi_2$$
$$\pi_2 \, M_3 = \pi_3$$
$$\vdots$$
$$\pi_{n-1} \, M_n = \pi_n$$

or from the sequences of mobility patterns,

$$\pi_0 \, M_1 = \pi_1$$
$$\pi_0 \, M_1 \, M_2 = \pi_2$$
$$\pi_0 \, M_1 \, M_2 \, M_3 = \pi_3$$
$$\vdots$$
$$\pi_0 \, M_1 \, M_2 \, M_3 \cdots M_{n-1} \, M_n = \pi_n.$$

4. Beyond the scope of the symbolic representations in equations (1) to (4), there lies the question of the further social structural consequences of changing occupational distributions. In other words, to what extent does the changing occupational distribution entail changing relationships between social roles or subsystems? The obverse of this question is: To what extent do changing relationships between occupational roles or occupational groups and the social structure generate mobility and changes in occupational distribution?

5. Also beyond the scope of our equations are the social psychological consequences of mobility. Many of the questions formulated in this area concern personal "adjustment," personal relationships, or mental health, and these clearly lie beyond the focus of this book. However, at least some social psychological correlates of mobility—for example, marriage and childbearing, change of residence, and school enrollment—have very broad and important implications for demography and social structure.

4. FACTORS AFFECTING THE PATTERN OF MOBILITY RATES

The General Approach to Individual Mobility

Discussions of factors affecting mobility rates are conventionally cast in terms of the conditions under which individuals are or are not occupationally mobile or in terms of the directions and distances of their mobility. Occasionally, the discussions concern the nature and conditions of recruitment into or out of specific occupations or occupational groupings, but only rarely do they envision a set of mobility rates as part of population process.

The discussion of individual mobility is always organized with reference to some set of categories. These may be as simple as the twofold "manual-nonmanual" scheme or the three-fold "manual-nonmanual-farm" scheme used in cross-national comparisons (see, for example, Lipset and Bendix, 1959), or they may be as elaborate as those used by Blau and Duncan (1967) and reproduced here in tables 10.1–10.5. Whatever categories are used, mobility is then considered in one of two ways. First, it may be viewed in terms of the chances of persons variously located in the social structure to achieve some specified occupational role or status. Alternatively, mobility may be viewed in terms of the chances that persons *beginning* their careers, or *beginning* their lives, at various locations in the social structure have of *improving upon their initial* occupational status or origins.

The characteristics found to bear upon an individual's chances of achieving any given occupational status include:

1. The individual's initial occupational status or the occupational status of his parents.
2. His education.
3. His residential history (e.g., farm origin or not, migrant or not).
4. The size of his family of orientation; his position among siblings.
5. His race, ethnicity, national origin, region, and community size or type.
6. His marital status; the size of his family of procreation.
7. His intelligence.
8. His motivation.
9. His age, year of birth, and year of entrance into the working force.

It is important to note that these variables have typically *not* been studied in connection with variations in mobility rates or patterns of rates, but only as personal characteristics of those achieving or retaining —or failing to achieve or retain—given types or levels of occupational status. We must recognize that, even if persons with higher educational achievement are more likely to be mobile or to achieve a given status than are persons with low educational achievement, *it does not necessarily follow* that societies or communities with high modal levels of educational attainment, or with extended compulsory school attendance, or with a high investment in education, will be characterized by higher rates or different directions of mobility than other communities. Similarly, even if sons of professionals and proprietors are more likely to achieve high status than the sons of others, it does not follow that societies with high proportions of professionals and proprietors necessarily have higher rates of mobility than others; and so forth. In other words, characteristics that bear upon individual rates or directions of mobility do not necessarily have corresponding "structural" effects for aggregate societal patterns of mobility.

Effects of Country of Origin upon the Mobility of Immigrants in Canada

In a study of social mobility among immigrants in Canada, A. H. Richmond (1964) obtained information on:

1. occupation of respondent's father;
2. respondent's own occupation in his former country;
3. respondent's first job in Canada;
4. respondent's occupation in Canada at the time of the survey (February 1961).

TABLE 10.6
Socioeconomic Status of Immigrants and Their Fathers

Code[a]	Father's Occupation		Former Occupation		First Job in Canada		Job: February 1961	
	No.	*Percent*	*No.*	*Percent*	*No.*	*Percent*	*No.*	*Percent*
	United Kingdom							
1	11	8.9	10	8.1	7	5.7	15	12.1
2	14	11.3	7	5.7	6	4.8	7	5.7
3	5	4.0	18	14.5	16	12.9	19	15.3
4	14	11.3	26	21.0	24	19.4	21	16.9
5	51	41.1	37	29.8	32	25.8	33	26.6
6	13	10.5	15	12.1	31	25.0	18	14.5
7	1	0.8	8	6.5	4	3.2	11	8.9
—	15	12.1	3	2.4	4	3.2	—	—
Total	124	100	124	100	124	100	124	100
	Non-United Kingdom							
1	29	8.2	10	2.8	5	1.4	11	3.1
2	28	7.9	21	5.9	14	4.0	19	5.4
3	15	4.2	16	4.5	6	1.7	12	3.4
4	20	5.6	37	10.5	10	2.8	30	8.5
5	105	29.7	94	26.6	70	19.8	116	32.8
6	110	31.1	119	33.6	218	61.6	151	42.7
7	2	0.6	33	9.3	10	2.8	15	4.2
—	45	12.7	24	6.8	21	5.9	—	—
Total	354	100	354	100	354	100	354	100

SOURCE: Richmond 1964, p. 544, table 1.

[a]Code: 1–Higher managerial   5–Highly skilled
           2–Higher professional   6–Other skilled, semiskilled, and unskilled
           3–Intermediate   7–Not in labor force and nonemployed, including students.
           4–Clerical and sales   —No reply

Table 10.6, which presents the data collected on all four points, distinguishes between British and non-British immigrants. Immigrants from the United Kingdom constituted about a quarter of the total immigrant population in Canada in 1961, and their social origins were generally higher than those of the immigrants from other countries. As the table shows, emigration to Canada from Britain took place mainly among persons with middle-class or upper working-class backgrounds. Only 12 percent of the British immigrants, compared to one-third of those from other countries, were in semiskilled or unskilled occupational categories before emigration.

Table 10.7 gives us some additional information: Among the British immigrants whose fathers were in the nonmanual, or white-collar, categories, two-thirds were themselves in nonmanual categories in the United Kingdom, and more than three-fourths (77 percent) had found white-

TABLE 10.7
Intergenerational Mobility of Postwar Immigrants in Canada (Outflow Analysis)

Father's Occupation[a]	1-4 Former Per-cent	1-4 Can. 1961 Per-cent	5 Former Per-cent	5 Can. 1961 Per-cent	6 Former Per-cent	6 Can. 1961 Per-cent	7 Former Per-cent	7 Can. 1961 Per-cent	Total Per-cent	Total No.
Non-United Kingdom Origin: Migrants' Occupations										
1-4	51	40	25	30	10	28	14	1	100	92
5	18	14	35	43	31	33	15	10	100	105
6	7	12	23	21	58	66	12	1	100	110
7	21	15	19	43	28	36	32	6	100	47
United Kingdom Origin: Migrants' Occupations										
1-4	66	77	16	7	9	9	9	7	100	44
5	37	37	37	43	16	14	10	6	100	51
6	31	31	54	38	15	31	—	—	100	13
7	56	31	25	19	6	19	13	31	100	16

SOURCE: Richmond 1964, p. 545, table 2.
 [a]Code: 1-4 Nonmanual
            5   Highly skilled
            6   Other skilled, semiskilled, and unskilled
            7   Not in labor force and not known: includes students and other nonemployed together with those about whom information was not available

collar employment in Canada. But among the immigrants from other countries, only half (51 percent) of those with fathers in white-collar categories were themselves in such categories abroad, and only 40 percent had obtained nonmanual employment in Canada.

Richmond summarizes these data as follows:

> In other words, the process of emigration had enabled the children of white-collar workers in the United Kingdom to retain or improve their position, whereas those from other countries fell in status. Clearly, this process was related to the question of language and of professional qualifications, both of which presented greater obstacles to the immigrant from Europe than from the United Kingdom. In the case of highly skilled workers there was almost exactly the same proportion of those from the United Kingdom and those from other countries who had the same status as their fathers in their former country. Furthermore, in the case of both United Kingdom immigrants and the others, the same proportion of those whose fathers were in highly skilled occupations achieved this status in Canada. However, of those who moved out of highly skilled occupations the majority of the United Kingdom immigrants moved up into white-collar employment, whereas the majority of other immigrants moved

down into semiskilled or unskilled types of employment. . . . Emigration from Britain is, principally, of people with middle-class or upper working-class backgrounds. Only 12 percent of the British immigrants, compared with one-third of those from other countries, were from semiskilled or unskilled occupations. [Richmond 1970, p. 546]

Richmond found that immigrants to Canada from the United Kingdom were much more likely than those from other countries to retain their pre-emigration occupational status (see table 10.8). Those from Britain whose occupational status declined in their first jobs in Canada were likely to lose less status than those from other countries; and they were more likely to regain their higher status in subsequent jobs.

Patterns of Societal Mobility Compared
Cross-Nationally or Over Time

THE "OPENNESS" OF AMERICAN SOCIETY. Discussions of mobility *rates* have frequently centered on two issues: (1) the trend over time in the United States, or in some other single country, in the rate of upward

TABLE 10.8
Intragenerational Mobility of Postwar Immigrants in Canada (Outflow Analysis)

Job in Country of Origin[a]	1–4 First Per-cent	1–4 1961 Per-cent	5 First Per-cent	5 1961 Per-cent	6 First Per-cent	6 1961 Per-cent	7 First Per-cent	7 1961 Per-cent	Total Per-cent	Total No.
Non-United Kingdom Origin: Job in Canada										
1–4	32	54	21	25	43	17	4	4	100	84
5	–	5	42	68	56	24	2	3	100	94
6	–	3	9	14	86	80	6	3	100	119
7	14	32	7	25	46	35	33	8	100	57
United Kingdom Origin: Job in Canada										
1–4	77	74	8	12	13	7	2	8	100	61
5	8	30	70	57	22	13	–	–	100	37
6	7	7	–	33	80	47	13	13	100	15
7	18	46	9	–	27	18	46	36	100	11

SOURCE: Richmond 1964, p. 553, table 8.
[a]Code: 1–4 Nonmanual
　　　　5　Highly skilled
　　　　6　Other skilled, semiskilled and unskilled
　　　　7　Not in labor force and not known: includes students and other nonemployed together with those about whom information was not available

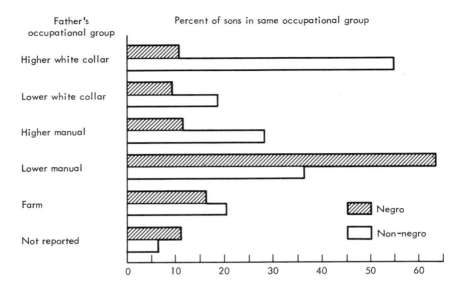

FIGURE 10.1. Transition percentages, father's occupation to 1962 occupation by race for civilian men aged 25–64 years, United States, 1962. Source: O. D. Duncan 1968, Table 6.

mobility ("Is America as 'open' a society as it was in the past?" "Is America still the 'land of opportunity'?"), and (2) the "openness" and social "opportunity" of the United States as compared to some one or several other countries. However, attempts to explore the variations and changes in "mobility regimes" and the correlates, causes, and consequences of such variations and changes have been few in number and limited in scope.

Most of the recent studies dealing with the topic seem to agree in concluding that the mobility rate—or "openness," or "opportunity"—of America has not declined or diminished in comparison to the rates that obtained earlier in this century or in the previous century. And as for differential mobility in the United States, social scientists and other observers have long believed that there are different "opportunity structures" (i.e., different mobility regimes) for different population groups, and especially for nonwhites, but such differences have only very recently been demonstrated and measured convincingly (Blau and Duncan 1967, chap. 2; Duncan 1969). Figure 10.1 demonstrates vividly the differential mobility of Negroes and non-Negroes in America.

Findings on the "openness" or "rigidity" of American society or of the American occupational structure as compared to other countries are much less conclusive, and there is no clear consensus among scholars as to whether America remains *the* country of more opportunity than the rest, if indeed it was so in the past. (For recent statements and findings, see Cutright 1968; Fox and Miller 1966). Cross-national comparisons of mobility have sometimes obscured rather than clarified the nature, volume, and directions of mobility processes, since a frequent requirement for making such comparisons has been that occupational categories be collapsed and reduced in number. Increasingly, however, such studies are illuminating the range of variation in mobility regimes and are beginning to deal empirically and analytically—rather than only speculatively—with the correlates, determinants, and consequences of such variations.

INTERSOCIETAL COMPARISONS BY LIPSET AND BENDIX. Among the first to attempt to use cross-national comparative mobility data in formulating generalizations about mobility patterns were Lipset and Bendix (1959). Their conclusions were that (1) Western countries are characterized by basically similar mobility patterns because (2) basically similar technological developments have operated to change their occupational structures in similar ways. Unfortunately, Lipset and Bendix indicated no clear procedure for measuring or comparing mobility patterns, so that there appear to be no solid criteria for determining the similarity or dissimilarity of the outflow tables presented. Moreover, although the distinction between "structural," or "forced," mobility and "exchange" mobility had long been made (see, for example, Lipset and Zetterberg 1966), no attempt was made in this study to separate them (see also, our discussion in chapter 5). Finally, the connections between occupational mobility and technologically induced changes in the occupational structure were merely *asserted,* with no support from either analysis or data.

INTERSOCIETAL COMPARISONS BY FOX AND MILLER. A study by Fox and Miller (1965) sought to investigate the relationship between mobility rates in twelve countries and the following five factors: (1) per capita gross national product; (2) percentage of population enrolled in school; (3) political stability; (4) percentage of population residing in cities of 20,000 or more; and (5) "achievement motivation." Mobility was measured in terms of (1) the proportion of persons with manual-occupation origins working in nonmanual occupations ("manual outflow mobility"), and (2) the proportion of persons with nonmanual-occupation origins working in manual occupations ("nonmanual outflow mobility"). These investigators concluded that political stability and educational enrollment were the most important factors—statistically, at least—for variations among the manual outflow mobility rates (upward mobility rates) of the different countries. "Achievement motivation" was found to be of minor importance, and urbanization and economic development (represented by per capita gross national product) worked differently as the effects of the other variables were held constant (negative partial correlation, regression coefficients) or not (positive simple correlation coefficient). The most important factors in accounting for variations in the nonmanual outflow (downward mobility rates) were found to be political stability and urbanization.

INTERSOCIETAL COMPARISONS BY CUTRIGHT. The Fox-Miller findings figure prominently in a study by P. Cutright (1968), which focuses upon intergenerational mobility and nonmobility in thirteen countries according to the manual-nonmanual distinction. Mobility here is studied in relation to four factors: (1) technology; (2) "stimulation and facilitation of selection by talent," i.e., the degree to which jobs are awarded, not on the basis of ascriptive characteristics (race, social class, etc.), but on the basis of the individual's talent, all as a result of the sophistication of the society's communications system, its availability of information about the job market, the prevalence of literacy, the state of its telephone and postage systems, etc.; (3) rural background, i.e., the proportion of sons with rural backgrounds, and (4) family size (with the gross reproduction rate as index). Cutright concludes that the first two factors, technology and communications, are so closely related as to be virtually inseparable, and that these, together with the rural-background factor, are most important in accounting for variations in mobility. The family-size factor is viewed as less important but not negligible. These conclusions hold for the urban populations taken alone. Citing the findings of Fox and Miller presented above, Cutright tries to show that they are consistent with and, largely subsumed by, his own.

RAMSØY'S STUDY OF DIFFERENT NORWEGIAN COMMUNITIES. Finally, we cite a study by Natalie Rogoff Ramsøy (1966) concerning the mobility of Norwegian males in communities differing greatly "in their division of labor at the starting point." Differentiating between "net mobility" (change in the proportions in the respective occupational categories) and "occupational exchange" (the reshuffling of the same jobs among different people), Ramsøy found that there was a high degree of occupational exchange, or "reciprocal" mobility, in urbanized and industrialized localities, but that in rural nonindustrial localities individual shifts were primarily unidirectional, those who moved not being replaced by others.

> At the urban-industrial extreme, [mobility] consists predominantly of mutually reciprocating moves with little effect on the total distribution of positions in the occupational structure, but considerable effect on the composition (at least the social origins) of persons in diverse occupational positions. At the rural-agricultural extreme mobility consists primarily of unreciprocated moves, tending to represent wholesale departure from agriculture and other extractive

occupations and a corresponding recruitment into industrial, clerical, and professional occupations previously represented in far
smaller numbers in these localities. Here it is far less the case that
the men who move away from their father's status are replaced by
and themselves replace men in other occupational origins; instead
the moves add up to pronounced changes in the occupational structure itself. [Ramsøy 1966, pp. 230–31]

Ramsøy's comparison of the occupational distributions of sons and
their fathers in the different communities (table 10.9) led her to conclude
that (1) the *direction* of change in the occupational structure was uniform
in the different localities—away from agricultural and unskilled occupations, and toward industrial, white collar, and professional occupations—
but that (2) the *rate* of change in occupational structure varied inversely,
and about proportionally, to the urban-industrial level of the locality;
thus, the higher the urbanism, the slower the change.

Mobility and the Occupational Structure

Studies of the factors influencing individual mobility in status
achievement and studies of mobility rates and patterns both have usually
assumed implicitly that mobility in a society is bounded by the net
changes that have occurred in occupational distribution. But even if this
is the case, it is very easy to show that a large variety of mobility-rate
patterns can satisfy a given condition of change in net occupational distribution, and that these patterns, in turn, may be characterized by either
high or low gross mobility, high or low degrees of occupational inheritance, and greater or smaller modal or mean distances of occupational
movement.

Occupations themselves may expand or contract over a given interval, and such changes may be associated with intergenerational or intragenerational inflow or outflows. Six possibilities have been distinguished
by Blau and Duncan (1967):

1. Expanding occupation: intergenerational inflow, intragenerational outflow—for example, among clerical workers, salesmen,
   operatives. These are occupational categories which are expanding, and they are categories *into which* sons of fathers not in
   these categories often move (hence; the intergenerational inflow); and at the same time these are categories *out of which*
   persons whose first jobs are here frequently move to other occupational categories (hence, the intragenerational outflow).
2. Expanding occupation: intergenerational outflow, intragenerational inflow—e.g., among managers, proprietors and officials,
   craftsmen, and service workers. Sons of fathers in these occupations frequently move *out* and into other occupational cate-

TABLE 10.9
Occupational Distribution of 19-Year-Old Men and their Fathers according to Place of Residence, Norway, 1950 (in percentages)

Occupational Status	Place of Residence							
	Capital City		Smaller Cities		Suburbs		Industrial Villages	
	Father	Son	Father	Son	Father	Son	Father	Son
Professionals, managers, & technicians	24.3	27.6	16.7	24.8	21.8	25.4	7.2	17.2
White-collar workers	6.8	17.8	6.1	15.1	4.5	12.1	2.1	7.0
Tradesmen	10.9	5.2	11.6	5.2	7.5	4.2	4.7	2.9
Craftsmen	9.3	10.7	12.9	12.2	8.7	11.6	12.4	14.7
Industrial workers	32.0	33.0	31.3	35.0	27.8	35.8	27.8	40.0
Unskilled labor	14.2	4.6	17.2	6.1	12.5	3.3	27.6	9.6
Farming, fishing, forestry	2.5	1.1	4.2	1.6	17.2	7.6	18.2	8.6
Total	100.0	100.0	100.0	100.0	100.0	100.0	100.0	100.0
Index of dissimilarity, fathers to sons	16.7		20.8		22.1		29.4	
No. of cases	1,310		2,911		1,146		1,469	

Occupational Status	Place of Residence							
	Mixed Villages		Agricultural Villages		Fishing Villages		All Communities	
	Father	Son	Father	Son	Father	Son	Father	Son
Professionals, managers, & technicians	5.9	12.3	4.7	10.2	3.5	8.8	9.3	15.9
White-collar workers	1.2	6.3	1.1	6.6	0.7	5.0	2.5	9.0
Tradesmen	4.1	3.3	2.9	3.0	4.0	2.8	5.5	3.6
Craftsmen	8.4	11.3	7.0	12.6	3.1	9.4	8.8	12.0
Industrial workers	12.2	34.3	8.8	27.2	3.8	25.9	17.1	32.5
Unskilled labor	13.2	5.7	9.2	4.8	5.5	4.3	13.3	5.5
Farming, fishing, forestry	55.0	26.8	66.3	35.6	79.4	43.8	43.5	21.5
Total	100.0	100.0	100.0	100.0	100.0	100.0	100.0	100.0
Index of dissimilarity, fathers to sons	36.5		35.1		38.0		31.7	
No. of cases	5,199		6,469		695		19,199	

SOURCE: Ramsøy 1966, pp. 220–21, table 1.

gories. Persons beginning their work careers elsewhere frequently move *into* these occupational categories.

3. Expanding occupation: intergenerational inflow, intragenerational inflow—e.g., among professional, technical, and kindred workers.

4. Contracting occupation: intergenerational outflow, intragenerational inflow—e.g., in farming.

5. Contracting occupation: intergenerational inflow, e.g., among laborers and farm laborers.
6. Contracting occupation: intergenerational outflow. No empirical cases.

In addition, occupations can be differentiated in accordance with patterns of recruitment into them and out of them. Here, Blau and Duncan use the terms "distributive of manpower" and "relatively self-contained." The first case describes occupations which recruit a great deal of manpower from different origins and supply disproportionate numbers of sons to different occupational destinations. The second describes occupations which neither recruit nor supply very much manpower. The growth or decline of an occupation, under recruitment to or from that occupation, is asymmetrical; and regardless of growth or decline, the number and variety of other occupation groups from which recruitment is drawn, or to which persons are recruited, are positively associated: in other words, the broader and more dispersed the occupational origins from which persons moving into an occupation are recruited, the broader and more dispersed the occupational destinations of those leaving it. Thus, Blau and Duncan illustrate, (*ibid.,* p. 423) the higher blue-collar groups—intermediate ranks in the occupational hierarchy—exhibit the most dispersion in both in-movement and out-movement. But higher white-collar strata and lower blue-collar and farm strata exhibit much more concentrated movements: from less-dispersed occupational origins *into* those occupational categories, and to less-dispersed occupational destinations *out of* them.

It has been widely asserted—and a number of attempts have been made to show analytically—that changing occupational distribution generates net occupational mobility. Then, the assertion continues, the patterns of recruitment characterizing the occupational groups generate differences between "gross" patterns of occupational mobility rates and net occupational mobility. The whole process, moreover, is mediated by patterns of differential fertility and differential entrance into the labor force (cf. Duncan 1966).

Because of the complexity of the process, these elements—changing occupational distributions, differential fertility, differential entrance into the labor force, and occupational mobility rates—have typically been examined separately. It is not ordinarily possible to show explicitly the connections between them. Thus, for example, we know about changes in the occupational distribution of American males since about 1870; we know something about entrance into the labor force of sons of fathers in different occupational groups; and we have a number of studies of intergenerational and intragenerational occupational mobility. But connecting these remains a matter of interpretation rather than of straightforward analysis. Recently, however, a number of analytical approaches have been proposed for the explicit representation of these relationships (Matras 1967).

A fundamental dimension of these analyses is their basic assumption that occupational distribution and changes in occupational distribution are processes *exogenous* to—i.e., determined by factors external to—the social structure and social mobility. In terms of the elements of equation (1), above, this assumption means that, given π_0 (the initial occupational distribution), the new occupational distribution, π_1, is determined by factors outside the mobility regime (for example, by the structure of consumer demand, or by production processes and technologies), M_1, and whatever goes into this regime; and that the mobility regime, M_1, is perforce bounded by π_0 *and* π_1, so as to conform to equation (1).[4]

But there are reasons to suppose that the very opposite may be the case. That is, the new occupational distribution may well be affected, (even if not entirely determined), by the occupational mobility regime, i.e., by the pattern of mobility rates. This is probably one of the important advantages of visualizing the mobility regime as a population process. We are accustomed to viewing population size and composition as determined by the processes of fertility and mortality, and we conventionally view the geographic distribution of the population as resulting from processes of migration in combination with differential natural increase. However, if the mobility regime is seen as a population process, there is a case to be made for viewing occupational distribution as determined—at least in large measure—by mobility processes in combination with differential natural increase and entrance into the labor force. We shall return to this point at the close of the chapter.

5. CONSEQUENCES OF MOBILITY PATTERNS

Social scientific interest in the consequences of mobility has been split fairly equally between behavioral or attitudinal consequences among individuals and the broader consequences of a social structural or demographic nature. In the discussion which follows, we shall examine the consequences of mobility from both points of view.

Western literature and historical writings have repeatedly focused on the upwardly or downwardly mobile individual, on the successful or unsuccessful aspirant, or on the triumphs and tribulations of the *parvenu*

---

4 Those familiar with matrix algebra will recognize here that there is no unique solution for M, given π_0 and π_1, that these bounds mean only that *net* occupational mobility—not the gross mobility—is determined. But this parallels our discussion above.

—Fitzgerald's *Great Gatsby,* Thackeray's *Vanity Fair,* and Eliot's *Middle-march* are but a few cases in point. And social science has followed suit, sometimes with attempts to systematize these inquiries but often with its own kinds of speculations.

Social scientific investigations generally confirm the repeated assumption in literature and the popularly held view that differences of social class pervade the individual's behavior, attitude, and management of social relationships (Bendix and Lipset 1966, part IV). It is therefore not surprising that social scientists should agree with literary and historical portrayals in anticipating that ambiguity, conflicting norms and habits, and a myriad of "cross-pressures" will confront individuals who are mobile. Moreover, sensing or "observing" widespread mobility and abundant norms and values of "success," social scientists have not failed to anticipate that situations of ambiguity, conflict, and "anomie" will characterize individuals who are *not* mobile.

Indeed, there are findings which support the notion that the fact of mobility, or of immobility, generates individual tensions and insecurity, or personal or interpersonal crises. But there are also findings that can be cited supporting the notion that mobility or immobility are of little if any consequence to psychological well-being (see the review of Lipset and Bendix 199, chap. IX; Kleiner and Parker 1963).

The Political Consequences of Mobility

The social structural consequences most frequently connected with patterns of mobility are those that pertain to political structure, fertility, family size, and population growth. The problem of political consequences has typically been cast either in terms of the recruitment of leadership and support for left or left-of-center political interests or in terms of the extent to which class-based politics and political cleavages flourish under different mobility regimes.

According to Lipset and Bendix, a regime characterized by high rates of individual social mobility—upward or downward rates or both—operates to deplete the support of left-of-center political movements and parties. (Lipset and Bendix 1959; Lipset 1959). In a society in which individuals hope and see a possibility for personal advancement independently of the fortunes of others in similar social straits, it is difficult to mobilize support for collective actions designed to bring about group or class mobility or otherwise to pursue class, estate, or status interests vis-à-vis an established class. Conversely, in a regime characterized by low rates of individual social mobility, political action is viewed as a means of collectively enhancing status, privileges, power, and economic benefit. Thus, in some countries institutions of individual mobility dominate, while in others institutions of group mobility hold sway. In the United States a host of institutions—not the least of which is lengthy, compulsory, and largely standardized education—are viewed as promoting the chances of individuals of modest origin; in Europe, on the other hand, political parties, trade unions, and social movements have been taken as the means for enhancing the chances of entire classes or categories of populations (cf. Ramsøy 1966).

The institutionalization of individual mobility in countries like the United States works to recruit able persons of modest or low social origins into high prestige and class roles—thus robbing the lower classes of talent and potential leadership. At the same time, downwardly mobile persons (those with previous attachments to higher classes) and lower-class persons with mobility aspirations are both frequently held to be oriented to conservative political movements or parties.

It is for reasons such as these, according to the Lipset (1959) analysis, that socialism has never taken hold in the United States (see also Lopreato 1967). However, these assertions are difficult to document or test empirically. Indeed, Lipset himself has concluded from a cross-national comparative study of mobility that mobility rates in Western Europe and the United States are basically similar in magnitude and direction.

A second type of political consequence of mobility concerns the composition of elites by social origin. Obviously, in a society characterized by high rates and a large volume of mobility at any moment in time, the body of political and social elites is composed of persons of heterogeneous social origins. Conversely, in societies characterized by low rates of mobility, elites tend to be homogeneous with respect to social origin (cf. Ramsøy 1966). Thus, it has been widely believed that American national and local legislatures include persons from a broader range of social origins than do, say, European parliaments and legislative bodies. Similarly, governmental and private bureaucracies in the United States have often been viewed as more representative of the various social, economic, regional, and ethnic groupings than is the case elsewhere. However, the documentation of these assertions has often been less than convincing.

Occupational and Social Consequences of Mobility

Just as the composition of elites is affected by elite mobility patterns, so the composition of occupational groups is determined largely by occupational mobility patterns. Where educational achievement has provided an entree to certain types of occupational roles, the increasing accessibility of educational opportunities to persons of all social origins is translated into an increasing heterogeneity of social origins in the respective occupational groupings. Conversely, in societies in which occupational inheritance is the dominant mode, occupational groups tend to be homogeneous with respect to their members' origins, training, and paths of career. In the United States, *some* occupations are characterized by a relative homogeneity of origins. The most obvious of these is farming, in which the majority employed are children of farmers or of agricultural workers and began their working lives in farm occupations. Self-employed professionals and clerical workers seem to be relatively heterogeneous (see table 10.3).

In periods of expansion, occupations are typically more heterogeneous with respect to social or occupational origins, although theoretically this need not be the case. Thus, the professions recruit not only sons of professionals but also sons of white-collar workers, merchants, and farmers; and semiskilled occupations recruit not only sons of semiskilled workers but sons of unskilled and farm workers as well. However, even in periods of expansion, farmers and farm laborers are recruited primarily from among persons of farm origins.

RELATIONSHIP BETWEEN OCCUPATIONAL OR SOCIAL MOBILITY AND KINSHIP, MIGRATION, AND POPULATION REDISTRIBUTION. In many respects, the relationship between social or occupational mobility and kinship structure is formally identical to the relationship between mobility and political structure. For many who have considered this question, the concept of individual mobility would appear to be the very antithesis of kinship. For while kinship is surely a system of stable, ascribed, role relationships, mobility represents the very departure from incumbency in one role and the assumption of incumbency in another. Thus, mobility assumes the disintegration of role relationships and the formation of new ones. In fact, however, mobility often does not challenge kinship relationships, and indeed, in some situations it actually sustains or reinforces them (see Goode 1966).

Because both social and occupational mobility very often entail a change in place of residence, mobility bears a special relationship to migration and population redistribution. As we indicated in the preceding chapter, economic factors are inevitably the first invoked in attempts to account for migratory shifts of population, and the economic dimension is typically expressed in job changes. For example, we know that migrants are more frequently upwardly mobile, occupationally, than are nonmigrants from the same areas of origin, but that they achieve lower average status than the nonmigrant residents of their places of destination (Blau and Duncan 1967, chap. 7).

Consequences for Fertility, Family Size, and Population Growth

Alongside the political consequences of mobility, the type of consequences most frequently mentioned and investigated pertain to fertility, family size, and population growth. The interest in this topic derives originally from the search for causes and remedies of the declining European and American birth rates, a decline that was especially notable between the two world wars. A familiar hypothesis held that both social and occupational mobility were inhibited by large families and by the responsibility of more, rather than fewer, children; and that, accordingly, couples or individuals actually or potentially mobile tended to limit more carefully and effectively their numbers of births. A somewhat different version of this hypothesis held that couples with few children were more likely to experience social and occupational mobility than were couples with many children. Both these relationships suggested inverse associations between fertility and upward mobility.

Such hypotheses have not found much empirical confirmation except as they apply to mobility away from the farm. In general, the relationship between upward mobility and fertility is weak; however, there is evidence that *both* upward and downward mobility are related to slightly diminished fertility, and that mobility from the farm is definitely related to lower fertility than that obtaining for individuals who remain on the farm. But no convincing support has yet accrued to the hypothesis that low-fertility couples are more likely to be mobile or to the hypothesis that mobile couples are more likely to control and depress family size.

Again, it is important to remark that the analyses of this issue have dealt with individual relationships between mobility and fertility. Virtually no study has asked whether high-mobility or low-mobility *aggregates* are characterized by high or low fertility rates. It is just such formulations and investigations that are sorely needed in studies of populations and societies.

6. CONCLUDING REMARKS: CHANGING SOCIAL AND OCCUPATIONAL STRUCTURE AS A CONSEQUENCE OF MOBILITY

We conclude by recapitulating and restating our position that mobility regimes should be seen as population transformations, for we regard this as the central issue for studies of mobility in populations and societies. Investigations of mobility have typically been divided according to whether they study "motivational" causes of mobility or whether they study causes of mobility which stem from the mobility process itself. The latter, in turn, have been viewed primarily as caused by, or at least as generated and minimally bound by, changes in the *supply* of social or occupational roles or statuses, and by regimes of recruitment to and from the various occupations or by patterns of exchange (or, more precisely, *interchange*) of ranks and roles. Thus, according to this way of viewing social life, the changing occupational distributions and occupational requirements of an economy may demand occupational shifts and so generate mobility patterns and institutions in order to promote such shifts (see, for example, Porter 1968; Coleman, in press).

But we have suggested that it is equally plausible to view a mobility regime, a pattern of mobility rates and institutions, as a process which *transforms* the occupational structure in a way consistent with the outputs of the mobility process. Occupational mobility and changing occupational structure are, in this view, a single population process and should be studied as such to discover: (a) what is stable and what changes, (b) the directions and reasons for changes (or for stabilities), (c) the general directions and paths of the occupational structure under different hypotheses, and (d) the exact way in which mobility and changing occupational structure are reciprocally related.

This problem has been examined by D. J. Treiman, who has suggested that shifts in occupational structure may result from pressure for expansion of the white-collar sector and pressure for reduction of the blue-collar sector, both types of pressure deriving from processes of mobility (Treiman 1970). Treiman summarizes his argument with the following tentative propositions:

> Rising levels of educational attainment create pressures toward an upward shift in the distribution of the labor force, of the following kind:
>
> A. An over-supply of white collar labor, which results from educational systems expanding too rapidly, drops the price of such labor, allowing low cost expansion of the white collar sector.
>
> B. Governments may enlarge the governmental bureaucracy to reduce the threat inherent in an unemployed highly-educated labor force.
>
> C. Educated individuals may become self-employed rather than accept employment in occupations not requiring education.
>
> D. An under-supply of adequate blue collar labor, which again would result from a too-rapidly expanding educational system, raises the price of blue collar labor, thus providing the incentive to replace the labor force with mechanical means of production. [Treiman 1970]

We shall try to cast this process somewhat differently, introducing here the notion of "available but untapped knowledge and ideas," which will play a central part later in our discussion of the consequences of population growth and transformation (Part III).

Mobility Processes—The Essential Ingredients for Socioeconomic Change

Any individual or collective human enterprise has access to some knowledge and ideas above and beyond those actually used, exploited, or implemented. Individuals and groups involved in production, in organization or management, and in social or economic activities generally *know about* possible alternative ways of doing things.

In particular, there is generally some acquaintance with ways of reforming, changing, reorganizing, or adopting innovations in economic activities of production and distribution. Some one or a combination of reasons may prevent the introduction of change: lack of capital, lack of supporting production or distribution services, the way in which consumption is structured or the size of the market, the lack of appropriate manpower, etc. But mobility processes—for example, education, training, recruitment of new people into occupational roles—often make it possible, practical, and profitable to adopt or introduce previously "available but untapped" knowledge, thus mobilizing the newly mobile manpower and restructuring the labor force and society.

Mobility and the shifts in occupational structure may indeed attract the other elements of innovation—the capital and the supporting services and institutions—whose absence otherwise contributes to the nonintroduction of innovation. What seems clear, in any case, is that the absence of supportive mobility institutions either obviates or severely limits the possibility of shifts in occupational structure and the industrialization and economic growth associated with such shifts.[5]

Thus, for the United States in the twentieth century, a major, if not *the* major, consequence of occupational mobility and of all the social institutions sustaining the mobility regime has been the changing occupational distribution of the economically active population. This changing distribution is represented very concisely in table 10.10. The changing occupational structure, in turn, has had vast consequences for the political, economic, and social structure of the country, as indeed for population growth and distribution. Finally, the relationships between roles themselves and between sets of roles—e.g., between and among clerks and craftsmen, between professionals and proprietors, between management and labor—and between families, schools, churches, and neighborhoods have been deeply affected by the changing absolute numbers and changing numerical relationships in the occupational structure.

---

5 For a discussion of how mobility patterns have been related to shifts in the occupational structure and industrialization of Israel, see Matras 1965, chap. 4.

TABLE 10.10

Experienced Civilian Labor Force in the United States: Percentage Distribution by Major Occupation Groups, 1900-1967

	Total	Professional, Technical, and Kindred Workers	Farmers and Farm Managers	Managers, Officials, and Proprietors, except Farm	Clerical and Kindred Workers	Sales Workers	Craftsmen Foremen, and Kindred Workers	Operatives and Kindred Workers	Private Household Workers	Service Workers, except Priv. Household	Farm Laborers and Foremen	Laborers, except Farm and Mine	Number in Experienced Civilian Labor Force*
		(1)	(2)	(3)	(4)	(5)	(6)	(7)	(8)	(9)	(10)	(11)	
Censuses													
1900	100.0	4.3	19.9	5.8	3.0	4.5	10.5	12.8	5.4	3.6	17.7	12.5	29,030
1910	100.0	4.7	16.5	6.6	5.3	4.7	11.6	14.6	5.0	4.6	14.4	12.0	37,291
1920	100.0	5.4	15.3	6.6	8.0	4.9	13.0	15.6	3.3	4.5	11.7	11.6	42,206
1930	100.0	6.8	12.4	7.4	8.9	6.3	12.8	15.8	4.1	5.7	8.8	11.0	48,686
1940	100.0	7.5	10.4	7.3	9.6	6.7	12.0	18.4	4.8	7.0	7.0	9.4	51,742
Current Population Survey													
1950	100.0	7.3	7.0	10.4	12.6	6.3	13.0	20.8	3.2	8.0	5.1	6.4	58,999
1954	100.0	8.9	6.0	9.8	13.1	6.4	13.6	20.7	2.9	8.2	4.1	6.3	64,103
1955	100.0	8.9	5.7	10.0	13.1	6.2	13.2	20.7	3.1	8.4	4.4	6.3	65,496
1956	100.0	9.2	5.5	9.8	13.5	6.3	13.4	20.1	3.3	8.6	4.5	5.9	67,210
1957	100.0	9.7	4.9	10.0	13.9	6.3	13.3	19.8	3.2	8.6	4.2	6.0	67,596
1958	100.0	10.4	4.5	10.1	14.0	6.4	13.3	18.8	3.4	8.9	3.9	6.2	68,213
1959	100.0	10.5	4.4	10.2	14.0	6.6	13.1	18.6	3.3	9.1	3.9	6.2	68,952
1960	100.0	10.8	4.0	10.2	14.5	6.5	12.9	18.6	3.3	9.3	3.9	6.0	70,156
1961	100.0	11.1	3.8	10.2	14.6	6.6	13.0	18.3	3.5	9.6	3.7	5.7	71,018
1962	100.0	11.5	3.6	10.5	14.8	6.4	12.8	18.3	3.5	9.7	3.3	5.7	71,315
1963	100.0	11.6	3.3	10.2	14.8	6.3	13.0	18.7	3.4	9.9	3.2	5.6	72,360
1964	100.0	11.8	3.2	10.3	15.0	6.3	12.7	18.8	3.3	10.0	3.1	5.5	73,614
1965	100.0	12.0	3.0	9.9	15.4	6.5	12.7	18.9	3.1	10.0	2.8	5.6	75,024
1966	100.0	12.5	2.8	9.9	16.1	6.2	13.1	19.2	2.6	10.2	2.2	5.1	75,299
1967	100.0	13.0	2.6	9.8	16.6	6.1	13.1	19.0	2.4	10.3	2.2	5.0	76,919

SOURCE: U.S. Bureau of the Census, *Historical Statistics* 1957.

*For 1900 to 1940: "economically active" population, i.e. number reporting "usually work."

417

Clearly, the changes in the occupational structure have come about not only because of intergenerational or intragenerational shifts of occupations or occupational roles. Differential fertility and mortality and differential patterns of entrance into, or departure from, the working force have also been important factors in the pattern of successive transformations of the occupational structure. If we express the occupational distributions in 1900, 1910 · · · 1966, 1967 as π_{1900} · · · π_{1967}, we can represent the sociodemographic processes transforming them as M_{1900}, M_{1910} · · · M_{1965}, M_{1966}, so that the process of change is represented as

$$1900 \text{ to } 1910: \quad \pi_{1900} \, M_{1900} = \pi_{1910}$$
$$1910 \text{ to } 1920: \quad \pi_{1910} \, M_{1910} = \pi_{1920}$$
$$\cdot$$
$$\cdot$$
$$\cdot$$
$$1966 \text{ to } 1967: \quad \pi_{1966} \, M_{1966} = \pi_{1967}$$

We know that the elements of the process represented by any M must include differential fertility and mortality, differential patterns of entrance into, and departure from, the working force, and rates and patterns of occupational mobility. In general, these data are not yet directly obtainable for 1900 and 1910 nor even for 1965 and 1966, and while the data of tables 10.1 through 10.5 are related to those needed, they are not identical to them. However, the data necessary for estimating occupational histories and the elements of the mobility processes are becoming increasingly available. Accordingly, progress will surely be made in the description and comparative analysis of such sociodemographic transformation processes.

Regardless of the current unavailability of appropriate data, it is important to recognize this phenomenon—the mobility-changing occupational structure—for the population transformation process that it is. In common with other processes of population transformation (e.g., fertility and mortality, marriage and divorce, and migration), it is deeply affected by social and by social-psychological factors. At the same time, it exerts a profound influence on the social structure. Conversely, no society can transform its technology, occupational structure, or social structure, as represented in π_{1900} · · · π_{1967}, without the mobility institutions underlying the mobility rates and patterns of working-force participation that comprise the elements of the transformation, M_{1900} · · · M_{1966}. Thus, without institutionalization of such processes as education, training, and recruitment, no society can change its social or occupational structure.

three

POPULATION GROWTH AND SOCIAL CHANGE

11

Social and Economic
Responses to
Population Growth

1. INTRODUCTORY REMARKS

In the first part of this volume we suggested that variations in population size, density, and structure are closely related to variations in social structure. In surveying world populations, we concluded that societies with distinctly different populations tend to differ in systematic ways. We pointed out later that some of the important taxonomies of societies are closely connected to the sizes and densities of their populations. Finally, we suggested that population growth, the responses of societies to actual or potential growth, and the "strategies" that societies adopt to assure their survival and material and nonmaterial adaptation in the face of population growth can usefully be viewed together as a fundamental cause of social change. In this connection we cited Durkheim's analysis, which sets forth the principle that the growth of population and social density gives rise to an increasing differentiation and division of labor, and that this, in turn, entails a new, symbiotic interdependency, or corporate basis of societal solidarity ("organic" solidarity), which replaces the earlier homogeneity, similarity, or categorical basis of solidarity ("mechanical" solidarity).

In this chapter we return to these ideas, try to explore them in more detail, and consider possible directions for the further study of ways in which population growth and pressure generate changes in social structure. We return to Durkheim's principle of the division of labor, exploring some of its reasons and some of its implications. In addition, we attempt to formulate—albeit in somewhat tentative fashion—two additional principles relating population growth to social change:

1. the expansion of social boundary systems, i.e., the increase in size, number of participants, range, or scope of social, economic, or political units; and
2. the adoption and institutionalization of innovations.

We shall try to show that these responses to population growth—division of labor, expansion of social boundary systems, and institutionalization of innovations—occur singly or in combination in all types of societies. In every case, their effect is to improve or to assure more decisively the survival and adaptation of the society under conditions of increased numbers in the population. We turn first to some general considerations of population growth and social structural change.

General Considerations of Population Growth and Social Structural Change

Sociological Approaches. Early sociologists viewed problems of social change and societal development as among the most important issues confronting their new discipline. They sought to develop explanations of individual cases of societal development, to explain historical changes in societies, and to discover and elucidate general principles and phenomena governing, causing, or generating societal change and patterns of development. Many of the principles and factors invoked by these sociologists to account for changing society and social structure remain issues in present-day sociology (for a compact summary, see Bottomore 1962, chap. 16).

Later schools of sociological thought have viewed the persistence of societies, of social structure, and of social patterns as the most crucial concern of sociology. Accordingly, their emphasis on social structure and on the functions of social relationships and patterns has been couched in efforts to account for the relative persistence over time of societies, social systems, social roles, societal institutions, and institutionalized relationships.

Sociological theory dealing with the persistence of social structure and social patterns has come under heavy criticism for its alleged absence of any serious attempt to account for social change. In particular, recent interest in the advancement of less developed or unindustrialized countries as well as attempts to analyze rapid urbanization and technological change in already industrialized countries have generated pressures for the analysis of change and have found structural-functional sociological theories seriously wanting in this respect (cf. Duncan and Schnore 1959, pp. 132–53; Bottomore 1962, pp. 278–79).

In recent years, sociologists working in the tradition of the structural-functional theories have sought to account more explicitly for social change and to develop a theory of social change within the framework of structural-functional analysis (Moore 1963; Eisenstadt 1964a, pp. 234–47; 1964b, pp. 375–86, and 1965, pp. 659–73; Parsons 1964, pp. 339–57; and 1966).

It has become increasingly clear that a comprehensive theory of societies and populations must deal both with the persistence and with the change of societies, social institutions, social systems, and social roles. Such a theory must identify, describe, and classify social patterns and forms which *recur* indicating the conditions under which they persist and those under which they change. As Nadel (1951) has suggested, the analysis of persisting social patterns and persisting aspects of social organization constitutes the *description* of society, social organization, and social structure, whereas the analysis of social change—of change in societies, social organization, and social structure—constitutes the *explanation* of these phenomena.

THE THREE GENERAL WAYS IN WHICH POPULATION PROCESSES GENERATE SOCIAL STRUCTURAL CHANGE. We have already suggested some ways in which population processes influence social structure and generate social structural change. It is appropriate at this point to return to the topic to add more detail. Very briefly, we can distinguish three broad ways in which population processes directly or indirectly generate social structural change:

1. by revising role relationships or by broadening institutionalized relationships between social roles and between social subsystems;
2. by directly redistributing the population, either geographically, or over social class, or over other social roles or role categories;
3. by establishing institutions or new institutionalized relationships for sustaining, controlling, integrating, or mobilizing increments to the population; or, alternatively, by controlling, diverting, or preventing the population increments themselves.

2. CHANGING POPULATION COMPOSITION BY ROLES: THE LABOR FORCE, AGE STRUCTURE, AND ECONOMIC GROWTH

The change in the composition of a population by social roles is accomplished in one or both of two ways: by differential growth of the numbers of incumbents of the different kinds of categories or social roles (e.g., by differential fertility or training and socialization), and by movement among social roles (e.g., by migration or social mobility).

We have discussed such processes fairly extensively in earlier chapters under the rubric of "population transformations," presenting as processes of transformation fertility, mortality, and changing size and sex-age composition of a population; migration and population redistribution; marriage and changing composition by marital status; and class or occupational mobility and changing occupational distribution. All these processes are alike in that they effect changes in role distribution. We shall restrict our discussion here to the type of population transformation which has recently received particular attention for its effect upon economic organization, production, and levels of living: the changing age structure of a population and its implications for changes in the absolute and relative size of the labor force, i.e., in the economic role distribution.

The key elements of our analysis are:

1. The population in the working or labor-force ages, usually taken as the population aged 15 to 64.
2. Dependency, taken usually as the ratio of persons under 15 and aged 65 or older to the population aged 15 to 64, but sometimes represented by the ratio of the *total* population to the population aged 15 to 64.
3. Density of the population, taken usually as the number of persons per unit of land area, or persons per units of arable land, but sometimes viewed in terms of the number of persons in the labor-force ages relative to land area or to other resources.

The Effect of Population Growth on the Economy of Underdeveloped Countries

Population growth and attendant changes in the labor force, in dependency, and in density affect the society's productivity and its levels of per capita income primarily via (1) the proportion of current national income that may be set aside for investment, and (2) the effectiveness with which available investment can be used to raise the productivity per worker.

The study of actual and alternative hypothetical population transformations in low-income, underdeveloped countries suggests that rapid population growth per se inhibits economic development and increased per capita income in such countries. (The pioneer and still the most detailed example of such an analysis is that of Coale and Hoover 1958.) The relationship is summarized very succinctly by F. Lorimer:

> Rapid population growth tends to reduce the proportion of current production that can be allocated to investment in new capital

equipment and other facilities due both to the larger volume of goods required for immediate consumption by individuals and to the larger public expenditures needed for transportation, communication, social services, etc. At the same time, in a population with a rapidly increasing labor force a larger proportion of current investment must be used *extensively,* to provide new workers with resources at the standards already in effect, so that less of current investment is available for *intensive* use in raising levels of productivity per worker. [Lorimer 1969, p. 178]

The study of population transitions and stable population models has shown conclusively that the central factor in the age distribution of a population is the schedule of fertility rates: high fertility implies a "young" age distribution (high proportions at pre-adult ages) and low fertility implies an "older" age distribution (high proportions at adult and older ages). Moreover, *changes* in mortality have only minor effects on the age distribution of a population, whereas *changes* in fertility affect it significantly and rapidly (Coale 1956).

Until the middle of the twentieth century, analyses of the effects of population upon the economy were conventionally cast in terms of relationships between population and natural resources, between population and the labor supply (primarily as affected by rates of economic activity or labor-force participation among both sexes at the various ages), and between population and consumption and markets.[1] In these analyses, the concept of dependency was introduced primarily with reference to aged persons, relatively little attention being given to the connection between fertility and dependent children.

The Case of India

In their *Population Growth and Economic Development in Low-Income Countries* (1958), A. J. Coale and E. M. Hoover apply the analysis of the relationship between fertility and age distribution to the measurement of effects of alternative patterns of fertility upon dependency and upon potentials for development and increase of per capita income. Carrying out alternative projections for India for 1951 through 1968, they show that the continuation of India's high fertility pattern implies *both* a continued rapid growth of the entire population *and* an increase in the already very high burden of dependency. If, however, fertility were reduced by 50 percent over a 25-year period, the rate of total population growth would decline very sharply and, no less important, the burden of dependency would diminish. Figure 11.1 and table 11.1 graphically illustrate these projections.

---

1 See especially the summary of such analysis in United Nations, "Determinants and Consequences" (1953), Part 3.

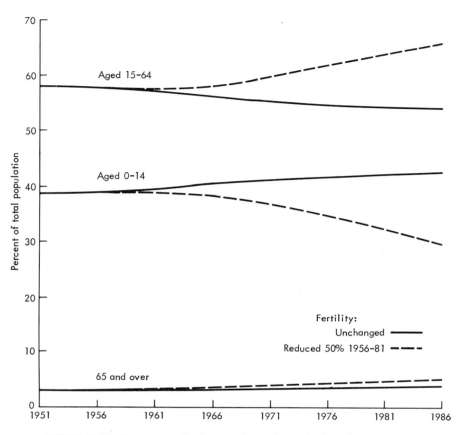

FIGURE 11.1. Percentage distribution of population by broad age groups under various assumptions, India, 1951–1986. Source: Coale and Hoover 1958, p. 41, Chart 4.

As K. Davis (1951) had previously observed in his study of the population there, the Indian subcontinent's rapid population growth attributable to high fertility yields an "unusual burden of young-age dependency," much of which is "wasted" in that "women are pregnant, give birth to, and nurse millions of babies each year who die before they reach a productive age. Energy, food, and supplies are wasted on them." Coale and Hoover are able to show that expenditures on the education, housing, social services, and consumption connected with high dependency operate to drain India's investment and development capability (see figures 11.2 and 11.3). Under conditions of continued high fertility, annual increases in income per consumer and in consumption per consumer are likely to be quite modest indeed, despite a substantial rate of

TABLE 11.1
*Approximate Number of Nonearning
Dependents per Earner under
Alternative Population Projections,
1956–1986*[a]

| | Projection | | |
	Low	Medium	High
1956	1.51	1.51	1.51
1961	1.53	1.55	1.55
1966	1.52	1.60	1.60
1971	1.46	1.60	1.63
1976	1.37	1.51	1.65
1981	1.29	1.37	1.69
1986	1.24	1.25	1.71

SOURCE: Coale and Hoover 1958, p. 235,
table 32.
[a]Assuming total number of full and part
earners is 68.4 percent of number of persons aged 15–64, as in 1951.

annual increase in national income. However, under conditions of medium or low fertility, not only would the annual rate of increase in national income be substantially higher, but the rate of increase in income
per consumer and in consumption per consumer would be three to four
times higher than under conditions of high fertility (table 11.2).

Similar analyses have been carried out for other underdeveloped
areas, and in each case the policy implications seem clear: countries seek-

FIGURE 11.2. Developmental expenditures as a proportion of national
income, with high and low fertility, India, 1956–1986. Source: Coale and
Hoover 1958, p. 276, Chart 11.

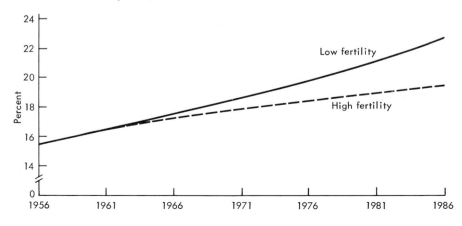

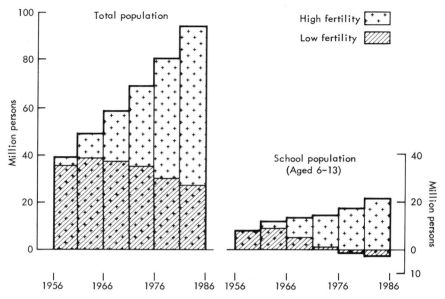

FIGURE 11.3.   Quinquennial increases in total population and in population of primary-school age, with high and low fertility, India, 1956–1986. Source: Coale and Hoover 1958, p. 265, Chart 9.

ing to promote rapid development and increased levels of living must seek ways to lower fertility, an insight which has been widely adopted in both popular and the scientific discussions of the "world population explosion" and the "world population crisis." However, there are other aspects of the relationship between population growth and development, and we return to this topic in the next section.

3. POPULATION PROCESSES, SOCIAL DISORGANIZATION, AND SOCIAL CHANGE

SOCIAL DISORGANIZATION.   Social disorganization here refers to an impairment in the functioning of a social system, that is, to the inability of a social system to attain its goals because of conflict, inconsistencies, or an absence of coordination among its elements (Matras 1965). As an example, we may take the family as a social system: thus, the family whose major earner is unemployed is unable to see to the welfare and sustenance of its members and hence may be said to be disorganized. Similarly, the community unable to perform an essential service for lack of leadership or resources, or the school unable to offer appropriate instruction by reason of overcrowding, may both be said to be disorganized.

TABLE 11.2
*Annual Rates of Increase in National Income, per Consumer Income,
and per Consumer "Consumption," by Five-Year Periods
(Projection 1)*

	Percentage Increase Per Annum					
	1956– *1961*	*1961–* *1966*	*1966–* *1971*	*1971–* *1976*	*1976–* *1981*	*1981–* *1986*
National Income						
High fertility	3.3	3.3	3.4	3.4	3.4	3.5
Medium fertility	3.3	3.3	3.4	3.5	3.7	4.0
Low fertility	3.3	3.5	3.7	3.9	4.2	4.5
Income per Consumer						
High fertility	1.4	1.2	1.0	1.0	0.9	0.9
Medium fertility	1.4	1.2	1.2	1.6	2.1	2.8
Low fertility	1.5	1.6	1.8	2.3	2.9	3.4
"Consumption" per Consumer						
High fertility	1.2	1.0	0.9	0.8	0.8	0.8
Medium fertility	1.2	1.0	1.0	1.4	1.9	2.5
Low fertility	1.3	1.4	1.6	2.0	2.6	3.0

SOURCE: Coale and Hoover 1958, p. 273, table 38.

The resolution of social disorganization, or "social reorganization," depends on social processes operating to diminish conflicts within the given social group, to increase coordination and solidarity within that group, and to enhance the group's ability to perform its functions and attain its goals. Such processes have long been viewed by social scientists as major stimulants to social structural change, for through them the content of roles is changed and role and subsystem relationships within groups, institutions, or communities change as well.[2]

POPULATION PROCESSES AS CAUSES OF SOCIAL DISORGANIZATION. Population processes may be the direct or indirect causes of social disorganization. Both the changing *size* of population elements and the changing absolute or relative numerical relationships between them may render a group, institution, or social system unable to function or pursue its goals. Population growth or changing age, class, or ethnic composition may render political institutions or decision-making processes inappropriate by making it impossible for them to serve their communities properly (cf. Hauser 1965). Thus, the "town meeting" form of decision-making becomes unwieldy when communities become large. Similarly, community

2 For the classic statements of this theory of social change, see Merton (1957) and Cohen (1955).

councils, assemblies, and legislative bodies with very heterogeneous constituencies cannot operate on an issue-by-issue basis but must form coalitions, political machines, and political exchange and trade-off routines. These, in turn, themselves become "disorganized" under changing population composition and must be periodically revamped.

Political elites typically are unable to remain "closed" under conditions of population growth and changing composition. Rather, they must either coopt new elements or "circulate"—give way to competitors—in their entireties. German, Irish, Jewish, and Italian immigrants, and Negroes and Puerto Ricans, have found their places in the political arenas of some—though not all—of the largest urban centers in the United States. And in much the same way, the Russian-Jewish immigrants originally monopolizing power in the Jewish community of pre-independence Palestine and of Israel have ultimately been obliged to share this power with Central and Western European immigrants, with Middle Eastern immigrants, with native Israelis, and, increasingly, with Arab groups in Israel.

Educational institutions provide another example of social systems disorganized by changing population composition. Primary and secondary schools serving pupils of one or a combination of several class, religious, ethnic, or racial origins, with whatever preschool socialization patterns are associated with these, are typically forced to introduce changes in curriculum and teaching routines when obliged to serve children with different origins and socialization histories. Thus, the migration and social mobility that affect a school district disorganize the school itself and make changes in procedures, and possibly in staff, imperative. Obviously the process of disorganization and change can extend to entire school systems in and outside "ghetto areas." Similarly, the disorganization can easily extend to other educational institutions as well, e.g., colleges and universities.

Similar processes might be outlined for churches, voluntary organizations, police forces, business and industry, communications, recreational institutions, etc. The changing composition of a population, whether it be by age, race ethnicity, religion, social class, or educational achievement, and changing size too, may well cause some institutionalized set of relationships to become disorganized—that is, to be unable to continue in the manner and direction in which they were previously stabilized—and thus force change in the content of roles and in the nature of social relationships.

How Changing Population Composition Can Disorganize the Economy. We return to a point made in the preceding chapter by considering the effect of changing population composition upon business and industry or upon the economy. The economy routinely and recur-

TABLE 11.3

*Educational Attainment of U.S. Males, 25–29 Years of Age, 1910–1960:
Percentage Distributions*

Date	Total	Completed Less Than Five Years of School	Completed Five or More Years of School; Did Not Complete High School	Completed High School or Beyond; Did Not Complete College	Completed College; Four Years or More	Median Number of School Years Completed
Census						
1960	100.0	3.4	22.5	59.7	14.4	12.3
1950	100.0	5.4	34.4	50.6	9.6	12.0
1940	100.0	6.9	50.2	36.0	6.9	10.1
Estimate						
1930	100.0	10.6	58.3	24.6	6.5	8.7
1920	100.0	16.7	59.2	19.2	4.9	8.4
1910	100.0	21.2	59.0	15.7	4.1	8.2

SOURCE: Adapted from Folger and Nam 1964, table 4.

rently becomes "disorganized" by the changing educational-achievement composition of successive cohorts of new entrants into the labor force. In the United States and in some other Western countries in recent years, each new cohort of job-seekers has been slightly different in composition from the cohort of persons leaving the labor force or dying. Table 11.3 and figure 11.4 show the difference in composition by educational attainment for U.S. labor-force entrants between 1910 and 1960.

No economy can integrate young persons with university degrees into the kinds of occupations and production arrangements in which persons with grade-school education have previously been functioning. Moreover, in addition to the disorganization brought on by differences in educational achievement, economies are probably likewise disorganized by the need to integrate the city-born and -bred into occupations and productive processes previously manned by the farm-born and -bred. Similarly, disorganization would probably attend the need to integrate persons born after World War II into jobs and work situations being vacated by persons born at the turn of the century. The economy, and every sector of the economy, must innovate and introduce changes, just as other social systems must. "Thus," as Ryder has put it, "social change occurs to the extent that successive cohorts do something other than merely repeat the patterns of behavior of their predecessors" (1964; see also Ryder 1965).

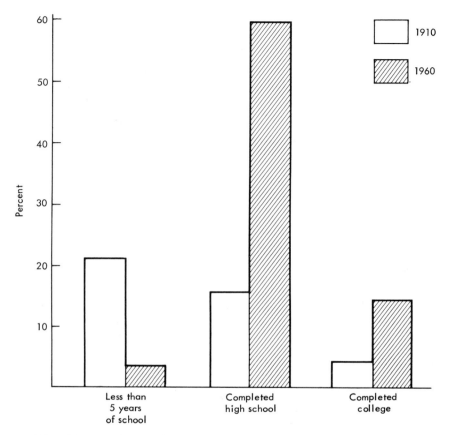

FIGURE 11.4. Educational attainment of U.S. males aged 25–29 in 1910 and 1960. Source: Table 11.3.

Of course, this is not an inevitable process: In societies with little migration, with little or no increase in educational opportunities, or with restricted social mobility, the composition of successive cohorts entering the working force is much more stable and most parts of the economy are less likely to be confronted by such disorganization. In such societies, there is less pressure for change and innovation in productive processes and in economic organization. But this is another way of making a point advanced in the previous chapter: technology, economic organization, and occupational distribution—far from being exogenous to social systems and social organization—are themselves a social system and deeply affected by the mobility regime and by population processes generally.

How Population Processes May Cause the Restructuring of Institutionalized Relationships. Population processes may cause a restructuring of institutionalized relations between groups, social systems, and subsystems whether accompanied or unaccompanied by conflict. This is because changing numerical relationships between aggregates of role incumbents—changes which occur as by-products of population processes —operate to change the nature and content of relationships between roles and between systems or roles quite apart from the presence or absence of institutional or systematic disorganization.

We may see this by considering the social and economic relationships between rural and urban populations as they have changed over time. Early in this century, the United States had a predominantly rural population. We may think of urban places at that time, and of the urban minority of the population, as organized basically to service the rural majority of the population, i.e., to provide commercial services and certain processed and fabricated products and to coordinate networks of communication in a vast agricultural society.

In 1900 there were about two urban dwellers for every 3 rural dwellers in the United States. By 1960, however, there were about seven urban dwellers for every 3 rural ones. The country had become largely an urban nation serviced, as it were, by a gradually shrinking rural population. The change in numbers alone has occasioned a restructuring of the relationship between urban and rural dwellers. The rural population today is organized basically to service the urban majority population instead of the reverse: it provides agricultural and other primary products for the pervasive—and, often, food-processing services—network of urban communities. Increasingly, however, the rural population provides also certain communications (road construction and maintenance, for example) and recreational services for the majority urban population as well. Both urban and rural economies and occupational structures, and the relationships between them, have been transformed in the wake of the population transformation and redistribution.

Let us consider next the role of the college teacher or professor and its relationship to the rest of the social structure. In 1900 a total of 7,000 persons out of some 29 million in the working force reported college teaching as their occupation. Thus, the college professor then was a rare and unusual person. By 1950, however, there were 127,000 college teachers and professors, although the working force had only doubled in size (to some 59 million). And by 1960 there were 177,000 college professors and teachers in an experienced working force of some 68 million. In the same period, the number of gasoline station proprietors and managers increased from 2,000 in 1900 to 186,000 in 1950, to 198,000 in 1960. Simultaneously, the number of blacksmiths, forgemen, and hammermen declined from 220,000 in 1900, to 60,000 in 1950, and to 33,000 in 1960 (U.S. Bureau of the Census, "Historical Statistics" 1960, and "Population Census" PC (2)–7A).

Between 1900 and 1960 the role of the college professor changed, and so did its relationship to the social structure—*in part* because of the large increase in the number of college teachers employed. Similarly, being a gasoline station operator or a blacksmith in the 1960s is different from what it was in 1900, in part because of the changing numbers in these occupations. Conversely, although the total number of physicians in the United States has increased in this century along with the rest of the population, the ratio of physicians to the rest of the population has changed but little. The nature of the physician's role, his status, and his relationship to the rest of the social structure varies in the different settings of the U.S. partly in accordance with the numerical physician-to-population ratio, an observation which clearly has not escaped the attention of those organized medical practitioners who oppose the expansion of medical education and an increase in number of colleagues.

Consider, finally, an urban community characterized by a given occupational and place-of-origin distribution and a given racial composition. The population process which brings into this community a large number of rural migrants of different occupational skills and different races of ethnic backgrounds changes the composition of the community *and* the relationships between its different occupational, ethnic, racial, duration-of-residence, or neighborhood groupings. Regardless of whether community or institution disorganization occurs, the balance and institutionalized relationships between the subsystems and groupings change. To the extent that one or more groups are dissatisfied with the changing relationships, social conflict may result.

Some social scientists have held that conflict *always* results in such a shifting of relationships between population groups and subsystems.[3] Whether or not this is true, it is important here to see that changes in the numerical relationships between population elements occupying different social roles and subsystems may have the effect of changing the nature and content of relationships between roles and between subsystems.

Population Growth and the Division of Labor

The "social division of labor," so central to Durkheim's analysis of societies and their variations, represents the first major response to popu-

---

3 The classic treatment of this problem is contained in the discussions of competition, conduct, accommodation, and assimilation in Park and Burgess (1921).

lation growth. Actually, the division of labor is a twofold process. It includes both the differentiation of individual social roles *and* the differentiation of subsystems in the society. Thus, for the absence or presence of the first kind of differentiation, we can contrast the society or community with little or no occupational differentiation—say, one in which all males are hunters and collectors and all females cultivators—with the society embracing a large variety of more specialized occupations: those engaging farmers, builders, rulers, traders, soldiers, drivers, machine operators, laborers, etc. As for systemic differentiation, we can contrast the society in which there is none—where the family or lineage is the sole unit of production, religious activity, defense, education, and so on—with the society in which there is extensive differentiation among subsystems: the family, the church, the army, the schools, the levels of government, etc., all separately identifiable.

The Effects of Population Size

It is the sheer *number* of persons belonging to a society which represents not only the totality of the society's human resources but also the *possibility,* in quantitative terms, of its social role differentiation, division of labor, variety and complexity of social relationships, tolerance for deviations from the mode, and multiplicity of values and interests. Moreover, the sheer *number* of persons belonging to a society is basic to the requirements of communication, the chain of power and authority, and the volume, range, and varieties of economic exchange.

Large population size renders individual eccentricities, idiosyncrasies, needs, and pursuits largely irrelevant to the survival, adaptation, and pursuit of the collective good which is the main business of any community *qua* community. If a total population represents a society's totality of human resources, then the larger the population the greater are both the *totality* of human resources and the *variety* of human resources, abilities, needs, and wishes. Larger population sizes permit a heterogeneity and differentiation of skills and needs, and they also allow the deviant and nonmodal to coexist with the modal.[4]

If mechanisms appear for mobilizing, organizing, and exploiting differences in taste, abilities, and activities, then production, consumption, and survival and adaptation are enhanced. Moreover, the principle of division of labor is recognized and institutionalized. Relationships among individuals and among social units (e.g., communities, cities, regions, nations) are thus symbiotic, being largely "exchange" relationships ("organic" rather than "mechanical," in Durkheim's terminology). Social

---

4 Ogburn and Duncan (1964) cite data in support of the idea that city size is directly related to tolerance of eccentricity, receptiveness to innovation, and overall inventiveness. See also the classic statement by Wirth (1938).

institutions—and by these we mean everything from motherhood, to the factory, to the political machine, to the international oil development countries—which are as purposive as societies themselves, can be analytically distinguished according to whether they are devoted to sustenance-producing activities (however elaborate the "sustenance" may turn out to be), or to the mediation of relationships among individuals and among "specialized" units or subsystems.

The multiplicity and mediational quality of institutions in communities and societies with large populations reflect the institutionalization of specialization and division of labor. An immediate consequence of population *size* is the absolute number of individual role and subsystem relationships which must be patterned and organized in some stable way so as to make possible the uninterrupted conduct of social relationships and of the society's affairs.

Social institutions are themselves confronted with conflicting exigencies the larger and more differentiated their population settings. First, they may be so small in size, or in number of roles, or in number of role incumbents, that individual eccentricities and differences of need, purpose, and behavior cannot be a matter of indifference. The reason for this is that individual institutions cannot sustain anything like the scale of deviance that an entire society or community can tolerate, and this is the case irrespective of the size of the population. Second, recalling our point about the large absolute number of mediating institutions in societies with large populations, it is clear that any social institution in a highly differentiated, multi-institutional community is inevitably *in competition with* other, more or less similar, social institutions in the same community to the extent that participation is voluntary. Institutions defecting from this competition risk extinction.

This "market" of institutionalized subsystems in competition with one another constitutes the setting for the interpersonal tensions and pressures on which Georg Simmel focused (Simmel 1950, especially his famous "Metropolis and Mental Life"). It can be viewed as a direct output of population size and the institutionalization of differentiation or division of labor. We shall return to this topic briefly in our discussion of population density.

The point to be made here is that social institutions must respond and change if they are to survive under conditions of large, highly differentiated, populations and under competition with alternative institutions. And more than this, they must build into themselves, or "institutionalize," an ongoing awareness and evaluation of the "competition" and an ability to respond and change. Many institutions have not done this. For example, a large variety of institutions of the home —from sewing and canning, to Bible instruction for children, to musical recitals and songfests—have disappeared or have been transferred else-

where. On the other hand, sex and childbearing, the nurture and socialization of young children, and the economic and social division of labor
among husband, wife, and other members remain family institutions.

The Effects of Population Density

If increasing population size generates the *possibility* of social differentiation, division of labor, and institutional variety and complexity,
then it is abundantly clear that it is increasing population *density* which
generates the *necessity* for differentiation and complexity. For high population density creates many social exigencies which do not necessarily
attend large population size alone. These include (1) a high frequency of
human contact by reason of simple propinquity; (2) a competition for
space; (3) a competition for *access* to places, activities, and institutions;
and (4) a competition for *priority* of attention and participation. In addition, high population density operates (5) to reduce costs and to simplify
exchange, two factors which together directly promote specialization, the
production for markets, and market relationships and institutions. Table
11.4 illustrates variations in density of cities in the different continents
and at different time points.

In chapter 2 we presented some simple calculations by P. M. Hauser
which indicated the notable increase in volume of possible daily contacts
associated with increased population density.[5] Thus, with increasing population density there is a greater need for institutionalized arrangements
and relationships able to mediate and regulate contacts and to assign
priorities. Moreover, the very volume and frequency of social contact
presses in the direction of enhancing the specificity, shortening the duration, and diminishing the information exchanged in each contact.

In communities of very low density, the number of potential contacts is small and an individual may have and maintain contact with
everyone "in contact range," i.e., with everyone in the community. Moreover, his contacts with another person may be long-lived over time and
may embrace different kinds of relationships. Thus, persons may be
more or less well-organized over the years in their business, friendship,
political, and neighborly contacts, but often a contact will cover several
of these areas at the same time.

Quite the reverse may be the case in high-density communities,
where the great majority of human contacts are very specific in nature and
purpose and very short-lived in time. Of course, *some* social relationships
are more diffuse, or more extended over time, even in high-density communities, but it is just such a process of sorting and assigning priorities
to social relationships which, we said earlier, was an imperative of the
high-density population.

5 For more elaborate presentations, see Simmel 1950, chap. 3; Hauser 1958.

TABLE 11.4

Density of Selected Cities in Various Years between 1822 and 1960

City	Date	Density per sq. mile	City	Date	Density per sq. mile
Asia			*Continental Europe*		
Calcutta	1881	73,815	Aarhus	1950	72,261
	1901	120,435	Berlin	1885	290,080
	1921	132,090		1900	409,220
	1951	217,560	Budapest	1935	279,720
Colombo		99,974	Copenhagen	1940	59,829
Djarkarta	—	33,152	Frankfurt	1890	142,450
Hong Kong	1931	802,900		1933	88,060
Hyderabad	1951	199,430	Oslo	1938	79,772
(Pakistan)			Paris	1817	450,660
Manila	—	72,520		1856	239,575
Nagoya	1950	30,044		1896	370,370
Okayama	1939	360,010		1931	471,380
	1953	240,870		1946	180,005
Osaka	1950	32,116	Stockholm	1940	110,075
Poona	1822	75,110	Vienna	1890	170,940
	1881	95,312	Zurich	1936	84,952
	1953	200,725			
Rangoon	1931	199,430	*United States*		
	1951	119,140	Allentown	1950	15,022
Sholapur	1869	42,735	Baltimore	1950	99,974
	1938	129,759	Birmingham	1950	10,101
Singapore	1953	660,450	Boston	1900	160,580
Tokyo	1950	60,088		1940	45,066
			Bridgeport	1950	59,570
Australia and New Zealand			Buffalo	1950	49,987
Brisbane	1901	17,094	Chicago	1880	97,125
	1933	24,864		1900	99,974
	1947	37,037		1940	71,225
Christchurch	1911	39,886		1956	63,455
	1936	39,886	Cleveland	1940	78,995
	1951	54,908	Dallas	1950	11,914
Dunedin	1911	11,137	Detroit	1950	50,505
	1936	9,065	Hartford	1950	29,785
	1951	8,029	Indianapolis	1950	20,202
Melbourne	1933	64,750	Los Angeles	1940	29,008
	1954	35,483	Minneapolis	1950	20,202
Sydney	1911	25,900	New Orleans	1950	59,570
	1947	34,965	New York	1900	178,710
	1954	24,087		1910	59,052
Wellington	1911	27,972		1925	81,326
	1936	24,864		1940	110,075
	1951	18,907		1950	239,575
			Omaha	1950	13,986
British Isles			Philadelphia	1900	112,147
				1940	55,944
Birmingham	1921	103,859	Rochester	1950	30,044
	1938	52,059	San Francisco	1960	40,145
Dublin	1936	69,930	Seattle	1950	40,145
Leeds	1951	30,044	St. Louis	1900	120,435
Liverpool	1921	330,225		1940	34,965
London	1801	269,360		1950	40,145
	1841	279,720	Washington	1948	32,116
	1871	224,035		1955	24,087
	1901	170,940	Youngstown	1950	59,570
	1921	114,737			
	1931	123,025	*Caribbean*		
	1939	82,880			
	1951	62,160	Kingston	1891	49,210
	1961	53,095		1911	68,376
Manchester	1939	37,037		1943	37,037
				1960	40,922

SOURCE: C. Clark 1967, pp. 349–50.

For ten cents the New York City resident can pick up a telephone, dial a number, and say, "Good morning" or, "How are you?" to any of several million other New Yorkers. He can buy or sell stocks through any of the scores of stock brokers or representatives. For the same price of a telephone call, he can order a sandwich, or reserve a dinner table, or have a new television set sent over, or arrange to try out the latest car model from Detroit—in each case through any of the several hundred establishments so engaged. He can invite any one or many of the other several millions to attend his daughter's wedding or debut or communion or piano recital, or his son's ball game or bar mitzvah.

It is the system of institutions which sort out social relationships and assign priorities to them which especially characterizes high-density communities. Thus, in big city neighborhoods nuclear and extended family groupings, schools, and industries all generate social settings within which recurring and diffuse relationships take place. But riding the subway or bus, buying the morning newspaper, getting "information" on the telephone, and any of the hundreds of other simple, everyday, transactions all comprise patterned social relationships which typically are of short duration, recur between the same role incumbents with only small probability, and the "anonymity," "isolation," and "atomization" characteristic of life in dense communities. There is, as Keyfitz has observed, a reciprocal *assumption*—rather than any actual knowledge—of the mutual competence of role incumbents engaged in social relationships and transactions with each other but unknown to one another beyond the confines of the specific instance at hand (Keyfitz 1965).

Since the amount of area per person in a population is, of course, the inverse of the number of persons per areal unit (the latter being the usual measure of population density), it is clear that space becomes a scarce commodity in direct proportion to the degree of population density. Aside from the sheer *amount* of space which may be available to each person, group, or activity, it is usually the case that locations are differentially *desirable* to the different persons and groups and for different reasons. Thus, the allocation of space in a community is necessarily more rigorously regulated the greater the population density, and it may be carried out through a number of institutionalized arrangements. A ruler or government may simply parcel out space on the basis of some specific criteria or with no basis other than momentary fancy. Or if private property is institutionalized in the society, there is likely to be a market and price mechanism strongly influencing the allocation of space. In many communities customs, tradition, or zoning laws regulate the use of space, regardless of whether or not there is a real property market. Thus, especially in high-density communities, there tends to be a real concentration and segregation of specific population types and of specific social and economic institutions and activities. There may be racial or ethnic segregation and there may be residential areas, business or industrial areas, hotel and transient areas, areas of growing families, areas with a large concentration of educational institutions, and areas devoted largely to entertainment establishments.

Competition for space is reflected not only in communities of the highest density but in smaller urban and in rural communities as well. However, in communities of lower density the competition for space takes a distinctly different form, being reflected primarily in different patterns of price, land use, and—in rural communities—in the different crops grown and density of cultivation rather than in different occupancy patterns.

In communities of the lowest density, nearly *all* persons are able to live in relatively uncongested surroundings; and regardless of the size or quality of the dwelling unit, it is likely to have windows and light on all sides and to be surrounded by at least some land unoccupied by other structures. Individual residential lots may vary in size, and dwellings may vary in size and facilities, but the residential areas do not tend to become highly differentiated with respect to population or occupancy types. Similarly, business and industrial properties may vary in size and facilities, but beyond there being a generalized "business center" and "industrial areas," these types of occupancy do not seem to be further differentiated.

By contrast, in the highest-density communities even persons or families who are quite well off may not be able to afford the luxury of a "detached" dwelling unit, that is, of a unit surrounded by at least some land area that is not built up. Moreover, there tend to arise blocks of homogeneous dwelling-unit types which, in turn, attract concentrations of occupant types: young married couples, unattached persons, retired persons, the rich, the newly married, etc. Similarly, there tend to be enclaves of homogeneous industrial or business properties— wholesalers, fish markets, garment industries, jewelers, importers, clothing retailers, book publishers—which tend to be located in distinctive areas. And among these dwelling units and commercial concentrations there tend to be corresponding enclaves of institutions serving, or composed of, the type of people living or working there.

Thus, we have the home-maintenance business, the do-it-yourself stores, the neighborhood improvement organizations, and the Welcome Wagon clubs for home owners; and the schools, the candy-and-ice cream shops, the boys' clubs, and the Girl Scout troops for the children and adolescents; and businesses-of-a-kind have purveyors and suppliers of specialized products and services nearby: restaurant suppliers or button-and-zipper purveyors, or iron-mongers for the workshops and ice-men for the fishmongers. The elderly have golden age clubs and churches

TABLE 11.5

*Median Commuting Time of Workers in New York
Metropolitan Region, by Job Type and Sex, 1956*

Job Type	Median Commuting Time (minutes)		
	Both sexes	Men	Women
Office & clerical	46	50	44
Executive & professional	44	—*	—*
Shop or factory	34	—*	—*
Retail sales	27	34	24

SOURCE: Hoover and Vernon 1962, p. 153.
    *Not calculated. Respondents in this category were predominantly male.

and health food stores and doctors' offices and group-practice clinics. And the young adults have eating places and clubs—commercial and private—for nourishment, amusement, and conversation.

Aside from the scarcity of space itself and the competition for *occupancy* of space in very high-density communities, there is the further problem of *access* to key areas, institutions, or activities. The network of transportation and communication in any society typically renders some locations more accessible than others. The problem of accessibility for workers in different occupations and of each sex is illustrated by the data in table 11.5.

As an institutionalized means of coping with problems of mutual accessibility, highways, public transportation, and communications media are more elaborate the greater the population density. Thus, high-density communities may have a multiplicity of newspapers and magazines, each serving a particular neighborhood, or the speakers of a particular foreign language, or a specialized industrial sector, or a particular occupation, or a single corporation. There are specialized fleets of messengers and vehicles, specialized telephone and teletype networks, and an increasing body of private-frequency radio communications—all with large numbers of persons engaged in their development and maintenance.

The relationship between income, residential density, and access to the metropolitan center has been compactly summarized by E. M. Hoover and R. Vernon for the New York Metropolitan Region in the 1950s:

> . . . Certain consistent and striking relations of income level to other community characteristics appear at once in table [11.6]. Higher-income places tend to be smaller in population, as roughly shown by the average number of dwelling units per place in the various income ranges.
>
> Net residential density declines consistently with rising income, that is, higher-income people buy more space per household. Associated with this density relation is the fact that the higher-

TABLE 11.6

Characteristics of Urban Places in the Land-Use Survey Area in Relation to Median 1949 Income of Families and Unrelated Individuals

Places According to Rank in 1949 Median Income	Median Income, 1949[a]	Average Number of Dwelling Units per place, 1954	Dwelling Units per Acre of Residentially Developed Land, 1954-55	Percent of Dwelling Units in Multifamily Structures, 1950[a]	Average Access-Zone Rating	Percent Increase in Dwelling Units, 1950-54
All places	$3,929	8,057	8.06	[b]	2.85	10%
Top fifth	5,128	3,510	3.69	12%	2.92	18
2nd fifth	4,288	4,040	4.94	13	3.12	12
3rd fifth	3,925	7,519	7.51	16	2.80	14
4th fifth	3,572	9,016	8.34	23	2.84	8
Bottom fifth	3,235	16,365	14.32	39	2.56	7
Bottom tenth[c]	3,078	24,476	19.10	39	2.23	4

SOURCE: Hoover and Vernon 1962, table 38, p. 160.

[a]Unweighted median of urban places in each group.

[b]Not calculated.

[c]Hoboken, Newark, Paterson, Orange, Union City, Edgewater, Jersey City, Guttenberg (Hudson), Harrison (Hudson), Passaic, Paramus (Bergen), Glen Cove (Nassau), and Washington Township (Bergen).

income places have a smaller proportion of their housing in multi-family structures. Commuting time to Manhattan tends to increase with higher income levels, though not at all sharply. For the highest-income fifth of these places, the access rating averages only about half a point more—equivalent to only 7 or 8 minutes' difference in commuting time—than for the lowest-income fifth.

Finally, higher income level appears to be associated with a higher recent rate of population growth and construction activity, as crudely measured by the estimated percentage increase in the number of dwelling units from 1950 to 1954. This reflects the fact that higher-income people tend to live in newer housing than lower-income people, and also the fact that the relatively spacious type of housing that higher-income people choose is more readily available in the kind of suburb in which there is still some space left for new construction.

Table [11.6] suggests, therefore, that higher-income people use their superior purchasing power to buy lower density, but at the cost of a longer journey to work. The relation is more clearly seen if we sort out the communities by *both* access and income level, as is done in table [11.7]. Reading up the columns of the table, we can see that for any given degree of access, higher income goes with lower density. Reading across the rows, we can see that for any given level of income, better access goes with higher density. Most of the exceptions are quantitatively insignificant. Finally, reading table [11.7] diagonally from lower right to upper left, one can discern a rough tendency for families with higher income to be closer to the center of the Region for any given level of density. Thus, only the two highest income groups get as far in as access zone 2 with densities of fewer than 8 dwelling units to the acre, settling in such places as Scarsdale, Bronxville, and Pelham Manor; lower-income communities tend to have such space standards only when they are substantially farther out. [Hoover and Vernon 1962, pp. 159–62]

The institutions for mitigating differences and competition notwithstanding, there remains in high-density communities considerable variation in accessibility to persons, institutions, activities, and information. Indeed, such variation constitutes an important axis of social differentiation in high-density communities and is related to other dimensions of social differentiation. Thus, for example, in high-density communities the lowest educational, income, or status groupings may have little if any direct access to the polity, that is, to the decision-making, resource-controlling, or value-formulating subsystems and roles in the society. However, institutions such as the political "machine," settlement houses, labor unions, churches, or voluntary organizations have sometimes afforded access to the polity to otherwise disenfranchised groups, thereby compensating in part for their disadvantage in the competition for access to power. Analogous situations obtain with respect to access to jobs, education, medical services, shopping, recreation, and relatively unpolluted air.

Finally, we may note that high population density, entailing as it does high frequency and a great variety of social interactions and relationships, operates to reduce the costs of exchange; and it operates more generally to simplify social and economic transactions, the division of labor, and coordination and corporate ventures of every sort. Not only are the mean costs of transferring commodities reduced by high population density, but, perhaps more important, the costs and delays of trans-

TABLE 11.7

Net Residential Density (Dwelling Units per Acre of Residentially Developed Land) in Urban Places in the Land-Use Survey Area, by Median 1949 Income and Access Zone

Median-Income Ranking	Access Zone				
	1	*2*	*3*	*4*	*5*
Top fifth	—	3.82 (2)[b]	3.86 (5)	3.26 (2)	—
2nd fifth	—	5.69 (3)	5.29 (5)	4.05 (2)	3.21 ([a])
3rd fifth	—	8.90 (11)	6.22 (4)	6.52 (3)	3.28 ([a])
4th fifth	7.80 (1)	9.61 (9)	8.48 (10)	5.39 (2)	4.31 ([a])
Bottom fifth	27.79 (26)	7.86 (5)	9.29 (8)	2.23 ([a])	3.83 (1)

SOURCE: Hoover and Vernon 1962, table 39, p. 161.

[a]Less than 0.5 per cent of total dwelling units.

[b]Figures in parentheses indicate what percentage of the 1,015,243 dwelling units is accounted for by places in each access-income category.

ferring information are substantially reduced as well. Thus, it is only in high-density communities that assembly lines can systematically replace fabrication in workshops and that production can be geared to an anonymous market rather than to the order of specific consumers. In places of very low density, e.g., Saudi Arabia, the expense of providing specialized teachers and educational facilities, and the difficulties and costs of communication entailed, have dampened the pace of institutionalization of formal education and of elaborate curative or preventive medical services. Conversely, in large American cities—high-density communities by all criteria—it has become increasingly evident that high schools and hospitals must be of some minimum size—that is, serve fairly large minimum numbers of pupils or patients—in order to operate reasonably efficiently in providing more or less standard services.

The low-density community may have its builder or building contractor, but in communities of the highest density even small structures are built by an elaborate system of architects, contractors, and subcontractors, each specializing in some particular facet of the operation. Such specialization and cooperation in erecting structures is possible only because high density initially places all elements in the transaction in close proximity and reduces the costs of meetings, informational exchange, and overall coordination.

Population Growth and the Expansion of Boundary Systems

THE CONCEPT OF SOCIAL BOUNDARY SYSTEMS. The concept of a "social boundary system" has been proposed and elaborated by the anthropologist Yehudi A. Cohen to designate a "structured system of relationships in which individuals are bound to one another by complex and ramifying ties," or "a network of social relations of the people who are required and permitted to engage in a sphere of social activity" (Cohen 1969). A social boundary system is distinguished from a social network or subsystem of social roles by the fact of being bounded. Thus, some social networks—a group riding a bus, a crowd watching an athletic event, drivers on a given stretch of highway—constitute subsystems that are not bounded, for anyone can enter or leave the network with very little ado. Other social networks—a married couple, a family, members of a political party, citizens of the United States—are bounded. In other words, they are set off from all other such units and have limits or demarcations—social boundaries—such that individuals and influences can pass across them or be excluded by them. According to Cohen, a network is "firmly bounded" to the extent that (1) persons and influences are excluded from it, and (2) admission to membership is determined by some "rite of passage" or ceremonial form (*ibid.*, p. 107). A bounded network not so characterized is said to be "weakly bounded."

Cohen proposes using the concept of "social boundary systems" as a central unit of analysis in exploring the following kinds of questions: How many groups and levels of organization—i.e., how many social boundary systems and levels of systems—can a society maintain? Can the same types of social relations be maintained in all of a society's groups? Can the same kinds of groups be maintained by societies at all stages of cultural-technological development? How do a society's groups affect each other and the society as a whole? What are the effects of a society's total organization on its component groups? What consequences do the directions of evolutionary change have on societies' groups and the organization of social relations within them?

Among the characteristics of social boundary systems to be investigated are the strength of the boundaries, the transposability of roles within boundary systems—i.e., the extent to which role relationships can be altered within the system—the differentiation of networks or subsystems within social boundary systems, the degree of dissent and heterogeneity obtaining within boundary systems, and the competition and conflict existing among boundary systems. Cohen advances the hypotheses that the strength, i.e., firmness, of the boundaries of a social boundary system is (1) directly related to transposability of roles within the system, (2) inversely related to the system's ability to tolerate sustained, outspoken dissent, and (3) inversely related to the strength of boundaries maintained by the system's component subsystems and directly related to the overall homogeneity of membership. Accepting the principle, as formulated earlier by Nadel, that social systems are purposive, Cohen suggests that social boundary systems conflict to the extent that their aims overlap, or conversely, that the greater the divergence in the aims of boundary systems, the greater their potential for mutual compatibility.

Finally, Cohen raises the issue of different bases of "boundedness" and of taxonomies of social boundary systems. For example, social networks or subsystems may be bounded on territorial, economic, ethnic, or religious bases, to name just a few. But this issue is postponed in Cohen's discussion.

THE EXPANSION OF BOUNDARY SYSTEMS AS A MAJOR RESPONSE TO POPULATION GROWTH. We may view boundary systems as a general phenomenon in societies and recognize that they include such concrete social systems as communities, polities, economies, regions, and occupational groups or classes. The *expansion* of a boundary system means not simply that additional members are absorbed into the system and that some one role or set of roles has an enlarged number of role incumbents, but also that the number of component subsystems within the boundary system is increased. We think of the expansion of, say, an economy, or a polity, or a metropolitan hinterland, or a religion as the inclusion of additional persons and, especially, of additional social units or subsystems. Such expansion involves exactly the opposite of the bifurcation sometimes associated with population growth: it involves the broader integration of subsystems previously coexisting but independent. Such integration may take place by means of competition and domination, annexation, or other forms of merger or affiliation.

The second major response to population growth, then, is the expansion of boundary systems. Clearly, its processes complement and support those of the first major response, the differentiation and division of labor. However, they have two types of results that are independent of the enhanced division of labor. In the first place, the expansion of boundary systems allows economies of scale: the same grocer can serve two to three times as many consumers; and the same or slightly larger church, voluntary organization, political party, or factory can serve larger clienteles, saving both material and human resources. In the second place, the total volume of whatever is done in the boundary system—production, social exchange, control, instruction, travel, etc.—increases by virtue of the expansion of the system. Under these circumstances, there is a change in the content of the system's roles and in the nature of relationships between the roles (cf. Boulding 1953; Kuznets 1960). Thus, the political regime sovereign over a million persons changes when its sovereignty expands to include two or three million, the city with a hinterland of 20 square miles changes when its hinterland expands to 100 square miles; the state university serving 10,000 students undergoes changes when its student body increases to 50,000; and the firm employing 1,000 workers changes when it grows to 100,000 workers and ten subsidiaries. In every case, the volume of activity, exchange, and social relationships in the system increases as the system expands.

Boundary systems are always associated with material or social resources. These are "scarce," at least in the sense that each system seeks to assure or enhance its own resources. Boundary systems of similar types —nations, regimes, industries, organizations, extended families, grocery stores—tend to compete with each other for scarce material and social resources, and they seek to control or neutralize competing boundary systems. Other things being equal, increasing numbers of population permitting initial economies of scale and enhanced efficiency improve the boundary system's position vis-à-vis competing systems. Merger with the advantaged boundary system allows a less-advantaged one to share—and indeed further enhance—the benefits of increased scale and efficiency.

Population Growth and the Adoption of Innovations

At any moment in time, societies, through their individual members and through various subsystems, possess some information or ideas concerning ways of doing things *other than those practiced* in them. Chiefs and kings and legislatures know about alternative ways of ruling; farmers know about different kinds of crops or cultivation practices; traders know about other ways of striking bargains; artisans know about alternative materials and techniques. A large number of factors combine with sheer inertia to render it unlikely that such alternatives will be adopted, whether they involve production, trade, distribution, social relations, or social control. In particular, instrumental criteria favoring the adoption of alternative ways of doing things are typically ignored in the face of normative prescription of the current, less efficient procedures or in the face of general support for them.

But population growth confronts a society with a kind of crisis: the society must make some adjustment in its "strategy of survival and adaptation," i.e., in its arrangements for producing and distributing sustenance and for pursuing its other goals. Failure to do so entails diminished levels of living, or increased mortality, or other dislocations and breakdowns. Under such circumstances, institutional resistances to change may be overcome and alternative ways of producing, organizing, or controlling things or relationships may be tried and ultimately adopted.

In some spheres of some societies there is always a search for, and a readiness to try, new and more efficient ways of doings things. However there is *no* reason to assume that this is a general characteristic of societies or of social systems. On the other hand, as we shall try to show more fully below, there *is* reason to hypothesize that population growth does have this effect of promoting the trial and adoption of innovation to enhance productivity and efficiency.

We may also note that this process of adopting innovations differs from processes of discovery, increase of scientific knowledge, or invention (cf. Kuznets 1962; Nelson 1962). The latter may take place independently of, or in conjunction with, the adoption of innovations. Also, the relationship between population growth and either discovery, increase of scientific knowledge, or invention would seem to be much more complex: a relationship probably exists to the extent that the social differentiation associated with population growth yields separate specialized institutions promoting knowledge, discovery, and invention, but the connection between population growth and the adoption of innovations is much more direct.

It is important to see that innovations generating an increased productivity of material goods and services extend far beyond the usual types popularly associated with invention and technological change. For these innovations include not only technical improvements in such spheres as energy conversion, production, cultivation, and the development of new materials or crops, but also innovations in such dimensions as systems of payment, work-sequence arrangements, legal concepts (e.g., the modern corporation), and systems and institutions of planning. Similarly, they can include marketing, storage, transport, and communications developments. All these innovations may substantially improve either productivity or the distribution of products and hence increase per capita consumption and levels of living.

It should also be seen that innovations in social relations and in social control extend far beyond the popularly recognized range of national and local political systems and beyond the substitution of non-family religious, educational, recreational, or welfare institutions for those previously contained in the family. For example, the institutionalization of bureaucracies or of hierarchical organizations or social relations in many spheres represents a distinct type of social structural innovation. Two other examples of social structural innovation would be the substitution of universalistic for ascriptive criteria in role allocation and social relations and the institutionalization of mobility processes (i.e., great changes in institutions and rates of mobility).

4. POPULATION GROWTH AND SOCIAL CHANGE

If suppositions in this chapter and in chapter 2 are correct, we should find this central hypothesis to be true: that population growth in every type of society and in every social setting is followed or accompanied by the mutually supportive kinds of social structural change noted under the rubrics of (1) differentiation and division of labor, (2) expansion of social boundary systems, and (3) adoption of innovations. Moreover, for societies initially at a given "evolutionary stage," an appropriate combination of such social changes should be found to propel the society to the next higher evolutionary stage.[6] We define these stages by the societal taxonomy used in chapter 2:

1. Nomadic hunting and food-gathering hands.
2. Nomadic hunting and food-gathering tribal societies.
3. Settled hunting and food-gathering societies.
4. Horticultural village and tribal societies.

6 Cf. Parsons's discussion of the "enhancement of the adaptive capacity" of societies (1966, chap. 2).

5. Nomadic, herding, tribal societies
6. Agricultural state societies.
7. Industrial, urban-dominated, state societies.
8. Metropolitan-megalopolitan societies.

In addition to agricultural state societies and to industrial, urban-dominated, state societies, we may distinguish between "rural" and "urban" sectors or communities. We would like, if possible, to show that population growth in each of these types of societies or social settings has the effects on social structure indicated above, namely, differentiation and division of labor, expansion of social boundary systems, and adoption of innovations. In addition, we would like to be able to study the variations in these processes and inquire about their causes and consequences.[7]

Unfortunately, there are enormous difficulties in carrying out such an analysis. In the first place, as we have already indicated, for most societies at most times there are neither systematic data nor any bases for estimating population size. And the opportunities for estimating population growth over any time interval are even fewer. Although historical accounts of one or another society often inform us that "the population increased," there are generally no means of rendering such accounts more precise.[8]

Second, even where data on population size exist and it is possible to estimate changes in size over time, *and* where data representing changing social structure, division of labor, or technology are available for the same intervals, it is extremely difficult to assess relationships between population change and other changes.[9] In particular, there are many problems involved in the effort to assign causality to any process of change over time. Bearing these difficulties in mind, we shall attempt below to bring some illustrative materials to bear upon the central hypothesis of this chapter.

The Effects of Population Growth on Hunting and Gathering Societies

In an observation similar to our own comments early in this book concerning the volume of prehistorical populations, Clark and Haswell (1967) have said that "by far the greatest part of the whole time which

---

[7] Of course, our scheme does not exclude the possibility—indeed, the fact—of social changes occurring because of factors other than population growth; nor does it exclude the effects of social changes upon population growth.

[8] But see, for example, Clark (1961), especially chapters 3 and 7, for an important suggestion on beginning this enterprise.

[9] This difficulty obtains for contemporary societies, virtually all of which have recent histories of both population growth *and* social change.

the human race has spent on this earth . . . has been passed in communities living solely by hunting, fishing, and the gathering of wild products." Our knowledge of these hunting and gathering populations is dominated by, although not limited to, what we have learned about hunting and gathering societies which have survived to recent times.

There is considerable evidence that hunting and gathering societies vary with respect to both population size and key elements of social structure and technology. In general, the smallest populations and lowest bonds of social, cultural, or political integration are associated with the simplest adaptive strategies and the least elaborate technologies and social organization (cf. Steward 1955, Part II; Service 1966).

Some time ago, Krzywicki (1934) assembled sets of population estimates for different dates for each of a large number of Australian and North American tribes. For the most part, these estimates show declining populations in periods of increasing contact with Europeans. However, it is usually difficult to determine whether an estimated change over time reflects differences in estimation procedures or actual changes in the size of the tribal population.

In his theory of the transformation of societies from lower to higher levels of sociocultural integration—i.e., from family units to such levels as bands, lineages, or clans—Steward (1955, chap. 9) attributes the transformation to (1) improvements in technology, productivity, and/or environment, which make possible (2) increasing population size and density entailing larger social groups, or more groups each occupying less territory, or else multilineage settlements, and eventually (3) an intermingling of groups, the adoption of common symbols, and the transfer of political autonomy from the localized lineage to a larger group, i.e., to a higher level of sociocultural integration. Finally, Semenov (1967) has concluded that paleolithic, mesolithic, and neolithic peoples were engaged in an ongoing development and continuous improvement of tools. Prehistoric man, according to this analysis, continuously sought ever more rational and effective means of controlling his environment, so that prehistoric technological progress, far from constituting a series of accidental discoveries, actually resulted from a perpetual process of inquiry and of experimentation with new materials and technologies.

The fact remains, however, that there have been very few opportunities to study directly the *changes* in population, social structure, or technology taking place within hunting and gathering societies.[10] The

---

[10] Numerous scholars dealing with the transition from food gathering to food production have been able to cite archaeological evidence of changes over time from big-game hunting to small-game hunting and trapping, and of the increasing importance over time of food gathering and collecting as opposed to hunting (see Braidwood and Willey 1962). However, here the question of identification and circumscription of populations or societies arises: it is not known whether archaeological data spanning long time periods for given locations can be associated with any one population or society (see, for example, Kenyon 1960, chaps. 1 and 2).

hypothesis that population growth is a central factor in the adoption of new technologies and social innovations, or in the division of labor, or in the expansion of different social boundary systems apparently can be neither verified nor rejected on the basis of the information currently available. Possibly, more systematic attention by historians, archaeologists, and anthropologists to changes and change processes in hunting and gathering societies would yield more insight and provide some test of the hypothesis.

Much greater interest has been attached to the transition from hunting and gathering strategies of adaptation to food-growing regimes. Clark and Haswell assert that "population growth appears to have been the motive force compelling our ancestors . . . to abandon the hunting life for the agricultural" (1967, p. 30). They are not able, however, to cite any convincing evidence for this assertion. Although food cultivation and the domestication of animals together have long been recognized as a great turning point in human history, the direct empirical study of their adoption is of very recent date, having begun for the most part after World War II (Adams 1964). Anthropologists and archaeologists investigating the subject have thus far been concerned primarily with the environmental conditions related to the adoption of agriculture.

In their summary of findings presented at an international symposium devoted to the transformation from hunting and gathering to food production, Braidwood and Willey say:

> The data on hand suggest that generally semi-arid regions (of temperate to tropical latitudes) with adequate but not over-abundant collectible food resources were the hearths of the most important beginnings of culivation and domestication. [Braidwood and Willey, 1962, p. 342]

But far from advancing an hypothesis of environmental determinism, they write:

> The favorable conditions for incipient cultivation and domestication must have obtained at least several times previous to the time in which they were taken advantage of in the various instances we cite. Why did incipient food production not come earlier? Our only answer at the moment is that culture was not yet ready to achieve it. [*Ibid.*]

The factor whose effect is, of course, absent from this summary is the pattern of population growth: incorporation of this factor into the analysis might reveal that population growth, or a *changing* rate of natural increase is one of the conditions for incipient cultivation and domestication. But appropriate data do not yet appear to be available for such an analysis.

Recurrent findings on the adoption of vegetative planting at different times and in different parts of the world have been (1) that the peoples concerned were sedentary or at least semisettled in small population agglomerations of one type or another—i.e., they did not live in isolated family groupings, (2) that they already had relatively stable and abundant food supplies, and (3) that a large proportion of their food supply consisted of wild food plants (cf. Clark 1962; Haury 1962; Collier 1962; Chang 1962; Caldwell 1962). Such findings are consistent with the hypothesis that population growth—to numbers and agglomerations exceeding those of nomadic food-gathering groupings—is a major factor in the transition to food cultivation. Of the American Southwest, E. W. Haury notes that

> on the local scene the level of cultural achievement, a subsistence economy that required maximum energy from a maximum number of people, must have been receptive to the addition of any resource to the cultural inventory that would ease the quest of food. [However, the] invention or acquisition of tools, the milling stones, and the mastery of their use . . . demanded no major overhauling of food-preparation practices when a new plant became available. [Haury 1962, p. 113]

Students of the process seem to agree that the adoption of food production did not entail an *immediate* cultural or social-structural transformation of any great magnitude. However, the relative stability of sustenance deriving from both food production and food *storage* (made possible especially by the adoption of pottery and other such innovations) eventually promoted increases in population size and density. Increased population size, together with greater control over the natural environment (or at least partial liberation from its constraints), ultimately generated the great transformations in patterns of settlement and in social, political, and economic structure denoted by Childe as the "urban revolution" (Childe 1952, 1950). R. McC. Adams eschews the hypothesis that population increases due to agriculture set the stage for urbanization. Rather, he feels that great population increase generally followed, not preceded, the core processes of the urban revolution. At the same time, however, he concedes that *some minimal population level* may have been necessary to set the process in motion (Adams 1966, p. 44; see also 1965, Part 2). Food-producing people did not inevitably become "urban societies," at least not within a short time after their adoption of agriculture, nor did their populations inevitably grow rapidly in size or density thereafter (cf. Rouse 1962). But it seems reasonable to suppose that a close connection exists between the adoption of agriculture and the onset of urbanization, reserving conclusions about causal relationships for future analysis.[11]

11 Cf. the analysis of the origins of Mesopotamian civilization in McNeill (1963, p. 30).

EFFECTS OF POPULATION DENSITY ON LEVEL OF POLITICAL INTE-GRATION. Closely related to this discussion is the question of how population density is related to the society's level of political integration. Among anthropologists studying the Western hemisphere, a widely held hypothesis supported by recurrent empirical results is that there is a positive correlation between population density and the presence of a state system of political organization. Moreover, a comparison of successive levels of sociocultural integration—band, tribe, chiefdom, state—reveals a corresponding order of population densities. Anthropological and archaeological findings which support this generalization vis-à-vis North and South America, Europe, and Asia have been cited and summarized by R. F. Stevenson (1968) in his own work dealing with the same relationship in tropical Africa.

On the other hand, in their discussion of a collection of studies on political organization in African societies, M. Fortes and E. E. Evans-Pritchard (1940) conclude that there is apparently no positive connection between population density and state societies among six African tribes compared, and that probably no such relationship obtains in Africa generally. This view has been the more important of the two, since the collection in which it appears has long been considered one of the authoritative works on African political organization. But Stevenson, challenging it, is able to make a strong case to the effect that Fortes and Evans-Pritchard misinterpreted their own data. Moreover, he mobilizes data for a large range of African societies in support of the hypothesis that, in Africa too, there is a positive relationship between population density and state political organization. However, Stevenson carefully avoids drawing strong causal inferences, concluding, on the contrary, that

> in the African cases the evidence would seem to indicate that . . . population density as such was not directly causative of the state formation process. Rather, in far the majority of cases, the process involved at least a threeway nexus between developing trade and trade routes, developing political and economic organization, and higher population densities . . . , all reciprocally interacting and feeding back upon each other. [Stevenson 1968, p. 232]

Stevenson does not actually describe or analyze this three-way nexus. However, a qualification which he appends to the hypothesis suggests that, at least chronologically, high population densities *precede* the formation of primitive state societies:

> My research would indicate that the hypothesis should be modified to acknowledge that along borders of states or within the interstices of states formally acephalous systems (leaderless, chiefless

groups) may develop or maintain quite high densities in small areas well in advance of the development of specialized political institutions of their own. [*Ibid.*]

The Effects of Population Growth on Horticultural or Agricultural Societies

Turning now to the question of social changes within horticultural or agricultural societies, it becomes much easier to relate changing food-cultivation practices to population growth. Probably the most important attempt to show these relationships systematically is the one made by E. Boserup (1965), who characterizes agricultural technologies in terms of intensity of land use, as follows:

1. *Forest-fallow cultivation:* plots of land cleared in the forest are sown and planted for a year or two, after which they are to lie fallow for some number of years sufficient for the forest to regain them (about 20 to 25 years). Once regained by the forest, they are cleared and planted anew, the whole cycle beginning again.

2. *Bush-fallow cultivation:* the same procedure as above, but with a period of between six and ten years, after which the land is covered with bush or small trees.[12]

3. *Short-fallow cultivation:* same as above, but with a fallow period of only one or two years.

4. *Annual cropping:* although this is not usually considered a "fallow-system," it may be classified as such since the land is left uncultivated for the months between the harvest of one crop and the planting of the next. This system includes procedures of annual crop rotation.

5. *Multi-cropping:* the most intensive system of land use, since the same plot bears two or more successive crops every year.

Analyzing patterns of agricultural development in Europe and elsewhere, Boserup concludes (1) that the typical sequence of development has been one of a gradual change from extensive to intensive types of land use, the change being more rapid in some regions than in others, and (2) that these shifts from extensive to intensive cultivation have occurred in the presence of increasing population size (Boserup 1965, pp. 16–18).

To show that changing agricultural methods are a consequence of population growth rather than the reverse (the latter being the Malthusian analysis), Boserup shows that virtually all cases of more intensive

12 Forest-fallow and bush-fallow cultivation are often not distinguished but denoted together as "long-fallow" or "shifting" cultivation.

cultivation entail, at least initially, a greater input of labor per unit of output. Thus, more intensive cultivation is typically not adopted except under the pressure of a rising population (*ibid.*, chap. 5).

In addition to causing the introduction or adoption of innovations in cultivation, the pressures of rural population growth have also been responsible for the introduction, or expansion and development, of rural industry in otherwise "preindustrial" societies. Both full-time and seasonal agricultural unemployment due to population growth or labor-saving innovations may create permanent or temporary surplus labor, and under conditions of fixed land area, population pressure and the resulting need to "import" food, such surplus labor can be mobilized into a rural industrial sector.

The short-term successes of such rural industrial sectors—due, for example, to improved terms of trade—have led to food surpluses for the rural population, and these, in turn, have encouraged earlier marriage and further population growth. Thus, population growth indeed results from improvements in the industrial sector, as Malthusian theory would have it, but it is the pressure of population growth itself that originally sets that very sector into operation. Such a process has been described and measured for preindustrial Flanders by F. F. Mendels:

> The Flemish population was thus embarked in an irreversible process of industrialization. Population pressure necessitated entrance into the nexus of foreign trade and the money economy; this caused an irreversible growth of population through a Malthusian process of myopic relaxation of restraints on marriage whenever a small surplus was left. [Mendels 1969]

Population growth need not, of course, entail more intensive cultivation or industrialization if there are opportunities for expanding the area of production by extension cultivation. Thus, Clark and Haswell point out that in Africa, south of the Sahara, the amount of land cultivated in any one year is probably about one-thirtieth of the potential cultivable land. Africans do cultivate very intensively indeed when hemmed in topographically, or by enemies, or when otherwise compelled to subsist on much smaller areas than they would like. But the system of shifting cultivation, rather than more intensive cultivation, is preferred. So long as abundant land is available, as it is in most of Africa, shifting cultivation yields better returns than settled agriculture in grain per unit of labor (Clark and Haswell 1967, pp. 50–51).

A similar but more elaborate analysis offered by Carneiro suggests conditions under which population pressure does or does not engender political and social-structural differentiation and development (1961, Supplement 2; 1968, Vol. 2). Carneiro first points out that although shifting, "slash-and-burn," cultivation [13] is by far the most common system found in tropical rain-forest environments, in fact (1) soils developed in tropical rain forests can support systems of cultivation more advanced than slash-and-burn, and (2) these more advanced systems arise in response to the increasing pressure of human numbers on the land. To illustrate the two propositions, Carneiro refers to the various horticultural systems maintained by Melanesian tribal societies. These systems range from rudimentary slash-and-burn cultivation to an intensive, semipermanent system employing irrigation, terracing, and the use of fertilizers.

According to Carneiro, an intensification of agriculture follows population increase in those regions in which the area of cultivable land is distinctly circumscribed and limited, e.g., in "narrow valleys sharply confined and delimited by mountains or deserts. It is in such areas that early advances in agriculture, *and in other aspects of culture,* took place" (Carneiro 1968, Vol. 2, p. 141; italics supplied). Conversely, regardless of their fertility, areas with broad expanses of arable land—e.g., the forested plains of northern Europe, the Russian steppes, the eastern woodlands and prairies of the United States—were not the initial areas of agricultural advance. Rather, they lagged behind the narrow river valleys and coastal regions in both their agricultural and cultural development. With extensive and unbroken agricultural land available, population increase resulted in the dispersion of peoples.

Where population growth entailed pressure on cultivable land, competition arose between groups, tribes, or societies, and the result was often warfare. However, such competitions were ultimately resolved, whether by warfare or by other means, and new and more complex political and social structural arrangements were institutionalized. For example, defeat in warfare might imply payment of tribute—and hence a need on the part of the losers to cultivate and exploit their land even more intensively in order to ensure a surplus. Where slavery was an outcome, the victorious society became stratified. Alternatively, alliances may have resulted from such competition, the result being an increase in the size of political units.

Finally, Carneiro postulates a general process of social and economic differentiation as the outcome of this scheme:

---

13 Under the slash-and-burn method, a ring is cut through the bark and cambium layer of each tree. This causes the tree to die. Once dead, the trees are either burned down or left standing (the latter being as effective as burning, since the trees, now leafless, cannot shade the ground). At this point the farmers plant around the dead stumps or trunks. Because of the difficult task of weeding, the area of planting is often abandoned after a few years and a new area subjected to the slash-and-burn technique (see Hoebel 1958, pp. 244–45).

Craft production would be immensely stimulated not only by the demands made on subject peoples for tribute and taxation, but also by the rise of a class of craft specialists. These artisans would come largely from landless segments of the population throughout the state, and they would gravitate toward the centers of political and religious activity. Their technical achievements, in ceramics, weaving, metallurgy, architecture, and the like, would enrich the culture of the state and enhance its prestige. The magnificence of the social and religious superstructure thus erected would obscure the origin of the state. It would be difficult to infer from the later history of the state that a shortage of land among simple farming peoples and the ensuing competition between them had given the original impetus to its formation. [Carneiro 1968, Vol. 2, pp. 142–43] [14]

Carneiro uses this analysis in contrasting the technological, social, economic, and cultural developments of the horticultural tribes of the Amazon basin with those of the tribes of the so-called Circum-Caribbean and Central Andean areas. In the first case, population increase in an area employing slash-and-burn agriculture did *not* result in any very dense concentration of population. Tendencies toward "overcrowding" were apparently met by migratory movements; and probably it is by this means that the tropical forest peoples and cultures spread throughout the vast area of the Amazon valley. In this area, the forms of social development—e.g., religious, political, socialization institutions—were more contingent upon processes of competition and conquest. In the Circum-Caribbean areas, however, the distinctive character of settlement involved areas of *circumscribed* arable land, e.g., the mountain valleys of Colombia, the coastal strips of Venezuela, and the islands of the Greater Antilles. Similarly, arable land in the central Andes was confined to the coastal valleys of Peru. The forms of social organization assumed by the Circum-Caribbean chiefdoms and by the Inca empire were outgrowths of this population increase in circumscribed areas and of the resulting intensification of agriculture, competition, political development, and social and economic differentiation (Carneiro 1968, Vol. 2, pp. 143–44).

The Relationship of Population Size to Social and Economic Characteristics

To conclude this chapter, we shall cite briefly some studies relating population size to variations in social and economic structure. The findings of these studies are consistent with the major hypotheses advanced earlier in this chapter, but they do not in any sense constitute "proof." Among these investigations are a number of large-scale, quantitative,

14 For a supporting viewpoint and analysis, cf. Orans (1966) and references cited therein.

multisocietal studies which have systematically measured relationships between population size and social institutions. In addition, the findings of a number of smaller-scale comparative studies have bearing on the discussion here, although these are not so readily quantifiable.

In a study of intercorrelations between social, economic, political, and other characteristics of 82 nations, each with a population greater than 800,000, Sawyer found that three factors—population size, per capita gross national product, and political institutions—sorted these nations into homogeneous groups. Size, wealth, and politics were shown to be highly correlated with a large number of other national characteristics (Sawyer 1967).

The greater the size of the national population, the greater tended to be the size of its army, its amount of arable land, its overall density of population, the stability of its governments (assessed according to the average period in office of the last two governments), the tendency toward federalist (as opposed to military) governmental arrangements, the number of nations to which it was contiguous. Conversely, the greater the size of the national population, the *smaller* the relative importance of trade and export to the gross national product, the smaller the extent to which the nation's largest city was numerically dominant (compared, for example, to the size of the next largest city), the smaller its amount of religious homogeneity, and the smaller the proportion of translated books among the total number of books produced (*ibid.*, table 3A).

A number of characteristics were found to be related to both population size and wealth (gross national product). Thus, local political autonomy—local elections of local and intermediate officials and legislators, rather than appointments by the center—were found to occur more frequently the larger the population *and* the greater the wealth. Similarly, the number of motor vehicles, the amount of air passenger travel, the number of foreign students in the country, the extent of foreign representation in the country and of national representation outside, and the production and consumption of energy were all positively related to both size and wealth (*ibid.*, table 3D).

In an investigation of smaller-scale, nonliterate, societies, Sawyer and Levine studied the relationship between societal characteristics and a number of variables, among them the size of the society (denoted as the extent of "political integration").[15] It was found that societies with relatively larger populations more frequently had established agricultural economies (especially cereal agriculture), animal husbandry as well as the domestication of animals, and a permanence and clustering of residences; on the other hand, they less frequently had food hunting and gathering activities. Moreover, these societies were more frequently characterized by

15 For a similar study, see Driver and Schuessler (1967).

male involvement in agriculture and in animal husbandry, whereas the rule in the smallest societies was of female involvement only. Finally and most important, the larger the population of the society, the more pronounced its social stratification.

Turning now to relationships between the population size and social institutions of local communities, we draw mainly upon a recent summary by W. F. Ogburn and O. D. Duncan (1964). This summary, like the cross-national comparison, concludes that population density is greater the larger the community. Related to this is the finding that residential land is more intensively utilized the larger the city's population, as indicated by the fact that the relative frequency of multiple-unit residential structures is greater the larger the city. Distances to work and presumably distance traveled in general (for shopping, recreation, etc.) are, on the average, greater the larger the community. Finally, the larger the population, the greater the number of specialized goods and service markets the city can support. For example, cities of 10,000 to 25,000 inhabitants are likely to be able to support eye, ear, nose, and throat specialists—but probably not pediatricians, who must locate themselves in cities of at least 50,000, and not dermatologists, who require cities of at least 100,000 (*ibid.*, table 6). Similarly, only very rarely can a city of 10,000 or less support an art museum, and very few such cities can support a college or university, but most cities of 250,000 or more have an art museum and virtually all have at least one college or university (Duncan 1956).

The number and variety of church denominations, voluntary organizations, work establishments, schools, health and medical organizations and practitioners, radio and television stations, and retail facilities are greater the larger the population of a community. So, too, average rentals, crime rates, certain accident rates, the cost of living, and incomes (*ibid.*). Finally, an extensive study based upon the 1950 U.S. Census of Population has shown that there is a definite relationship between a city's population size and the composition of its population, its marriage, divorce, and fertility rates, its employment and labor force characteristics, and other of its aggregate social characteristics (Duncan and Reiss 1958).

However, despite the extensive documentation that social institutions vary concomitantly with variations in population size, our knowledge is far from complete. Direct studies of the relationships between population size and a large number of social institutions have yet to be carried out. For example, we still do not know what effect population size has on the organization of work and on occupational prestige and mobility; on patterns of matchmaking, marriage, marital dissolution, and remarriage; on religious rituals, roles, and beliefs; on educational roles and on the organization and availability of education; and on the organization of power, access to local or national power, and on the roles of decision-making or value-formulation.

12

Demographic
Responses
to Population Growth

1. INTRODUCTORY REMARKS

In chapter 2 we indicated that the responses of societies to actual or potential population growth may be social organizational, economic, or demographic. Now, having considered social and economic responses in chapter 11, we turn to demographic ones. As will be demonstrated below, demographic responses to population growth can be distinguished according to whether they are *distributional responses,* which entail some change in the geographic or spatial distribution of the population, or whether they are *growth-control responses,* which entail some form of social intervention in the processes of population replacement and growth. We have talked about such responses before, although not precisely in those terms. In this chapter we shall discuss and illustrate them in more detail, and we shall consider conditions under which one or another type of response is likely to occur.

The treatment of "demographic" responses—population redistribution and growth control—as separate from social and economic responses is artificial and undertaken for analytic purposes only. The point is particularly relevant here, for one of the purposes of this book has been to show that population changes (such as redistribution or a change in growth rate) themselves generate social structural changes. Accordingly, the abstraction here of "demographic responses" should be viewed in the context of our overall discussion of responses to population pressure, change, and growth.

Bearing this in mind, it is important to see that the two general demographic strategies of dealing with population growth are vastly different in nature. The first type—redistribution—is basically a positive response, reflecting the society's institutionalized acceptance of population growth. The second—growth control—is basically a negative response, reflecting an institutionalized rejection, or at least only a qualified acceptance, of population growth. Unfortunately, we are still far from capable of analyzing inductively the correlates and causes of institutionalized acceptance or rejection of population growth. Still, it is important to consider as far as possible the alternatives and circumstances associated with societies opting for one or the other response.

In chapter 8 we cited a number of theories of fertility change and earlier yet mentioned the problem of describing and analyzing variations in demographic transitions. Now, once more, we shall find that population studies are in need of a more elaborate and more detailed theory of population transitions.

One of the schemes we cited in chapter 8 was K. Davis's theory (1963) of a "multiphasic demographic response" to declining mortality and sustained population growth. This theory represents one of the most important efforts yet made to analyze demographic responses to population growth, and it is appropriate that we review its elements in the present context. Davis first points out that the importance in post-World War II Japan of induced abortion as a factor in the decline of fertility has had its counterparts in western and eastern Europe, just as factors connected with the control of population growth in Europe—contraception, postponement of marriage, and international migration—have been observed for Japan as well. These similarities lead Davis to hypothesize that a common battery of demographic responses is stimulated under conditions of sustained population growth—low or declining mortality and high or medium fertility—but not under the threat of imminent poverty. On the contrary, the European and Japanese cases show that these responses typically occur under conditions of increasing prosperity. Moreover, they are *individual* responses to opportunities for enhancing status or levels of living.

From our point of view, however, the theory of multiphasic response raises as many questions as it answers. Of course, it is extremely important to know not only that individuals can solve their personal status or level-of-living problems by one or another "response," and that they all thereby contribute, "as if by invisible hand," to an aggregate dampening of population growth. But from the point of view of the social structural as well as demographic implications of the process, it is more important to know which response will be adopted—i.e., what will be the modal response or the distribution of responses—in different populations, just as it is important to know what the timing of the responses will be in relation to the stimuli for population growth, and what the differential patterns of response are in different sectors of a population. But perhaps most important, we need to know what factors—social structural, historical, economic, and environmental—are connected with different patterns of demographic responses to population growth.

2. POPULATION GROWTH AND REDISTRIBUTION: OUT-MIGRATION AND BIFURCATION VERSUS INVOLUTION

Out-Migration and Bifurcation

It is already abundantly clear that a society confronted with population growth must either export or otherwise rid itself of the population increment or else expand its base of sustenance. Otherwise, it faces lower average levels of living or worse. To the extent that a base of sustenance is closely circumscribed territorially, it is obvious that the expansion of settlement or control is one means of dealing with the problem. But "exportation" of the population increment by emigration is equivalent to the expansion of territorial settlement or control in the sense that the population increment is sustained by some territorial base of sustenance above and beyond that already existing for the initial population. Thus, out-migration or territorial expansion can be viewed as a generalized strategy for the survival of population increments.[1] This strategy, in turn, may take a number of forms:

1. Expansion of the area of settlement or control
2. Emigration of the population increment to join a different, already organized, population or society
3. Migration of the population increment to form a new, separately organized, population or society

The virtual Europeanization of the world, depicted graphically in figure 12.1 took all three of these general forms.

Examples of areal expansion—following or associated with population growth—are recorded for every type of society, from hunting and gathering bands to urban-industrial nation-states. However, regardless of type, a society may find itself facing any one of a variety of contingencies

[1] Cf. Petersen's important analysis, "The General Determinants of Migration," in Petersen (1969) and Petersen (1958) in which he elaborates upon connections between migration and population growth.

with respect to the opportunities and potentialities for expanding its area of settlement or control. Some of these have been mentioned already in chapter 2 and need not be recapitulated. It suffices to note that only in the case of small, low-density populations is the expansion of areas of settlement or control likely to be uncomplicated by the economics and politics of intersocietal relations, and that only in low-density areas comprising *only* small, low-density, populations may such areal expansions go unchallenged.

Under even the most favorable conditions, the extent to which a society can expand areally is limited by the potentiality for transport, communication, and economic and political integration over the expanded area. Historically, societies have varied widely in their degrees of success in colonizing and in adapting their political, economic, and social institutions to greatly expanded areal settings. The social, economic, or political disorganization and disintegration associated with failure to extend the control and institutional arrangement of the "mother" society may bring to an end the very population growth that initiated the expansion. Spain in the modern period is a case in point. However, alternative demographic responses to population growth may be available even in such circumstances.

Examples of the transfer and resettlement of parts of populations accompanying or following substantial population growth are known for virtually all types of societies. By transfer and resettlement, as opposed to "expansion of settlement," we mean the effective departure of a population subgroup from membership in the "mother" society to somewhere outside that society's political control and institutional sphere. One example would be the Irish emigration to North America. Population subgroups so "departing" and transferring out of the initial population may be more or less organized as social groupings; moreover, after their departures they may or may not organize themselves.

In transferring and resettling themselves, population subgroups may reorganize into autonomous social groupings or independent societies. Thus, we know of the frequent occurrence of growth and bifurcation among hunting and gathering bands, and even among settled tribal societies. Similarly, we associate much premodern and modern exploration, colonization, and population transfer with the founding of new societies and nations.

Alternatively, transferred and resettled population subgroups may join some already existing, relatively highly organized, society. Thus, the "great Atlantic migration" from Europe to America in the nineteenth and early twentieth centuries involved population subgroups joining, essentially, an existing and ongoing nation. Similarly, the extensive population transfers following World War II (with the possible exception of the migration to the State of Israel) involved groups departing from their

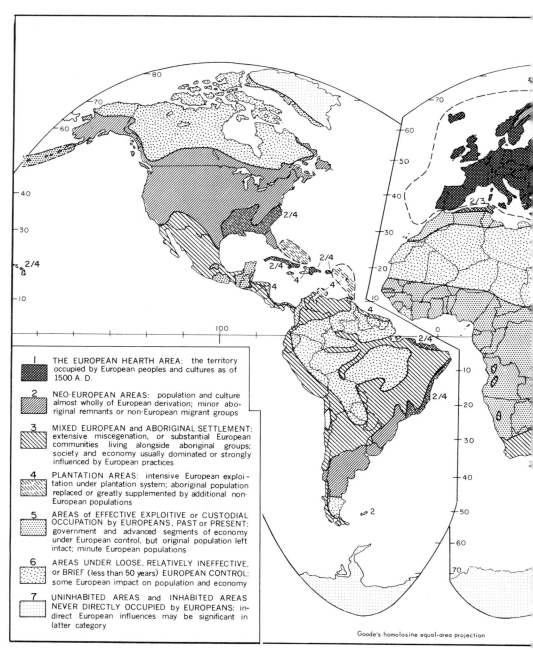

1 THE EUROPEAN HEARTH AREA: the territory occupied by European peoples and cultures as of 1500 A. D.

2 NEO-EUROPEAN AREAS: population and culture almost wholly of European derivation; minor aboriginal remnants or non-European migrant groups

3 MIXED EUROPEAN and ABORIGINAL SETTLEMENT: extensive miscegenation, or substantial European communities living alongside aboriginal groups; society and economy usually dominated or strongly influenced by European practices

4 PLANTATION AREAS: intensive European exploitation under plantation system; aboriginal population replaced or greatly supplemented by additional non-European populations

5 AREAS of EFFECTIVE EXPLOITIVE or CUSTODIAL OCCUPATION by EUROPEANS, PAST or PRESENT: government and advanced segments of economy under European control, but original population left intact; minute European populations

6 AREAS UNDER LOOSE, RELATIVELY INEFFECTIVE, or BRIEF (less than 50 years) EUROPEAN CONTROL: some European impact on population and economy

7 UNINHABITED AREAS and INHABITED AREAS NEVER DIRECTLY OCCUPIED by EUROPEANS: indirect European influences may be significant in latter category

Goode's homolosine equal-area projection

FIGURE 12.1. The Europeanization of the world. Source: Zelinsky 1966, pp. 74–75, Figure 5.

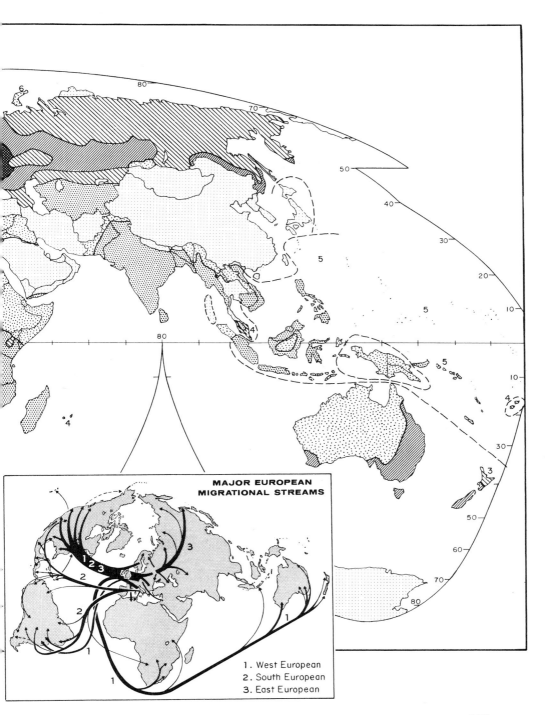

MAJOR EUROPEAN MIGRATIONAL STREAMS

1. West European
2. South European
3. East European

societies of origin and "joining" already existing societies of destination shortly thereafter. Thus, for example, many Germans left Germany and moved to South American countries; and large numbers emigrated from countries of Southern Europe to Australia and to Canada. The directions and political and economic outcomes of population transfers are related to the sizes and densities of populations outside that of the "home" society, as well as to general intersocietal relationships, communication, and exchange.

Population transfer originating as an expansion of settlement or as colonization on the part of the "home" society has often resulted in bifurcation, i.e., in the "independence" of the newly-transferred and re-settled population. At the same time, the newly-settled societies, if small or sparsely populated, have often actually recruited or sought otherwise to promote substantial population transfers and increments (notable examples are Australia, Canada, and New Zealand).

It seems clear that both expansion of settlement and the territorial transfer of parts of a population are demographic responses to population growth which permit problems of sustenance to be resolved *without* necessarily entailing great immediate social reorganization or technological changes in the original society. On the other hand, there are minimum conditions for these responses: the availability of some territorial destination and the physical and political access to it. For the society confronted by a growing population, emigration is a *relatively painless* solution—provided there is a place to which to emigrate.

Involution

Exactly the opposite conditions from those described in the paragraph above characterize the alternative demographic response to population growth—population involution. This response, which involves agglomeration or increased density of settlement as well as an intensification of exploitation, has virtually immediate effects upon, and implications for, social and political organization. (Some of these have been discussed or touched upon in the previous chapter.) Moreover, population involution may occur independently of the intersocietal demographic and political setting.

Population involution *means* the adaptation and extraction of sustenance for a larger population occupying the same territorial unit as that of the original population, or occupying progressively smaller territorial units. This alone implies some change in production, distribution, and exchange and in the processes of social control. Thus, theories or analyses which assume that societal inertia has always been the preferred strategy, or that societies "opt for" the status quo or for stability rather than change, would indicate that population involution is a demographic response to population growth *only* where less disorganizing responses, such as out-migration, are ruled out on geographical, political, or other grounds. But this, as we hope to show, is not true.

We have already cited in the previous chapter Carneiro's contention that societies with access to great territorial range—e.g., those in the Amazon Basin—respond to population growth and pressure by expanding their areas of settlement, whereas those more rigidly circumscribed geographically tend to respond to population growth by exploiting their environments more intensively. A somewhat similar note is sounded by Geertz in his analysis of contrasts in the agricultural and social organization of various Indonesian population groups (Geertz 1963).

Historically, as mankind has increasingly populated the earth, the alternatives open to population groupings seeking to emigrate have become progressively narrower and more rigidly enforced. Thus, the societal strategy of survival and adaptation has increasingly entailed an involutional response to growth. However, as we shall try to show in the concluding chapter, using the case of the United States, societies turn to involution as a demographic response to population growth despite the opportunities for further expansion of settlement. Thus, *some* societies "opt for" the path of social structural, economic, and political change connected with population involution despite the absence of constraints on the presumably preferred nonchange strategy of expansion of settlement.

We shall delay consideration of the reason why societies adopt one response rather than another for the last section of this chapter. We close the present section by pointing out that the notion of population involution is extremely broad and includes virtually every change in population density. Thus, both more intensive and more dense agricultural exploitation and settlement, as well as urbanization, metropolitanization, and megalopolitanization, can be viewed as involutional responses to population growth. And, of course, these responses themselves vary quite broadly over societies and historically within societies.

Again, the notion of a population transformation and of sequences of population transformations can serve us well in conceptualizing the demographic responses to population growth. In the case of involution, it is clear that the main elements in the process are natural increase (fertility and mortality) and migration streams; and that it is multi-interval sequences of transformations which are of concern. For a population experiencing substantial growth in an initial interval, we are interested in learning the patterns of gross and net migration in the following intervals. Increasingly, data portraying such sequences of transformations are becoming available (Taeuber and Matras 1969), so that hopefully, our description and understanding of these sequences will be advanced considerably.

3. CONTROL OF POPULATION GROWTH

It will be recalled that in the chapters concerning mortality, marriage, and fertility, we took note of the variability in the extent to which societies institutionalize mechanisms of controlling mortality, timing and matchmaking in marriage, and fertility. We reconsider this variability now in the context of demographic responses to population growth. In our previous discussions we mentioned a number of social and economic factors in connection with this variability and to these we now add one more: recent patterns of population growth.

It is clear that in virtually all societies the volume and rate of population growth are not ordinarily ignored but, rather, are recognized and observed on a more or less ongoing basis. Moreover, the relationships between births, marriages, deaths, health and illness, and population growth are also recognized, if not always analyzed with the precision with which we like to credit ourselves. To the extent that means, technologies, or social arrangements of intervening in and controlling the elements of natural increase are known by a society, it seems reasonable to hypothesize that one or a combination of these may be invoked in response to actual or immediately potential population growth or pressure. However, no body of propositions or theory yet exists to predict whether or not a society confronted with a growing population will institutionalize intervention into natural increase, or, if it does, what form the intervention will take and what vital area (mortality, marriage, or fertility) it will involve.

The Noncontrol of Mortality

The classic Malthusian statement holds that *since* the production of sustenance cannot keep up with the growth of population, increases in population must inevitably be followed and "balanced" by the "positive check" of increased mortality. A much less rigid statement, suggested in Hawley's discussion of "population balance" (1950), is that *if* production or distribution of sustenance cannot keep up with population growth (and if no avenues of migration are possible), then mortality is likely to rise.

But our concern here is with another problem: does population growth unaccompanied by increased production of sustenance induce societies to intervene in the direction of increasing, or allowing, higher mortality, and does population decline induce them to intervene in the direction of controlling and decreasing mortality? We considered the second part of the queston in chapter 6, when we speculated on the conditions under which societies do or do not institutionalize efforts to control mortality. That societies may also institutionalize the noncontrol of mortality is consistent with the observation of (1) fluctuations in mortality in primitive societies and (2) patterns reflecting such intervention in agrarian and preindustrial societies. Although noting the poor quality of the data, Kryzwicki is nevertheless able to remark that while infant and child mortality in primitive tribes is higher than in European civilization, it is not uniformly high, and he cites examples of both quite low and quite high mortality (Kryzwicki 1934, pp. 226–43). E. A. Wrigley (1968) examining the preindustrial mortality history of Colyton, Devon, in England, notes that there were instances and periods of extremely low—as well as quite high—infant and child mortality in the sixteenth, seventeenth, and eighteenth centuries, and that there was considerable variation in adult mortality as well. Wrigley suggests that these fluctuations may have been closely related to living standards, to short-term weather, harvest, or epidemic conditions, or to longer-term economic circumstances, density of settlement, changes in virulence of diseases, or changes in genetic characteristics. This may be true, but they may also have reflected responses to population growth and to the changing circumstances of the survival and adaptation of population increments. That even societies not actually practicing infanticide and similar means of population control may manipulate mortality is suggested in Colin Clark's characterization of 1953 Lebanese infant mortality rates—195 and 315 for males and females, respectively—as reflecting the operation of a principle on the order of "thou shalt not kill but need not strive officiously to keep alive" (Clark 1967, p. 44).

Societal Control of Marital Fertility—General Considerations

Malthus's prescription for the control of population growth entailed, essentially, the control of marriage. We have already noted some of the axes of variation in patterns of frequency and age at marriage. However, there seems thus far to have been little or no attempt made to investigate the relationship—direct or indirect—between population growth and patterns of marriage, except insofar as certain patterns of growth in combination with patterns of age-assortative marriage generate "marriage squeezes."[2] Nor has there been much attention paid to the relationship between patterns of migration, population redistribution, and marriage. Nevertheless, there can be little doubt that norms and practices of marriage, divorce, and remarriage are related to the efforts of societies to control their amounts or rates of population growth, although the exact connections remain to be determined. Perhaps the most

2 This is discussed in detail in Hirschman and Matras (1971).

convincing evidence of this are the declines in age at marriage and the
increases in proportions ever married associated, at least chronologically,
with the recent spread and institutionalization of fertility control. In
other words, with the advent of effective, institutionalized, techniques of
fertility control, marriage appears to have been freed from its bondage to
the exigencies of societal control of population growth.[3]

One of the great problems confronting contemporary population
studies concerns the extent to which, and the manner in which, societies
institutionalize control of marital fertility in response to population
growth and other changes. In the chapter on fertility, we argued that the
recent widespread interest in individual behavior vis-à-vis fertility and in
individual responses to social, economic, or demographic contingencies
to fertility is probably of only limited promise. Of more importance, we
suggested, is the subject of the societal institutionalization of norms and
patterns of marital fertility in response to social, economic, or demographic contingencies. Summarizing findings to date of what is probably
the most extensive, ambitious, and geographically detailed historical
study of marriage and marital fertility, A. J. Coale notes that there is still
no possibility of formulating a "grand generalization that will provide a
compact and widely valid explanation of the decline of marital fertility
in Europe" (Coale 1969). More precisely, although a relationship between
declining mortality and fertility is often advanced, it is clear that in
Spain, Bulgaria, and other southern and eastern European countries,
fertility in fact declined in the last decades of the nineteenth and first
decades of the twentieth centuries while mortality was still high.

The relationship between patterns of fertility control and *changes*
in population size, density, distribution, composition, or mobility awaits
direct systematic study. Tentatively, we may view societal intervention to
control marital fertility as a special case of social innovation, and we may
hypothesize that population growth and increasing density are likely to
promote the adoption of this particular—and demographically crucial—
innovation.

4. DEMOGRAPHIC RESPONSES IN SELECTED
INDUSTRIALIZED COUNTRIES

We conclude this chapter by reviewing the important study by D. Fried-
lander of alternative demographic responses to population growth in
Europe in the late eighteenth, nineteenth, and early twentieth centuries
(Friedlander 1969). Noting that these responses to persistently high rates

---

3 For some evidence, see Matras (1965), van de Walle (1968), and Coale (1969,
p. 26).

of natural increase are believed to have included (1) higher age at marriage and lower proportions marrying, (2) intervention for the purpose of controlling marital fertility, (3) external migration, and (4) rural-urban migration or population redistribution (involution, in our terms), Friedlander attempts to analyze the conditions under which one or another, or some combination of them, occurred.

During the European population transitions, some societies were structured economically and demographically in such a way as to have a high capacity for population growth, whereas others were structured so as to have an extremely low capacity. These capacities depended upon the extent to which population growth could be accompanied by a constant population redistribution involving shifts from agriculture to industry, from rural to urban residence, etc. Taking examples from both sides of the Atlantic, the United States at the turn of the nineteenth century had a higher capacity to absorb extra numbers than did most European countries, and in Europe, England had a higher capacity than Sweden. In all three of these cases, it was the urban sector which expanded and absorbed the bulk of the population growth; in the rural sectors, population growth did not persist long after modernization began. Thus, during the periods of great national population growth in these countries, the rural populations reached their peaks, stabilizing or even declining thereafter, whereas the urban areas continued to broaden their absorptive capacities (see Friedlander, 1969, for statistical documentation).

Some Representative Demographic Responses

For populations with initially high proportions in rural areas, declining urban birth rates, and no rural-urban differences in death rates or in pattern of decline, three demographic responses may occur in different combinations and sequences: (1) declining rural birth rates, (2) rural-to-urban migration, and (3) external migration. Thus, a rapidly industrializing society may be characterized by early rural-to-urban migration *and* some external migration, followed by greatly intensified rural-to-urban migration accompanied by moderate external migration, followed finally by continued, intensive, rural-to-urban migration, a rather intensive decline in rural fertility, and no further external migration. This pattern, which we shall call Model I, resembles the transition in England and Wales.

A slowly industrializing society may be characterized by early, moderate, rural-to-urban migration, followed by continued moderate rural-to-urban migration and by fairly intensive declines in rural birth rates, followed finally by a very intensive decline in rural birth rates with neither external migration nor further rural-to-urban internal migration.

Summary of Response Pattern: Model I

Period (years)	Pattern of Response		
	Declining birth rates in rural areas	*Rural-to-urban migration*	*External migration*
0–50		X	X
50–100		XXX	X
100–140	XX	XXX	

Note: X means a "weak response"; XX is a response of medium intensity; XXX is a response of strong intensity.

Thus, this transition is characterized mainly by declining rural fertility and only to a small extent by rural-to-urban migration. Shown below, as Model II, it resembles the transition in France.

Summary of Response Pattern in France: Model II

Period (years)	Pattern of Response		
	Declining birth rates in rural areas	*Rural-to-urban migration*	*External migration*
0–50		X	
50–100	XX	X	
100–140	XXX		

The demographic transitions in the countries of eastern Europe involved only slow declines in rural fertility, moderate levels of rural-to-urban migration, and extremely high levels of external migrations (Model III). The "New Overseas Societies" (for example, the United States) were characterized by only slow declines in rural birth rates, by moderate rural-to-urban migration, and by "inward" external migration to the frontiers.

Summary of Typical Response Pattern in Eastern Europe: Model III

Period (years)	Pattern of Response		
	Declining birth rates in rural areas	*Rural-to-urban migration*	*External migration*
0–50			XX
50–100	X	X	XXX
100–120	XX	X	XXX
120–150	XXX	XX	

Summary Pattern for New Overseas Societies: Model IV

Period (years)	Pattern of Response		
	Declining birth rates in rural areas	Rural-to-urban migration	External migration
0–50	X	X	X
50–100	XX	X	XXX
100–150	XX	XX	XX

A COMPARISON OF TWO DEMOGRAPHIC TRANSITIONS. Having presented the schemes described above, Friedlander goes on to compare the demographic transition in England and Wales with that of Sweden. With Sweden's more rapid decline in rural birth rates, her population growth was much slower than that of England and Wales. And while both countries underwent transitions from "rural" to "urban" and from "high balance" (high death and birth rates; little or no net natural increase) to "low balance," (low death and birth rates; little or no net natural increase) the rural-to-urban transition was completed much later in Sweden (half of it occurring after 1930, compared to practically all of it completed before 1900 in England and Wales). It was England's rapid industrialization that provided the necessary conditions for her early rural-to-urban migration and relatively slow decline in rural population growth. With practically all the surplus rural population able to move to the cities, birth rates (and therefore natural increase) in the rural sector could continue to be high for a fairly long period. In rural Sweden, on the other hand, birth rates *had* to decline much earlier, since slow industrialization did not provide the necessary conditions for rural-to-urban migration. Rural England was a pool which could overflow into its fast-expanding urban sector, while in Sweden the "pool" had to be controlled from within, that is, by the reduction of fertility.

For England, external migration was a "delayed response" (as were declining birth rates in rural areas); that is, it became significant only

Summary of Response Pattern in England and Wales: Model V

Period	Pattern of Response		
	Declining birth rates in rural areas	Rural-to-urban migration	External migration
1800–1830		X	
1830–1880		XXX	X
1880–1930	XXX	X	X

Summary of Response Pattern in Sweden:
Model VI

Period	Pattern of Response		
	Declining birth rates in rural areas	Rural-to-urban migration	External migration
1800–1860		X	X
1860–1890	XX	X	XX
1890–1930	XXX	XX	X

after the rate of urbanization had begun to decline. Compared to the country's rural-to-urban migration in the nineteenth century, or to its declining rural fertility in the twentieth, this external migration was never a very important demographic response. By contrast, overseas migration from rural Sweden was a very significant demographic response and in some periods, indeed, was the most important factor in Sweden's demographic transition. Only after the 1920s did rural-to-urban migration become more significant in Sweden.

General Conclusion

A general conclusion emerging from Friedlander's analysis is that demographic responses to population growth are mediated in significant ways by social and economic responses to the same or to earlier patterns of population growth. A similar type of conclusion may be drawn from R. A. Easterlin's study (1961) of the post-World War II "baby boom" in the United States. Easterlin found that the fertility of urban native whites, the most important component in the "baby boom," responded positively to the strong economic expansion reflected in exceptionally favorable job-market conditions for those in the family-building ages. In the past, the fertility of urban native whites had not responded so strongly to economic expansion because the influence of the economy on the job market was offset by (a) foreign immigration and entrance into the job market, and (b) high rates of entry into the labor force of the native-born population itself. However, the post-World War II period was one of very restricted immigration to the United States *and* of unusually low rates of entrance into the labor force, the latter due to the low levels of fertility that had prevailed during the Great Depression of the 1930s. Both the restricted immigration and low entrance into the labor force reflected past demographic responses to population growth and economic trends. Thus, the resulting sustained high employment and rising incomes promoted the high fertility that continued in a population now characterized by extended growth *and* by the very widespread knowledge and practice of family planning.

The kinds of questions posed at the beginning of the chapter about demographic transitions and responses to population growth remain largely unanswered in any great detail. The description, classification, and analysis of demographic transitions and the study of their relationships to population and to social transformations represent one of the major frontiers in demographic and population research.[4]

---

[4] For some tentative formulations about demographic transitions, see Taeuber (1967).

13

A Case Study:
Population and
Society in
the United States

1. INTRODUCTION

In this chapter, we shall apply concepts and approaches presented earlier to a very concise review of major changes in population and social structure in the United States. The present section introduces the main theme of the analysis, the interaction of population trends with technology and with the changing societal strategy of settlement and adaptation. The second section reviews population growth and expansion of settlement prior to the Civil War, and the third summarizes the social patterns and institutional features associated with these prewar trends. In the fourth section we summarize the changing patterns of post-Civil War population growth and settlement that were associated with the introduction of new technologies, on the one hand, and with shifting sources and volumes of immigration, on the other; and in the fifth we examine the social patterns and institutional features associated with the postwar population and technological trends. Finally, the last two sections review the trends and implications of America's more recent economic organization and megalopolitan settlement.

The growth of the population of the United States and the development of American society originated not in societies and social processes indigenous to the American continent but rather as a consequence of European population growth and the migration of Europeans to the relatively unsettled Western Hemisphere. However, although the American colonies were initially part of Europe's hinterland, their distance from the more developed European origins and centers, combined with their size and density of population and great natural wealth, allowed them relatively early economic and political independence from Europe. Thus, post-independence patterns of settlement, and to some extent even colonial patterns, are legitimately viewed as largely indigenous to the new American nation, and so, too, are their accompanying forms of social and economic organization.[1]

The main outlines of the analysis presented in this chapter may be sketched with reference to the data in table 13.1. In the first two columns of the table, the growth of the total land area and population of the United States is shown for the census dates from 1790 to 1950. By 1850, the United States had made virtually all its land acquisitions, and its total land area had more than tripled since 1790. Thus, although the population had increased almost sixfold in the same period, 1790 to 1850, population density in 1860, on the eve of the Civil War, was only slightly more than double the density at the time of the first U.S. census. Most important, in the pre-Civil War period, 1790 to 1860, the great bulk of the increase in population—some 78 percent of it—was accounted for, or absorbed by, an increase in the *rural* population. The pre-Civil War strategy of survival and adaptation in the face of a very sharply increasing population was expansion of rural settlement and of agriculture, forestry, mining, and other primary extractive economic activities.

Between approximately 1860 and 1870, the decade of the Civil War, the overall strategy of adaptation of America's still increasing population changed to one of urbanization, great expansion of existing urban centers, and rapid growth of new urban agglomerations. Between 1860 and 1950, the total population of the United States almost quintupled. Of the total population increase in this period, some 69 percent can be accounted for by the growth of the urban population.

Because the land area of the United States remained fixed while the total population virtually quintupled, the total population density also increased nearly fivefold, from 10.6 persons per square mile in 1860 to

1 In recent years there has appeared an important series of historical studies dealing with the prerevolutionary population and society of the United States. A major concern of these studies is the direct connection of patterns of population growth and density of agricultural settlement in the colonies—mainly New England, so far—to family structure and inheritance, local political and economic organization, and, ultimately, migration and frontier resettlement. See, for example, K. B. Lockridge (1968), P. J. Greven, Jr. (1970) and J. Demos (1968).

TABLE 13.1

Population of the United States, Urban and Rural, and Intercensal Change, 1790–1960

Year	Total land area (rounded to thousand sq. miles)	Population (millions)			Intercensal Increase (millions)			Population Density (total pop. per sq. mile)	Rural Population per Sq. Mile
		Total	Urban	Rural	Total	Urban	Urban as percentage of total		
1790	865	3,929,000	0.2	3.7	—	—	—	4.5	4.3
1800	865	5,308,000	0.3	5.0	1.4	0.1	6.9	6.1	5.8
1810	1,682	7,240,000	0.5	6.7	1.9	0.2	10.5	4.3	4.0
1820	1,749	9,638,000	0.7	8.9	2.4	0.2	7.0	5.5	5.1
1830	1,749	12,866,000	1.1	11.8	3.2	0.4	13.4	7.4	6.7
1840	1,749	17,069,000	1.8	15.3	4.2	0.7	17.1	9.8	8.7
1850	2,940	23,192,000	3.5	19.7	6.1	1.7	27.7	7.9	6.7
1860	2,970	31,443,000	6.2	25.2	8.3	2.7	32.4	10.6	8.5
1870	2,970	38,558,000	9.9	28.7	7.1	3.7	51.8	13.0	9.6
1880	2,970	50,156,000	14.1	36.1	11.6	4.2	36.5	16.9	12.1
1890	2,970	62,948,000	22.1	40.3	12.8	8.0	62.4	21.2	13.6
1900	2,970	75,995,000	30.2	45.8	13.0	8.1	61.7	25.6	15.4
1910	2,970	91,972,000	42.0	50.0	16.0	11.8	74.1	31.0	16.8
1920	2,969	105,711,000	54.2	51.5	13.7	12.2	88.5	35.6	17.3
1930	2,947	122,775,000	69.0	53.8	17.1	14.8	86.7	41.2	18.1
1940	2,977	131,669,000	74.4	57.3	8.9	5.5	61.5	44.2	19.2
1950	2,975	150,697,000	89.7	60.9	19.0	15.3	76.2	50.7	20.9
1960	2,971	178,464,000	112.5	65.9	27.8	22.8	82.0	60.1	22.2

SOURCE: U.S. Bureau of the Census, *Census of Population 1960: Characteristics of the Population*, Vol. 1, Part 1, tables 2–3.

50.7 persons per square mile in 1950. However, rural population density only doubled, from 8.5 to 20.9 persons per square mile.

Thus, American population and society are viewed here basically in terms of the changing strategy of settlement, absorption, and adaptation undertaken by a rapidly growing population and in terms of the social and economic accompaniments to this change. Of course, the change did not take place uniformly or simultaneously throughout the country. The flow of immigrants entered the country on the eastern seaboard, and both rural and urban settlement and population growth took place there first. However, it is clear, on the one hand, that urban concentrations have nearly always existed in the United States despite the early, predominantly rural, character of the country as a whole, and on the other hand, that many areas of the United States are still predominantly rural, despite the overall urban character of the population and the low proportion now engaged in, or directly supported by, agriculture or other primary economic activities.

Correspondingly, parts of the American economy—or, perhaps more correctly, certain local or regional American economies—have always been market economies of a quite highly differentiated and interdependent nature, whereas others began as extremely localized subsistence economies and only gradually became integrated into progressively larger, more differentiated, and more interdependent regional or national complexes. Such differences in patterns of settlement and in scope of economy have always been associated with sectional differences, competition, and tension in national politics. Moreover, in regional and national politics, urban and rural differences have always been sources of cleavage and conflict. As for local politics, these have been characterized by competition between specific economic and social classes, and between ethnic, religious, racial, or neighborhood groups, the competition in many instances having been affected by patterns of immigration, absorption of immigrants, and differential fertility.

Finally, family formation and population growth itself have been affected by the change in the societal strategy of survival and adaptation. Both urbanization and the correlates of technological change and social differentiation—education and mobility—have affected both the size and composition of the nuclear family and its relationship to the other institutions of American society. And it was these same factors—education and mobility—that generated the shift in the American strategy of survival and adaptation from expansion of rural settlement, spectacularly rapid industrialization, expansion of the economy to national and international dimensions, and the megalopolitanization of American population and society.

2. POPULATION GROWTH AND EXPANSION
OF SETTLEMENT, 1790–1860

Between 1790 and 1800, the population of the United States grew from 3,929,000 to 5,308,000, an increase of 35.1 percent. In this decade there was no increase in the nation's land area, and the increase in population was divided almost equally between the northwestern states and the South, some 93 percent of the growth occurring in the rural population. The North Central states had a population of about 51,000 in 1800.

In the next decade, the territory of the United States practically doubled because of the Louisiana Purchase. In this period, too, the total population grew by some 36.4 percent, from 5,308,000 in 1800 to 7,240,000 in 1810. Again, the bulk of the growth—about 90 percent—took place in the rural population, and the total increase was divided about equally between the northeastern states and the South. But the population of the North Central states increased almost sixfold, numbering about 292,-000 by 1810.

The following three decades—1810 to 1820, 1820 to 1830, and 1830 to 1840—were characterized by a steady growth of population at an average rate of some 3.3 percent per annum, reaching 17,069,000 by the time of the 1840 census. The land area of the nation increased slightly during this period, primarily because of the acquisition of Florida and other areas ceded by Spain. Beginning in 1819, a count was maintained of overseas immigrants to the United States; and in the years between 1819 and 1840 their number totaled some 750,000. In these decades, 1810 to 1840, the populations of the northeastern and southern regions both increased by nearly 200 percent, but the population of the North Central states, the frontier of the early nineteenth century, grew more than elevenfold, from 292,000 in 1810 to 3,352,000 in 1840. Again, the bulk of the growth was absorbed by the rural population. However, the total number of urban places increased from only 46 in 1810 to 131 in 1840, the latter count including three cities with more than 100,000 inhabitants each and nine with more than 25,000 (but less than 100,000).

In the period between 1840 and 1860, the bulk of the territorial expansion of the United States was completed with the acquisition of Texas, Oregon, the Mexican Cession, and the Gadsden Purchase. The total population grew by 83 percent, from 17,069,000 in 1840 to 31,443,000 in 1860. It was in this period that the settlement of the West began, the population there reaching some 619,000 by 1860, and by 1860, too, the population of the North Central states nearly equaled that of the Northeast. Overseas immigration from 1840 to 1860 totaled some 4,311,000 persons, and in these two decades the urban population began to absorb a substantial part of the overall population increase (28 percent between 1840 and 1850, and 32 percent between 1850 and 1860). By 1860 the number of urban places had increased to 392, including nine cities of 100,000 residents or more and 26 cities of 25,000 or more (but less than 100,000).

3. FAMILIES AND ECONOMIC, SOCIAL, AND POLITICAL INSTITUTIONS OF NINETEENTH-CENTURY RURAL AMERICA

Contemporary America has an extremely rich heritage of literature and lore originating in colonial and nineteenth-century rural American society. In addition, it is widely held that many of the nation's most deeply cherished traditions, institutions, and values are rooted in frontier life and in the rural social, economic, and political organization of the late nineteenth and early twentieth centuries. However, the study of pre-World War I rural social structure through the systematic analysis of events and documents has been limited to the activities of historians, who, for the most part, have not made much use of sociological or ecological concepts and styles of analysis, although they have often employed national and local census materials to good advantage.

The discipline of rural sociology in the United States has been closely connected with the agricultural extension services and agricultural research conducted in the country's Land Grant colleges and universities. Rural sociological research has been carried out mostly with reference to contemporary, or almost contemporary, rural life, and however fruitful, interesting, and important this research has been to rural sociologists themselves, it deals with a rural society which is both highly mechanized and capitalized and which maintains very intense and intimate social, economic, and political relationships with the growing urban-industrial society and its technology and institutions.[2] Thus, although the concepts, approaches, and methods of contemporary sociology are relevant to the study of the social structure of nineteenth-century rural America, the actual research, descriptive accounts, and findings of the discipline have only a limited bearing on the subject.

A number of historical studies of rural communities in the nineteenth century or earlier do employ sociological or ecological concepts, and these, combined with other historical analyses and census and other data, allow us to sketch a partial portrayal of some of the main features of social structure in premechanized rural America.

---

2 For a good introduction to rural sociological research, see Kolb and de Brunner (1935). It is worth noting, too, that modern human ecology has strong roots in the tradition of rural sociology.

Three Salient Aspects of Rural Settlement in America

In considering the major social institutions of nineteenth-century rural America, it is important to bear in mind three separate aspects of the history of the nation's rural settlement. In the first place, any area of settlement always included a large proportion of migrants—either from areas of the United States farther east or northeast, or from foreign countries. Population turnover in any given rural area was, in the nineteenth century, generally quite high: some migrants remained only briefly in an area and then moved on to new or more promising places; others remained for a number of years and then moved; and in many areas only a small minority of migrants ever settled permanently. Thus, many areas were quite heterogeneous with respect to national, ethnic, or linguistic origins, and more often than not with respect to their residents' period of arrival or length of stay. Accordingly, those social institutions that involved members of many families tended to be characterized by changing numbers and composition.

In the second place, inasmuch as land—or at least frontier land—was cheap, and, in the eastern United States, an extremely promising investment, settlers sought to claim or purchase the largest homestead or farm which they could afford, regardless of their ability, experience, or expectation concerning actual cultivation. In contrast both to European rural settlement and to the earliest forms of agricultural settlement in New England, most of the rural settlement in the United States took place on relatively isolated farms or homesteads, with each settler family physically isolated from other settler families. Villages, which abounded in rural America no less than in rural areas elsewhere, were generally not the farmers' places of residence, but rather places of business and of residence for the nonagricultural rural population engaged in one or another service to the agricultural population. Thus, farm families in the United States were characterized by considerable physical isolation, and certain types of family self-sufficiency were in fact demanded by this isolation. However, a characteristic feature of rural communities throughout the United States was the organization of social, economic, or political units whose main purposes included the reduction of the physical isolation of these families through the development of road networks and transportation and communication services.

Finally, rural settlement in the United States did not ordinarily, if ever, occur spontaneously. Rather, it was organized and promoted by various individuals, groups, and agencies interested, for a variety of reasons, first in the settlement of the Western frontier areas and later in the more dense or intensive settlement of nonfrontier areas. National and local governments, land and real estate speculators and promoters, merchants, traders, and transportation companies all were involved in promotional schemes for settlement. For the most part, the promoting agents understood the necessity for organizing both personal services and services essential to farm maintenance and development. In addition, they generally understood the necessity for organizing those marketing and retailing services that would give access to the eastern or overseas market and to urban manufacturers and services.

It follows that "subsistence agriculture," although frequent enough, was hardly ever a "way of life" in rural America. Rather, it was a transitional stage between initial settlement on the land and the development of the communication, transportation, and institutions that provided access to neighboring or distant markets and sources. American farmers generally were well acquainted with the more elaborate socioeconomic organization of the more densely settled and already partially urbanized East, or with the more densely settled and elaborately organized European countries of origin. The isolation of large Western holdings implied, perhaps, the promise of eventual wealth and security, but in fact rural settlement in the United States was promoted and developed in the direction of intricate social, economic, and political relationships within larger regional and national economies.

The Family

The basic family unit in rural America was the nuclear family. Broader kinship ties were also recognized, but they never formed the basis of rural residence units. Again, a very large proportion of the rural families were migrant families or families which had been formed by migrants at the new places of settlement. Migration took place almost exclusively among single persons, or among nuclear family groups, but almost never among extended families (cf. Eblen 1965). Rural American families tended to be quite large, due to the combination of relatively early marriage, high fertility, and low child mortality. In the United States and Canada, marriage has always occurred earlier among rural than among urban females. This contrasts with the pattern in, say, Scandinavia or Ireland, where the reverse is true, or in England, where there are no substantial urban-rural differences in age at marriage.

Families in rural areas were, as indicated above, typically physically isolated from one another and from the institutions of villages and towns. Partly in consequence of their isolation, and presumably partly because of traditional family patterns, the American rural family was what may be termed a "multifunctional" family. Not only was it the social institution in which legitimate sex and childbearing and child-rearing were carried out, but it was also a production and consumption unit, a religious unit, a recreational unit, and an associational unit mediating a very large proportion of the individual member's contacts with the outside world. Age-sex differentiation was, as in families universally, the rule in American rural families, but there was relatively little internal differentiation among age-sex categories with respect to occupations, interests, religious activities, social associations, and the allocation of time. Family members were typically all involved—to the extent that their individual ages and sex permitted—in the production activities of the farm or, if a village family, of the family business. Family members typically shared the same small social world of contacts with other families, school, church, business establishments, and community agencies and institutions. The same life cycle was more or less repeated by each family member in the relatively small and undifferentiated social world of the rural American community. And, with little or no individual or personal access to private transportation or communication, there was little opportunity for different family members to embark on separate social paths.

The Economy

Rural communities generally embraced three overlapping and interrelated economies, each of different range: that of the household, the village, and the region. In any given area, the relative importance of each of these economies and the closeness of the relationship between them were generally associated with the quality of communication and transportation and only secondarily with the elaborateness of mediating economic institutions—e.g. brokerages, banking, transport, or marketing institutions. In general, economic institutions as elaborate as necessary were founded as soon as political and communication conditions permitted their operation, and the establishment of modern economic institutions—be they factories, storage and distribution firms, or transport companies—typically did not have to overcome obstacles of any traditional sort but only those of a very pragmatic nature.

THE HOUSEHOLD ECONOMY. The household economy produced some combination of cash crops and products for home consumption, and it consumed some combination of home-produced and other products purchased outside. The nature of the overall combination varied with the possibility of producing cash crops for a market—a function of the individual farm family, its land, and its access to the knowledge, techniques, and equipment necessary for such production—and with the family's physical and economic capability of gaining access to the market. To the extent that the farm was physically isolated, it could produce little or nothing for a market, regardless of its own production potential; thus, being unable either to reach the market physically or to earn money to buy the items necessary for its own subsistence, the household itself had to produce all the goods it required. Alternatively, to the extent that a farm family could produce items for a cash market but had little or no access to other market products of routine home consumption, it could market a considerable portion of its output but was still obliged to produce for its own consumption.

Thus, regardless of the tendency in literature, and sometimes in history books, to glorify the self-sufficiency and home production of rural families, the extent to which the household economy relied on the market or on home production tended to vary in accordance with the accessibility of the market or with the socioeconomic situation of the household. If Granny could earn more cash or goods by manufacturing flower pots than by baking pies *and* if she could buy the equivalent or near-equivalent pies in the local grocery store, she generally gave up baking pies, switched to flower pots, and pocketed the difference.

THE VILLAGE ECONOMY.   The village in rural America consisted of a number of small businesses (usually family-owned and family-operated), some personal and professional services, and some community institutions such as schools, churches, and hospitals—all serving the farm families of the more or less immediately surrounding area. Although the villagers were often only part-time tradesmen, physicians, clergymen, or merchants—being part-time farmers as well—the American village was almost never a self-sufficient unit; rather, it was part of a village economy involving farmers, villagers, and often external markets or sources of goods and services. In many areas of the United States, villages were deliberately planned and constructed by railroads, land speculators, promoters, etc., to enhance the attractiveness of the surrounding farm lands.

The typical village business was owned and operated by a family living on the same or nearby property. The village family was similar to the farm family in a number of ways, but particularly relevant to business was its similarity in size and in the entire family's economic involvement in the business. Village businesses might be engaged in mediating exchange among the farmers; in providing services to the farmers (transportation, construction, contracting, milling, storage, the marketing or brokerage of local crops into the regional or national system, etc.); in the local distribution of outside, especially manufactured, products; and in providing personal and household services through such specialists as physicians, barbers, and blacksmiths. In addition, villages typically included people engaged in public services—in churches, newspapers, schools, and, occasionally, commercial entertainment.

THE REGIONAL ECONOMY.   The regional economy embraced that town or city which was the major marketing, transportation, or manufacturing center of the area and the surrounding village economies connected with it, usually by waterways or by rail. The regional centers processed rural products or marketed them to their nearby or far-flung consumers, and they processed and fabricated raw materials into consumer products, distributing them throughout the region. Although the regional center was not, of course, characterized by rural patterns of social structure, it was always a fundamental part of the rural economy. Again, migration and new rural settlement in the United States did not take place for the purpose of helping migrants establish some elementary level of subsistence: typically, they had enjoyed that modicum of sustenance or more in their places of origin. Rather, migrants sought to *better* their styles of life, and in agricultural settlement this always involved the production of cash crops for a market, the market usually being at least regional in scope.

Of course in many areas conditions were such that farm families had no alternative but to engage in subsistence farming. In these cases, the absence of knowledge, capital, or tools, or the fact of poor land, or the socioeconomic characteristics of the communities in which the people were born or settled, rendered anything other than subsistence farming impossible. In the United States there have always been impoverished rural families and, indeed, impoverished rural areas. But the nation's rural agricultural settlement—to the extent that it was planned or guided at all—was always organized with reference to some potential or expected *market,* usually regional in scope.

Social Institutions

SCHOOLS. A large number of laws and ordinances made the public school—accessible, in principle if not always in fact, to all children regardless of social or economic status, creed, language, or origin—a major American institution. Typically, state or territorial constitutions required local authorities (county or township) to organize school districts for the purpose of levying school taxes and building, staffing, and maintaining public schools. Such laws were implemented to a greater or lesser degree, depending upon local conditions, available state aid, and the enthusiasm of the various persons and public agencies involved.

In general, rural primary schools in the nineteenth century suffered from inadequate physical facilities, untrained and poorly paid teachers, and indifference or systematic attempts to cut school costs and budgets on the part of the population charged with their support. Worse than that, the typical school term in rural areas was very short—as brief as one month per year and seldom longer than four months—and many school-aged children were not enrolled in the schools, many enrolled children did not attend the schools, and teachers of any calibre were difficult to mobilize at any price.

Nevertheless, tens of thousands of schools were built and attended by millions of children, and virtually every rural community had at least a one-room schoolhouse. Only very much later—well into the twentieth century, when the organization of free bus transportation made it possible to consolidate rural schools into institutions serving much greater areas—did rural schools become substantially improved. The teachers' standards and salaries were raised, their working conditions were improved, and the educational opportunities available to rural children were made comparable to those available to urban youngsters.

CHURCHES. The rural church typically enjoyed considerably more support than did the school, perhaps because it made fewer demands upon the working time of the farm families. Rural churches were ordinarily quite small, serving very specific congregations. Often the church would be a rural neighborhood one, located in open country, while a rural village might contain three or four churches of different denominations.

No religion practiced in rural America ever became the indigenous or established religion of the country or of any of the areas in it. Rather, migrating families tended to bring their religious practices and beliefs with them, and small numbers of families with the same beliefs or religious background sufficed to give birth to a church, often with a part-time preacher who, like his flock, farmed on weekdays.

Many churches were born, and many died, in nineteenth-century rural America. In any given region, a number of Protestant sects or denominations might establish churches in competition with one another, and some or several of them would not survive. Typically, different ethnic or language groups formed their own churches, and many of these were incapable of surviving even minor population movements. Most important, improvements in roads and transportation rendered many neighborhood churches superfluous and brought larger numbers of worshippers to the villages.

VOLUNTARY ORGANIZATIONS. Rural America was characterized even in the nineteenth century by innumerable voluntary organizations, whether of a mutual-aid, civic, or recreational nature. These catered to a variety of interests—athletic, educational, fraternal, musical, patriotic, youth-serving, etc.—and they might be entirely indigenous to the local area or represent carry-overs brought in by migrants from some common place of origin.

The outstanding characteristic of voluntary organizations in rural America was their instability (Kolb and de Brunner 1935). Even more than churches, many organizations were born and many died. However, at any point in time and in any given community of rural America, it was possible to find a substantial number of organizations to which individuals, families, couples, or children might belong and in which social relationships of various types obtained. Later on, rural services were organized in many places on a township, county, or statewide basis, and many of the voluntary organizations received professional or semiprofessional assistance and some financial support, ultimately achieving a considerable measure of stability.

Political Institutions

Although settlers on the American frontier are often held to have universally initiated local democratic institutions and self-government, in point of fact the ordinances and legislation providing for local self-government generally preceded the arrival and settlement of newcomers. Territorial ordinances and state constitutions, codes, and statutes, usually patterned after those of eastern seaboard states, defined the state, county, township, and village organs of government, the key administrative and judicial roles, the institutions of the town meeting, and the organs for electing and controlling officials and reviewing their activities. It was the restriction upon state codes and constitutions imposed by the national Constitution, and the patterning of so many state codes on a few New England and Middle Atlantic state constitutions which accounted for the standardization of political institutions and patterns over such a large part of rural America.

Villages or townships were ordinarily the smallest or "most local" political units, and in many states these were established by law, complete with governing machinery that usually consisted of a periodic town or village meeting and the election of committees and officials. Official roles might include those of the town clerk, the town assessor, the justice of the peace, the town treasurer, and the town supervisors, among others, and typically the requirements and duties of these roles were spelled out in considerable detail by statute. Township or village business included the building of roads and bridges, the provision of schools, assistance to the needy, the licensing of businesses, and the registering of mortgages and deeds.

In the sparsely settled rural areas, county government was also quite "localized," and a considerable part of the economic welfare of individuals was associated with the county's road-opening and road-maintenance services. In addition, the county had broad judicial, administrative, educational, law enforcement, and social welfare functions. In most areas, the county was quite wealthy in comparison to individuals and even to other corporate groups, and it was often the area's most important employer, consumer, and entrepreneur.

State government was generally far more removed from the rural community than was either the township or county government, and of course the federal government was even more distant. Nevertheless, local people often participated with a lively interest in elections, referenda, and attempts to influence state and national governing bodies.

Political parties operated on the local level in each county and often in each township. Of course the various population groups were differentially attracted to the separate political parties, and there were differences, too, in the degree to which various groups backed candidates and participated in political campaigns. However, researchers have apparently found it difficult to make any generalizations about the directions of these differences. In particular, the social bases of political cleavage are difficult to determine.

Social Differentiation

Generally, the rural population of the country as a whole, and of individual states and countries as well, was characterized by only limited social differentiation, along a number of separate, although not entirely independent, axes. In the first place, "new settlers" were inevitably differentiated from "old settlers," at least in terms of local political power and influence and very often in terms of economic well-being. Second, the settlers' places of origin and such related characteristics as language, literacy, and skill were also sources of differentiation. In the community itself, open-country settlers or farmers were ordinarily distinguished from village settlers, and in the village there was some occupational differentiation.

How meaningful these differentiating characteristics were in terms of prestige or social standing cannot be assessed in any comprehensive fashion, nor is it easy to determine how rigid the distinctions were. A part of the American creed holds that mobility and self-improvement are possible for any man or his sons, but the extent to which this was actually the case in nineteenth-century rural America is not easy to ascertain.

4. POPULATION GROWTH AND REDISTRIBUTION, 1870-1950

The main trends in the development of the U.S. population since the Civil War are fairly well known and have been described in considerable detail elsewhere (Bogue 1959; U.S. Bureau of the Census, "Historical Statistics," 1960; Taeuber and Taeuber 1958). We review here only the highlights of these trends.

The nation's population virtually doubled between 1870 and 1900, from about 38.6 million to nearly 76.0 million, and it doubled again after 1900 to reach about 150.7 million in 1950 (table 13.1). However, with

TABLE 13.2
Increase in Population, Net Arrivals (Foreign-Born Immigrants), and Natural Increase: 1810–1950

Period	Total Increase		Natural Increase	Net Arrivals
	Number	*% over initial population*		
1810–1820	2,399	33.1	2,328	71
1820–1830	3,228	33.5	3,105	123
1830–1840	4,203	32.7	3,710	493
1840–1850	6,122	35.9	4,702	1,420
1850–1860	8,251	35.6	5,614	2,593
1860–1870	8,375	26.6	6,291	2,102
1870–1880	10,337	26.0	7,675	2,622
1880–1890	12,792	25.5	7,527	4,966
1890–1900	13,047	20.7	9,345	3,711
1900–1910	15,978	21.0	9,656	6,294
1910–1920	13,738	14.9	11,489	2,484
1920–1930	17,064	16.1	14,500	3,187
1930–1940	8,894	7.2	9,962	85
1940–1950	19,028	14.5	17,666	1,326

SOURCE: C. Taeuber and Taeuber 1958, table 91.

the exception of a small gain between 1920 and 1930, the rate of increase declined steadily from 1870 until 1940 (table 13.2, column 2). Beginning in 1840, foreign immigration became a major component of population growth. The net number of immigrants reached a peak of 6.3 million in the years from 1900 to 1910, accounting for about 39 percent of the decade's total population increase of about 16 million.

The contribution of foreign-born immigrants to the growth of the population can be only partially assessed from the census statistics. Aside from their own addition to the population, immigrants also contributed births to the "native-born" population. Although these were separately identifiable in U.S. censuses as "native of foreign-born or mixed parentage" (or, together with immigrants, as the so-called "foreign stock"), *their* children were "native-born of native parentage" and therefore indistinguishable in the census data.

The second half of the nineteenth century witnessed the settlement and development of the North Central region and the beginning of the settlement of the West. Whereas the total population of the U.S. grew by some 228 percent in the period from 1850 to 1900, the population of the North Central states increased almost fivefold, from 5.4 million in 1850 to 26.3 million in 1900. In the same period the population of the West increased from only 179,000 to four million.

In the first half of the twentieth century, the population of the North Central states grew at a rate lower than that of the rest of the country, whereas the population of the West continued to grow at a rate several times higher (table 13.3). The settlement of the North Central

TABLE 13.3

Population of Regions and States: 1850 to 1950

Region and State	Population (thousands)			Percentage increase	
				1850 to 1900	1900 to 1950
	1850	1900	1950	1850 to 1900	1900 to 1950
United States	23,192	75,995	150,697	228	98
Regions					
Northeast	8,627	21,047	39,478	144	88
North Central	5,404	26,333	44,461	387	69
South	8,983	24,524	47,197	173	93
West	179	4,091	19,562	2,188	378
States					
Maine	583	694	914	19	32
New Hampshire	318	412	533	29	30
Vermont	314	344	378	9	10
Massachusetts	995	2,805	4,691	182	67
Rhode Island	148	429	792	191	85
Connecticut	371	908	2,007	145	121
New York	3,097	7,269	14,830	135	104
New Jersey	490	1,884	4,835	285	157
Pennsylvania	2,312	6,302	10,498	173	67
Ohio	1,980	4,158	7,947	110	91
Indiana	988	2,516	3,934	155	56
Illinois	851	4,822	8,712	466	81
Michigan	398	2,421	6,372	509	163
Wisconsin	305	2,069	3,435	578	66
Minnesota	6	1,751	2,982	28,720	70
Iowa	192	2,232	2,621	1,061	17
Missouri	682	3,107	3,955	356	27
North Dakota	—	319	620	—	94
South Dakota	—	402	653	—	63
Nebraska	—	1,066	1,326	—	24
Kansas	—	1,470	1,905	—	30
Delaware	92	185	318	102	72
Maryland	583	1,188	2,343	104	97
District of Columbia	52	279	802	439	188
Virginia	1,119	1,854	3,319	66	79
West Virginia	302	959	2,006	217	109
North Carolina	869	1,894	4,062	118	115
South Carolina	669	1,340	2,117	101	58
Georgia	906	2,216	3,445	145	55
Florida	87	529	2,771	504	424
Kentucky	982	2,147	2,945	119	37
Tennessee	1,003	2,021	3,292	102	63
Alabama	772	1,829	3,062	137	67
Mississippi	607	1,551	2,179	156	41
Arkansas	210	1,312	1,910	525	46
Louisiana	518	1,382	2,684	167	94
Oklahoma	—	790	2,233	—	183
Texas	213	3,049	7,711	1,334	153
Montana	—	243	591	—	143
Idaho	—	162	589	—	264
Wyoming	—	93	291	—	214
Colorado	—	540	1,325	—	146
New Mexico	62	195	681	217	249
Arizona	—	123	750	—	510
Utah	11	277	689	2,332	149
Nevada	—	42	160	—	278
Washington	1	518	2,379	43,039	359
Oregon	12	414	1,521	3,320	268
California	93	1,485	10,586	1,504	613

SOURCE: Adapted from C. Taeuber and Taeuber 1958, table 2.

TABLE 13.4
Number of Urban Places by Population Size: Selected Years,
1850–1960

Size of Place	1850	1900	1930	1950	1960
Total – 2,500 and over	236	1,737	3,165	4,284	5,445
1,000,000 or more	—	3	5	5	5
500,000 to 1,000,000	1	3	8	13	16
250,000 to 500,000	—	9	24	23	30
100,000 to 250,000	5	23	56	65	81
50,000 to 100,000	4	40	98	126	201
25,000 to 50,000	16	82	185	252	432
10,000 to 25,000	36	280	606	778	1,134
5,000 to 10,000	85	465	851	1,176	1,394
2,500 to 5,000	89	832	1,332	1,846	2,152

SOURCE: U.S. Bureau of the Census, U.S. Census of Population, 1950,
Vol. II, and 1960, Vol. I.

and western regions occurred largely as a consequence of westward, and
some northward, migration.

In addition to interstate movements of population, two other kinds
of geographic movements have characterized the post-Civil War century:
(1) off-the-farm migration; and (2) the suburbanization of metropolitan
areas.

Since 1870, urban population growth has accounted for more than
half of the nation's total population increase (table 13.1). However,
estimates of the volume of rural-to-urban migration are available only
for the period after 1920. Between 1920 and 1930, it is estimated, net
migration from rural to urban areas amounted to 5.7 million persons,
or 11 percent of the total rural population in 1920 (Taeuber and Taeuber
1958). In a 1958 study of residence histories, it was found that 62 percent
of all farm-born adults in the U.S. were no longer living on farms, the
breakdowns in this figure ranging from 53 percent among 18–24 year olds
to 68 percent among those aged 65 and older (Taeuber, Chiazze, and
Haenszel 1968). Because of this rural-to-urban movement, 16 percent of
all nonfarm residents in 1958 were persons of farm origin.

Movement off the farm as well as accelerated foreign migration continued in the post-Civil War period to populate a rapidly-increasing
number of urban places and to increase population size and density in
the existing cities (see table 13.4). Thus, although cities of 100,000 persons or more contained only five percent of the population in 1850, they
accounted for about 19 percent in 1900 and about 30 percent in 1930.

Immigrants have always been heavily represented in urban places
generally and in the largest cities in particular. In 1900, two-thirds of the
foreign-born population—compared to only 40 percent of the total population—lived in urban places. In 1950, more than half the foreign-born,

but less than one-fourth of the native-born whites, lived in urbanized areas of one million or more, and more than a third of the foreign-born lived in areas of three million or more.

Especially since 1920 there has been large scale movement of city dwellers to the peripheries of urban areas, "suburbanization" in the largest cities in the U.S. The notion of the "metropolitan area," which includes a "central city" and a "satellite area" (or "metropolitan ring") of socially and economically related places and population, has enjoyed wide use and application, especially in view of the frequently arbitrary nature of the administrative boundaries delineating cities, townships, or counties and their limitations for analytical purposes.

Metropolitan growth in most recent decades has taken place largely as a twofold process of migration: (1) the movement of large numbers of migrants from outside the metropolitan area to the largest cities, and (2) the accompanying displacement and exodus of urban dwellers to the peripheries, suburbs, or metropolitan ring (Bogue 1953; Bogue and Hawley 1956).

Thus, movement off the farm, foreign immigration, and the high fertility of both the rural-to-urban migrants and the foreign-born combined to produce the nation's tremendous urban growth—from under ten million in 1870 to 69 million in 1930 and 89 million in 1950. Moreover, together with great investment and development, they transformed a rural, agriculturally oriented, America into the urban-industrial society that it is today. By 1870, nearly half (47 percent) of the total number of gainfully employed were in nonagricultural occupations, and by 1920 the proportion had risen to nearly three-fourths (73 percent).

The Changing Strategy of Adaptation:
Variations in Time and Space

It is important to see that the change from a rural to urban absorption of population growth—what we have termed the changing societal strategy of adaptation—did not occur uniformly in time or space in the United States. To be sure, it is only since 1870 that the bulk of the country's population increase has been accounted for by urban growth; and the industrialization of the United States is conventionally studied as a manifestation of the post-Civil War period (partly because relevant data on occupations and industries are not generally available for the years before 1870). In addition, the major developments in the mechanization of agriculture did not actually get under way in the United States until after the Civil War.

However, the urbanization of several of the northeastern and Middle Atlantic states began several decades before 1870. More than half the population of Massachusetts and Rhode Island was urban by 1850.

Moreover, in the decade between 1850 and 1860, almost all the population growth of Massachusetts (97 percent) was accounted for by urban growth; and in the same period Rhode Island actually experienced a decline in rural population, its total and urban populations growing by some 27,000 and 28,000 respectively (table 13.5).

In the same decade, 1850 to 1860, the urban population absorbed 75 percent of the total population growth in Connecticut, 85 percent of the growth in New York, and 73 percent of the growth in New Jersey. Thus, although only some 20 percent of the total population of the U.S. was urban at the onset of the Civil War, important areas of the country were already characterized by an "urban strategy" of adaptation and population absorption and by substantially higher proportions of urban, rather than rural, residents.

5. FAMILIES AND ECONOMIC, SOCIAL, AND POLITICAL INSTITUTIONS OF TWENTIETH-CENTURY URBAN AMERICA

The post-Civil War population trends represented in table 13.1 have had major implications for American social structure. Technological changes and increasing population density have multiplied greatly the number of different social roles and, concomitantly, have greatly multiplied and diversified the nation's social institutions.

The Family

The urban American family remains, basically, a conjugal or nuclear family unit, but, especially since the spread of birth-control practices, it has become small. Although marriage in urban places is generally undertaken later than in rural places, it still takes place at relatively early ages. Childbearing tends to be concentrated in the earliest years of marriage, and the combination of early marriage, small planned families completed early in marriage, and increased longevity of both husbands and wives has both lengthened the family cycle and tended to compartmentalize it.

The American urban family cycle now often includes a period of childbearing and a period in which the couple is still relatively young but already relatively free of childbearing duties. Women are increasingly active in the labor force, and both the joint retirement of couples and the individual retirement of widowers or widows are prolonged. Thus, at any moment in time a cross-section of urban American families probably includes families in a wider range of family-cycle types than was the case among rural families in the previous century (Glick and Parke, Jr. 1965; Uhlenberg 1969).

TABLE 13.5

*Total and Urban Population Growth: Selected States,
1850–1860*

State	% Urban		1850–1860 Increase (in thousands)		% Urban
	1850	1860	Total	Urban	
U.S. total	15	20	8,300	2,700	32
Massachusetts	51	60	236	229	97
Rhode Island	56	63	27	28	104
Connecticut	16	26	89	67	79
New York	28	39	764	651	85
New Jersey	18	33	183	134	73
Pennsylvania	24	31	584	350	60
Maryland	32	34	104	45	42
Ohio	12	17	360	158	44

SOURCE: U.S. Bureau of the Census, U.S. Census of Population,
1950, Vol. II.

Urban families are *physically* not at all isolated from other families or from other elements of the social structure. However, the urban family per se is neither integrated into, nor isolated from, the rest of society; rather, families are characterized by varying degrees of integration or isolation. Of course, different subgroups or categories of families may be characterized by more or less integration or isolation, and such patterns of differentiation are important topics of research.

The urban family's physical proximity to, or non-isolation from, the rest of the social structure is associated with its changing functions or, most often, with its *diminishing* functions. Sex, childbearing, child-rearing, and child socialization remain key family functions. However, the urban family is rarely a production unit, and its function as a consumption unit is less than that of the rural family; often, too, it is neither a religious, recreational, political, nor other social unit. Individual family members develop their own relationships to the economy through occupational choice and individual paths of education and employment. Individuals also account for much of the total consumption, although the family remains a very important consumption unit. Individual family members often seek their own entertainment, religious experiences, and political and social activities outside the home.

The Economy

The same technological developments which led to the new social strategy of settlement and to accelerating urbanization—the mechanization of agriculture and the spread of cheap and efficient land transport—operated also to alter significantly the local and regional economies and their institutions. The mechanization of agriculture freed resources and labor from primary agricultural and extractive activities for employment in secondary, and increasingly in tertiary, sectors of the economy. The development of cheap land transport promoted both rural agricultural *and* urban specialization as well as those social and economic institutions devoted to the mediation of exchange and interdependence. These developments led to the emergence of the regional economy, dominated usually by some regional metropolis with its smaller satellite cities and surrounding rural areas, the functions of the rural villages becoming increasingly superfluous (Bogue 1950). Both the cities and the rural areas were functionally specialized in the regional economy, with the internal structure of a city or rural community strongly influenced by the nature of its function or *specialized economic base*.

The urban-regional economy is characterized by relatively large establishments, especially in the manufacturing, distribution, transport, and finance sectors, and these in turn operate over large areas. Ownership, management, and work are often—perhaps usually—differentiated and bureaucratized, so that any individual's role in the economy tends to be highly specialized. However, the urban scene is characterized by a very large variety of types, sizes, and proprietary arrangements of economic activity, and the internal organization of establishments ranges from one-person neighborhood businesses to giant corporations. Individual attachment to economic activity also varies widely in the urban economy, from casual or temporary employment, the shaping of careers, to proprietorship.

Social Institutions

SCHOOLS. The schools of twentieth-century urban America are much more "important" in every respect than their nineteenth-century rural predecessors were. They are larger, have absolutely and relatively far more resources invested in them, account for a much greater proportion of the time and life cycle of children, and are much more intimately connected with other facets of the social and economic structure.

In the first place, the time of urban children is not ordinarily taken up with chores or with involvement in a family economic enterprise. In terms of time, then, children are free to attend school; and in most American communities throughout most of the twentieth century, children of certain ages have been obliged by law to do so. In the second place, in contrast to occupational roles in the agricultural sector, urban occupational roles typically demand some minimal skill in the manipulation of words, numbers, and abstractions, and more often require considerably more than elementary skill in reading and arithmetic. Finally, in contrast to the social and economic situation in which successful farming, increased land holdings, or successful merchandising were the keys to mobility and social and economic advancement, the urban path to success much more frequently involves a hierarchy of skills or of professional or technical competence. In other words, it is a path that can be traveled only with considerable formal education.

Accordingly, urban American schools are key institutions, and access to them and the opportunities offered by such access have been the theme of major social movements and issues. Probably the best indication of the integration of schools and educational institutions into the rest of the economy and social structure is the tendency on the part of both economists and laymen to view the schools increasingly as a community "investment" rather than as an item of "consumption." [3]

CHURCHES. The distinguishing feature of the churches of twentieth-century America is probably the fact that they must compete with other social and economic institutions in making claims upon, or offering entertainment and diversion to, the urban population. Thus, the twentieth-century urban American church may sponsor the Thursday night bingo game, lectures on everything from sex to social justice, dances and church suppers, nursery schools, theatre groups and summer camps for children. Not only did the rural church meet with relatively little serious competition for the attention of the family, but it was often able to benefit from local legislation effectively restraining, or barring entirely, all potential competition by stores and places of amusement. The so-called "blue laws," for example, prohibited work, commerce, and amusement on Sundays. Churches in many urban communities are still able to benefit from such "blue laws" and enjoy a partial monopolization of the sabbath, but individuals and families are typically much more mobile and may develop more effective strategies for finding nonchurch sabbath diversions than was the case in the past.

Of course the relationship of very large numbers of individuals to churches is often basically one of religious belief and practice, a phenomenon whose relative frequency probably varies among the different religious groups and denominations. But urban churches have typically sought to attract the less enthusiastic and less deeply committed believers and practitioners of the religion, rather than depend entirely upon the support of the very religious.

Urban churches of all denominations tend to be quite large, and, like other institutions, have a large number and variety of roles. These

[3] For a very critical review of modern patterns of interrelationships between schools and the social structure, see Illich (1970).

in turn are divided between clerical and lay roles, with different churches having different internal organizations. Large cities may have churches of many different sizes, resources, and volumes of activity, ranging from the once-a-week storefront church with an unpaid or even itinerant preacher to the vast and complex operations of a Catholic diocese. The latter typically includes not only the conventional pursuits of religion but also its own school system, social welfare system, youth and lay adult movements and organizations, property interests, and recreational, cultural, and political activities.

VOLUNTARY ORGANIZATIONS. Voluntary organizations are like other social institutions in twentieth-century America in that they range in internal organization and intensity of interest and activity. Thus, the urban organization with a large membership may have an extremely active nucleus, a larger number of moderately active members, and an even larger number of members who are normally indifferent or passive and only occasionally aroused to greater interest or involvement, or vice versa. In either case, urban organizations are more capable than their earlier rural counterparts of withstanding such changes without great disturbance.

The very heterogeneity of urban society serves as the *raison d'être* for a large number of voluntary organizations: individuals of similar characteristics or interests seek each other out and, upon finding others, institutionalize organized social contact and activities. Urban voluntary organizations include not only the same types found in rural communities, although in larger variety, but also a large number of types peculiar to the urban setting itself. Groups interested in particular facets of music, science, literature, art, and sports, etc., thrive in the urban setting. Foreign-language groups and ethnic associations of mutual aid *(landsmannschaften)* are ordinarily found only in cities, as are foreign-language newspapers and other publications and foreign-language theater. The labor union in the United States has thus far been limited mostly to cities and to one-industry rural communities.

Urban voluntary organizations are much more stable than their rural counterparts, at least potentially, again because of their size and the differentiation among their memberships. An organization may be entirely local in nature or it may be connected to regional or national parent organizations. For individuals, organizational membership is a key avenue of communication and of integration into the larger social structure.

Political Institutions

Many of the institutions of local, state, and national government in twentieth-century urban America duplicate in *form* their rural counterparts of the nineteenth century. However, the changes in population size and distribution and in economic structure have generated some extremely far-reaching *functional* changes in these institutions and in the political structure generally.

Probably the greatest change is the increase in size and function enjoyed by the federal and municipal governments. In addition to its traditional responsibility for defense, foreign trade, international relations, and immigration, the federal government has assumed the initiative for establishing and regulating important matters concerning the economy and trade, resource development and conservation, and social welfare and health, mobilizing and channeling enormous resources comprising a considerable proportion of the total national product. City governments, for their part, have become deeply involved in matters of health, welfare, housing, local transportation, delinquency, social disorganization, education, and the promotion of the local economy. The intermediate levels of administration and government, such as townships and counties, have become increasingly superfluous.

Both the size of the federal and effective urban governments and the decline of smaller local governments have made direct individual participation in politics relatively less influential than organizational participation. In urban America, individual political participation is typically organized and mediated by voluntary associations, political parties and clubs, labor unions, and professional groups commanding far more resources than any individual. The political parties and organizations themselves are very complex and elaborate in the urban setting, having to contend both with the complexities of government and with the problem of reaching, or being reached by, large numbers and many different types of constituents and supporters.

6. COMMUNITY, ETHNICITY, AND SOCAL CLASS: CHANGING AXES OF SOCIAL SOLIDARITY AND POLITICAL CLEAVAGE

Those differences in social characteristics, behavior, interaction, and solidarity that are associated with community size and type (residence), race, religion, or national origin (ethnicity), and socioeconomic status (social class) have been clearly recognized and documented empirically in American social science generally and in sociology in particular. Such differences are reflected in the earliest U.S. censuses, which distinguish between urban and rural populations, whites and nonwhites, freemen and slaves, and the native-born and foreign-born, although never between the different religious groupings. Censuses, government and private surveys, community studies, historical studies, and case studies have all revealed residential, ethnic, and class-based variations in all types of social phenomena: marriage and fertility, socialization and education, employment and consumption, voting and political participation, and so on. Often these have been found to overlap: e.g., residential differences in employment characteristics are often due to the educational, ethnic, color, or social class differences between residential categories. Ethnic group differences in fertility may sometimes be due to the differences in social class composition or to differential roles of women's employment in the respective ethnic categories. But geographic and residential, racial and ethnic, and social status differences are often found to persist even when the other variables are taken into account.

America: "Melting Pot" or Pluralistic Society?

A major problem in American sociology is: To what extent are residence, ethnicity, and class eroding or strengthening as bases of social differentiation and solidarity under the impact of population transformations and social change? Subsumed under this comprehensive question are more particular ones: To what extent does migration and improved transportation undermine regional, urban-rural, size-of-place, or community and neighborhood differences in social relations and behavior? To what extent do legal equality and processes of assimilation render race, religion, or national origin socially—and sociologically—irrelevant? To what extent do occupational and status mobility neutralize social-class differences in behavior, associations, and political activity? [4]

The answers to such questions are neither easy to suggest nor tidily documented. Theories (or ideologies) of "melting pots"—of ethnic amalgamation, acculturation, or assimilation—anticipate a convergence of the characteristics and behavior of the different racial, religious, and national-origin groups. As far as white Protestants are concerned, it is probably the case that those of the different national origins (Scandinavian, British, German, etc.) are much less dissimilar today than they were two generations—or even one generation—ago, and, indeed, it is probable that a considerable amount of intermarriage has taken place between native-born members of white Protestant ethnic groups. Similarly, it is probably the case that white Catholics of different national origins (Irish, Polish, Italian, German, etc.) are less dissimilar than in the past, although they are probably less characterized by intermarriage than Protestants have been. But white Catholics remain "different" from white Protestants and in many respects socially segregated from them; and Jews, by and large, remain "different" and socially segregated from Christians of both groups. (Table 13.6 shows the estimated composition of the population by religious denominations in 1957, and table 13.7 shows the differences in age structure among the major religious denominations. Median age is

---

4 For a penetrating analysis of this question, see Gordon (1964).

TABLE 13.6
Religion Reported for Persons Aged 14 and Over, by Color and Sex: U.S. Civilian Population, March 1957

Religion	Total	White		Nonwhite		Percentage Distribution				
							White		Nonwhite	
		Male	Female	Male	Female	Total	Male	Female	Male	Female
Total, 14 years and over	119,333,000	51,791,000	55,570,000	5,679,000	6,293,000	100.0	100.0	100.0	100.0	100.0
Protestant	78,952,000	32,320,000	36,155,000	4,851,000	5,626,000	66.2	62.4	65.1	85.4	89.4
Baptist	23,525,000	7,822,000	8,450,000	3,354,000	3,899,000	19.7	15.1	15.2	59.1	62.0
Lutheran	8,417,000	4,084,000	4,301,000	17,000	15,000	7.1	7.9	7.7	0.3	0.2
Methodist	16,676,000	6,788,000	7,821,000	968,000	1,099,000	14.0	13.1	14.1	17.0	17.5
Presbyterian	6,656,000	3,000,000	3,549,000	57,000	50,000	5.6	5.8	6.4	1.0	0.8
Other Protestant	23,678,000	10,626,000	12,034,000	455,000	563,000	19.8	20.5	21.7	8.0	8.9
Roman Catholic	30,669,000	14,396,000	15,499,000	361,000	413,000	25.7	27.8	27.9	6.4	6.6
Jewish	3,868,000	1,860,000	1,999,000	1,000	8,000	3.2	3.6	3.6	—	0.1
Other religion	1,545,000	688,000	676,000	88,000	93,000	1.3	1.3	1.2	1.5	1.5
No religion	3,195,000	2,015,000	730,000	306,000	108,000	2.7	4.0	1.3	5.4	1.7
Religion not reported	1,104,000	476,000	511,000	72,000	45,000	0.9	0.9	0.9	1.3	0.7

SOURCE: U.S. Bureau of the Census, "Current Population Reports," Series P-20, No. 79 (1958), table 1.
Note: The "civilian population" includes about 809,000 members of the armed forces living off post or with their families on post, but excludes all other members of the armed forces. Four largest Protestant groups shown separately. Percentage not shown where less than 0.1.

TABLE 13.7
Age and Sex of Persons Aged 14 and Over, by Reported Religion: U.S. Civilian Population, March 1957

Religion and Sex	Total, 14 Years and Over	14 to 19 Years	20 to 24 Years	25 to 34 Years	35 to 44 Years	45 to 64 Years	65 Years and Over	Median Age (years)
Male	57,470,000	6,843,000	4,419,000	11,368,000	11,269,000	16,817,000	6,754,000	40.4
Protestant	37,171,000	4,536,000	2,788,000	7,232,000	7,152,000	10,898,000	4,565,000	40.6
White	32,320,000	3,812,000	2,325,000	6,211,000	6,237,000	9,611,000	4,124,000	41.1
Nonwhite	4,851,000	724,000	463,000	1,021,000	915,000	1,287,000	441,000	37.4
Roman Catholic	14,757,000	1,817,000	1,209,000	3,163,000	3,118,000	4,042,000	1,408,000	38.8
Jewish	1,861,000	160,000	127,000	309,000	337,000	698,000	230,000	44.9
Other religion and not reported	1,324,000	138,000	110,000	220,000	230,000	431,000	195,000	43.4
No religion	2,357,000	192,000	185,000	444,000	432,000	748,000	356,000	43.3
Female	61,863,000	7,117,000	5,324,000	12,069,000	11,844,000	17,582,000	7,927,000	40.4
Protestant	41,781,000	4,798,000	3,544,000	7,956,000	7,767,000	12,009,000	5,707,000	40.9
White	36,155,000	4,038,000	2,963,000	6,705,000	6,662,000	10,570,000	5,217,000	41.6
Nonwhite	5,626,000	760,000	581,000	1,251,000	1,105,000	1,439,000	490,000	37.0
Roman Catholic	15,912,000	1,890,000	1,466,000	3,392,000	3,289,000	4,224,000	1,651,000	38.7
Jewish	2,007,000	190,000	106,000	351,000	392,000	695,000	273,000	44.1
Other religion and not reported	1,325,000	142,000	99,000	204,000	252,000	416,000	212,000	43.6
No religion	838,000	97,000	109,000	166,000	144,000	238,000	84,000	38.3

SOURCE: U.S. Bureau of the Census, "Current Population Reports," Series P-20, No. 79 (1958), table 5.

lowest for Catholics, and nonwhite Protestants, highest for Jews, and intermediate for Protestants.) Clearly, Negroes and other nonwhites remain even more "different," and, even worse, they remain segregated residentially, occupationally, and socially from whites of all religions and types.

There are some similar conclusions to be drawn with regard to social class. The skilled-worker and craftsmen groups are overtaking the lower clerical and sales groups in income levels and consumption, and the styles of life of these and other groups are exhibiting increasing similarities. In addition, as we indicated in chapter 8, social-class fertility differentials have diminished greatly (Ryder and Westoff 1971; Kiser et al. 1968). But the social and occupational classes remain distinct with respect to marriage, child-rearing, child-socialization, and participation in voluntary organizations, and with respect also to political orientation and participation at both the community and national levels.

Finally, although the rural population has declined proportionally and absolutely, what we refer to as the "urban" population remains differentiated with respect to city size, proximity to the metropolitan centers, and the city's "functional class" (i.e., whether predominantly manufacturing, commercial, administrative, etc.). Thus, though rural, urban, and size-of-place fertility differences and differences in numbers marrying have diminished, there remain differences in age at marriage, in labor-force participation and employment, in political organization, in types of economic and voluntary organizations, and in types of public institutions.

Population Transformations: Their Bearing on Ethnicity, Social Class, and Community Organization

We may invoke two general characteristics of population transformations, the first to explain why such transformations do not effectively eliminate ethnicity, social class, or residence as axes of social organization, and the second to indicate the ways these bases of social solidarity and political cleavage do change under population transformations.

In the first place, movements of population among places, states, role, or social locations tend to be highly concentrated in the relatively "short-distance" or "similar-category" streams of movement. Thus, in a matrix representing migration, mate-selection, or social-mobility in any single time interval, the population will tend to be highly concentrated around the diagonal, whereas movement over "long-distances," i.e., between quite dissimilar categories, will be relatively less frequent. In sequences of time intervals, "longer-distance" movement will take place in stages, of course. This process assures that the interchange of population among places of residence, or in the ethnically organized marriage market, or among social classes, will never really be complete, and that there will always be a certain amount of stability over time in the various residential, ethnic, or social-class subgroups.

In the second place, the generally increasing absolute size and density of the various residential, ethnic, or social-class groups preserves, and indeed increases, heterogeneity and differentiation *within* each group. Thus Negroes—or Jews, or Catholics—who were previously relatively homogeneous with respect to occupation, style of life, and the other dimensions of social class, are now characterized by a broader spectrum of social roles, statuses, and social-class attachments *and* by vertical mobility. Similarly, the ethnic groups and population categories previously relatively concentrated and homogeneous with respect to residence types (at least in so far as they were less dispersed and heterogeneous residentially than the native white Protestants were) are now more similar residentially to the total population—if only because native white Protestants and Negroes have moved to cites and metropolitan areas and now resemble more closely the white ethnic groups. Thus, geographic migration may typically be from one ethnic enclave to another enclave of the same ethnic group—usually of the same social class with the ethnic group—and need not entail any departure or severing of ethnic ties at all. For this reason, there has been an increasing development of *national* and geographically diffuse networks of ethnic solidarity and identification. Residence, voluntary organization, and political participation remain organized largely along ethnic lines, and marraige is generally ethnically endogamous as well as class-endogamous within the larger ethnic group.

Such phenomena as physical propinquity, neighborliness, and the general persistence of neighborhood schools, along with the fact that residential patterns often overlap ethnic and class patterns, all combine to retain an important role for residence and community in social organization. In powerful support of this is the retention of the district and residential basis of political organization at all levels.

Beyond the family, then, community ethnic-class subgroups may be among the most elementary of the solidary social units. These subgroups, in turn, may be interrelated along community, ethnic, or class lines, and they may join forces, as it were, for different purposes and in different circumstances. The important changes in these axes of social organization are therefore changes of internal differentiation: as communities, ethnic groups, and social classes each become more and more differentiated internally, they nevertheless continue as bases of solidarity, political cleavage, and social interaction, even under the impact of sequential population growth and transformation.

7. CONCLUSION

Social Change as a Permanent Fixture of American Society

Careful study of United States Census data would almost surely reveal that *some* counties or areas of the United States, in *some* period of three or four decades, did *not* undergo substantial change either in population size, distribution, and composition, or in number, size, and economic sector of business establishments, or in size, occupational distribution, or industrial composition of the labor force. But such instances of stability are clearly exceptional in the United States and in any case do not necessarily reflect social stability. For more likely than not, seemingly stable areas have been deeply affected by population changes and related social transformations occurring in both neighboring and distant parts of the country. Moreover, even in areas of unchanging population size and composition, we can be sure that some typically have had more schooling than their fathers, that transportation and communication must have changed radically over any generation, and that methods of work and production, whether within or outside of agriculture, have changed considerably. Thus, with few or no reservations, it may be said that social change itself has been the most enduring aspect of American social structure.

Any description of the social structural features of nineteenth-century rural America, or of twentieth-century urban America, is misleading then, unless understood as an ideal type or analytical model.

At no time did the social structure of the United States correspond perfectly, or even approximately, to our description of rural social structure in the nineteenth century—and it does not now, nor will it probably ever, correspond to our description of urban social structure in the twentieth century. However, the different parts of the United States did at different times have social structures characterized by the features we have described for twentieth-century urban America, and for at least some parts of America, the change from a nineteenth-century rural social structure to a twentieth-century urban one indeed corresponds to the social changes that have already occurred or are even now taking place. Hopefully, more precise concepts and methods of describing the nature, amount, and direction of change will emerge, for an extensive field of study awaits them both in American society, where social change is a permanent fixture, and in other societies as well.

Megalopolis and Beyond

The United States Census of 1970 recorded continued population growth, increased metropolitan concentration, and increased suburbanization, and subsequent population surveys carried out by the Bureau of the Census have revealed a continuation of the same trends. Although there is good reason to anticipate some tapering off of the overall growth rate, there is at present no reason to expect any diminishing of the trends towards metropolitan concentration and suburbanization along what we called earlier the "megalopolitan belt," that is, along the main arteries of the megalopolitan network.

An eastern seaboard megalopolis has already been identified and described in great detail, and, as we have indicated (in chapter 2), a number of inland megalopolitan networks and one on the western seaboard are also identifiable. Unfortunately, no attempt has yet been made to analyze systematically and empirically just how and why a megalopolitan network differs from any single metropolitan area or set of such areas, to what extent its social structural, demographic, and population growth characteristics are different from those of other metropolitan communities, and what, if any, special consequences of further megalopolitanization may be anticipated.

Analyses of such similarities and differences are urgently needed and must adhere to a basic framework for megalopolitan studies. Such a framework for megalopolitan studies would include rules for classifying the points and lines of the megalopolitan network by size and function and rules for describing relationships between the various points within the network and between points within and outside the network. Once such a framework is developed, we will be able to study and describe megalopolitan networks of cities, suburbs, and urbanized bands with reference to their internal structure, their changes over time, and their similarities or dissimilarities to one another and to nonmegalopolitan societies and populations.

Appendix A

| This leaflet shows the content of the questionnaires being used in the 1970 Census of Population and Housing. See explanatory notes on the page 1 flap. |

UNITED STATES CENSUS

This is your Official Census Form

Please fill it out and mail it back
on Census Day, Wednesday,
April 1, 1970

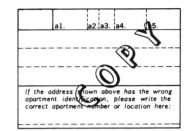

a1.   a2. a3. a4.   a5.

If the address shown above has the wrong apartment identification, please write the correct apartment number or location here:

How To Fill This Form

1. **Use a black pencil to answer the questions.**

   This form is read by an electronic computer. Black pencil is better to use than ballpoint or other pens.

   Fill circles "○" like this: ●

   The electronic computer reads every circle you fill. If you fill the wrong circle, erase the mark completely, then fill the right circle.

   When you write an answer, print or write clearly.

2. **See the filled-in example on the yellow instruction sheet.**

   This example shows how to fill circles and write in answers. If you are not sure of an answer, give the best answer you can.

   If you have a problem, look in the instruction sheet.

   All instructions are numbered the same as the questions on the Census form.

   If you need more help, call the Census office.

   You can get the number of the local office from telephone "Information" or "Directory assistance."

3. **Your answers are CONFIDENTIAL. The law (Title 13, United States Code) requires that you answer the questions to the best of your knowledge.**

   Your answers will be used only for statistical purposes and cannot, by law, be disclosed to any person outside the Census Bureau for any reason whatsoever.

   The householder should make sure that the information is shown for everyone here.

   If a boarder or roomer or anyone else prefers not to give the householder all his information to enter on the form, the householder should give at least his name, relationship, and sex in questions 1 to 3, then mail back the form. A Census Taker will call to get the rest of the information directly from the person.

4. **Check your answers. Then, mail back this form on Wednesday, April 1, or as soon afterward as you can. Use the enclosed envelope; no stamp is needed.**

   Your cooperation in carefully filling out the form and mailing it back will help make the census successful. It will save the government the expense of calling on you for the information.

PLEASE CONTINUE

U.S. Department of Commerce
Bureau of the Census
Form D-60

5. Answer the questions in this order:

Questions on page 2 about the people in your household.

Questions on page 3 about your house or apartment.

6. In Question 1 on page 2, please list each person who was living here on Wednesday, April 1, 1970, or who was staying or visiting here and had no other home.

EXPLANATORY NOTES

This leaflet shows the content of the 1970 census questionnaires. The content was determined after review of the 1960 census experience, extensive consultation with many government and private users of census data, and a series of experimental censuses in which various alternatives were tested.

Three questionnaires are being used in the census and each household has an equal chance of answering a particular form.

80 percent of the households answer a form containing only the questions on pages 2 and 3 of this leaflet.

15 percent and **5 percent** of the households answer forms which also contain the specified questions on the remaining pages of this leaflet. The 15-percent form does not show the 5-percent questions, and the 5-percent form does not show the 15-percent questions. On both forms, population questions 13 to 41 are repeated for each person in the household but questions 24 to 41 do not apply to children under 14 years of age.

The same sets of questions are used throughout the country, regardless of whether the census in a particular area is conducted by mail or house-to-house canvass. An illustrative example is enclosed with each questionnaire to help the householder complete the form.

80, 15, and 5 percent (100 percent)

1. WHAT IS THE NAME OF EACH PERSON

who was living here on Wednesday, April 1, 1970 or
who was staying or visiting here and had no other home?

DO NOT MARK THIS COL-UMN

Line No.

Print names in this order

Head of the household
Wife of head
Unmarried children, oldest first
Married children and their families
Other relatives of the head
Persons not related to the head

2. HOW IS EACH PERSON RELATED TO THE HEAD OF THIS HOUSEHOLD?

Fill one circle.

If "Other relative of head," also give exact relationship, for example, mother-in-law, brother, niece, grandson, etc.

If "Other not related to head," also give exact relationship, for example, partner, maid, etc.

---

(1) Last name _____

First name _____ Middle initial ____

- ○ Head of household
- ○ Wife of head
- ○ Son or daughter of head
- ○ Other relative of head— *Print exact relationship* →
- ○ Roomer, boarder, lodger
- ○ Patient or inmate
- ○ Other not related to head— *Print exact relationship* ↗

---

(2) Last name _____

First name _____ Middle initial ____

- ○ Head of household
- ○ Wife of head
- ○ Son or daughter of head
- ○ Other relative of head— *Print exact relationship* →
- ○ Roomer, boarder, lodger
- ○ Patient or inmate
- ○ Other not related to head— *Print exact relationship* ↗

---

(3) Last name _____

First name _____ Middle initial ____

- ○ Head of household
- ○ Wife of head
- ○ Son or daughter of head
- ○ Other relative of head— *Print exact relationship* →
- ○ Roomer, boarder, lodger
- ○ Patient or inmate
- ○ Other not related to head— *Print exact relationship* ↗

---

(4) Last name _____

First name _____ Middle initial ____

- ○ Head of household
- ○ Wife of head
- ○ Son or daughter of head
- ○ Other relative of head— *Print exact relationship* →
- ○ Roomer, boarder, lodger
- ○ Patient or inmate
- ○ Other not related to head— *Print exact relationship* ↗

---

(5) Last name _____

First name _____ Middle initial ____

- ○ Head of household
- ○ Wife of head
- ○ Son or daughter of head
- ○ Other relative of head— *Print exact relationship* →
- ○ Roomer, boarder, lodger
- ○ Patient or inmate
- ○ Other not related to head— *Print exact relationship* ↗

---

(6) Last name _____

First name _____ Middle initial ____

- ○ Head of household
- ○ Wife of head
- ○ Son or daughter of head
- ○ Other relative of head— *Print exact relationship* →
- ○ Roomer, boarder, lodger
- ○ Patient or inmate
- ○ Other not related to head— *Print exact relationship* ↗

---

(7) Last name _____

First name _____ Middle initial ____

- ○ Head of household
- ○ Wife of head
- ○ Son or daughter of head
- ○ Other relative of head— *Print exact relationship* →
- ○ Roomer, boarder, lodger
- ○ Patient or inmate
- ○ Other not related to head— *Print exact relationship* ↗

---

(8) Last name _____

First name _____ Middle initial ____

- ○ Head of household
- ○ Wife of head
- ○ Son or daughter of head
- ○ Other relative of head— *Print exact relationship* →
- ○ Roomer, boarder, lodger
- ○ Patient or inmate
- ○ Other not related to head— *Print exact relationship* ↗

---

9. If you used all 8 lines —**Are there any other persons in this household?**   ○ Yes   ○ No

Do not list the others; we will call to get the information.

10. Did you leave anyone out of Question 1 because you were not sure if he should be listed—for example, a new baby still in the hospital, or a lodger who also has another home?   ○ Yes   ○ No

On back page, give name(s) and reason left out.

512

3. SEX	4. COLOR OR RACE	DATE OF BIRTH				8. WHAT IS EACH PERSON'S MARITAL STATUS?
		5. Month and year of birth and age last birthday	6. Month of birth	7. Year of birth		
Fill one circle	Fill one circle. If "Indian (American)," also give tribe. If "Other," also give race.	Print	Fill one circle	Fill one circle for first three numbers	Fill one circle for last number	Fill one circle

| Male ○ / Female ○ | ○ White / ○ Negro or Black / ○ Indian (Amer.) Print tribe → | ○ Japanese ○ Hawaiian / ○ Chinese ○ Korean / ○ Filipino ○ Other– Print race | Month ____ / Year ____ / Age ____ | ○ Jan.-Mar. / ○ Apr.-June / ○ July-Sept. / ○ Oct.-Dec. | ○ 186- ○ 192- / ○ 187- ○ 193- / ○ 188- ○ 194- / ○ 189- ○ 195- / ○ 190- ○ 196- / ○ 191- ○ 197- | ○ 0 ○ 5 / ○ 1 ○ 6 / ○ 2 ○ 7 / ○ 3 ○ 8 / ○ 4 ○ 9 | ○ Now married / ○ Widowed / ○ Divorced / ○ Separated / ○ Never married | Make no mark in this margin |

| Male ○ / Female ○ | ○ White / ○ Negro or Black / ○ Indian (Amer.) Print tribe → | ○ Japanese ○ Hawaiian / ○ Chinese ○ Korean / ○ Filipino ○ Other– Print race | Month ____ / Year ____ / Age ____ | ○ Jan.-Mar. / ○ Apr.-June / ○ July-Sept. / ○ Oct.-Dec. | ○ 186- ○ 192- / ○ 187- ○ 193- / ○ 188- ○ 194- / ○ 189- ○ 195- / ○ 190- ○ 196- / ○ 191- ○ 197- | ○ 0 ○ 5 / ○ 1 ○ 6 / ○ 2 ○ 7 / ○ 3 ○ 8 / ○ 4 ○ 9 | ○ Now married / ○ Widowed / ○ Divorced / ○ Separated / ○ Never married |

| Male ○ / Female ○ | ○ White / ○ Negro or Black / ○ Indian (Amer.) Print tribe → | ○ Japanese ○ Hawaiian / ○ Chinese ○ Korean / ○ Filipino ○ Other– Print race | Month ____ / Year ____ / Age ____ | ○ Jan.-Mar. / ○ Apr.-June / ○ July-Sept. / ○ Oct.-Dec. | ○ 186- ○ 192- / ○ 187- ○ 193- / ○ 188- ○ 194- / ○ 189- ○ 195- / ○ 190- ○ 196- / ○ 191- ○ 197- | ○ 0 ○ 5 / ○ 1 ○ 6 / ○ 2 ○ 7 / ○ 3 ○ 8 / ○ 4 ○ 9 | ○ Now married / ○ Widowed / ○ Divorced / ○ Separated / ○ Never married |

| Male ○ / Female ○ | ○ White / ○ Negro or Black / ○ Indian (Amer.) Print tribe → | ○ Japanese ○ Hawaiian / ○ Chinese ○ Korean / ○ Filipino ○ Other– Print race | Month ____ / Year ____ / Age ____ | ○ Jan.-Mar. / ○ Apr.-June / ○ July-Sept. / ○ Oct.-Dec. | ○ 186- ○ 192- / ○ 187- ○ 193- / ○ 188- ○ 194- / ○ 189- ○ 195- / ○ 190- ○ 196- / ○ 191- ○ 197- | ○ 0 ○ 5 / ○ 1 ○ 6 / ○ 2 ○ 7 / ○ 3 ○ 8 / ○ 4 ○ 9 | ○ Now married / ○ Widowed / ○ Divorced / ○ Separated / ○ Never married |

| Male ○ / Female ○ | ○ White / ○ Negro or Black / ○ Indian (Amer.) Print tribe → | ○ Japanese ○ Hawaiian / ○ Chinese ○ Korean / ○ Filipino ○ Other– Print race | Month ____ / Year ____ / Age ____ | ○ Jan.-Mar. / ○ Apr.-June / ○ July-Sept. / ○ Oct.-Dec. | ○ 186- ○ 192- / ○ 187- ○ 193- / ○ 188- ○ 194- / ○ 189- ○ 195- / ○ 190- ○ 196- / ○ 191- ○ 197- | ○ 0 ○ 5 / ○ 1 ○ 6 / ○ 2 ○ 7 / ○ 3 ○ 8 / ○ 4 ○ 9 | ○ Now married / ○ Widowed / ○ Divorced / ○ Separated / ○ Never married |

| Male ○ / Female ○ | ○ White / ○ Negro or Black / ○ Indian (Amer.) Print tribe → | ○ Japanese ○ Hawaiian / ○ Chinese ○ Korean / ○ Filipino ○ Other– Print race | Month ____ / Year ____ / Age ____ | ○ Jan.-Mar. / ○ Apr.-June / ○ July-Sept. / ○ Oct.-Dec. | ○ 186- ○ 192- / ○ 187- ○ 193- / ○ 188- ○ 194- / ○ 189- ○ 195- / ○ 190- ○ 196- / ○ 191- ○ 197- | ○ 0 ○ 5 / ○ 1 ○ 6 / ○ 2 ○ 7 / ○ 3 ○ 8 / ○ 4 ○ 9 | ○ Now married / ○ Widowed / ○ Divorced / ○ Separated / ○ Never married |

| Male ○ / Female ○ | ○ White / ○ Negro or Black / ○ Indian (Amer.) Print tribe → | ○ Japanese ○ Hawaiian / ○ Chinese ○ Korean / ○ Filipino ○ Other– Print race | Month ____ / Year ____ / Age ____ | ○ Jan.-Mar. / ○ Apr.-June / ○ July-Sept. / ○ Oct.-Dec. | ○ 186- ○ 192- / ○ 187- ○ 193- / ○ 188- ○ 194- / ○ 189- ○ 195- / ○ 190- ○ 196- / ○ 191- ○ 197- | ○ 0 ○ 5 / ○ 1 ○ 6 / ○ 2 ○ 7 / ○ 3 ○ 8 / ○ 4 ○ 9 | ○ Now married / ○ Widowed / ○ Divorced / ○ Separated / ○ Never married | Make no mark in this margin |

| Male ○ / Female ○ | ○ White / ○ Negro or Black / ○ Indian (Amer.) Print tribe → | ○ Japanese ○ Hawaiian / ○ Chinese ○ Korean / ○ Filipino ○ Other– Print race | Month ____ / Year ____ / Age ____ | ○ Jan.-Mar. / ○ Apr.-June / ○ July-Sept. / ○ Oct.-Dec. | ○ 186- ○ 192- / ○ 187- ○ 193- / ○ 188- ○ 194- / ○ 189- ○ 195- / ○ 190- ○ 196- / ○ 191- ○ 197- | ○ 0 ○ 5 / ○ 1 ○ 6 / ○ 2 ○ 7 / ○ 3 ○ 8 / ○ 4 ○ 9 | ○ Now married / ○ Widowed / ○ Divorced / ○ Separated / ○ Never married |

11. Did you list anyone in Question 1 who is away from home now— for example, on a vacation or in a hospital? ○ Yes ○ No *On back page, give name(s) and reason person is away.*

12. Did anyone stay here on Tuesday, March 31, who is not already listed? ○ Yes No *On back page, give name of each visitor for whom there is no one at his home address to report him to a census taker.*

26:1

513

Please answer questions
10, 11, and 12 at the
bottom of page 2.

80, 15, and 5 percent (100 percent)

Page 3

A. How many living quarters, occupied and vacant, are at this address?

- ○ One
- ○ 2 apartments or living quarters
- ○ 3 apartments or living quarters
- ○ 4 apartments or living quarters
- ○ 5 apartments or living quarters
- ○ 6 apartments or living quarters
- ○ 7 apartments or living quarters
- ○ 8 apartments or living quarters
- ○ 9 apartments or living quarters
- ○ 10 or more apartments or living quarters
- ○ This is a mobile home or trailer

Answer these questions for your living quarters

H1. Is there a telephone on which people in your living quarters can be called?

- ○ Yes → What is
- ○ No   the number? _____
         Phone number

H2. Do you enter your living quarters—

- ○ Directly from the outside or through a common or public hall?
- ○ Through someone else's living quarters?

H3. Do you have complete kitchen facilities?
Complete kitchen facilities are a sink with piped water, a range or cook stove, and a refrigerator.

- ○ Yes, for this household only
- ○ Yes, but also used by another household
- ○ No complete kitchen facilities for this household

H4. How many rooms do you have in your living quarters?
Do not count bathrooms, porches, balconies, foyers, halls, or half-rooms.

- ○ 1 room
- ○ 2 rooms
- ○ 3 rooms
- ○ 4 rooms
- ○ 5 rooms
- ○ 6 rooms
- ○ 7 rooms
- ○ 8 rooms
- ○ 9 rooms or more

H5. Is there hot and cold piped water in this building?

- ○ Yes, hot and cold piped water in this building
- ○ No, only cold piped water in this building
- ○ No piped water in this building

H6. Do you have a flush toilet?

- ○ Yes, for this household only
- ○ Yes, but also used by another household
- ○ No flush toilet

H7. Do you have a bathtub or shower?

- ○ Yes, for this household only
- ○ Yes, but also used by another household
- ○ No bathtub or shower

H8. Is there a basement in this building?

- ○ Yes
- ○ No, built on a concrete slab
- ○ No, built in another way *(include mobile homes and trailers)*

H9. Are your living quarters—

- ○ Owned or being bought by you or by someone else in this household? *Do not include cooperatives and condominiums here.*
- ○ A cooperative or condominium which is owned or being bought by you or by someone else in this household?
- ○ Rented for cash rent?
- ○ Occupied without payment of cash rent?

H10a. Is this building a one-family house?

- ○ Yes, a one-family house
- ○ No, a building for 2 or more families or a mobile home or trailer

b. If "Yes"— Is this house on a place of 10 acres or more, or is any part of this property used as a commercial establishment or medical office?

- ○ Yes, 10 acres or more
- ○ Yes, commercial establishment or medical office
- ○ No, none of the above

H11. If you live in a one-family house which you own or are buying—
What is the value of this property; that is, how much do you think this property (house and lot) would sell for if it were for sale?

- ○ Less than $5,000
- ○ $5,000 to $7,499
- ○ $7,500 to $9,999
- ○ $10,000 to $12,499
- ○ $12,500 to $14,999
- ○ $15,000 to $17,499
- ○ $17,500 to $19,999
- ○ $20,000 to $24,999
- ○ $25,000 to $34,999
- ○ $35,000 to $49,999
- ○ $50,000 or more

If this house is on a place of 10 acres or more, or if any part of this property is used as a commercial establishment or medical office, do not answer this question.

H12. Answer this question if you pay rent for your living quarters.

a. If rent is paid by the month—
What is the monthly rent?

Write amount here → $ _____ .00 *(Nearest dollar)*

and

Fill one circle →

- ○ Less than $30
- ○ $30 to $39
- ○ $40 to $49
- ○ $50 to $59
- ○ $60 to $69
- ○ $70 to $79
- ○ $80 to $89
- ○ $90 to $99
- ○ $100 to $119
- ○ $120 to $149
- ○ $150 to $199
- ○ $200 to $249
- ○ $250 to $299
- ○ $300 or more

b. If rent is not paid by the month—
What is the rent, and what period of time does it cover?

$ _____ .00 per
(Nearest dollar) *(Week, half-month, year, etc.)*

H13. *Answer question H13 if you pay rent for your living quarters.*

In addition to the rent entered in H12, do you also pay for—

a. Electricity?

- ○ Yes, average monthly cost is → $ _____ .00
  Average monthly cost
- ○ No, included in rent
- ○ No, electricity not used

b. Gas?

- ○ Yes, average monthly cost is → $ _____ .00
  Average monthly cost
- ○ No, included in rent
- ○ No, gas not used

c. Water?

- ○ Yes, yearly cost is ——→ $ _____ .00
  Yearly cost
- ○ No, included in rent or no charge

d. Oil, coal, kerosene, wood, etc.?

- ○ Yes, yearly cost is ——→ $ _____ .00
  Yearly cost
- ○ No, included in rent
- ○ No, these fuels not used

H14. How are your living quarters heated?
Fill one circle for the kind of heat you use most.

- ○ Steam or hot water system
- ○ Central warm air furnace with ducts to the individual rooms, or central heat pump
- ○ Built-in electric units *(permanently installed in wall, ceiling, or baseboard)*

- ○ Floor, wall, or pipeless furnace
- ○ Room heaters <u>with</u> flue or vent, burning gas, oil, or kerosene
- ○ Room heaters <u>without</u> flue or vent, burning gas, oil, or kerosene *(not portable)*

- ○ Fireplaces, stoves, or portable room heaters of any kind

  In some other way—*Describe* ——→ _____

- ○ None, unit has no heating equipment

H15. About when was this building originally built? *Mark when the building was first constructed, not when it was remodeled, added to, or converted.*

- ○ 1969 or 1970   ○ 1950 to 1959
- ○ 1965 to 1968   ○ 1940 to 1949
- ○ 1960 to 1964   ○ 1939 or earlier

H16. Which best describes this building?
Include all apartments, flats, etc., even if vacant.

- ○ A one-family house detached from any other house
- ○ A one-family house attached to one or more houses
- ○ A building for 2 families
- ○ A building for 3 or 4 families
- ○ A building for 5 to 9 families
- ○ A building for 10 to 19 families
- ○ A building for 20 to 49 families
- ○ A building for 50 or more families

- ○ A mobile home or trailer

  Other—
  Describe _____

H17. Is this building—

- ○ On a city or suburban lot?— *Skip to H19*
- ○ On a place of less than 10 acres?
- ○ On a place of 10 acres or more?

H18. Last year, 1969, did sales of crops, livestock, and other farm products from this place amount to—

- ○ Less than $50 (or None)   ○ $2,500 to $4,999
- ○ $50 to $249   ○ $5,000 to $9,999
- ○ $250 to $2,499   ○ $10,000 or more

H19. Do you get water from—

- ○ A public system *(city water department, etc.)* or private company?
- ○ An individual well?
- ○ Some other source *(a spring, creek, river, cistern, etc.)*?

H20. Is this building connected to a public sewer?

- ○ Yes, connected to public sewer
- ○ No, connected to septic tank or cesspool
- ○ No, use other means

H21. How many bathrooms do you have?
A complete bathroom is a room with flush toilet, bathtub or shower, and wash basin with piped water.

A half bathroom has at least a flush toilet <u>or</u> bathtub or shower, but does <u>not</u> have all the facilities for a complete bathroom.

- ○ No bathroom, or only a half bathroom

- ○ 1 complete bathroom
- ○ 1 complete bathroom, plus half bath(s)

- ○ 2 complete bathrooms
- ○ 2 complete bathrooms, plus half bath(s)

- ○ 3 or more complete bathrooms

H22. Do you have air-conditioning?

- ○ Yes, 1 individual room unit
- ○ Yes, 2 or more individual room units
- ○ Yes, a central air-conditioning system
- ○ No

H23. How many passenger automobiles are owned or regularly used by members of your household?
Count company cars kept at home.

- ○ None
- ○ 1 automobile
- ○ 2 automobiles
- ○ 3 automobiles or more

515

H24a. How many stories (floors) are in this building?

- ○ 1 to 3 stories
- ○ 4 to 6 stories
- ○ 7 to 12 stories
- 13 stories or more ■

b. *If 4 or more stories—*
Is there a passenger elevator in this building?

○ Yes   ○ No

H25a. Which fuel is used most for cooking? ■

Gas { From underground pipes serving the neighborhood. ○
Bottled, tank, or LP .... ○

Electricity .... ○

Fuel oil, kerosene, etc. .... ○

Coal or coke ○
Wood ...... ○
Other fuel .. ○
No fuel used ○

b. Which fuel is used most for house heating? ■

Gas { From underground pipes serving the neighborhood. ○
Bottled, tank, or LP .... ○

Electricity .... ○

Fuel oil, kerosene, etc. .... ○

Coal or coke ○
Wood ...... ○
Other fuel .. ○
No fuel used ○

c. Which fuel is used most for water heating? ■

Gas { From underground pipes serving the neighborhood. ○
Bottled, tank, or LP .... ○

Electricity .... ○

Fuel oil, kerosene, etc. .... ○

Coal or coke ○
Wood ...... ○
Other fuel .. ○
No fuel used ○

H26. How many bedrooms do you have?
Count rooms used mainly for sleeping even if used also for other purposes.

- ○ No bedroom   ○ 3 bedrooms
- ○ 1 bedroom   ■   ○ 4 bedrooms
- ○ 2 bedrooms   ○ 5 bedrooms or more

H27a. Do you have a clothes washing machine?

- ○ Yes, automatic or semi-automatic
- ○ Yes, wringer or separate spinner
- ○ No

b. Do you have a clothes dryer?

- ○ Yes, electrically heated
- ○ Yes, gas heated
- ○ No   ■

c. Do you have a dishwasher *(built-in or portable)*?

○ Yes   ○ No

d. Do you have a home food freezer which is separate from your refrigerator?

○ Yes   ○ No

H28a. Do you have a television set? *Count only sets in working order.*

- ○ Yes, one set
- ○ Yes, two or more sets
- ○ No

b. *If "Yes"—* **Is any set equipped to receive UHF broadcasts, that is, channels 14 to 83?**

○ Yes   ○ No   ■

H29. Do you have a battery-operated radio?
Count car radios, transistors, and other battery-operated sets in working order or needing only a new battery for operation.

○ Yes, one or more   ○ No

H30. Do you (or any member of your household) own a second home or other living quarters which you occupy sometime during the year?

○ Yes   ○ No

5 percent

516

15 and 5 percent

Name of person on line ① of page 2

Last name   First name   Initial

13a. Where was this person born? *If born in hospital, give State or country where mother lived. If born outside U.S., see instruction sheet; distinguish Northern Ireland from Ireland (Eire).*

○ This State

OR

_____
(Name of State or foreign country; or Puerto Rico, Guam, etc.)

5 percent

b. Is this person's origin or descent— *(Fill one circle)*

○ Mexican   ○ Central or South American
○ Puerto Rican   ○ Other Spanish
○ Cuban   ○ No, none of these

15 percent

14. What country was his father born in?

○ United States

OR

_____
(Name of foreign country; or Puerto Rico, Guam, etc.)

15. What country was his mother born in?

○ United States

OR

_____
(Name of foreign country; or Puerto Rico, Guam, etc.)

5 percent

16. *For persons born in a foreign country—*

a. Is this person naturalized?

○ Yes, naturalized
○ No, alien ■
○ Born abroad of American parents

b. When did he come to the United States to stay?

○ 1965 to 70   ○ 1950 to 54   ○ 1925 to 34
○ 1960 to 64   ○ 1945 to 49   ○ 1915 to 24
○ 1955 to 59   ○ 1935 to 44   ○ Before 1915

15 percent

17. What language, other than English, was spoken in this person's home when he was a child? *Fill one circle.*

○ Spanish ■   ○ Other—
○ French   *Specify* _____
○ German   ○ None, English only

18. When did this person move into this house (or apartment)? *Fill circle for date of last move.*

○ 1969 or 70   ○ 1965 or 66   ○ 1949 or earlier
○ 1968   ○ 1960 to 64   ○ Always lived in
○ 1967 ■   ○ 1950 to 59   this house or apartment

19a. Did he live in this house on April 1, 1965? *If in college or Armed Forces in April 1965, report place of residence there.*

○ Born April 1965 or later ⎤
○ Yes, this house .... ⎬ *Skip to 20*
○ No, different house   ⎦

b. Where did he live on April 1, 1965?

(1) State, foreign country,
U.S. possession, etc. _____

(2) County _____

(3) Inside the limits of a city, town, village, etc.?
○ Yes   ○ No

(4) If "Yes," name of city,
town, village, etc.

---

15 percent

20. Since February 1, 1970, has this person attended regular school or college at any time? *Count nursery school, kindergarten, and schooling which leads to an elementary school certificate, high school diploma, or college degree.*

○ No ■
○ Yes, public
○ Yes, parochial
○ Yes, other private

15 and 5 percent

21. What is the highest grade (or year) of regular school he has ever attended?

Fill one circle. If now attending, mark grade he is in.

○ Never attended school— *Skip to 23*
○ Nursery school
○ Kindergarten ■

Elementary through high school (grade or year)
1 2 3 4 5 6   7 8   9 10 11 12
○ ○ ○ ○ ○ ○ ○ ○ ○ ○ ○ ○

College (academic year)
1 2 3 4 5 6 or more
○ ○ ○ ○ ○ ○

22. Did he finish the highest grade (or year) he attended?

○ Now attending this grade (or year)
○ Finished this grade (or year)
○ Did not finish this grade (or year)

23. When was this person born?

○ Born before April 1956— *Please go on with questions 24 through 41.*

○ Born April 1956 or later— *Please omit questions 24 through 41 and go to the next page for the next person.*
● ■   ■

5 percent

24. *If this person has ever been married—*

a. Has this person been married more than once?

○ Once   ○ More than once

b. When did he   **When did he get married**
get married?   **for the first time?**

_____   _____
Month   Year   Month   Year

c. *If married more than once—* **Did the first marriage end because of the death of the husband (or wife)?**

○ Yes   ○ No ■

15 and 5 percent

25. *If this is a girl or a woman—*
How many babies has she ever   1 2 3 4 5 6 7 8
had, not counting stillbirths?   ○ ○ ○ ○ ○ ○ ○ ○
Do not count her stepchildren
or children she has adopted.   9 10 11 12 or   None
                                      ○ ○ ○ ○ more   ○

15 percent

26. *If this is a man—*

a. Has he ever served in the Army, Navy, or other Armed Forces of the United States? ■

⎡ ○ Yes
⎣ ○ No

b. Was it during— *(Fill the circle for each period of service.)*

Vietnam Conflict *(Since Aug. 1964)* .... ○
Korean War *(June 1950 to Jan. 1955)* .... ○
World War II *(Sept. 1940 to July 1947)* .... ○
World War I *(April 1917 to Nov. 1918)* .... ○
Any other time .... ○

517

27a. Has this person ever completed a vocational training program?

For example, in high school; as apprentice; in school of business, nursing, or trades; technical institute; or Armed Forces schools.

○ Yes   ○ No— *Skip to 28*

b. What was his main field of vocational training? *Fill one circle.*

○ Business, office work
○ Nursing, other health fields
○ Trades and crafts *(mechanic, electrician, beautician, etc.)*
○ Engineering or science technician; draftsman
○ Agriculture or home economics
○ Other field— *Specify* ⌐

_ _ _ _ _ _ _ _ _ _ _ _ _ _ _ _ _ _ _ _

28a. Does this person have a health or physical condition which limits the <u>kind</u> or <u>amount</u> of work he can do at a job?

If 65 years old or over, skip to question 29.

○ Yes
○ No

b. Does his health or physical condition keep him from holding <u>any</u> job at all?

○ Yes
○ No

c. If "Yes" in a or b— How long has he been limited in his ability to work?

○ Less than 6 months   ○ 3 to 4 years
○ 6 to 11 months   ○ 5 to 9 years
○ 1 to 2 years   ○ 10 years or more

QUESTIONS 29 THROUGH 41 ARE FOR ALL PERSONS BORN BEFORE APRIL 1956 INCLUDING HOUSEWIVES, STUDENTS, OR DISABLED PERSONS AS WELL AS PART-TIME OR FULL-TIME WORKERS

29a. Did this person work at any time <u>last week</u>?

○ Yes— *Fill this circle if this person did full- or part-time work.*

(Count part-time work such as a Saturday job, delivering papers, or helping without pay in a family business or farm; and active duty in the Armed Forces)

○ No— *Fill this circle if this person did not work, or did only own housework, school work, or volunteer work.*

Skip to 30

b. How many hours did he work <u>last week</u> (at all jobs)?

Subtract any time off and add overtime or extra hours worked.

○ 1 to 14 hours   ○ 40 hours
○ 15 to 29 hours   ○ 41 to 48 hours
○ 30 to 34 hours   ○ 49 to 59 hours
○ 35 to 39 hours   ○ 60 hours or more

---

c. Where did he work <u>last week</u>?

If he worked in more than one place, print where he worked most last week.

If he travels about in his work or if the place does not have a numbered address, see instruction sheet.

(1) Address *(Number and street name)* _ _ _ _ _ _ _ _ _ _ _

(2) Name of city, town, village, etc. _ _ _ _ _ _ _ _ _ _

(3) Inside the limits of this city, town, village, etc.?
○ Yes
○ No

(4) County _ _ _ _ _ _ _ _ _ _ _ _ _ _ _

(5) State   (6) ZIP Code

d. How did he get to work <u>last week</u>? *Fill one circle for chief means used on the last day he worked at the address given in 29c.*

○ Driver, private auto   ○ Taxicab
○ Passenger, private auto   ○ Walked only
○ Bus or streetcar   ○ Worked at home
○ Subway or elevated   ○ Other means— *Specify* ⌐
○ Railroad

_ _ _ _ _ _ _ _ _ _ _ _ _ _ _ _ _ _

After completing question 29d, skip to question 33.

---

30. Does this person have a job or business from which he was temporarily absent or on layoff <u>last week</u>?

○ Yes, on layoff
○ Yes, on vacation, temporary illness, labor dispute, etc.
○ No

31a. Has he been looking for work during the past 4 weeks?

○ Yes   ○ No— *Skip to 32*

b. Was there any reason why he could not take a job <u>last week</u>?

○ Yes, already has a job
○ Yes, because of this person's temporary illness
○ Yes, for other reasons (in school, etc.)
○ No, could have taken a job

---

32. When did he last work at all, even for a few days?

○ In 1970 ┊ ○ 1964 to 1967 ┊ ○ 1959 or earlier ⎰ *Skip*
○ In 1969 ┊ ○ 1960 to 1963 ┊ ○ Never worked ⎱ *to 36*
○ In 1968

– continued –

33-35. Current or most recent job activity

Describe clearly this person's chief job activity or business last week, if any. If he had more than one job, describe the one at which he worked the most hours.

If this person had no job or business last week, give information for last job or business since 1960.

33. Industry

a. For whom did he work? *If now on active duty in the Armed Forces, print "AF" and skip to question 36.*

(Name of company, business, organization, or other employer)

b. What kind of business or industry was this?
Describe activity at location where employed.

(For example: Junior high school, retail supermarket, dairy farm, TV and radio service, auto assembly plant, road construction)

c. Is this mainly— *(Fill one circle)*

- ○ Manufacturing
- ○ Wholesale trade
- ○ Retail trade
- ○ Other *(agriculture, construction, service, government, etc.)*

34. Occupation

a. What kind of work was he doing?

(For example: TV repairman, sewing machine operator, spray painter, civil engineer, farm operator, farm hand, junior high English teacher)

b. What were his most important activities or duties?

(For example: Types, keeps account books, files, sells cars, operates printing press, cleans buildings, finishes concrete)

c. What was his job title?

35. Was this person— *(Fill one circle)*

Employee of private company, business, or individual, for wages, salary, or commissions... ○

Federal government employee .... ○
State government employee................... ○
Local government employee *(city, county, etc.)*... ○

Self-employed in own business, professional practice, or farm— ■
    Own business not incorporated .... ○
    Own business incorporated .... ○

Working without pay in family business or farm ○

36. In April 1965, what State did this person live in?

○ This State

OR

(Name of State or foreign country; or Puerto Rico, etc.)

GPO 902-842

37. In April 1965, was this person— *(Fill three circles)*

a. Working at a job or business *(full or part-time)*?
    ○ Yes   ○ No

b. In the Armed Forces?
    ○ Yes   ○ No

c. Attending college? ■
    ○ Yes   ○ No

38. If "Yes" for "Working at a job or business" in question 37—
Describe this person's chief activity or business in April 1965.

a. What kind of business or industry was this?

b. What kind of work was he doing (occupation)?

c. Was he—
An employee of a private company or government agency... ○
Self-employed or an unpaid family worker .... ○

39a. Last year (1969), did this person work at all, even for a few days?
    ○ Yes   ○ No— *Skip to 41*

b. How many weeks did he work in 1969, either full-time or part-time?
Count paid vacation, paid sick leave, and military service.

- ○ 13 weeks or less ■
- ○ 14 to 26 weeks
- ○ 27 to 39 weeks
- ○ 40 to 47 weeks
- ○ 48 to 49 weeks
- ○ 50 to 52 weeks

40. Earnings in 1969— Fill parts a, b, and c for everyone who worked any time in 1969 even if he had no income.
(If exact amount is not known, give best estimate.)

a. How much did this person earn in 1969 in wages, salary, commissions, bonuses, or tips from all jobs?
(Before deductions for taxes, bonds, dues, or other items.)
$ _____ .00
(Dollars only)
OR ○ None

b. How much did he earn in 1969 from his own nonfarm business, professional practice, or partnership?
(Net after business expenses. If business lost money, write "Loss" above amount.) ■
$ _____ .00
(Dollars only)
OR ○ None

c. How much did he earn in 1969 from his own farm?
(Net after operating expenses. Include earnings as a tenant farmer or sharecropper. If farm lost money, write "Loss" above amount.)
$ _____ .00
(Dollars only)
OR ○ None

41. Income other than earnings in 1969— Fill parts a, b, and c.
(If exact amount is not known, give best estimate.)

a. How much did this person receive in 1969 from Social Security or Railroad Retirement?
$ _____ .00
(Dollars only)
OR ○ None

b. How much did he receive in 1969 from public assistance or welfare payments?
Include aid for dependent children, old age assistance, general assistance, aid to the blind or totally disabled. ■
Exclude separate payments for hospital or other medical care.
$ _____ .00
(Dollars only)
OR ○ None

c. How much did he receive in 1969 from all other sources?
Include interest, dividends, veterans' payments, pensions, and other regular payments.
(See instruction sheet.)
$ _____ .00
(Dollars only)
OR ○ None

FORM CPS—1
9 7 70
28:1

U.S. DEPARTMENT OF COMMERCE
Bureau of the Census

CURRENT POPULATION SURVEY

Form Approved   NOVEMBER 1970
Budget Bureau No. 41 - R1202.14

1. INTERVIEWER CHECK ITEM

Only CPS—1 for household .... ○   (Fill all applicable
First CPS—1 of continuation h'hld . ○   items on this page)
Second CPS—1 of continuation h'hld ○   (Transcribe Items 2-16
Third, fourth, etc. CPS—1........ ○   from first CPS—1)

2. CONTROL NUMBER

3. SAMPLE
A   C
○   ○

4a. (Transcribe from Control Card items 10a, 11 or 12)
A B C D E
○ ○ ○ ○ ○

6. PSU NO.

7. SERIAL NO.

8. IDEN. CODE

9. HOUSE-HOLD NO.

10. SEGMENT NO.

5. TYPE OF LIVING QUARTERS

HOUSING UNIT

House, apartment, flat.......... ○
HU in nontransient hotel, motel, etc. ○
HU, permanent, in transient hotel, motel, etc.... ○
HU in rooming house .... ○
Trailer, permanent .... ○
Trailer, mobile .... ○
HU not specified above .... ○
(Describe below)

OTHER UNIT

Quarters not HU in rooming or boarding house ...... ○
Unit not permanent in transient hotel, motel, etc.. ○
Tent site or trailer site..... ○
Other not HU .... ○
(Describe below)

FILL FOR SPECIAL DWELLING PLACE

11a. NAME OF PLACE

11b. TYPE OF PLACE CODE

12a. SAMPLE UNIT NO. 12b. DESCRIPTION OF SAMPLE UNIT (Room no., bed no., etc.)

13. INTERVIEWER   CODE
A B C D E F G H J K L M
○ ○ ○ ○ ○ ○ ○ ○ ○ ○ ○ ○

14. DATE COMPLETED:

15. LINE NO. H'HLD. RESP.
1 2 3 4 5 6 +
Non. h'hld resp .... ○
(Specify)

16a. TYPE INTERVIEW
Personal ... ○
Tel-coll back ○
ICR filled .. ○
Noninterview ○ (Fill 17)
Tel-regular.. ○

17. NONINTERVIEW (Mark one reason in Item 17a or 17b. If Item 17a marked, fill Race of Head. If Item 17b marked, fill Items 17c-e, as applicable.)

17a. TYPE A
(Mark noninterview reason and race of head below.)

REASON
No one home ○
Temporarily absent .. ○
Refused .. ○
Other-Occ. ○
(Describe below)

RACE OF HEAD
White ○
Negro ○
Other ○

17b. TYPE B OR C

Vacant - regular .... ○
Vacant - storage of h'hld furniture .... ○
Temp. occ. by persons with URE .... ○

Unfit or to be demolished................ ○
Under construction, not ready .... ○
Converted to temp. business or storage ...... ○
Occ. by Armed Force members or persons under 14 ○
Unoccupied tent site or trailer site .... ○
Permit granted, construction not started ...... ○
Demolished........................... ○
House or trailer moved .... ○
Outside segment .... ○
Converted to permanent business or storage .... ○
Merged .... ○
Condemned .... ○
Built after April 1, 1960 .... ○
Other (Specify below)................... ○

T Y P E B

T Y P E C

(Fill 17c)

(Omit 17c-e)

17c. SEASONAL STATUS

Year round ..... ○   (Fill HVS if HU in Item 5)

Migratory workers ○   (Fill Items 17d and 17e
Seasonal .... ○   below if HU in Item 5)

17d. Is this unit usually occupied:

Summers only ... ○   (Transcribe to back
Winters only .... ○   of Control Card
Other........ ○   first time unit is
(Describe below)   vacant during a
                    4-month
                    enumeration
                    period.)

(Transcribe from back of Control Card in each succeeding month unit is vacant in the same 4-month enumeration period.)

17e. CONDITION OF UNIT

Sound .... ○
Deteriorating.... ○
Dilapidated..... ○

51. LENGTH OF INTERVIEW
Minutes

52. Total number of children under 18 years of age, related to the head.

+

53. TOTAL FAMILY INCOME
(From CC item 33)
A ○   G ○
B ○   H ○
C ○   I ○
D ○   J ○
E ○   K ○
F ○

INTERVIEWER TRANSCRIPTION ITEMS
(For continuation households, fill on all CPS-1's)

NOTES

18. Line No.

19. What was . . . doing most of LAST WEEK—
- Working
- Keeping house
- Going to school
- or something else?

Working (Skip to 20A) .. WK ○
With a job but not at work J ○
Looking for work ..... LK ○
Keeping house .... H ○
Going to school ...... S ○
Unable to work (Skip to 24) U ○
Other (Specify) ...... OT ○

---

20. Did . . . do any work at all LAST WEEK, not counting work around the house?
(Note: If farm or business operator in hh., ask about unpaid work)

Yes ○   No ○ (Go to 21)

20A. How many hours did . . . work LAST WEEK at all jobs?

20B. INTERVIEWER CHECK ITEM

49+ (Skip to item 23)
1-34 (Go to 20C)
35-4B (Go to 20D)

20C. Does . . . USUALLY work 35 hours or more a week at this job?

Yes ○ What is the reason . . . worked less than 35 hours LAST WEEK?

No ○ What is the reason . . . USUALLY works less than 35 hours a week?
(Mark the appropriate reason)

Slack work ○
Material shortage .... ○
Plant or machine repair ..... ○
New job started during week . ○
Job terminated during week . ○
Could find only part-time work ○
Holiday (Legal or religious) .. ○
Labor dispute .... ○
Bad weather .... ○
Own illness .... ○
On vacation .... ○
Too busy with housework, school, personal bus.,etc. ○
Did not want full-time work .. ○
Full-time work week under 35 hours .. ○
Other reason (Specify) ..... ○

(Skip to 23 and enter job worked at last week)

20D. Did . . . lose any time or take any time off LAST WEEK for any reason such as illness, holiday or slack work?

Yes ○ How many hours did . . . take off?

No ○
(Correct 20A if lost time not already deducted; if 20A reduced below 35, correct 20B and fill 20C; otherwise, skip to 23.)

20E. Did . . . work any overtime or at more than one job LAST WEEK?

Yes ○ How many extra hours did . . . work?

No ○
(Correct 20A and 20B as necessary if extra hours not already included and skip to 23.)

(Skip to 23)

---

21. (If J in 19, skip to 21A.) Did . . . have a job or business from which he was temporarily absent or on layoff LAST WEEK?

Yes ○   No ○ (Go to 22)

21A. Why was . . . absent from work LAST WEEK?

Own illness .... ○
On vacation .... ○
Bad weather.... ○
Labor dispute .. ○
New job to begin within 30 days ○ (Skip to 22B and 22C2)
Temporary layoff (Under 30 days) ○
Indefinite layoff (30 days or more or no def. recall date) ○ (Skip to 22C3)
Other (Specify).. ○

21B. Is . . . getting wages or salary for any of the time off LAST WEEK?

Yes .... ○
No......... ○
Self employed ○

21C. Does . . . usually work 35 hours or more a week at this job?

Yes ○
No ○

(Skip to 23 and enter job held last week)

---

22. (If LK in 19, skip to 22A.) Has . . . been looking for work during the past 4 weeks?

Yes ○   No ○ (Go to 24)

22A. What has . . . been doing in the last 4 weeks to find work? (Mark all methods used; do not read list.)

Checked with— pub.employ.agency ○
pvt.employ.agency ○
employer directly . ○
friends or relatives ○
Placed or answered ads .... ○
Nothing (Skip to 24) ○
Other (Specify in notes, e.g., MDTA, union or prof. register, etc.) ○

22B. Why did . . . start looking for work? Was it because . . . lost or quit a job at that time (pause) or was there some other reason?

Lost job .... ○
Quit job .... ○
Left school .... ○
Wanted temporary work ○
Other (Specify in notes) ○

22C. 1) How many weeks has . . . been looking for work?

2) How many weeks ago did . . . start looking for work?

3) How many weeks ago was . . . laid off?

22D. Has . . . been looking for full-time or part-time work?

Full ○   Part ○

22E. Is there any reason why . . . could not take a job LAST WEEK?

Yes ○   Already has a job ○
No ○   Temporary illness ○
Going to school . ○
Other (Specify in notes) ○

22F. When did . . . last work at a full-time job or business lasting 2 consecutive weeks or more?

1965 or later (Write month and year).. ○
_____ (Month and year)
Before 1965.................. ○
Nev. worked full-time 2 wks. or more ○
Never worked at all .... ○
(Skip to 23 and enter last full-time civilian job lasting 2 weeks or more, job from which laid off, or "Never Worked")

OFFICE USE ONLY

INDUSTRY	OCCUPATION
0 ○○ A ○	0 ○○○○ N ○
1 ○○ B ○	1 ○○○○ P ○
2 ○○ C ○	2 ○○○○ Q ○
3 ○○ D ○	3 ○○○○ R ○
4 ○○ E ○	4 ○○○○ S ○
5 ○○ F ○	5 ○○○○ T ○
6 ○○ G ○	6 ○○ U ○
7 ○○ H ○	7 ○○ V ○
8 ○○ J ○	8 ○○ W ○
9 ○○ K ○	9 ○○ X ○
L ○	Y ○
M ○	Z ○

---

23. DESCRIPTION OF JOB OR BUSINESS

23A. For whom did . . . work? (Name of company, business, organization or other employer.)

23B. What kind of business or industry is this? (For example: TV and radio mfg., retail shoe store, State Labor Dept., farm.)

23C. What kind of work was . . . doing? (For example: electrical engineer, stock clerk, typist, farmer.)

23D. Was this person

An employee of PRIVATE Co., bus., or individual for wages, salary or comm P ○
A GOVT. employee (Federal, State, or local)........................ G ○
Self-empl in OWN bus., prof. practice, or farm.................... O ○   } (If not a farm) Is the business incorporated? Yes ○ No ○
Working WITHOUT PAY in fam. bus., or farm................... WP ○
NEVER WORKED .... NEV ○

---

24. INTERVIEWER CHECK ITEM

Unit in rotation group:
(Mark one circle only)

○ 2, 3, 4, 6, 7 or 8 (End questions)
○ 1 or 5 (Go to 24A)

24A. When did . . . last work for pay at a regular job or business, either full- or part-time?

Within past 12 months ○
1 up to 2 years ago ○
2 up to 3 years ago ○ } (Go to 24B)
3 up to 4 years ago ○
4 up to 5 years ago ○
5 or more years ago ○ } (Skip to 24C)
Never worked ..... ○

24B. Why did . . . leave that job?

Personal, family (Incl. pregnancy) or school .. ○
Health................... ○
Retirement or old age .... ○
Seasonal job completed ..... ○
Slack work or business conditions ... ○
Temporary nonseasonal job completed ..... ○
Unsatisfactory work arrangements (Hours, pay, etc.) ○
Other.................... ○

24C. Does . . . want a regular job now, either full- or part-time?

Yes .... ○   } (Go to 24D)
Maybe-it depends (Specify in notes). ○
No .... ○   } (Skip to 24E)
Don't know .... ○

24D. What are the reasons . . . is not looking for work? (Mark each reason mentioned)

• Believes no work available in line of work or area .... ○
• Couldn't find any work .... ○
• Lacks nec. schooling, training, skills or experience .... ○
• Employers think too young or too old .... ○
• Other pers. handicap in finding job .... ○
• Can't arrange child care .... ○
• Family responsibilities ..... ○
• In school or other training .... ○
• Ill health, physical disability ○
• Other (Specify in notes)..... ○
• Don't know .... ○

24E. Does . . . intend to look for work of any kind in the next 12 months?

Yes.................. ○
It depends (Specify in notes) ○
No .... ○
Don't know .... ○

(If entry in 24B, describe job in 23)

---

25. LINE NO.

26. RELATIONSHIP TO HOUSEHOLD HEAD

Head with other relatives (incl. wife) in household ○
Head with no other relatives in household .... ○
Wife of head.......... ○
Other relative of head ...... ○
Non-rel. of head with own rels. (incl. wife) in h'hld. ○
Nonrelative of head with no own relatives in h'hld .. ○

27. AGE

28. MARITAL STATUS

Married-civilian spouse present ... ○
Married-Armed Force spouse present ... ○
Married-spouse absent— (include separated).. ○
Widowed or divorced.. ○
Never married .... ○

29. RACE

White ○
Negro ○
Other ○

30. SEX AND VETERAN STATUS

Male
Vietnam Era . ○
Korean War .. ○
World War 11. ○
World War 1.. ○
Other Service ○
Nonveteran.. ○
Female .... ○

31. HIGHEST GRADE ATTENDED

E H C

None

32. GRADE COMPLETED

Yes ○
No ○

33.

DO NOT WRITE IN THIS SPACE

34. INTERVIEWER CHECK ITEM *(Mark one item and proceed accordingly)*

○ Entry in item 20A and P or G (including Incorp. "Yes") in item 23D — *(Ask item 35)*

○ Entry in item 20A and O or WP (excluding Incorp. "Yes") in item 23D — *(Ask item 39)*

○ Entry in item 21A — *(Ask item 41)*

○ All other cases — *(Skip to 45)*

---

35. How much does ... usually earn per week at this job before deductions?

Under $25 ○	$80–$89 ○
$25–$39 ○	$90–$99 ○
$40–$49 ○	$100–$124 ○
$50–$59 ○	$125–$149 ○
$60–$69 ○	$150–$199 ○
$70–$79 ○	$200+ ○

(Ask 36)

36. Did ... work for more than one employer LAST WEEK?

Yes ○ *(Skip to 42)*

No ○ *(Ask 37)*

37. In addition to working for wages or salary, did ... operate his own farm, business, or profession LAST WEEK?

Yes ○ *(Skip to 42)*

No ○ *(Ask 38)*

38. Did ... have any other job LAST WEEK at which he did not work at all?
(If "Yes," indicate whether paid for time off.)

Yes-Paid ... ○ } *(Skip to 42)*
Yes-Not Paid ○ }

No .... ○ *(Skip to 45)*

---

39. In addition to this work, did ... do any work for wages or salary LAST WEEK?

Yes ○ *(Skip to 42)*

No ○ *(Ask 40)*

40. Did ... have a job LAST WEEK at which he did not work at all?
(If "Yes," indicate whether paid for time off.)

Yes-Paid ... ○ } *(Skip to 42)*
Yes-Not Paid ○ }

No .... ○ *(Skip to 45)*

DESCRIBE 2ND JOB IF "YES" IN ANY OF 36 – 41

NOTE: Mark whether second job is same as or different from job in item 23B-D. Describe if different.

42. What was ...'s second job LAST WEEK?

Same as 23B-D ○ *(Skip to 43)*

Different from 23 B-D ○ *(Describe below and go to 43)*

A. NAME OF EMPLOYER

B. INDUSTRY

C. OCCUPATION

D. CLASS OF WORKER
Private .... ○
Gov't .... ○
Self-emp .... ○ *(If not a farm)* Inc. } Yes ○ *(Ask 43)*
No ○
Without Pay .... ○

43. How many hours did ... work at his second job LAST WEEK?

0 ○ ○
1 ○ ○
2 ○ ○
3 ○ ○
4 ○ ○
5 ○ ○
6 ○ ○
7 ○ ○
8 ○ ○
9 ○ ○

(Ask 44)

44. How many hours did ... work at his principal job (Item 23) LAST WEEK?

0 ○ ○
1 ○ ○
2 ○ ○
3 ○ ○
4 ○ ○
5 ○ ○
6 ○ ○
7 ○ ○
8 ○ ○
9 ○ ○

(Skip to 45)

---

41. In addition to this job, did ... have some other job LAST WEEK at which he did not work at all?

Yes ○ *(Ask 42)*

No ○ *(Skip to 45)*

FOR OFFICE USE ONLY

INDUSTRY

0 ○   A ○
1 ○ ○   B ○
2 ○ ○   C ○
3 ○ ○   D ○
4 ○ ○   E ○
5 ○ ○   F ○
6 ○ ○ ○ G ○
7 ○ ○ ○ H ○
8 ○ ○ ○ J ○
9 ○ ○ ○ K ○
        L ○
        M ○

OCCUPATION

0 ○ ○ ○ N ○
1 ○ ○ ○ P ○
2 ○ ○ ○ Q ○
3 ○ ○ ○ R ○
4 ○ ○ ○ S ○
5 ○ ○ ○ T ○
6 ○ ○ ○ U ○
7 ○ ○ ○ V ○
8 ○ ○ ○ W ○
9 ○ ○ ○ X ○
        Y ○
        Z ○

---

45. INTERVIEWER CHECK ITEM

In what State is this household located? *(Mark one circle and proceed accordingly)*

All states except Georgia, Kentucky, Alaska, or Hawaii ○ ↓	Georgia or Kentucky ○ ↓	Alaska ○ ↓	Hawaii ○ ↓
Is this person 21 years old or over?	Is this person 18 years old or over?	Is this person 19 years old or over?	Is this person 20 years old or over?
Yes ○ / No ○	Yes ○ / No ○	Yes ○ / No ○	Yes ○ / No ○
(Ask 46) / *(Go to next person)*	*(Ask 46)* / *(Go to next person)*	*(Ask 46)* / *(Go to next person)*	*(Ask 46)* / *(Go to next person)*

---

46. This month we have some questions about whether people voted in the recent Congressional election. Did ... vote in the election held on November 3rd *(pause)* or did something keep ... from voting?

Voted ○ *(Skip to 49)*
Did not vote ○ *(Ask 47)*
Don't know ○ *(Ask 47)*

47. Was ... registered to vote in that election?

Yes ○ *(Skip to 49)*
No ○ *(Ask 48)*
Don't know ○ *(Skip to 49)*

---

48. What was the main reason ... was not registered to vote? *(Mark one circle)*

- Not a citizen of the United States .... ○
- Had not lived here long enough to be qualified to vote .... ○
- Not interested, just never got around to it, dislikes politics, etc. .... ○
- Unable to register because of illness, no transportation, couldn't take time off from work, etc. ... ○
- Other reason *(Specify below)* .... ○ } *(Ask 49)*

- Don't know .... ○

49. Thinking back to 1968, did ... vote in the Presidential election that year?

Yes ○ } *(Fill 50)*
No ○
Don't know ○

50. INTERVIEWER CHECK ITEM

Who reported on voting for this person?

Self ○
Other ○

(Go to next person)

Bibliography

ADAMS, R. McC. 1966. *The Evolution of Urban Society: Early Mesopotamia and Pre-Hispanic Mexico.* Chicago: Aldine Publishing Co.

———. 1965. *Land Beyond Baghdad.* Chicago: University of Chicago Press.

———. 1964. The origins of agriculture. In S. Tax, ed., *Horizons of Anthropology.* Chicago: Aldine Publishing Co.

ABU-LUGHOD, J. 1955. The emergence of differential fertility in urban Egypt. *Milbank Memorial Fund Quarterly,* Vol. 63, No. 1, Part 1.

ALBRIGHT, W. F. 1965. Some remarks on the archaeological chronology of Palestine before about 1500 B.C. In R. W. Ehrich, ed., *Chronologies in Old World Archaeology.* Chicago: University of Chicago Press.

ALTERMAN, H. 1969. *Counting People: The Census in History.* New York: Harcourt, Brace and World.

BACHI, R. 1963. Standard distance measures and related methods for spatial analysis. Regional Science Association: Papers, 1962, Vol. 10.

———. 1958. Statistical analysis of geographical series. *Bulletin de l'Institut International de Statistique,* Vol. 36, Part 2.

——— and MATRAS, J. 1964. Family size preferences of Jewish maternity cases in Israel. *Milbank Memorial Fund Quarterly,* April.

BANKS, J. A. 1954. *Prosperity and Parenthood: A Study of Family Planning Among the Victorian Middle Classes.* London: Routledge and Kegan Paul.

BARBER, E. G. 1955. Changing patterns of mobility. In *The Bourgeoisie in 18th Century France*. Princeton: Princeton University Press. Reprinted in W. J. Goode, ed., *Readings on the Family*. Englewood Cliffs, N.J.: Prentice-Hall, Inc., 1964.

BECKER, G. S. 1960. An economic analysis of fertility. In the *National Bureau of Economic Research, Demographic and Economic Change in Developed Countries*. Princeton: Princeton University Press.

BEHRMAN, S. J., CORSA, L., and FREEDMAN, R. 1969. *Fertility and Family Planning: A World View*. Ann Arbor: University of Michigan Press.

BELOCH, J. 1886. *Die Bëvolkerung in Griechisch-Römanish Alterum*. Leipzig.

BENDIX, R., and LIPSET, S. M., eds. 1966. *Class, Status and Power*. 2nd ed. New York: The Free Press.

————. 1953. *Class, Status and Power*. Glencoe, Illinois: The Free Press.

BERARD, J. 1960. *L'Expansion et la Colonisation Grecques jusqu'aux Guerres Médiques*. Paris: Aubier.

BERELSON, B., ET AL., eds. 1966. *Family Planning and Population Programs*. Chicago: University of Chicago Press.

BERENT, J. 1970a. Causes of fertility decline in Eastern Europe and the Soviet Union. Part I. The influence of demographic factors. *Population Studies*, Vol. 24, No. 1, March.

————. 1970b. Causes of fertility decline in Eastern Europe and the Soviet Union. Part II. Economic and social factors. *Population Studies*, Vol. 24, No. 2, July.

BESHERS, J. M. 1967. *Population Processes in Social Systems*. New York: The Free Press.

————, and NISHIURA, E. N. 1960. A theory of internal migration differentials. *Social Forces*, Vol. 39.

BETTLEHEIM, C., and FRERE, S. 1950. *Une Ville Francaise Moyenne: Auxerre en 1950*. Paris: Armand Colin. Cited in T. Caplow, Urban structure in France. *American Sociological Review*, Vol. 17, 1952. Reprinted in P. Meadows and E. H. Mizruhi, eds., *Urbanism, Urbanization, and Change: Comparative Perspectives*. Reading, Massachusetts: Addison-Wesley, 1969.

BLAKE, J. 1965. Demographic science and population policy. In M. C. Sheps and J. C. Ridley, eds., *Public Health and Population Change*. Pittsburgh: University of Pittsburgh Press.

BLAU, P. M. 1960. Structural effects. *American Sociological Review*, Vol. 25.

————. 1957. Formal organizations: dimensions of analysis. *American Journal of Sociology*, Vol. 63, July.

————, and DUNCAN, O. D. 1967. *The American Occupational Structure*. New York: Wiley and Sons.

BOGUE, D. J. 1959a. *The Population of the United States*. Glencoe, Illinois: The Free Press.

————. 1959b. Internal migration. In P. M. Hauser and O. D. Duncan, eds., *The Study of Population*. Chicago: University of Chicago Press.

————. 1953. *Population Growth in Standard Metropolitan Areas, 1900–1950.* Washington: Government Printing Office.

————. 1952. *A Methodological Study of Migration and Labor Mobility in Michigan and Ohio in 1947.* Oxford, Ohio: Scripps Foundation, Miami University.

————. 1949. *The Structure of the Metropolitan Community, A Study of Dominance and Subdominance.* Ann Arbor: Horace H. Rackham School of Graduate Studies, University of Michigan.

BONILLA, F. 1961. Rio's Favelas. *American Universities Field Staff Reports,* East Coast South America Series, Vol. 8, No. 3. Reprinted in W. Mangin, ed., *Peasants in Cities, Readings in the Anthropology of Urbanization.* Boston: Houghton Mifflin Co., 1970.

BORGATTA, E., ed. 1969. *Sociological Methodology.* San Francisco: Jossey-Bass.

BOSERUP, E. 1965. *The Conditions of Agricultural Growth.* Chicago: Aldine Publishing Co.

BORRIE, W. D., and SPILLIUS, J. 1957. The population of Tikopia, 1929 and 1952. *Population Studies,* Vol. 10, No. 3, March.

BOTTOMORE, T. B. 1962. *Sociology.* London: Allen and Unwin.

BOULDING, K. E. 1953. Towards a general theory of growth. *Canadian Journal of Economics and Political Science,* Vol. 19; 326–340. Reprinted in J. J. Spengler and O. D. Duncan, eds., *Demographic Analysis.* Glencoe: The Free Press, 1956.

BOURGEOIS-PICHAT, J. 1965. The general development of the population of France since the 18th century. In D. V. Glass and D. E. C. Eversley, eds., *Population in History.* Chicago: Aldine Publishing Co.

BRAIDWOOD, R. J. 1960. The agricultural revolution. *Scientific American* (September).

————, and WILLEY, G. R., eds. 1962. *Courses Toward Urban Life: Archaeological Considerations of Some Cultural Alternates.* Viking Fund Publications in Anthropology, No. 32. Chicago: Aldine Publishing Co.

BURGESS, E. W., and BOGUE, D. J., eds. 1964. *Contributions to Urban Sociology.* Chicago: The University of Chicago Press.

————, and NEWCOMB, C. 1930. *Census of the City of Chicago, 1930.* Chicago: University of Chicago Press.

BUTZER, K. W. 1964. *Environment and Archaeology: An Introduction to Pleistocene Geography.* Chicago: Aldine Publishing Co.

CALDWELL, J. R. 1962. Eastern North America. In R. J. Braidwood and G. R. Willey, eds., *Courses Toward Urban Life: Archaeological Considerations of Some Cultural Alternates.* Viking Fund Publications in Anthropology, No. 32. Chicago: Aldine Publishing Co.

CAMPBELL, A. A. 1965. Recent fertility trends in the United States and Canada. U.N. World Population Conference, 1965, *Proceedings,* Vol. II.

CARNEIRO, R. L. 1961. Slash and burn cultivation among the Kuikura and its implications for cultural development in the Amazon Basin. *Antropologica,* Supplement No. 2, September. Reprinted in Y. A. Cohen, ed.,

Man in Adaptation. Vol. 2: The Cultural Present. Chicago: Aldine Publishing Co., 1968.

CARR-SAUNDERS, A. M. 1936*a*. Estimate of the population of the world and its continents from 1650 to 1900. In United Nations Department of Social Affairs, Population Division, The Determinants and Consequences of Population Trends. *Population Studies,* No. 17. New York: United Nations, 1953.

————. 1936*b. World Population.* Oxford: Clarendon Press.

CHANG, K. 1962. China. In R. J. Braidwood and G. R. Willey, eds., *Courses Toward Urban Life: Archaeological Considerations of Some Cultural Alternates.* Viking Fund Publications in Anthropology, No. 32. Chicago: Aldine Publishing Co.

CHASE, H. C. 1969. Registration completeness and international comparisons of infant mortality. *Demography,* Vol. 6, No. 4, November.

————. 1967. *International comparison of perinatal and infant mortality: the United States and six west European countries.* National Center for Health Statistics, Vital and Health Statistics, Series 3, No. 6. Washington: Public Health Service.

CHILDE, V. G. 1952. *New Light on the Most Ancient East.* London: Routledge and Kegan Paul.

————. 1951. *Man Makes Himself.* London: Watts and Co.

————. 1950. The urban revolution. *Town Planning Review,* Vol. 21.

CHO, LEE-JAY, GRABILL, W. H., and BOGUE, D. J. 1970. *Differential Current Fertility in the United States.* Chicago: Community and Family Study Center, University of Chicago.

CIPOLLA, C. M. 1965. Four centuries of Italian demographic development. In D. V. Glass and D. E. C. Eversley, *Population in History.* Chicago: Aldine Publishing Co.

CLARK, C. 1967. *Population Growth and Land Use.* London: Macmillan.

————, and HASWELL, M. 1967. *The Economics of Subsistence Agriculture.* 3rd ed. London: St. Martin's Press.

CLARK, G. 1947. *Archaeology and Society.* 2nd ed. London: Methuen and Co.

CLARK, J. D. 1962. Africa south of the Sahara. In R. J. Braidwood and G. R. Willey, eds., *Courses Toward Urban Life: Archaeological Considerations of Some Cultural Alternates.* Viking Fund Publications in Anthropology, No. 32. Chicago: Aldine Publishing Co.

CLARK, J. G. D. 1952. *Prehistoric Europe, The Economic Basis.* London: Methuen and Co., Ltd.

COALE, A. J. 1969. The decline of fertility in Europe from the French Revolution to World War II. In S. J. Behrman, L. Corsa, Jr., and R. Freedman, eds., *Fertility and Family Planning: A World View.* Ann Arbor: University of Michigan Press.

————. 1963. Population and economic development. In P. M. Hauser, ed., *The Population Dilemma.* Englewood Cliffs, N.J.: Prentice-Hall, Inc.

————. 1956. The effects of changes in mortality and fertility on age composition. *Milbank Memorial Fund Quarterly,* Vol. 34, No. 1, January.

————, and HOOVER, E. M. 1958. *Population Growth and Economic Development in Low-Income Countries.* Princeton: Princeton University Press.

COHEN, A. K. 1955. *Delinquent Boys.* Glencoe, Illinois: The Free Press.

COHEN, Y. A. 1969. Social boundary systems. *Current Anthropology,* Vol. 10, No. 1, February.

————, ed. 1968. *Man in Adaptation.* Vol. 2: *The Cultural Present.* Chicago: Aldine Publishing Co.

COLEMAN, J. S. (in press) Demand and supply considerations in mobility. In R. McGinnis (ed.), *Proceedings of Cornell Conference on Human Mobility,* 1968.

COLLIER, D. 1962. The central Andes. In R. J. Braidwood and G. R. Willey, eds., *Courses Toward Urban Life: Archaeological Considerations of Some Cultural Alternates.* Viking Fund Publications in Anthropology, No. 32. Chicago: Aldine Publishing Co.

CONCEPCION, M. B. 1967. The effect of current social and economic changes in differential fertility. In U.N., World Population Conference, 1965, *Proceedings,* Vol. II. New York: United Nations.

CORSA, L., JR. 1966. The United States. In B. Berelson et al., eds., *Family Planning and Population Programs.* Chicago: University of Chicago Press.

COX, P. 1959. *Demography.* Cambridge: Cambridge University Press.

CUTRIGHT, P. 1968. Occupational inheritance: a cross-national analysis. *American Journal of Sociology,* Vol. 73, No. 4, January.

DARAGAN, M. V. 1967. Economic development and internal migration. In U.N., World Population Conference, 1965, *Proceedings,* Vol. 4. New York: United Nations.

DAVIS, J. A., SPAETH, J. L., and HUSON, C. 1961. A technique for analyzing the effect of group composition. *American Sociological Review,* Vol. 20, April.

DAVIS, K. 1969. *World Urbanization 1950–1970.* Vol. 1: *Basic Data for Cities, Countries, and Regions.* Berkeley: Institute for International Studies, University of California.

————. 1963. Theory of change and response in modern demographic history. *Population Index,* Vol. 29, No. 4, October. Reprinted in T. R. Ford and G. F. DeJong, eds., *Social Demography.* Englewood Cliffs, N.J.: Prentice-Hall, Inc., 1970.

————. 1951. *The Population of India and Pakistan.* Princeton: Princeton University Press.

————. 1950. Statistical perspectives on marriage and divorce. *Annals of the American Academy of Political and Social Science,* Vol. 272, November. Reprinted in J. J. Spengler and O. D. Duncan, eds., *Demographic Analysis.* Glencoe, Illinois: The Free Press, 1956.

————, and BLAKE, J. 1956. Social structure and fertility: an analytic framework. *Economic Development and Cultural Change,* Vol. 4, April.

DEEVEY, E. S., JR. 1960. The human crop. *Scientific American,* September.

DEMOS, J. 1968. Families in colonial Bristol, Rhode Island: an exercise in historical demography. *William and Mary Quarterly,* Vol. 25.

DENIEL, R., and HENRY, L. 1965. La population d'un village du nord de la France: Sainghin-en-Mélantois, de 1665 à 1851. *Population,* Vol. 20.

DEPREZ, P. 1965. The demographic development of Flanders in the eighteenth century. In D. V. Glass and D. E. C. Eversley, eds., *Population in History.* Chicago: Aldine Publishing Co.

DIA, O. 1967. The urban growth of Cap-Vert, Dakar. In U.N. World Population Conference, 1965, *Proceedings,* Vol. 4. New York: United Nations.

DOLL, R., and HILL, A. B. 1956. Lung cancer and other causes of death in relation to smoking: 2nd report on mortality of British doctors. *British Medical Journal,* Vol. 2.

DORN, H. F. 1963. World population growth. In P. M. Hauser, ed., *The Population Dilemma.* Englewood Cliffs, N.J.: Prentice-Hall, Inc.

———. 1959. Tobacco consumption and mortality from cancer and other diseases. *Public Health Reports,* Vol. 74.

DRIVER, H. E., and SCHUESSLER, K. F. 1967. Correlational analysis of Murdock's 1957 ethnographic sample. *American Anthropologist,* Vol. 69, No. 3–4, June-August.

DUESENBERRY, J. S. 1960. Comment. In National Bureau of Economic Research, *Demographic and Economic Change in Developed Countries.* Princeton: Princeton University Press.

DUNCAN, B., and HAUSER, P. M. 1960. *Housing a Metropolis—Chicago.* Glencoe, Illinois: The Free Press.

DUNCAN, O. D. 1969. Inequality and opportunity. *Population Index,* Vol. 35, No. 4.

———. 1968. Patterns of occupational mobility among Negro men. *Demography,* Vol. 5, No. 1.

———. 1966. Methodological issues in the analysis of social mobility. In N. J. Smelser and S. M. Lipset, eds., *Social Structure and Mobility in Economic Development.* Chicago: Aldine Publishing Co.

———. 1965. Farm background and differential fertility. *Demography,* Vol. 2.

———. 1964. Social organization and ecosystem. In R. E. L. Faris, ed., *Handbook of Modern Sociology.* Chicago: Rand McNally and Co.

———. 1959. Human ecology and population studies. In P. M. Hauser and O. D. Duncan, eds., *The Study of Population.* Chicago: University of Chicago Press.

———. 1957. Population distribution and community structure. *Cold Spring Harbor Symposia on Quantitative Biology,* Vol. 22.

———. 1956. Optimum size of cities. In J. J. Spengler and O. D. Duncan, eds., *Demographic Analysis.* Glencoe, Illinois: The Free Press.

———, CUZZORT, R. P., and DUNCAN, B. 1961. *Statistical Geography.* Glencoe, Illinois: The Free Press.

DUNCAN, O. D., and DUNCAN, B. 1955. Residential distribution and occupational stratification. *American Journal of Sociology,* Vol. 60, March.

DUNCAN, O. D., and PFAUTZ, H. W., 1960. Translator's preface. In M. Halbwachs, *Population and Society: Introduction to Social Morphology.* Translated by O. D. Duncan and H. W. Pfautz. Glencoe, Illinois: The Free Press.

DUNCAN, O. D., and REISS, A. J. 1956. *Social Characteristics of Urban and Rural Communities, 1950.* New York: John Wiley and Sons.

DUNCAN, O. D., and SCHNORE, L. F. 1959. Cultural, behavioral, and ecological perspectives in the study of social organization. *American Journal of Sociology,* Vol. 65, September.

DUNCAN, O. D., ET AL. 1960. *Metropolis and Region.* Baltimore: Johns Hopkins University Press.

DURKHEIM, E. 1951. *Suicide: A Study in Sociology.* Translated by J. A. Spaulding and G. Simpson. Glencoe, Illinois: The Free Press.

———. 1933, *The Division of Labor in Society.* Translated by G. Simpson. New York: Macmillan.

EASTERLIN, R. A. 1969. Towards a socioeconomic theory of fertility: a survey of recent research on economic factors in American fertility. In S. J. Behrman, R. Corsa, and R. Freedman, eds., *Fertility and Family Planning: A World View.* Ann Arbor: University of Michigan Press.

———. 1967. Effects of population growth on the economic growth of developing countries. *Annals of the American Academy of Political and Social Science,* January. Reprinted in T. R. Ford and G. F. DeJong, eds., *Social Demography.* Englewood Cliffs, N.J.: Prentice-Hall, Inc., 1970.

———. 1961. The American baby boom in historical perspective. *American Economic Review,* Vol. 51, December. Reprinted in D. M. Heer, ed., *Readings in Population.* Englewood Cliffs, N.J.: Prentice-Hall, Inc., 1968.

EBLEN, J. E. 1965. An analysis of nineteenth-century frontier populations. *Demography,* Vol. 2.

EHRICH, R. W., ed. 1965. *Chronologies in Old World Archaeology.* Chicago: University of Chicago Press.

EISENSTADT, S. N. 1965. The MacIver lecture: transformation of social, political and cultural orders in modernization. *American Sociological Review,* Vol. 30.

———. 1964a. Institutionalization and change. *American Sociological Review,* Vol. 29.

———. 1964b. Social change, differentiation and evolution. *American Sociological Review,* Vol. 29.

———. 1954. *The Absorption of Immigrants.* Glencoe, Illinois: The Free Press.

EL-BADRY, M. A. 1969. Higher female than male mortality in some countries of south Asia: a digest. *Journal of the American Statistical Association,* Vol. 64, December.

ELDRIDGE, H. T., and THOMAS, D. S. 1964. *Population Redistribution and Economic Growth, United States 1870–1950,* Vol. III: *Demographic Analyses and Interrelations.* Philadelphia: American Philosophical Society.

ELIZAGU, J. C. 1966. A study of migration to greater Santiago (Chile). *Demography,* Vol. 3, No. 2.

EVERSLEY, D. E. C. 1965a. Population, economy, and society. In D. V. Glass and D. E. C. Eversley, eds., *Population in History.* Chicago: Aldine Publishing Co.

————. 1965b. Mortality in Britain in the eighteenth century: problems and prospects. In P. Harsin and E. Hélin, eds., *Actes du Colloque International de Démographie Historique Liege 18–20 Avril, 1963.* Paris. Ed. M. Th. Genin.

————. 1959. *Social Theories of Fertility and the Malthusian Debate.* London: Oxford University Press.

FARIS, R. E. L., ed. 1964. *Handbook of Modern Sociology.* Chicago: Rand McNally and Co.

FARLEY, R. 1970. *Growth of the Black Population, A Study of Demographic Trends.* Chicago: Markham Publishing Co.

————. 1965. The demographic rates and social institutions of the 19th century Negro population: a stable population analysis. *Demography,* Vol. 2.

FEDERICI, N. 1968. *Lezioni di Demografia.* 3rd ed. Rome: Edizioni E. De Santis.

FENNESSEY, J. 1968. The general linear model: a new perspective in some familiar topics. *American Journal of Sociology,* Vol. 74, No. 1, July.

FOLGER, J. K., and NAM, C. B. 1964. Educational trends from census data. *Demography,* Vol. 1, No. 1. Reprinted in C. B. Nam, ed., *Population and Society.* Boston: Houghton Mifflin, 1968.

FORD, T. R., and DEJONG, G. F., eds. 1970. *Social Demography.* Englewood Cliffs, N.J.: Prentice-Hall, Inc.

FORDE, C. D. 1964. *Habitat, Economy, and Society.* London: Methuen and Co.

FORM, W. H., ET AL. 1954. The compatibility of alternative approaches to the delimitation of urban sub-areas. *American Sociological Review,* Vol. 19, No. 4, August. Reprinted in J. P. Gibbs, ed., *Urban Research Methods.* Princeton: D. Van Nostrand Inc., 1961.

FORTES, M. 1950. Kinship and marriage among the Ashanti. In A. R. Radcliffe-Brown and D. Forde, *African Systems of Kinship and Marriage.* London: Oxford University Press.

————, and EVANS-PRITCHARD, E. E., eds. 1940. *African Political Systems.* London: Oxford University Press.

FOURASTIÉ, J. 1959. De la vie traditionelle a la vie tertiare. *Population,* Vol. 14, No. 3.

FOX, T. G., and MILLER, S. M. 1966. Intra-country variations: occupational stratification and mobility. In R. Bendix and S. M. Lipset, eds., *Class, Status and Power.* 2nd ed. New York: The Free Press.

————. 1965. Economic, political, and social determinants of mobility: an international cross-sectional analysis. *Acta Sociologica*, Vol. 9, No. 1–2.

FREEDMAN, R., ed. 1964. *Population, The Vital Revolution*. New York: Anchor Books.

————. 1963. Norms for family size in underdeveloped areas. *Proceedings of the Royal Society*, B. Vol. 159. Reprinted in D. M. Heer, ed., *Readings on Population*. Englewood Cliffs, N.J.: Prentice-Hall, Inc., 1968.

————. 1962. American studies of family planning and fertility: a review of major trends and issues. In C. V. Kiser, ed., *Research in Family Planning*. Princeton: Princeton University Press.

————, TAKESHITA, J. Y., and SUN, T. H. 1964. Fertility and family planning in Taiwan. A case study of the demographic transition. *American Journal of Sociology*, Vol. 69, No. 1, July.

FREEDMAN, R., and TAKESHITA, J. Y. 1965. Studies of fertility and family limitation in Taiwan. In M. C. Sheps and J. C. Ridley, eds., *Public Health and Population Change*. Pittsburgh: University of Pittsburgh Press.

FREEDMAN, R., WHELPTON, P. K., and CAMPBELL, A. A. 1959. *Family Planning, Sterility and Population Growth*. New York: McGraw-Hill.

FREEMAN, L. C. 1965. *Elementary Statistics in the Behavioral Sciences*. New York: John Wiley and Sons.

FREZEL-LOZEY, M. 1969. *Histoire Démographique d'un Village en Bearn: Bilheres-d'Ossau (XVIII–XIX Siecles)*. Bordeaux.

FRIEDLANDER, D. 1970. The spread of urbanization in England and Wales 1851–1951. *Population Studies*, Vol. 24, No. 3, November.

————. 1969. Demographic responses and population change. *Demography*, Vol. 6, No. 4, November.

GABRIEL, K. R. 1960. *Nuptiality and Fertility in Israel*. In Hebrew, with English summary. Jerusalem.

GANIAGE, J. 1963. *Trois Villages d'Ille-de-France au XVIII Siecle*. Paris: INED.

GAUTIER, E., and HENRY, L. 1958. *La Population de Crulai, Paroisse Normande*. Paris: Presses Universitaires de France.

GEERTZ, C. 1963. *Agricultural Involution: The Process of Ecological Change in Indonesia*. Berkeley: University of California Press.

GERMANI, G. 1965. Migration and acculturation. In P. M. Hauser, ed., *Handbook of Social Research in Urban Areas*. Paris: UNESCO.

GIBBS, J. P., ed. 1961. *Urban Research Methods*. Princeton: D. Van Nostrand, Inc.

————, and DAVIS, K. 1958. Conventional versus metropolitan data in the international study of urbanization. *American Sociological Review*, Vol. 23, No. 5, October. Reprinted in J. P. Gibbs, ed., *Urban Research Methods*. Princeton: D. Van Nostrand, Inc., 1961.

————, and SCHNORE, L. F. 1960. Metropolitan growth: an international study. *American Journal of Sociology*, Vol. 66.

GILLE, H. 1949. Demographic history of the Northern European countries in the 18th century. *Population Studies,* Vol. 3, No. 1, June.

GIRARD, P. 1959. Aperçus de la démographie de Sotteville-les-Rouen vers la fin du XVIII siècle. *Population,* Vol. 14.

GLASS, D. V. 1968. Fertility trends in Europe since the Second World War. *Population Studies,* Vol. 22, No. 1, March.

————. 1965. Population growth and population policy. In M. C. Sheps and J. C. Ridley, *Public Health and Population Change.* Pittsburgh: University of Pittsburgh Press.

————, ed. 1953. *Introduction to Malthus.* New York: John Wiley & Sons, Inc.

————, and EVERSLEY, D. E. C., eds. 1965. *Population in History.* Chicago: Aldine Publishing Co.

GLICK, P. C. 1962. The 1960 census as a source for social research. *American Sociological Review,* Vol. 27.

————, and PARKE, R., JR. 1965. New approaches to studying the life cycle of the family. *Demography,* Vol. 2.

GOLDBERG, D. 1965. Fertility and fertility differentials: some observations on recent changes in the United States. In M. C. Sheps and J. C. Ridley, eds., *Public Health and Population Change.* Pittsburgh: University of Pittsburgh Press.

————. 1960. Another look at the Indianapolis fertility data. *Milbank Memorial Fund Quarterly,* Vol. 38, January.

————. 1959. The fertility of two-generation urbanites. *Population Studies,* Vol. 12, March.

GOLDBERG, S. 1958. *Introduction to Difference Equations.* New York: John Wiley & Sons, Inc.

GOLDSCHEIDER, C. 1971. *Population, Modernization, and Social Structure.* Boston: Little, Brown and Co.

————. 1967. Fertility of the Jews. *Demography,* Vol. 4, No. 1.

————. 1965. Socio-economic status and Jewish fertility. *Jewish Journal of Sociology,* Vol. 7.

GOLDSCHMIDT, W. 1959. *Man's Way: A Preface to the Understanding of Human Society.* New York: Henry Holt.

GOLDSTEIN, S. 1969. Completed and expected fertility in an American Jewish community. Paper presented at Demographic Section, Fifth World Congress of Jewish Studies, Jerusalem.

————. 1965. Rural-suburban-urban population redistribution in Denmark. *Rural Sociology,* Vol. 30, No. 3, September.

————. 1964. The extent of repeated migration: an analysis based on the Danish population register. *Journal of the American Statistical Association,* Vol. 59, December.

————. 1963. Some economic consequences of suburbanization in the Copenhagen metropolitan area. *American Journal of Sociology,* Vol. 68, No. 5, March.

————. and GOLDSCHEIDER, C. 1968. *Jewish Americans*. Englewood Cliffs, N.J.: Prentice-Hall, Inc.

GOODE, W. J. 1966. Family and mobility. In R. Bendix and S. M. Lipset, eds., *Class, Status and Power*. 2nd ed. New York: The Free Press.

————, ed. 1964. *Readings on the Family*. Englewood Cliffs, N.J.: Prentice-Hall, Inc.

————. 1963. *World Revolution and Family Patterns*. New York: The Free Press.

GOODMAN, L. A. 1959. Some alternatives to ecological correlations. *American Journal of Sociology*, Vol. 64.

————, and KRUSKAL, W. 1954 and 1959. Measures of Association for cross-classifications, I and II. *Journal of the American Statistical Association*.

GORDON, M. M. 1964. *Assimilation in American Life*. New York: Oxford University Press.

GOTTMAN, J. 1961. *Megalopolis: The Urbanized Northeastern Seaboard of the United States*. New York: Twentieth Century Fund.

GRABILL, W. F. 1959. The fertility of the United States population. In D. J. Bogue, *The Population of the United States*. Glencoe, Illinois: The Free Press.

GRAUMAN, J. V. 1965. Fertility and population density: a macro-demographic approach. Paper presented at 1965 Meetings of the Population Association of America. Abstracted in *Population Index*, Vol. 31, No. 3, July 1968.

————. 1959. Population estimates and projections. In P. M. Hauser and O. D. Duncan, eds., *The Study of Population*. Chicago: University of Chicago Press.

GRAUNT, J. 1939. *Natural and Political Observations . . . Made Upon the Bills of Mortality* (London, 1662). American edition. Edited by J. B. Hollander. Baltimore: Johns Hopkins Press.

Great Britain: Registrar General. 1954. *Decennial Supplement, England and Wales, 1951*. Part 1. Occupational Mortality. London: H.M.S.O.

GREBENIK, E. 1959. The development of demography in Great Britain. In P. M. Hauser and O. D. Duncan, eds., *The Study of Population*. Chicago: University of Chicago Press.

GREEN, H. L. 1961. Hinterland boundaries of New York City and Boston in southern New England. In J. P. Gibbs, ed., *Urban Research Methods*. New York: D. Van Nostrand Co., Inc.

GREENE, G. 1962. *World Prehistory: An Outline*. Cambridge: Cambridge University Press.

GREVEN, P. J., JR. 1970. *Four Generations: Population, Land, and Family in Colonial Andover, Massachusetts*. Ithaca: Cornell University Press.

GREVILLE, T. N. E. 1943. Short methods of constructing abridged life tables. *The Record of the American Institute of Actuaries*, Vol. 23, Part 1, No. 65, June.

GUILLAUME, P., and POUSSOU, J.-P. 1970. *Démographie Historique*. Paris: Armand Colin.

HACKENBERG, R. A. 1962. Economic alternatives in arid lands: a case study of the Pima and Papago Indians. *Ethnology*, Vol. 1. Reprinted in Y. A. Cohen, ed., *Man in Adaptation, The Cultural Present*. Chicago: Aldine Publishing Co., 1968.

HAENSZEL, W., ed. 1966. *Epidemiological Approaches to the Study of Cancer and Other Diseases*. National Cancer Institute Monograph No. 19. Washington: Government Printing Office.

HAJNAL, J. 1965. European marriage patterns in perspective. In D. V. Glass and D. E. C. Eversley, *Population in History*. Chicago: Aldine Publishing Co.

————. 1953a. The marriage boom. *Population Index*, Vol. 19, No. 2. Reprinted in J. S. Spengler and O. D. Duncan, eds., *Demographic Analysis*. Glencoe, Illinois: The Free Press, 1956.

————. 1953b. Age at marriage and proportions marrying. *Population Studies*, Vol. 7, No. 2.

HALBWACHS, M. 1960. *Population and Society: Introduction to Social Morphology*. Translated by O. D. Duncan and H. W. Pfautz. Glencoe, Illinois: The Free Press.

HAMMOND, E. C. 1966. Smoking in relation to the death rates of one million men and women. In W. Haenszel, ed., *Epidemiological Approaches to the Study of Cancer and Other Diseases*. National Cancer Institute Monograph No. 19. Washington: Government Printing Office.

HANSEN, M. H., HURWITZ, W. N., and PRITZKER, L. 1953. The accuracy of census results. *American Sociological Review*, Vol. 18.

HARSIN, P., and HELIN, E. eds. 1965. *Actes du Colloque International de Démographie Historique Liege 18–20 Avril, 1963*. Paris: Ed. M. Th. Genin.

HAURY, E. W. 1962. The greater American southwest. In R. J. Braidwood and G. R. Willey, eds., *Courses Toward Urban Life: Archaeological Considerations of Some Cultural Alternates*. Viking Fund Publications in Anthropology, No. 32. Chicago: Aldine Publishing Co.

HAUSER, P. M., ed. 1965a. *Handbook of Social Research in Urban Areas*. Paris: UNESCO.

————. 1965b. Urbanization: an overview. In P. M. Hauser and L. F. Schnore, eds., *The Study of Urbanization*. New York: John Wiley & Sons, Inc.

————. 1963a. *The Population Dilemma*. Englewood Cliffs, N.J.: Prentice-Hall, Inc. 2nd ed., 1969.

————. 1963b. Statistics and society. *Journal of the American Statistical Association*, Vol. 58, No. 301.

————, ed. 1961. *Urbanization in Latin America*. Paris: UNESCO.

————. 1958. On the impact of urbanism on social organization, human nature, and the political order. *Confluence*, Vol. 7, No. 1, Spring.

————, and DUNCAN, O. D. 1959a. The data and methods. In P. M. Hauser and

O. D. Duncan, eds., *The Study of Population*. Chicago: University of Chicago Press.

————. 1959*b*. Demography as a body of knowledge. In P. M. Hauser and O. D. Duncan, eds., *The Study of Population*. Chicago: University of Chicago Press.

————. 1959*c*. The nature of demography. In P. M. Hauser and O. D. Duncan, eds., *The Study of Population*. Chicago: University of Chicago Press.

————, eds. 1959*d*. *The Study of Population*. Chicago: University of Chicago Press.

HAUSER, P. M., and MATRAS, J. 1965. Primary analytical units. In P. M. Hauser, ed., *Handbook of Social Research in Urban Areas*. Paris: UNESCO.

HAUSER, P. M., and SCHNORE, L. F., eds. 1965. *The Study of Urbanization*. New York: John Wiley & Sons, Inc.

HAWLEY, A. H. 1959. Population composition. In P. M. Hauser and O. D. Duncan, eds., *The Study of Population*. Chicago: University of Chicago Press.

————. 1956. *The Changing Shape of Metropolitan America: Deconcentration Since 1920*. Glencoe, Illinois: The Free Press.

————. 1950. *Human Ecology: A Theory of Community Structure*. New York: Ronald Press Co.

————, and PRACHUABMOH, V. 1966. Family growth and family planning: responses to a family-planning action program in a rural district in Thailand. *Demography*, Vol. 3, No. 2.

HAWTHORN, G. 1970. *The Sociology of Fertility*. London: Collier-Macmillan Ltd.

HEER, D. M., ed. 1968. *Readings in Population*. Englewood Cliffs, N.J.: Prentice-Hall, Inc.

————. 1967. Fertility differences in Andean countries: a reply to W. H. James. *Population Studies*, Vol. 2, No. 1, July.

————. 1966. Births necessary to assure desired survivorship of sons under differing mortality conditions. Paper presented to the Annual Meetings of the Population Association of America, New York, April.

————, and SMITH, D. O. 1969. Mortality level, desired family size, and population increase: a further variant on a basic model. *Demography*, Vol. 6, No. 2, May.

————. 1967. Mortality level and desired family size. *Contributed Papers of the Sydney Conference of the International Comm. for the Scientific Study of Population*.

HELLEINER, K. F. 1957. The vital revolution reconsidered. *Canadian Journal of Economics and Political Science*, Vol. 23, No. 1. Reprinted in D. V. Glass and D. E. C. Eversley, eds., *Population in History*. Chicago: Aldine Publishing Co., 1965.

HENRIPIN, J. 1954. *La Population Canadienne au Debut du XVIII Siècle*. Paris: Presses Universitaires de France.

HENRY, L. 1969. Schemas de nuptialité: deséquilibre des sexes et age au marriage. *Population,* Vol. 24, No. 6.

————. 1965. French statistical research in natural fertility. In M. C. Sheps and J. C. Ridley, eds., *Public Health and Population Change.* Pittsburgh: University of Pittsburgh Press.

————. 1956. *Anciennes Familles Genèvoises.* Paris: Presses Universitaires de France.

HERRICH, B. H. 1965. *Urban Migration and Economic Development in Chile.* Cambridge, Massachusetts: The M.I.T. Press.

HERTZLER, J. O. 1961. *American Social Institutions.* Boston: Allyn and Bacon, Inc.

HILL, R., STYCOS, J. M., and BACK, K. 1959. *The Family and Population Control.* Chapel Hill, North Carolina: University of North Carolina Press.

HIMES, N. E. 1963. *Medical History of Contraception.* Reprinted. New York: Gamut Press.

HIRSCHMAN. C., and MATRAS, J. 1971. A new look at the marriage market and nuptiality rates, 1915–1958. *Demography,* Vol. 8, No. 4, November.

HOBHOUSE, L. T. 1924. *Social Development, Its Nature and Conditions. Hobhouse's Principles of Sociology,* Vol. IV. New York: Reprinted. London: Allen and Unwin, 1966.

————, WHEELER, G. C., and GINSBERG, M. 1915. *The Material Culture and Social Institutions of Simpler Peoples.* Reprinted. London: Routledge and Kegan Paul, 1965.

HODGE, P. L., and HAUSER, P. M. 1968. *The Challenge of America's Metropolitan Population Outlook 1960–1985.* New York: Frederick A. Praeger.

HOEBEL, E. A. 1958. *Anthropology.* New York: McGraw-Hill.

HOLLINGSWORTH, T. H. 1969. *Historical Demography.* London: Source of History Ltd.

HOOVER, E. M., and VERNON, R. 1962. *Anatomy of a Metropolis.* New York: Anchor Books.

HOPKINS, M. K. 1965. The age of Roman girls at marriage. *Population Studies,* Vol. 18, No. 3, March.

HUTCHINSON, E. P. 1959. Swedish population thought in the eighteenth century. *Population Studies,* Vol. 13, No. 1, July.

ILLICH, I. 1970. *Deschooling Society.* New York: Harper & Row.

Israel: Central Bureau of Statistics. 1961 Census of Population. *Families in Israel, 1961.* Jerusalem: Israel Central Bureau of Statistics, 1968.

————. 1961 Census of Population. *Languages, Literacy, and Education,* Parts I, II, and III, Census Publications Nos. 15, 29, and 30. Jerusalem: Israel Central Bureau of Statistics, 1968.

————. *Statistical Abstract of Israel,* No. 20, 1969.

JAFFE, A. J. 1951. *Handbook of Statistical Methods for Demographers: Selected Problems in the Analysis of Census Data.* Washington: U.S. Bureau of the Census.

JAMES, W. H. 1966. The effect of altitude on fertility in Andean countries. *Population Studies,* Vol. 20, No. 1, July.

JOHNSON, G. Z. 1960. Differential fertility in European countries. In National Bureau of Economic Research, *Demographic and Economic Change in Developed Countries.* Princeton: Princeton University Press.

JUTIKKALA, E. 1965. Finland's population movement in the 18th century. In D. V. Glass and D. E. C. Eversley, eds., *Population in History.* Chicago: Aldine Publishing Co.

KENDALL, P. L., and LAZARSFELD, P. F. 1955. The relation between individual and group characteristics in the American soldier. In P. F. Lazarsfeld and M. Rosenberg, eds., *The Language of Social Research.* Glencoe, Illinois: The Free Press.

KENYON, K. M. 1960. *Archaeology in the Holy Land.* New York: Praeger Paperbacks.

KEYFITZ, N. 1968. *Introduction to the Mathematics of Population.* Reading, Massachusetts: Addison-Wesley Publishing Co., Inc.

————. 1966. How many people have lived on the earth. *Demography,* Vol. 3, No. 2.

————. 1965. Population density and the style of social life. *Bioscience,* Vol. 16, No. 12, December.

————. 1952. Differential fertility in Ontario: application of a factorial design to a demographic problem. *Population Studies,* Vol. 6, No. 2, November.

KIRK, D. 1969. Natality in the developing countries: recent trends and prospects. In S. J. Behrman, Leslie Corsa, Jr., and Ronald Freedman, *Fertility and Family Planning: A World View.* Ann Arbor: University of Michigan Press.

KISER, C. V. 1967. The growth of American family studies: an assessment of significance. *Demography,* Vol. 4, No. 1.

————, ed. 1962. *Research in Family Planning.* Princeton: Princeton University Press.

————, GRABILL, W. H., and CAMPBELL, A. A. 1968. *Trends and Variations in Fertility in the United States.* Cambridge, Massachusetts: Harvard University Press.

KISER, C. V., and WHELPTON, P. K. 1958. Social and psychological factors affecting fertility, XXXIII. Summary of chief findings and implications for future studies. *Milbank Memorial Fund Quarterly,* Vol. 36, No. 2, July. Reprinted in C. V. Kiser and P. K. Whelpton, eds., *Social and Psychological Factors Affecting Fertility,* Vol. 5. New York: Milbank Memorial Fund.

————, eds. 1958. *Social and Psychological Factors Affecting Fertility,* Vols. 1–5. New York: Milbank Memorial Fund.

KITAGAWA, E. M., and HAUSER, P. M. 1968. Education differentials in mortality by cause of death, United States, 1960. *Demography,* Vol. 5, No. 1.

————. 1963. Methods used in a current study of social and economic differentials in mortality. In *Emerging Techniques in Population Research.* New York: Milbank Memorial Fund.

KITAGAWA, E. M., and TAEUBER, K. E. 1963. *The 1960 Local Community Fact Book Chicago Metropolitan Area.* Chicago: University of Chicago Press.

KLEINER, R. J., and PARKER, S. 1963. Goal striving, social status, and mental disorder: a research review. *American Sociological Review,* Vol. 28, April.

KOLB, J. H., and BRUNNER, DE S. 1935. *A Study of Rural Society, Its Organization and Changes.* Boston: Houghton Mifflin.

KRZYWICKI, L. 1934. *Primitive Society and Its Vital Statistics.* Warsaw: Mianowski Institute.

KUZNETS, S. 1962. Inventive activity: problems of definition and measurement. In National Bureau of Economic Research, *The Rate and Direction of Inventive Activity: Economic and Social Factors.* Princeton: Princeton University Press.

————. 1960. Population change and aggregate output. In National Bureau of Economic Research, *Demographic and Economic Change in Developed Countries.* Princeton: Princeton University Press.

————, MILLER, A. R., and EASTERLIN, R. A. 1960. *Population Redistribution and Economic Growth, United States 1870–1950,* Vol. II: *Analyses of Economic Change.* Philadelphia: American Philosophical Society.

LADINSKY, J. 1967. Sources of geographic mobility among professional workers: a multivariate analysis. *Demography,* Vol. 4, No. 2.

LAMPARD, E. E. 1965. Historical aspects of urbanization. In P. M. Hauser and L. F. Schnore, eds., *The Study of Urbanization.* New York: John Wiley & Sons, Inc.

LAZARSFELD, P. F., and ROSENBERG, M., eds. 1955. *The Language of Social Research.* Glencoe, Illinois: The Free Press.

LEASURE, J. W. 1963. Malthus, marriage, and multiplication. *Milbank Memorial Fund Quarterly,* Vol. 41, No. 4, October.

LEE, E. S., ET AL. 1957. *Population Redistribution and Economic Growth, United States,* Vol. I: *Methodological Considerations and Reference Tables.* Philadelphia: American Philosophical Society.

LEE, R. B., and DEVORE, I., eds. 1968. *Man the Hunter.* Chicago: Aldine Publishing Co.

LEWIS-FANING, E. 1949. Report on an inquiry into family limitation and its influence on human fertility during the past fifty years. *Papers of the Royal Commission Population,* Vol. 1. London: HMSO.

LIEBENSTEIN, H. 1957. *Economic Backwardness and Economic Growth.* New York: John Wiley & Sons, Inc.

LIEBERSON, S. 1961. The impact of residential segregation on ethnic assimilation. *Social Forces,* Vol. 40, No. 1, October.

LINDER, F. E. 1959. World demographic data. In P. M. Hauser and O. D. Duncan, eds., *The Study of Population.* Chicago: University of Chicago Press.

LINTON, R. 1936. *The Study of Man.* New York: Appleton-Century-Crofts.

LIPSET, S. M. 1960. *Political Man*. Garden City, New York: Doubleday.

————, and BENDIX, R. 1959. *Social Mobility in Industrial Society*. Berkeley: University of California Press.

LIPSET, S. M., and ZETTERBERG, H. L. 1966. A theory of social mobility. In R. Bendix and S. M. Lipset, eds., *Class, Status and Power*. 2nd ed. New York: The Free Press.

LOCKRIDGE, K. B. 1968. Land, population, and the evolution of New England society, 1630–1790. *Past and Present*, Vol. 39, April.

LOPREATO, J. 1967. Upward social mobility and political orientation. *American Sociological Review*, Vol. 32, No. 4, August.

LORIMER, F. 1969. Issues in population policy. In P. M. Hauser, ed., *The Population Dilemma*. 2nd ed. Englewood Cliffs, N.J.: Prentice-Hall, Inc.

————. 1967. The economics of family formation under different conditions. U.N. World Population Conference, *Proceedings*, 1965, Vol. II. New York: United Nations.

————. 1959. The development of demography. In P. M. Hauser and O. D. Duncan, eds., *The Study of Population*. Chicago: University of Chicago Press.

————. 1954. *Culture and Human Fertility*. Paris: UNESCO.

LOWRY, I. S. 1966. *Migration and Metropolitan Growth: Two Analytical Models*. San Francisco: Chandler Publishing Co.

LUNDE, A. S. 1965. White-nonwhite fertility differentials in the United States. *Health, Education and Welfare Indicators*, September. U.S. Department of Health, Education and Welfare.

MACDONALD, J. S., and MACDONALD, L. D. 1964. Chain migration, ethnic neighborhood formation, and social networks. *Milbank Memorial Fund Quarterly*, Vol. 62, No. 1, January.

McGINNIS, R. M., ed. In press. *Proceedings of Cornell Conference on Human Mobility*, 1968.

McKEOWN, T. 1965. Medicine and world population. In M. C. Sheps and J. C. Ridley, eds., *Public Health and Population Change*. Pittsburgh: University of Pittsburgh Press.

————, and BROWN, R. G. 1955. Medical evidence related to English population changes in the eighteenth century. *Population Studies*, Vol. 9, Part 2, November.

McKEOWN, T., and RECORD, R. G. 1962. Reasons for the decline of mortality in England and Wales during the nineteenth century. *Population Studies*, Vol. 16, Part 2, November.

McNEIL, W. H. 1963. *The Rise of the West*. Chicago: University of Chicago Press.

MALTHUS, T. R. 1958. *An Essay on the Principle of Population*, 2 Vols. Everyman's Library. London: Dent & Sons (reprinted).

————. 1829. *A Summary View of the Principle of Population*. Supplement to Encyclopaedia Britannica.

MANGRIN, W., ed. 1970. *Peasants in Cities, Readings in the Anthropology of Urbanization.* Boston: Houghton Mifflin Co.

MATRAS, J. In press. Mobility, marriage, and natural increase: a further variant in the linear model. In R. M. McGinnis, ed. *Proceedings of Cornell Conference on Human Mobility, 1968.* Ithaca: Cornell University Press.

————. 1968. *Families in Israel, 1961,* Part II. Israel 1961 Census of Population No. 39. Jerusalem: Israel Central Bureau of Statistics.

————. 1967. Social mobility and social structure: some insights from the linear model. *American Sociological Review,* Vol. 32, No. 4, August.

————. 1966. Social strategies of family formation: urban-rural, size-of-city, provincial, and major city variations among Canadian female cohorts. *Canadian Review of Sociology and Anthropology,* Vol. 3, No. 3, August.

————. 1965a. The social strategy of family formation: some variations in time and space. *Demography,* Vol. 2.

————. 1965b. Social strategies of family formation: some comparative data for Scandinavia, the British Isles, and North America. *International Social Science Journal,* Vol. 17, No. 2.

————. 1965c. *Social Change in Israel.* Chicago: Aldine Publishing Co.

————. 1965d. Social and personal disorganization. In P. M. Hauser, ed., *Handbook of Social Research in Urban Areas.* Paris: UNESCO.

————, and AUERBACH, C. 1962. On rationalization of family formation in Israel. *Milbank Memorial Fund Quarterly,* Vol. 40, No. 4, October.

MATRAS, J., ROSENFELD, J. M., and SALZBERGER, L. 1969. On the predicaments of Jewish families in Jerusalem. *International Journal of Comparative Sociology,* Vol. 10, No. 3.

MATRAS, J., and WINSBOROUGH, H. H. 1969. On the empirical study of population transformations. Paper presented to the Second Conference on Mathematical Demography. Berkeley and Asilomar, California, August.

MAY, D. A., and HEER, D. M. 1968. Son survivorship and family size in India: a computer simulation. *Population Studies,* Vol. 22, No. 2, July.

MAYER, A. J., and HAUSER, P. M. 1953. Class differentials in expectation of life at birth. In R. Bendix and S. M. Lipset, eds., *Class, Status and Power.* Glencoe, Illinois: The Free Press.

MEAD, M. 1950. *Sex and Temperament in Three Primitive Societies.* New York: New American Library.

MEADOWS, P., and MIZRUHI, E. H., eds. 1969. *Urbanism, Urbanization, and Change: Comparative Perspectives.* Reading, Massachusetts: Addison-Wesley.

MENDELS, F. F. 1969. Population pressure and rural industrialization in a preindustrial society. Paper read at General Assembly, International Union for the Scientific Study of Population, London, September.

MERTON, R. K. 1962. *Social Structure and Social Change.* 2nd ed. Glencoe, Illinois: The Free Press.

MEUVRET, J. 1965. Demographic crises in France from the sixteenth to eighteenth century. In D. V. Glass and D. E. C. Eversley, eds., *Population in History*. Chicago: Aldine Publishing Co.

MICKLEWRIGHT, F. H. A. 1961. The rise and decline of English neo-Malthusianism. *Population Studies*, Vol. 15, No. 1, July.

MIRO, C. A. 1964. The population of Latin America. *Demography*, Vol. 1, No. 1.

MOORE, W. E. 1963. *Social Change*. Englewood Cliffs, N.J.: Prentice-Hall, Inc.

MORIYAMA, I. M., and GURALNICK, L. 1956. Occupational and social class differences in mortality. In *Trends and Differentials in Mortality*. New York: Milbank Memorial Fund.

MORONI, A. 1969. Historical demography, human ecology, and consanguinity. Paper presented to World Population Conference, London, September.

MURDOCK, G. P. 1949. *Social Structure*. New York: Macmillan Co.

————, and WHITING, J. W. M. 1968. Are the hunter-gatherers a cultural type? In R. B. Lee and I. Devore, eds., *Man the Hunter*. Chicago: Aldine Publishing Co.

NADEL, S. F. 1957. *The Theory of Social Structure*. Glencoe, Illinois: The Free Press.

————. 1951. *Foundations of Social Anthropology*. Glencoe, Illinois: Glencoe Free Press.

————. 1950. Dual descent in the Nuba Hills. In A. R. Radcliffe-Brown and D. Forde, eds., *African Systems of Kinship and Marriage*. London: Oxford University Press.

NAG, M. 1962. *Factors Affecting Human Fertility in Non-industrial Societies: A Cross-cultural Study*. Yale University Publications in Anthropology, No. 66. New Haven: Department of Anthropology, Yale University.

NAM, C. B., ed. 1968. *Population and Society*. Boston: Houghton Mifflin.

National Bureau of Economic Research. 1962. *The Rate and Direction of Inventive Activity: Economic and Social Factors*. Princeton: Princeton University Press.

————. 1960. *Demographic and Economic Change in Developed Countries*. Princeton: Princeton University Press.

NELSON, R. R. 1962. Introduction. In National Bureau of Economic Research, *The Rate and Direction of Inventive Activity: Economic and Social Factors*. Princeton: Princeton University Press.

NOUGIER, L. R. 1954. Essai sur le peuplement pre-historique de la France. *Population*, Vol. 9, No. 2, April-June.

Office of Population Research. 1969a. *Population Index*, Vol. 35, January-March. Princeton: Princeton University Press.

————. 1969b. *Population Index*, Vol. 35, April-June. Princeton: Princeton University Press.

————. 1969c. *Population Index*, Vol. 35, July-September. Princeton: Princeton University Press.

————. 1969*d*. *Population Index,* Vol. 35, October-December. Princeton: Princeton University Press.

————. 1965. *Population Index,* Vol. 31, October-December. Princeton: Princeton University Press.

————. 1964. *Population Index,* Vol. 30, July-September. Princeton: Princeton University Press.

OGBURN, W. F., and DUNCAN, O. D. 1964. City size as a sociological variable. In E. W. Burgess and D. J. Bogue, eds., *Contributions to Urban Sociology.* Chicago: University of Chicago Press.

O'LESSKER, K. 1968. Who voted for Hitler? A new look at the class basis of Nazism. *American Journal of Sociology,* Vol. 74, No. 1, July.

ORANS, M. 1966. Surplus. *Human Organization,* Vol. 25, No. 1. Reprinted in Y. A. Cohen, ed., *Man in Adaptation: The Cultural Present.* Chicago: Aldine Publishing Co., 1968.

OTTENBERG, S., and OTTENBERG, P. 1960. *Cultures and Societies of Africa.* New York: Random House.

The Oxford Shorter English Dictionary. 1964. 3rd revised ed. London: Oxford University Press.

PARK, R. E. 1952. *Human Communities, The City, and Human Ecology.* Glencoe, Illinois: The Free Press.

————. 1925. Community organization and juvenile delinquency. In R. E. Park, E. W. Burgess, and R. D. McKenzie, *The City.* Chicago: University of Chicago Press. Reprinted in R. E. Park, *Human Communities, The City and Human Ecology.* Glencoe, Illinois: The Free Press, 1952.

————, and BURGESS, E. W. 1921. *Introduction to the Science of Sociology.* Chicago: University of Chicago Press.

————, and McKENZIE, R. D. 1925. *The City.* Chicago: University of Chicago Press.

PARSONS, T. 1966. *Societies: Evolutionary and Comparative Perspectives.* Englewood Cliffs, N.J.: Prentice-Hall, Inc.

————. 1964. Evolutionary universals in society. *American Sociological Review,* Vol. 29.

PAUL, B. D., ed. 1955. *Health, Culture and Community.* New York: Russell Sage Foundation.

PELLER, S. 1965. Births and deaths among Europe's ruling families since 1500. In D. V. Glass and D. E. C. Eversley, eds., *Population in History.* Chicago: Aldine Publishing Co.

————. 1948. Mortality, past and future. *Population Studies,* Vol. 1, No. 4, March.

PETERSEN, W. 1971. The Malthus-Godwin debate, then and now. *Demography,* Vol. 8, No. 1, February.

————. 1969. *Population.* 2nd ed. New York: Macmillan Co.

————. 1964. *The Politics of Population.* New York: Doubleday.

————. 1961. *Population.* New York: The Macmillan Co.

———. 1958. A general typology of migration. *American Sociological Review,* Vol. 23, No. 3, June. Reprinted in W. Petersen, *The Politics of Population.* New York: Doubleday, 1964.

PORTER, J. 1968. The future of upward mobility. *American Sociological Review,* Vol. 33, No. 2, February.

POWERS, M. G. 1968. Class, ethnicity and residence in metropolitan America. *Demography,* Vol. 5, No. 1.

PRESSAT, R. 1972. *Demographic Analysis.* Translated by J. Matras. Chicago: Aldine Publishing Co.

———. 1970. *Population.* London: C. A. Watts and Co., Ltd.

PRICE, C. A. 1963. *Southern Europeans in Australia.* Melbourne: Oxford University Press.

RADCLIFFE-BROWN, A. R., and FORDE, D., eds. 1950. *African Systems of Kinship and Marriage.* London: Oxford University Press.

RAINA, B. L. 1966. India. In B. Berelson, et al., eds., *Family Planning and Population Programs.* Chicago: University of Chicago Press.

RAINWATER, L. 1965. *Family Design, Marital Sexuality, Family Size, and Contraception.* Chicago: Aldine Publishing Co.

———. 1960. *And the Poor Get Children.* Chicago: Quadrangle Books.

RAMSØY, N. R. In press. Social mobility in Europe: a brief review of the 1960's. In R. McGinnis, ed., *Proceedings of Cornell Conference on Human Mobility,* 1968.

———. 1966. Changes in rates and forms of mobility. In N. J. Smelser and S. M. Lipset, eds., *Social Structure and Mobility in Economic Development.* Chicago: Aldine Publishing Co.

REINHARD, M. R., and ARMENGAUD, A. 1961. *Histoire Generale de la Population Mondiale.* Paris: Editions Montchrestien.

RELE, J. R. 1965. Trends and differentials in the American age at marriage. *Milbank Memorial Fund Quarterly,* Vol. 43, No. 2, April.

RICHMOND, A. H. 1964. Social mobility of immigrants in Canada. *Population Studies,* Vol. 18, July. Reprinted in T. R. Ford and G. F. DeJong, eds., *Social Demography.* Englewood Cliffs, N.J.: Prentice-Hall, Inc., 1970.

RILEY, M. W. 1964. Sources and types of sociological data. In R. E. L. Faris, ed., *Handbook of Modern Sociology.* Chicago: Rand McNally & Company.

ROBINSON, W. C. 1950. Ecological correlations and the behavior of individuals. *American Sociological Review,* Vol. 15, June.

ROGOFF, N. 1953. *Recent Trends in Occupational Mobility.* Glencoe, Illinois: The Free Press.

ROSEN, B. C., and SIMMONS, A. B. 1971. Industrialization, family, and fertility: a structural-psychological analysis of the Brazilian case. *Demography,* Vol. 8, No. 1, February.

ROSS, E. A. 1927. *Standing Room Only.* New York: Century Co.

ROSSI, P. H. 1955. *Why Families Move.* New York: The Free Press.

ROSTOW, W. W. 1960. *The Stages of Economic Growth, A Non-Communist Manifesto*. Cambridge: Cambridge University Press.

————. 1956. The take-off into self-sustained growth. *Economic Journal*, March.

ROUSE, I. 1962. The intermediate area, Amazonia and the Caribbean areas. In R. J. Braidwood and C. N. Willey, eds., *Courses Toward Urban Life: Archaeological Considerations of Some Cultural Alternates*. Viking Fund Publications in Anthropology, No. 32. Chicago: Aldine Publishing Co.

ROWNTREE, G., and PIERCE, R. M. 1961. Birth control in Britain. Parts I and II. *Population Studies*, Vol. 15, Nos. 1 and 2, July and November.

RYDER, N. B. 1965. The cohort as a concept in the study of social change. *American Sociological Review*, Vol. 30, December. Reprinted in T. R. Ford and G. F. DeJong, eds., *Social Demography*. Englewood Cliffs, N.J.: Prentice-Hall, Inc., 1970.

————. 1964. Notes on the concept of a population. *American Journal of Sociology*, Vol. 69, March.

————. 1959. Fertility. In P. M. Hauser and O. D. Duncan, eds., *The Study of Population*. Chicago: University of Chicago Press.

————, and WESTOFF, C. F. 1971. *Reproduction in the United States, 1965*. Princeton: Princeton University Press.

————. 1969. Fertility planning status: United States, 1965. *Demography*, Vol. 6, No. 4, November.

ST. ERLICH, V. 1966. *Family in Transition, A Study of 300 Yugoslav Villages*. Princeton: Princeton University Press.

SAUVY, A. 1954. *Théorie Génerale de la Population*, Vol. II. Paris: Presses Universitaires de France.

SAWYER, J. 1967. Dimensions of nations: size, wealth, and politics. *American Journal of Sociology*, Vol. 73, No. 2, September.

————, and LEVINE, R. A. 1966. Cultural dimensions: a factor analysis of the world ethnographic sample. *American Anthropologist*, Vol. 68, No. 3, June.

SCHNORE, L. F., ed. 1967. *Social Science and the City: A Survey of Urban Research*. New York: Frederick A. Praeger.

————. 1961. Social mobility in demographic perspective. *American Sociological Review*, Vol. 26, No. 3, June.

————. 1958. Social morphology and human ecology. *American Journal of Sociology*, Vol. 63.

————, and PINKERTON, J. R. 1966. Residential redistribution of socio-economic strata in metropolitan areas. *Demography*, Vol. 3, No. 2.

SCHUESSLER, K. F. 1969. Covariance analysis in sociological research. In E. F. Borgatta, ed., *Sociological Methodology*. San Francisco: Jossey-Bass.

SCHWIRIAN, K. P., and RICO-VALASCO, J. 1971. The residential distribution of status groups in Puerto Rico's metropolitan areas. *Demography*, Vol. 8, No. 1, February.

SEMENOV, A. 1964. *Prehistoric Technology.* Translated from Russian by M. W. Thompson. London: Barnes and Noble.

SERVICE, E. R. 1966. *The Hunters.* Englewood Cliffs, N.J.: Prentice-Hall, Inc.

SHAHAR, J. 1971. *Feuchtwanger Collection: Jewish Art and Tradition.* Jerusalem: Israel Museum. In Hebrew.

SHANNON, L. W., and SHANNON, M. 1967. The assimilation of migrants to cities. In L. F. Schnore, ed., *Social Science and the City: A Survey of Urban Research.* New York: Frederick A. Praeger.

SHAPIRO, S. 1954. Recent testing of birth registration completeness in the United States. *Population Studies,* Vol. 8.

SHEPS, M. C., and RIDLEY, J. C., eds. 1965. *Public Health and Population Change, Current Research Issues.* Pittsburgh: University of Pittsburgh Press.

SHRYOCK, H. S., JR. 1964. *Population Mobility Within the United States.* Chicago: Community and Family Study Center.

SIMMEL, G. 1950. *The Sociology of Georg Simmel.* Translated and edited by K. H. Wolf. New York: Free Press of Glencoe.

SJOBERG, G. 1964. The rural-urban dimension in pre-industrial, transitional, and industrial societies. In R. E. L. Faris, ed., *Handbook of Modern Sociology.* Chicago: Rand McNally.

SMELSER, N. J., and LIPSET, S. M., eds. 1966. *Social Structure and Mobility in Economic Development.* Chicago: Aldine Publishing Co.

SOUTHAM, A. L. 1966. Contraceptive methods: use, safety, and effectiveness. In B. Berelson et al., eds., *Family Planning and Population Programs.* Chicago: University of Chicago Press.

SPENGLER, J. J. 1971. Malthus on Godwin's 'Of Population.' *Demography,* Vol. 8, No. 1, February.

————, and DUNCAN, O. D., eds. 1956. *Demographic Analysis.* Glencoe, Illinois: The Free Press.

SPIEGELMAN, M. 1968*a.* Mortality in the United States: a review and evaluation of special reports of the National Center for Health Statistics. *Demography,* Vol. 5, No. 1.

————. 1968*b. Introduction to Demography.* Revised ed. Cambridge: Harvard University Press.

STEVENSON, R. F. 1968. *Population and Political Systems in Tropical Africa.* New York: Columbia University Press.

STEWARD, J. H. 1955. *Theory of Culture Change.* Urbana: University of Illinois Press.

STINCHCOMBE, A. L. 1968. *Constructing Social Theories.* New York: Harcourt, Brace & World, Inc.

STOLNITZ, G. J. 1965. Recent mortality trends in Latin America, Asia and Africa. *Population Studies,* Vol. 19, No. 2 .

STOUFFER, S. 1940. Intervening opportunities: a theory relating mobility and distance. *American Sociological Review,* Vol. 5.

Stycos, J. M. 1961. Social class and differential fertility in Peru. Document No. 34, submitted to the International Population Conference. Cited in C. A. Miro, The population of Latin America. *Demography*, Vol. 1, No. 1, 1964.

Süssmilch, J. P. 1761–62. *Die Gottliche Ordnung in der Veranderungen des Menschlichen Geschlicts aus der Gebunt, dem Tode, und der Fortpflanzung desselben Orwiesen.* 2nd ed., 2 Vols. Berlin.

Taeuber, C. 1964. Taking an inventory of 180 million people: the U.S. census. In R. Freedman, ed., *Population, The Vital Revolution.* New York: Anchor Books.

—————, and Hansen, M. H. 1964. A preliminary evaluation of the 1960 census of population and housing. *Demography*, Vol. 1, No. 1.

Taeuber, C., and Taeuber, I. B., 1958. *The Changing Population of the United States.* New York: John Wiley & Sons, Inc.

Taeuber, I. B. 1967. Demographic transitions and population problems of the United States. *The Annals of the American Academy of Political and Social Science,* Vol. 369, January.

Taeuber, K. E., Chiazze, L., Jr., and Haenzel, W. 1968. *Migration in the United States: An Analysis of Residence Histories.* Public Health Monograph No. 77. Washington: U.S. Government Printing Office.

Taeuber, K. E., and Matras, J. 1969. A new look at twentieth century migration and population redistribution in the United States. Presented at 1969 meetings of the Population Association of America, Atlantic City, New Jersey, April.

Taeuber, K. E., and Taeuber, A. F. 1965. *Negroes in Cities.* Chicago: Aldine Publishing Co.

—————. 1964. The Negro as an immigrant group: recent trends in racial and ethnic segregation in Chicago. *American Journal of Sociology,* Vol. 69, No. 4.

Tax, S., ed. 1964. *Horizons of Anthropology.* Chicago: Aldine Publishing Co.

Textor, R. B. 1967. *A Cross Cultural Survey.* New Haven: HRAF Press.

Thomas, D. S. 1941. *Social and Economic Aspects of Swedish Population Movements, 1750–1933.* New York: Macmillan.

Thomas, E. M. 1959. *The Harmless People.* New York: Alfred A. Knopf, Inc.

Thomas, W. I., and Znaniecki, F. 1958. *The Polish Peasant in Europe and America.* 2 Vols. New York: Owen Publications.

Thomlinson, P. 1965. *Population Dynamics.* New York: Random House.

Thompson, W. S., and Whelpton, P. K. 1933. *Population Trends in the U.S.A.* New York: McGraw-Hill.

Tietze, C. 1965. Induced abortion and sterilization as methods of fertility control. In M. C. Sheps and J. C. Ridley, eds., *Public Health and Population Change.* Pittsburgh: University of Pittsburgh Press.

Treiman, D. J. 1970. Issues in the comparative study of social stratification. *Sociological Inquiry,* Summer.

Uhlenberg, P. R. 1969. A study of cohort life cycles: cohorts of native-born Massachusetts women, 1830–1920. *Population Studies,* Vol. 23, November.

United Nations. 1958. *Recent Trends in Fertility in Industrialized Countries.* New York: United Nations.

U.N. Department of Economic and Social Affairs. 1970. Statistical Office. *Demographic Yearbook: 1969.* New York: United Nations.

————. 1969. Statistical Office. *Demographic Yearbook: 1968.* New York: United Nations.

————. 1968a. *Compendium of Social Statistics: 1967.* New York: United Nations.

————. 1968b. Statistical Office. *Demographic Yearbook: 1967.* New York: United Nations.

————. 1967. Statistical Office. *Demographic Yearbook: 1966.* New York: United Nations.

————. 1966. Statistical Office. *Demographic Yearbook: 1965.* New York: United Nations.

————. 1963a. Statistical Office. *Demographic Yearbook: 1962.* New York: United Nations.

————. 1963b. *Population Bulletin, No. 7.* New York: United Nations.

————. 1962. *Population Bulletin, No. 6.* New York: United Nations.

————. 1953. *Population Studies, No. 17. The determinants and consequences of population trends.* New York: United Nations.

UNESCO. 1967. *World Social Situation.* New York: United Nations.

U.S. Bureau of the Census. 1969. *Statistical Abstract of the United States: 1969.* Washington: U.S. Government Printing Office.

————. 1965. *Current Population Reports.* Population Estimates, Series P-25, No. 310. Estimates of the population of the United States and components of change, by age, color, and sex, 1950 to 1960. Washington: U.S. Government Printing Office.

————. 1964a. *U.S. Census of Population: 1960.* Vol. I. *Characteristics of the Population.* Part 1, United States Summary. Washington: U.S. Government Printing Office.

————. 1964b. *Current Population Reports,* Series P-23, No. 11. Lifetime occupational mobility of adult males, March 1962. Washington: U.S. Government Printing Office.

————. 1963a. Working Paper No. 16. *Procedural Report on the 1960 Censuses of Population and Housing.* Washington: U.S. Government Printing Office.

————. 1963b. *U.S. Census of Population: 1960.* Subject Reports. *Occupational Characteristics. Final Report* PC (2)–7A. Washington: U.S. Government Printing Office.

————. 1963c. *U.S. Census of Population: 1960.* Subject Reports *Occupation by Earnings and Education.* Final Report PC (2)–7B. Washington: U.S. Government Printing Office.

————. 1960. Historical Statistics of the U.S., *Colonial Times to 1957.* Washington: U.S. Government Printing Office.

————. 1958. *Current Population Reports,* Series P-20, No. 79. Religion reported by the civilian population of the United States: March 1957. Washington: U.S. Government Printing Office.

————. 1952. *U.S. Census of Population: 1950.* Vol. II. *Characteristics of the Population.* Washington: U.S. Government Printing Office.

————. 1943. *U.S. Census of Population: 1940.* Special Reports. *Age of Migrants.* Washington: U.S. Government Printing Office.

————. 1933. *U.S. Census of Population: 1930.* Washington: U.S. Government Printing Office.

U.S. Department of Health, Education, and Welfare. 1969a. Public Health Service. *Vital Statistics of the United States: 1967.* Volume I—*Natality.* Washington: U.S. Government Printing Office.

————. 1969b. Public Health Service. *Vital Statistics of the United States: 1967.* Vol. II—*Mortality.* Washington: U.S. Government Printing Office.

————. 1964. Report of the Advisory Committee to the Surgeon General of the Public Health Services. PHS Publication 1103. *Smoking and Health.* Washington: U.S. Government Printing Office.

U.S. National Center for Health Statistics. 1967. Public Health Service Publication No. 1000, Series 21, No. 11. *Natality Statistics Analysis, 1964.* Washington: U.S. Government Printing Office.

UTTERSTROM, G. 1965a. A discussion of some current issues. In D. V. Glass and D. E. C. Eversley, eds. *Population in History.* Chicago: Aldine Publishing Co.

————. 1965b. An outline of some population changes in Sweden 1660–1750. In D. V. Glass and D. E. C. Eversley, eds., *Population in History.* Chicago: Aldine Publishing Co.

VALLIN, J. 1968. La mortalité dans les pays du tiers monde: évolution et perspectives. *Population,* Vol. 23, No. 5, September-October.

VALMARY, P. 1965. *Familles Paysannes au XVIII Siècle en Bas-Quercy.* Paris: INED.

VAN DE WALLE, E. 1968. Marriage and marital fertility. In *Daedalus,* Historical Population Studies, Spring.

WARREN, D. I. 1965. Structural effects: index of social structure or statistical artifact? Paper presented at annual meetings of the American Sociological Association, Chicago, September.

WATSON, P. J. 1965. The chronology of North Syria and North Mesopotamia from 10,000 B.C. to 2,000 B.C. In R. W. Ehrich, ed., *Chronologies in Old World Archaeology.* Chicago: University of Chicago Press.

WEBER, M. 1968. *The City.* Translated by D. Martindale and G. Neuwirth. Glencoe, Illinois: The Free Press.

————. 1961. *General Economic History.* Translated by F. H. Knight. New York: Collier Books.

WELLIN, E. 1955. Water boiling in a Peruvian town. In B. D. Paul, ed., *Health, Culture and Community.* New York: Russell Sage Foundation.

WESTOFF, C. F., POTTER, R. G., and SAGI, P. C. 1964. Some selected findings of the Princeton fertility study, 1963. *Demography,* Vol. 1, No. 1.

————. 1963. *The Third Child.* Princeton: Princeton University Press.

WESTOFF, C. F., and MISHLER, E. G. 1961. *Family Growth in Metropolitan America.* Princeton: Princeton University Press.

WESTOFF, C. F., and RYDER, N. B. 1969. Practice of contraception in the U.S.A. In S. J. Behrman, L. Corsa, Jr., and R. Freedman, eds., *Fertility and Family Planning: A World View.* Ann Arbor: University of Michigan Press.

WHELPTON, P. K., CAMPBELL, A. A., and PATTERSON, J. E. 1966. *Fertility and Family Planning in the United States.* Princeton: Princeton University Press.

WHITE, H. C. 1963. *An Anatomy of Kinship.* Englewood Cliffs, N.J.: Prentice-Hall, Inc.

WILLCOX, W. F. 1939. "Introduction" to J. Graunt, *Natural and Political Observations . . . Made Upon the Bills of Mortality* (London, 1662). American edition. Edited by J. B. Hollander. Baltimore: Johns Hopkins Press.

————. 1931. Estimate of the population of the world and its continents from 1650 to 1900. In United Nations, Department of Social Affairs, Population Division, *The Determinants and Consequences of Population Trends.* Population Studies, No. 17. New York: United Nations, 1953.

WILSON, M. 1950. Nyakyusha kinship. In A. R. Radcliffe-Brown and D. Forde, eds., *African Systems of Kinship and Marriage.* London: Oxford University Press.

WIRTH, L. 1945. The problem of minority groups. In R. Linton, ed., *The Science of Man in the World Crisis.* New York: Columbia University Press. Reprinted in A. J. Reiss, Jr., ed., *Louis Wirth on Cities and Social Life.* Chicago: University of Chicago Press, 1964.

————. 1938. Urbanism as a way of life. *American Journal of Sociology,* Vol. 44, July.

WOLFENDEN, H. H. 1954. *Population Statistics and Their Compilation.* Chicago: University of Chicago Press.

WOYTINSKY, W. S., and WOYTINSKY, E. S. 1953. *World Population and Production, Trends and Outlook.* New York: Twentieth Century Fund, Inc.

WRIGLEY, E. A. 1968. Mortality in pre-industrial England: the example of Colyton, Devon, over three centuries. *Daedalus,* Historical Population Studies, Spring.

————. 1966*a*. Family limitation in pre-industrial England. *Economic History Review,* 2nd series, Vol. 18.

————, ed. 1966*b*. *An Introduction to English Historical Demography.* New York: Basic Books.

YAM, J. 1965. *An Introduction to Demography,* Vol. I. Jerusalem: Academon. In Hebrew.

YAUKEY, D. 1961. *Fertility Differences in a Modernizing Country.* Princeton: Princeton University Press.

YOUNG, P. V. 1949. *Scientific Social Surveys and Research.* Englewood Cliffs, N.J.: Prentice-Hall, Inc.

ZACHARIAH, K. C. 1966. Bombay migration study: a pilot analysis of migration to an Asian metropolis. *Demography,* Vol. 3, No. 2.

————. 1964. *A Historical Study of Internal Migration in the Indian Sub-continent 1901–1931.* London: Asia Publishing House.

ZELDITCH, M., JR. 1964. Family, marriage and kinship. In R. E. L. Faris, ed., *Handbook of Modern Sociology.* Chicago: Rand McNally and Co.

ZELINSKY, W. 1966. *A Prologue to Population Geography.* Englewood Cliffs, N.J.: Prentice-Hall, Inc.

ZELNIK, M. 1966. Fertility of the American Negro in 1830 and 1950. *Population Studies,* Vol. 20, No. 1, July.

Index

POPULATION INFORMATION FOR 145 COUNTRIES

Region or Country	Population Estimates Mid-1971 (millions) †	Annual Births per 1,000 Population ‡	Annual Deaths per 1,000 Population ‡	Annual Rate of Population Growth (percent) °	Number of Years to Double Population □	Annual Infant Mortality (Deaths under one year per 1,000 Live Births) ‡	Population under 15 Years (percent) ▲	Population Projections to 1985 (millions) †	Per Capita Gross National Product (US $) §
NORTHERN AMERICA	229[2]	18	9	1.2	58	—	30	280	—
Canada	21.8	17.6	7.3	1.7	41	20.8	33	27.3	2,460
United States [3]	207.1	18.2	9.3	1.1	63	19.8	30	241.7	3,980
LATIN AMERICA	291[2]	38	9	2.9	24	—	42	435	—
MIDDLE AMERICA	70	43	9	3.4	21	—	46	112	—
Costa Rica	1.9	45	8	3.8	19	60	48	3.2	450
El Salvador	3.6	47	13	3.4	21	63	45	5.9	280
Guatemala	5.3	42	13	2.9	24	94	46	7.9	320
Honduras	2.8	49	16	3.4	21	—	51	4.6	260
Mexico	52.5[4]	42	9	3.4	21	66	46	84.4	530
Nicaragua	2.1	46	16	3.0	24	—	48	3.3	370
Panama	1.5	41	8	3.3	21	41	43	2.5	580
CARIBBEAN	26	34	10	2.2	32	—	40	36	—
Barbados	0.3	21	8	0.8	88	42	38	0.3	440
Cuba	8.6	27	8	1.9	37	40	37	11.0	310
Dominican Republic	4.4[4]	48	15	3.4	21	64	47	7.3	290
Guadeloupe*	0.4	32	8	2.4	29	35	42	0.5	510
Haiti	5.4	44	20	2.5	28	—	42	7.9	70
Jamaica	2.0	33	8	2.1	33	39	41	2.6	460
Martinique*	0.4	30	8	1.9	37	34	42	0.5	610
Puerto Rico*	2.9	24	6	1.4	50	29	39	3.4	1,340
Trinidad & Tobago	1.1	30	7	1.8	39	37	43	1.3	870
TROPICAL SOUTH AMERICA	155	39	9	3.0	24	—	43	236	—
Bolivia	4.8	44	19	2.4	29	—	44	6.8	150
Brazil	95.7	38	10	2.8	25	170	43	142.6	250
Colombia	22.1	44	11	3.4	21	78	47	35.6	310
Ecuador	6.3	45	11	3.4	21	86	48	10.1	220
Guyana	0.8	37	8	2.9	24	40	46	1.1	340
Peru	14.0	43	11	3.1	23	62	45	21.6	380
Surinam*	0.4	41	7	3.2	22	30	46	0.6	430
Venezuela	11.1	41	8	3.4	21	46	46	17.4	950
TEMPERATE SOUTH AMERICA	40	26	9	1.8	39	—	33	51	—
Argentina	24.7	22	9	1.5	47	58	29	29.6	820
Chile	10.0[4]	34	11	2.3	31	92	40	13.6	480
Paraguay	2.5	45	11	3.4	21	52	45	4.1	230
Uruguay	2.9	21	9	1.2	58	50	28	3.4	520
EUROPE	466[2]	18	10	0.8	88	—	25	515	—
NORTHERN EUROPE	81	16	11	0.6	117	—	24	90	—
Denmark	5.0	14.6	9.8	0.5	140	14.8	24	5.5	2,070
Finland	4.7	14.5	9.8	0.4	175	13.9	27	5.0	1,720
Iceland	0.2	20.7	7.2	1.2	58	11.7	34	0.3	1,680
Ireland	3.0	21.5	11.5	0.7	100	20.6	31	3.5	980
Norway	3.9	17.6	9.9	0.9	78	13.7	25	4.5	2,000
Sweden	8.1	13.5	10.4	0.5	140	13.0	21	8.8	2,620
United Kingdom	56.3	16.6	11.9	0.5	140	18.6	23	61.8	1,790